Handbook of Practical Gear Design

Darle W. Dudley
Dudley Engineering Co.

McGraw-Hill Book Company

New York St. Louis San Francisco Auckland
Bogotá Hamburg Johannesburg London Madrid
Mexico Montreal New Delhi Panama Paris
São Paulo Singapore Sydney Tokyo Toronto

Library of Congress Cataloging In Publication Data

Dudley, Darle W.
Handbook of practical gear design.

Rev. ed. of: Practical gear design. 1st ed. 1954.
Includes index.
1. Gearing—Handbooks, manuals, etc. I. Dudley,
Darle W. Practical gear design. II. Title.
TJ184.D784 1984 621.8'33 84-3860
ISBN 0-07-017951-4

A revision of *Practical Gear Design.*

2 3 4 5 6 7 8 9 0 DOC/DOC 8 9 8 7 6 5

ISBN 0-07-017951-4

The editors for this book were Patricia Allen-Browne and Sheila H. Gillams, the designer was Mark E. Safran, and the production supervisor was Thomas G. Kowalczyk. It was set in Baskerville by Byrd Data Imaging Group.

Printed and bound by R. R. Donnelley & Sons Company.

Dedicated to Laurence J. Collins, General Electric Company, retired. Larry Collins first assigned me to gear research and development work, and it was he who first encouraged me to write a book on gear design. Larry Collins contributed greatly to the development of both technology and personnel in the gear industry. I am, like many others, very grateful for his guidance and encouragement.

contents

Foreword *xiii*
Preface *xv*

chapter 1
GEAR-DESIGN TRENDS *1.1*

Manufacturing Trends *1.4*
1.1 Small, Low-Cost Gears for Toys, Gadgets, and Mechanisms *1.5*
1.2 Appliance Gears *1.7*
1.3 Machine Tools *1.9*
1.4 Control Gears *1.9*
1.5 Vehicle Gears *1.12*
1.6 Transportation Gears *1.14*
1.7 Marine Gears *1.16*
1.8 Aerospace Gears *1.19*
1.9 Industrial Gearing *1.21*
1.10 Gears in the Oil and Gas Industry *1.23*
1.11 Mill Gears *1.24*

Selection of the Right Kind of Gear *1.26*

1.12 External Spur Gears *1.27*
1.13 External Helical Gears *1.30*
1.14 Internal Gears *1.31*
1.15 Straight Bevel Gears *1.33*
1.16 Zerol Bevel Gears *1.36*
1.17 Spiral Bevel Gears *1.37*
1.18 Hypoid Gears *1.38*
1.19 Face Gears *1.40*
1.20 Crossed-Helical Gears (Nonenveloping Worm Gears) *1.41*
1.21 Single-Enveloping Worm Gears *1.43*
1.22 Double-Enveloping Worm Gears *1.47*
1.23 Spiroid Gears *1.49*

chapter 2
PRELIMINARY DESIGN CONSIDERATIONS *2.1*

Stress Formulas *2.1*

2.1 Calculated Stresses *2.4*
2.2 Gear-Design Limits *2.5*
2.3 Gear-Strength Calculations *2.7*
2.4 Gear Surface-Durability Calculations *2.14*
2.5 Gear Scoring *2.24*
2.6 Thermal Limits *2.32*

Preliminary Estimate of Gear Size *2.34*

2.7 Gear Specifications *2.35*
2.8 Size of Spur and Helical Gears by *Q*-Factor Method *2.36*
2.9 Indexes of Tooth Loading *2.41*
2.10 Estimating Spur- and Helical-Gear Size by *K*-Factor *2.44*
2.11 Estimating Bevel-Gear Size *2.47*
2.12 Estimating Worm-Gear Size *2.51*
2.13 Estimating Spiroid-Gear Size *2.53*

Data Needed for Gear Drawings *2.55*

2.14 Gear Dimensional Data *2.55*
2.15 Gear-Tooth Tolerances *2.65*
2.16 Gear Material and Heat Treat Data *2.67*
2.17 Enclosed Gear Unit Requirements *2.68*

chapter 3
DESIGN FORMULAS *3.1*

Calculation of Gear-Tooth Data *3.1*

3.1 Number of Pinion Teeth *3.3*
3.2 Hunting Teeth *3.8*
3.3 Spur-Gear-Tooth Proportions *3.9*
3.4 Root Fillet Radii of Curvature *3.12*

3.5 Long-Addendum Pinions *3.14*
3.6 Tooth Thickness *3.19*
3.7 Chordal Dimensions *3.21*
3.8 Degrees Roll and Limit Diameter *3.23*
3.9 Form Diameter and Contact Ratio *3.29*
3.10 Spur-Gear Dimension Sheet *3.31*
3.11 Internal-Gear Dimension Sheet *3.33*
3.12 Helical-Gear Tooth Proportions *3.39*
3.13 Helical-Gear Dimension Sheet *3.43*
3.14 Bevel-Gear Tooth Proportions *3.45*
3.15 Straight-Bevel-Gear Dimension Sheet *3.51*
3.16 Spiral-Bevel-Gear Dimension Sheet *3.54*
3.17 Zerol-Bevel-Gear Dimension Sheet *3.56*
3.18 Hypoid-Gear Calculations *3.58*
3.19 Face-Gear Calculations *3.59*
3.20 Crossed-Helical-Gear Proportions *3.62*
3.21 Single-Enveloping-Worm-Gear Proportions *3.65*
3.22 Single-Enveloping Worm Gears *3.66*
3.23 Double-Enveloping Worm Gears *3.69*

Gear-Rating Practice *3.73*

3.24 General Considerations in Rating Calculations *3.74*
3.25 General Formulas for Tooth Bending Strength and Tooth Surface Durability *3.78*
3.26 Geometry Factors for Strength *3.88*
3.27 Overall Derating Factor for Strength *3.93*
3.28 Geometry Factors for Durability *3.108*
3.29 Overall Derating Factor for Surface Durability *3.112*
3.30 Load Rating of Worm Gearing *3.115*
3.31 Design Formulas for Scoring *3.128*
3.32 Trade Standards for Rating Gears *3.141*
3.33 Vehicle Gear-Rating Practice *3.143*
3.34 Marine Gear-Rating Practice *3.146*
3.35 Oil and Gas Industry Gear Rating *3.148*
3.36 Aerospace Gear-Rating Practices *3.150*

chapter 4
GEAR MATERIALS *4.1*

Steels for Gears *4.4*

4.1 Mechanical Properties *4.5*
4.2 Heat-Treating Techniques *4.6*
4.3 Heat-Treating Data *4.11*
4.4 Hardness Tests *4.13*

Localized Hardening of Gear Teeth *4.16*

4.5 Carburizing *4.17*
4.6 Nitriding *4.24*
4.7 Induction Hardening of Steel *4.30*
4.8 Flame Hardening of Steel *4.38*

4.9 Combined Heat Treatments *4.39*
4.10 Metallurgical Quality of Steel Gears *4.40*

Cast Irons for Gears *4.47*

4.11 Gray Cast Iron *4.48*
4.12 Ductile Iron *4.51*
4.13 Sintered Iron *4.52*

Nonferrous Gear Metals *4.53*

4.14 Kinds of Bronze *4.54*
4.15 Standard Gear Bronzes *4.57*

Nonmetallic Gears *4.57*

4.16 Thermosetting Laminates *4.58*
4.17 Nylon Gears *4.61*

chapter 5
GEAR-MANUFACTURING METHODS *5.1*

Gear-Tooth Cutting *5.3*

5.1 Gear Hobbing *5.4*
5.2 Shaping—Pinion Cutter *5.10*
5.3 Shaping—Rack Cutter *5.16*
5.4 Cutting Bevel Gears *5.23*
5.5 Gear Milling *5.26*
5.6 Broaching Gears *5.31*
5.7 Punching Gears *5.34*
5.8 G-TRAC Generating *5.36*

Gear Grinding *5.38*

5.9 Form Grinding *5.39*
5.10 Generating Grinding—Disc Wheel *5.46*
5.11 Generating Grinding—Bevel Gears *5.51*
5.12 Generating Grinding—Threaded Wheel *5.53*
5.13 Thread Grinding *5.57*

Gear Shaving, Rolling, and Honing *5.59*

5.14 Rotary Shaving *5.60*
5.15 Rack Shaving *5.65*
5.16 Gear Rolling *5.66*
5.17 Gear Honing *5.70*

Gear Measurement *5.72*

5.18 Gear Accuracy Limits *5.73*
5.19 Machines to Measure Gears *5.80*

Gear Casting and Forming *5.86*

5.20 Cast and Molded Gears *5.86*

5.21 Sintered Gears *5.88*
5.22 Cold-Drawn Gears and Rolled Worm Threads *5.89*

chapter 6
DESIGN OF TOOLS TO MAKE GEAR TEETH *6.1*

6.1 Shaper Cutters *6.2*
6.2 Gear Hobs *6.10*
6.3 Spur-Gear Milling Cutters *6.27*
6.4 Worm Milling Cutters and Grinding Wheels *6.29*
6.5 Gear-Shaving Cutters *6.36*
6.6 Punching Tools *6.39*
6.7 Sintering Tools *6.40*

chapter 7
THE KINDS AND CAUSES OF GEAR FAILURES *7.1*

Analysis of Gear-System Problems *7.2*
7.1 Determining the Problem *7.2*
7.2 Possible Causes of Gear-System Failures *7.3*
7.3 Incompatibility in Gear Systems *7.7*
7.4 Investigation of Gear Systems *7.9*

Analysis of Tooth Failures and Gear Bearing Failures *7.11*
7.5 Nomenclature of Gear Failure *7.11*
7.6 Tooth Breakage *7.17*
7.7 Pitting of Gear Teeth *7.19*
7.8 Scoring Failures *7.22*
7.9 Wear Failures *7.24*
7.10 Gearbox Bearings *7.28*
7.11 Rolling-Element Bearings *7.29*
7.12 Sliding-Element Bearings *7.32*

Some Causes of Gear Failure other than Excess Transmitted Load *7.35*
7.13 Overload Gear Failures *7.35*
7.14 Gear Casing Problems *7.37*
7.15 Lubrication Failures *7.39*
7.16 Thermal Problems in Fast-Running Gears *7.47*

chapter 8
SPECIAL DESIGN PROBLEMS *8.1*

8.1 Center Distance Problems *8.1*
8.2 Profile Modification Problems *8.12*
8.3 Load Rating Problem *8.22*

chapter 9
APPENDIX MATERIAL *9.1*

9.1 Introduction to Gears (Supplement to Chap. 1) *9.1*
9.2 Dynamic Load Theory (Supplement to Chap. 2) *9.9*
9.3 Highest and Lowest Points of Single-Tooth Contact (Supplement to Chaps. 2 and 3) *9.15*
9.4 Layout of Large Circles by Calculation (Supplement to Chaps. 2 and 3) *9.17*
9.5 Special Calculations for Spur Gears (Supplement to Chap. 3) *9.19*
9.6 Special Calculations for Internal Gears (Supplement to Chap. 3) *9.27*
9.7 Special Calculations for Helical Gears (Supplement to Chap. 3) *9.31*
9.8 Summary Sheets for Bevel Gears (Supplement to Chap. 3) *9.36*
9.9 Complete AGMA and ISO Formulas for Bending Strength and Surface Durability (Supplement to Chap. 3) *9.37*
9.10 Profile Modification Calculation Procedure (Supplement to Chap. 3) *9.48*
9.11 The Basics of Gear-Tooth Measurement for Accuracy and Size (Supplement to Chap. 5) *9.50*
9.12 Shaper-Cutter Tooth Thickness (Supplement to Chap. 6) *9.54*
9.13 General Method for Determining Tooth Thicknesses When Helical Gears Are Operated on Spread Centers (Supplement to Chap. 8) *9.59*
9.14 Calculation of Geometry Factor for Scoring (Supplement to Chap. 3) *9.63*

References
Index

foreword

At a time when the gear industry is sorely in need of design and manufacturing engineers, Darle Dudley's book arrives as a source of new information for the student and professional alike.

This major work points up the challenge of an industry that will be with us for many generations. It should become the bible of the industry, and its guidelines will serve the engineering body responsible for present and future standards of gearing.

Most textbooks published on the art of gearing are over 30 years old. This treatise encompasses years of development in which Mr. Dudley has faithfully participated and recorded. Recognized nationally and internationally as one of the foremost contributors to the advancement of gear design, Mr. Dudley has also received the E. P. Connell Award, which is the highest honor of the American Gear Manufacturers Association.

In these pages, the reader will discover Mr. Dudley's contribution to the state of the art of gearing.

December 1983
Arlington, Virginia

WILLIAM W. INGRAHAM
Executive Director
American Gear Manufacturers Association

preface

This is a revision of the book *Practical Gear Design*, published by the McGraw-Hill Book Company in 1954. This work is now called a "handbook" because of its broader coverage of subjects pertaining to gear design and the recognition that the content of the original book made it a *lasting* reference that saw constant use in day-to-day gear work.

Although this revision is broader in scope and has more pages, the plan of the book and the way many aspects of the gear art are treated has been kept just the same. Those familiar with *Practical Gear Design* will find themselves right at home as they read the *Handbook of Practical Gear Design*. The main difference is that new things learned in the 1960s and 1970s about how to better design, build, and use gears are included in this book. Gear technology has made rapid progress, just as space technology and computer technology have made rapid progress in the same time period.

This book has been written with the general engineer or technician in mind. It is my hope that alert shop planning engineers, tool engineers, engineering students, cost analysts, shop supervisors, and progressive machine-tool operators will find this book of value and assistance when confronted with problems involving gear design or manufacture or involving failure in service.

The scope of the work includes the geometry of gear design, manufacturing methods, and causes of gear installation failures. A gear design is not good design unless it is practical and economical to manufacture and unless it is well enough thought out to meet all the hazards of service in the field. It has been my aim to show how a *practical* gear design must be based on the limitations and availability of machine tools and tooling setups.

As in most phases of engineering, there are often divergent methods advocated to gain a given result. The gearing art is no exception. For instance, in Chapter 5, equations are given to calculate the length of time required to make gear teeth by various processes. Several experts in the gear field reviewed the data and equations in this chapter. Their comments indicated that the data would be very helpful to most designers, but they also pointed out that some gear designs would be difficult to manufacture and a shop might—through no fault of its own—be unable to meet production rates estimated by the material in this chapter.

In spite of all that has been learned about how to design gears, how to rate them for load-carrying capacity, and how to use them properly in service, there is still an urgent need to do more bench testing, to make better analyses of gear-tooth stresses, and to learn more about effects of lubricants, variations in gear material quality, and peculiarities of the environment (corrosion, dirt in the oil, temperature transients, load transients, etc.) in which the gears operate.

This book refers to many standards for gears that are in current use. It can be expected that present standards will be revised and enlarged as gear technology progresses. This book, in several places, advises the reader to expect more and better standards for gear work as the years go by. The book gives practical advice about what to do, but it also cautions the reader to always consider the latest rules and data in a constantly changing array of gear trade standards.

ACKNOWLEDGEMENTS

The writing of a technical book covering a whole field of work is a very sizable project. The author is faced not only with organizing and writing the text material and equations, but also with computing data, preparing tables and figures, and locating good reference data for a multiplicity of items.

I wish to wholeheartedly thank all of the people who have helped prepare this work.

The initial typing and equation work was done by Mrs. M. Irene Galarneau (a longtime secretary of mine), Mrs. Violet Daughters, and Mrs. Dorothy Dudley (my wife). The final typing, proofreading, and preparation of illustrations was done by Mrs. Carolyn Strickland (a technical assistant). She also wrote Section 9.1.

Many of the illustrations in the book have been furnished by companies which have also helped me get items of technical data. (Note the company names given in the figure legends.) The assistance of all of these companies is greatly appreciated.

The American Gear Manufacturers Association (AGMA) has been most helpful to me. The officers and staff are dedicated to the advancement of gear technology and have long provided forums for the discussion and evaluation of gear experience. The great body of standards that have been issued by AGMA is of immense reference value. The reader will note that this book has made much use of AGMA standards.

I wish to particularly acknowledge the assistance of a few individuals with unusual knowledge and experience in the gear trade.

Dr. Hans Winter of the Technical University of Munich in Germany (Technische Universität München) has reviewed parts of this book and has helped me obtain data and a better understanding of the many aspects of gear research and gear rating.

Dr. Giovanni Castellani, a gear consultant in Modena, Italy, has helped me in comparing European and American gear rating practices and gear-tooth accuracy limits.

Mr. Eugene Shipley of Mechanical Technology Inc. in Latham, New York, has helped me—on the basis of his worldwide experience with gears in service—in many discussions about gear wear and gear failures.

Dr. Daniel Diesburg of the Climax Molybdenum Company in Ann Arbor, Michigan, was most helpful in reviewing data on gear metals and gear heat-treating procedures.

Mr. Dennis Townsend of the NASA Lewis Research Center in Cleveland, Ohio, has done unusual research work and also has brought together many key people in the gear trade under the auspices of ASME international meetings. The international ASME gear meeting in Chicago, Illinois, in 1977 was of much value to me.

Dr. Aizoh Kubo of Kyoto University in Kyoto, Japan, has directly contributed to this book in the section on dynamic loading. Indirectly, he has helped me greatly in getting to know the leading people in gear research in Japan.

While I acknowledge with much thanks the assistance of these and many other experts during this work, I must accept the responsibility for having made the final decisions on the technical content of this book. I have tried to present a fair consensus of opinion and the best gear design guidance from all the somewhat divergent theories and practices in the gear field.

San Diego, California
December 7, 1983

DARLE W. DUDLEY

chapter 1

Gear-Design Trends

Gears are used in most types of machinery. Like nuts and bolts, they are a common machine element which will be needed from time to time by almost all machine designers. Gears have been in use for over three thousand years,* and they are an important element in all manner of machinery used in current times.

Gear design is a highly complicated art. The constant pressure to build less expensive, quieter running, lighter weight, and more powerful machinery has resulted in a steady change in gear designs. At present much is known about gear load-carrying capacity, and many complicated processes for making gears are available.

The industrialized nations are all doing gear research work in university laboratories and in manufacturing companies. Even less-developed countries are doing a certain amount of research work in the mathematics of gears and in gear applications of particular interest. At the 1981 International Sympo-

*The book *Evolution of the Gear Art*, 1969, by D. W. Dudley gives a brief review of the history of gears through the ages. Consult the reference section at the end of the book for complete data on this book and on other important references.

TABLE 1.1 Glossary of Gear Nomenclature, Chap. 1

Gear A geometric shape that has teeth uniformly spaced around the circumference. In general, a gear is made to mesh its teeth with another gear. (A *sprocket* looks like a gear but is intended to drive a chain instead of another gear.)
Pinion When two gears mesh together, the *smaller* of the two is called the *pinion.* The larger is called the *gear.*
Ratio *Ratio* is an abbreviation for gear-tooth ratio, which is the number of teeth on the gear divided by the number of teeth on its mating pinion.
Module A measure of tooth size in the metric system. In units, it is millimeters of pitch diameter *per tooth.* As the tooth size increases, the module also increases. Modules usually range from 1 to 25.
Diametral pitch A measure of tooth size in the English system. In units, it is the *number of teeth* per inch of pitch diameter. As the tooth size increases, the diametral pitch *de*creases. Diametral pitches usually range from 25 to 1.
Circular pitch The circular distance from a point on one gear tooth to a like point on the next tooth, taken along the *pitch circle.* Two gears must have the same circular pitch to mesh with each other. As they mesh, their pitch circles will be tangent to one another.
Pitch diameter The diameter of the pitch circle of a gear.
Addendum The radial height of a gear tooth above the pitch circle.
Dedendum The radial depth of a gear tooth below the pitch circle.
Whole depth The total radial height of a gear tooth. (Whole depth = addendum + dedendum.)
Pressure angle The slope of the gear tooth at the pitch-circle position. (If the pressure angle were 0°, the tooth flank would be radial.)
Helix angle The inclination of the tooth in a lengthwise direction. (If the helix angle is 0°, the tooth is parallel to the axis of the gear—and is really a spur-gear tooth.)
Spur gears Gears with teeth straight and parallel to the axis of rotation.
Helical gears Gears with teeth that spiral around the body of the gear.
External gears Gears with teeth on the outside of a cylinder.
Internal gears Gears with teeth on the inside of a hollow cylinder. (The mating gear for an internal gear must be an external gear.)
Bevel gears Gears with teeth on the outside of a conical-shaped body (normally used on 90° axes).
Worm gears Gearsets in which one member of the pair has teeth wrapped around a cylindrical body like screw threads. (Normally this gear, called the *worm,* has its axis at 90° to the worm-gear axis.)
Face gears Gears with teeth on the *end* of the cylinder.
Spiroid gears A family of gears in which the tooth design is in an intermediate zone between bevel-, worm-, and face-gear design. The Spiroid design is patented by the Spiroid Division of Illinois Tool Works, Chicago, Illinois.
Transverse section A section through a gear *perpendicular to the axis* of the gear.
Axial section A section through a gear in a lengthwise direction that *contains the axis* of the gear.
Normal section A section through the gear that is *perpendicular to the tooth* at the pitch circle. (For spur gears, a normal section is also a transverse section.)

Notes:
1. For terms relating to gear materials, see Chap. 4.
2. For terms relating to gear manufacture, see Chap. 5.
3. For terms relating to the specifics of gear design and rating, see Chaps. 2 and 3.
4. For a simple introduction to gears, see Chap. 9, Sec. 9.1.

TABLE 1.2 Gear Terms, Symbols, and Units, Chap. 1

Term	Metric		English		First reference or definition
	Symbol	Units*	Symbol	Units*	
Module	m	mm	—	—	Eq. (1.1)
Pressure angle	α	deg	ϕ	deg	Figs. 1.18, 1.33
Number of teeth or threads	z	—	N	—	
Number of teeth, pinion	z_1	—	N_P or n	—	Eq. (1.7)
Number of teeth, gear	z_2	—	N_G or N	—	Eq. (1.7)
Ratio (gear or tooth ratio)	u	—	m_G	—	$u = z_2/z_1$ ($m_G = N_G/N_P$)
Diametral pitch	—	—	P_d or P	in.$^{-1}$	Eq. (1.1)
Pi	π	—	π	—	$\pi \cong 3.1415927$
Pitch diameter, pinion	d_{p1}	mm	d	in.	Fig. 1.18, Eq. (1.3)
Pitch diameter, gear	d_{p2}	mm	D	in.	Fig. 1.18, Eq. (1.3)
Base (circle) diameter, pinion	d_{b1}	mm	d_b	in.	Fig. 1.18
Base (circle) diameter, gear	d_{b2}	mm	D_b	in.	Fig. 1.18
Outside diameter, pinion	d_{a1}	mm	d_o	in.	Fig. 1.18 (abbrev. O.D.)
Outside diameter, gear	d_{a2}	mm	D_o	in.	Fig. 1.18
Form diameter	d'_f	mm	d_f	in.	Fig. 1.18
Circular pitch	p	mm	p	in.	Fig. 1.18, Eq. (1.2)
Addendum	h_a	mm	a	in.	Fig. 1.18
Dedendum	h_f	mm	b	in.	Fig. 1.18
Face width	b	mm	F	in.	Fig. 1.18
Whole depth	h	mm	h_t	in.	Fig. 1.18
Working depth	h'	mm	h_k	in.	Fig. 1.18
Clearance	c	mm	c	in.	Fig. 1.18
Chordal thickness	$\bar{s}$	mm	t_c	in.	Fig. 1.18
Chordal addendum	$\bar{h}_a$	mm	a_c	in.	Fig. 1.18
Tooth thickness	s	mm	t	in.	Fig. 1.18
Center distance	a	mm	C	in.	Eq. (1.4)
Circular pitch, normal	p_n	mm	p_n	in.	Fig. 1.19, Eq. (1.5)
Circular pitch, transverse	p_t	mm	p_t	in.	Fig. 1.19, Eq. (1.5)
Lead angle	γ	deg	λ	deg	Fig. 1.19, Eq. (1.33)
Helix angle	β	deg	ψ	deg	Fig. 1.19, Eq. (1.8)
Pitch, base or normal	p_b or p_{bn}	mm	p_b or p_N	in.	Fig. 1.19
Diametral pitch, normal	—	—	P_n	in.$^{-1}$	Eq. (1.10)
Axial pitch	p_x	mm	p_x	in.	Eq. (1.11)
Inside (internal) diameter	d_i	mm	D_i	in.	Fig. 1.20, (abbrev. I.D.)
Root diameter, pinion	d_{f1}	mm	d_R	in.	Fig. 1.29
Root diameter, gear	d_{f2}	mm	D_R	in.	Fig. 1.20
Pitch angle, pinion	δ'_1	deg	γ	deg	Fig. 1.21, Eq. (1.16)
Pitch angle, gear	δ'_2	deg	Γ	deg	Fig. 1.21, Eq. (1.16)
Root angle, pinion	δ_{f1}	deg	γ_R	deg	Fig. 1.21
Root angle, gear	δ_{f2}	deg	Γ_R	deg	Fig. 1.21
Face angle, pinion	δ_{a1}	deg	γ_o	deg	Fig. 1.21
Face angle, gear	δ_{a2}	deg	Γ_o	deg	Fig. 1.21
Dedendum angle	θ_f	deg	δ	deg	Fig. 1.21
Shaft angle	Σ	deg	Σ	deg	Fig. 1.21, Eq. (1.18)
Cone distance	R	mm	A	in.	Fig. 1.21
Circular (tooth) thickness	s	mm	t	in.	Fig. 1.21
Backlash	j	mm	B	in.	Fig. 1.21
Throat diameter of worm	d_{t1}	mm	d_t	in.	Fig. 1.29
Throat diameter of worm gear	d_{t2}	mm	D_t	in.	Fig. 1.29
Lead of worm	p_{zW}	mm	L_W	in.	Eq. (1.32)

*Abbreviations for units: mm = millimeters, in. = inches, deg = degrees.

sium on Gearing and Power Transmissions in Tokyo, Japan, 162 papers were presented by delegates from 24 nations. After excellent world gear conferences in Paris, France, in 1977 and Dubrovnik, Yugoslavia, in 1978, the even larger Tokyo gear conference in 1981 was a high-water mark in the gear art.

Most machine designers do not have the time to keep up with all the developments in the field of gear design. This makes it hard for them to quickly design gears which will be competitive with the best that are being used in their field. There is a great need for *practical* gear-design information. Even though there is a wealth of published information on gears, gear designers often find it hard to locate the information they need quickly. This book is written to help gear designers get the vital information they need as easily as possible.

Those who are just starting to learn about gears need to start by learning some basic words that have special meanings in the gear field. The glossary in Table 1.1 is intended to give simple definitions of these terms as they are understood by gear people. Table 1.2 shows the metric and English gear symbols for the terms which are used in Chap. 1. The Chap. 5 glossary (Table 5.1) defines gear-manufacturing terms. See AGMA 112.05 (1976)* and AGMA 600.01 (1979) for English and metric gear nomenclature.

In the last chapter—an appendix chapter—Sec. 9.1 gives a simple explanation of some basics of gearing. Beginners will probably find it helpful to read Sec. 9.1 and the tables mentioned above before they continue with the Chap. 1 text.

MANUFACTURING TRENDS

Before plunging into the formulas for calculating gear dimensions, it is desirable to make a brief survey of how gears are presently being made and used in different applications.

The methods used to manufacture gears depend on design requirements, machine tools available, quantity required, cost of materials, and *tradition*. In each particular field of gear work, certain methods have become established as the *standard* way of making the gears. These methods tend to change from time to time, but the tradition of the industry tends to act as a brake to restrain any abrupt changes that result from technological devel-

*AGMA stands for the American Gear Manufacturers Association, and AGMA 112.05 refers to a specific published standard of AGMA. Complete titles of AGMA standards mentioned in the text are given in the references at the end of the book.

opments. The gear designer, studying gears as a whole, can get a good perspective of gear work by reviewing the methods of manufacture in each field.

1.1 Small, Low-Cost Gears for Toys, Gadgets, and Mechanisms

There is a large field of gear work in which tooth stresses are of almost no consequence. Speeds are slow, and life requirements do not amount to much. Almost any type of "cog" wheel which could transmit rotary motion might be used. In this sort of situation, the main thing the designer must look for is low cost and high volume of production.

The simplest type of gear drive—such as those used in toys—frequently uses punched gears. Pinions with small numbers of teeth may be die-cast or extruded. If loads are light enough and quietness of operation is desired, injection-molded gears and pinions may be used. Molded-plastic gears from a toy train are shown in Fig. 1.1. Things like film projectors, oscillating fans, cameras, cash registers, and calculators frequently need quiet-running gears to transmit insignificant amounts of power. Molded-plastic gears are widely used in such instances. It should be said, though, that the devices just mentioned often need precision-cut gears where loads and speeds become appreciable.

Die-cast gears of zinc alloy, brass, or aluminum are often used to make

FIG. 1.1 Plastic gears in a toy.

small, low-cost gears. This process is particularly favored where the gear wheel is integrally attached to some other element, such as a sheave, cam, or clutch member. The gear teeth and the special contours of whatever is attached to the gear may all be finished to close accuracy merely by die-casting the part in a precise metal mold. Many low-cost gadgets on the market today would be very much more expensive if it were necessary to machine all the complicated gear elements that are in them.

Metal forming is more and more widely used as a means of making small gear parts. Pinions and gears with small numbers of teeth may be cut from rod stock with cold-drawn or extruded teeth already formed in the rod. Figure 1.2 shows some rods with cold-drawn teeth. Small worms may have cold-rolled threads. The forming operations tend to produce parts with very smooth, work-hardened surfaces. This feature is important in many devices

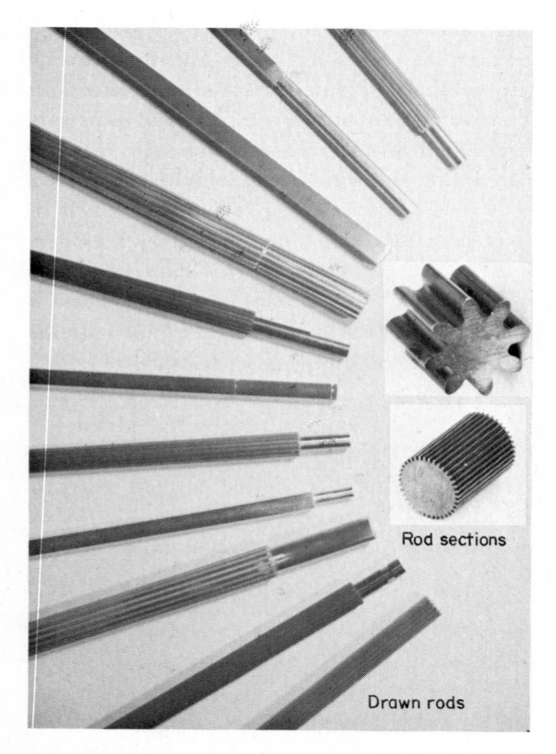

FIG. 1.2 Samples of cold-drawn rod stock for making gears and pinions. (*Courtesy of Rathbone Corp., Palmer, MA, U.S.A.*)

FIG. 1.3 Assortment of gears used in small mechanisms. (*Courtesy of Winzeler Manufacturing and Tool Co., Chicago, IL, U.S.A.*)

where the friction losses in the gearing tend to be the main factor in the power consumption of the device.

Figure 1.3 shows an assortment of stamped and molded gears used in small mechanisms.

1.2 Appliance Gears

Home appliances like washing machines, food mixers, and fans use large numbers of small gears. Because of competition, these gears must be made for only a relatively few cents apiece. Yet they must be quiet enough to suit a discriminating homemaker and must be able to endure for many years with little or no more lubrication than that given to them at the factory.

Medium-carbon-steel gears finished by conventional cutting used to be the standard in this field. Cut gears are still in widespread use, but the cutting is often done by high-speed automatic machinery. The worker on the cutting machine does little more than bring up trays of blanks and take away trays of finished parts.

Modern appliances are making more and more use of gears other than cut steel gears. Figure 1.4 shows some sintered-iron gears from an automatic washer. Sintered-iron gears are very inexpensive (in large quantities), run quietly, and frequently wear less than comparable cut gears. The sintered metal is porous and may be impregnated with a lubricant. It may also be

FIG. 1.4 Sintered-iron gears used in an automatic washing machine.

impregnated with copper to improve its strength. Gear teeth and complicated gear-blank shapes may all be completely finished in the sintering process. The tools needed to make a sintered gear may cost as much as $50,000, but this does not amount to much if 100,000 or more gears are to be made on semiautomatic machines.

Laminated gears using phenolic resins and cloth or paper have proved very good where noise reduction is a problem. The laminates in general have much more load-carrying capacity than molded-plastic gears. Nonmetallic gears with cut teeth do not suffer nearly so much from tooth inaccuracy as do metal gears. Under the same load, a laminated phenolic-resin gear tooth will bend about thirty times as much as a steel gear tooth! It has often been possible to take a set of steel gears which were wearing excessively because of tooth-error effects, replace one member with a nonmetallic gear, and have the set stand up satisfactorily.

Nylon gear parts have worked very well in situations in which wear resulting from high sliding velocity is a problem. The nylon material seems to have some of the characteristics of a solid lubricant. Nylon gearing has been used in some processing equipment where the use of a regular lubricant would pollute the material being processed.

1.3 Machine Tools

Accuracy and power-transmitting capacity are quite important in machine-tool gearing. Metal gears are usually used. The teeth are finished by some precise metal-cutting process.

The machine tool is often literally full of gears. Speed-change gears of the spur or helical type are used to control feed rate and work rotation. Index drives to work or table may be worm or bevel. Sometimes they are spur or helical. Many bevel gears are used at the right-angle intersections between shafts in bases and shafts in columns. Worm gears and spiral gears are also commonly used at these places.

Machine-tool gearing is often finish-machined in a medium-hard condition (250 to 300 HV or 25 to 30 HRC). Mild-alloy steels are frequently used because of their better machinability and physical properties. Cast iron is often favored for change gears because of the ease in casting the gear blank to shape, its excellent machinability, and its ability to get along with scanty lubrication.

The higher cutting speeds involved in cutting with tungsten carbide tools have forced many machine-tool builders to put in harder and more accurate gears. Shaving and grinding are commonly used to finish machine-tool gears to high tooth accuracy. In a few cases, machine-tool gears are being made with such top-quality features as full hardness (700 HV or 60 HRC), profile modification, and surface finish of about 0.5 μm or 20 μin.

The machine-tool designer has a hard time calculating gear sizes. Loads vary widely depending on feeds, speeds, size of work, and material being cut. It is anybody's guess what the user will do with the machine. Because machine tools are quite competitive in price, the overdesigned machine may be too expensive to sell. In general, the designer is faced with the necessity of putting in gears which have more capacity than the average load, knowing that the machine tool is apt to be neglected or overloaded on occasions.

Figure 1.5 shows an example of machine-tool gears.

1.4 Control Gears

The guns on ships, helicopters, and tanks are controlled by gear trains with the backlash held to the lowest possible limits. The primary job of these gears is to transmit motion. What power they may transmit is secondary to their job of precise control of angular motion. In power gearing, a worn-out gear is one with broken teeth or bad tooth-surface wear. In the control-gear field, a worn-out gear may be one whose thickness has been reduced by as small an amount as 0.01 mm (0.0004 in.)!

FIG. 1.5 Example of change gears on a machine tool. (*Courtesy of Warner & Swasey Co., Cleveland, OH, U.S.A.*)

Some of the most spectacular control gears are those used to drive radio telescopes and satellite tracking antennas. These gears are so large that the only practical way to make them is to cut rack sections and then bend each section into an arc of a circle. Figure 1.6 shows an example of a very large antenna drive made this way. The teeth on the rack sections are cut so that they will have the correct tooth dimensions when they are bent to form part of the circular gear.

The radar units on an aircraft carrier use medium-pitch gears of fairly large size. Radar-unit gearing is generally critical on backlash, must handle rather high momentary loads, and must last for many years with somewhat marginal lubrication. (Radar gears are often somewhat in the open, and therefore can only use grease lubrication.)

Control gears are usually spur, bevel, or worm. Helical gears are used to a limited extent. Control gears are often in the fine-pitch range—1.25 module (20 diametral pitch) or finer. Figure 1.7 shows a control device with many small gears.

In a few cases, control gears become quite large. The gears which train a main battery must be very rugged. The reaction on the gears when a main battery is fired can be terrific.

Control gears are usually made of medium-alloy, medium-carbon steels. In many cases, they are hardened to a medium hardness before final machining. In other cases, they are hardened to a moderately high hardness after final machining. These gears need hardness mainly to limit wear. Any hardening done after final finishing of the teeth must be done in such a way as to give only negligible dimensional change or distortion. To eliminate backlash, it is necessary to size the gear teeth almost perfectly (or use special "antibacklash" gear arrangements).

Shaving and/or grinding are used to control tooth thickness to the very close limits needed in control gearing. The inspection of control gears is usually based on checking machines which measure the variation in center distance when a master pinion or rack is rolled through mesh with the gear being checked. A spring constantly holds the master and the gear being checked in tight mesh. The chart obtained from such a checking machine gives a very clear picture of both the tooth thickness of the gear being checked and the variations in backlash as the gear is rolled through mesh. If

FIG. 1.6 Gears are used to position large radio telescopes. (*Courtesy of Harris Corporation, Melbourne, FL, U.S.A.*)

FIG. 1.7 Control device with many small gears.

the backlash variation can be held to acceptable limits in control-gear sets, there is usually no need to know the exact involute and spacing accuracy. In some types of radar and rocket-tracking equipment, control-gear teeth must be spaced very accurately with regard to accumulated error. For instance, it may be necessary to have every tooth all the way around a gear wheel within its true position within about 10 seconds of arc. On a 400-mm (15.7-in.) wheel, this would mean that every tooth had to be correctly spaced with respect to every other tooth within 0.01 mm (0.0004 in.). This kind of accuracy can be achieved only by special gear-cutting techniques. Inspection of such gears generally requires the use of gear-checking machines that are equipped to measure accumulated spacing error. The equipment commonly used will measure any angle to within 1 second of arc or better.

1.5 Vehicle Gears

The automobile normally uses spur and helical gears in the transmission and bevel gears in the rear end. If the car is a front-end drive, bevel gears may still be used or helical gears may be used. Automatic transmissions are now widely used. This does not eliminate gears, however. Most automatic transmissions have more gears than manual transmissions.

Automotive gears are usually cut from low-alloy-steel forgings. At the time of tooth cutting, the material is not very hard. After tooth cutting, the gears are case-carburized and quenched. Quenching dies are frequently used to minimize distortion. The composition of heats (batches) of steel is watched carefully, and all steps in manufacture are closely controlled with the aim of having each gear in a lot behave in the same way when it is carburized and quenched. Even if there is some distortion, it can be compensated for in machining, provided that each gear in a lot distorts uniformly and by the same amount. Since most automotive-gear teeth are not ground or machined after final hardening, it is essential that the teeth be quite accurate in the as-quenched condition. The only work that is done after hardening is the grinding of journal surfaces and sometimes a small amount of lapping. Finished automotive gears usually have a surface hardness of about 700 HV or 60 HRC and a core hardness of 300 HV or 30 HRC.

A variety of machines are used to cut automotive-gear teeth. In the past, shapers, hobbers, and bevel-gear generators were the conventional machines. New types of these machines are presently favored. For instance, multistation shapers, hobbers, and shaving machines are used. A blank is loaded on the machine at one station. While the worker is loading other stations, the piece is finished. This means that the worker spends no time waiting for work to be finished.

There is a wide variety of special design machines to hob, shape, shave, or grind automotive gears. The high production of only one (or two or three) gear design makes it possible to simplify a general-purpose machine tool and then build a kind of *processing center* where these functions are performed:

Incoming blank is checked for correct size.

Incoming blank is automatically loaded into the machine.

Teeth are cut (or finished) very rapidly.

Finished parts are checked for accuracy and sorted into categories of accept, rework, or reject.

Outgoing parts are loaded onto conveyor belts.

Sometimes the processing center may be developed to the point where cutting, heat treating, and finishing are all done in one processing center.

The gears for the smaller trucks and tractors are made somewhat like automotive gears, but the volume is not quite so great and sizes are larger. Examples of large-vehicle gears are shown in Figs. 1.8 and 1.9. Large tractors, large trucks, and "off-the-road" earth-moving vehicles use much larger gears and have much lower volume than automotive gears. More conventional machine tools are used. Special-purpose processing centers are generally not used.

Vehicle gears are heavily loaded for their size. Fortunately, their heaviest loads are of short duration. This makes it possible to design the gears for limited life at maximum motor torque and still have a gear that will last many years under average driving torque.

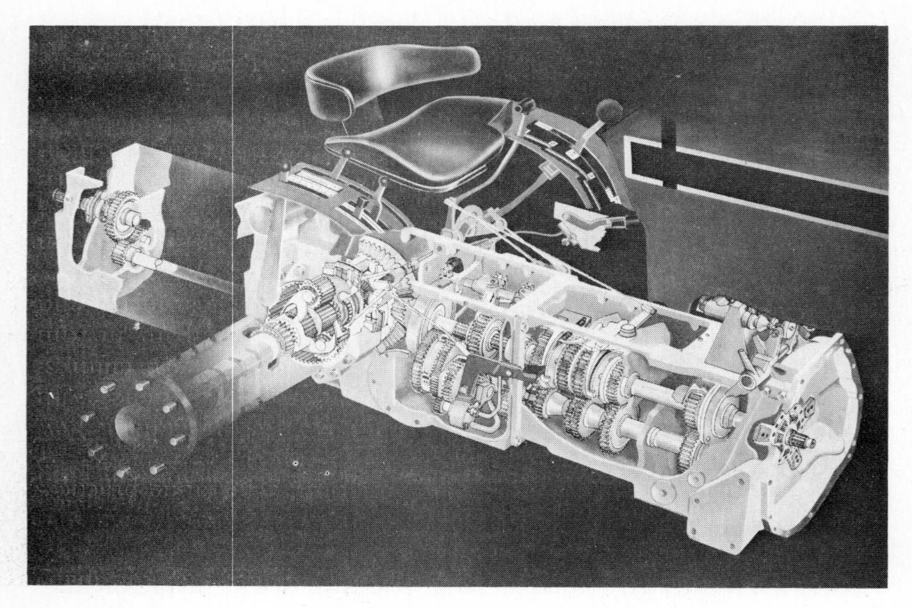

FIG. 1.8 Tractor power train. (*Courtesy of International Harvester Co., Chicago, IL, U.S.A.*)

Although carburizing has been widely used as a means of hardening automotive gears, other heat treatments are being used on an increased scale. Combinations of carburizing and nitriding are used. Processes of this type produce a shallower case for the same length of furnace time, but tend to make the case harder and the distortion less. Induction hardening is being used on some flywheel-starter gears as well as some other gears. Flame hardening is also used to a limited extent.

1.6 Transportation Gears

Buses, subways, mine cars, and railroad diesels all use large quantities of spur and helical gears. The gears range up to 0.75 meter (30 in.) or more in diameter. See Fig. 1.10. Teeth are sometimes as coarse as 20 module ($1\frac{1}{4}$ diametral pitch). Plain carbon and low-alloy steels are usually used. Much of the gearing is case-carburized and ground. Through-hardening is also used extensively. A limited use is being made of induction-hardened gears.

Transportation gears are heavily loaded. Frequently their heaviest loads last for a long period of time. Diesels that pull trains over high mountain ranges have long periods of operation at maximum torque. In some appli-

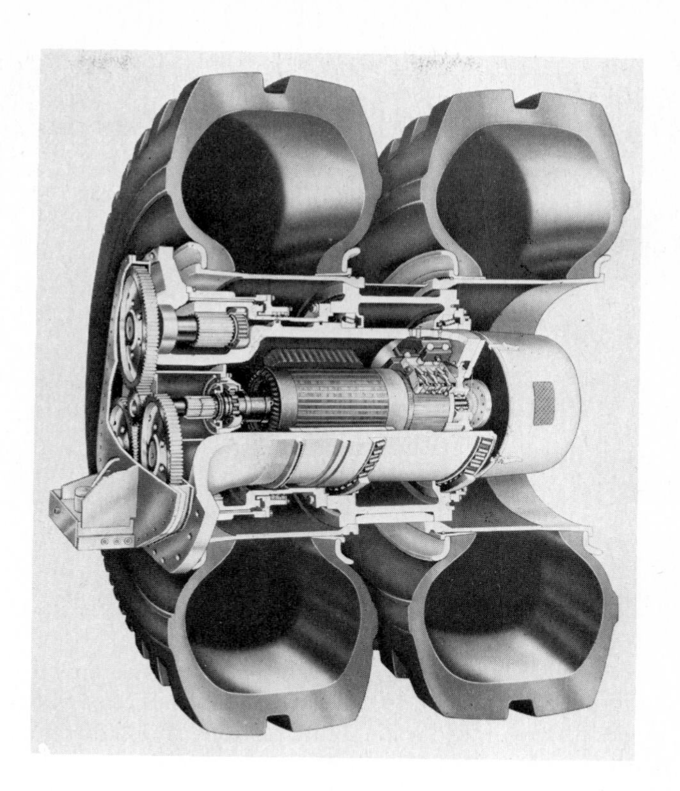

FIG. 1.9 Motorized wheels drive large earth-moving trucks. (*Courtesy of General Electric Co., Erie, PA, U.S.A.*)

FIG. 1.10 Railroad wheel drive. (*Courtesy of Electro-Motive Div., General Motors Corp., La Grange, IL, U.S.A.*)

cations, severe but infrequent shock loads are encountered. Shallow-hardening, medium-carbon steels seem to resist shock better than gears with a fully hardened carburized case. Both furnace and induction-hardening techniques are used to produce shallow-hardened teeth with high shock resistance.

Gear cutting is done mostly by conventional hobbing or shaping machines. Some gears are shaved and then heat-treated, while others are heat-treated after cutting and then ground. In this field of work, the volume of production is much lower and the size of parts is much larger than in the vehicle-gear field. Both these conditions make it harder to keep heat-treat distortion so well under control that the teeth may be finished before hardening.

The machine tools used to make transportation gears are quite conventional in design. The volume of production in this field is not large enough to warrant the use of the faster and more elaborate types of machine tools used in the vehicle-gear field.

1.7 Marine Gears

Powerful, high-speed, large-sized gears power merchant marine and navy fighting ships. Propeller drives on cargo ships use bull gears up to 5 meters (200 in.) in diameter. First reduction pitch-line speeds on some ships go up to 100 m/s (meters per second) or 20,000 fpm (feet per minute). Single propeller drives in a navy capital ship go up to 40,000 or more kW (kilowatts) of power. Some of the new cargo ships now in service have 30,000 kW [40,000 hp (horsepower)] per screw. Figure 1.11 shows a typical marine gear unit.

Marine gears are almost all made by finishing the teeth after hardening. Extreme accuracy in tooth spacing is required to enable the gearing to run satisfactorily at high speed. As many as 6000 pair of teeth may go through one gear mesh in a second's time!

There is an increasing use of carburized and ground gears in the marine field. The fully hard gear is smaller and lighter. This lowers pitch-line velocity and helps to keep the engine room reasonably small. Hard gears resist pitting and wear better than medium-hard gears (through-hardened gears).

Single helical gears have long been used for electric-power-generating equipment. Double helical gears have generally been used for the main propulsion drive of large ships. Single helical gears—with special thrust runners on the gears themselves—are coming into fairly common use even on larger ships.

FIG. 1.11 Partially assembled double-reduction marine gear unit. (*Courtesy of Transamerica Delaval Inc., Trenton, NJ, U.S.A.*)

Spur and bevel gear drives are often used on small ships, but they are seldom used on large turbine-drive ships. (Some slower-speed diesel-drive ships use spur gearing.)

Marine gears generally use a medium-alloy carbon steel. It is difficult or impossible to heat-treat plain carbon and low-alloy carbon steels in large sizes and get hardnesses over about 250 HV (250 HB) and a satisfactory metallurgical structure. Special welding techniques for large gear wheels make it possible to use medium-alloy steels and get good through-hardened gears up to 5 meters (200 in.) with gear-tooth hardness at 320 HV (300 HB) or higher. The smaller pinions are not welded and can usually be made up to 375 HV (350 HB) or higher in sizes up to 0.75 meter (30 in.).

There is growing use of carburized and ground gears for ship propulsion. Some of these gears are now being made as large as 2 meters (80 in.) in size. In a very large marine drive, it is quite common to have fully hard, carburized gears in the first reduction and medium-hard, through-hardened gears in the second reduction. Figure 1.12 shows a large marine drive unit being lowered into position.

The designer of marine gearing has to worry about both noise and load-

FIG. 1.12 Lowering a very powerful marine gear unit into the engine space of a supertanker. (*Courtesy of Transamerica Delaval Inc., Trenton, NJ, U.S.A.*)

carrying capacity. Although the tooth loads are not high compared with those on aircraft or transportation gearing, the capacity of the medium-hardness gearing to carry load is not high either. Considering that during its lifetime a high-speed pinion on a cargo ship may make 10 to 11 billion cycles of operation at full-rated torque, it can be seen that load-carrying capacity is very important.

Gear noise is a more or less critical problem on all ship gearing. The auxiliary gears that drive generators are frequently located quite close to passenger quarters. The peculiar high-pitched whine of a high-speed gear has a damaging effect on either an engine-room operator or a passenger who may be quartered near the engine room.

On fighting ships, there is the added problem of keeping enemy submarines from picking up water-borne noises and of operating your own ship quietly enough to be able to hear water-borne noises from an enemy.

Quietness is achieved on marine gears by making the gears with large numbers of teeth and cutting the teeth with extreme accuracy. A typical marine pinion may have around 60 teeth and a tooth-to-tooth spacing accuracy of 5 μm (0.0002 in.) maximum. A pinion of the same diameter used in a railroad-gear application would have about 15 teeth and a tooth-spacing accuracy of 12 μm (0.0005 in.). In the comparison just made, the marine-gear teeth would be only one-quarter the size of the railroad-gear teeth.

1.8 Aerospace Gears

Gears are used in a wide variety of applications on aircraft. Propellers are usually driven by single- or double-reduction gear trains. Accessories such as generators, pumps, hydraulic regulators, and tachometers are gear-driven. Many gears are required to drive these kinds of accessories even on *jet* engines—which have no propellers. Additional gears are used to raise landing wheels, open bomb-bay doors, control guns, operate computers for gun- or bomb-sighting devices, and control the pitch of propellers. Helicopters have a considerable amount of gearing to drive main rotors and tail rotors. (See Fig. 1.13.) Space vehicles often use power gears between the turbine and the booster fuel pumps.

The most distinctive types of aircraft gears are the power gears for propellers, accessories, and helicopter rotors. The control and actuating types of gears are not too different from what would be used for ground applications of a similar nature (except that they are often highly loaded and made of extra hard, high-quality steel).

Aircraft power gears are usually housed in aluminum or magnesium casings. The gears have thin webs and light cross sections in the rim or hub. Accessory gears are frequently made integral with an internally splined hub.

FIG. 1.13 Cutaway view of a helicopter gear unit. The last two stages are epicyclic. The first stage is spiral bevel. (*Courtesy of Bell Helicopter Textron, Fort Worth, TX, U.S.A.*)

Spur or bevel gears are usually used for accessory drives. Envelope clearances required to mount the accessory driven by the gear often make it necessary to use large center distance but narrow face width. This fact plus the thrust problem tends to rule out helical accessory gears. Propeller-drive gears have wider face widths. Spur, bevel, and helical gear drives are all currently in use. To get maximum power capacity with small size and lightweight gearboxes, it is often desirable to use an epicyclic gear train. In this kind of arrangement, there is only one output gear, but several pinions drive against it.

Aerospace power gears are usually made of high-alloy steel and fully hardened (on the tooth surface) by either case carburizing or nitriding. In some designs it is feasible to cut, shave, case-carburize, and grind only the journals. Many designs have such thin, nonsymmetrical webs as to require grinding after hardening. In general, piston-engine gearing runs more slowly than gas-turbine gearing. This makes some difference in the required accuracy. So far, many more piston-engine gears have been successfully finished before hardening than have gas-turbine gears.

The tooth loads and speeds are both very high on modern aircraft gears. The designer must achieve high tooth strength and high wear resistance. In addition, the thin oils used for low-temperature starting of military aircraft make the scoring type of lubrication failure a critical problem. Several special things are done to meet the demands of aircraft-gear service. Pinions are often made *long* addendum and gears *short* addendum to adjust the tip sliding velocities and to strengthen the pinion. Pinion tooth thicknesses are often increased at the expense of the gear to strengthen the pinion. High pressure angles, such as $22\frac{1}{2}°$, 25°, and $27\frac{1}{2}°$, are often used to reduce the contact stress on the tooth surface and increase the width of the tooth at the base. Involute-profile modifications are generally used to compensate for bending and to keep the tips from cutting the mating part.

The most highly developed aerospace gears are those used in rocket engines. The American projects *Vanguard*, *Mercury*, *Gemini*, and *Apollo* succeeded in boosting heavy payloads into orbit and eventually putting men on the moon. Unusual aerospace-gear capability was developed to meet the special requirements of power gears and control gears in space vehicles.

Materials and dimensional tolerances must be held under close control. A gear failure can frequently result in the loss of human life. The gear designer and builder both have a grave responsibility to furnish gears that are always sure to work satisfactorily. Extensive ground and flight testing are required to prove new designs.

The machine tools used to make aircraft gears are conventional hobbers, shapers, bevel-gear generators, shavers, and gear grinders. For the close tolerances, the machinery must be in the very best condition and precision tooling must be used. A complete line of checking equipment is needed so that involute profile, tooth spacing, helix angle, concentricity, and surface finish can be precisely measured.

1.9 Industrial Gearing

A wide range of types and sizes of gears that are used in homes, factories, and offices come under the "industrial" category (see examples in Figs. 1.14 and 1.15). In general, these gears involve electric power from a motor used to drive something. The driven device may be a pump, conveyor, or liquid stirring unit. It may also be a garage door opener, an air compressor for office refrigeration, a hoist, a winch, or a drive to mix concrete on a truck hauling the concrete to the job.

Industrial gearing is relatively low speed and low horsepower. Typical

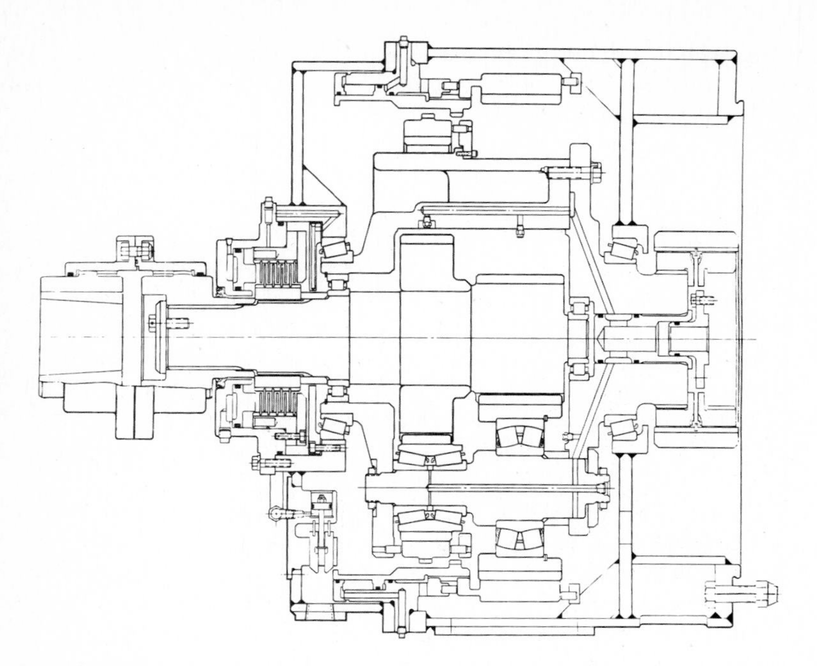

FIG. 1.14 Truck-mounted, two-speed gear unit used to drive a piston pump for oil-well fracturing. (*Courtesy of Sier-Bath Gear Co., Inc., North Bergen, NJ, U.S.A.*)

pitch-line speeds range from about 0.5 m/s to somewhat over 20 m/s (100 fpm to 4000 fpm). The types of gears may be spur, helical, bevel, worm, or Spiroid.* The power may range from less than 1 kW up to a few hundred kW. Typical input speeds are those of the electric motor, like 1800, 1500, 1200 and 1000 rpm (revolutions per minute).

The industrial field also includes drives with hydraulic motors. The field is characterized more by relatively low pitch-line speeds and power inputs than by the means of making or using the power.

Much of the gearing used in industrial work is made with through-hardened steel used *as cut*. There is, though, growing use of fully hardened gears where the size of the gearing or the life of the gearing is critical.

In the past, industrial gearing has not generally required long life or high reliability. The trend now—in the more important factory installations—is to obtain gears for moderately long life and reliability. For instance, a pump

*Spiroid is a registered trademark of the Spiroid Division of the Illinois Tool Works, Chicago, IL, U.S.A.

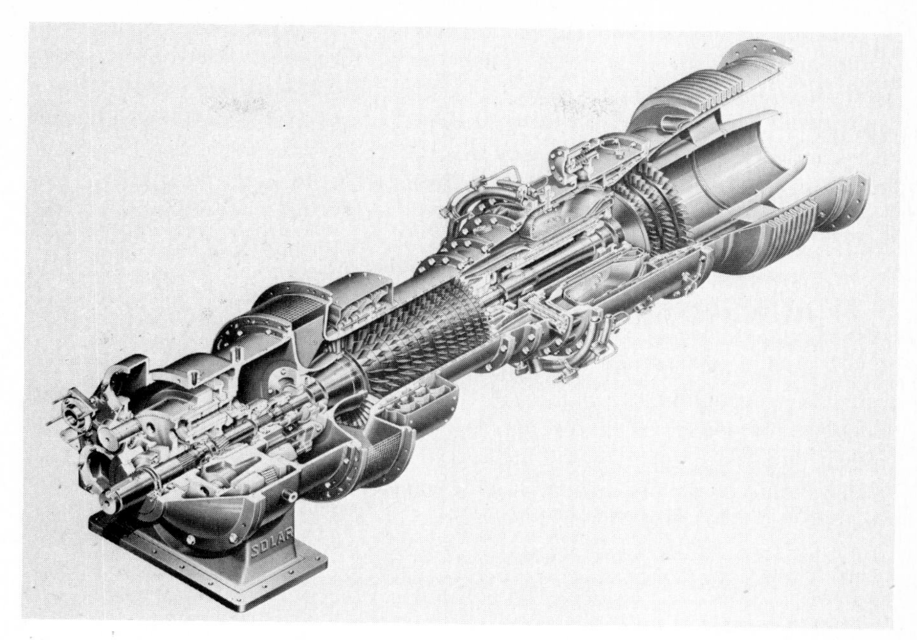

FIG. 1.15 Two-stage epicyclic gear, close-coupled to a high-speed gas turbine. This unit is used to drive a generator. (*Courtesy of Solar Turbines Incorporated, San Diego, CA, U.S.A.*)

drive with an 80 percent probability of running OK for 1000 hours might have been quite acceptable in the 1960s. The pump buyer in the 1980s may be more concerned with the cost of *downtime* and parts replacement, and may want to get gears good enough to have a 95 percent probability of lasting for 10,000 hours at rated load.

1.10 Gears in the Oil and Gas Industry

The production of petroleum products for the energy needs of the world requires a considerable amount of high-power, high-speed gearing. Gear units are used on oil platforms, pumping stations, drilling sites, refineries, and power stations. Usually the drive is a turbine, but it may be a large diesel engine. The power range goes from about 750 kW to over 50,000 kW. Pitch-line speeds range from 20 to 200 m/s (4000 to 40,000 fpm).

Bevel gears are used to a limited extent. Sometimes a stage of bevel gearing is needed to make a 90° turn in a power drive. (As an example, a horizontal-axis turbine may drive a vertical-axis compressor.)

Hardened and ground gears are widely used. With better facilities to grind and measure large gears and better equipment to case-harden large gears has come a strong tendency to design the powerful gears for turbine and diesel applications with fully hardened teeth. This reduces weight and size considerably. Pitch-line speeds become lower. Less space and less frame structure is required in a power package with the higher-capacity, fully hardened gears.

1.11 Mill Gears

Large mills make cement, grind iron ore, make rubber, roll steel, or do some other basic function. See Fig. 1.16. It is common to have a few thousand kilowatts of power going through two or more gear stages to drive some massive processing drum or rolling device.

The mill is usually powered by electric motors, but diesel engines or turbines may be used. The characteristic of mill drives is high power (and frequently unusually high torques).

A process mill will often run continuously for months at a time. Down-

FIG. 1.16 Large mill gear drive. Note twin power paths to bull gear. (*Courtesy of the Falk Corporation, Milwaukee, WI, U.S.A.*)

FIG. 1.17 Jumbo-size drive gear for a large mill application. (*Courtesy of David Brown Gear Industries, Huddersfield, England*)

time is critical because the output ceases completely when a mill unit is shut down.

Spur and helical gears are generally used. Pitch-line speeds are usually quite low. A first stage may be going around 20 m/s (4000 fpm), but the final stage in a mill may run as slowly as 0.1 to 1.0 m/s (20 to 200 fpm). Some bevel gears are also used—where axes must be at 90°.

The larger mill gears are generally made medium hard, but they may even be of a low hardness. The very large sizes involved often make it impractical to use the harder gears. There is an increasing use, though, of fully hardened mill gears up to gear pitch diameters of about 2 meters.

Mill gears are commonly made in sizes up to 11 meters. Such giant gears have to be made in two or more segments. Figure 1.17 shows a large two-segment mill gear. The segments are bolted together for cutting and then unbolted for shipping. (It is impractical to ship round pieces of metal over about 5 meters in diameter.)

SELECTION OF THE RIGHT KIND OF GEAR

The preceding sections gave some general information on how gears are made and used in different fields. In this part of the chapter, we shall concentrate on the problem of selecting the *right* kind of gear. The first step in designing a set of gears is to pick the right kind.

In many cases, the geometric arrangement of the apparatus which needs a gear drive will considerably affect the selection. If the gears must be on parallel axes, then spur or helical gears are the ones to use. Bevel and worm gears can be used if the axes are at right angles, but they are not feasible with parallel axes. If the axes are nonintersecting and nonparallel, then crossed-helical gears, hypoid gears, worm gears, or Spiroid gears may be used. Worm gears, though, are seldom used if the axes are not at right angles to each other. Table 1.3 shows in more detail the principal kinds of gears and how they are mounted.

There are no dogmatic rules that tell the designer just which gear to use. Frequently the choice is made after weighing the advantages and disadvantages of two or three kinds of gears. Some generalizations, though, can be made about gear selection.

In general, external helical gears are used when both high speeds and high horsepowers are involved. External helical gears have been built to carry as much as 45,000 kW of power on a single pinion and gear. And this is not the limit for designing helical gears—bigger ones could be built if anyone needed them. It is doubtful if any other kind of gear could be built and used successfully to carry this much power on a single mesh.

Bevel gears are ordinarily used on right-angle drives when high efficiency is needed. These gears can usually be designed to operate with 98 percent or better efficiency. Worm gears often have a hard time getting above 90 percent efficiency. Hypoid gears do not have as good efficiency as bevel gears, but they make up for this by being able to carry more power in the same space—provided the speeds are not too high.

TABLE 1.3 Kinds of Gears in Common Use

Parallel axes	Intersecting axes	Nonintersecting nonparallel axes
Spur external	Straight bevel	Crossed-helical
Spur internal	Zerol bevel	Single-enveloping worm
Helical external	Spiral bevel	Double-enveloping worm
Helical internal	Face gear	Hypoid
		Spiroid

Worm gears are ordinarily used on right-angle drives when very high ratios are needed. They are also widely used in low to medium ratios as packaged speed reducers. Single-thread worms and worm gears are used to provide the indexing accuracy on many machine tools. The critical job of indexing hobbing machines and gear shapers is nearly always done by a worm-gear drive.

Spur gears are relatively simple in design and in the machinery used to manufacture and check them. Most designers prefer to use them wherever design requirements permit.

Spur gears are ordinarily thought of as slow-speed gears, while helical gears are thought of as high-speed gears. If noise is not a serious design problem, spur gears can be used at almost any speeds which can be handled by other types of gears. Aircraft gas-turbine spur gears sometimes run at pitch-line speeds above 50 m/s (10,000 fpm). In general, though, spur gears are not used much above 20 m/s (4000 fpm).

1.12 External Spur Gears

Spur gears are used to transmit power between parallel shafts. They impose only radial loads on their bearings. The tooth profiles are ordinarily curved in the shape of an involute. Variations in center distance do not affect the trueness of the gear action unless the change is so great as to either jam the teeth into the root fillets of the mating member or withdraw the teeth almost out of action.

Spur-gear teeth may be hobbed, shaped, milled, stamped, drawn, sintered, cast, or shear-cut. They may be given a finishing operation such as grinding, shaving, lapping, rolling, or burnishing. Speaking generally, there are more kinds of machine tools and processes available to make spur gears than to make any other gear type. This favorable situation often makes spur gears the choice where cost of manufacture is a major factor in the gear design.

The standard measure of spur-gear tooth size in the metric system is the *module*. In the English system, the standard measure of tooth size is *diametral pitch*. The meanings are:

Module is millimeters of pitch diameter per tooth.

Diametral pitch is number of teeth per inch of pitch diameter (a reciprocal function).

Mathematically,

$$\text{Module} = \frac{25.400}{\text{diametral pitch}} \tag{1.1}$$

or
$$\text{Diametral pitch} = \frac{25.400}{\text{module}}$$

Curiously, module and diametral pitch are size dimensions which cannot be directly measured on a gear. They are really reference values used to calculate other size dimensions which are measurable.

Gears can be made to any desired module or diametral pitch, provided that cutting tools are available for that tooth size. To avoid purchasing cutting tools for too many different tooth sizes, it is desirable to pick a progression of modules and design to these except where design requirements force the use of special sizes. The following commonly used modules are recommended as a start for a design series: 25, 20, 15, 12, 10, 8, 6, 5, 4, 3, 2.5, 2.0, 1.5, 1, 0.8, 0.5. Many shops are equipped with English-system diametral pitches in this series: 1, $1\frac{1}{4}$, $1\frac{1}{2}$, $1\frac{3}{4}$, 2, $2\frac{1}{2}$, 3, 4, 5, 6, 8, 10, 12, 16, 20, 24, 32, 48, 64, 128. Considering the trend toward international trade, it is desirable to purchase new gear tools in standard metric sizes, so that they will be handy for gear work going to any part of the world. *(The standard measuring system of the world is the metric system.)*

Most designers prefer a 20° pressure angle for spur gears. In the past the $14\frac{1}{2}°$ pressure angle was widely used. It is not popular today because it gets into trouble with undercutting much more quickly than the 20° tooth when small numbers of pinion teeth are needed. Also, it does not have the load-carrying capacity of the 20° tooth. A pressure angle of $22\frac{1}{2}°$ or 25° is often used. Pressure angles above 20° give higher load capacity but may not run quite as smoothly or quietly.

Figure 1.18 shows the terminology used with a spur gear or a spur rack (a rack is a section of a spur gear with an *infinitely* large pitch diameter).

The following formulas apply to spur gears in all cases:

$$\text{Circular pitch} = \text{pi} \times \text{module} \qquad \text{Metric} \quad (1.2a)$$
$$= \text{pi} \div \text{diametral pitch} \qquad \text{English} \quad (1.2b)$$
$$\text{Pitch diameter} = \text{no. of teeth} \times \text{module} \qquad \text{Metric} \quad (1.3a)$$
$$= \text{no. of teeth} \div \text{diametral pitch} \qquad \text{English} \quad (1.3b)$$

The *nominal* center distance is equal to the sum of the pitch diameter of the pinion and the pitch diameter of the gear divided by 2:

$$\text{Center distance} = \frac{\text{pinion pitch dia.} + \text{gear pitch dia.}}{2} \qquad (1.4)$$

Since the center distance is a machined dimension, it may not come out to be exactly what the design calls for. In addition, it is common practice to use a slightly larger center distance to increase the operating pressure angle. For instance, if the actual center is made 1.7116 percent larger, gears cut

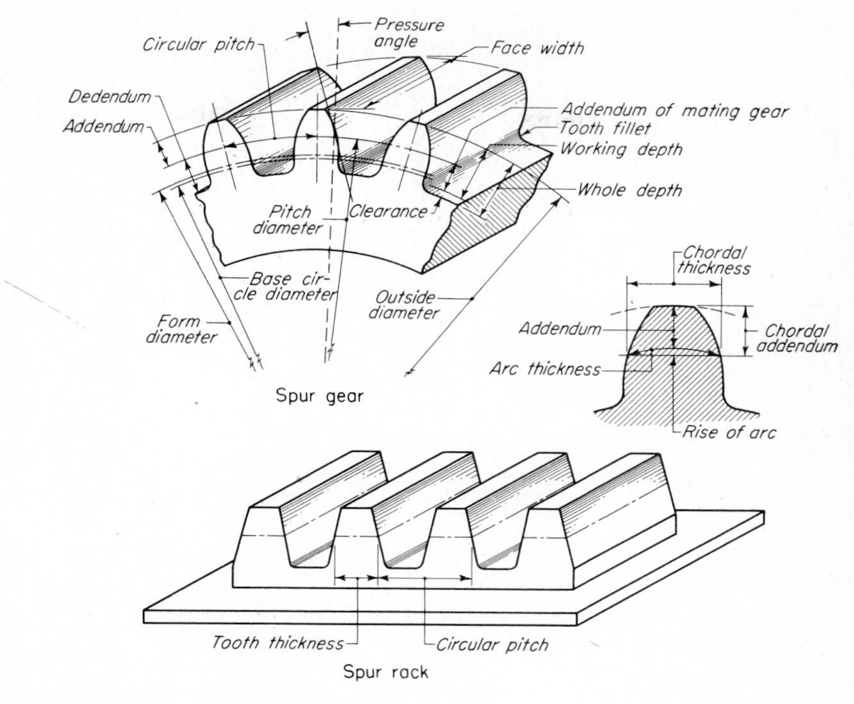

FIG. 1.18 Spur-gear and rack terminology.

with 20° hobs or shaper-cutters will run at $22\frac{1}{2}°$ pressure angle. (See Sec. 8.1 for methods of design for special center distances.)

For the reasons just mentioned, it is possible to have two center distances, a *nominal* center distance and an *operating* center distance. Likewise, there are two pitch diameters. The pitch diameter for the tooth-cutting operation is the nominal pitch diameter and is given by Eq. (1.3). The operating pitch diameter is

$$\text{Pitch dia. (operating) of pinion} = \frac{2 \times \text{operating cent. dist.}}{\text{ratio} + 1} \tag{1.5}$$

$$\text{Pitch dia. (operating) of gear} = \text{ratio} \times \text{pitch dia. (operating) of pinion} \tag{1.6}$$

where

$$\text{Ratio} = \frac{\text{no. gear teeth}}{\text{no. pinion teeth}} \tag{1.7}$$

1.13 External Helical Gears

Helical gears are used to transmit power or motion between parallel shafts. The helix angle must be the same in degrees on each member, but the hand of the helix on the pinion is opposite to that on the gear. (A RH pinion meshes with a LH gear, and a LH pinion meshes with a RH gear.)

Single helical gears impose both thrust and radial load on their bearings. Double helical gears develop equal and opposite thrust reactions which have the effect of canceling out the thrust load. Usually double helical gears have a gap between helices to permit a runout clearance for the hob, grinding wheel, or other cutting tool. One kind of gear shaper has been developed that permits double helical teeth to be made *continuous* (no gap between helices).

Helical-gear teeth are usually made with an involute profile in the *transverse* section (the transverse section is a cross section perpendicular to the gear axis). Small changes in center distance do not affect the action of helical gears.

Helical-gear teeth may be made by hobbing, shaping, milling, or casting. Sintering has been used with limited success. Helical teeth may be finished by grinding, shaving, rolling, lapping, or burnishing.

The size of helical-gear teeth is specified by module for the metric system and by diametral pitch for the English system. The helical tooth will frequently have some of its dimensions given in the *normal section* and others given in the *transverse section.* Thus standard cutting tools could be specified for either section—but not for *both* sections. If the helical gear is small (less than 1 meter pitch diameter), most designers will use the same pressure angle and standard tooth size in the normal section of the helical gear as they would use for spur gears. This makes it possible to hob helical gears with standard spur gear hobs. (It is not possible, though, to cut helical gears with standard spur-gear shaper-cutters.)

Helical gears often use 20° as the standard pressure angle in the normal section. However, higher pressure angles, like $22\frac{1}{2}°$ or 25°, may be used to get extra load-carrying capacity.

Figure 1.19 shows the terminology of a helical gear and a helical rack. In the transverse plane, the elements of a helical gear are the same as those of a spur gear. Equations (1.1) to (1.7) apply just as well to the transverse plane of a helical gear as they do to a spur gear. Additional general formulas for helical gears are:

$$\text{Normal circ. pitch} = \text{circ. pitch} \times \text{cosine helix angle} \tag{1.8}$$

$$\text{Normal module} = \text{transverse module} \times \text{cosine helix angle} \tag{1.9}$$

$$\text{Normal diam. pitch} = \text{trans. diam. pitch} \div \text{cosine helix angle} \tag{1.10}$$

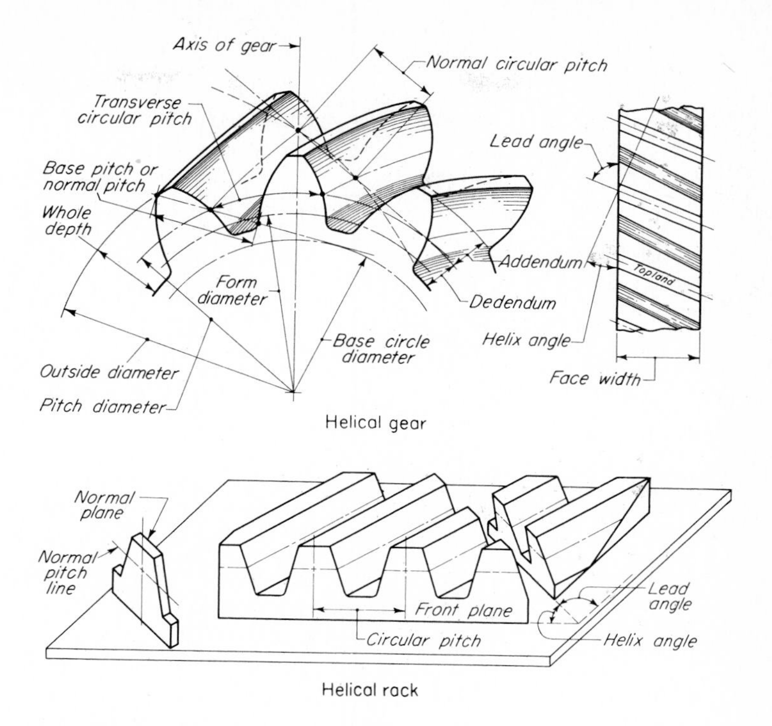

FIG. 1.19 Helical-gear and rack terminology.

$$\text{Axial pitch} = \text{circ. pitch} \div \text{tangent helix angle} \tag{1.11}$$

$$= \text{norm. circ. pitch} \div \text{sine helix angle} \tag{1.12}$$

1.14 Internal Gears

Two internal gears will not mesh with each other, but an external gear may be meshed with an internal gear. The external gear must not be larger than about two-thirds the pitch diameter of the internal gear when full-depth 20° pressure angle teeth are used. The axes on which the gears are mounted must be parallel.

Internal gears may be either spur or helical. Even double helical internal gears are used occasionally.

An internal gear is a necessity in an epicyclic type of gear arrangement. The short center distance of an internal gearset makes it desirable in some applications where space is very limited. The shape of an internal gear forms

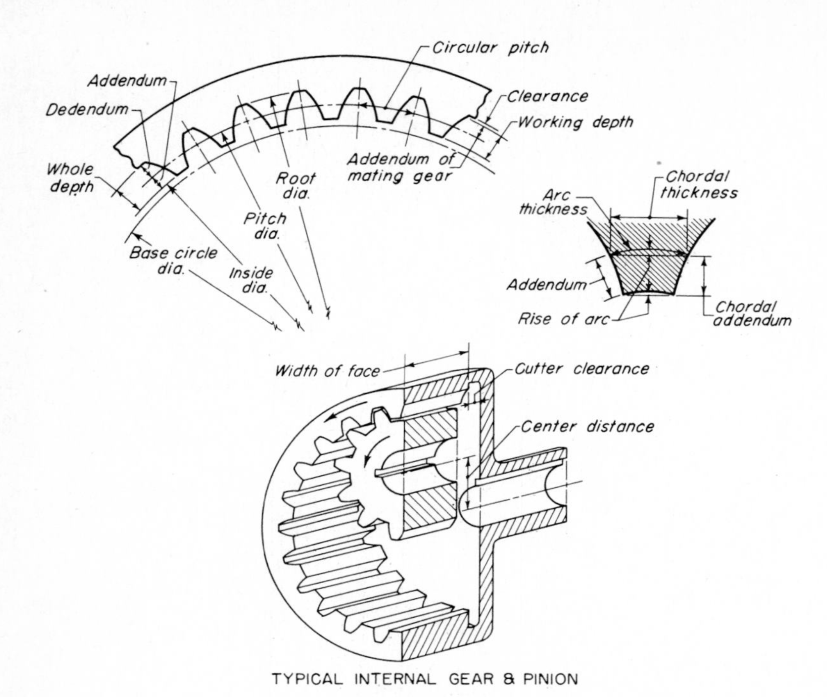

FIG. 1.20 Internal-gear terminology.

a natural guard over the meshing gear teeth. This is very advantageous for some types of machinery.

Internal gears have the disadvantage that fewer types of machine tools can produce them. Internal gears cannot be hobbed.* They can be shaped, milled, or cast. In small sizes they can be broached. Both helical and spur internals can be finished by shaving, grinding, lapping, or burnishing.

An internal gear has the same helix angle in degrees and the same hand as its mating pinion (right-hand pinion meshes with right-hand gear and vice versa).

Figure 1.20 shows the terminology used for a spur internal gear. All the previously given formulas apply to internal gearing except those involving center distance [Eqs. (1.4), (1.5), and (1.6) do not hold for internals]. Formulas for internal-gear center distance are

$$\text{Center distance} = \frac{\text{pitch dia. of gear} - \text{pitch dia. of pinion}}{2} \tag{1.13}$$

*Some very special hobs and hobbing machines have been used—to a rather limited extent—to hob internal gears.

$$\text{Pitch dia. (operating) of pinion} = \frac{2 \times \text{op. cent. dist.}}{\text{ratio} - 1} \tag{1.14}$$

$$\text{Pitch dia. (operating) of gear} = \frac{2 \times \text{op. cent. dist.} \times \text{ratio}}{\text{ratio} - 1} \tag{1.15}$$

1.15 Straight Bevel Gears

Bevel gear blanks are conical in shape. The teeth are tapered in both tooth thickness and tooth height. At one end the tooth is large, while at the other end it is small. The tooth dimensions are usually specified for the *large* end of the tooth. However, in calculating bearing loads, the central-section dimensions and forces are used.

The simplest type of bevel gear is the *straight* bevel gear. These gears are commonly used for transmitting power between intersecting shafts. Usually the shaft angle is 90°, but it may be almost any angle. The gears impose both radial and thrust load on their bearings.

Bevel gears must be mounted on axes whose shaft angle is almost exactly the same as the design shaft angle. Also, the axes on which they are mounted must either intersect or come very close to intersecting. In addition to the accuracy required of the axes, bevel gears must be mounted at the right distance from the cone center. The complications involved in mounting bevel gears make it difficult to use sleeve bearings with large clearances (which is often done on high-speed, high-power spur and helical gears). Ball and roller bearings are the kinds commonly used for bevel gears. The limitations of these bearings' speed and load-carrying capacity indirectly limit the capacity of bevel gears in some high-speed applications.

Straight bevel teeth are usually cut on bevel-gear generators. In some cases, where accuracy is not too important, bevel-gear teeth are milled. Bevel teeth may also be cast. Lapping is the process often used to finish straight bevel teeth. Shaving is not practical for straight bevel gears, but straight bevels may be ground.

The size of bevel-gear teeth is defined in module for the metric system and in diametral pitch for the English system. The specified size dimensions are given for the large end of the tooth. A bevel gear tooth which is 12 module at the large end may be only around 10 module at the small end. The commonly used modules (or diametral pitches) are the same as those used for spur gears (see Sec. 1.12). There is no particular advantage to using standard tooth sizes for bevel gears. A set of cutting tools will cut more than a single pitch.

The two views of bevel gears in Fig. 1.21 show bevel-gear terminology. Bevel-gear teeth have profiles which closely resemble an involute curve. The

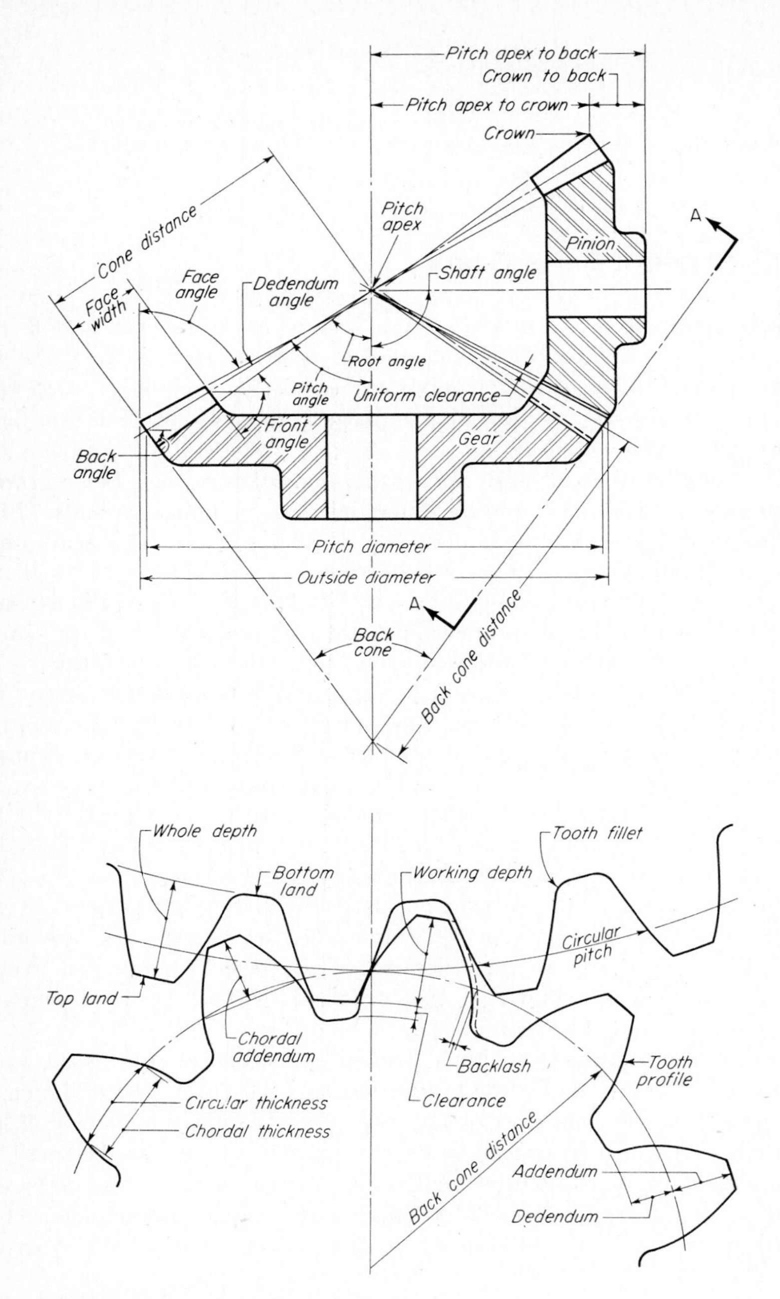

FIG. 1.21 Bevel-gear terminology.

shape of a straight bevel-gear tooth (in a section *normal* to the tooth) closely approximates that of an involute spur gear with a larger number of teeth. This larger number of teeth, called the *virtual number of teeth*, is equal to the actual number of teeth divided by the cosine of the pitch angle.

Straight bevel-gear teeth have been commonly made with $14\frac{1}{2}$, $17\frac{1}{2}$, and 20° pressure angles. The 20° design is the most popular.

The pitch angle of a bevel gear is the angle of the pitch cone. It is a measure of the amount of taper in the gear. For instance, as the taper is reduced, the pitch angle approaches zero and the bevel gear approaches a spur gear.

The pitch angles in a set of bevel gears are defined by lines meeting at the cone center. The root and face angles are defined by lines which *do not* hit the cone center (or apex). In old-style designs these angles did meet at the apex, but modern designs make the outside cone of one gear parallel to the root cone of its mate. This gives a constant clearance and permits a better cutting-tool design and gear-tooth design than the old-style design with its tapering clearance.

The circular pitch and the pitch diameters of bevel gears are calculated the same as for spur gears. [See Eqs. (1.1) to (1.3).] The pitch-cone angles may be calculated by one of the following sets of equations:

$$\text{Tan pitch angle, pinion} = \frac{\text{no. teeth in pinion}}{\text{no. teeth in gear}} \tag{1.16}$$

$$\text{Tan pitch angle, gear} = \frac{\text{no. teeth in gear}}{\text{no. teeth in pinion}} \tag{1.17}$$

When the shaft angle is less than 90°,

$$\text{Tan pitch angle, pinion} = \frac{\text{sin shaft angle}}{\text{ratio} + \text{cos shaft angle}} \tag{1.18}$$

$$\text{Tan pitch angle, gear} = \frac{\text{sin shaft angle}}{1/\text{ratio} + \text{cos shaft angle}} \tag{1.19}$$

When the shaft angle is over 90°,

$$\text{Tan pitch angle, pinion} = \frac{\sin\,(180° - \text{shaft angle})}{\text{ratio} - \cos\,(180° - \text{shaft angle})} \tag{1.20}$$

$$\text{Tan pitch angle, gear} = \frac{\sin\,(180° - \text{shaft angle})}{1/\text{ratio} - \cos\,(180° - \text{shaft angle})} \tag{1.21}$$

In all the above cases,

$$\text{Pitch angle, pinion} + \text{pitch angle, gear} = \text{shaft angle} \tag{1.22}$$

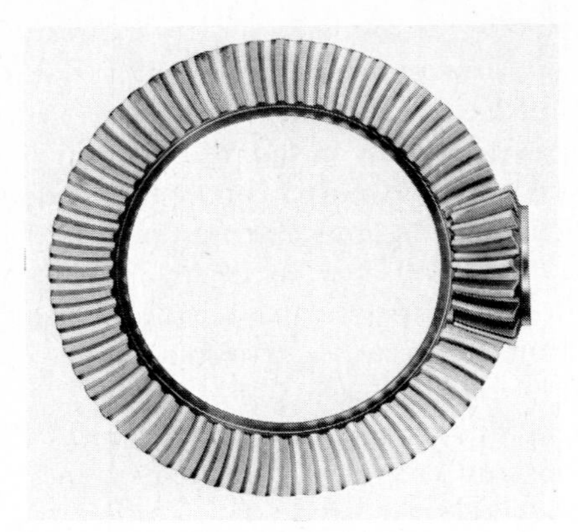

FIG. 1.22 A pair of Zerol bevel gears. (*Courtesy of the Gleason Works, Rochester, NY, U.S.A.*)

1.16 Zerol Bevel Gears

Zerol* bevel gears are similar to straight bevel gears except that they have a curved tooth in the lengthwise direction. See Fig. 1.22. Zerol bevel gears have 0° spiral angle. They are made in a different kind of machine from that used to make straight bevel gears. The straight-bevel-gear-generating machine has a cutting tool which moves back and forth in a straight line. The Zerol is generated by a rotary cutter that is like a face mill. It is the curvature of this cutter that makes the lengthwise curvature in the Zerol tooth.

The Zerol gear has a profile which somewhat resembles an involute curve. The pressure angle of the tooth varies slightly in going across the face width. This is caused by the lengthwise curvature of the tooth.

Zerol gear teeth may be finished by grinding or lapping. Since the Zerol gear can be ground, it is favored over straight bevel gears in applications in which both high accuracy and full hardness are required. Even in applications in which cut gears of machinable hardness can be used, the Zerol may be the best choice if speeds are high. Because of its lengthwise curvature, the Zerol tooth has a slight overlapping action. This tends to make it run more smoothly than the straight-bevel-gear tooth. A cut Zerol bevel gear is usually more accurate than a straight bevel gear.

In making a set of Zerol gears, one member is made first, using theoretical machine settings. Then a second gear is finished in such a way that its

*Zerol is a registered trademark of the Gleason Works, Rochester, NY, U.S.A.

profile and lengthwise curvature will give satisfactory contact with the first gear. Several trial cuts and adjustments to machine settings may be required to develop a set of gears which will conjugate properly. If a number of identical sets of gears are required, a matching set of test gears is made. Then each production gear is machined so that it will mesh satisfactorily with one or the other of the test gears. In this way a number of sets of interchangeable gears may be made.

Zerol gears are usually made to a 20° pressure angle. In a few ratios where pinion and gear have small numbers of teeth, $22\frac{1}{2}$° or 25° is used.

The calculations for pitch diameter and pitch-cone angle are the same for Zerol bevel gears as for straight bevel gears.

1.17 Spiral Bevel Gears

Spiral bevel gears have a lengthwise curvature like Zerol gears. However, they differ from Zerol gears in that they have an appreciable angle with the axis of the gear. See Fig. 1.23. Although spiral bevel teeth do not have a true helical spiral, a spiral bevel gear looks somewhat like a helical bevel gear.

Spiral bevel gears are generated by the same machines that cut or grind Zerol gears. The only difference is that the cutting tool is set at an angle to the axis of the gear instead of being set essentially parallel to the gear axis.

Spiral bevel gears are made in matched sets like Zerol bevel gears. Different sets of the same design are not interchangeable unless they have been purposely built to match a common set of test gears.

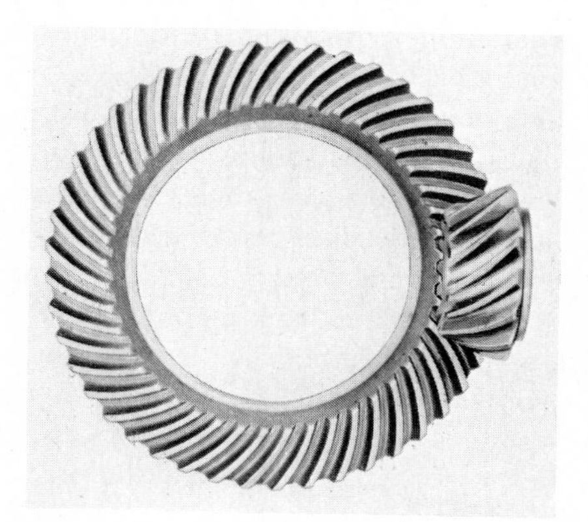

FIG. 1.23 A pair of spiral bevel gears. (*Courtesy of the Gleason Works, Rochester, NY, U.S.A.*)

Generating types of machines are ordinarily used to cut or grind spiral-bevel-gear teeth. In some high-production jobs, a special kind of machine is used which cuts the teeth without going through a generating motion. Spiral-bevel-gear teeth are frequently given a lapping operation to finish the teeth and obtain the desired tooth bearing.

In high-speed gear work, the spiral bevel is preferred over the Zerol bevel because its spiral angle tends to give the teeth a considerable amount of overlap. This makes the gear run more smoothly, and the load is distributed over more tooth surface. However, the spiral bevel gear imposes much more thrust load on its bearings than does a Zerol bevel gear.

Spiral bevel gears are commonly made to 16°, $17\frac{1}{2}$°, 20°, and $22\frac{1}{2}$° pressure angles. The 20° angle has become the most popular. It is the only angle used on aircraft and instrument gears. The most common spiral angle is 35°.

1.18 Hypoid Gears

Hypoid gears resemble bevel gears in some respects. They are used on crossed-axis shafts, and there is a tendency for the parts to taper as do bevel gears. They differ from true bevel gears in that their axes do not intersect. The distance between a hypoid pinion axis and the axis of a hypoid gear is called the *offset*. This distance is measured along the perpendicular common to the two axes. If a set of hypoid gears had *no offset*, they would simply be spiral bevel gears. See Fig. 1.24 for *offset* and other terms.

Hypoid pinions may have as few as five teeth in a high ratio. Since the various kinds of bevel gears do not often go below 10 teeth in a pinion, it can be seen that it is easier to get high ratios with hypoid gears.

Contrary to the general rule with spur, helical, and bevel gears, hypoid pinions and gears *do not* have pitch diameters which are in proportion to their numbers of teeth. This makes it possible to use a large and strong pinion even with a high ratio and only a few pinion teeth. See Fig. 1.25.

Hypoid teeth have unequal pressure angles and unequal profile curvatures on the two sides of the teeth. This results from the unusual geometry of the hypoid gear rather than from a nonsymmetrical cutting tool.

Hypoid gearsets are matched to run together, just as Zerol or spiral gearsets are matched. Interchangeability is obtained by making production gears fit with test masters.

Hypoid gears and pinions are usually cut on a generating type of machine. They may be finished by either grinding or lapping.

The hypoid gears for passenger cars and for industrial drives usually have a basic pressure angle of 21°15′. For tractors and trucks the average pressure angle is 22°30′. Pinions are frequently made with a spiral angle of 45° or 50°.

In hypoid gearing, module and diametral pitch are used for the gear *only*.

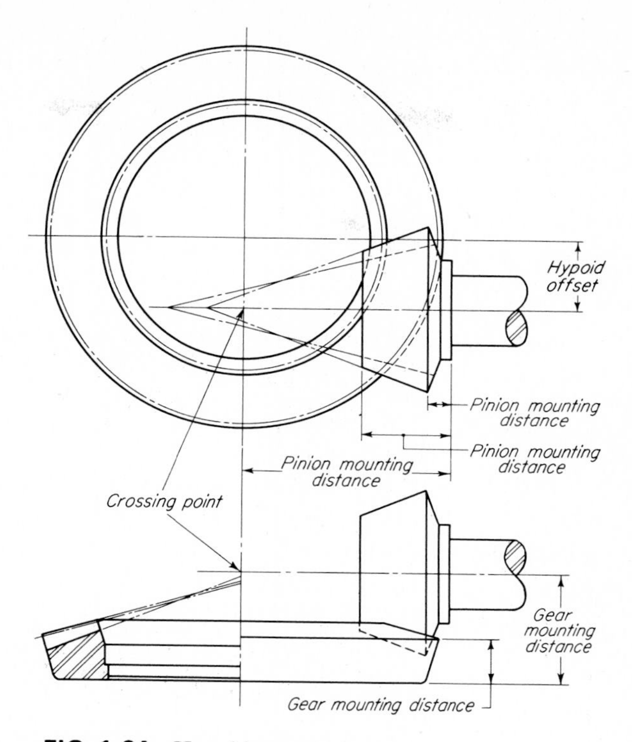

FIG. 1.24 Hypoid-gear arrangement.

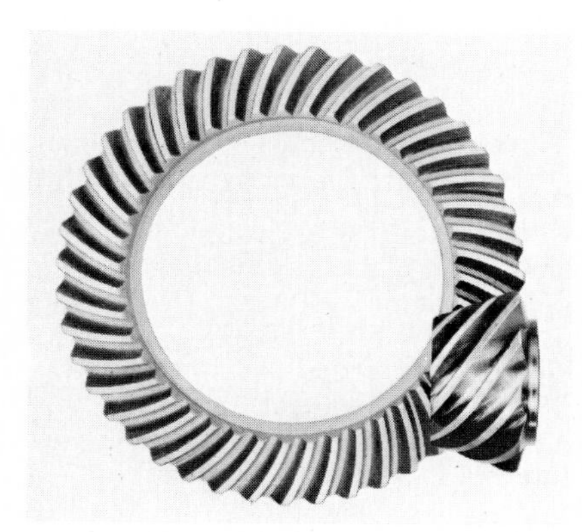

FIG. 1.25 A pair of hypoid gears (*Courtesy of the Gleason Works, Rochester, NY, U.S.A.*)

Likewise, the pitch diameter and the pitch angle are figured for the gear only. If a pitch were used for the pinion, it would be smaller than that of the gear. The size of a hypoid pinion is established by its outside diameter and its number of teeth. The geometry of hypoid teeth is defined by the various dimensions used to set up the machines to cut the teeth.

1.19 Face Gears

Face gears have teeth cut on the end face of a gear, just as the name "face" implies. They are not ordinarily thought of as bevel gears, but functionally they are more akin to bevel gears than to any other kind.

A spur pinion and a face gear are mounted—like bevel gears—on shafts that intersect and have a shaft angle (usually 90°). The pinion bearings carry mostly radial load, while the gear bearings have both thrust and radial load. The mounting distance of the pinion from the pitch-cone apex is not critical, as it is in bevel or hypoid gears. Figure 1.26 shows the terminology used with face gears.

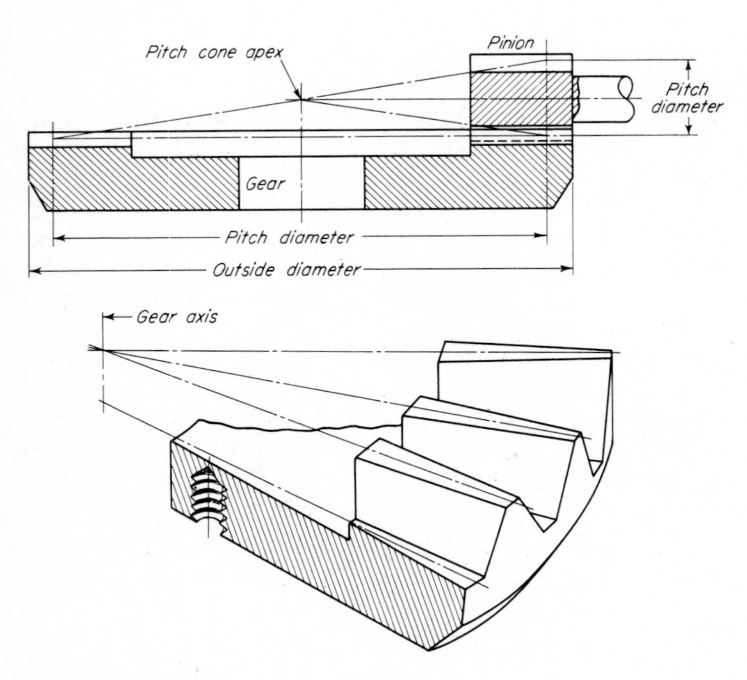

FIG. 1.26 Face-gear terminology.

The pinion that goes with a face gear is usually made spur, but it can be made helical if necessary. The formulas for determining the dimensions of a pinion to run with a face gear are no different from those for the dimensions of a pinion to run with a mating gear on parallel axes. The pressure angles and pitches used are similar to spur-gear (or helical-gear) practice.

The pinion may be finished or cut by all the methods previously mentioned for spur and helical pinions. The gear, however, must be finished with a shaper-cutter which is almost the same size as the pinion. Equipment to grind face gears is not available. The teeth can be lapped, and they might be shaved without too much difficulty, although ordinarily they are not shaved.

The face-gear tooth changes shape from one end of the tooth to the other. The face width of the gear is limited at the outside end by the radius at which the tooth becomes pointed. At the inside end, the limit is the radius at which undercut becomes excessive. Practical considerations usually make it desirable to make the face width somewhat short of these limits.

The pinion to go with a face gear is usually made with 20° pressure angle.

1.20 Crossed-Helical Gears (Nonenveloping Worm Gears)

The word "spiral" is rather loosely used in the gear trade. The word may be applied to both helical and bevel gears. In this section we shall consider the special kind of worm gear that is often called a "spiral gear." More correctly, though, it is a *crossed-helical* gear.

Crossed-helical gears are essentially *nonenveloping* worm gears. Both members are cylindrically shaped. (See Fig. 1.27.) In comparison, the *single-enveloping* worm gearset has a cylindrical worm, but the gear is throated so that it tends to wrap around the worm. The *double-enveloping* worm gearset goes still further; both members are throated, and both members wrap around each other.

Crossed-helical gears are mounted on axes that do not intersect and that are at an angle to each other. Frequently the angle between the axes is 90°. The bearings for crossed-helical gears have both thrust and radial load.

A *point contact* is made between two spiral gear teeth in mesh with each other. As the gears revolve, this point travels across the tooth in a sloping line. After the gears have worn in for a period of time, a shallow, sloping line of contact is worn into each member. This makes the original point contact increase to a line as long as the width of the sloping band of contact. The load-carrying capacity of crossed-helical gears is quite small when they are new, but if they are worn in carefully, it increases quite appreciably.

Crossed-helical gearsets are able to stand small changes in center distance and small changes in shaft angle without any impairment in the accuracy

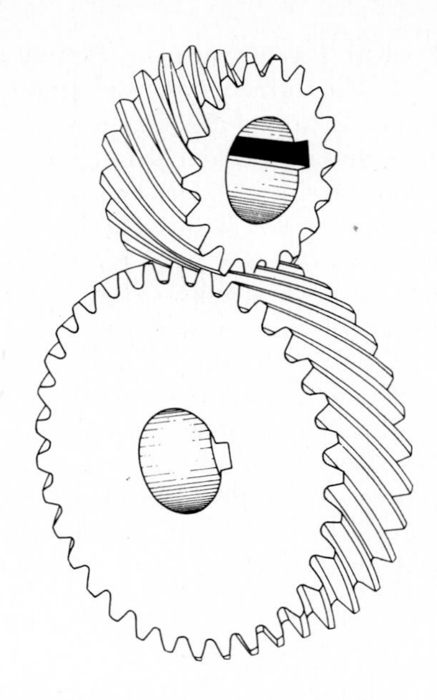

FIG. 1.27 Crossed-helical-gear drive.

with which the set transmits motion. This fact, and the fact that shifting either member endwise makes no difference in the amount of contact obtained, makes this the easiest of all gears to mount. There is no need to get close accuracy in center distance, shaft alignment, or axial position—provided the teeth are cut with reasonably generous face width and backlash.

Crossed-helical gears may be made by any of the processes used to make single helical gears. Up to the point of mounting the gear in a gearbox, there is no difference between a crossed-helical gear and a helical gear.

Usually a crossed-helical gear of one hand is meshed with a crossed-helical gear of the same hand. It is not necessary, though, to do this. If the shaft angle is properly set, it is possible to mesh opposite hands together. Thus the range of possibilities is

RH driver with RH driven

LH driver with LH driven

RH driver with LH driven

LH driver with RH driven

The pitch diameters of crossed-helical gears—like those of hypoid gears—are not in proportion to the tooth ratio. This makes the use of the word "pinion" for the smaller member of the pair inappropriate. In a crossed-helical gearset, the small *pinion* might easily have more teeth than the *gear*! The two members of a crossed-helical set are described as *driver* and *driven.*

The same helix angle in degrees does not have to be used for each member. Whenever different helix angles are used, the module (or diametral pitch) for two crossed-helical gears that mesh with each other is not the same. The thing that is the same in all cases is the normal module (and the normal circular pitch). This makes the normal module (or normal diametral pitch) the most appropriate measure of tooth size.

Designers of crossed-helical gears usually get the best results when there is a contact ratio in the normal section of at least 2. This means that in all positions of tooth engagement, the load will be shared by at least two pair of teeth. To get this high contact ratio, a low normal pressure angle and a deep tooth depth are needed. When the helix is 45°, a normal pressure angle of $14\frac{1}{2}°$ gives good results.

Some of the basic formulas for crossed-helical gears are

$$\text{Shaft angle} = \text{helix angle of driver} \pm \text{helix angle of driven} \tag{1.23}$$

$$\text{Normal module} = \text{normal circ. pitch} \div \text{pi} \tag{1.24}$$

$$\text{Normal diam. pitch} = \frac{\text{pi}}{\text{normal circ. pitch}} \tag{1.25}$$

$$\text{Pitch dia.} = \frac{\text{no. of teeth} \times \text{normal module}}{\text{cosine of helix angle}} \tag{1.26}$$

$$\text{Center distance} = \frac{\text{pitch dia. driver} + \text{pitch dia. driven}}{2} \tag{1.27}$$

$$\text{Cosine of helix angle} = \frac{\text{no. teeth} \times \text{normal circ. pitch}}{\text{pi} \times \text{pitch dia.}} \tag{1.28}$$

1.21 Single-Enveloping Worm Gears

Figure 1.28 shows a single-enveloping worm gear. Worm gears are characterized by one member having a screw thread. Frequently the thread angle (lead angle) is only a few degrees. The worm in this case has the outward appearance of the thread on a bolt, greatly enlarged. When a worm has multiple threads and a lead angle approaching 45°, it may be (if it has an involute profile) geometrically just the same as a helical pinion of the same lead angle. In this case the only difference between a worm and a helical pinion would be in their usage.

Worm gears are usually mounted on nonintersecting shafts which are at a 90° shaft angle. Worm bearings usually have a high thrust load. The worm-

FIG. 1.28 Single-enveloping worm gearset. (*Courtesy of Transamerica Delaval, Delroyd Worm Gear Div., Trenton, NJ, U.S.A.*)

gear bearings have a high radial load and a low thrust load (unless the lead angle is high).

The single-enveloping worm gear has a line contact which extends either across the face width or across the part of the tooth that is in the zone of action. As the gear revolves, this line sweeps across the whole width and height of the tooth. The meshing action is quite similar to that of helical gears on parallel shafts, except that much higher sliding velocity is obtained for the same pitch-line velocity. In a helical gearset, the sliding velocity at the tooth tips is usually not more than about one-fourth the pitch-line velocity. In a high-ratio worm gearset, the sliding velocity is greater than the pitch-line velocity of the worm.

Worm gearsets have considerably more load-carrying capacity than crossed-helical gearsets. This results from the fact that they have *line* contact instead of *point* contact. Worm gearsets must be mounted on shafts that are very close to being correctly aligned and at the correct center distance. The axial position of a single-enveloping worm is not critical, but the worm gear must be in just the right axial position so that it can wrap around the worm properly.

Several different kinds of worm-thread shapes are in common use. These are

Worm thread produced by straight-sided conical milling or grinding wheel

Worm thread straight-sided in the axial section

Worm thread straight-sided in the normal section

Worm thread an involute helicoid shape

The shape of the worm thread defines the worm-gear tooth shape. The worm gear is simply a gear element formed to be "conjugate" to a specified worm thread.

A worm and a worm gear have the same hand of helix. A RH worm, for example, meshes with a RH gear. The helix angles are usually very different for a worm and a worm gear. Usually the worm has a more than 45° helix angle, and the worm gear has a less than 45° helix angle. Customarily the *lead angle*—which is the complement of the helix angle—is used to specify the angle of the worm thread. See Fig. 1.29 for a diagram of the worm gear and its terminology. When the worm gearset has a 90° shaft angle, the worm lead angle is numerically equal to the worm-gear helix angle.

The *axial pitch* is the dimension that is used to specify the size of worm threads. It is the distance from thread to thread measured in an axial plane. When the shaft angle is 90°, the axial pitch of the worm is numerically equal to the worm-gear circular pitch. In the metric system, popular axial pitch values are 5, $7\frac{1}{2}$, 10, 15, 20, 30, and 40 mm. In the English system, commonly used values have been 0.250, 0.375, 0.500, 0.750, 1.000, 1.250, and 1.500 in. Fine-pitch worm gears are often designed to standard lead- and pitch-diameter values so as to obtain even lead-angle values (see AGMA* standard 374.04).

Worm threads are usually milled or cut with a single-point lathe tool. In fine pitches, some designs can be formed by rolling. Grinding is often employed as a finishing process for high-hardness worms. In fine pitches, worm threads are sometimes ground from the solid.

Worm-gear teeth are usually hobbed. The cutting tool is essentially a duplicate of the mating worm in size and thread design. New worm designs should be based on available hobs wherever possible to avoid the need for procuring a special hob for each worm design.

*The abbreviation AGMA stands for the American Gear Manufacturers Association.

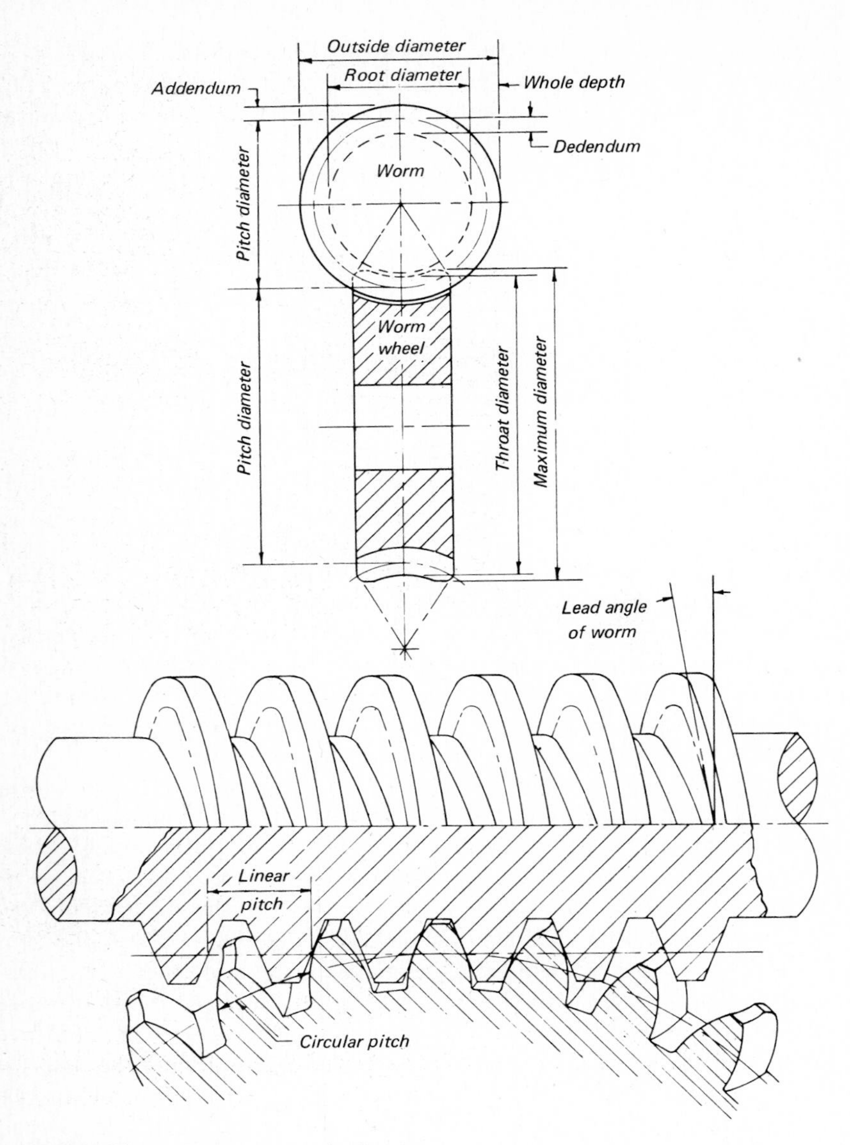

FIG. 1.29 Worm-gear terminology.

A variety of pressure angles are used for worms. Single-thread worms used for indexing purposes frequently have low axial pressure angles, like $14\frac{1}{2}°$. Multiple-thread worms with high lead angles like 30 or 40° are often designed with about 30° axial pressure angles.

The following formulas apply to worm gears which are designed to run on 90° axes:

$$\text{Axial pitch of worm} = \text{circ. pitch of worm gear} \tag{1.29}$$

$$\text{Pitch dia. of gear} = \frac{\text{no. of teeth} \times \text{circ. pitch}}{\text{pi}} \tag{1.30}$$

$$\text{Pitch dia. of worm} = 2 \times \text{center distance} - \text{pitch dia. of gear} \tag{1.31}$$

$$\text{Lead of worm} = \text{axial pitch} \times \text{no. of threads} \tag{1.32}$$

$$\text{Tan lead angle} = \frac{\text{lead of worm}}{\text{pitch dia.} \times \text{pi}} \tag{1.33}$$

$$\text{Lead angle of worm} = \text{helix angle of gear} \tag{1.34}$$

1.22 Double-Enveloping Worm Gears

The double-enveloping worm gear is like the single-enveloping worm gear except that the worm envelops the worm gear. Thus both members are throated. See Fig. 1.30.

Double-enveloping worm gears are used to transmit power between non-intersecting shafts, usually those at a 90° angle. Double-enveloping worm gears load their bearings with thrust and radial loads the same as single-enveloping worm gears do.

Double-enveloping worm gears should be accurately located on all mounting dimensions. Shafts should be at the right shaft angle and at the right center distance.

The double-enveloping type of worm gear has more tooth surface in contact than a single-enveloping worm gear. Instead of line contact, it has *area* contact at any one instant in time. The larger contact area of the

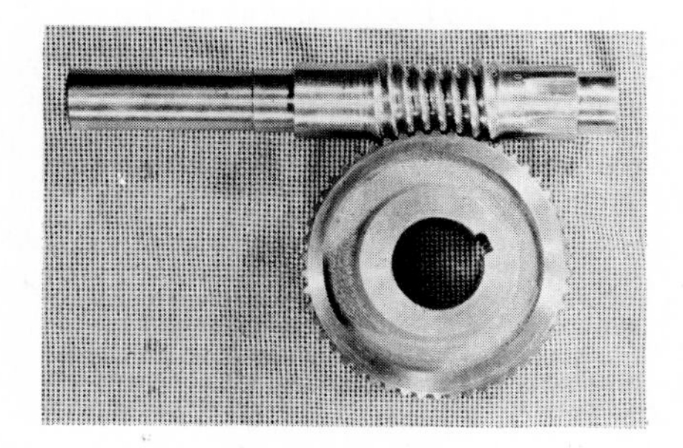

FIG. 1.30 Double-enveloping worm gear-set. (*Courtesy of Ex-Cell-O Corp., Cone Drive Div., Traverse City, MI, U.S.A.*)

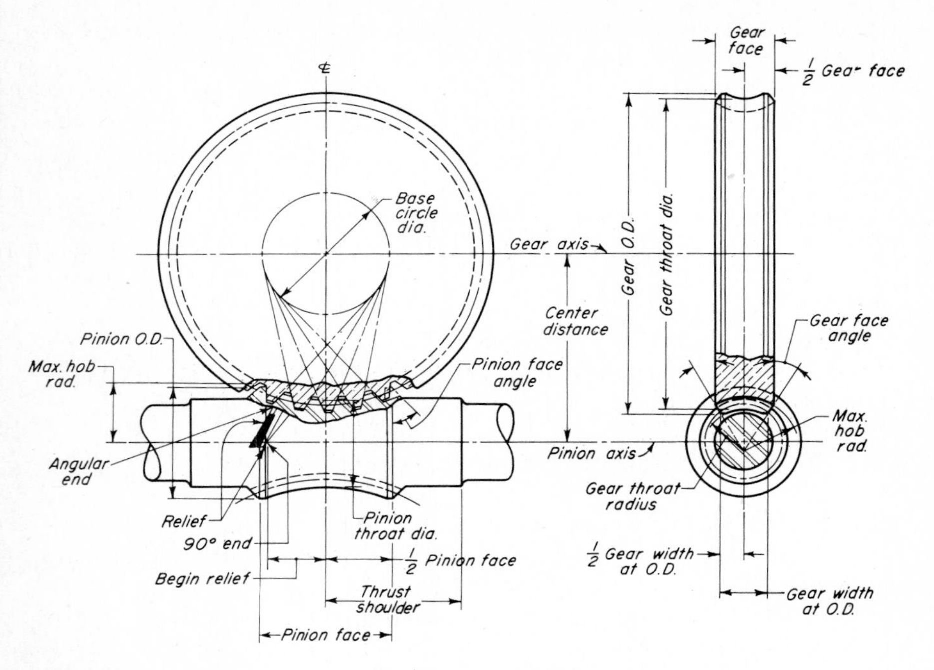

FIG. 1.31 Terminology of Cone-Drive worm gears.

double-enveloping worm gear increases the load-carrying capacity. On most double-enveloping worm gearsets, the worm rubbing speed is below 10 m/s (2000 fpm). Above 10 m/s, it is possible to get good results with oil lubrication, using a circulating system and coolers. The lubrication system must be good enough to prevent scoring and overheating.

The only double-enveloping worm gear that is in widespread use today is the Cone-Drive* design. Figure 1.31 shows the terminology used with Cone-Drive worm gears.

The Cone-Drive worm has a straight-sided profile in the axial section, but this profile changes its inclination as you move along the thread. At any one position, this slope is determined by a line which is tangent to the *base cylinder* of the gear. The base cylinder of a Cone-Drive gear is like an involute base circle in that it is an imaginary circle used to define a profile. Geometrically, though, the base circle of a Cone-Drive gear is not used in the same way as the base circle of an involute gear.

*Cone-Drive is a registered trademark of the Ex-Cell-O Corp., Cone-Drive Div., Traverse City, Michigan, U.S.A.

The size of Cone-Drive gear teeth is measured by the circular pitch of the gear.

The normal pressure angle is ordinarily 20° or 22°. The Cone-Drive worm and gear diameters are not in proportion to the ratio. With low ratios, it is possible (although not recommended) to have a worm which is larger than the gear!

Equations (1.30) and (1.31) apply to Cone-Drive gears as well as to regular worm gears. The other formulas for single-enveloping worm gears apply only to the center of the Cone-Drive worm, since it does not have a fixed axial pitch and lead like a cylindrical worm.

In both single-enveloping worm gears and Cone-Drive gears, it is generally recommended that the worm or pinion diameter be made a function of the center distance (see AGMA 342.02). Thus

$$\text{Pitch dia. of worm} = \frac{(\text{center distance})^{0.875}}{2.2} \tag{1.35}$$

Following the recommendation of Eq. (1.35) is, of course, not necessary. This formula merely recommends a good proportion of worm to gear diameter for best power capacity. In instrument and control work, the designer may not be interested in power transmission at all. In such cases, it may be desirable to depart considerably from Eq. (1.35) in picking the size of a worm or pinion. In fact, AGMA 374.04 shows a whole series of worm diameters for fine-pitch work which do not agree with Eq. (1.35).

When a worm diameter is picked in accordance with Eq. (1.35), the gear diameter and the circular pitch may be obtained by working backward through Eqs. (1.31), (1.30), and (1.29).

The helix angle of a worm gear or a Cone-Drive gear may be obtained from the following general formula:

$$\text{Tan center helix angle of gear} = \frac{\text{pitch dia. of gear}}{\text{pitch dia. of worm} \times \text{ratio}} \tag{1.36}$$

1.23 Spiroid Gears

The Spiroid family of gears operates on nonintersecting, nonparallel axes. The most famous family member is called Spiroid. It involves a tapered pinion that somewhat resembles a worm (see Fig. 1.32). The gear member is a face gear with teeth curved in a lengthwise direction; the inclination to the tooth is like a helix angle—but not a true helical spiral.

FIG. 1.32 Double-reduction Spiroid linear actuator unit. (*Courtesy of Spiroid Div. of Illinois Tool Works, Inc., Chicago, IL, U.S.A.*)

Figure 1.33 shows the schematic relation of the Spiroid type of gear to worm gears, hypoid gears, and bevel gears.

The Spiroid family has Helicon* and Planoid* types as well as the Spiroid type. The Helicon is essentially a Spiroid with no taper in the pinion. The Planoid is used for lower ratios than the Spiroid, and its offset is lower—more in the range of the hypoid gear.

The Spiroid pinions may be made by hobbing, milling, rolling, or thread chasing. Spiroid gears are typically made by hobbing, using a specially built (or modified) hobbing machine and special hobs. The gear may be made with molded or sintered gear teeth using tools (dies or punches) that have teeth resembling hobbed gears. Shaping and milling are not practical to use in making Spiroid gears.

The Spiroid gears may be lapped as a final finishing process. Special "shaving" type hobs may also be used in a finishing operation.

Spiroid gears are used in a wide variety of applications, ranging from aerospace actuators to automotive and appliance uses. The combination of a high ratio in compact arrangements, low cost when mass-produced, and good load-carrying capacity makes the Spiroid-type gear attractive in many situations. The fact that the gearing can be made with lower-cost machine tools and manufacturing processes is also an important consideration.

*Helicon and Planoid are registered trademarks of Illinois Tool Works Inc., Chicago, IL, U.S.A., as is the term Spiroid.

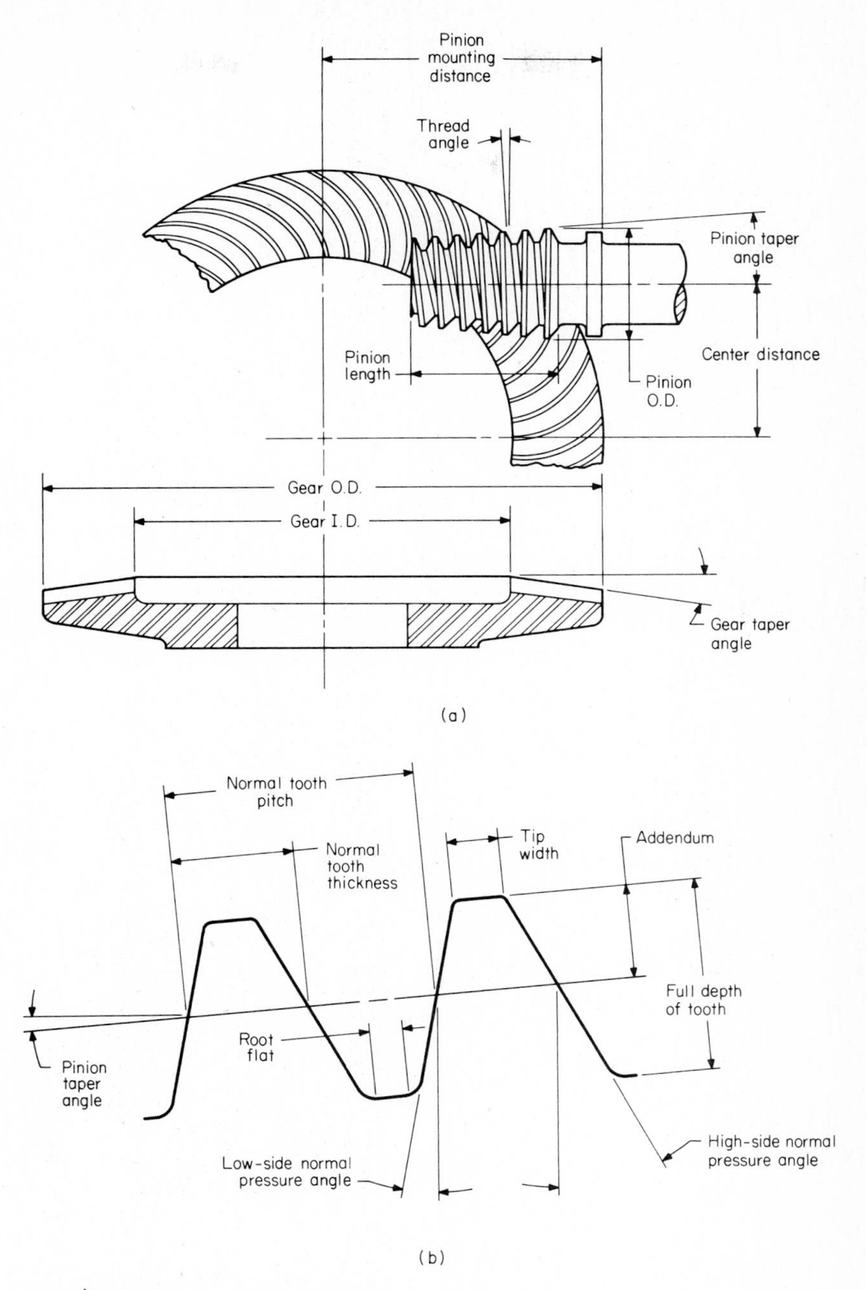

FIG. 1.33 Spiroid-gear terminology.

chapter 2

Preliminary Design Considerations

In the first chapter, we reviewed the design trends in different fields of gear work. General information was given that would help the designer pick the kind of gear that might be most suitable for a particular application.

In this chapter we shall begin to get into the detail work of designing a gear. Usually the gear designer roughs out a preliminary design before doing all the work involved in a final design. The preliminary design stage involves consideration of the kinds of stresses in the gears, an estimate of the approximate gear size, and consideration of the kind of data that will be required on the gear drawings. Each of these preliminary design considerations will be discussed in this chapter. Tables 2.1 and 2.2 are included for easy reference to the important gear nomenclature and symbols used in Chap. 2.

STRESS FORMULAS

The gear designer's first problem is to find a design which will be able to carry the power required. The gears must be big enough, hard enough, and accurate enough to do the job required.

TABLE 2.1 Glossary of Gear Nomenclature, Chap. 2

Backlash The amount by which the sum of the circular tooth thicknesses of two gears in mesh is less than the circular pitch. Normally backlash is thought of as the freedom of one gear to move while the mating gear is held stationary.

Bottom land The surface at the bottom of the space between adjacent teeth.

Crown A modification that results in the flank of each gear tooth having a slight outward bulge in its center area. A crowned tooth becomes gradually thinner toward each end. A *fully crowned* tooth has a little extra material removed at the tip and root areas also. See Fig. 5.50 for the shape of a crowned helix. The purpose of crowning is to ensure that the center of the flank carries its full share of the load even if the gears are slightly misaligned or distorted.

Face width The length of the gear teeth as measured along a line parallel to the gear axis. (A gap between the helices of double helical gears is excluded unless "total face width" is specified.)

Fillet The rounded portion at the base of the gear tooth between the tooth flank and the bottom land.

Flank The working, or contacting, side of the gear tooth. The flank of a spur gear usually has an involute profile in a transverse section.

Form diameter The diameter set by the gear designer as the limit for contact with a mating part. Gears are manufactured so that the tooth profile is suitable to transmit load between the tip of the tooth and the form diameter.

Involute curve A mathematical curve which is commonly specified for gear-tooth profiles. See Sec. 9.1 for details.

Journal surfaces The finished surface of the part of a gear shaft which has been prepared to fit inside a sleeve bearing or ball bearing.

***K* factor** An index of the intensity of tooth load from the standpoint of surface durability. See Eqs. (2.22), (2.61), and (3.50).

Overhung A gear with two bearings (for support) at one end of the face width and no bearings at the other end.

Pi A dimensionless constant which is the ratio of the circumference of a circle to its diameter. Pi is denoted by the Greek letter π and is approximately equal to 3.14159265.

Pitch-line velocity The linear speed of a point on the pitch circle of a gear as it rotates. Pitch-line velocity is equal to rotational speed multiplied by the pitch-circle circumference.

***Q* factor** A quantity factor for the weight of a gearset, defined by Eq. (2.47).

Sliding velocity The linear velocity of the sliding component of the interaction between two gear teeth in mesh. The rate of sliding changes constantly; it is zero at the pitch line, and it increases as the contact point travels away from the pitch line in either direction.

Straddle mount A method of gear mounting in which the gear has a supporting bearing at each end of the face width.

Throated A gear is throated when the gear blank has a smaller diameter in the center than at the ends of the "cylinder." This concave shape causes the gear to partially envelop its mate and thus increases the area of contact between them. This design is often used to increase the load-carrying capacity of worm gearsets.

Top land The top surface of a gear tooth. See Fig. 1.21.

Undercut When part of the involute profile of a gear tooth is cut away near its base, the tooth is said to be *undercut*. See Fig. 3.4. Undercutting becomes a problem when the numbers of teeth are small. See Sec. 3.5 for more details. Also, preshave or pregrind may be designed to produce undercut, even when no undercut would be present because of the small number of teeth.

TABLE 2.2 Gear Terms, Symbols, and Units, Chap. 2

Term	Metric		English		Reference or comment
	Symbol	Units	Symbol	Units	
Module, transverse	m_t	mm	—	—	$m_t = 25.4 \div P_t$
Module, normal	m_n	mm	—	—	Eq. (2.53)
Diametral pitch, transverse	—	—	P_t or P_d	in.$^{-1}$	$P_t = 25.4 \div m_t$
Diametral pitch, normal	—	—	P_{nd}	in.$^{-1}$	Eq. (2.53)
Circular pitch	p	mm	p	in.	Eq. (2.4)
Pitch diameter, pinion	d_{p1}	mm	d	in.	
Pitch diameter, gear	d_{p2}	mm	D	in.	
Pitch radius, pinion	r_{p1}	mm	r	in.	Fig. 2.14
Pitch radius, gear	r_{p2}	mm	R	in.	Fig. 2.14
Outside radius, pinion	r_{a1}	mm	r_o	in.	Fig. 2.14
Outside radius, gear	r_{a2}	mm	R_o	in.	Fig. 2.14
Face width	b	mm	F	in.	Eq. (2.18)
Ratio (tooth or gear)	u	—	m_G	—	No. gear teeth ÷ no. pinion teeth
Center distance	a	mm	C	in.	Fig. 2.14, Eq. (2.34)
Pressure angle	α	deg	ϕ	deg	Fig. 2.10, Eq. (2.14)
Helix angle (or spiral)	β	deg	ψ	deg	Eq. (2.23)
Pitch angle, pinion	δ'	deg	γ	deg	Fig. 2.21
Outer cone distance	R_a	mm	A_o	in.	Fig. 2.21
Bending stress	s_t	N/mm^2	s_t	psi	Sec. 2.3
Contact stress (hertz)	s_c	N/mm^2	s_c	psi	Compressive stress also. Sec. 2.4
Modulus of elasticity	x_E	N/mm^2	E	psi	Eq. (2.9)
Poisson's ratio	v	—	v	—	Eq. (2.9)
Load	W	N	W	lb	Sec. 2.3
Tangential load (force)	W_t	N	W_t	lb	Fig. 2.4
Power	P	kW	P	hp	Eq. (2.51)
Torque	T	N · m	T	in.-lb	Eq. (2.35)
Radius of curvature	ρ	mm	ρ	in.	Eqs. (2.14), (2.32)
of root fillet	ρ_f	mm	ρ_f	in.	Fig. 2.6
Roll angle (involute)	θ_r	deg	ε_r	deg	Fig. 2.10
Zone of action	g_α	mm	Z	in.	Fig. 2.14, Eq. (2.34)
Rotational speed, pinion	n_1	rpm	n_P	rpm	Eq. (2.41)
Rotational speed, gear	n_2	rpm	n_G	rpm	Eq. (2.42)
Pitch-line velocity	v_t	m/s	v_t	fpm	Rotational speed × pitch circumference
Sliding velocity	v_s	m/s	v_s	fpm, fps	Sec. 2.5, Eq. (2.40)
Number of cycles	n_c	—	n_c	—	Sec. 2.4
Size factor for gearbox	Q	—	Q	—	Sec. 2.8
Loading index for strength	U_ℓ	N/mm^2	U_ℓ	psi	Sec. 2.9
Loading index for surface durability	K	N/mm^2	K	psi	Sec. 2.9
Scoring criterion number	Z_c	°C	Z_c	°F	Eq. (2.44)
Contact ratio (profile)	ε_α	—	m_p	—	Eq. (2.39)
Band of contact width (between two cylinders)	—	—	B	in.	Fig. 2.11, Eq. (2.43)
Specific film thickness	—	—	Λ	—	Eq. (2.31)
Oil-film thickness (EHD)	h_{min}	μm	h_{min}	μin.	Eq. (2.31), Fig. 2.11
Surface roughness	S	μm	S	μin.	Eq. (2.31)

Note: Abbreviations for units are as follows:

Metric system		English system	
mm	millimeters	in.	inches
deg	degrees	deg	degrees
N	newtons	lb	pounds
N · m	newton-meters	in. · lb	inch-pounds
N/mm^2	newtons per square millimeter	psi	pounds per square inch
kW	kilowatts	hp	horsepower
rpm	revolutions per minute	rpm	revolutions per minute
m/s	meters per second	fpm	feet per minute
		fps	feet per second
°C	degrees Celsius	°F	degrees Fahrenheit
μm	microns (10^{-6} meters)	μin.	microinches (in./10^6)

There are several kinds of stresses present in loaded and rotating gear teeth. The designer must consider all the possibilities so that the gears are proportioned to keep all the stresses within design limits.

2.1 Calculated Stresses

The stresses calculated in gear-design formulas are not necessarily *true* stresses. For instance, the tensile stress at the root of a gear tooth might be calculated at 275 N/mm^2 (40,000 psi) using the formula for a cantilever beam. If the tooth was very hard and there were a large number of cycles, there might be an effective stress-concentration factor of about 2 to 1. This would tend to raise the stress to an effective value of perhaps 550 N/mm^2 (80,000 psi) in this example. If the part was case-hardened, there might be a residual compressive stress in the outer fiber of the root fillet of as much as 140 N/mm^2 (20,000 psi). If the root fillet was large and well polished and the number of cycles was low, the effective stress concentration might be as low as 1.0. In this case, a calculated stress of 275 N/mm^2 (40,000 psi) might be effectively reduced to as little as 140 N/mm^2 (20,000 psi)!

It can be seen from the example just considered that things like stress concentration and residual stress can make it difficult to get correct answers about gear-tooth stresses.

Other things also make it hard to get correct calculated stresses. The load that the gear teeth are transmitting may be known. However, whether this load is uniformly distributed (see Fig. 2.1) across the face width and whether this load is properly shared by the two or more pairs of teeth that are in

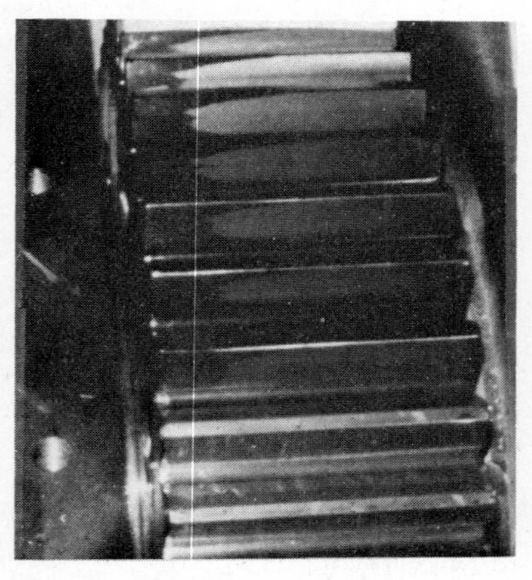

FIG. 2.1 Contact checks at full torque for two sets of gears. Left-hand view shows misalignment resulting in overload at end of tooth more than twice what it should be. Right-hand view shows essentially uniform load distribution across the face width.

mesh at the same time may not be known. Errors in tooth spacing not only disrupt the sharing of tooth loads but may cause accelerations and decelerations which will cause a dynamic overload. The masses of the rotating gears and connected apparatus resist velocity changes. Tachometer gears made of hardened steel have been known to pit in high-speed aircraft applications even when the transmitted load was negligible.

Several assumptions have to be made to permit the calculation of stresses in gear teeth. It can be seen from the previous discussion that it is difficult to make assumptions that will properly allow for such things as stress concentration, residual stress, misalignment, and tooth errors. This means that the stress calculated is probably not the true stress.

Once a "stress" is calculated, there is usually no sure way of knowing how this stress is related to the physical properties of the material. Ordinarily the only properties of a gear material known with some certainty are the ultimate strength and the yield point. Endurance-limit values may be available, but these will usually be taken from reverse-bending tests of small bars. The gear tooth is essentially a cantilever beam which is bent in *one direction only*. This is not so hard on the tooth as fully reversed bending would be.

Laboratory fatigue tests are made on small test specimens with a uniform and smoothly polished test section. In contrast, the actual gear tooth is usually a part of a large piece of metal of more or less nonuniform structure. The critical section of the gear tooth may have tear marks, rough finish, and possibly corrosion on the surface. Its failure is usually a *fatigue* failure. All these things make it hard for the gear designer to take ordinary handbook data on the strength of materials and design gears. The best way to find out how much load gears will carry is to build and test gears. Then the designer can work backward and calculate what "stress" was present when the gear worked properly.

2.2 Gear-Design Limits

In spite of the difficulty of calculating true stresses, gear-stress formulas are a valuable and necessary design tool. When materials, quality of manufacture, and kind of design stay quite constant, formulas can be used quite successfully to determine the proper size of new designs. Essentially the formula is used as a yardstick to make a new design a scale model of an old design which was known to be able to carry a certain load successfully.

It is particularly important to base new designs on old designs which have been successful. If the designer has an application which is not similar to anything built in the past, it is important to realize that a *new* design cannot be rated with certainty. Formulas may be used to estimate how much the new gear will do. However, it should be kept in mind that one can *only estimate* the performance of a new gear design. Field experience will be required to give the final answer about what the gears will do. In many cases, it has been possible to raise the power rating of gearsets after a sufficient amount of field experience was obtained. Several aircraft engines today have gears in them which are running at 25 to 50 percent more power than the gears were rated at when they were first designed.

The design engineer is obligated to design a gear unit so that all criteria are met in a reasonable fashion. Besides stress limits, there are temperature limits and oil-film-thickness limits. In addition to these first-order requirements, there are secondary considerations like vibration, noise, and environment.

The general procedure in design is to first make the gears large enough to keep the tooth-bending stresses and surface compressive stresses within allowable limits. Further calculations are made to check the risks of scoring and over-temperature. Frequently, refinements in details of tooth design, kind of lubricant, temperature of lubricant, and accuracy of the gear tooth are required to meet all the design limits.

Table 2.3 outlines the design limits generally used. Sections 2.3 to 2.6 explain these limits and present background information about how the limits have developed.

TABLE 2.3 Gear-Design Limits

Item	Symbol		Prime variables	Cross references in this book
	Metric	English		
Tooth bending stress	s_t	s_t	Size of teeth, metal hardness, tooth design, tooth accuracy	Sec. 3.25
Surface contact stress	s_c	s_c	Pinion diameter, ratio of pinion to gear, metal hardness, tooth design, tooth accuracy	Sec. 3.25
Oil-film thickness	$h_{\min}$	$h_{\min}$	Pitch-line speed, oil viscosity, pinion diameter, ratio, load intensity	Eq. (3.82)
Specific film thickness	—	Λ	Surface finish, oil-film thickness	Eq. (3.88)
Blank temperature	T_b	T_b	Oil inlet temperature, temperature rise of part	Sec. 3.31
Flash temperature	T_F	T_F	Blank temperature, tooth loading, pinion rotational speed, tooth-design details, tooth size	Sec. 3.31

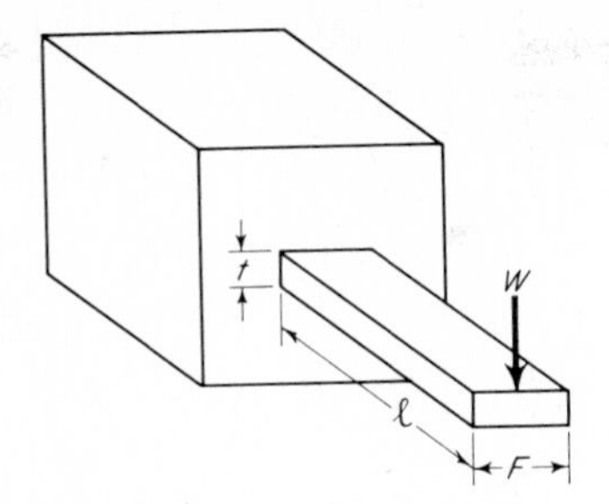

FIG. 2.2 A loaded cantilever beam.

2.3 Gear-Strength Calculations

A gear tooth is essentially a stubby cantilever beam. At the base of the beam, there is tensile stress on the loaded side and compressive stress on the opposite side. When gear teeth break, they usually fail by a crack at the base of the tooth on the tensile-stress side. The ability of gear teeth to resist tooth breakage is usually referred to as their *beam strength* or their *flexural strength.*

The flexural strength of gear teeth was first calculated to a close degree of accuracy by Wilfred Lewis* in 1893. He conceived the idea of inscribing a parabola of uniform strength inside a gear tooth. It happens that when a parabola is made into a cantilever beam, the stress is *constant* along the surface of the parabola. By inscribing the largest parabola that will fit into a gear-tooth shape, one immediately locates the most critically stressed position on the gear tooth. This position is at the point at which the parabola of uniform strength becomes *tangent* to the surface of the gear tooth.

The Lewis formula can be derived quite simply from the usual textbook formula for the stress at the root of a cantilever beam. Figure 2.2 shows a rectangular cantilever beam. The tensile stress at the root of this beam is

$$s_t = \frac{6Wl}{Ft^2} \tag{2.1}$$

If we substitute a gear tooth for the rectangular beam, we can find the critical point in the root fillet of the gear by inscribing a parabola. This is point a in Fig. 2.3.

The next step is to draw some construction lines to get a dimension x. By

*The Lewis paper and other references that apply to this chapter are given in the reference list at the end of the book.

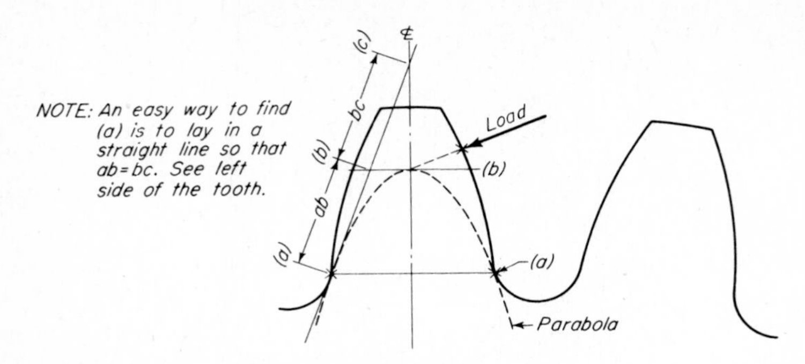

FIG. 2.3 When gear tooth is loaded at point b, point a is the most critically stressed point. Inscribed parabola is tangent to root fillet at point a and has its origin where load vector cuts the center line.

similar triangles in Fig. 2.4, it is apparent that

$$x = \frac{t^2}{4l} \tag{2.2}$$

By substituting x into Eq. (2.1), we get

$$s_t = \frac{W}{F(2x/3)} \tag{2.3}$$

The circular pitch p may be entered into both the numerator and the denominator without changing the value of the equation. This gives

$$s_t = \frac{Wp}{F(2x/3)p} \tag{2.4}$$

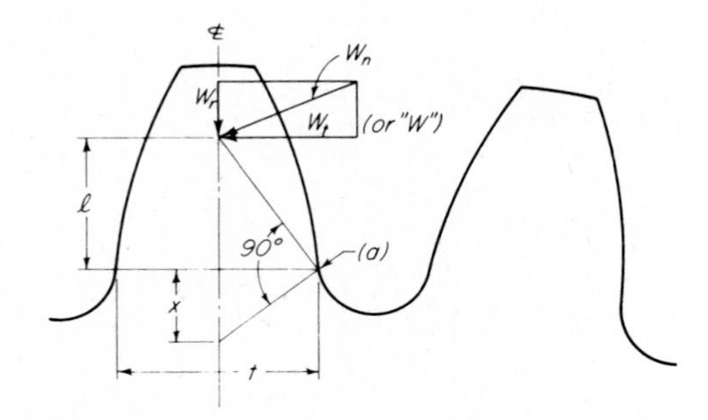

FIG. 2.4 Determination of x dimension from a gear-tooth layout.

The term $2x/3p$ was called y by Lewis. This was a factor that could be determined by a layout of the gear tooth. Since the factor was *dimensionless*, it could be tabulated and used for any pitch.

Using y, the Lewis formula may be written as

$$s_t = \frac{W}{Fpy} \qquad \text{or} \qquad W = s_t pFy \tag{2.5}$$

In present-day work, most engineers prefer to use module or diametral pitch instead of circular pitch in making stress calculations. This can be done by substituting Y for y ($Y = \pi y$) and P_d for p ($P_d = \pi/p$). This makes the Lewis formula become

$$s_t = \frac{WP_d}{FY} \quad \text{psi} \tag{2.6}$$

The original Lewis formula was worked out for the transverse component of the applied load. In Fig. 2.4, it is apparent that the load normal to the tooth surface has a tangential and a radial component. The radial component produces a small compressive stress across the root of the gear tooth. When this component is considered, the tensile stress is reduced by a small amount, and the compressive stress on the opposite side of the tooth is increased by a slight amount. Seemingly this would indicate that the tooth would be most critically stressed on the compression side. This is not the case, however. In most materials, a tensile stress is more damaging than a somewhat higher compressive stress.

Lewis took the application of load to be at the tip of the tooth. In his day, even the best gears were not very accurate. This meant that the load was usually carried by a single tooth instead of being shared between two teeth on a gear. If a single tooth carried full load, it is obvious that the greatest stress would occur when the tooth had rolled to a point at which the tip was carrying the load.

Worst Load. When gears are made accurate enough for the teeth to share load, the tip-load condition is not the most critical. In nearly all gear designs, the contact ratio is high enough to put a second pair of teeth in contact when one pair has reached the tip-load condition on one member. The *worst-load* condition occurs when a single pair of teeth carry full load and the contact has rolled to a point at which a second pair of teeth is just ready to come into contact. Figure 2.5 shows how to locate the worst-load condition on a spur pinion. Note that the contact point has advanced to where it is just one base pitch away from the first point of contact.

In spur gears, the worst-load condition can be used in the Lewis formula by simply making the tooth layout with the load applied at the *worst point*

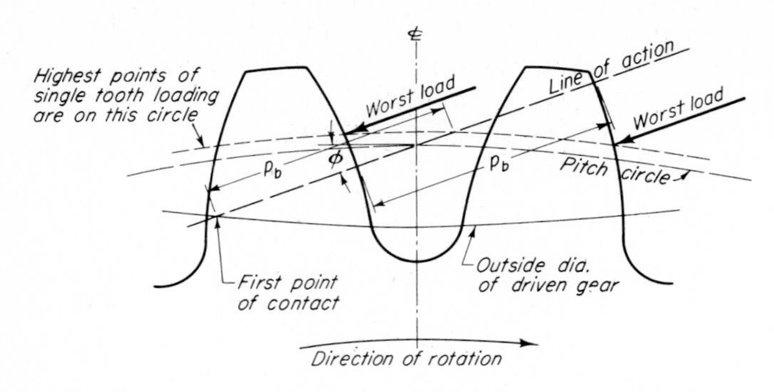

FIG. 2.5 Worst application of beam loading on precision spur gears is one base pitch above the first point of contact.

instead of at the *tip*. This gives a larger *Y* factor. Table 2.4 shows how this affects the *Y* factor for a few 20° spur pinions made to a standard depth of 2.250 in. for 1 pitch. The addendum is 1.000 in. for 1 pitch.

In helical and spiral bevel gears, the teeth are usually accurate enough to share load. The geometry of the teeth, however, is such as to make any position of load which can accurately be labeled the "worst application" of load impossible to find. In all positions of contact, the design usually makes it possible for two or more pair of teeth to share the load. This situation is handled by calculating a *geometry factor* for strength. See Sec. 2.9 for further details.

Stress Concentration. In Lewis' time, stress-concentration factors were not used in engineering calculations. In present gear work, almost all design-

TABLE 2.4 *Y* Factors for Standard 20° Spur Pinions

		Y factor	
No. pinion teeth	No. gear teeth	Tip load	Worst load
20	20	0.287	0.527
20	60	0.287	0.577
20	120	0.287	0.600
25	25	0.310	0.583
25	60	0.310	0.657
25	120	0.310	0.693
30	30	0.332	0.640
30	60	0.332	0.673
30	120	0.332	0.740

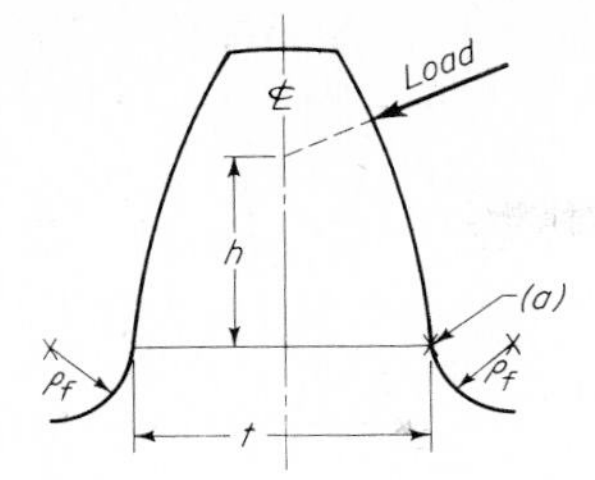

FIG. 2.6 Dimensions used to calculate stress concentration.

ers realize the necessity of using a stress-concentration factor. Dolan and Broghamer (1942) have made an extensive study of photoelastic stress-concentration factors in plastic models of gear teeth. Their work has been widely used in recent years.

Figure 2.6 shows the dimensions used to calculate stress concentration. The equations established from the experimental work of Dolan and Broghamer are

$$K_r = 0.18 + \left(\frac{t}{\rho_f}\right)^{0.15}\left(\frac{t}{h}\right)^{0.45} \tag{2.7}$$

for 20° involute spur teeth, and

$$K_r = 0.22 + \left(\frac{t}{\rho_f}\right)^{0.20}\left(\frac{t}{h}\right)^{0.40} \tag{2.8}$$

for $14\frac{1}{2}°$ involute teeth.

In the above equations, K_r is the stress-concentration factor. The radius ρ_f is the radius of curvature of the root fillet at the point at which the fillet joins the root diameter.

Tests of actual metal gear teeth show that the real stress-concentration factor is not the same as the photoelastic value determined on models made of plastic material.* If the root fillet has deep scratches and toolmarks, it may be higher. Some materials are more brittle than others. In general, high-hardness steels show more stress-concentration effects than low-hardness steels. Some of the case-hardened and induction-hardened steels are an exception to this, however. When a high residual compressive stress is obtained in the surface layer of the material, stress-concentration effects are reduced.

Stress concentration is also influenced by the number of cycles. Some of the low-hardness steels show little or no effect of stress concentration when

*The Drago paper P229.24 (1982) gives some very interesting research test data on stresses in gear-tooth samples.

loaded to destruction statically. Yet when fatigued for a million or more cycles, they show a definite reduction in strength due to stress concentration.

Load Distribution. The face width used by Lewis was the *full* face width. Actual gears are seldom loaded uniformly across the face width. Errors in shaft alignment and helix angles tend to increase the load on one end of the tooth or the other. Present practice is to use a *load-distribution factor* to account for the extra load imposed somewhere in the face width as a result of nonuniform load distribution.

Dynamic Load. The load applied to the gear tooth is greater than the transmitted load based on horsepower. In general, the faster the gears are running, the more shock due to tooth errors and the more dynamic effects due to imbalance and torque variations in the driving and driven apparatus. Lewis intended to allow for this situation by reducing the safe working stress as pitch-line velocity was increased.

A considerable amount of research has been carried out to determine the amount of *dynamic* gear-tooth loads. A research committee of the American Society of Mechanical Engineers—headed by Earle Buckingham—published the first authoritative work on dynamic loads in 1931. This work gave what was believed to be an accurate method for calculating dynamic load. A simplified formula that makes possible a quick but approximate calculation of dynamic load was developed from this work. This method has been widely published and used.

In his most recent work, Buckingham has given equations that permit dynamic load to be calculated using actual shaft stiffnesses and inertias. This work covers dynamic-load calculations on several kinds of gear teeth.

The problem of gear-tooth dynamic load received much attention during the 1950s and 1960s. Many papers were published showing test data. The latest and probably the most technically accurate data is the work done by Dr. Aizoh Kubo* and others.

In design work, the overload on gear teeth is often handled by a *dynamic factor*. This factor is used as a multiplier of the transmitted load.

A. Tucker and many others (including Buckingham) point out that the dynamic overload is really an *incremental* amount of load that is *added* to the transmitted load rather than being a multiplier of the transmitted load. For instance, low-hardness gears idling at little or no transmitted load may be inaccurate enough to develop such serious dynamic loads that they fail prematurely!

Using the dynamic overload as an adder is somewhat unhandy in rating equations. The usual rating formula is worked out for full rated power, and the dynamic factor—used as a multiplier—adds on what is considered to be

*See Sec. 9.2 for a review of Kubo's dynamic-load work.

the extra amount for dynamic load. Such rating formulas, of course, give the wrong answer at light loads, but they can be quite accurate at full load.

Finite Element. The German practice in calculating tooth strength has developed into taking the tangency point of a 30° angle as the critical stress point on the root fillet. Stress-concentration effects are determined by the *finite element* method of stress analysis instead of by photoelastic results.

The proposed International Standards Organization (ISO) method of gear rating for tooth strength uses the 30° angle and equations for stress concentration based on finite element studies of gear teeth. The standards of the American Gear Manufacturers Association (AGMA) use strength formulas derived from the work of Lewis and Dolan/Broghamer.

German gear people feel that the 30° angle method is simpler than the inscribed parabola method and that the results are close enough to be suitable for any normal design work. The finite element method of getting stress-concentration values, though, gives results that are often considerably different from those found using the Dolan/Broghamer method. Figure 2.7 shows a comparison of the 30° angle method and the inscribed parabola method.

In 1980 Dr. Giovanni Castellani and Mr. V. Parenti Castelli made a considerable study of the proposed ISO strength rating method compared with established AGMA standard methods. They presented comparative geometry factors for strength based on several spur- and helical-gear designs. The differences in results were so great that it is now felt that more test work must be done.

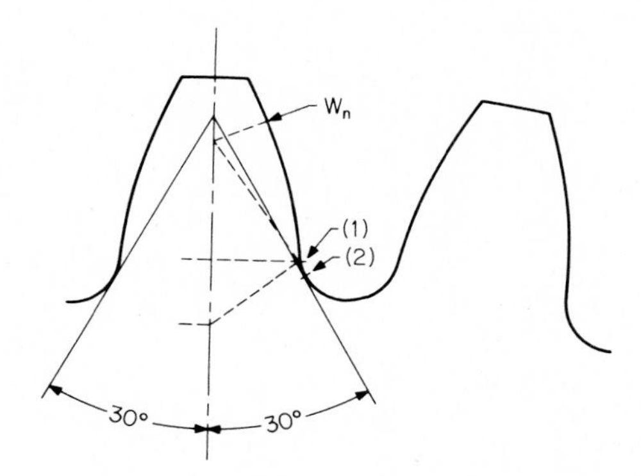

(1) Most critically stressed point by inscribed parabola method
(2) Most critically stressed point by 30° angle method

FIG. 2.7 Comparison of 30° method of finding most critically stressed point with inscribed parabola method.

2.4 Gear Surface-Durability Calculations

Gears fail by pitting and wear as well as by tooth breakage. Frequently gears will wear to the point where they begin to run roughly. Then the increased dynamic load plus the stress-concentration effects of the worn tooth surface cause the teeth ultimately to fail by breakage. Figure 2.8 shows the kinds of stresses that are present in the region of the contact band. In the center of the band, there is a point of maximum compressive stress. Directly underneath this point, there is a maximum subsurface shear stress. The depth to the point of maximum shear stress is a little more than one-third the width of the band of contact.

The gear-tooth surfaces move across each other with a combination of rolling and sliding motion. The sliding motion plus the coefficient of friction tends to cause additional surface stresses. Just ahead of the band of contact, there is a narrow band of compression. Just behind the band of contact, there is a narrow region of tensile stress.

A bit of metal on the surface of a gear tooth goes through a cycle of compression and tension each time a mating gear tooth passes over it. If the tooth is loaded heavily enough, there will usually be evidence of both surface cracks and plastic flow on the contacting surface. There may also be a rupturing of the metal as a result of subsurface shear stresses.

Hertz Derivations. The stresses on the surface of gear teeth are usually determined by formulas derived from the work of H. Hertz (of Germany). Frequently these stresses are called *hertz* stresses.

Hertz determined the width of the contact band and the stress pattern

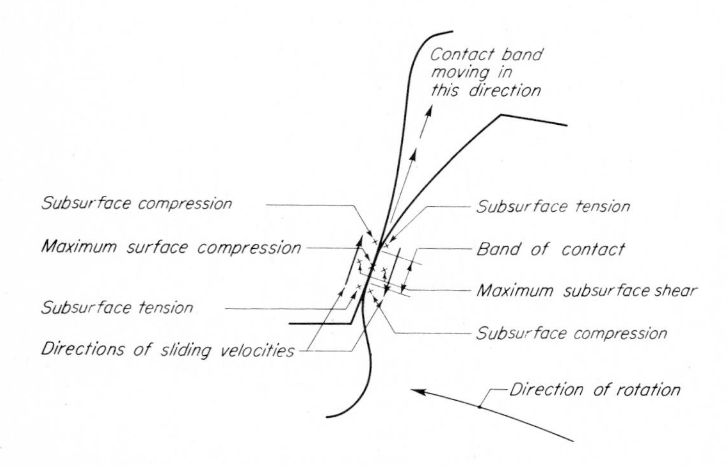

FIG. 2.8 Stresses in region of tooth contact.

when various geometric shapes were loaded against each other. Of particular interest to gear designers is the case of two cylinders with parallel axes loaded against each other.

Figure 2.9 shows the case of two cylinders with parallel axes. The applied force is F pounds and the length of the cylinders is L inches. The width of the band of contact is B inches.

The hertz formula for the width of the band of contact is

$$B = \sqrt{\frac{16F(K_1 + K_2)R_1R_2}{L(R_1 + R_2)}} \tag{2.9}$$

where

$$K_1 = \frac{1 - v_1^2}{\pi E_1}$$

$$K_2 = \frac{1 - v_2^2}{\pi E_2}$$

In the above equations, v is Poisson's ratio and E is the modulus of elasticity.

The maximum compressive stress is

$$s_c = \frac{4F}{L\pi B} \tag{2.10}$$

The maximum shear stress is

$$s_s = 0.295s_c \tag{2.11}$$

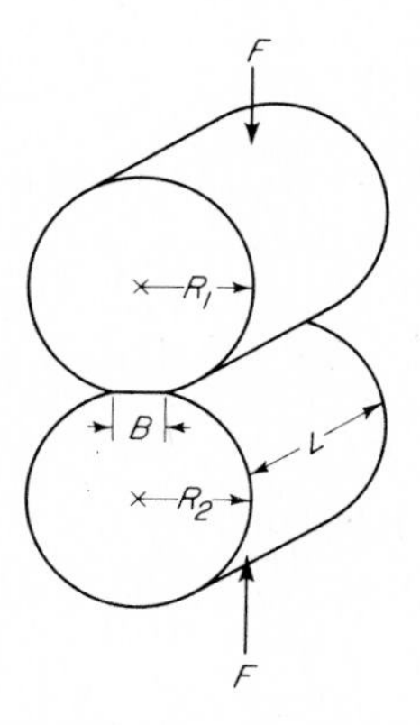

FIG. 2.9 Parallel cylinders in contact and heavily loaded.

The depth to the point of maximum shear is

$$Z = 0.393B \tag{2.12}$$

Equations (2.9) and (2.10) may be combined and simplified to give the following when Poisson's ratio is taken as 0.3:

$$s_c = \sqrt{0.35 \frac{F(1/R_1 + 1/R_2)}{L(1/E_1 + 1/E_2)}} \tag{2.13}$$

The hertz formulas can be applied to spur gears quite easily by considering the contact conditions of gears to be equivalent to those of cylinders that have the same radius of curvature at the point of contact as the gears have. This is an approximation because the radius of curvature of an involute tooth will change while going across the width of the band of contact. The change is not too great when contact is in the region of the pitch line. However, when contact is near the base circle, the change is rapid, and contact stresses calculated by the hertz method for cylinders are not very accurate.

Figure 2.10 shows how the radius of curvature may be determined at any point on an involute curve. At the pitch line, the radius of curvature is

$$\rho = \frac{d \sin \phi}{2} \tag{2.14}$$

At any other diameter, such as d_1, the radius of curvature is

$$\rho_1 = \frac{d_1 \sin \phi_1}{2} \tag{2.15}$$

The angle ϕ_1 can be found by the relation

$$\cos \phi_1 = \frac{d \cos \phi}{d_1} \tag{2.16}$$

The compressive stress at the pitch line of a pair of spur gears can be obtained by substituting the following into Eq. (2.13):

$$F = \frac{W_t}{\cos \phi} \tag{2.17}$$

$$L = F$$

$$R_1 = \frac{d \sin \phi}{2} \qquad R_2 = m_G R_1 \tag{2.18}$$

Note: At this point, we are switching from the symbols of conventional mechanics to the symbols used by gear engineers. This can be confusing, unfortunately, because F is *applied force* in Eqs. (2.9) to (2.17), but F is *face width* in Eq. (2.18) and following equations.

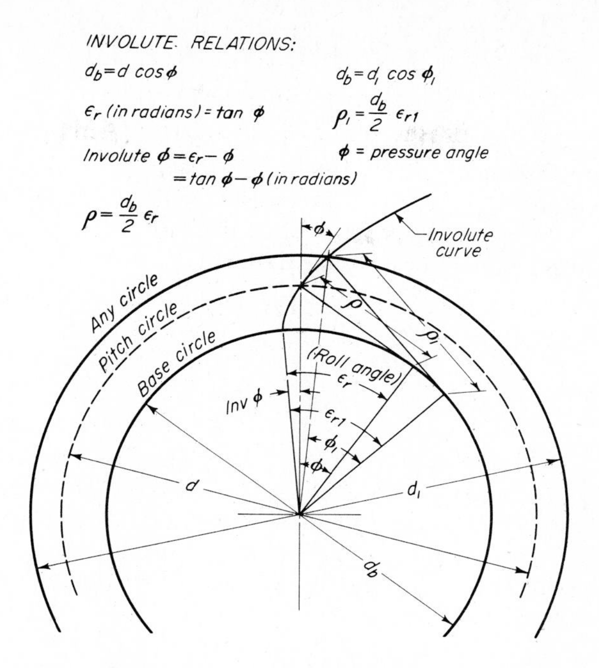

FIG. 2.10 Radius of curvature of an involute and other basic relations of the involute curve.

In the Eq. (2.17) W_t is the tangential driving pressure in pounds. It can be obtained by dividing the pinion torque by the pitch radius of the pinion. In Eq. (2.18), F is the face width in inches, and d is the pitch diameter of the pinion. The ratio of gear teeth to pinion teeth is m_G. Combining Eqs. (2.13), (2.17), and (2.18) gives

$$s_c = \sqrt{\frac{0.70}{(1/E_1 + 1/E_2) \cos\phi \sin\phi}} \sqrt{\frac{W_t}{Fd}\left(\frac{m_G + 1}{m_G}\right)} \tag{2.19}$$

K-Factor Derivation. For a steel spur pinion meshing with a steel gear, we may substitute the nominal value of 30,000,000 for E. Then

$$s_c = 5715 \sqrt{\frac{W_t}{Fd}\left(\frac{m_G + 1}{m_G}\right)} \tag{2.20}$$

when the teeth have a 20° pressure angle.

Many gear designers have found it convenient to call the term under the square-root sign in Eq. (2.20) the K factor. This makes it possible to reduce Eq. (2.20) to

$$s_c = 5715 \sqrt{K} \tag{2.21}$$

where

$$K = \frac{W_t}{Fd}\left(\frac{m_G + 1}{m_G}\right) \qquad (2.22)$$

The compressive stress on helical-gear teeth can be obtained by finding the radius of curvature of the teeth in a section *normal* to the pitch helix. This section has a *pitch ellipse* instead of a pitch circle. Using an equation for an ellipse, we can get values to use for the R values in Eq. (2.13). These are

$$R_1 = \frac{d \sin \phi_n}{2 \cos^2 \psi}$$
$$R_2 = m_G\left(\frac{d \sin \phi_n}{2 \cos^2 \psi}\right) \qquad (2.23)$$

In accurate helical gears, the load is shared by several pair of teeth. The average length of tooth working is equal to the face width multiplied by the contact ratio and divided by the cosine of the helix angle. The *normal* load (load in *normal section*) applied is equal to the tangential load in the transverse plane divided by the cosine of the helix and divided by the cosine of the normal pressure angle. Substituting these values into Eq. (2.19) gives a basic equation for the compressive stress in helical-gear teeth:

$$s_c = \sqrt{\frac{0.70 \cos^2 \psi}{(1/E_1 + 1/E_2) \cos \phi_n \sin \phi_n m_p}} \sqrt{\frac{W_t}{Fd}\left(\frac{m_G + 1}{m_G}\right)} \qquad (2.24)$$

where m_p is the profile contact ratio.

By introducing the K factor and a constant C_k, most of the terms in the equation can be eliminated. This gives us a simplified equation*

$$s_c = C_k \sqrt{\frac{K}{m_p}} \quad \text{psi} \qquad (2.25)$$

Table 2.5 gives some values of C_k and m_p for typical helical gears made to full-depth proportions in the normal section. The profile-contact-ratio values were calculated for a 25-tooth pinion meshing with a 100-tooth gear. For other numbers of teeth, the contact ratio will change by a small amount; however, it makes very little difference in Eq. (2.25), since the contact-ratio term is *under* the square-root sign.

Bevel and worm gears can be handled in a somewhat similar manner.

Worst-Load Position. In most cases, the compressive stress on spur-gear teeth is calculated at the lowest point on a pinion tooth at which full load is carried by a single pair of teeth. This situation cannot occur in wide-face

*This equation illustrates the derivation of rating formulas, but is now obsolete. Do not use it for design.

TABLE 2.5 Value of C_k and m_p for Helical Gears

Normal pressure angle ϕ_n	Spur		15° helix		30° helix		45° helix	
	C_k	m_p	C_k	m_p	C_k	m_p	C_k	m_p
$14\frac{1}{2}°$	6581	2.10	6357	2.01	5699	1.71	4653	1.26
$17\frac{1}{2}°$	6050	1.88	5844	1.79	5240	1.53	4278	1.13
20°	5715	1.73	5520	1.65	4949	1.41	4041	1.05
25°	5235	1.52	5057	1.45	4534	1.25	3702	0.949

Note: The above values are illustrative of the development of gear-rating equations, but should not be used for design purposes. Chapter 3 gives different values that are appropriate for actual design work.

helicals, but it can occur in narrow helicals, bevels, and spur gears. Theoretically, if one pair of teeth carries full load and the position of loading is at the lowest possible position on the pinion, there is a *worst-load* condition for hertz stress corresponding to the *worst-load* position for strength described in the preceding section.

Different formulas for contact stress may include factors to account for the increase in load due to velocity and tooth inaccuracy. The same questions of dynamic load and misalignment across the face width are present in calculating contact stress as in calculating the root stress. Service factors allow for torque pulsations and the length of service required from the gears.

Endurance Limit. The tendency of gear teeth to pit has traditionally been thought of as a surface fatigue problem in which the prime variables were the compressive stress at the surface, the number of repetitions of the load, and the endurance strength of the gear material. In steel gears the surface endurance strength is quite closely related to hardness, and so stress, cycles, and hardness then become the key items.

It was also believed that there was an *endurance limit* for surface durability at about ten million cycles (10^7 cycles). For case-carburized steel gears, fully hardened, typical design values were:

Item	Metric*		English	
	Symbol	Value	Symbol	Value
Maximum allowable stress	s_c	1724 N/mm²	s_c	250,000 psi
Number of cycles	n_c	10^7	n_c	10^7
Surface hardness	HV	700 min.	HRC	60 min.

*In Chap. 2, most of the data will be given in English units to agree with previously published derivations. From Chap. 3 onward, the data will be primarily given in the metric system. For the convenience of readers, equivalent English values will often be given as a second set of values.

Gear work in the 1970s led to two very important conclusions. (These conclusions had been suspected in the 1960s.):

1 Pitting is very much affected by the lubrication conditions.

2 There is no endurance limit against pitting.

Work on the theory of elastohydrodynamic lubrication (EHD) showed that gears and rolling-element bearings often developed a very thin oil film that tended to separate the two contacting surfaces so that there was little or no metallic contact. When this favorable situation was obtained, the gear or the bearing could either carry *more load* without pitting or run for a *longer time* without pitting at a given load.

The idea that there was an endurance-limit pitting grew up from test-stand data, where tests were generally discontinued after 10^7 cycles or 2×10^7 cycles. (If a test is being run at 1750 cycles per minute, it takes 190 hours to reach 2×10^7 cycles.)

Real gears in service frequently run for several thousand hours before pitting starts—or becomes serious. A gear can often run for up to a billion (10^9) cycles with little or no pitting, but after 2 or 3 billion (2 or 3×10^9) cycles, pitting—and the wear* resulting from pitting—makes the gears unfit for further service.

Regimes of Lubrication. To handle the problem of EHD lubrication effects, the designer needs to think of three *regimes* of lubrication. These are:

Regime I: No appreciable EHD oil film (boundary)

Regime II: Partial EHD oil film (mixed)

Regime III: Full EHD oil film (full film)

In Regime I, the gears may be thought of as running wet with oil, but the thickness of the EHD oil film developed is quite small compared with the surface roughness. Essentially full metal-to-metal contact is obtained in the hertzian contact band area. Regime I is typical of slow-speed, high-load gears running with a rough surface finish. Hand-operated gears in winches, food presses, and jacking devices are typical of slow-speed Regime I gears.

Regime II is characterized by partial metal-to-metal contact. The asperities of the tooth surfaces hit each other, but substantial areas are separated by a thin film. Regime II is typical of medium-speed gears, highly loaded, running with a relatively thick oil and fairly good surface finish. Most vehicle gears are in Regime II. (Tractors, trucks, automobiles, and off-road equipment are vehicle gear applications.)

In Regime III the EHD oil film is thick enough to essentially avoid

*The ASME *Wear Control Handbook*, pp. 755–830, discusses gear wear in depth. See Ref. 130.

metal-to-metal contact. Even the asperities generally miss each other. The well-designed and well-built high-speed gear is generally in Regime III. Turbine-gear applications in ship drives, electric generators, and compressors are good examples of high-speed gears. In the aerospace gearing field, turboprop drives are high-speed and in Regime III. Helicopter main rotor gears are in the high-speed gear region, except for some final-stage gears that may be slow enough to be out of the high-speed domain and into medium speed with Regime II conditions. (Some of the best pioneering work in defining regimes of lubrication was done by the late Charles Bowen, working on helicopter-gear development.)

Figure 2.11 shows a schematic representation of the three regimes of lubrication. Note the details of the hertzian contact band for each regime. Figure 2.12 shows the "nominal" zones for the three regimes.

The quality of the surface finish of the new gear, the degree of finish improvement achieved in breaking in new gears, the thickness and kind of

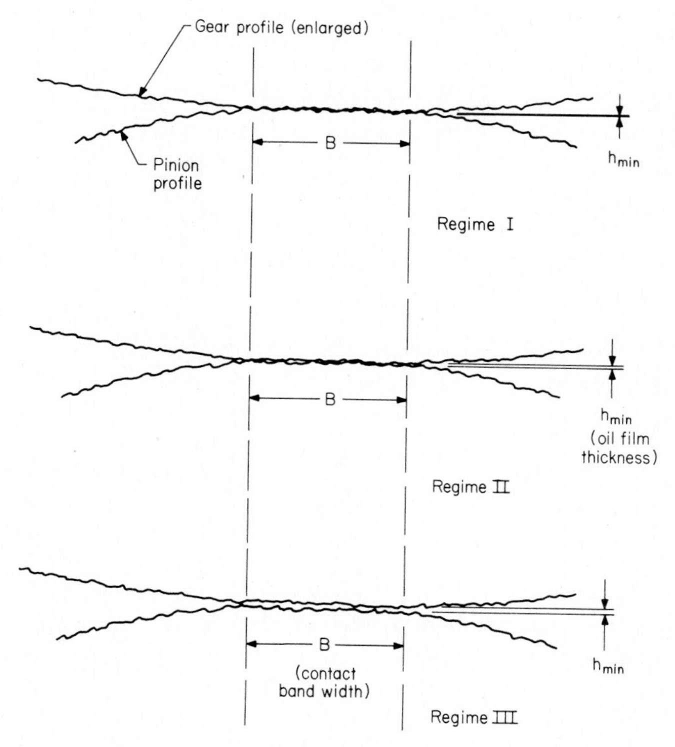

FIG. 2.11 Schematic representation of the three regimes of gear-tooth lubrication.

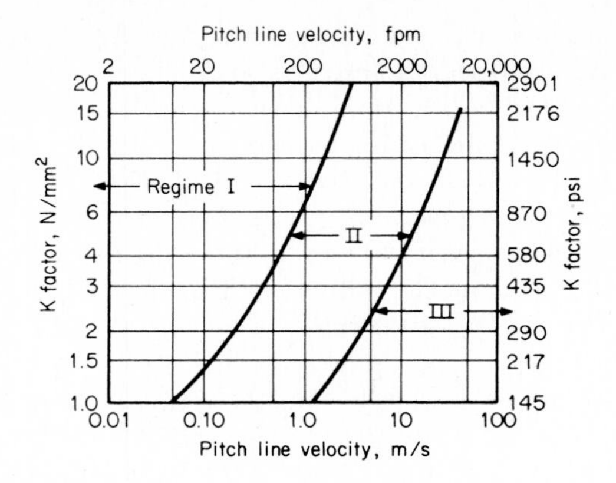

FIG. 2.12 Location of regimes of lubrication for average gears. (*Reprinted from "Characteristics of Regimes of Gear Lubrication" by permission of the Japanese Society of Mechanical Engineers. See Ref. 131.*)

lubricant, the operating temperature, the pitch-line velocity, and the load intensity all enter into the determination of which regime the gear pair operates in. Means of calculating EHD oil-film thickness and design for different regimes of lubrication are given in Chap. 3. Figure 2.12 should be used only as a rough guide.

The surface durability in the different regimes of lubrication varies considerably. Figure 2.13 shows the general trend* of surface contact stress capacity at different numbers of cycles for each of the three regimes of lubrication. The three curves have these equations at 10^7 cycles:

$$\frac{L_b}{L_a} = \left(\frac{K_a}{K_b}\right)^{3.2} \qquad \text{Regime I} \qquad (2.26)$$

$$\frac{L_b}{L_a} = \left(\frac{K_a}{K_b}\right)^{5.3} \qquad \text{Regime II} \qquad (2.27)$$

$$\frac{L_b}{L_a} = \left(\frac{K_a}{K_b}\right)^{8.4} \qquad \text{Regime III} \qquad (2.28)$$

where L_b = cycles (any number from 10^6 to 10^8)
$L_a = 10^7$ cycles
K_a = allowable load intensity at 10^7 cycles
K_b = allowable load intensity at L_b cycles

*Figure 2.13 is a nominal curve intended to show average conditions for reasonably good steel and nominal quality. These curves should not be used for final design.

The contact stress s_c is proportional to the square root of the load intensity. For simplified gear rating,

$$s_c = C_k(KC_d)^{0.50} \tag{2.29}$$

where C_k = tooth geometry constant for the particular design

$$K = \frac{W_t}{Fd}\left(\frac{m_G + 1}{m_G}\right) \quad \text{external teeth}$$

$$= \frac{W_t}{Fd}\left(\frac{m_G - 1}{m_G}\right) \quad \text{internal teeth} \tag{2.30}$$

W_t = tangential driving force

$= \text{torque} \times \dfrac{2}{d}$

C_d = overall derating factor for gear and gearbox design imperfections

The data shown in Fig. 2.13 can be interpreted to show the results of Table 2.6.

Table 2.6 shows the substantial difference in load-carrying capacity of the different regimes. Regime I loses over 50 percent of its capacity every time there is a tenfold increase in life (number of cycles). Regime II loses about 35 percent of its load capacity for a tenfold increase. In comparison, Regime III loses only about 24 percent of its capacity with a tenfold increase.

The damaging situation in Regime I can be considerably offset by substituting a *chemical additive* film on the tooth surfaces for an EHD oil film. Special EP (extreme pressure) oils have been developed for slow-speed, highly loaded vehicle gears. These oils develop chemical compounds on the contacting gear-tooth surfaces. When the lubricant additive is working, it is possible for the gear-tooth operation to shift from Regime I to Regime

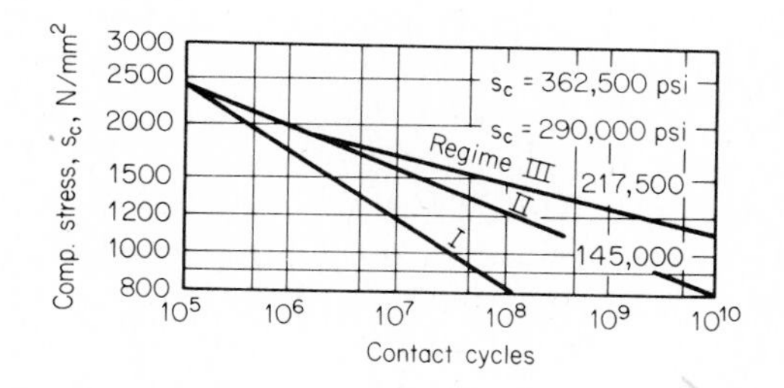

FIG. 2.13 Trend of contact stress for Regimes I, II, and III. Carburized gears. (*Reprinted from "Characteristics of Regimes of Gear Lubrication" by permission of the Japanese Society of Mechanical Engineers.*)

TABLE 2.6 Nominal Comparison of Load-Carrying Capacity of the Regimes of Lubrication

	Load capacity for different regimes		
No. cycles	I	II	III
10^5	100%	100%	100%
10^6	48.7%	64.8%	76.0%
10^7	23.7%	41.9%	57.8%
10^8	—	27.2%	44.9%
10^9	—	—	33.4%
10^{10}	—	—	25.4%

II—with load-carrying capacity improving to Regime II. Likewise, appropriate additives can help gear teeth in Regime II move over into Regime III. This subject will be treated in more depth in Secs. 3.31, 7.8, and 7.15.

2.5 Gear Scoring

When excessive compressive stresses are carried on a gear tooth for a long period of time, pits will develop. If the gear is kept in operation after pitting starts, the whole surface of the tooth will eventually be worn away. Severe pitting leads to rough running and "hammering" of the gear teeth. This in turn leads to other types of surface wear, such as scoring, swaging, and abrasion. *Scoring* is characterized by radial scratch lines, *swaging* is an upsetting process similar to cold rolling, while *abrasion* is the tearing away of small particles when rough surfaces are rubbed across each other.

Gear teeth may score when no pitting has taken place. This may occur when the gears are first put into operation. Sometimes the cause of scoring—when gears have not pitted first—is simply that the accuracy is not sufficient. The teeth do not have a good enough surface finish or good enough spacing and profile accuracy.

Aircraft gears and other types of heavily loaded high-speed gears tend to fail by scoring even when accuracy is good. Apparently the combination of high surface pressure and high sliding velocity can be severe enough to vaporize the oil film and cause instantaneous welding of the surfaces. The continued rotation of the gear teeth causes a radial tearing action which makes the characteristic score marks.

Hot and Cold Scoring. The scoring problem is not limited to high-speed gears. Slow-speed gears may also score. The score marks on slow-speed gears look somewhat different. The failure mechanism seems to be more one of filing or abrading away the metal rather than welding and tearing. European gear people—with some reason—call the slow-speed scoring *cold scuffing** and the high-speed scoring *hot scuffing*.

Cold scoring is basically a problem of gears that are running in Regime I or Regime II conditions with an oil that does not have enough chemical additives to protect the surface. The key variable is *specific film thickness* Λ, which is defined as

$$\Lambda = \frac{h_{\min}}{S'} \tag{2.31}$$

where $h_{\min}$ = EHD oil-film thickness
S' = composite surface roughness of the gear pair
$= (S_1^2 + S_2^2)^{0.50}$
S_1 = surface roughness of pinion
S_2 = surface roughness of gear

The surface roughness values used for S_1 and S_2 are normally the arithmetic-average (AA) values. Formerly, root-mean-square (rms) values were used for surface finish. The rms value for finish is normally about 1.11 times the AA value.

The surface roughness that is used may be different from the value measured on new gears just finished in the gear shop. Most gears will wear in and improve their finish in the first 100 or so hours of operation. This process is helped by not loading the gears too heavily or running them at maximum temperature until they are well broken in. A special lubricant with extra additives or more viscosity may also be used to help lessen the danger of scoring when new gears are first put into service.

Assuming that a favorable break-in will be achieved, in Eq. (2.31) the designer can use the surface roughness values after break-in rather than those from the gear shop. For instance, a precision-ground gear with a 20 AA surface roughness may wear into a 15 AA finish.

It is necessary to calculate a *scoring factor* that will evaluate the combined effects of surface pressure, sliding velocity, coefficient of friction, kind of metals, and kind of oil from the standpoint of scoring.

The gear trade has used several methods of calculating scoring risk. No method has yet proved to be entirely reliable. The principal methods that have been used are shown in Table 2.7.

The remainder of this section will cover the basics of PVT, flash temperature, and scoring index. Specific design recommendations will be given in Sec. 3-31.

*The terms "scuffing" and "scoring" are used somewhat interchangeably. AGMA practice recommends the word "scoring." Other engineering groups in the U.S.A. and abroad often prefer "scuffing" over "scoring."

TABLE 2.7 Scoring Calculation Methods

Name of method	When developed	Kind of scoring	Where covered in this book
PVT	1940s	Hot scoring	Chap. 2
Flash temperature	1940s 1950s	Hot scoring	Chaps. 2, 3
Scoring criterion	1960s	Hot scoring	Chaps. 2, 3
Specific film thickness	1960s 1970s	Cold scoring	Chaps. 2, 3
Integral temperature	1970s	Hot scoring	Chaps. 2, 3

PVT Formula. A PVT formula was used with considerable success in designing small aircraft gears to be built by automotive-gear manufacturers. During World War II, a number of automotive-gear plants made large numbers of aircraft gears. The PVT formula developed as a result of this wartime experience.

The factors in PVT are as follows*:

P—hertz contact pressure. This is usually figured for the tip of the pinion and figured again for the root of the pinion (tip of the gear). The applied load is divided by the profile contact ratio to approximate the way load is shared by two pairs of teeth.

V—sliding velocity in feet per second at the point at which *P* is figured.

T—distance along the line of action from the pitch point to the point at which *P* is calculated.

The quantity *PVT* is always zero at the pitch point on spur or helical gears. It increases steadily as contact moves away from the pitch point, reaching a maximum at the point at which contact is at the tip of the tooth. For this reason, PVT is ordinarily calculated only for the tips of the teeth.

The equations and nomenclature used in the following equations follow the procedure customarily used by automotive-gear designers. The reader will recognize that general equations like (2.13) and (2.15) could have been used as well.

The calculation of PVT involves solving a series of equations. First, the radius of curvature at the pinion tip is calculated (see Fig. 2.14):

$$\rho_p = \sqrt{r_0^2 - (r \cos \phi_t)^2} \tag{2.32}$$

*PVT nomenclature was established in the early 1940s and does not agree with current nomenclature. See Table 2.2 for symbols in use now.

Similarly, the radius of curvature at the gear tip is

$$\rho_G = \sqrt{R_0^2 - (R \cos \phi_t)^2} \tag{2.33}$$

The length of the line of action is

$$Z = \rho_P + \rho_G - C \sin \phi_t \tag{2.34}$$

The hertz compressive stress for the tip of the pinion is

$$P_P = 5740 \sqrt{\frac{T_P}{FZN_P} \frac{C \sin \phi_n}{\rho_P(C \sin \phi_t - \rho_P)}} \tag{2.35}$$

where T_P = pinion torque, in.-lb
F = face width, in.
N_P = number of pinion teeth
C = center distance

Similarly, the stress at the gear tip is

$$P_G = 5740 \sqrt{\frac{T_P}{FZN_P} \frac{C \sin \phi_n}{\rho_G(C \sin \phi_t - \rho_G)}} \tag{2.36}$$

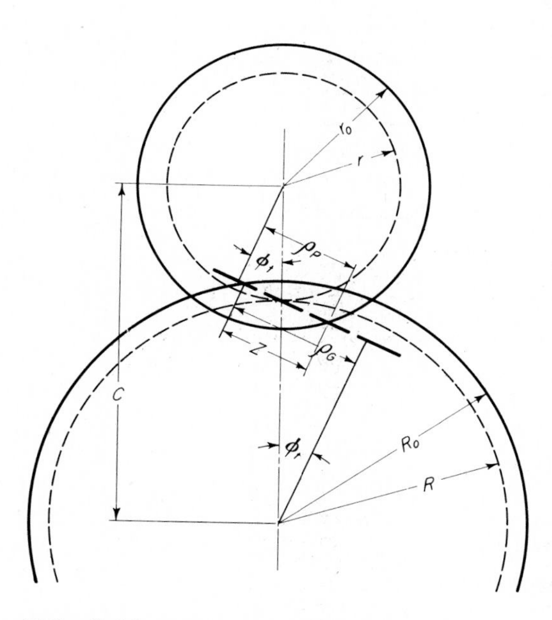

FIG. 2.14 Dimensions used in scoring-factor calculation.

The scoring factor for the pinion tip is

$$\mathrm{PVT}_P = \frac{\pi n_P}{360}\left(1 + \frac{N_P}{N_G}\right)(\rho_P - r \sin \phi_t)^2 P_P \tag{2.37}$$

where n_P = pinion speed, rpm.

At the gear tip, the scoring factor is

$$\mathrm{PVT}_G = \frac{\pi n_P}{360}\left(1 + \frac{N_P}{N_G}\right)(\rho_G - R \sin \phi_t)^2 P_G \tag{2.38}$$

These equations will work for either spur or helical gears. In the case of spur gears, there is only one pressure angle. This makes $\phi_n = \phi_t$.

The profile contact ratio can be obtained easily from the Z value in Eq. (2.34). Since this value is needed frequently, we shall give an equation for it here:

$$m_P = \frac{Z N_P}{2 \cos \phi_t \pi r} \tag{2.39}$$

Equation (2.39) holds for either spur or helical gears. Literally the contact ratio represents the length* of the line of action divided by the base pitch. It is the *average* number of teeth that are in contact in the transverse plane. When the contact ratio comes out to some number like 1.70, it does not actually mean that 1.70 teeth are working. If the ratio is between 1 and 2, there are alternately one pair and two pair of teeth working. From a *time* standpoint, though, it would work out that on the *average* there were 1.70 pair of teeth working.

A design limit of 1,500,000 has been used frequently for a safe limit on PVT. This value works reasonably well with case-hardened gears that are of good accuracy and are lubricated with a medium-weight petroleum oil. Pitch-line velocity should be above 2000 fpm.

Flash Temperature. The concept of flash temperature was first presented by Professor Harmen Blok. The basics of this formula are

$$T_f = T_b + \frac{c_f f W_t (v_1 - v_2)}{\cos \phi_t F_e (\sqrt{v_1} + \sqrt{v_2})\sqrt{B/2}} \tag{2.40}$$

where T_f = flash temperature, °F

T_b = temperature of blank surface in contact zone (often taken as inlet oil temperature), °F

c_f = material constant for conductivity, density, and specific heat

f = coefficient of friction

*Length between the first point of contact and the last point of contact is the *length* used here.

W_t = tangential driving load, lb
v_1 = rolling velocity of pinion at point of contact, fps
v_2 = rolling velocity of gear at point of contact, fps
$v_s = v_1 - v_2$, sliding velocity, fps
ϕ_t = transverse pressure angle, degrees
F_e = face width in contact, in.
B = width of band of contact, in.

The rolling velocities may be obtained from the rpm of the pinion or gear by

$$v_1 = \frac{n_P \pi \rho_1}{360} \tag{2.41}$$

$$v_2 = \frac{n_G \pi \rho_2}{360} \tag{2.42}$$

Originally flash temperatures were calculated for the pinion tip and the gear tip. In this case,

Pinion tip

$\rho_1 = \rho_P$ [see Eq. (2.32)]

$\rho_2 = \rho_G - Z$ (see Fig. 2.14)

Gear tip

$\rho_1 = \rho_G$ [see Eq. (2.33)]

$\rho_2 = \rho_P - Z$ (see Fig. 2.14)

Later development of the flash-temperature formula led to scoring being considered most apt to occur at the *lowest point of single* tooth contact on the pinion or the *highest point of single* tooth contact on the pinion. This situation is most apt to occur when very accurate aircraft spur gears have a small amount of profile modification at the tip to relieve tip loading.

Figure 2.15 shows the location of the highest and lowest points of single tooth contact for the pinion. Normally, scoring calculations are made for the *pinion only*. The gear is handled indirectly, since the pinion can score only when in contact with the gear. (If the pinion is OK, the gear should be OK.)

Table 2.8 shows how to calculate the radii of curvature of the highest and lowest points of single tooth contact.

The material constant c_f was taken as 0.0528 for straight petroleum oils. The coefficient of friction was taken as 0.06.

The width of the band of contact for steel gears was obtained from

$$B = 0.00054\left[\frac{W_t \rho_1 \rho_2}{\cos \phi_t F_e(\rho_1 + \rho_2)}\right]^{0.50} \tag{2.43}$$

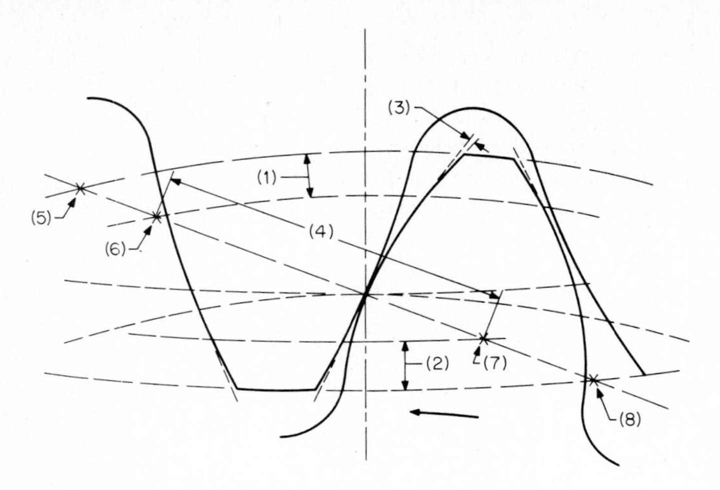

(1) Depth to start modification for pinion
(2) Depth to start modification for gear
(3) Exaggerated profile modification
(4) Zone of contact, unmodified involute profiles
(5) A most critical scoring point if pinion has little or no modification
(6) Most critical scoring point with appropriate profile modification of pinion
(7) Most critical scoring point with appropriate profile modification of gear
(8) A most critical scoring point if gear has little or no profile modification

FIG. 2.15 Layout of teeth to locate critical points for scoring calculations.

Table 2.9 shows some typical design values for maximum flash temperatures used in the 1950s. These values are of some historical importance, but they are not recommended for current designs. More complex procedures, involving surface finish, overload of teeth due to errors, special lubricant effects, and other such factors are needed. (See Chap. 3, Sec. 3.31.)

TABLE 2.8 Radii of Curvature of Involute Spur or Helical Teeth

Contact position	Pinion curvature ρ_1	Gear curvature ρ_2
Lowest single tooth contact	$\sqrt{r_o^2 - (r \cos \phi_t)^2} - p \cos \phi_t$	$C \sin \phi_t - \rho_1$
Highest single tooth contact	$C \sin \phi_t - \rho_2$	$\sqrt{R_o^2 - (R \cos \phi_t)^2} - p \cos \phi_t$

Note: In this table, the outside radius of the pinion is r_o and the pitch radius is r. Radii for the gear are capitalized. The circular pitch is p.

TABLE 2.9 Maximum Design Limit of Flash Temperatures to Prevent Scoring of Spur Gears

Kind of oil	Specification	T_f, °F
Petroleum	SAE 10	250
	SAE 30	375
	SAE 60	500
	SAE 90 (gear lubricant)	600
Diester, compounded	75 SUS at 100°F	330
Petroleum	SAE 30 plus mild EP	425

Scoring Criterion. Some gears have a high risk of hot scoring, while others have little or no risk of hot scoring. To judge the risk of scoring, the *scoring criterion* was developed by Dudley.

The formula for this index number is

$$\text{Scoring-criterion number} = \left(\frac{W_t}{F_e}\right)^{3/4} \frac{n_P^{1/2}}{P_d^{1/4}} \tag{2.44}$$

Table 2.10 shows scoring-criterion numbers published in 1964. If the calculated scoring value exceeds those in Table 2.10, there is a risk of scoring, and more complex calculations should be made. If the value is below

TABLE 2.10 Critical Scoring-Criterion Numbers

Blank temperature, °F	100°	150°	200°	250°	300°
Kind of oil	Critical scoring-index numbers				
AGMA 1	9,000	6,000	3,000	—	—
AGMA 3	11,000	8,000	5,000	2,000	—
AGMA 5	13,000	10,000	7,000	4,000	—
AGMA 7	15,000	12,000	9,000	6,000	—
AGMA 8A	17,000	14,000	11,000	8,000	—
Grade 1065, Mil-O-6082B	15,000	12,000	9,000	6,000	—
Grade 1010, Mil-O-6082B	12,000	9,000	6,000	2,000	—
Synthetic (Turbo 35)	17,000	14,000	11,000	8,000	5,000
Synthetic Mil-L-7808D	15,000	12,000	9,000	6,000	3,000

Notes: 1. See Sec. 3.31 for more data on rating gears for scoring and the use of the scoring-criterion number.

2. See Sec. 7.15 for general data on gear lubricants and the hazard of lubrication failures.

3. See AGMA 250.04 and 251.02 for general data on industrial lubricants.

4. This table is reproduced by permission from the *Gear Handbook*, Chap. 13.

those in the table, the risk of scoring is low, but it may still exist as a result of such things as poor finish, appreciable overload due to inaccuracy, and inadequate lubricant proportions.

The scoring-criterion number is a useful guide for spur, helical, and spiral bevel gears.

The scoring criterion was derived from the flash-temperature equation, Eq. (2.40). By mathematical manipulation it is possible to write the flash-temperature equation in the form

$$T_f = T_b + Z_t\left(\frac{W_t}{F_e}\right)^{3/4} \frac{n_P^{1/2}}{P_d^{1/4}} \tag{2.45}$$

where

$$Z_t = 0.0175 \frac{[\sqrt{\rho_1} - \sqrt{\rho_2/m_G}]P_d^{1/4}}{(\cos \phi_t)^{3/4}[\rho_1\rho_2/(\rho_1 + \rho_2)]^{1/4}} \tag{2.46}$$

The constant Z_t is dimensionless when used with the scoring-criterion number. This makes it possible to tabulate Z_t values for different proportions and styles of tooth design. The term Z_t can be thought of as a *tooth geometry factor** for scoring.

2.6 Thermal Limits

The design of gear drives involves more than just making the gear teeth able to carry bending stresses and contact stresses and to resist scoring. Along with such things as bearing capacity, shaft design, and spline capacity, the designer must consider the thermal limits.

Small gear drives (particularly those under 200 hp) are often splash-lubricated by a quantity of liquid oil in the gearbox. Without a pumped oil system and oil coolers, the gearbox is cooled by the surrounding air. Such a gear drive will have a *thermal rating* as well as a mechanical rating. The application of the gear unit to a job should be such that neither the thermal rating nor the mechanical rating is exceeded.

Customary procedure in calculating thermal ratings is based on finding the maximum horsepower that a unit can carry for 3 hours without the sump temperature exceeding 93°C (200°F) when the ambient air temperature is not over 38°C (100°F).

Long trade experience has led to the development of a great deal of expertise in the thermal capacity of helical-gear units, spiral-bevel-gear

*See Sec. 9.15 for a general calculation method for Z_t which can be used to obtain values at any point on the tooth profile.

units, and worm-gear units. Trade practices have developed to set approximate methods of calculation for a standard thermal rating. No doubt further experience will develop ways of handling thermal ratings that are more complex than those now used. (For instance, special steels and oils can be used at quite high temperatures, and so trade practices may change to recognize special designs that can run hotter than is common in industrial gearing today.)

Equations and calculation procedures for setting thermal ratings will not be given in this book. Instead, Table 2.11 is a rough guide to what is involved in thermal rating.

The prime variables in determining thermal capacity are the gearbox size, the input pinion speed, and the ratio. Table 2.11 shows that if a gear unit is built twice as large, the thermal rating increases about 3 to 1. The mechanical rating increases almost 8 to 1 when the size doubles, so this predicts that large gear units will be short of thermal capacity.

Table 2.11 shows that for the same size unit, the thermal rating drops quite rapidly as the speed is increased. In contrast, the mechanical rating increases somewhat in proportion to an increase in speed.

There is an influence from the ratio, but it is quite mild. From Table 2.11, at 400 rpm it might be possible to design medium-hard gears up to 600 mm (24 in.) center distance and still have enough thermal rating to match the mechanical rating. At 1200 rpm, though, it would probably not be possible to exceed 200 mm (8 in.) center distance and still have enough thermal capacity to match the mechanical capacity.

TABLE 2.11 Some Approximate Values of Thermal Rating in Horsepower

	Center distance, in.			
Pinion speed, rpm	4	8	16	24
	Ratio, 2 to 1			
400	80	240	720	1200
1200	40	110	315	500
2400	12	30	80	55
	Ratio, 4 to 1			
400	80	240	720	1200
1200	42	115	325	525
2400	15	40	110	85

When the normal thermal capacity is exceeded, the thermal capacity may be improved by using one or more fans mounted on input shafts. A favorable fan arrangement can as much as double the normal thermal capacity.

For the larger and more powerful gear units, the thermal capacity is completely inadequate. Pumped-oil lubrication systems with oil coolers must be used.

With a pumped-oil system, calculations must be made to assure that the bearings and gear teeth are fed enough oil to adequately cool and lubricate all parts. The design of gear-lubrication systems will not be covered here. Some general information on this subject is given in Chap. 15 of the *Gear Handbook*.

Thermal Limits at High Speed. When spur-gear teeth run faster than 10 m/s (2000 fpm) or helical teeth run faster than 100 m/s (20,000 fpm), there may be problems with the trapping of air and oil in the gear mesh. Special design features have allowed small spur teeth in aerospace applications to run up to around 100 m/s reasonably successfully. Likewise, special designs of helical gears have permitted successful operation up to 200 m/s.

Some further data on problems with fast-running gears are given in Sec. 7.16 (Chap. 7) of this book. In general, though, the design of gearing that is critical from a speed standpoint is too complex to cover in this book. Several references give special information on this subject. The Martinaglia paper (ASME 1972) and the Akazawa paper (ASME 1980) are particularly useful.

PRELIMINARY ESTIMATE OF GEAR SIZE

The first part of the chapter has shown the general nature of the various kinds of stress formulas that may be used in designing a gearset. This material will probably help the reader to understand the problem of designing a gearset, but it does not give much help in knowing what to do *first* in designing a set after choosing the kind of gear.

There are many ways to start the design of a set. Perhaps the easiest way is to skip all the detail design work and immediately estimate how big the gears must be. If a size that is close to being right can be chosen in the beginning, the designer can work through the dimensional calculations with the prospect of only minor adjustments after the design is checked with appropriate rating formulas.

In this part of the chapter we shall take up the problem of estimating gear size.

2.7 Gear Specifications

Gears are used to transmit power from one shaft to another and to change rotational speed. The designer needs to have specifications for:

1 The amount of power to be transmitted

2 The pinion speed (or gear speed)

3 The required ratio of input and output speeds

4 The length of time the gears must operate

Frequently it is hard to find out how much power a gearset must carry. Take the example of a gear driven by a 10-hp motor. In some applications the motor might be expected to run every day of the year at 10 hp. In other cases the motor might run only intermittently at powers well below 10 hp. In still others the motor might be started every day and have to pull up to 20 hp for a short period of time while the driven machinery was warming up.

The example just cited shows that the gear designer's first problem may be to establish a proper power specification. In doing this, it is necessary to check both the driving and driven apparatus. It may be that the driven apparatus tends to stall or suffer severe shock at infrequent intervals. This might give rise to peak torques as much as five or ten times the full-load torque capacity of the driving motor. Although the gearset does not have to be the strongest of the three connected pieces of apparatus, neither should it be the weakest—unless there is good reason.

Where power and speeds may be quite variable, the designer should strive to reduce the specifications to simple conditions. First, the maximum *continuous* load that the gear might be expected to handle should be established. Next, the maximum *torque* should be determined. This load will probably last for only a short period of time. In many designs, it is necessary to make stress calculations for only these two conditions. In some cases, though, there may be a high *intermediate* load which is less than the maximum but does not last so long as the continuous load. Here it is necessary to calculate stresses for the intermediate load also.

In complex design situations, it is necessary to construct a gear *histogram*. The best procedure is to calculate the pinion torque for each design condition. The results are plotted on log-log graph paper, with the highest loads being put at the lowest number of cycles. Figure 2.16 shows two examples of load histograms. For the vehicle gear shown, it turns out that the critical design condition is low gear and maximum torque. In comparison, the turbine application has its most critical situation at the maximum continuous torque, not the highest torque seen under starting conditions.

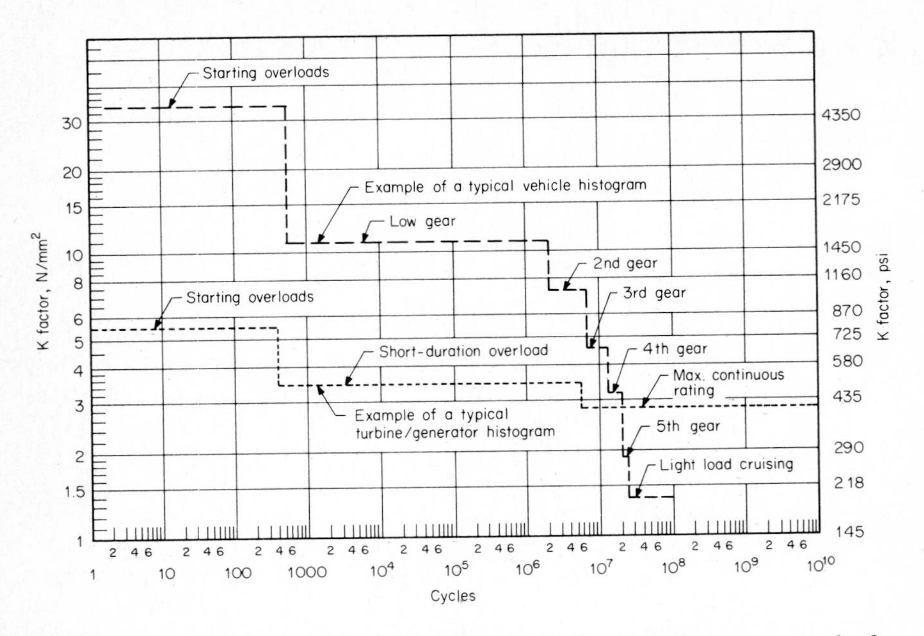

FIG. 2.16 Histograms of load intensity (K factor) plotted against contact cycles for a vehicle gear mesh and a turbine gear mesh. Note that the vehicle is critical for the low gear rating and the turbine is critical for its maximum continuous rating.

2.8 Size of Spur and Helical Gears by *Q*-Factor Method

It is fairly easy to estimate the sizes of spur and helical gears. After the proper gear specifications have been established, a tentative gear size can be obtained by the *Q-factor method.* This method was originally developed to estimate gear weights. It is very handy, though, in estimating center distance and face width.

The Q-factor method of estimating gear size is simply a method whereby the power, speed, and ratio of a gearset are all reduced to a single number. This number, called Q for quantity, is a measure of the size of the job the gear has to do. The value of the Q factor as an index can be demonstrated quite readily from the weight curves shown in Figs. 2.17 and 2.18. These show how the average weight of complete single-reduction gearsets compares with calculated Q factors:

$$Q = \frac{\text{kW power}}{\text{pinion rpm}} \times \frac{(u+1)^3}{u} \qquad \text{metric} \qquad (2.47a)$$

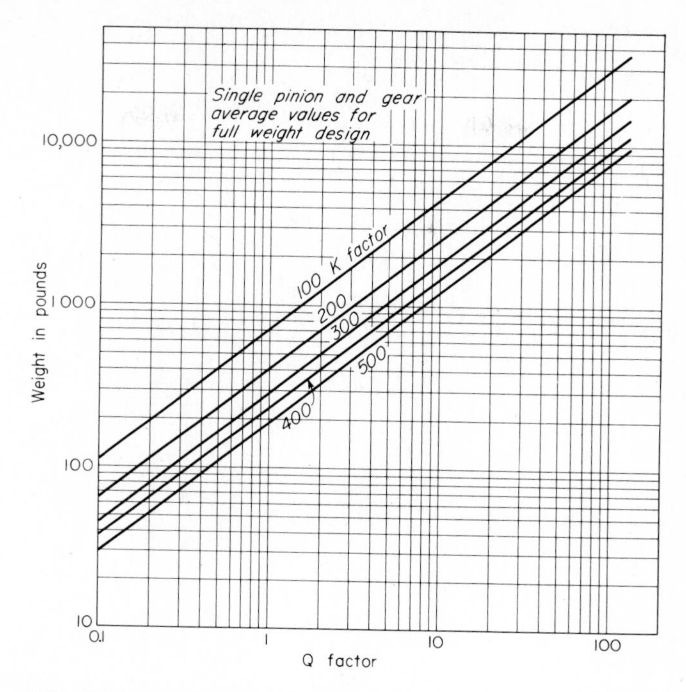

FIG. 2.17 Gear weights plotted against Q factor for different intensities of tooth loading. (English units.)

$$Q = \frac{\text{horsepower}}{\text{pinion rpm}} \times \frac{(m_G + 1)^3}{m_G} \qquad \text{English} \qquad (2.47b)$$

The ratio factor in Eq. (2.47) has been tabulated in Table 2.12 for ratios from 1 to 10.

The required center distance and face width can be obtained from the Q factor as soon as the designer decides how heavily it is safe to load the gears. For spur and helical gears, the K factor is a convenient index for measuring the intensity of tooth loads. Equations (2.54) and (2.55) define* the K factor, and Table 2.15 gives some values of K factor that can be used for preliminary estimates of gearset sizes. (See Sec. 2.10.)

As soon as the amount of K factor has been decided on, the following

*The derivation of K factor is given in Sec. 2.4. For estimating gear size, disregard the equations in Sec. 2.4 and work with the material in this section. Do the final design using the methods in Chap. 3.

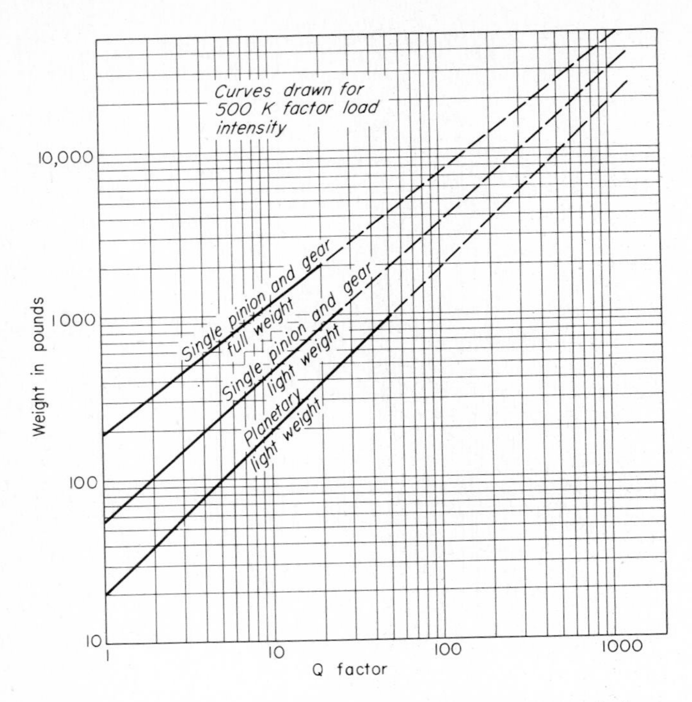

FIG. 2.18 Comparisons of gear weights for different designs.

equation can be solved:

$$a^2b = \frac{4,774,650Q}{K} \qquad \text{metric} \qquad (2.48a)$$

$$C^2F = \frac{31,500Q}{K} \qquad \text{English} \qquad (2.48b)$$

Face-Width Considerations. In spur or single helical gears, using a face width which exceeds the pinion pitch diameter is often not advisable. If the face width is wider, torsional twist concentrates the load quite heavily on one end. In many applications, it is not even possible to effectively use a face width as wide as the pinion diameter. Errors in tooth alignment and shaft alignment may make it impossible to get tooth contact across this much face width.

When a face width equal to the pinion diameter is intended, Eq. (2.48) may be modified to the following:

$$a^3 = \frac{2,387,325Q(u+1)}{K} \qquad \text{metric} \qquad (2.49a)$$

$$C^3 = \frac{15{,}750Q(m_G + 1)}{K} \qquad \text{English} \quad (2.49b)$$

In double helical gears, the face width may be as wide as 1.75 times the pinion pitch diameter before the problems of torsional twist and beam bending get too serious. This results from the fact that double helical pinions shift axially under load to equalize the loading on each helix. This shifting compensates for most of the torsional twist.

With both single- and double-helix gears, the face width can be made relatively wide, provided proper helix modification is made to compensate for the deflections involved.

Table 2.13 shows guideline information on how to make an initial choice of face width. A constant is also given to permit the center distance to be immediately obtained from the Q factor for the chosen aspect ratio. Use this constant in Eq. (2.49) in place of the numerical constant shown.

After the center distance is obtained, the pitch diameters are obtained by Eqs. (1.4) and (1.5).

Weight from Volume. When other than simple gear pairs or simple planetary units are involved, the Q-factor method of weight estimating becomes rather impractical. A simple alternative based on a summation of the face widths multiplied by the pitch diameters squared works quite well. In 1963 R. J. Willis published a paper showing how to pick gear ratios and gear arrangements for the lightest weight. His work was based on this concept. The basic weight equation is

$$\sum \left(\frac{bd_p^2 \times \text{weight constant}}{36{,}050} \right) = \text{weight, kg} \qquad \text{metric} \quad (2.50a)$$

$$\sum (Fd^2 \times \text{weight constant}) = \text{weight, lb} \qquad \text{English} \quad (2.50b)$$

TABLE 2.12 Ratio Factors for Single-Reduction Gears

Speed ratio u	Ratio factor $(u + 1)^3 \div u$	Speed ratio u	Ratio factor $(u + 1)^3 \div u$
1.00	8.000	3.00	21.333
1.20	8.873	3.50	26.036
1.40	9.874	4.00	31.250
1.60	10.985	4.50	36.972
1.80	12.195	5.00	43.200
2.00	13.500	6.00	57.167
2.20	14.895	7.00	73.143
2.40	16.377	8.00	91.125
2.60	17.945	9.00	111.11
2.80	19.597	10.00	133.10

TABLE 2.13 Guide for Choice of Face Width in Spur or Helical Gears

Aspect ratio m_a b/d_{p1} (metric) F/d (English)	Situation	Numerical constant for center distance, Eq. (2.49)	
		Metric	English
0.4	Lower-accuracy gears, appreciable error in mounting dimensions. May need crowning, but helix modification not needed	59,683,125	39,375
1.0	Medium accuracy, good mounting accuracy. Helix modification generally not needed. May need crowning	2,387,325	15,750
1.5	High-accuracy parts and mounting. Helix modification generally not needed	1,591,550	10,500
1.75	Very high accuracy. Probably need helix modification for single helical gears. May not need for double helix	1,364,186	9,000
2.00	Very high accuracy. Will need helix modification in single-helix designs, and will probably need helix modification in double-helix designs	1,193,662	7,875
2.25	Very high accuracy. May not be practical to use, due to criticalness of helix modification required	1,061,033	7,000

TABLE 2.14 Weight Constants for Use in Preliminary Estimates

Application	Factor	Typical conditions
Aircraft	0.25 to 0.30	Magnesium or aluminum casings; limited-life design; high stress levels; rigid weight control
Hydrofoil	0.30 to 0.35	Lightweight steel casings; relatively high stress levels; limited-life design; rigidity desired
Commercial	0.60 to 0.625	Cast or fabricated steel casings; relatively low stress levels; unlimited-life design; solid rotors and shafts

Note: Use these factors in Eq. (2.50).

The weight constant to be used is the same for metric or English units and is given in Table 2.14.

Figure 2.19 shows in schematic form a few of the many possible gear arrangements. To get a rough approximation of the weight, pitch diameters and face widths are obtained for all gear parts. Then Eq. (2.50) is used to get the summation of the face widths times the pitch diameters squared.

Table 2.14 shows some typical values of the weight constant needed for Eq. (2.50). The data in this table are based on general experience in gear design. Special situations, of course, may make the real weight of a well-designed unit quite different from the first estimate. For instance, a gearbox may support the motor or engine and need extra weight for the frame structure. Extra weight may be needed for oil-pump equipment or other accessory parts added to the primary gear unit.

When weight is critical, special design efforts that use lightweight bearings, hollow shafts, thin casing walls, and gears with all excess material removed from the gear bodies may achieve surprisingly low weights.

2.9 Indexes of Tooth Loading

There are two indexes of tooth loading that are very important in gear design. *Unit load* is an index of tooth loading from the standpoint of tooth strength. The *K factor* is an index of tooth loading from the standpoint of tooth surface durability. To say it another way, the higher the unit load, the

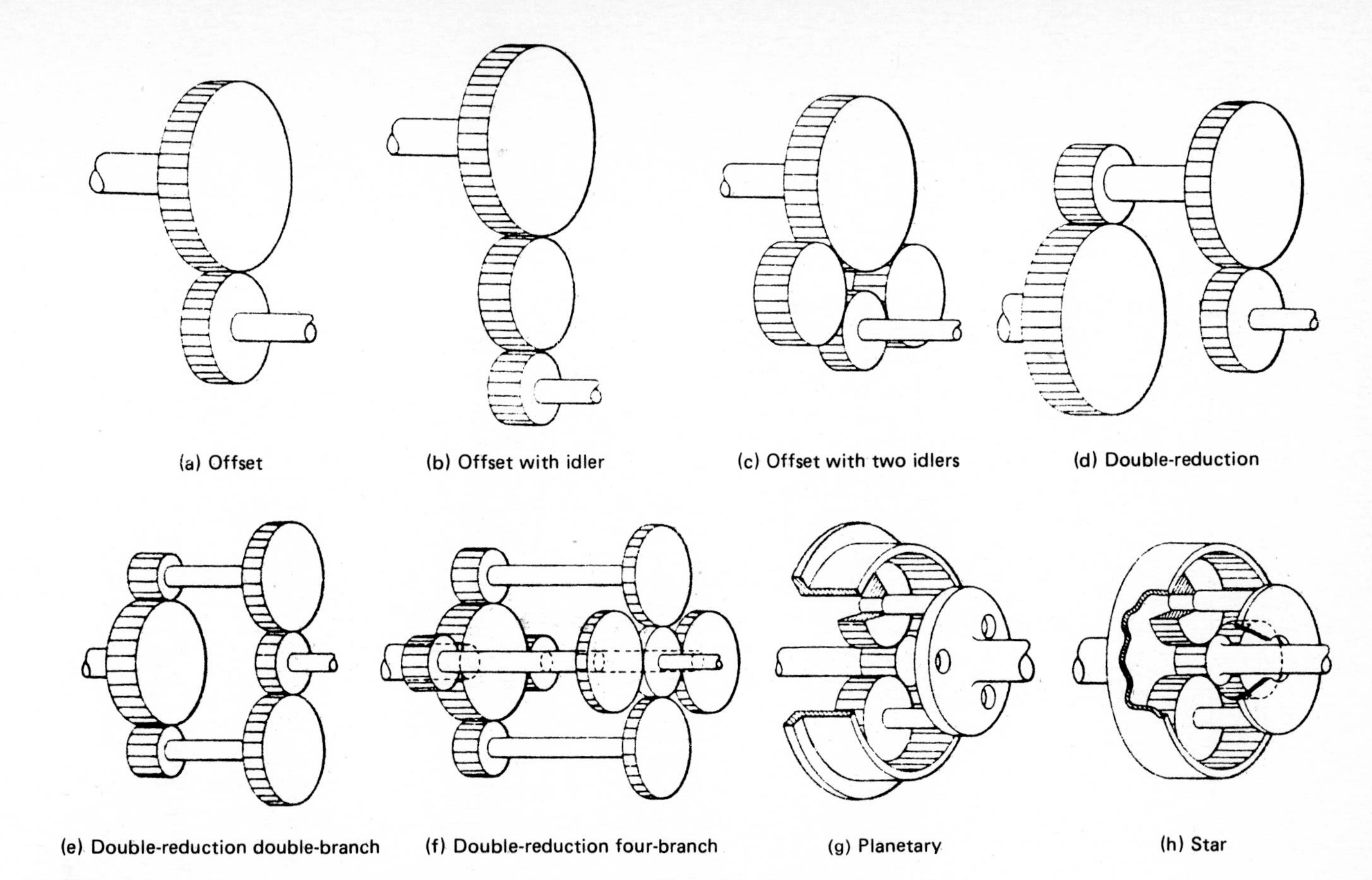

FIG. 2.19 Eight kinds of gear arrangements for spur or helical gears. *(Reprinted from "Product Engineering," January 21, 1963. Copyright © 1963 McGraw-Hill Publishing Co., Inc.)*

more risk of tooth breakage, and the higher the K factor, the more risk of tooth pitting.

Both of these index numbers are calculated from the transmitted power. The normal calculation method for spur or helical gears is

$$\text{Torque } T_P = \frac{P \times 9549.3}{n_1} \quad \text{N}\cdot\text{m} \quad \text{metric} \quad (2.51a)$$

where P = power in kilowatts.

$$\text{Torque } T_P = \frac{P \times 63{,}025}{n_P} \quad \text{in.-lb} \quad \text{English} \quad (2.51b)$$

where P = horsepower.

$$\text{Tangential driving load } W_t = T_p \times \frac{2000}{d_{p1}} \quad \text{N} \quad \text{metric} \quad (2.52a)$$

$$= T_P \times \frac{2}{d} \quad \text{lb} \quad \text{English} \quad (2.52b)$$

where d_{p1} = pinion pitch diameter, mm
d = pinion pitch diameter, in.

The unit load index is derived from the Lewis formula for tooth strength. [See Eq. (2.6).] It is

$$U_\ell = \frac{W_t}{b} \times m_n \quad \text{N/mm}^2 \quad \text{metric} \quad (2.53a)$$

$$= \frac{W_t}{F} \times P_{nd} \quad \text{psi} \quad \text{English} \quad (2.53b)$$

The K factor is based on the hertz stress formula. It was first shown in Eq. (2.22). It will now be given in both metric and English forms and for both external and internal gearsets.

External:

$$K = \frac{W_t}{d_{p1} b}\left(\frac{u+1}{u}\right) \quad \text{N/mm}^2 \quad \text{metric} \quad (2.54a)$$

$$K = \frac{W_t}{dF}\left(\frac{m_G+1}{m_G}\right) \quad \text{psi} \quad \text{English} \quad (2.54b)$$

Internal:

$$K = \frac{W_t}{d_{p1} b}\left(\frac{u-1}{u}\right) \quad \text{N/mm}^2 \quad \text{metric} \quad (2.55a)$$

$$K = \frac{W_t}{dF}\left(\frac{m_G-1}{m_G}\right) \quad \text{psi} \quad \text{English} \quad (2.55b)$$

The load indexes show the *intensity* of loading that the teeth are trying to carry. They are based on real quantities, and they measure what the user of gearing is getting out of the mesh. For instance, a K factor of 5 means that a gear mesh is carrying 5 newtons of tooth load for each millimeter of pinion pitch diameter and each millimeter of face width in contact, with an appropriate adjustment for the relative size of the gear that is in mesh with the pinion.

The gear user can understand unit load and K factor as measures of how much load is being carried per unit of size in the gear mesh, from bending strength and surface loading viewpoints. In comparison, the stress formulas have factors in them that are related to the quality and geometry of the application. The calculated stress number is, of course, very useful, but it does not directly tell the user the relative intensity of loading. For instance, a high stress may occur in a situation in which a moderate load intensity is coupled with a poor geometric design and low quality. Obviously less gear-unit size is needed if acceptable stress levels can be achieved when the design has a relatively high intensity of loading and good enough quality and geometric design of teeth to keep these factors favorable.

The general procedure in preliminary design is to size the gears based on the K factor. Then the tooth size in module (or pitch) is determined by figuring the unit load and making the teeth large enough to get an acceptable unit-load value. For instance, a spur pinion with 36 teeth might be OK on K factor but too high on unit load. If 18 teeth were put on the same pitch diameter (tooth size twice as great), the unit load is reduced 2 to 1 (50 percent as much unit load).

2.10 Estimating Spur- and Helical-Gear Size by *K* Factor

Since the K factor is so important in determining gear size, it is necessary to know how much K factor can be carried in different applications.

The teeth of low- and medium-hard-steel gears usually have more strength than they have capacity to resist pitting. Hence the index of surface durability becomes the limiting factor in determining the load-carrying capacity of the gears. If a very thin oil is used or there is inadequate provision to cool the gearset, scoring might be a limiting condition. Generally, though, the designer will use a heavy enough oil and provide enough cooling to get all the capacity out of the gears that is in the metal. Oil and oil-cooling systems are usually cheaper than larger-sized gears.

In fully hardened gearing, the strength of the teeth may become as important as, or even more important than, surface durability. Even in this case, the gear designer can often so proportion the design that there will be

TABLE 2.15 Indexes of Tooth Loading for Preliminary Design Calculations

Application	Minimum hardness of steel gears		No. pinion cycles	Accuracy	*K* factor		Unit load	
	Pinion	Gear			N/mm²	psi	N/mm²	psi
Turbine driving a generator	225 HB	210 HB	10^{10}	High precision	0.69	100	45	6,500
	335 HB	300 HB	10^{10}	High precision	1.04	150	59	8,500
	59 HRC	58 HRC	10^{10}	High precision	2.76	400	83	12,000
Internal combustion engine driving a compressor	225 HB	210 HB	10^9	High precision	0.48	70	31	4,500
	335 HB	300 HB	10^9	High precision	0.76	110	38	5,500
	58 HRC	58 HRC	10^9	High precision	2.07	300	55	8,000
General-purpose industrial drives, helical (relatively uniform torque for both driving and driven units)	225 HB	210 HB	10^8	Medium high precision	1.38	200	38	5,500
	335 HB	300 HB	10^8	Medium high precision	2.07	300	48	7,000
	58 HRC	58 HRC	10^8	Medium high precision	5.52	800	69	10,000
Large industrial drives, spur—hoists, kilns, mills (moderate shock in driven units)	225 HB	210 HB	10^8	Medium precision	0.83	120	24	3,500
	335 HB	300 HB	10^8	Medium precision	1.24	180	31	4,500
	58 HRC	58 HRC	10^8	Medium precision	3.45	500	41	6,000
Aerospace, helical (single pair)	60 HRC	60 HRC	10^9	High precision	5.86	850	117	17,000
Aerospace, spur (epicyclic)	60 HRC	60 HRC	10^9	High precision	4.14	600	76	11,000
Vehicle transmission, helical	59 HRC	59 HRC	4×10^7	Medium high precision	6.20	900	124	18,000
Vehicle final drive, spur	59 HRC	59 HRC	4×10^6	Medium high precision	8.96	1300	124	18,000
Small commercial (pitch-line speed less than 5 m/s)	320 HB	Phenolic laminate	4×10^7	Medium precision	0.34	50	—	—
	320 HB	Nylon	10^7	Medium precision	0.24	35	—	—
Small gadget (pitch-line speed less than 2.5 m/s)	200 HB	Zinc alloy	10^6	Medium precision	0.10	15	—	—
	200 HB	Brass or aluminum	10^6	Medium precision	0.10	15	—	—

Notes: 1. The above indexes of tooth loading assume average conditions. With a special design and a favorable application, it may be possible to go higher. With an unfavorable application and/or a design that is not close to optimum, the indexes of tooth loading shown will be too high for good practice.

2. The table assumes that the controlling load must be carried for the pinion cycles shown.

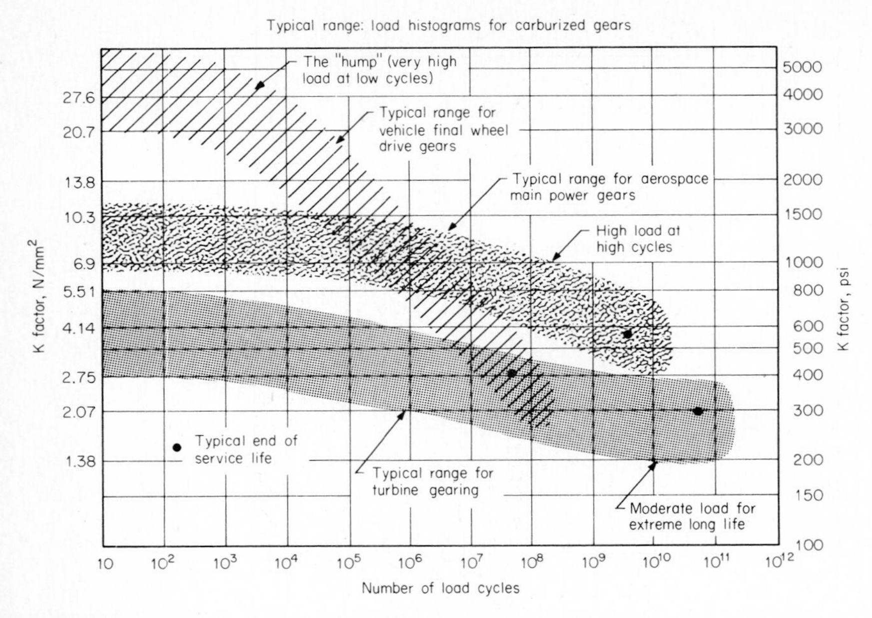

FIG. 2.20 Rough comparison of design K factors for carburized gears used in vehicle, aerospace, and turbine applications. The bandwidths result from quality of gearing, tooth design, application, level of risk, etc.

enough strength available to match the capacity of the teeth to withstand pitting. If strength is more limiting than wear, a proper reduction in K factor can still aid in obtaining teeth of adequate strength. With this in mind, it is possible to use appropriate K factors as a measure of the amount of load that can be carried on many types of spur and helical gears.

Table 2.15 shows a study of K-factor and unit-load values that are typical of nominal design practice for a variety of gear applications. These values are intended for use in the preliminary sizing of a gearset. Figure 2.20 shows in pictorial fashion the nominal design range for vehicle, aerospace, and turbine gears.

After the preliminary sizing of gears, detail design work must be done to establish the pressure angle, helix angle, tooth addenda, tooth whole depth, and tooth thickness. Then, when complete tooth geometry has been picked, the designer should calculate tooth stresses and compare them with allowable values for the material being used and the degree of reliability required. Chapter 3 covers the determination of gear-tooth geometry and the calculation of load-carrying capacity to meet appropriate gear-rating criteria. In this chapter, the data on how to use index values to size gears are intended only as a means of establishing the first approximation of an appropriate gear size.

2.11 Estimating Bevel-Gear Size

It is possible to estimate bevel-gear sizes by the Q-factor method. So far this method has had limited usage. It appears that the method will work fairly well for bevel gears but will not give quite as good results as for spur and helical gears.

The geometry of bevel gears is more complicated than that of spur or helical gears. Under load, bevel gears tend to shift position more than gears on parallel shafts. It is frequently necessary to design a "mismatch" into the teeth. The mismatch concentrates the tooth load in the center of the face width and allows some shifting of shaft alignment to occur before the load is concentrated too heavily at one end of the tooth. These things make it hard for a simple formula to estimate capacity correctly.

Some changes are required before the formulas in Sec. 2.8 can be applied to bevel gears. Bevel gears do not have any *center-distance* dimension. This means that center distance must be removed from Eq. (2.48). This can be done with the help of Eq. (1.5). The result is

$$d_{p1}^2 b = \frac{1.91 \times 10^7 Q}{(u + 1)^2 K} \qquad \text{metric} \qquad (2.56a)$$

$$d^2 F = \frac{126{,}000 Q}{(m_G + 1)^2 K} \qquad \text{English} \qquad (2.56b)$$

Equation (2.56) can be used for both bevel and spur gears. It is handy to use when the design requirements have been reduced to a Q factor, but the designer has not yet decided whether spur, helical, or bevel gears are to be used. This equation can help the designer estimate the sizes of all three kinds.

The calculation of unit load and K factor for bevel gears is somewhat different than for spur and helical gears. Figure 2.21 shows how these are calculated for the bevel gearset.

The K factor in Eq. (2.56) is the same value that was used previously. However, it is sometimes necessary to use lower values than those shown in Table 2.15 to compensate for some of the special problems in bevel gears. For instance, if mountings do not maintain good tooth contact at full load, the K factor should be reduced.

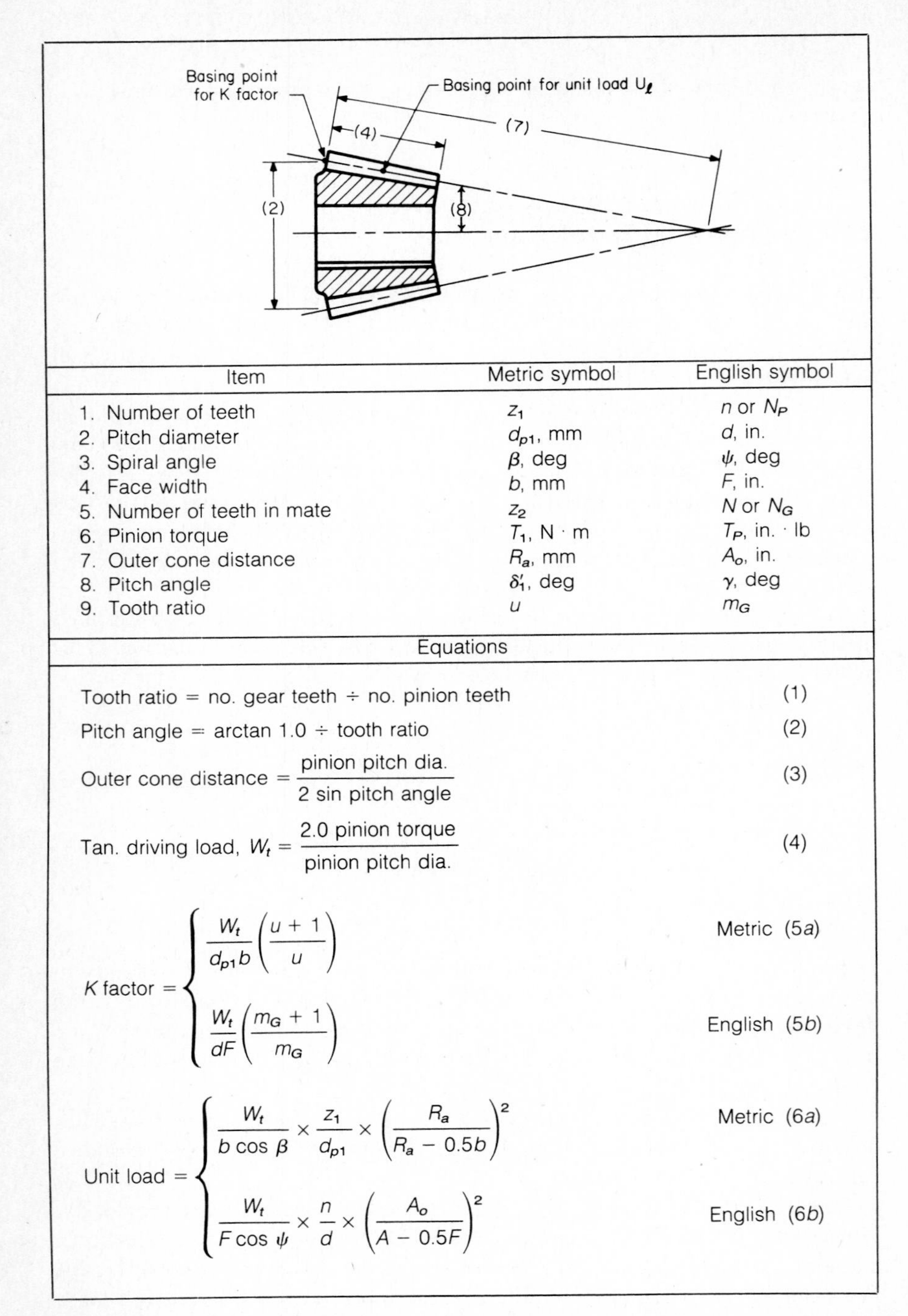

Item	Metric symbol	English symbol
1. Number of teeth	z_1	n or N_P
2. Pitch diameter	d_{p1}, mm	d, in.
3. Spiral angle	β, deg	ψ, deg
4. Face width	b, mm	F, in.
5. Number of teeth in mate	z_2	N or N_G
6. Pinion torque	T_1, N · m	T_P, in. · lb
7. Outer cone distance	R_a, mm	A_o, in.
8. Pitch angle	δ_1', deg	γ, deg
9. Tooth ratio	u	m_G

Equations

Tooth ratio = no. gear teeth ÷ no. pinion teeth (1)

Pitch angle = arctan 1.0 ÷ tooth ratio (2)

$$\text{Outer cone distance} = \frac{\text{pinion pitch dia.}}{2 \sin \text{pitch angle}} \tag{3}$$

$$\text{Tan. driving load, } W_t = \frac{2.0 \text{ pinion torque}}{\text{pinion pitch dia.}} \tag{4}$$

$$K \text{ factor} = \begin{cases} \dfrac{W_t}{d_{p1} b}\left(\dfrac{u+1}{u}\right) & \text{Metric (5}a\text{)} \\[2ex] \dfrac{W_t}{dF}\left(\dfrac{m_G+1}{m_G}\right) & \text{English (5}b\text{)} \end{cases}$$

$$\text{Unit load} = \begin{cases} \dfrac{W_t}{b \cos \beta} \times \dfrac{z_1}{d_{p1}} \times \left(\dfrac{R_a}{R_a - 0.5b}\right)^2 & \text{Metric (6}a\text{)} \\[2ex] \dfrac{W_t}{F \cos \psi} \times \dfrac{n}{d} \times \left(\dfrac{A_o}{A - 0.5F}\right)^2 & \text{English (6}b\text{)} \end{cases}$$

FIG. 2.21 The method for calculating indexes of tooth loading for straight or spiral bevel gears at a 90° shaft angle.

TABLE 2.16 Approximate *K*-Factor Values for Bevel Gears

Pinion pitch diameter		Gear ratio	Pitch-line speed			
			5 m/s	1000 fpm	20 m/s	4000 fpm
			K factor			
mm	in.	z_2/z_1 (N_G/N_P)	N/mm^2	psi	N/mm^2	psi
Case 1. Industrial spiral bevel gears at HRC 58						
50	2.0	1	3.93	570	3.45	500
		3	3.38	490	2.96	430
100	5.0	1	3.27	475	2.90	420
		3	2.79	405	2.48	360
250	10.0	1	2.72	395	2.41	350
		3	2.38	345	2.10	305
Case 2. Industrial spiral bevel gears, pinion BHN 245, gear BHN 210						
50	2.0	1	1.83	265	1.62	235
		3	1.65	239	1.46	212
100	5.0	1	1.41	205	1.24	180
		3	1.23	179	1.08	157
250	10.0	1	1.12	163	0.99	143
		3	0.94	137	0.83	120
Case 3. Industrial straight bevel gears, pinion BHN 245, gear BHN 210						
50	2.0	1	0.86	125	—	— (See Note 1)
		3	0.77	112	—	—
100	5.0	1	0.83	120	—	—
		3	0.76	110	—	—
250	10.0	1	0.79	115	—	—
		3	0.72	105	—	—

Notes:

1. Straight bevel gears are usually not used above 10 m/s (2000 fpm). At 20 m/s (4000 fpm), spiral bevel gears are the normal choice.
2. The above *K*-factor values assume average conditions. With a special design and a favorable application, it may be possible to go higher. With an unfavorable application and/or a design that is not close to being optimum, the *K*-factor values shown will be too high for good practice.
3. The above *K*-factor values are based on 10^8 cycles and an application factor K_a of 1.5. This is equivalent to an electric motor driving a piece of equipment that has mild shock.

Bevel-gear designers have tended to reduce capacity for both size of pinion and increase in pitch-line velocity.

Table 2.16 shows a study of bevel-gear K factors based on load-rating formulas in current use. These values represent averages of different ratio designs for a *uniform* power source and a *mild shock* power-absorbing device (like an electric motor driving a well-designed pump).

If the designer has already decided to use a bevel gearset, it is not necessary to go to the trouble of calculating a Q factor. The equation can be simplified to

$$d_{p1}^2 b = \frac{1.910}{K} \times \frac{10^7\ P}{n_1} \frac{(u+1)}{u} \qquad \text{metric} \qquad (2.57a)$$

$$d^2 F = \frac{126{,}000}{K} \frac{P}{n_P} \frac{(m_G+1)}{m_G} \qquad \text{English} \qquad (2.57b)$$

Both Eqs. (2.57*a*) and (2.57*b*) determine the quantity pitch diameter squared times face width. To get a complete solution, it is necessary to know the relation of pitch diameter to face width. The Gleason Works recommends that the face width of straight and spiral bevel gears not exceed 0.3 times the cone distance or 10 in. divided by the diametral pitch. For Zerol gears, the only difference in the limits is that the cone-distance constant is 0.25 instead of 0.3.

Table 2.17 shows how these limits work out in terms of pitch diameter of the pinion for different ratios. A shaft angle of 90° is assumed.

Table 2.17 shows that the face width for a low ratio like 1 to 1 will probably be limited by the cone distance. For a high ratio like 5 to 1, the

TABLE 2.17 Ratio of Maximum Face Width to Bevel-Pinion Pitch Diameter

Ratio	Face width based on 0.3 cone distance	Face width based on 10 in. per diametral pitch		
		15 teeth	20 teeth	25 teeth
1	0.212d*	0.667d	0.500d	0.400d
1.5	0.270d	0.667d	0.500d	0.400d
2	0.335d	0.667d	0.500d	0.400d
3	0.474d	0.667d	0.500d	0.400d
4	0.618d	0.667d	0.500d	0.400d
5	0.765d	0.667d	0.500d	0.400d
6	0.912d	0.667d	0.500d	0.400d
7	1.061d	0.667d	0.500d	0.400d

*d is the pinion pitch diameter.

pitch will probably limit the face width. An appropriate value of face width can be picked from Table 2.17. Then this value can be used to solve Eq. (2.57).

Hypoid gears are hard to estimate. As a general rule, a hypoid pinion will carry about the same power as a bevel pinion. Since the hypoid pinion is bigger—for the same ratio—than a bevel pinion, the hypoid set will carry more power as a set.

Face gears may be handled somewhat similarly to straight bevel gearsets. Generally it will be necessary to use less face width for the face gear than would be allowed as a maximum for the same ratio of bevel gears (see Sec. 3.19).

2.12 Estimating Worm-Gear Size

It is much harder to estimate the capacity of worm gears. In spur, helical, and bevel gears, the magnitude of the surface compressive stress is the major thing that determines capacity. The limits of strength and scoring seldom determine the gear size—unless the set is poorly proportioned. In worm gearing, the tendency to score is often as important as the tendency to pit in determining capacity. Since scoring depends on both compressive stress and rubbing (or sliding) velocity, a rating formula has to be based on more than a K factor.

Worm-gear sizes can be estimated reasonably well from a table of power vs. center distance for a series of worm speeds. Table 2.18 shows the nominal capacity of a range of sizes of single-enveloping worm gears. It is assumed that the worm is case-hardened and ground to good accuracy and finish. To meet the table specifications, the worm gear should be made of a good grade of chill-cast phosphor bronze and cut to give a good bearing with the worm. The ratings in the table should be regarded as *nominal*. Several manufacturers have been able to carry up to 100 percent more load than that shown in the table by the use of special materials and by obtaining a very high degree of precision in the worm and gear. Conversely, when accuracy has not been the best and when operating conditions have not been good (when such conditions as shock loads, vibration, or overheating have been present), it has been necessary to rate worm gearsets substantially lower than the values shown in Table 2.18.

The nominal capacity of double-enveloping worm gears of the Cone-Drive design is shown in Table 2.19.

Tables 2.18 and 2.19 are intended for worm gears subject to shock-free loading and in service for not more than 10 hours per day. If service is 24 hours per day with some shock loading, the table ratings should be reduced to about 75 percent of the values shown.

TABLE 2.18 Nominal Capacity of Cylindrical Worm Gearing

Ratio m_G	Center distance C, in.	Worm pitch diameter d, in.	Effective face width F_e, in.	Lead angle λ, degrees	Rpm of worm: 100	720	1750	3600	10,000
					Output hp at different worm speeds				
5	2	0.825	0.46875	37.6	0.19	1.2	2.1	2.9	4.4
8	2		0.500	25.7	0.15	0.90	1.7	2.3	3.6
15	2		0.46875	14.4	0.08	0.51	0.95	1.3	2.1
25	2		0.46875	8.75	0.05	0.31	0.59	0.83	1.3
50	2		0.46875	4.40	0.02	0.15	0.28	0.39	0.62
5	4	1.525	0.875	40.3	1.6	8.0	12	17	22
8	4		0.9375	28.0	1.2	6.4	9.9	14	19
15	4		0.9375	15.8	0.72	3.9	6.1	8.7	12
25	4		0.9375	9.64	0.44	2.4	3.8	5.4	7.4
50	4		0.9375	4.85	0.21	1.2	1.8	2.6	3.6
5	8	2.800	1.6875	43.3	11	39	60	75	—
8	8		1.8125	30.5	8.1	33	50	64	—
15	8		1.8125	17.4	4.8	21	31	41	—
25	8		1.8125	10.7	3.0	13	19	26	—
50	8		1.8125	5.39	1.4	6.2	9.3	12	—
5	16	5.100	3.125	46.5	63	186	254	—	—
8	16		3.375	33.4	50	156	221	263	—
15	16		3.375	19.4	30	98	143	169	—
25	16		3.375	11.9	19	62	90	107	—
50	16		3.375	6.02	8.9	30	43	52	—

Notes: 1. Service factor K_s has a value of 1.0 for this table. (See service factors in Table 3.47.)
2. Sliding velocity not over 6000 fpm.

The horsepower ratings shown in Tables 2.18 and 2.19 are *mechanical* ratings. The mechanical rating is the amount of power that the set is expected to carry without excessive wear or tooth breakage when the set is kept reasonably cool. In many cases, worm gearsets will overheat because there is not enough cooling of the gear case or the oil supply to remove the heat generated by the set. This makes it necessary to calculate a *thermal* rating. The thermal rating is the maximum amount of power that the set can carry before a dangerous operating temperature is reached. Quite obviously the thermal rating depends as much on casing design and lubrication system as it does on the size of the gears themselves. In many cases a worm-gear design will not carry so much thermal rating as mechanical rating. However, if adequate oil pumps, heat exchangers, and oil jets are used, it should be possible to operate any worm gearset up to its full mechanical rating. AGMA 440.04 shows standard thermal ratings for cylindrical worm gearsets.

TABLE 2.19 Nominal Capacity of Double-Enveloping Worm Gearing

Ratio m_G	Center distance C, in.	Worm pitch diameter d, in.	Rpm of worm: 100	720	1750	3600	10,000
			Input hp at different worm speeds				
5	2	0.830	0.40	2.19	3.82	5.53	7.93
15	2	0.830	0.17	0.99	1.79	2.61	3.83
50	2	0.850	0.05	0.31	0.56	0.82	1.22
5	4	1.730	3.65	16.9	26.6	34.6	—
15	4	1.550	1.65	8.15	13.1	17.3	22.9
50	4	1.660	0.52	2.56	4.11	5.47	7.28
5	8	3.450	25.9	95.2	135	163	—
15	8	2.940	11.8	48.1	70.7	90.9	—
50	8	2.900	3.67	15.2	22.5	28.9	—
5	16	5.143	180	513	678	—	—
15	16	5.143	83.2	273	369	439	—
50	16	5.143	26.1	87.1	119	140	—
5	24	7.333	473	1194	1488	—	—
15	24	7.333	227	636	829	—	—
50	24	7.333	71.7	204	270	—	—

Notes: 1. Service factor K_s is 1.0. (See service factors in Table 3.52.)
2. Sliding velocity not over 6000 fpm.

In each of the designs shown in the tables, an arbitrary size of worm was used. The size chosen represents good design practice. In many instances, though, it will be necessary to use different-sized worms. Often a worm is made to a "shell" design to slip over a large shaft. Large turbine shafts may have large worms mounted on them to drive small worm gears attached to oil pumps or governors. Good designs of this type can be made, but they are not so efficient as worm gearsets in which the worm and gear sizes can be more properly proportioned.

2.13 Estimating Spiroid-Gear Size

Spiroid gears have less sliding than worm gears but much more sliding than spur or helical gears. It is not practical to estimate their size by a Q-factor method.

In general, both members of the Spiroid set are carburized. Final finishing is done by grinding or lapping. Normally the lubrication is handled by extreme pressure (EP) lubricants.

Table 2.20 shows the nominal capacity of a range of Spiroid gearset sizes. This table can be used to make a preliminary estimate of the size needed for a Spiroid gearset.

TABLE 2.20 Nominal Capacity of Spiroid Gears (Pinion and Gear Case-Hardened, 60 Rockwell C min.)

Ratio m_G	Center distance C	Pinion O.D. d_o	Gear O.D. D_o	Rpm of pinion 100	720	1750	3600	10,000
				Hp at different pinion speeds				
10.250	0.500	0.437	1.500	0.0142	0.0697	0.129	0.1948	0.3354
14.667	0.500	0.421	1.500	0.0120	0.0589	0.109	0.1645	0.2834
25.500	0.500	0.423	1.500	0.0088	0.0432	0.080	0.1208	0.2080
47.000	0.500	0.427	1.500	0.0064	0.0313	0.058	0.0876	0.1508
10.250	1.000	0.853	3.000	0.0937	0.4601	0.852	1.287	
14.667	1.000	0.821	3.000	0.0759	0.3726	0.690	1.042	
25.500	1.000	0.827	3.000	0.0550	0.2700	0.500	0.7550	
47.000	1.000	0.837	3.000	0.0377	0.1852	0.343	0.5179	
71.000	1.000	0.761	3.000	0.0299	0.1469	0.272	0.4107	
10.250	1.875	1.507	5.625	0.4961	2.435	4.51	6.810	
14.667	1.875	1.463	5.625	0.4125	2.025	3.75	5.663	
25.500	1.875	1.435	5.625	0.2915	1.431	2.65	4.002	
47.000	1.875	1.448	5.625	0.1804	0.8856	1.64	2.476	
71.000	1.875	1.308	5.625	0.1441	0.7074	1.31	1.978	
106.000	1.875	1.215	5.625	0.1188	0.5832	1.08	1.631	
10.200	3.250	2.395	9.750	2.101	10.31	19.0		
14.667	3.250	2.465	9.750	1.760	8.64	16.0		
25.500	3.250	2.319	9.750	1.21	5.94	11.0		
47.000	3.250	2.344	9.750	0.7205	3.537	6.55		
71.000	3.250	2.090	9.750	0.5544	2.722	5.04		
106.000	3.250	1.933	9.750	0.4455	2.187	4.05		
10.167	5.125	3.342	15.375	7.007	34.40	63.7		
14.250	5.125	3.342	15.375	5.918	29.05	53.8		
25.333	5.125	3.092	15.375	3.949	19.39	35.9		
47.500	5.125	2.910	15.375	2.255	11.07	20.5		
71.000	5.125	3.097	15.375	1.727	8.478	15.7		
106.000	5.125	2.841	15.375	1.386	6.804	12.6		

Notes:
1. Class 1 AGMA service.
2. Pitch-line speed not over 1700 fpm.
3. No allowance for shock loads, $K_s = 1.0$.
4. Based on tooth proportions recommended by Spiroid Division of Illinois Tool Works, Chicago, IL, U.S.A.

DATA NEEDED FOR GEAR DRAWINGS

After the size of a gear train has been determined, the designer must work out all the dimensional specifications and tolerances that are necessary to define exactly the gears required. Data on the gear material required and the heat treatment must also be given.

Many years ago it was customary to specify only a few major dimensions, such as pitch, number of teeth, pressure angle, and face width. It was assumed that the skilled mechanic in the shop would know what tooth thickness, whole depth, addendum, and degree of accuracy were required. Little or no consideration was given to such things as root fillet radius, surface finish, and profile modification.

Today the designer of gears for a highly developed piece of machinery such as an airplane engine, an ocean-going ship, or an automobile finds it necessary to specify dimensions and tolerances covering all features of the gear in close detail. There is often the risk that a buyer of gears will purchase thousands of dollars worth of gears and find that their quality is unsuitable for the application.

2.14 Gear Dimensional Data

The dimensional data which may be required to make a gear drawing can be broken down into blank dimensions and tooth data. The blank dimensions are usually shown in cross-sectional views. The tooth data are either tabulated or shown directly on an enlarged view of one or more teeth. Some of the common blank dimensions are

Outside diameter
Face width
Outside cone angle (bevel gears)
Back cone angle (bevel gears)
Throat diameter (worm gears)
Throat radius (worm gears)
Root diameter
Bore diameter (internal gears)
Mounting distance (bevel gears)
Inside rim diameter
Web thickness
Journal diameter

The tabulated gear-tooth data will cover such items as

Number of teeth
Module (or diametral pitch)
Pitch diameter
Circular pitch
Linear pitch (worm gears)
Pressure angle
Normal pressure angle (helical gears)
Normal circular pitch (helical gears)
Normal module or pitch (helical gears)
Addendum
Whole depth
Helix angle
Hand of helix
Lead angle (worm gears)
Pitch cone angle (bevel gears)
Root cone angle (bevel gears)
Tooth thickness
Lead (worm gears)

Special views of gear teeth may be used to show things like minimum root fillet radius, form diameter, tip radius, end radius, and surface finish. Notes may be added to the drawing to specify the heat treatment and to define the accuracy limits for checking the gear teeth. Further notes often define the reference axis used in checking and refer to drawings of cutting tools or processing procedures needed to make the gear come out right.

The description just given of what may go on a gear drawing may leave the impression that gear drawings have to be very complicated. This is not necessarily the case. The designer should consider the gear quality required to meet design requirements, together with the responsibility that the shop making the gear will assume for making gears that will work satisfactorily. If the gear shop will assume responsibility for making a gear that will operate satisfactorily, and they understand the design requirements, a very simple drawing may be sufficient. Many fine gears are made from drawings that are very simple. The problem of the gear designer is to determine just how detailed the drawing must be *to give the gear maker the responsibility for producing a gear that will do the job.*

Figure 2.22 shows how a complex drawing is made for a pinion used with a high-speed turbine. These aspects of the drawing shown in Fig. 2.22 are worth noting:

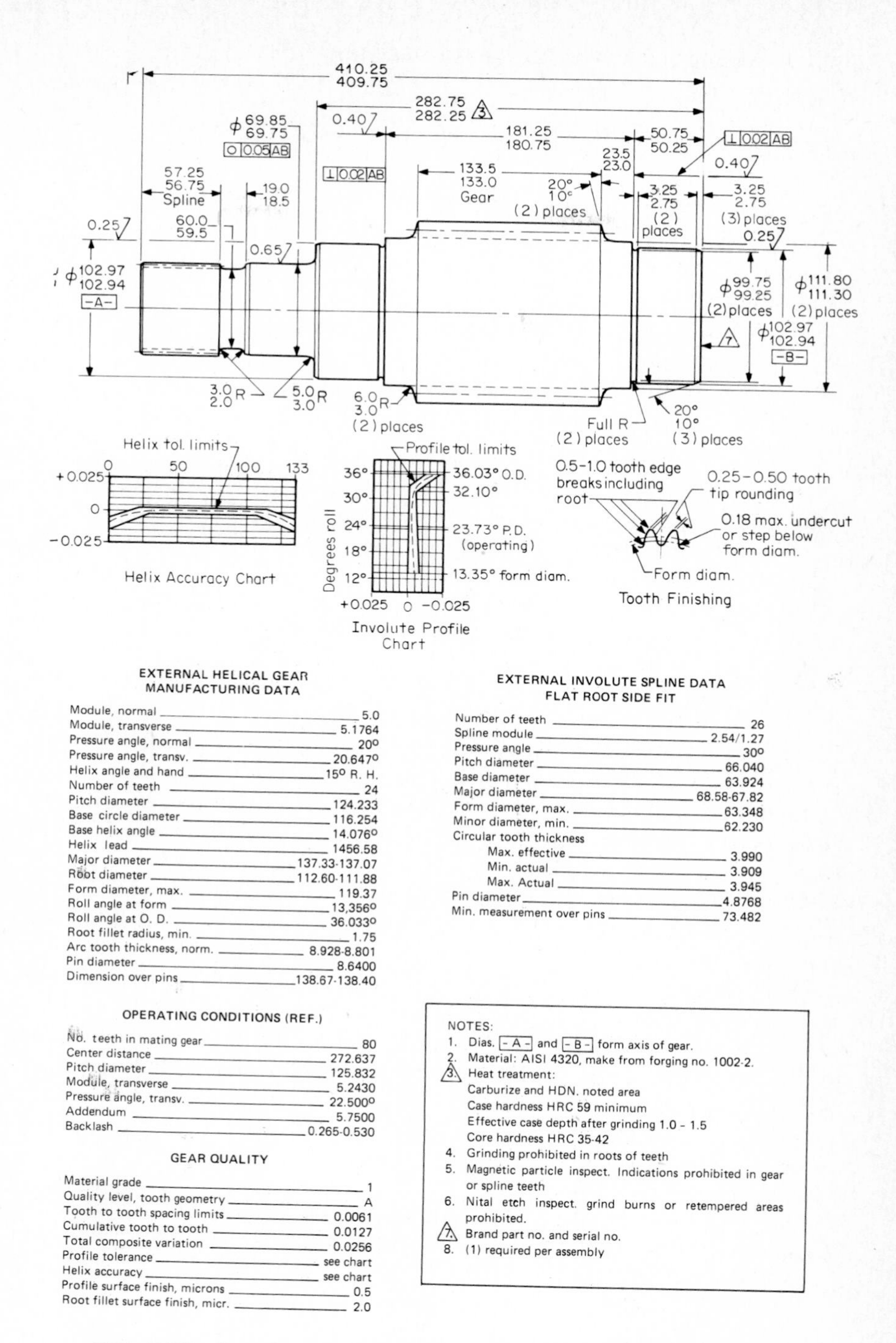

EXTERNAL HELICAL GEAR MANUFACTURING DATA

Module, normal	5.0
Module, transverse	5.1764
Pressure angle, normal	20°
Pressure angle, transv.	20.647°
Helix angle and hand	15° R. H.
Number of teeth	24
Pitch diameter	124.233
Base circle diameter	116.254
Base helix angle	14.076°
Helix lead	1456.58
Major diameter	137.33-137.07
Root diameter	112.60-111.88
Form diameter, max.	119.37
Roll angle at form	13,356°
Roll angle at O. D.	36.033°
Root fillet radius, min.	1.75
Arc tooth thickness, norm.	8.928-8.801
Pin diameter	8.6400
Dimension over pins	138.67-138.40

EXTERNAL INVOLUTE SPLINE DATA FLAT ROOT SIDE FIT

Number of teeth	26
Spline module	2.54/1.27
Pressure angle	30°
Pitch diameter	66.040
Base diameter	63.924
Major diameter	68.58-67.82
Form diameter, max.	63.348
Minor diameter, min.	62.230
Circular tooth thickness	
Max. effective	3.990
Min. actual	3.909
Max. Actual	3.945
Pin diameter	4.8768
Min. measurement over pins	73.482

OPERATING CONDITIONS (REF.)

No. teeth in mating gear	80
Center distance	272.637
Pitch diameter	125.832
Module, transverse	5.2430
Pressure angle, transv.	22.500°
Addendum	5.7500
Backlash	0.265-0.530

GEAR QUALITY

Material grade	1
Quality level, tooth geometry	A
Tooth to tooth spacing limits	0.0061
Cumulative tooth to tooth	0.0127
Total composite variation	0.0256
Profile tolerance	see chart
Helix accuracy	see chart
Profile surface finish, microns	0.5
Root fillet surface finish, micr.	2.0

NOTES:

1. Dias. -A- and -B- form axis of gear.
2. Material: AISI 4320, make from forging no. 1002-2.
3. (△) Heat treatment:
   Carburize and HDN. noted area
   Case hardness HRC 59 minimum
   Effective case depth after grinding 1.0 - 1.5
   Core hardness HRC 35-42
4. Grinding prohibited in roots of teeth
5. Magnetic particle inspect. Indications prohibited in gear or spline teeth
6. Nital etch inspect. grind burns or retempered areas prohibited.
7. (△) Brand part no. and serial no.
8. (1) required per assembly

FIG. 2.22 Sample gear drawing for high-precision turbine gear work.

Basic tooth data for gear teeth and spline teeth are shown in tabular form.

A cross-sectional view (and an end view if needed) shows the body dimensions of the gear.

Enlarged tooth views may be needed to define finish, critical radii, and instructions on where grinding is permitted.

Special rounding or breaking of sharp end corners is covered in an enlarged tooth view.

A series of notes covers requirements of accuracy, metallurgy, and (perhaps) special processing procedures.

For several years, a major effort has been made to establish drafting standards for gears. This work has led to gear and spline standards issued as American National Standards Institute (ANSI) document 14.7.*

Figure 2.23 shows an example from ANS Y14.7.1 for a spur gear and a helical gear. Note that formats A, B, C, and D are recognized, and that there are quite a few special instructions for those who do the design and drafting work.

Examples of a straight bevel gear and a spiral bevel gear from ANS Y14.7.2 are shown in Figs. 2.24 and 2.25. Note the long list of tabulated data items. Also note the special data shown in the cross-sectional view to define *crossing point*, *face apex*, and other things peculiar to bevel gears.

Standard worm and worm-gear drawing examples from ANS Y14.7.3 are shown in Figs. 2.26 and 2.27. Note the difference in practice between single-enveloping worm gearing and double-enveloping worm gearing.

Spiroid and Helicon gears also need special drafting treatment. Figure 2.28 shows an example from ANS Y14.7.3 for a Spiroid pinion and a Spiroid gear.

Those involved in the details of gear and spline† drafting should study carefully all the special data and instructions given in ANS Y14.7.1 to Y14.7.4. After years of work, a general agreement has been reached on an international practice on defining and depicting the whole family of gears and splines.

* Figures 2.23 to 2.28 are extracted from American National Standard Drafting Practices, Gear Drawing Standards (ANS Y14.7.1 to Y14.7.3) with the permission of the publisher, The American Society of Mechanical Engineers, United Engineering Center, 345 East 47th Street, New York, N.Y. 10017.

†The spline with gear teeth is closely related to gearing in its design and manufacture. Functionally, though, the spline is a joint connection rather than a gear mesh.

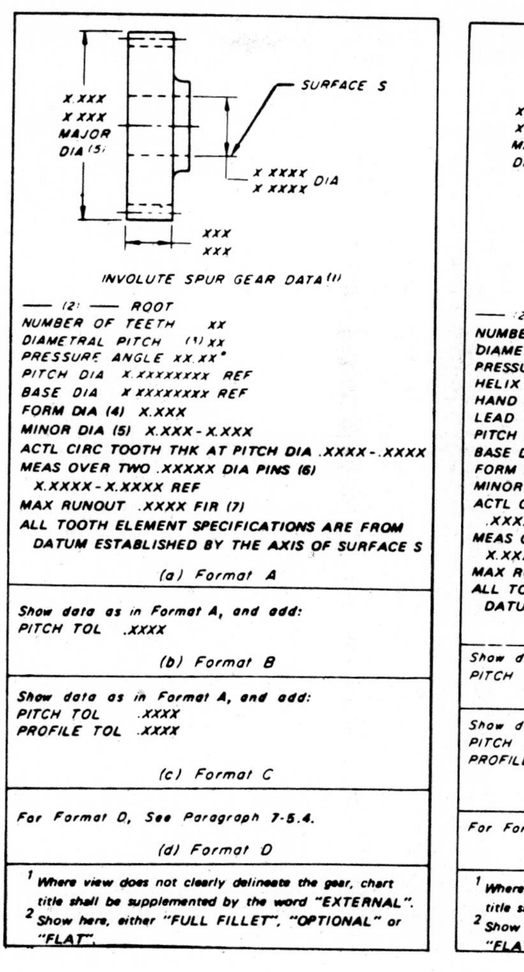

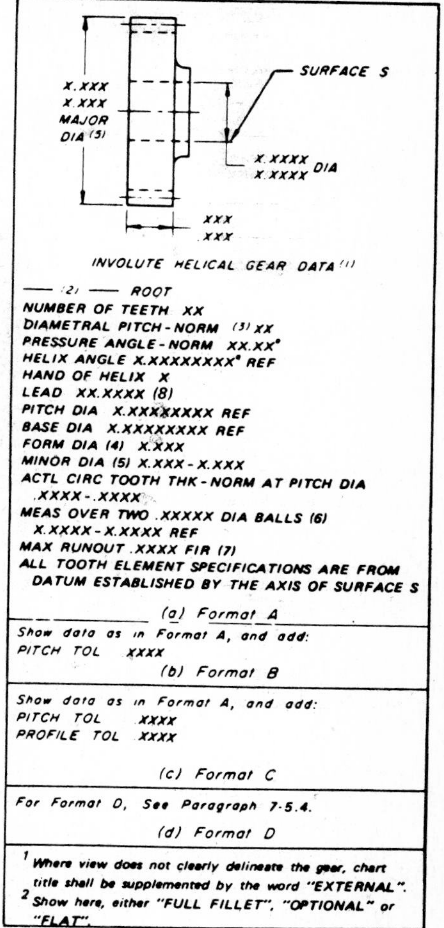

FIG. 2.23 Standard drawing formats for spur and helical gears. *(Extracted from American National Standard Drafting Practices, Gear Drawing Standards (ANS Y14.7.1) with the permission of the publisher, The American Society of Mechanical Engineers. United Engineering Center, 345 East 47th Street, New York, NY 10017.)*

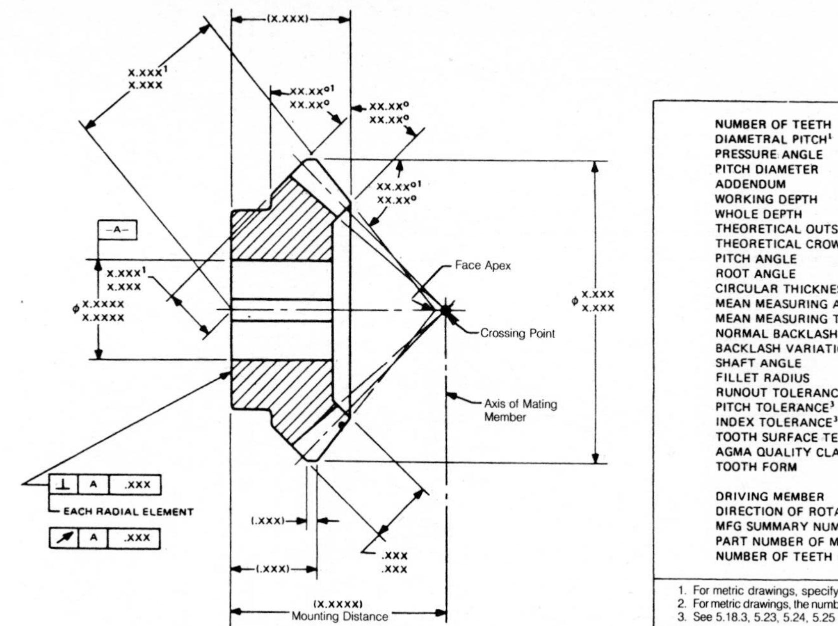

NUMBER OF TEETH	XX
DIAMETRAL PITCH[1]	(XX.XXX)
PRESSURE ANGLE	(XX.XX°)
PITCH DIAMETER	(X.XXXX)
ADDENDUM	(.XXX)[2]
WORKING DEPTH	(.XXX)[2]
WHOLE DEPTH	.XXX-.XXX[2]
THEORETICAL OUTSIDE DIAMETER	(X.XXX)[2]
THEORETICAL CROWN TO BACK	(X.XXX)[2]
PITCH ANGLE	(XX.XX°)[2]
ROOT ANGLE	(XX.XX°)
CIRCULAR THICKNESS	(.XXXX)[2]
MEAN MEASURING ADDENDUM	.XXX[2]
MEAN MEASURING THICKNESS	.XXX-.XXX[2]
NORMAL BACKLASH WITH MATE	.XXX-.XXX[2]
BACKLASH VARIATION TOLERANCE[3]	.XXXX
SHAFT ANGLE	(XX.XX°)
FILLET RADIUS	.XXX-.XXX[2]
RUNOUT TOLERANCE[3]	.XXXX
PITCH TOLERANCE[3]	.XXXX
INDEX TOLERANCE[3]	.XXXX
TOOTH SURFACE TEXTURE	XX AA OR R_a
AGMA QUALITY CLASS	XX
TOOTH FORM	CONIFLEX® OR REVACYCLE®
DRIVING MEMBER	PINION OR GEAR
DIRECTION OF ROTATION	CW AND/OR CCW
MFG SUMMARY NUMBER	XXXXXX
PART NUMBER OF MATE	XXXXXX
NUMBER OF TEETH IN MATE	XX

1. For metric drawings, specify module in place of diametral pitch.
2. For metric drawings, the number of decimal places to the right of the decimal point should be reduced by one.
3. See 5.18.3, 5.23, 5.24, 5.25 and 5.26 concerning when to specify these values on the gear drawing.

1. When face angle distance and back angle distance are used for dimensioning the gear blank, the face angle and the back angle should be given as reference dimensions on the drawing, without a tolerance.

FIG. 2.24 Standard drawing format for straight bevel gears. *(Extracted from American National Standard Drafting Practices, Gear Drawing Standards (ANS Y14.7.2) with the permission of the publisher, The American Society of Mechanical Engineers, United Engineering Center, 345 East 47th Street, New York, NY 10017.)*

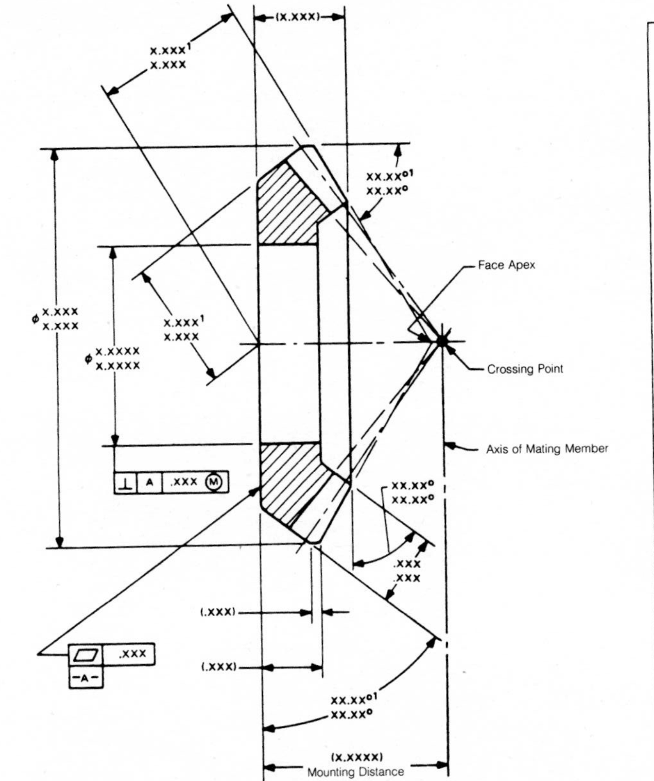

1. When face angle distance and back angle distance are used for dimensioning the gear blank, the face angle and the back angle should be given as reference dimensions on the drawing, without a tolerance.

NUMBER OF TEETH	XX
DIAMETRAL PITCH[1]	(XX.XXX)
NORMAL PRESSURE ANGLE	(XX.XX°)
MEAN SPIRAL ANGLE	(XX.XX°)
HAND OF SPIRAL	LH OR RH
PITCH DIAMETER	(X.XXXX)
ADDENDUM	(.XXX)[2]
WORKING DEPTH	(.XXX)[2]
WHOLE DEPTH	(.XXX)[2]
THEORETICAL OUTSIDE DIAMETER	(X.XXX)[2]
THEORETICAL CROWN TO BACK	(X.XXX)[2]
PITCH ANGLE	(XX.XX°)
ROOT ANGLE	(XX.XX°)
CIRCULAR THICKNESS	(.XXXX)[2]
MEAN MEASURING ADDENDUM	.XXX[2]
MEAN MEASURING THICKNESS	.XXX-.XXX[2]
MEAN MEASURING DEPTH	.XXX-.XXX[2]
NORMAL BACKLASH WITH MATE	.XXX-.XXX[2]
BACKLASH VARIATION TOLERANCE[3]	.XXXX[2]
SHAFT ANGLE	(XX.XX°)
FILLET RADIUS	.XXX-.XXX[2]
RUNOUT TOLERANCE[3]	.XXXX
PITCH TOLERANCE[3]	.XXXX
INDEX TOLERANCE[3]	.XXXX
TOOTH SURFACE TEXTURE	XX AA OR R_a
AGMA QUALITY CLASS	XX
TOOTH FORM	GENERATED OR FORMATE® OR HELIXFORM®
DRIVING MEMBER	PINION OR GEAR
DIRECTION OF ROTATION	CW AND/OR CCW
MFG SUMMARY NUMBER	XXXXXX
PART NUMBER OF MATE	XXXXXX
NUMBER OF TEETH IN MATE	XX

V AND H CHECK IN THOUSANDTHS OF AN INCH (OR HUNDREDTHS OF A MILLIMETER) FOR FINISHED GEARS[4]

GEAR CONVEX	TOE	HEEL	TOTAL		GEAR CONCAVE	TOE	HEEL	TOTAL
V	XX	XX	XX		V	XX	XX	XX
H	XX	XX	XX		H	XX	XX	XX

1. For metric drawings, specify module in place of diametral pitch.
2. For metric drawings, the number of decimal places to the right of the decimal point should be reduced by one.
3. See 5.18.3, 5.23, 5.24, 5.25 and 5.26 concerning when to specify these values on the gear drawing.
4. May be optional for matched sets. Specify on matched set drawing.

FIG. 2.25 Standard drawing format for spiral bevel gears. *(Extracted from American National Standard Drafting Practices, Gear Drawing Standards (ANS Y14.7.2) with the permission of the publisher, The American Society of Mechanical Engineers, United Engineering Center, 345 East 47th Street, New York, NY 10017.)*

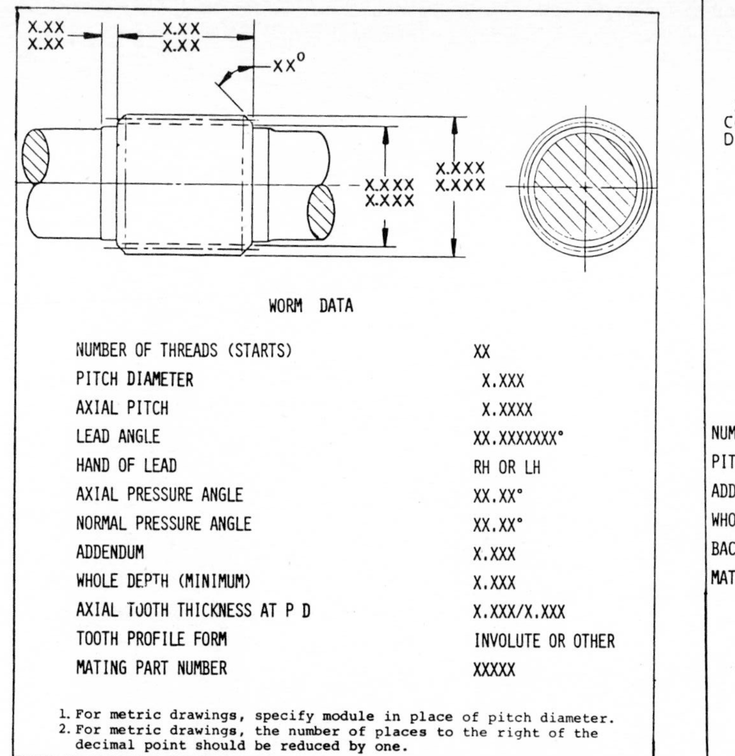

FIG. 2.26 Standard drawing format for single-enveloping worm gears. *(Extracted from American National Standard Drafting Practices, Gear Drawing Standards (ANS Y14.7.3) with the permission of the publisher, The American Society of Mechanical Engineers, United Engineering Center, 345 East 47th Street, New York, NY 10017.)*

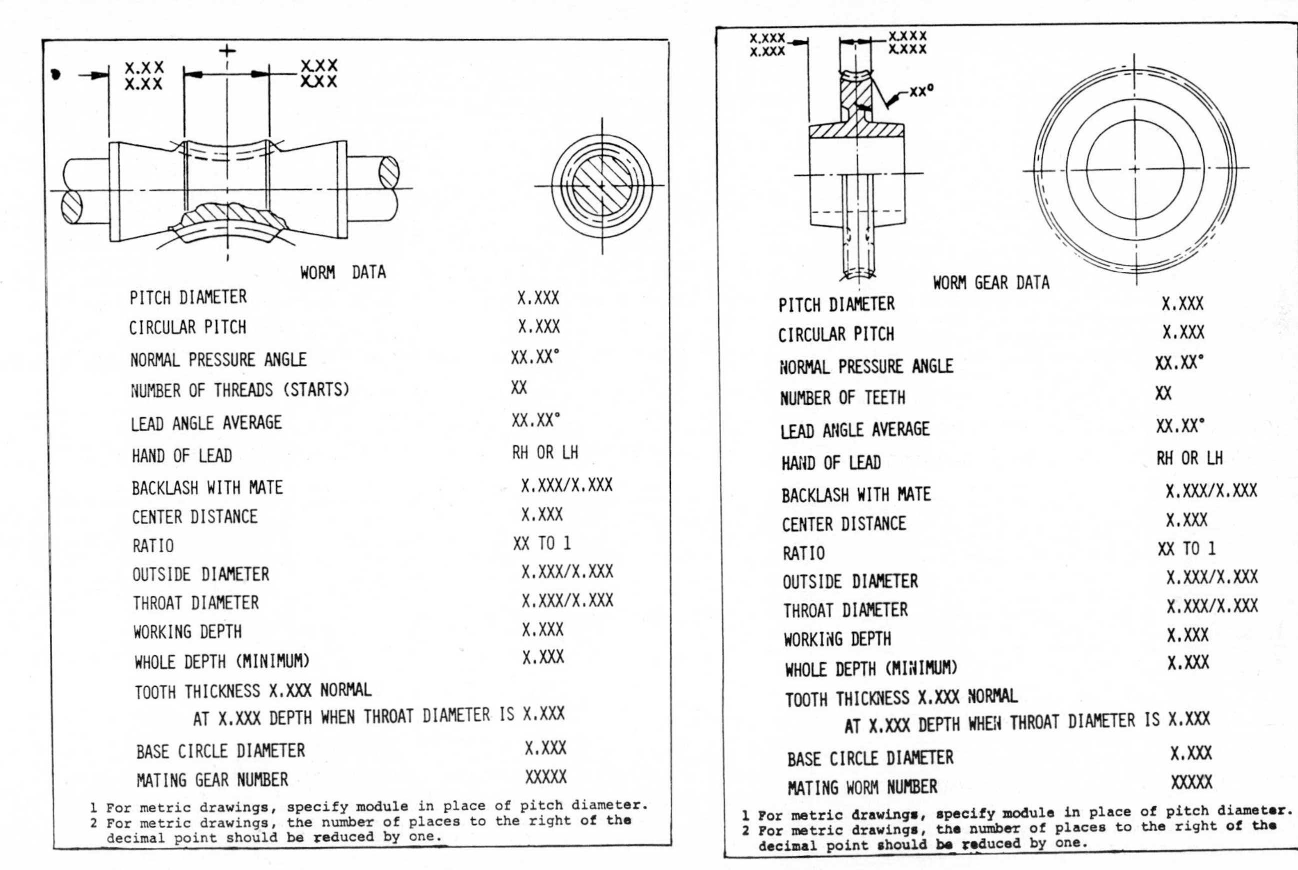

FIG. 2.27 Standard drawing format for double-enveloping worm gears. *(Extracted from American National Standard Drafting Practices, Gear Drawing Standards (ANS Y14.7.3) with the permission of the publisher, The American Society of Mechanical Engineers, United Engineering Center, 345 East 47th Street, New York, NY 10017.)*

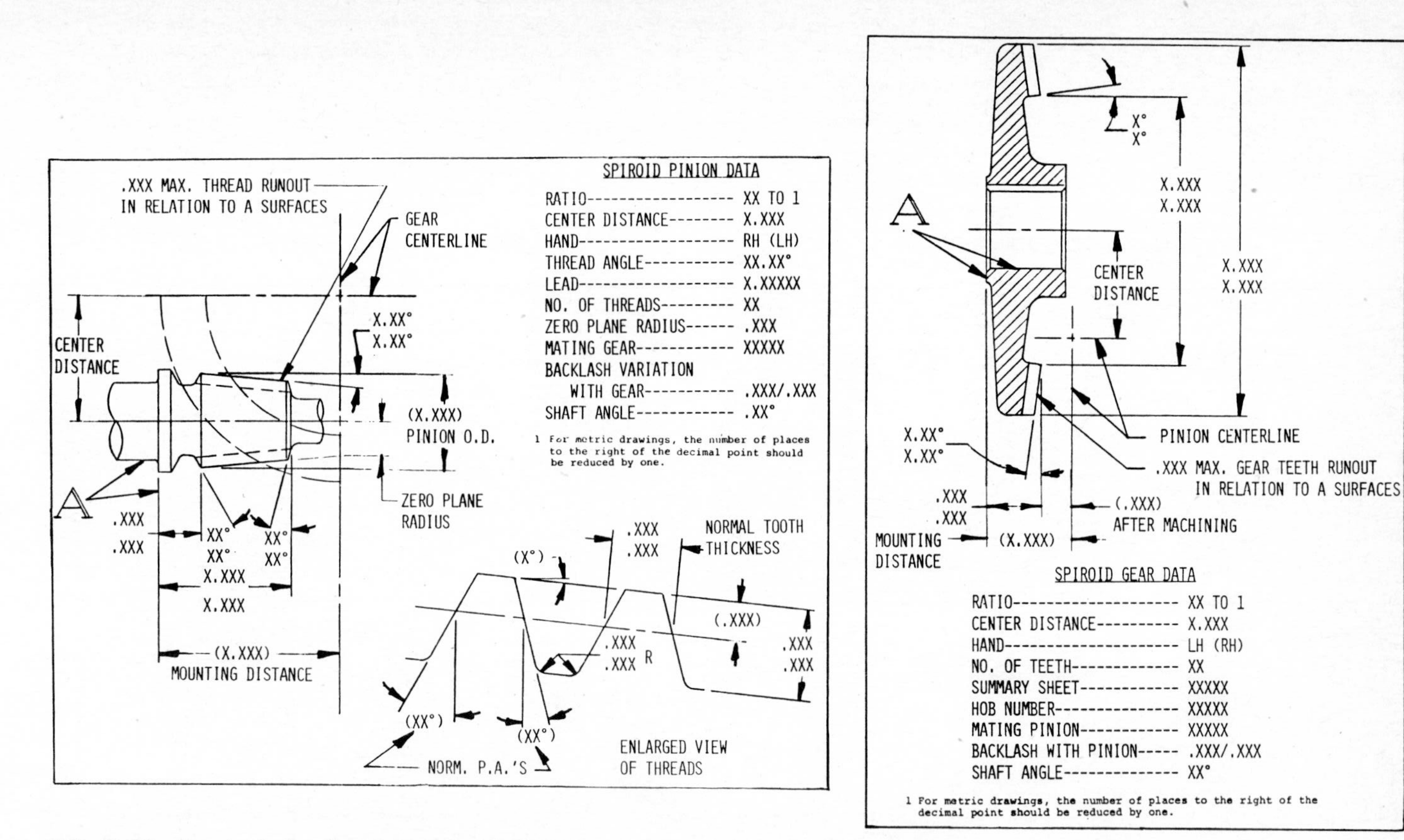

FIG. 2.28 Standard drawing format for Spiroid gears. *(Extracted from American National Standard Drafting Practices, Gear Drawing Standards (ANS Y14.7.3) with the permission of the publisher, The American Society of Mechanical Engineers, United Engineering Center, 345 East 47th Street, New York, NY 10017.)*

2.15 Gear-Tooth Tolerances

This is a difficult and controversial subject. Much has been written about gear tolerances, and yet there are no clear-cut answers. Space will not permit a detailed study of tolerances in this book.

From a general standpoint, tolerances on a gear must meet two kinds of requirements:

1. The tolerances must be broad enough to be met by the method of manufacture and the craftsmanship of the plant undertaking the manufacture.
2. The tolerances must be close enough so that the gears will carry the required loads for a sufficient length of time and without objectionable noise or vibration. In timing and control applications, suitable accuracy of motion and freedom from "lost motion" on reversal must be obtained.

The designer has several sources of information on tolerances. If the product is in production, the accuracy already achieved and the performance in the field can be studied. This should give an answer to the questions of what can be done and what is needed. On entirely new products, studies of dynamic loads, effects of misalignment, and effects of surface finish may be required. Sections 3.27 and 3.28 in Chap. 3 and Sec. 5.18 in Chap. 5 show some of the considerations that will help a designer estimate accuracy requirements. Trade standards, such as AGMA 390.03 and DIN 3961, are very helpful in showing trade practices in regard to tolerances and inspection of different kinds of gears. Machine-tool builders can usually give good data as to the accuracy that their products can produce.

The quality of gear teeth cannot be completely controlled until appropriate tolerances are specified on the following items:

Tooth spacing
Tooth profile
Concentricity of teeth with axis
Tooth alignment (or lead or helix)
Tooth thickness (or backlash)
Surface finish of flank and fillet

The best tooth-to-tooth spacing accuracy obtainable is about 2.5 μm (0.0001 in.). Very careful grinding or very good cutting and shaving is required to get this extreme degree of accuracy. Only a few of the best-designed machine tools are capable of this kind of work. This kind of accuracy is needed in a few very high-speed gears for marine and industrial uses. Tooth-to-tooth accuracy of most *precision* gear applications is of the order of

5 μm (0.0002 in.) or 8 μm (0.0003 in.). Good commercial gears range from 12 μm (0.0005 in.) to 40 μm (0.0016 in.) in tooth-to-tooth accuracy.

In a few cases, the involute profile is held to 5 μm (0.0002 in.) variation. Most precision gears have their involutes true within 12 μm (0.0005 in.). Good general-purpose gears range from 25 to 12 μm on involute. Concentricity of control gears of small size is held to 12 μm for some applications. Most precision gears are in the range of 25 to 50 μm. Good commercial gears range up to about 120 μm. *Concentricity* is ordinarily measured as *twice* the eccentricity (full indicator reading used).

Tooth alignment in very critical applications is held to as little as 15 μm and 10 μm over 250 to 500 mm. Extraordinary equipment and effort are required to hold a tight control over wide-face-width gears like the 500-mm-per-helix gears used in ship propulsion. Many commercial gears are held to limits like 12 to 20 μm for 25-mm face width.

Power gears allow from 50 to 120 μm (0.002 to 0.005 in.) tooth-thickness variation. This variation, of course, is *not within one* gear but from one gear to another. All teeth of one gear will be very close to the same size if tooth spacing is close. Some control gears are ground or shaved to as little as 5 μm tooth-thickness tolerance. This is very hard to do.

Tooth-surface finish can be held within 0.4 μm (16 μin.) AA by very skilled shaving or grinding. Many precision gears are held to about 0.8 μm AA. Commercial gears are apt to be around 1.2 to 2 μm or more.

There is a general trend to use limits-of-accuracy sheets to define tolerances. This saves writing out all the tolerances on each drawing. All that has to be put on the drawing is the limits column that the gear is to be checked to.

When a company issues its own engineering limits for gear accuracy, several things can be covered:

Several classes or grades of accuracy can be set. High accuracy grades can be set for long-life, high-speed gears. Lower accuracy grades will cover medium- or slow-speed gears.

Things not covered in trade standards on accuracy can be covered. These may be things like root fillet radii tolerances, allowable mismatch between side of tooth profile and root fillet, or allowable waviness or irregularity in profile and helix.

An engineering limits document can define checking machine procedures to get tooth-to-tooth spacing, accumulated spacing, and runout readings. Procedures can be defined to handle allowed error in master gears used to check production gears. Stylus size, stylus pressure, and other mechanics of checking can be defined to fit the checking machinery intended to be used in manufacture.

Many major companies that build a goodly volume of important geared machinery have found a well-developed engineering document on gear checking essential.

Trade standards like AGMA 390.03 and DIN 3961 are valuable guidelines for setting company engineering standards for gears. And, of course, it is quite appropriate to work directly to trade standards on gearing without special extra data that may be peculiar to an individual company.

Table 2.21 shows typical AGMA gear tolerances for quality numbers 9 to 13. In comparison, Table 2.22 shows DIN tolerances from 10 to 3. Both AGMA 390.03 and the DIN document show a considerable amount of additional gear tolerance and inspection data. Also, these documents are updated every few years. Those designing and building gears are strongly advised to get the latest issues of these standards and keep abreast of the best current practices in gear inspection.

In many cases, gear quality can be measured by simple functional tests. In some applications, the ability to run quietly in a noise-testing machine is a good check. Some power gearing is checked by running at full load and full speed for a period of time. If the gear runs smoothly and the surface polishes up without wear, it can be assumed that the gear will do its job in service. In control gearing, the measurement of backlash in different positions may serve to control quality. Since it costs a lot to give gears detailed checks, the designer should choose the least expensive checking system which will ensure proper quality. Then the gear drawing should be toleranced in keeping with the inspection that is planned.

2.16 Gear Material and Heat-Treat Data

Historically, the geometric quality of gears (tooth tolerances) received much attention between 1940 and 1980. As Sec. 2.15 has just described, there are trade standards for gear accuracy and a well-developed gear industry practice. The *metallurgical* quality of gears has not (so far) received equal attention.

The best gear people around the world are now coming to realize that metallurgical quality is just as important as geometric quality. A gear of good accuracy made from material that has a poor hardness pattern or substantial metallurgical flaws will not last as long as it should or will be unable to carry full load without serious distress.

Take the case-hardened gear, for example. If the case is too thin, the tooth strength and wear resistance will be unsatisfactory. If the case is too deep, the tooth is apt to be too brittle and subject to high internal stresses (the case will tend to break away from the core material). If the carburizing gas is too rich, the outer case will contain too much carbon and is apt to

TABLE 2.21 Typical AGMA Gear Tolerances for Quality Numbers 9 to 13

		Runout tolerance										Pitch tolerance				
AGMA quality number	Normal diametral pitch	Pitch diameter (inches)										Pitch diameter (inches)				
		3/4	1½	3	6	12	25	50	100	200	400	3/4	1½	3	6	12
9	1/2					104.7	124.7	147.0	173.4	204.5	241.2					13.4
	1				63.5	74.8	89.1	105.1	124.0	146.2	172.4				10.2	11.5
	2			38.5	45.4	53.5	63.7	75.2	88.6	104.5	123.3			7.7	8.7	9.8
	4		23.3	27.5	32.4	38.3	45.6	53.7	63.4	74.7	88.1		5.8	6.6	7.4	8.4
	8	14.1	16.7	19.7	23.2	27.4	32.6	38.4	45.3	53.4	63.0	4.4	5.0	5.6	6.4	7.2
	12	11.6	13.7	16.2	19.1	22.5	26.8	31.6	37.2	43.9	51.8	4.0	4.6	5.1	5.8	6.6
	20	9.1	10.7	12.6	14.9	17.6	20.9	24.7	29.1	34.3	40.4	3.6	4.1	4.6	5.2	5.9
10	1/2					74.8	89.0	105.0	123.8	146.1	172.3					9.4
	1				45.3	53.5	63.7	75.1	88.5	104.4	123.2				7.2	8.1
	2			27.5	32.4	38.2	45.5	53.7	63.3	74.7	88.1			5.4	6.1	6.9
	4		16.7	19.6	23.2	27.3	32.5	38.4	45.3	53.4	63.0		4.1	4.6	5.2	5.9
	8	10.1	11.9	14.0	16.6	19.5	23.3	27.4	32.4	38.2	45.0	3.1	3.5	4.0	4.5	5.1
	12	8.3	9.8	11.5	13.6	16.1	19.1	22.6	26.6	31.4	37.0	2.8	3.2	3.6	4.1	4.6
	20	6.5	7.6	9.0	10.6	12.5	14.9	17.6	20.8	24.5	28.9	2.5	2.9	3.2	3.7	4.1
11	1/2					53.4	63.6	75.0	88.5	104.3	123.0					6.6
	1				32.4	38.2	45.5	53.6	63.2	74.6	88.0				5.0	5.7
	2			19.6	23.1	27.3	32.5	38.3	45.2	53.3	62.9			3.8	4.3	4.9
	4		11.9	14.0	16.6	19.5	23.2	27.4	32.3	38.1	45.0		2.9	3.3	3.7	4.2
	8	7.2	8.5	10.0	11.8	14.0	16.6	19.6	23.1	27.3	32.2	2.2	2.5	2.8	3.2	3.6
	12	5.9	7.0	8.2	9.7	11.5	13.7	16.1	19.0	22.4	26.4	2.0	2.3	2.6	2.9	3.3
	20	4.6	5.5	6.4	7.6	9.0	10.7	12.6	14.8	17.5	20.6	1.8	2.0	2.3	2.6	2.9
12	1/2					38.1	45.4	53.6	63.2	74.5	87.9					4.7
	1				23.1	27.3	32.5	38.3	45.2	53.3	62.8				3.5	4.0
	2			14.0	16.5	19.5	23.2	27.4	32.3	38.1	44.9			2.7	3.0	3.4
	4		8.5	10.0	11.8	13.9	16.6	19.6	23.1	27.2	32.1		2.0	2.3	2.6	2.9
	8	5.2	6.1	7.2	8.5	10.0	11.9	14.0	16.5	19.5	23.0	1.5	1.7	2.0	2.2	2.5
	12	4.2	5.0	5.9	6.9	8.2	9.8	11.5	13.6	16.0	18.9	1.4	1.6	1.8	2.0	2.3
	20	3.3	3.9	4.6	5.4	6.4	7.6	9.0	10.6	12.5	14.7	1.3	1.4	1.6	1.8	2.0
13	1/2					27.2	32.4	38.3	45.1	53.2	62.8					3.3
	1				16.5	19.5	23.2	27.4	32.3	38.1	44.9				2.5	2.8
	2			10.0	11.8	13.9	16.6	19.6	23.1	27.2	32.1			1.9	2.1	2.4
	4		6.1	7.2	8.4	10.0	11.9	14.0	16.5	19.5	22.9		1.4	1.6	1.8	2.1
	8	3.7	4.3	5.1	6.0	7.1	8.5	10.0	11.8	13.9	16.4	1.1	1.3	1.4	1.6	1.8
	12	3.0	3.6	4.2	5.0	5.9	7.0	8.2	9.7	11.4	13.5	1.0	1.1	1.3	1.4	1.6
	20	2.4	2.8	3.3	3.9	4.6	5.4	6.4	7.6	8.9	10.5	0.9	1.0	1.1	1.3	1.4

Notes: 1. Tolerance values are in ten-thousandths of an inch.

2. Extracted from AGMA Handbook for Unassembled Gears, Volume 1, Gear Classifications, Materials, and Inspection (AGMA 390.03, 1971), with the permission of the publisher, the American Gear Manufacturers Association, Suite 1000, 1901 North Forth Myer Drive, Arlington, VA 22209, U.S.A.

Pitch tolerance					Profile tolerance										Lead tolerance				
Pitch diameter (inches)					Pitch diameter (inches)										Face width (inches)				
25	50	100	200	400	3/4	$1\frac{1}{2}$	3	6	12	25	50	100	200	400	1 and less	2	3	4	5
15.3	17.3	19.5	22.1	24.9					30.4	34.1	37.9	42.2	46.9	52.2					
13.1	14.8	16.7	18.9	21.4				20.2	22.5	25.2	28.1	31.2	34.7	38.6					
11.2	12.7	14.3	16.2	18.3			13.5	15.0	16.7	18.6	20.7	23.1	25.7	28.6					
9.6	10.8	12.2	13.8	15.7		8.9	10.0	11.1	12.3	13.8	15.3	17.1	19.0	21.1	4	7	9	11	13
8.2	9.3	10.5	11.9	13.4	5.9	6.6	7.4	8.2	9.1	10.2	11.4	12.6	14.1	15.6					
7.5	8.5	9.6	10.8	12.2	5.0	5.5	6.2	6.9	7.6	8.6	9.5	10.6	11.8	13.1					
6.7	7.6	8.5	9.7	10.9	4.0	4.4	4.9	5.5	6.1	6.8	7.6	8.5	9.4	10.5					
10.8	12.2	13.7	15.5	17.6					21.7	24.3	27.1	30.1	33.5	37.3					
9.2	10.4	11.8	13.3	15.0				14.5	16.1	18.0	20.0	22.3	24.8	27.6					
7.9	8.9	10.1	11.4	12.9			9.6	10.7	11.9	13.3	14.8	16.5	18.3	20.4					
6.7	7.6	8.6	9.8	11.0		6.4	7.1	7.9	8.8	9.9	11.0	12.2	13.6	15.1	3	5	7	9	10
5.8	6.5	7.4	8.3	9.4	4.2	4.7	5.3	5.9	6.5	7.3	8.1	9.0	10.0	11.2					
5.3	6.0	6.7	7.6	8.6	3.6	4.0	4.4	4.9	5.5	6.1	6.8	7.6	8.4	9.4					
4.7	5.3	6.0	6.8	7.7	2.9	3.2	3.5	3.9	4.4	4.9	5.4	6.1	6.7	7.5					
7.6	8.6	9.7	10.9	12.4					15.5	17.4	19.3	21.5	24.0	26.7					
6.5	7.3	8.3	9.4	10.6				10.3	11.5	12.9	14.3	15.9	17.7	19.7					
5.6	6.3	7.1	8.0	9.1			6.9	7.6	8.5	9.5	10.6	11.8	13.1	14.6					
4.8	5.4	6.1	6.9	7.8		4.6	5.1	5.6	6.3	7.0	7.8	8.7	9.7	10.8	3	4	6	7	8
4.1	4.6	5.2	5.9	6.6	3.0	3.4	3.8	4.2	4.6	5.2	5.8	6.4	7.2	8.0					
3.7	4.2	4.7	5.4	6.1	2.5	2.8	3.1	3.5	3.9	4.4	4.9	5.4	6.0	6.7					
3.3	3.7	4.2	4.8	5.4	2.0	2.3	2.5	2.8	3.1	3.5	3.9	4.3	4.8	5.4					
5.3	6.0	6.8	7.7	8.7					11.1	12.4	13.8	15.4	17.1	19.0					
4.6	5.2	5.8	6.6	7.5				7.4	8.2	9.2	10.2	11.4	12.7	14.1					
3.9	4.4	5.0	5.6	6.4			4.9	5.5	6.1	6.8	7.6	8.4	9.4	10.4					
3.3	3.8	4.3	4.8	5.5		3.3	3.6	4.0	4.5	5.0	5.6	6.2	6.9	7.7	2	3	5	6	7
2.9	3.2	3.7	4.1	4.7	2.2	2.4	2.7	3.0	3.3	3.7	4.1	4.6	5.1	5.7					
2.6	3.0	3.3	3.8	4.3	1.8	2.0	2.2	2.5	2.8	3.1	3.5	3.9	4.3	4.8					
2.3	2.6	3.0	3.4	3.8	1.5	1.6	1.8	2.0	2.2	2.5	2.8	3.1	3.4	3.8					
3.8	4.2	4.8	5.4	6.1					7.9	8.9	9.9	11.0	12.2	13.6					
3.2	3.6	4.1	4.6	5.3				5.3	5.9	6.6	7.3	8.1	9.0	10.1					
2.8	3.1	3.5	4.0	4.5			3.5	3.9	4.3	4.9	5.4	6.0	6.7	7.4					
2.4	2.7	3.0	3.4	3.8		2.3	2.6	2.9	3.2	3.6	4.0	4.4	4.9	5.5	2	3	4	4	5
2.0	2.3	2.6	2.9	3.3	1.5	1.7	1.9	2.1	2.4	2.7	3.0	3.3	3.7	4.1					
1.8	2.1	2.4	2.7	3.0	1.3	1.4	1.6	1.8	2.0	2.2	2.5	2.8	3.1	3.4					
1.6	1.9	2.1	2.4	2.7	1.0	1.2	1.3	1.4	1.6	1.8	2.0	2.2	2.5	2.7					

TABLE 2-22 Typical DIN Gear Tolerances for Grades 10 to 3

DIN grade no.	Normal tooth size		Pitch diameter, mm (in.)																	
			Over 50 to 125 (over 2 to 4.9)						Over 125 to 280 (over 4.9 to 11)						Over 280 to 560 (over 11 to 22)					
			Runout		Spacing				Runout		Spacing				Runout		Spacing			
					t-to-t		cum.				t-to-t		cum.				t-to-t		cum.	
	Module	Diam. pitch	μm	10^{-4} in.	μm	10^{-4} in.	μm	10^{-4} in.	μm	10^{-4} in.	μm	10^{-4} in.	μm	10^{-4} in.	μm	10^{-4} in.	μm	10^{-4} in.	μm	10^{-4} in.
10	10–16	1.6–2.5	110	43	63	25	140	55	125	49	71	28	180	71	140	55	71	28	200	79
	6–10	2.5–4.2	100	39	56	22	140	55	110	43	56	22	160	63	125	49	63	25	180	71
	3.55–6	4.2–7.15	90	35	50	20	125	49	100	39	50	20	140	55	110	43	56	22	180	71
	2–3.55	7.15–12.7	80	31	40	16	125	49	90	35	45	18	140	55	100	39	45	18	160	63
9	10–16	1.6–2.5	80	31	40	16	90	35	90	35	45	18	110	43	100	39	45	18	125	49
	6–10	2.5–4.2	71	28	36	14	90	35	80	31	36	14	100	39	90	35	40	16	110	43
	3.55–6	4.2–7.15	63	25	32	13	80	31	71	28	32	13	90	35	80	31	36	14	110	43
	2–3.55	7.15–12.7	56	22	25	10	71	28	63	25	28	11	90	35	71	28	28	11	100	39
8	10–16	1.6–2.5	56	22	32	13	63	25	63	25	32	13	80	31	71	28	36	14	90	35
	6–10	2.5–4.2	50	20	25	10	63	25	56	22	25	10	71	28	63	25	28	11	80	31
	3.55–6	4.2–7.15	45	18	20	8	56	22	50	20	22	9	71	28	56	22	25	10	80	31
	2–3.55	7.15–12.7	40	16	18	7	50	20	45	18	20	8	63	25	50	20	20	8	71	28
7	10–16	1.6–2.5	40	16	22	9	45	18	45	18	22	9	56	22	50	20	25	10	63	25
	6–10	2.5–4.2	36	14	18	7	45	18	40	16	18	7	56	22	45	18	20	8	63	25
	3.55–6	4.2–7.15	32	13	16	6	40	16	36	14	16	6	45	18	40	16	18	7	56	22
	2–3.55	7.15–12.7	28	11	12	5	36	14	32	13	14	5.5	45	18	36	14	16	6	50	20
6	10–16	1.6–2.5	28	11	16	6	32	13	32	13	16	6	40	16	36	14	18	7	45	18
	6–10	2.5–4.2	25	10	12	5	32	13	28	11	14	5.5	36	14	32	13	14	5.5	40	16
	3.55–6	4.2–7.15	22	9	11	4	28	11	25	10	11	4	36	14	28	11	12	5	40	16
	2–3.55	7.15–12.7	20	8	9	3.5	28	11	22	9	10	4	32	13	25	10	10	4	36	14
5	10–16	1.6–2.5	20	8	11	4	25	10	22	9	11	4	28	11	25	10	12	5	32	13
	6–10	2.5–4.2	18	7	9	3.5	22	9	20	8	10	4	25	10	22	9	10	4	28	11
	3.55–6	4.2–7.15	16	6	8	3	20	8	18	7	9	3.5	25	10	20	8	9	3.5	28	11
	2–3.55	7.15–12.7	14	5.5	6	2	20	8	16	6	8	3	22	9	18	7	8	3	25	10
4	10–16	1.6–2.5	14	5.5	8	3	18	7	16	6	8	3	20	8	18	7	9	3.5	22	9
	6–10	2.5–4.2	12	5	6	2	16	6	14	5.5	7	3	20	8	16	6	8	3	22	9
	3.55–6	4.2–7.15	11	4	5	2	16	6	12	5	5.5	2	18	7	14	5.5	6	2	20	8
	2–3.55	7.15–12.7	10	4	4.5	2	14	5.5	11	4	5	2	16	6	12	5	5	2	18	7
3	10–16	1.6–2.5	10	4	5.5	2	12	5	11	4	5.5	2	14	5.5	12	5	6	2	16	6
	6–10	2.5–4.2	9	3.5	4.5	2	11	4	10	4	5	2	14	5.5	11	4	5	2	16	6
	3.55–6	4.2–7.15	8	3	4	1.5	10	4	9	3.5	4	1.5	12	5	10	4	4.5	2	14	5.5
	2–3.55	7.15–12.7	7	3	3	1	10	4	8	3	3.5	1	12	5	9	3.5	3.5	1	14	5.5

Notes:
1. Tolerance values above are given in both microns (μm) and ten-thousandths of an inch (10^{-4} in.).
2. For definition of tolerances, see Fig. 5-50.
3. t-to-t = tooth-to-tooth spacing tolerance
   cum. = cumulative spacing tolerance
4. Runout values are about 10% lower than concentricity values determined with a master gear.
5. Tolerance values in this table were extracted from DIN Standard 3962 (1978), Beuth Verlag GmbH, Berlin 30 und Koen 1, German Federal Republic.

Pitch diameter, mm (in.)														Face width							
Over 560 to 1000 (over 22 to 39)						Over 1000 to 1600 (over 39 to 63)								20–40 mm (0.8–1.6 in.)		40–100 mm (1.6–3.9 in.)		100–160 mm (3.9–6.3 in.)		160+ mm (6.3+ in.)	
Runout		Spacing				Runout		Spacing				Profile slope (total)		Helix slope (total)							
		t-to-t		cum.				t-to-t		cum.											
μm	10^{-4} in.	μm	10^{-4} in.	μm	10^{-4} in.	μm	10^{-4} in.	μm	10^{-4} in.	μm	10^{-4} in.	μm	10^{-4} in.	μm	10^{-4} in.	μm	10^{-4} in.	μm	10^{-4} in.	μm	10^{-4} in.
160	63	80	31	220	87	180	71	80	31	250	98	90	35	50	20	63	25	80	31	80	31
140	55	71	28	200	79	160	63	71	28	220	87	71	28								
125	49	56	22	200	79	140	55	63	25	220	87	56	22								
110	43	50	20	180	71	125	49	56	22	200	79	45	18								
110	43	50	20	140	55	125	49	50	20	160	63	56	22	32	13	40	16	50	20	50	20
100	39	40	16	125	49	110	43	45	18	140	55	45	18								
90	35	36	14	125	49	100	39	40	16	140	55	36	14								
80	31	32	13	110	43	90	35	36	14	125	49	28	11								
80	31	36	14	100	39	90	35	36	14	110	43	40	16	20	8	25	10	32	13	32	13
71	28	28	11	90	35	80	31	32	13	100	39	32	13								
63	25	25	10	90	35	71	28	28	11	100	39	25	10								
56	22	22	9	80	31	63	25	25	10	90	35	20	8								
56	22	25	10	71	28	63	25	28	11	80	31	28	11	15	6	18	7	22	9	22	9
50	20	20	8	71	28	56	22	22	9	71	28	22	9								
45	18	20	8	63	25	50	20	20	8	71	28	18	7								
40	16	16	6	56	22	45	18	18	7	63	25	14	5.5								
40	16	18	7	50	20	45	18	20	8	56	22	22	9	10	4	12	5	16	6	16	6
36	14	14	5.5	45	18	40	16	16	6	50	20	16	6								
32	13	14	5.5	45	18	36	14	16	6	50	20	12	5								
28	11	11	4	40	16	32	13	12	5	45	18	10	4								
28	11	12	5	36	14	32	13	14	5.5	40	16	16	6	8	3	10	4	12	5	12	5
25	10	11	4	32	13	28	11	11	4	36	14	12	5								
22	9	10	4	32	13	25	10	10	4	36	14	9	3.5								
20	8	8	3	28	11	22	9	9	3.5	32	13	7	3								
20	8	9	3.5	25	10	22	9	10	4	28	11	11	4	6	2	8	3	10	4	10	4
18	7	8	3	25	10	20	8	9	3.5	28	11	8	3								
16	6	7	3	22	9	18	7	8	3	25	10	7	3								
14	5.5	5.5	2	20	8	16	6	7	3	22	9	5	2								
14	5.5	6	2	18	7	16	6	7	3	20	8	8	3	5	2	6	2	8	3	8	3
12	5	5.5	2	18	7	14	5.5	6	2	18	7	6	2								
11	4	5	2	16	6	12	5	5	2	18	7	5	2								
10	4	4.5	2	16	6	11	4	5	2	18	7	4	1.5								

spall under heavy load. If the gas is too lean, the tooth surface will not develop full hardness and wear resistance.

If the case-carburized gear is unprotected just prior to quench, it may "out gas" carbon and have deficient hardness right at the surface. If the quench is too slow for the alloy content and the size of the part, the core may lack strength and hardness and be unable to support the case under severe load conditions.

The raw steel used to make forgings for carburized gears may be dirty or nonhomogeneous. The best carburizing possible will not make a good gear if the machined forging has serious internal flaws before the final heat-treating operation.

Those making drawings for carburized gears need to cover items like these:

Steel composition (maximum and minimum limits for all elements and impurities)

Cleanness of steel (vacuum-arc-remelt steel is often used where even the best air-melt steel is not clean enough)

Case depth (control is needed at tip, flank, and root)

Case and core hardness

Test for grinding burns

Metallurgical structure (proper martensitic quality is needed in both case and core)

Through-hardened gears have their own metallurgical problems. If the quench is not fast enough for the size and alloy content of the gear part, there is apt to be a lack of hardness in the tooth root area. The structure may also be improper.

General information on materials and heat treatments for gears will be given in Chap. 4. See in particular Sec. 4.10 for detailed information on gear material quality.

2.17 Enclosed-Gear-Unit Requirements

The gear designer has much more to do than just design gear teeth and gear parts. The gear unit will have gear casings, shafts, bearings, seals, and a lubrication system. All these things are part of the gear product and therefore become the responsibility of the gear designer.

Those in gear-design work soon find that they have to become highly skilled in bearing selection, bearing design, and the fit of bearings on shafts and into casings.

The load on the bearings from a gear mesh is not a steady load like a weight load, but a somewhat pulsating load because of tooth-error effects and tooth-stiffness effects as pairs of teeth roll through the meshing zone. Wear particles from contacting gear teeth tend to get into the lubricant and go through the bearings. Temperature changes resulting from changing gear loads or changing ambient conditions cause somewhat nonuniform expansions and contractions that disturb the rather critical gear-bearing fits. All these things make the design of gear bearings more critical than the design of bearings for a machinery application usually is.

The lubrication system for a gear unit needs to keep all the tooth surfaces wet with lubricant and reasonably cool. In high-horsepower, high-speed gear units, oil-jet design, oil cooling by heat exchangers, oil-pump design, and oil-filter provisions to remove dirt and wear particles all become very critical. Even in slow-speed designs with heavy oil or grease lubrication, where a pumped system is not needed, keeping the teeth wet and providing a lubricant that will work over a wide temperature range (from start-up on a cold day to maximum continuous load on a hot day) may be critical.

It is beyond the scope of this book to go into gear lubrication in detail. The *Gear Handbook* has a whole chapter on gear lubrication. Section 7.15 of this book covers some of the lubrication problems that lead to gear failures.

The gear casing must support the gears and provide accurate alignment. For face widths up to about 100 mm, it is usually possible to make the gears and casing accurate enough to achieve satisfactory alignment with parts made to normal gear trade tolerances. Above 100 mm this becomes difficult, and at 250 mm face width it is usually impossible to be assured of a satisfactory tooth fit just by making all gears, bearings, and casings to close tolerances.

The solution to this problem is to assemble a gear unit and check contact across the face width. In a critical application, contact checks may be needed at no load, 1/4 load, 1/2 load, 3/4 load, and full load. (When allowance for deflections under load is made by changing the helix angle, full contact under light load is not wanted, since the parts are meant to deflect and shift contact to achieve the desired load distribution as torque is increased.)

When contact checks show an unsatisfactory condition under torque, the pinion or gear may be recut to better fit its mate. Sometimes casing bores are scraped or remachined to correct small errors in the original casing boring.

In some situations, there may be several gear casings and several sets of gears available on the assembly floor. If the first gearset in a casing does not fit quite right, a second or third set may be tried. With selective assembly, it is often possible to fit up most of the units without doing any corrective work on gear parts or casings.

In addition to fitting all right under torque loads, a critical gear unit may need to be tested at full speed to make sure that it runs without undue vibration and that all bearing temperatures and gear-part temperatures are OK. In addition, the run test will show whether or not the gear teeth are tending to score or have some serious local misfit condition. (Generally, after full-speed power testing, the unit is disassembled and all gear parts and bearings are inspected carefully by someone experienced with gears to see if there is any evidence of serious distress—that requires correction—in either the gear teeth or the bearings.)

Those designing gear units have the responsibility of determining what testing may be needed to get satisfactory tooth alignment and to prove out whether or not the gear unit runs satisfactorily under power. (Of course, if the gear unit is small and does not run too fast, the risk of an assembled unit not being OK when all parts are appropriately checked to part drawings may be relatively negligible.)

To summarize this section, the gear unit designer has these major tasks:

Design of gear parts

Design of casing structures

Design of bearings

Design of lubrication system

Design of seals, bolts, dowell pins, etc.

Specification of assembly procedures

Specification of gear running test procedures

Definition of acceptable or unacceptable results from run tests and inspection of parts after testing

chapter 3

Design Formulas

The material presented so far has shown how to choose a kind of gear and how to make a preliminary estimate of the gear size required. The general nature of the detail information required on gear drawings has also been discussed.

In this chapter we shall take up the calculation of the detail dimensions and the checking of the design against gear-rating formulas. The designer following this procedure should get almost the right size design on the first try. If the load-rating calculations show that the design is not quite right, it will usually be possible to make only one or two changes, such as a change in pitch or a change in face width, to adjust the capacity within the proper limits. It should not be necessary for the designer to scrap the whole design and start over from scratch after checking the load rating.

CALCULATION OF GEAR-TOOTH DATA

In this part of the chapter, we shall go over all the numbers and dimensions that will be needed on the drawings of the various kinds of gears. Designers who are not familiar with the limitations on gear size and shape that differ-

TABLE 3.1 Glossary of Gear Nomenclature, Chap. 3

Approach action Involute action before the point of contact between meshing gears has reached the pitch point. (A *driving* pinion has approach action on its dedendum.)

Breakage A gear tooth or portion of a tooth breaking off. Usually the failure is from fatigue; pitting, scoring, and wear may weaken a tooth so that it breaks even though the stresses on the tooth were low enough to present no danger of tooth breakage when it was new. Sometimes a relatively new tooth will break as a result of a severe overload or a serious defect in the tooth structure.

Derating Reducing the power rating of a gearset to compensate for tooth errors and for irregularities in the power transmission into and out of the gear drive. (When derated 2 to 1, a gear unit is rated to transmit only one-half the power that it might have transmitted under perfect conditions.)

Edge radius A radius of curvature at the end corner or top corner of a gear tooth.

End easement A tapering relief made at each end of a gear tooth while the middle portion of the tooth length is made to the true helix angle. The relief stops at some specified distance from the tooth end, such as one-eighth to one-sixth of the face width. End easement protects the teeth from misalignment and from stress concentrations peculiar to tooth ends. End easement is used on wide-face-width gears, while crowning may be used on narrow gears. (See Fig. 5.50 for a comparison.)

Flash temperature The temperature at which a gear-tooth surface is calculated to be hot enough to destroy the oil film and allow instantaneous welding at the contact point.

Full-depth teeth Gear teeth with a working depth of 2.0 times the normal module (or 2.0 divided by the normal diametral pitch).

Helix correction or **helix modification** When pinions are wide in face width for their diameter, there is appreciable bending and twisting of the pinion in mesh. A small change in helix angle (called helix correction or helix modification) may be used to compensate for the bending and twisting. This correction tends to give better load distribution across the face width.

Hunting ratio A ratio of numbers of gear and pinion teeth which ensures that each tooth in the pinion will contact *every* tooth in the gear before it contacts any gear tooth a second time. (13 to 48 is a hunting ratio; 12 to 48 is not a hunting ratio.)

Lead The axial advance of a thread or a helical spiral in 360° (one turn about the shaft axis).

Lead angle The inclination of a thread at the pitch line from a line at 90° to the shaft axis.

Limit diameter The diameter at which the outside diameter of the mating gear crosses the line of action. The limit diameter can be thought of as a *theoretical* form diameter. See Fig. 3.11.

Pitch point The point on a gear-tooth profile which lies on the pitch circle of that gear. At the moment that the pitch point of one gear contacts its mating gear, the contact occurs at the pitch point of the mating gear, and this common pitch point lies on a line connecting the two gear centers.

Pitting A fatigue failure of a contacting tooth surface which is characterized by little bits of metal breaking out of the surface.

Profile modification Changing a part of the involute profile to reduce the load in

TABLE 3.1 Glossary of Gear Nomenclature, Chap. 3 (*Continued*)

that area. Appropriate profile modifications help gears to run more quietly and better resist scoring, pitting, and tooth breakage.
Recess action Involute action after the point of contact between meshing gears has passed the pitch point. (A *driving* pinion has recess action on its addendum.)
Runout A measure of eccentricity relative to the axis of rotation. Runout is measured in a radial direction, and the amount is the difference between the highest and lowest reading in 360° (one turn). For gear teeth, runout is usually checked by either putting pins between the teeth or using a master gear. Cylindrical surfaces are checked for runout by a measuring probe that reads in a radial direction as the part is turned on its specified axis.
Scoring A failure of a tooth surface in which the asperities tend to weld together and then tear, leaving radial scratch lines. Scoring failures come quickly and are thought of as lubrication failures rather than metal fatigue failures.
Zone of action The distance, on the line of action between two gears, from the start of contact to the end of contact for each tooth.

ent materials or different manufacturing equipment may impose should consider the design worked out in this chapter as *tentative* until they have considered the things brought up in the later chapters of the book.

Table 3.1 is a glossary of gear terms used in Chap. 3. Table 3.2 shows the metric and English symbols for the principal terms used in calculating gear data. (Many secondary terms are defined in figures and tables used for specific calculations.)

3.1 Number of Pinion Teeth

In general, the more teeth a pinion has, the more quietly it will run and the better its resistance to wear will be. On the other hand, a smaller number of pinion teeth will give increased tooth strength, lower cutting cost, and larger tooth dimensions. In spur work, for instance, a seven-tooth pinion of 64 diametral pitch has been found quite useful in some fractional-horsepower applications.

Spur pinions used on railroad traction motors usually have from 12 to 20 teeth. High-load, high-speed aircraft pinions run from about 18 to 30 teeth. High-speed helical pinions for ship propulsion frequently have from 35 to 60 teeth.

In general, low-ratio sets can stand more teeth than high-ratio sets. A 1 to 1 ratio set with 35 teeth will have about the same tooth strength as a 5 to 1 ratio set with 24 pinion teeth.

TABLE 3.2 Gear Terms, Symbols, and Units Used in the Calculation of Gear Dimensional Data

Term	Metric		English		Reference or formula
	Symbol	Units	Symbol	Units	
Number of teeth, pinion	z_1	—	N_P or n	—	Sec. 3.1
Number of teeth, gear	z_2	—	N_G or N	—	Secs. 3.1, 3.2
Number of threads, worm	z_1	—	N_W	—	Table 3.29
Number of crown teeth	z	—	N_c	—	Eq. (3.29) and following
Tooth ratio	u	—	m_G	—	z_2/z_1 (or N_G/N_P)
Addendum, pinion	h_{a1}	mm	a_P	in.	Secs. 3.3, 3.5
Addendum, gear	h_{a2}	mm	a_G	in.	Secs. 3.3, 3.5
Addendum, chordal	$\bar{h}_a$	mm	a_c	in.	Fig. 3.7, Eq. (3.4), Sec. 3.15
Rise of arc	—	mm	—	in.	Fig. 3.7
Dedendum	h_f	mm	b	in.	Eq. (3.1)
Working depth	h'	mm	h_k	in.	2.0 × module (for full-depth teeth)
Whole depth	h	mm	h_t	in.	Sec. 3.3, Eq. (3.33)
Clearance	c	mm	c	in.	Eq. (3.33), Sec. 3.22
Tooth thickness	s	mm	t	in.	Sec. 3.6
Arc tooth thickness, pinion	s_1	mm	t_P	in.	Secs. 3.6, 3.11
Arc tooth thickness, gear	s_2	mm	t_G	in.	Secs. 3.6, 3.14, Eq. (3.23)
Tooth thickness, chordal	$\bar{s}$	mm	t_c	in.	Fig. 3.7, Eq. (3.5), Sec. 3.15, Eq. (3.24)
Backlash, transverse	j	mm	B	in.	Sec. 3.6, Table 3.21
Backlash, normal	j_n	mm	B_n	in.	Sec. 3.6
Pitch diameter, pinion	d_{p1}	mm	d	in.	Table 3.11
Pitch diameter, gear	d_{p2}	mm	D	in.	Table 3.11
Pitch diameter, cutter	d_{po}	mm	d_c	in.	Eq. (3.36)
Base diameter, pinion	d_{b1}	mm	d_b	in.	Table 3.11
Base diameter, gear	d_{b2}	mm	D_b	in.	Table 3.11
Outside diameter, pinion	d_{a1}	mm	d_o	in.	Pitch diameter + (2 × addendum)
Outside diameter, gear	d_{a2}	mm	D_o	in.	Pitch diameter + (2 × addendum)
Inside diameter, face gear	d_{i2}	mm	D_i	in.	Eq. (3.31)
Root diameter, pinion or worm	d_{f1}	mm	d_R	in.	Eq. (3.39)
Root diameter, gear	d_{f2}	mm	D_R	in.	Eq. (3.39)
Form diameter	d'_f	mm	d_f	in.	Secs. 3.9, 3.11
Limit diameter	d_ℓ	mm	d_ℓ	in.	Fig. 3.11, Sec. 3.8
Excess involute allowance	Δd_ℓ	mm	Δd_ℓ	in.	Allows for runout, Δ center distance, Secs. 3.9, 3.11
Ratio of diameters	ε	—	m	—	Ratio, any diameter to pitch diameter
Center distance	a	mm	C	in.	Secs. 2.7 to 2.13
Face width	b	mm	F	in.	Sec. 2.8
Net face width	b'	mm	F_e	in.	Meshing face width
Module, transverse	m or m_t	mm	—	—	mm of pitch diameter per tooth

TABLE 3.2 Gear Terms, Symbols, and Units Used in the Calculation of Gear Dimensional Data (*Continued*)

Term	Metric		English		Reference or formula
	Symbol	Units	Symbol	Units	
Module, normal	m_n	mm	—	—	Module in normal section
Diametral pitch, transverse	—	—	P_d or P_t	in.$^{-1}$	Teeth per in. of pitch diameter
Diametral pitch, normal	—	—	P_n	in.$^{-1}$	Diametral pitch in normal section
Circular pitch	p	mm	p	in.	Pitch-circle arc length per tooth
Circular pitch, transverse	p_t	mm	p_t	in.	
Circular pitch, normal	p_n	mm	p_n	in.	
Base pitch	p_b	mm	p_b	in.	Eq. (3.17)
Axial pitch	p_x	mm	p_x	in.	$p_n \div$ sin of helix angle
Lead (length)	p_z	mm	L	in.	$p_x \times$ no. of threads
Pressure angle	α or α_t	deg	ϕ or ϕ_t	deg	Sec. 3.3
Pressure angle, normal	α_n	deg	ϕ_n	deg	Sec. 3.12
Pressure angle, axial	α_x	deg	ϕ_x	deg	Eq. (3.40)
Pressure angle of cutter	α_0	deg	ϕ_c	deg	Sec. 3.22
Helix angle	β	deg	ψ	deg	Sec. 3.12
Lead angle	γ	deg	λ	deg	Complement of helix angle
Shaft angle	Σ	deg	Σ	deg	Angle between gear shaft and pinion shaft
Roll angle	θ_r	deg	ε_r	deg	Involute roll angle
Pitch angle, pinion	δ'_1	deg	γ	deg	Eq. (3.27)
Pitch angle, gear	δ'_2	deg	Γ	deg	Eq. (3.26)
Pi	π	—	π	—	Constant, about 3.14159265
Contact ratio	ε_α	—	m_p	—	Sec. 3.9
Zone of action	g_α	mm	Z	in.	Fig. 3.12
Edge radius, tool	r_{a0}	mm	r_T	in.	Generating tool, Eqs. (3.1), (3.22)
Radius of curvature, root fillet	ρ_f	mm	ρ_f	in.	Generated root radius, Eqs. (3.1), (3.22)
Circular thickness factor	k	—	k	—	(Bevel gears), Sec. 3.14
Cone distance	R	mm	A	in.	(Bevel gears), Table 3.23
Outer cone distance	R_a	mm	A_o	in.	Table 3.23
Mean cone distance	R_m	mm	A_m	in.	$\dfrac{R_a + R_f}{2} \left(\text{or } \dfrac{A_o + A_i}{2} \right)$
Inner cone distance	R_f	mm	A_i	in.	$R_a - b$ (or $A_o - F$)

Notes: 1. Abbreviations for units: mm = millimeters, in. = inches, deg = degrees.
2. See Table 3.33 for terms, symbols, and units used in load rating of gears.

TABLE 3.3 General Guide to Selection of Number of Pinion Teeth

No. pinion teeth	Design considerations
7	Requires at least 25° pressure angle and special design to avoid undercutting. Poor contact ratio. Use only in fine pitches
10	Smallest practical number with 20° teeth. Takes about 145 percent long addendum to avoid undercut. Poor wear characteristics
15	Used where strength is more important than wear. Requires long addendum
19	No undercutting with 20° standard-addendum design
25	Good balance between strength and wear for hard steels. Contact kept away from critical base-circle region
35	Strength may be more critical than wear on hard steels—about even on medium-hard steels
50	Probably critical on strength on all but low-hardness pinions. Excellent wear resistance. Favored in high-speed work for quietness

Note: The data given in Table 3.3 are rather general in nature. They are intended to give the reader a general view of the considerations involved in picking numbers of teeth. For somewhat more specific guidance in designing spur or helical gears, Table 3.4 shows how the choice tends to shift as hardness and ratio are varied.

Table 3.3 may be used as a general guide for numbers of teeth for spur and helical gears.

Table 3.4 is worked out to give an approximate balance between gear-surface-durability capacity and gear-tooth-strength capacity. To understand this table, let's consider a high-speed gear drive at 3 to 1 ratio with case-hardened and ground teeth at a surface hardness of 60 HRC (equivalent to about 600 HB or about 725 HV). The table says that a 25/75 tooth ratio ought to be OK. This means that when a large enough center distance and face width are picked based on surface-durability calculations, further calculations on tooth strength ought to be OK if the module (or pitch) is chosen to get 25 pinion teeth. Gear people would say that it was a "balanced design between durability and strength."

For our 3 to 1 example with fully hard gears, the balance would be reasonably good in short-life vehicle gears or somewhat longer-life aircraft gears. For turbine power gears that would run for many more hours and would need a capability of around 10^{10} or more pinion cycles, the durability calculations would considerably reduce the intensity of tooth loading. A balanced design might then be achieved at higher numbers of teeth, like 30 to 38 pinion teeth.

TABLE 3.4 Guide to Selecting Number of Pinion Teeth z_1 (or N_P) for Good Durability and Adequate Strength

Ratio	Long-life, high-speed gears				Vehicle gears, short life at maximum torque			
u	Brinell hardness				Brinell hardness			
(m_G)	200	300	400	600	200	300	400	600
1	80	50	39	35	50	37	29	26
1.5	67	45	32	30	45	30	24	22
2	60	42	28	27	42	27	21	20
3	53	37	25	25	37	24	18	18
4	49	34	24	24	34	23	17	17
5	47	32	23	23	32	22	17	17
7	45	31	22	22	31	21	16	16
10	43	30	21	21	30	20	16	16

Notes: 1. Typical high-speed applications that fit this table are turbine-driven helicopter gears. For turbine-driven industrial gears, more pinion teeth can be used because of lower allowable surface loading. (About 25% more is typical.)

2. Typical vehicle gears are spur and helical gears used in final wheel drives. (Considerably fewer pinion teeth are used in hypoid and spiral bevel final drives.)

In high-speed turbine gearing, scoring hazards and noise and vibration considerations make it desirable to use as small a tooth size as possible. The designer might get a good durability/strength balance at something like 35 teeth for the 3 to 1 example, but decide to go up to 40 pinion teeth and put a little more face width and/or center distance in to keep the rating within acceptable limits. This design would not have the lightest weight possible, but would compromise enough to avoid scoring and noise hazards reasonably well.

In contrast to the example of high-speed turbine gears just cited, a vehicle designer with hard gears at a 3 to 1 ratio might go as low as 20/60 teeth rather than 25/75. The much shorter life, slow-speed vehicle gears can stand quite a little surface damage, but a broken tooth puts the gear drive out of action immediately. The designer of vehicle gears needs extra strength and can get it by using fewer and larger teeth. There is often a scoring hazard in vehicle gears, but this is handled more by using special extreme pressure (EP) lubricants than by using smaller teeth.

To sum it up, Table 3.4 is a general guide to where to start on tooth numbers, but a complete design study may show that it is desirable to use pinion tooth numbers that differ from the table by a modest amount.

3.2 Hunting Teeth

The numbers of pinion and gear teeth *must* be whole numbers. It is generally desirable—particularly with low-hardness parts—to obtain a *hunting* ratio between gear and pinion teeth. With a hunting ratio, any tooth on one member will—in time—contact *all* the teeth on the mating part. This tends to equalize wear and improve spacing accuracy.

To illustrate this point, let us consider a tooth ratio of 21 to 76. The factors of 21 are 3 and 7. The factors of 76 are 2, 2, and 19. This ratio will hunt because *the parts have no common factor*. The gear should not be cut with a double-thread hob. A shaving cutter with 57 teeth would be a poor choice for either part. The cutter has factors of both 3 and 19.

As a general rule, tooth numbers should be selected so that there is no common factor between the number of teeth of a pinion and a gear that mesh together, and there should be no common factor between the number of teeth of a gear and of a cutting tool that has a gearlike meshing action with the part being cut.

Recent technical studies by Ishibashi and by Ichimaru (ASME 1980)* show that in certain cases, improved gear load-carrying capacity can be obtained with a nonhunting ratio. Tests were made of spur gears having a hunting ratio of 25/27 and an integer ratio of 26/26. Pitch-line speed was about 7 m/s (1400 fpm).

At a low hardness of 185 HV (about 185 HB), Ishibashi found that the 26/26 ratio would carry a little over 1000 N/mm^2 surface compressive stress before pitting, while the 25/27 ratio would only carry about 800 N/mm^2 before pitting. The pitting limit was defined as the highest loading the gear pair would carry for 10^7 cycles without pitting. The numbers just quoted are based on a part being considered "pitted" when 1 percent of the contact area is pitted.

To say it another way, the tests showed that the integer ratio could carry about 25 percent more hertz stress. Since hertz stress is proportional to the square root of K factor, the integer ratio carried about 60 percent more K factor. At a higher hardness of 300 HB for one part and over 600 HB for the other part, the hunting ratio carried about 6 percent more stress or about 12 percent more K factor.

The Ichimaru work showed somewhat similar results. Of particular interest in this paper were the data on how the surface finish wore in and how an EHD oil film was formed quickly with the integer ratio but slowly with the hunting ratio.

The explanation seems to be that a single pair of teeth meshing with each other wear down asperities (or "coin" a fit between the surfaces) quite

*See references at the end of the book.

TABLE 3.5 Hunting Tooth Considerations

Approximate hardness, HB		Lubrication regime		
Pinion	Gear	I	II	III
200	200	#1	#2	#3
300	300	#4	#5	#6
600	300	#7	#8	#9
600	600	#10	#11	#12

	Situation
#1, 2, 4, 5	Substantial gain in load capacity with integer ratio. After serious pitting, failure may be hastened as a result of growth of spacing errors and rough running of integer ratio.
#3, 6	Hunting ratio probably best if parts kept in service after some teeth pitted more than 1%. No data available to prove gain in load carrying for integer ratio parts to be taken out of service when a "worst" tooth pits more than 5%.
#7, 8	Substantial gain in load capacity with integer ratio. After serious pitting, failure may be quick as a result of spacing error effects.
#9	Hunting ratio probably best. Worst error spots on lower-hardness gear will have fewer cyles and more chance to be worked into a fit by the hard pinion teeth.
#10, 11	Possibly a small gain in load capacity with integer ratio. Hunting ratio probably best. Wear-in effects will be quite small.
#12	Worst tooth pair (with highest stresses resulting) will contact much less frequently.

quickly. In the hunting ratio, a tooth on one part has to get worn and wear *all* the teeth on the other part into a fit with itself. Thus a full fit cannot occur until all pinion teeth are worn alike, all gear teeth are worn alike, and the pinion-worn profile is a very close surface fit to the gear-worn profile.

The decision on whether or not to use hunting ratios becomes much more complex. Several pros and cons need to be considered. Table 3.5 shows the range of considerations.

3.3 Spur-Gear-Tooth Proportions

The proportions of addendum equal to $1.000m_n$ and whole depth equal to $2.250m_n$ have been used for many years. This design allows only a very small root fillet radius of curvature, and it is a hard design to work with when designing shaper cutters, preshave hobs, or shaving cutters.

Table 3.6 shows the more popular spur-gear-tooth proportions. Note that teeth finished by shaving or grinding require more whole depth than gears finished by cutting only (hobbing, shaping, or milling).

When maximum load capacity is desired, the teeth need as large a root

TABLE 3.6 Spur-Gear Proportions

Use	Pressure angle α (ϕ)	Working depth h' (h_k)	Whole depth h (h_t)	Edge radius of generating rack r_{a0} (r_T)
General purpose	20	2.000	2.250	0.300
Extra depth for shaving	20	2.000	2.350	0.350
Aircraft, full fillet, high fatigue strength	20	2.000	2.400	0.380
Alternative high-strength design	25	2.000	2.250	0.300
Fine-pitch gears	20	2.000	2.200 + * (constant)	—

*The extra amount of whole depth is 0.05 mm or 0.002 in. This constant is added to the calculated whole depth for small teeth 1.27 module or smaller. (In the English system fine pitch is 20 pitch and larger pitch numbers.)

Notes: For metric design, the depth values and tool radius are in millimeters and for 1 module. (For other modules, multiply by module.)

For English design, the depth values and tool radius are in inches and for 1 diametral pitch. (For other diametral pitches, divide by pitch.)

fillet radius as possible. This in turn leads to a need for more whole depth and a relatively large corner radius on the hob, grinding wheel, or other tool used to make the root area of the tooth.

The most common pressure angle now in use for spur gears is 20°. Case-hardened aircraft or vehicle gears very often use a 25° pressure angle. The 25° form makes the teeth thicker at the base, and this improves the bending strength. In addition, the 25° teeth have larger radii of curvature at the pitch line, and this enables more load to be carried before the contact stress exceeds allowable limits.

The 25° teeth generally run with more noise, as a result of the lower contact ratio. The tips of the teeth are thinner, and this may lead to fracturing of the tip when case-hardened teeth are cased too deep or the metallurgical structure is faulty.

When made just right, and when the application can stand somewhat rougher running, the 25° tooth form will carry about 20 percent more torque (or power in kilowatts) than a 20° tooth form.

A good compromise design that is easier to make successfully than 25° and has more capacity than 20° is a $22\frac{1}{2}$° tooth form. This design has about 11 percent more capacity than a 20° design.

Figure 3.1 shows some comparisons of tooth forms when they are cut with a rack (tooth number = ∞).

In the gear trade, there was considerable use of *stub* teeth in early days. A

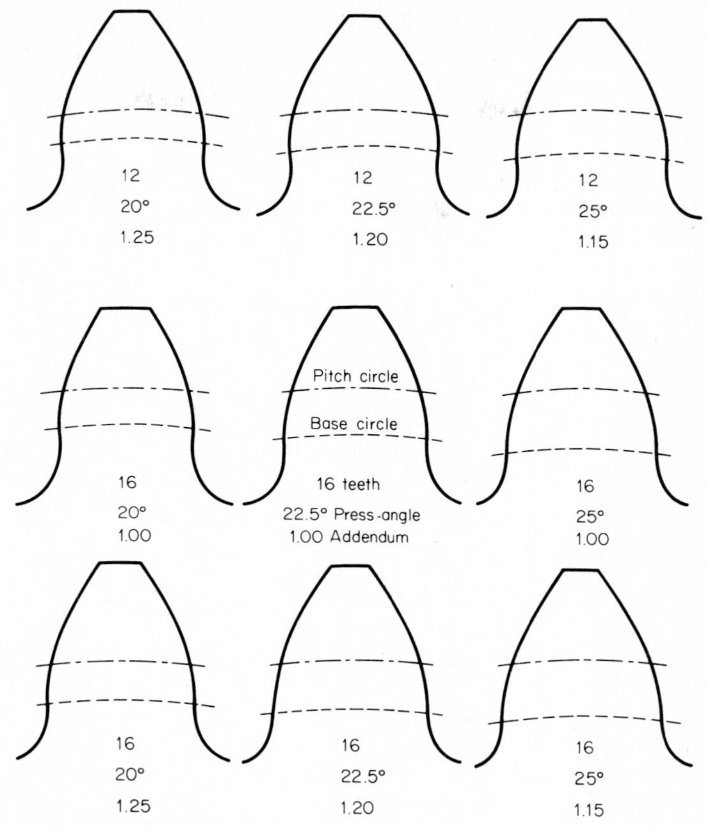

FIG. 3.1 Comparison of tooth forms.

typical stub tooth would have a working depth of around 1.60 ($1.60 \times m$). When teeth are quite inaccurate, load sharing between two pair of teeth in the meshing zone may not exist. This means that one pair has to carry full load right out to the very tip of the pinion or gear. In such a situation, it is obvious that a shorter and stubbier tooth can take more load without breakage than a taller, full-depth tooth.

The use of stub teeth has declined to where they are seldom used. In general, gear teeth are designed and built accurately enough to share load when they should. Test data and field experience show that full-depth teeth, made accurately, will carry more load and/or last longer than stub teeth.

This leads to the consideration of *extra-depth* teeth. (If accurate full-depth teeth are better than stub teeth, why not go on to even deeper teeth than full-depth teeth?)

Some gears are in production and doing very well with a whole depth as great as 2.30. At this much depth, a 25° pressure angle is impossible and $22\frac{1}{2}°$ is difficult. Pressure angles in the $17\frac{1}{2}°$ to 20° range are reasonably practical with 2.30 working depth.

The extra-depth teeth have problems with thin tips and smaller root fillet radii. Also, the effect on radii of curvature of the lower pressure angle somewhat offsets the gain from the higher contact ratio of the extra depth. In addition, very-high-speed extra-depth teeth are more sensitive to scoring troubles.

In some situations, a less than 20° pressure angle may be used to get smoother and quieter running. If the pinion has more than 30 teeth, fairly good load capacity can be obtained with a pressure angle as low as $14\frac{1}{2}°$. Also, in instrument and control gears, center-distance changes have less effect on backlash at $14\frac{1}{2}°$ than at 20°.

Stub teeth, extra-depth teeth, and low-pressure-angle teeth all have possible advantages for limited applications. For general use, though, the full-depth 20° design represents the best compromise.

3.4 Root Fillet Radii of Curvature

To get adequate tooth strength, it is desirable to cut or grind gear teeth to get either a full-radius root fillet or one that is almost full radius.

Figure 3.2 shows an example of a 25-tooth pinion with a $22\frac{1}{2}°$ pressure angle as it would be cut with a hob having a 0.36 edge radius (0.36 × module). The pinion has a whole depth of 2.35 and a long addendum of 1.2. Note the shape of the trochoidal root fillet and the path of the hob tip. Note also that the generated fillet of this type has its smallest radius of curvature near the root diameter.

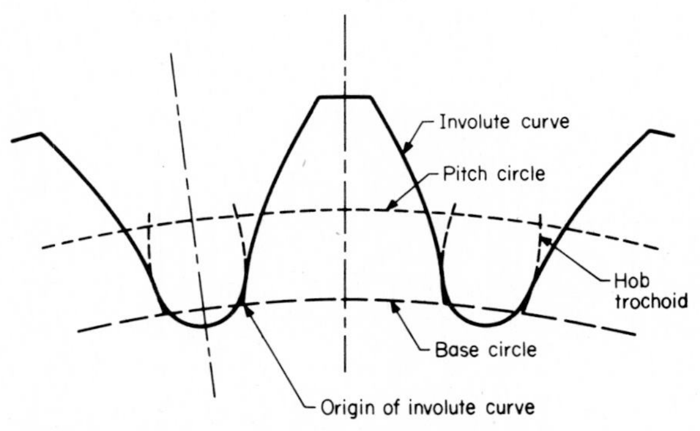

FIG. 3.2 25-tooth pinion with $22\frac{1}{2}°$ pressure angle.

For design purposes, a $22\frac{1}{2}°$ spur tooth would not be made exactly as shown in Fig. 3.2. A slightly smaller whole depth of 2.3 and a preshave or pregrind edge radius of 0.35 would be used. These changes facilitate the overall tool design and make it possible to use normal tolerances. The fillet obtained is still very good and has a relatively low stress-concentration factor.

The formula for calculating the minimum radius of curvature produced by hobbing or generating grinding is

$$\rho_f = r_{a0} + \frac{(h_f - r_{a0})^2}{d_{p1}/2 + (h_f - r_{a0})} \qquad \text{metric} \qquad (3.1a)$$

$$\rho_f = r_T + \frac{(b - r_T)^2}{d/2 + (b - r_T)} \qquad \text{English} \qquad (3.1b)$$

The term ρ_f is the *minimum* radius of curvature in the generated trochoidal fillet. The edge radius of the hob or grinding tool is r_{a0} (or r_T). The dedendum of the part is h_f (or b). For a list of gear symbols and units used in this chapter, see Tables 3.2 and 3.33.

For general-purpose work, the value of the minimum root fillet radius on the drawing should not be more than about 70 percent of the calculated minimum. This allows the toolmaker a reasonable margin of error in not obtaining the design tool radius.

When gears are shaped, form ground, or milled, it is possible to get about the same minimum radius as would be obtained in hobbing. The shape of the fillet will be slightly different, though. From a practical standpoint, the designer can design to the method shown above and be assured that the gears can be produced by any of the cutting methods if the tools are properly designed.

Figure 3.3 shows curve sheets based on Eq. (3.1) for teeth with 20° and 25° pressure angles. Values for $22\frac{1}{2}°$ are about midway between the values for 20° and 25°.

Figure 3.3 shows an example of special curve sheet paper used by the author to plot gear data. The abscissa distance is proportional to the *reciprocal* of the tooth number. Note that the distance from 12 to ∞ is just *twice* the distance from 24 to ∞.

The effect* of tooth numbers on many variables having to do with involute curvature or trochoidal curvature is somewhat proportional to the reciprocal of the tooth number. Hence this graph paper results in relatively straight-line curves for many tooth variables.

*The reader should note from this graph paper that a change of *one* tooth at the 12-tooth point means a change of more than *20* teeth at the 80-tooth point!

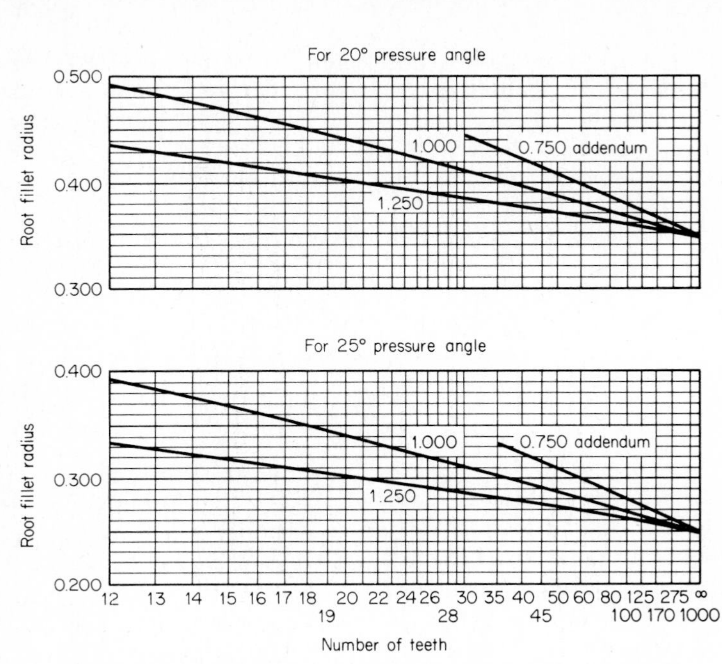

Notes: The above curves are for 1 module if metric or for 1 diametral pitch if English.

At 20° the tip radius of the generating rack is 0.350 mm (metric) or 0.350 in (English).

At 25° the tip radius is 0.250.

Read values in millimeters or in inches.

FIG. 3.3 Minimum root fillet radius graphs.

3.5 Long-Addendum Pinions

A *long-addendum pinion* is one that has an addendum which is longer than that of the mating gear. Since the working depth is 2.000*m* for full-depth teeth, long-addendum pinions—in a full-depth design—have an addendum *greater* than 1.000*m*.

Long-addendum pinions mate with "short-addendum" gears. The standard design practice is to make the gear addendum short by the same amount that the pinion addendum is made long.

The most compelling reason to use long-addendum pinions is to avoid undercut.* An undercut design is bad for several reasons. From a load-carrying standpoint, the undercut pinion is low in strength and wears easily at the point at which the undercut ends. In addition, there is the danger of *interference*. If the cutting tool does not make a big enough undercut, the

*See Fig. 8.1 for an example of a 16-tooth standard-addendum pinion that is undercut.

FIG. 3.4 How long addendum eliminates undercut. Pinion at left, with an addendum of 0.100 in., is badly undercut, but pinion at right, with 0.135-in. addendum, has no undercut. Both of these 10-pitch, 12-tooth pinions were cut with the same hob and shaving cutter to the same whole depth.

mating gear may try to enlarge the undercut. Since the mating gear is not a cutting tool, it does a poor job of removing metal. It tends to bind in the undercut. This creates an interference condition which is very detrimental.

The more teeth on the cutting tool, the greater the undercut. Since a hob corresponds to a rack (a *rack* is a section of a gear with an infinite number of teeth), the hob produces the most undercut. As a general rule, it can be stated that *hobbed* teeth will not have interference due to lack of undercut.

Besides avoiding undercut with low numbers of teeth, the long-addendum tooth has other advantages. In general, the pinion tooth tends to be weaker than the gear. A long-addendum design, together with a proportional increase in tooth thickness at the pitch line [see Eq. (3.3)], makes the pinion tooth stronger and the gear tooth weaker. Thus a long addendum can be used to balance strength. Figure 3.4 shows the remarkable difference that a 35 percent long addendum makes on a 12-tooth pinion.

The highest sliding velocity and the greatest compressive stress occur at the bottom of the pinion tooth. This condition can be helped by using a long-addendum design to get the start of the active involute farther away from the pinion base circle.

Figure 3.5 shows a curve sheet giving amounts of addendum for 20° standard teeth. The dashed curve on the left-hand side shows the bare minimum which is necessary to avoid undercut. No gear or pinion should have less addendum than that given by this curve.

The solid lines in Fig. 3.5 show the addendum for both pinion and gear. Suppose a 20-tooth pinion was meshing with a 50-tooth gear. The curve would be read for 20 meshing with 50, and then again for 50 meshing with 20. The answers would be $1.16m$ for the pinion and $0.84m$ for the gear.

If the dashed curve is read for pinion addendum, there is no place to read

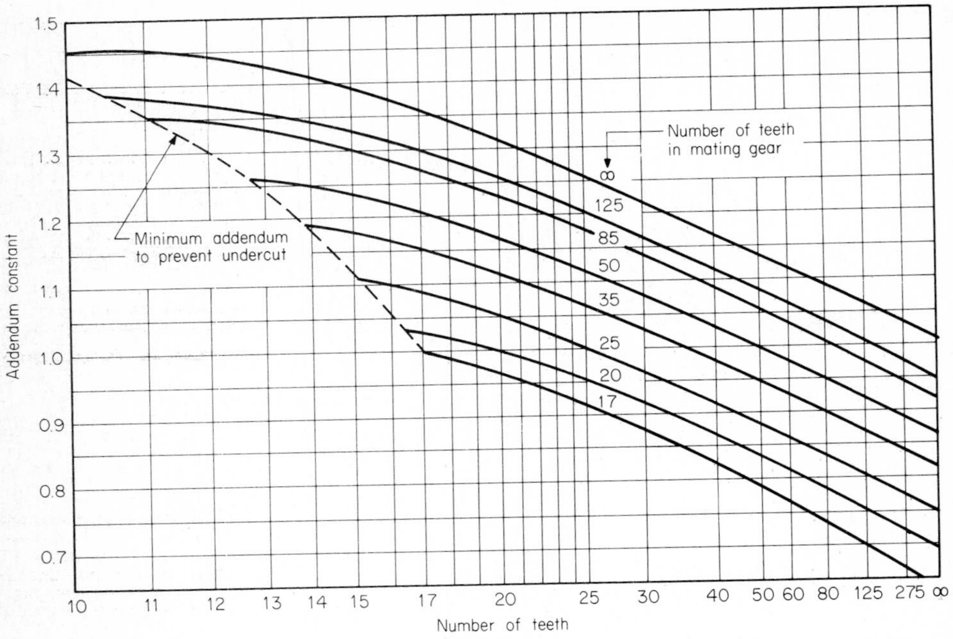

FIG. 3.5 Recommended addendum constant for pinions and gears of 20° pressure angle. The addendum constant is for 1 module or for 1 diametral pitch.

the gear addendum. In this case the designer should *subtract from the gear addendum the same amount that is added to the pinion addendum.* The sum of the pinion addendum and the gear addendum must always equal the working depth.

The curve sheet of Fig. 3.5 was drawn to give an approximate balance between the strength of the pinion and the strength of the gear. It also took care of the problem of pinion undercut.

The problem of undercut is not as critical with $22\frac{1}{2}°$ teeth, and it almost ceases to exist with 25° teeth. The general formula to find the minimum number of teeth needed to avoid undercut in spur gears is

$$z = \frac{2h_{fx}}{m(\sin \alpha)^2} \qquad \text{metric} \quad (3.2a)$$

where $h_{fx} = h_f - r_{a0}(1 - \sin \alpha)$.

$$N = \frac{2XP_t}{(\sin \phi)^2} \qquad \text{English} \quad (3.2b)$$

where $X = b - r_T(1 - \sin \phi)$.

When the pinion has a standard addendum of $1.000m$ and the spur teeth are designed to the proportions shown in Table 3.6, the minimum number of teeth that can be used without undercut is

20° pressure angle	19 teeth
$22\frac{1}{2}$° pressure angle	15 teeth
25° pressure angle	13 teeth

When using a long addendum to avoid undercut, the amounts of long addendum shown in Table 3.7 are needed.

TABLE 3.7 Amount of Long Addendum to Avoid Undercut with Hobbed Teeth

Pressure angle	At 10 teeth	At 12 teeth	At 15 teeth
20°	1.50	1.40	1.27
$22\frac{1}{2}$°	1.37	1.22	1.00 OK
25°	1.20	1.03	1.00 OK

Note: For metric design the addendum of the pinion is the long addendum given above multiplied by the module. The gear addendum = 2.00*m* − pinion addendum. For English design, divide the number given by the diametral pitch for the pinion addendum. For gear addendum, divide 2.00 by diametral pitch and subtract pinion addendum.

When the pinion has enough teeth to avoid undercut, the question of how much long addendum to use becomes more complex. A modest amount of long addendum will tend to balance strength between the pinion and the gear. Some benefit also results from the standpoint of surface durability and scoring.

If a large amount of long addendum is used, the pinion is apt to be substantially stronger than the gear, and the tendency to score at the pinion tip becomes much greater.

Some gear designers have used and advocated a 200 percent pinion addendum and a 0 percent gear addendum. This kind of design has all *recess* action* when the pinion drives and no *approach* action. If gears are somewhat inaccurate, they will run more smoothly and quietly as the arc of recess is increased and the arc of approach decreased.

There are special cases in which the design of a gearset justifies a very long pinion addendum and a very short gear addendum. For most designs of power gears, I recommend only a modest amount of long addendum. This somewhat balances pinion and gear strength and gives favorable results from the standpoint of surface durability and scoring. In service, the dedendum of

*See Fig. 9.15 for definition of arc of approach and arc of recess.

TABLE 3.8 Long and Short Addendum for Speed-Reducing Spur Gears

	$\alpha = 20°$ ($\phi = 20°$)		$\alpha = 25°$ ($\phi = 25°$)	
Tooth ratio z_1/z_2 (N_P/N_G)	Pinion addendum h_{a1} (a_P)	Gear addendum h_{a2} (a_G)	Pinion addendum h_{a1} (a_P)	Gear addendum h_{a2} (a_G)
12/35	1.24	0.76	1.16	0.84
12/50	1.32	0.68	1.22	0.78
12/75	1.38	0.62	1.25*	0.75
12/125	1.44	0.56	1.25*	0.75
12/∞	1.48	0.52	1.25*	0.75
16/35	1.15	0.85	1.10	0.90
16/50	1.22	0.78	1.15	0.85
16/75	1.27	0.73	1.18	0.82
16/125	1.32	0.68	1.21	0.79
16/∞	1.36	0.64	1.24	0.76
24/35	1.06	0.94	1.04	0.96
24/50	1.11	0.89	1.08	0.92
24/75	1.15	0.85	1.10	0.90
24/125	1.20	0.80	1.13	0.87
24/∞	1.24	0.76	1.16	0.84

*It is not practical to use more addendum here because the tip of the tooth is as thin as good practice will allow.

Note: Data in millimeters for 1-module teeth. (For 1-pitch teeth, read addendum data in inches.)

the pinion and gear may pit extensively. (See Chap. 7.) If the gear dedendum is not unduly large, the gear can survive heavy pitting fairly well.

Table 3.8 shows some guideline values for amounts of long addendum. These relatively low amounts of long addendum will give good results in rating calculations. From a practical standpoint, these gears will run backwards (gear driving rather than pinion) relatively well. Most gear drives have a power reversal under "coast" conditions, so the ability to run in reverse is usually a design requirement. In addition, the gear dedendum is not large enough to be a major problem when the gear member happens to have premature pitting.

In *speed-increasing* drives, the gear is the driver. A long pinion addendum (in this case) makes the drive run more roughly and noisily. As a general rule, only enough long addendum is used to avoid undercut. Generally it is possible—and also advisable—to design the speed-increasing drive with enough pinion teeth to be out of the undercut problem area. This means that speed-increasing gear drives will usually have the same addendum for the pinion and the gear.

3.6 Tooth Thickness

The tooth thickness of standard-addendum pinions and gears can be obtained by subtracting the minimum backlash from the circular pitch and dividing by 2. When long- and short-addendum proportions are used, it is necessary to adjust the tooth thicknesses. Usually this adjustment is made with a formula which will permit a standard hob to cut the set. There is no simple formula that will permit a shaper cutter to cut long and short proportions just as well as it cuts standard proportions (see Sec. 9.12). However, if the tooth thicknesses are adjusted for hobbing, it is usually possible to shape them with standard shaping tools and have only a small error in whole depth. With this thought in mind, the following formula for hobbed teeth is a good one to use to design all kinds of gears:*

$$s = \frac{p_t - j}{2} + \Delta h(2 \tan \alpha) \qquad \text{metric} \qquad (3.3a)$$

where $p_t = \pi m$

j = backlash

$\Delta h_a = h_a - \dfrac{h'}{2}$

$$t = \frac{p_t - B}{2} + \Delta a(2 \tan \phi) \qquad \text{English} \qquad (3.3b)$$

where $p_t = \dfrac{\pi}{P_d}$

B = backlash

$\Delta a = a - \dfrac{h_k}{2}$

The tooth-thickness values obtained from Eq. (3.3) are *arc tooth thickness*. See Sec. 3.7 for chordal tooth-thickness values.

Backlash. The design amount of backlash j (or B) should be chosen to meet the requirements of the application. In power gearing, it is usually a good policy to use relatively generous backlash. The amount should be at least enough to let the gears turn freely when they are mounted on the shortest center distance and are subject to the worst condition of temperature and tooth error. In control gearing, the design usually can have but

*Unfortunately, a small s is used for both tooth thickness and stress in the metric system. The reader needs to be aware that some symbols can have double meanings.

For involute helical teeth, use normal module, normal circular pitch, and normal pressure angle. The tooth thickness obtained is in the normal section. (For English calculation, use similar normal-section values and the result will be normal tooth thickness.) The normal circular pitch $p_n = p_t \cos \psi$ for English.

very little backlash. Some binding of the teeth as a result of eccentricity and tooth error may be preferable to designing so that there is appreciable lost motion due to backlash.

TABLE 3.9 Suggested Backlash When Assembled

Metric		English	
Module	Backlash, mm	Diametral pitch	Backlash, inches
25	0.63–1.02	1	0.025–0.040
18	0.46–0.69	1½	0.018–0.027
12	0.35–0.51	2	0.014–0.020
10	0.28–0.41	2½	0.011–0.016
8	0.23–0.36	3	0.009–0.014
6	0.18–0.28	4	0.007–0.011
5	0.15–0.23	5	0.006–0.009
4	0.13–0.20	6	0.005–0.008
3	0.10–0.15	8 and 9	0.004–0.006
2	0.08–0.13	10–13	0.003–0.005
1	0.05–0.10	14–32	0.002–0.004

Table 3.9 shows amounts of backlash as a guide for gear design with spur, helical, bevel, and spiral bevel gears. When the gears are not running fast and there are relatively small temperature changes, the table is useful for determining the minimum amount of backlash to use—assuming that extra backlash represents lost motion and may be somewhat undesirable from a performance standpoint. (A *reversing* gear drive, for instance, should not have any more backlash than necessary.)

In epicyclic gears, it may be necessary to use a low backlash to keep "floating" suns or ring gears from floating too far and causing high vibration at light load. Table 3.9 is again useful as a guide.

Although Table 3.9 is based on general practice, it should be kept in mind that the values are suggested values and must be used with discretion. Where gears have large center distance or where the casing material has a different rate of expansion from that of the gears, some of the values shown are risky. For instance, 2.5-module high-speed gears used for either marine or aircraft applications will need a minimum backlash of the order of 0.15 or 0.20 mm (0.006 or 0.008 in.) to operate satisfactorily under all temperature conditions.

Tolerances on Tooth Thickness. The variation in backlash will depend considerably on the tooth-thickness tolerance. In hobbing or shaping teeth, a tolerance of 0.05 mm (0.002 in.) on thickness represents close work. Adding

TABLE 3.10 Tolerances on Tooth Thickness

Method of cutting	Degree of care					
	Very best		Close work		Easy to meet	
	mm	in.	mm	in.	mm	in.
Grinding	0.005	0.0002	0.013	0.0005	0.05	0.002
Shaving	0.005	0.0002	0.013	0.0005	0.05	0.002
Hobbing	0.013	0.0005	0.05	0.002	0.10	0.004
Shaping	0.018	0.0007	0.05	0.002	0.10	0.004

tolerances for the pinion and gear, a backlash variation of 0.10 mm (0.004 in.) is obtained from cutting alone! Obviously it would not be good policy to design gear teeth so that the backlash tolerances made the tooth-cutting costs prohibitive. Table 3.10 shows a study of tooth-thickness tolerances for different cutting methods for teeth in the 2- to 5-module range. These values should be considered when setting ranges of backlash and tooth-thickness tolerances.

3.7 Chordal Dimensions

The tooth thickness of a spur or helical gear is often measured with calipers. This instrument is set for a depth corresponding to the *chordal addendum*, and it measures a width corresponding to the *chordal tooth thickness*. Figure 3.6 shows the tooth thickness being measured. Figure 3.7 defines the chordal dimensions.

The chordal addendum is obtained by adding the *rise of arc* to the addendum. The equation generally used is

$$\bar{h}_a = h_a + \frac{s^2 \cos^2 \beta}{4d_p} \qquad \text{metric} \qquad (3.4a)$$

$$a_c = a + \frac{t^2 \cos^2 \psi}{4d} \qquad \text{English} \qquad (3.4b)$$

Equation (3.4) works for both helical and spur gears. In helical gears, the tooth thickness used should be the *normal tooth thickness*.

Figure 3.8 shows the rise of arc for a range of diameters and tooth thicknesses. For helical gears, curve readings are multiplied by the cosine squared of the helix.

Chordal tooth thicknesses are obtained by subtracting a small amount from the arc tooth thickness. This arc-to-chord correction is so small that it can be neglected in many gear designs. The calculation should always be

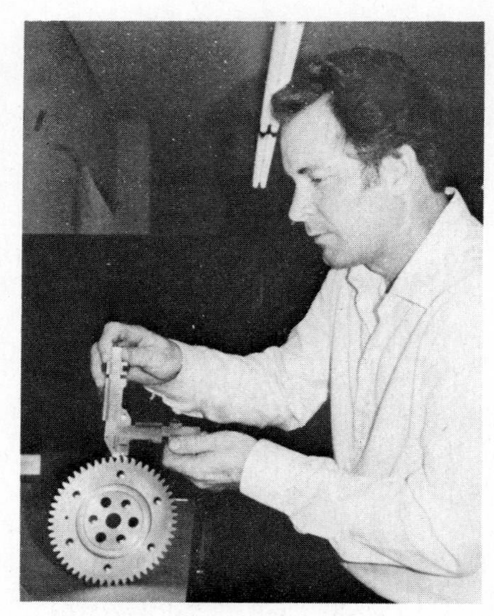

FIG. 3.6 Measuring tooth thickness with gear tooth calipers. (*Courtesy of Vi-Star Gear Co., Inc., Paramount, CA, U.S.A.*)

made, though, for coarse-pitch pinions, master gears, and gear-tooth gages. The approximate equation which is usually used is

$$\bar{s} = s - \frac{s^3 \cos^4 \beta}{6d_p^2} \qquad \text{metric} \quad (3.5a)$$

$$t_c = t - \frac{t^3 \cos^4 \psi}{6d^2} \qquad \text{English} \quad (3.5b)$$

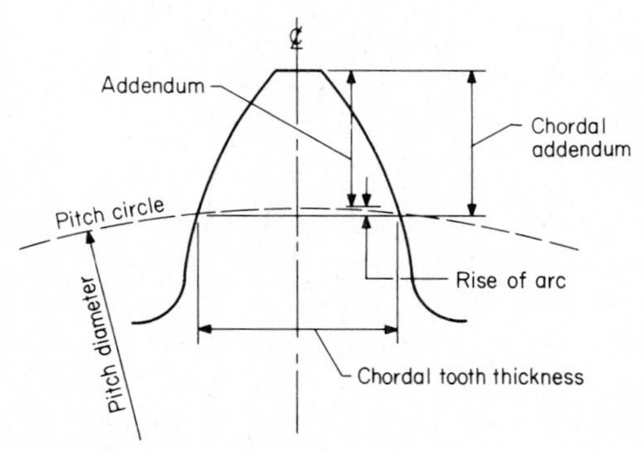

FIG. 3.7 Chordal dimensions of a gear or pinion tooth.

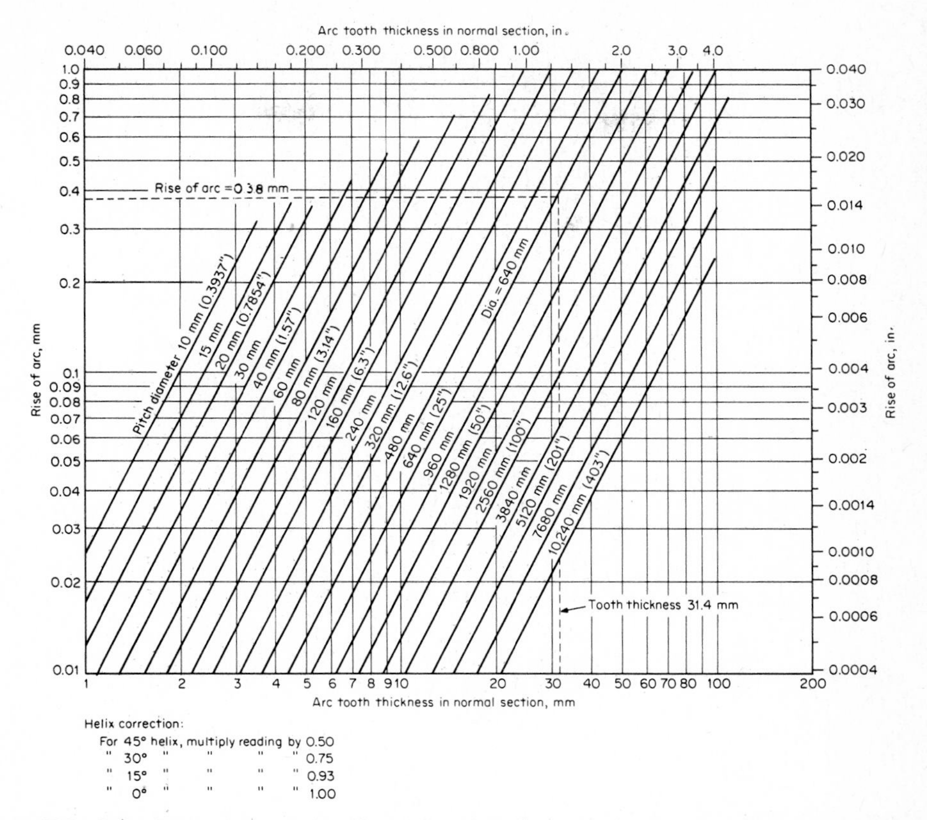

FIG. 3.8 Rise of arc graph. Read the rise of arc as shown, and then correct for helix angle.

For helical gears, the normal tooth thickness should be used in Eq. (3.5). The arc-to-chord correction s_c is plotted in Fig. 3.9 for a range of diameters and tooth thicknesses. Multiplying constants are shown to take care of helical gears.

3.8 Degrees Roll and Limit Diameter

The checking machines used to measure the involute profile of spur and helical gears usually record error in involute against *degrees roll*. This makes it necessary in many cases to determine the degrees roll at the start of active profile and at the end of active profile. The start of active profile—so far as checking goes—is at the form diameter. The end of active profile is at the outside diameter.

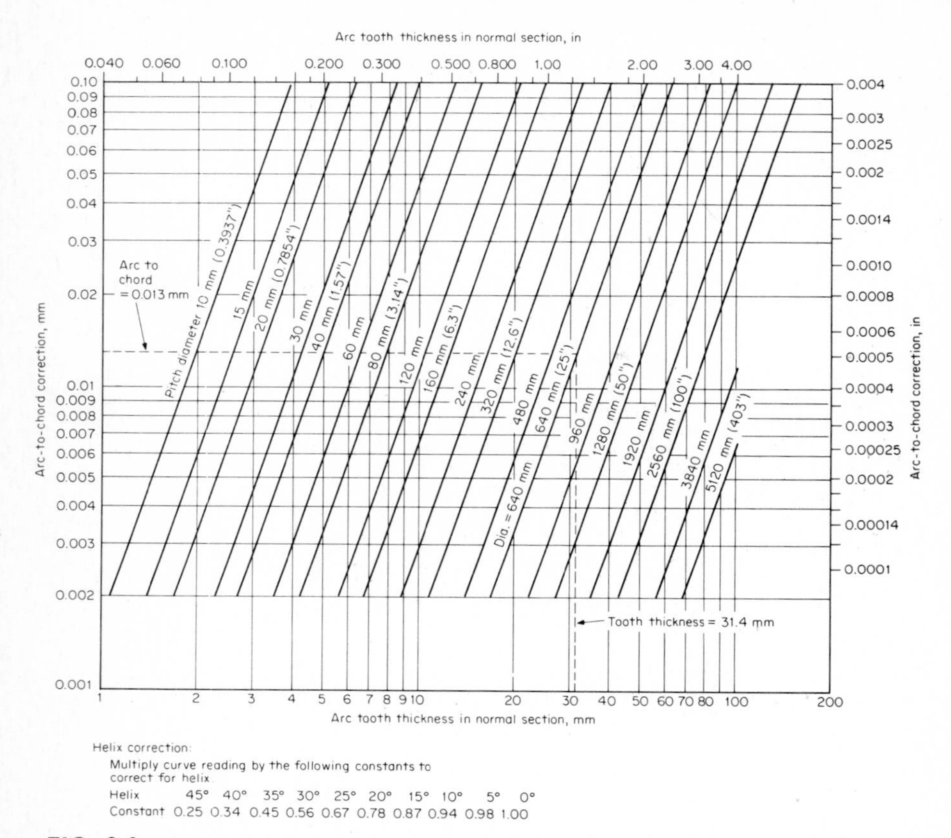

FIG. 3.9 Arc-to-chord correction graph. Read the arc-to-chord correction as shown, and then correct for helix angle.

Figure 2.10 showed the basic involute relations in the English system. Figure 3.10 is a similar diagram showing basic involute relations in the metric system. In Fig. 3.10 the roll angle to the pitch circle (or to the *pitch point*) is the angle designated θ_r. The roll angle to "any point" on the involute curve is θ_{r1}.

The solution of the roll angle problem lies in the fact that the length of the line unwrapped from the base cylinder is equal to the arc length from the origin of the involute to the tangency point of the involute action line to the base cylinder. An angle in *radians* is equal to the arc length of the angle divided by the radius. These relations plus other obvious triangular relations lead to the basic relations of the involute shown in Fig. 3.10 (or in Fig. 2.10).

The degrees roll at the outside diameter may be calculated by solving the

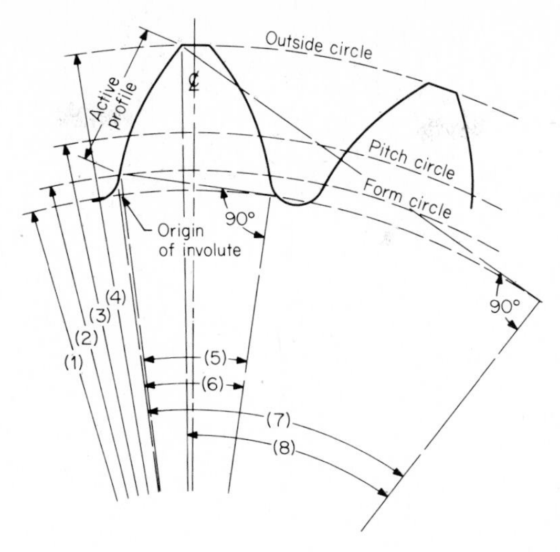

Item	Name	Symbol Metric	Symbol English
(1)	Base diameter	d_b	d_b
(2)	Form diameter	d'_f	d_f
(3)	Pitch diameter	d_p	d
(4)	Outside diameter	d_a	d_o
(5)	Pressure angle, form diameter	α_f	ϕ_f
(6)	Roll angle, form diameter	θ_{rf}	ϵ_{rf}
(7)	Roll angle, outside diameter	θ_{ra}	ϵ_{ro}
(8)	Pressure angle, outside diameter	α_a	ϕ_o

FIG. 3.10 Roll angles which define the active profile of the gear.

following equations:

Metric	English	
$\varepsilon_\alpha = \dfrac{d_a}{d_p}$	$m_o = \dfrac{d_o}{d}$	(3.6)
$\cos \alpha_a = \dfrac{\cos \alpha_t}{\varepsilon_a}$	$\cos \phi_o = \dfrac{\cos \phi_t}{m_o}$	(3.7)
$\theta_{ra} = \dfrac{180° \tan \alpha_a}{\pi}$	$\varepsilon_{ro} = \dfrac{180° \tan \phi_o}{\pi}$	(3.8)

The angle θ_{ra} (ε_{ro}) is the degrees roll at the outside diameter. The roll angle at the limit diameter is calculated in a similar manner.

The *limit diameter* is the diameter at which the outside diameter of the

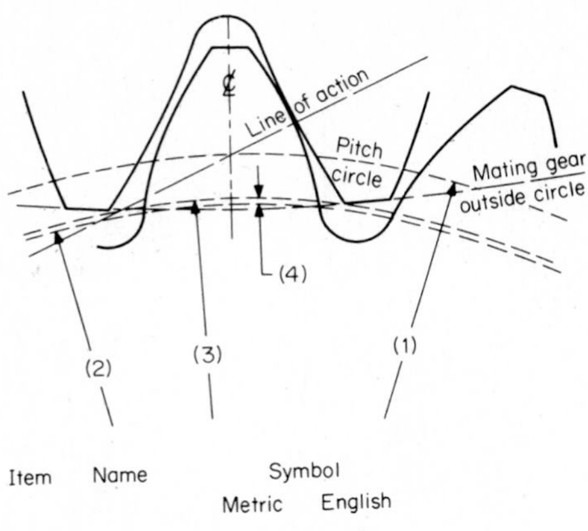

Item	Name	Symbol Metric	Symbol English
(1)	Pitch diameter	d_p	d
(2)	Form diameter	d'_f	d_f
(3)	Limit diameter	d_ℓ	d_ℓ
(4)	Extra involute	$\frac{d_\ell - d'_f}{2}$	$\frac{d_\ell - d_f}{2}$

FIG. 3.11 Limit diameter and form diameter. The allowance for extra involute should be large enough to allow for center-distance variations and variations in outside diameter of the mating gear.

mating gear crosses the line of action. See Fig. 3.11. Roll angles for limit diameter or form diameter can be obtained by:

Metric	English	
$\varepsilon_\ell = \dfrac{d_\ell}{d_p}$	$m_\ell = \dfrac{d_\ell}{d}$	(3.9)
$\cos \alpha_\ell = \dfrac{\cos \alpha_t}{\varepsilon_\ell}$	$\cos \phi_\ell = \dfrac{\cos \phi_t}{m_\ell}$	(3.10)
$\theta_{r\ell} = \dfrac{180^\circ \tan \alpha_\ell}{\pi}$	$\varepsilon_{r\ell} = \dfrac{180^\circ \tan \phi_\ell}{\pi}$	(3.11)
$\varepsilon_f = \dfrac{d'_f}{d_p}$	$m_f = \dfrac{d_f}{d}$	(3.12)
$\cos \alpha_f = \dfrac{\cos \alpha_t}{\varepsilon_f}$	$\cos \phi_f = \dfrac{\cos \phi_t}{m_f}$	(3.13)
$\theta_{rf} = \dfrac{180^\circ \tan \alpha_f}{\pi}$	$\varepsilon_{rf} = \dfrac{180^\circ \tan \phi_f}{\pi}$	(3.14)

Calculation Table 3.11 gives the step-by-step procedure for calculating all

TABLE 3.11 Calculation Sheet for the Meshing-Zone Dimensions for a Pair of Involute Gear Teeth
(See Fig. 3.12 for identification of items in this table)

Basic data		
1. Pressure angle, transverse	20	
2. Cosine, pressure angle	0.939693	
3. Tangent, pressure angle	0.363970	
4. Circular pitch	9.424778	
5. Base pitch, (2) × (4)	8.856394	
Calculations	**Pinion**	**Gear**
6. Number of teeth	25	96
7. Addendum	3.54	2.46
8. Pitch diameter, (4) × (6) ÷ π	75.00	288.00
9. Outside diameter, (8) + 2 × (7)	82.08	292.92
10. Base diameter, (8) × (2)	70.47695	270.63148
11. (9) ÷ (10)	1.164636	1.082357
12. (11) × (11)	1.356377	1.171498
13. $[(12) - 1.0000]^{0.50}$	0.596973	0.414123
14. (13) − (3)	0.233003	0.050153
15. (6) ÷ 6.283185	3.978873	15.27887
16. Contact ratio, addendum, (14) × (15)	0.92709	0.76628
17. Contact ratio, pair, $(16)_1 + (16)_2$	1.69337	
18. Line of action, addendum, (16) × (5)	8.21067	6.78647
19. Zone of action, $(18)_1 + (18)_2$	14.99715	
20. 0.5 × (10) × (3)	12.82575	49.25090
21. Line of action, total, (18) + (20)	21.03642	56.03737
22. (21) − (19)	6.03927	41.04022
23. $[2 \times (22)]^2$	145.89113	6737.1986
24. Limit diameter, $[(23) + (10)^2]^{0.50}$	71.50449	282.80487
25. (10) ÷ (9)	0.858637	0.923909
26. Pressure angle, OD, arccos (25)	30.836078	22.495559
27. Roll angle, OD, 57.29578 × tan (26)	34.204057	23.727487
28. (10) ÷ (24)	0.985630	0.956955
29. Pressure angle, LD, arccos (28)	9.725034	16.872143
30. Roll angle, LD, 57.29578 × tan (29)	9.819514	17.377365

Notes:
1. This table can be calculated in the metric system by using millimeters for all dimensions. Columns 1 and 2 show a metric example of 25 teeth meshing with 96 teeth.
2. This table can be calculated in the English system by using inches for all dimensions.
3. All angles are in degrees.

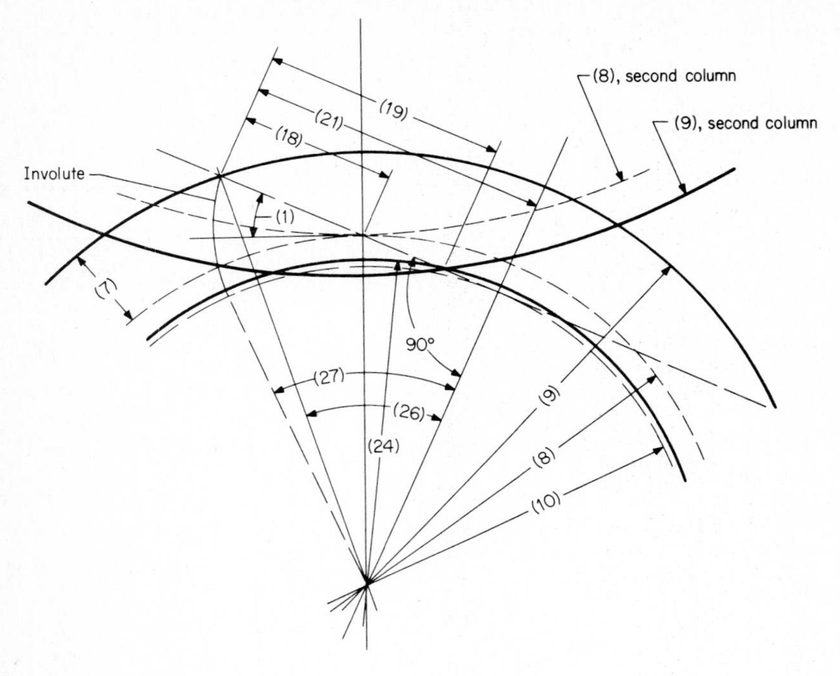

Item	Name	Symbol Metric	Symbol English
(1)	Pressure angle	α	ϕ
(7)	Addendum	h_a	a
(8)	Pitch diameter	d_p	d
(9)	Outside diameter	d_a	d_o
(10)	Base diameter	d_b	d_b
(18)	Line of action, addendum	g_a	Z_r
(19)	Zone of action	g_α	Z
(21)	Line of action, total	g_t	Z_t
(24)	Limit diameter	d_ℓ	d_ℓ
(26)	Pressure angle at O.D.	α_a	ϕ_o
(27)	Roll angle to O.D.	θ_{ra}	ϵ_{ro}

FIG. 3.12 Identification of dimensions used in calculations for the meshing of a pair of involute gear teeth. The numbers correspond to the line numbers in Table 3.11.

the dimensions in the zone of action. The following items are of particular interest:

Line of action for the addendum (18)

Zone of action (19)

Line of action, total (21)

Limit diameter (24)

Roll angle, outside diameter (27)

Roll angle, limit diameter (30)

This calculation sheet is illustrated by an example worked out for 25 pinion teeth meshing with 96 gear teeth with a pressure angle of 20°. The teeth are 3 module and spur. The constant 57.29578 is 180° divided by pi (3.14159265).

Figure 3.12 illustrates the dimensions that are calculated in Table 3.11. This table works for either metric or English dimensions.

3.9 Form Diameter and Contact Ratio

The *form diameter* of a gear is that diameter which represents the design limit of involute action. A theoretical limit diameter d_ℓ is first obtained, then a practical value is obtained by subtracting an allowance Δd_ℓ for outside-diameter runout and center-distance tolerance.

Limit diameter may be calculated graphically or by solving a series of equations. The preceding section gave the necessary equations, and Table 3.11 showed a sample calculation.

After d_ℓ is obtained, the form diameter is

$$d'_f = d_\ell - \Delta d_\ell \tag{3.15}$$

The allowance Δd_ℓ should be large enough to accommodate the effect of various tooth errors in extending the contact below the theoretical point plus the effect of tooth bending under load in extending the contact deeper. For general applications the value of $0.05m_t$ has worked out quite well. If the pinion has a small number of teeth, so that the limit diameter is close to the base circle, little or no allowance can be used. Since *involute* action ends at the base circle, a form diameter that is below the base circle should never be specified. With a standard-addendum pinion of 20° pressure angle, an allowance for excess involute as large as $0.05m_t$ should be used only when there are 25 or more teeth in the pinion.

The value of $0.05m_t$ (m_t = transverse module) has an English equivalent of 0.050 in./P_d. Some sample values are:

Tooth size	Δd_ℓ
1 module	0.05 mm
5 module	0.25 mm
20 module	1.00 mm
20 pitch	0.0025 in.
5 pitch	0.010 in.
1 pitch	0.050 in.

For calculation purposes, it is handy to make the excess involute a function of the circular pitch (instead of a function of the module or an *inverse* function of the diametral pitch). On this basis, it works out that

$$\Delta d_\ell = 0.016 \times \text{circular pitch}$$

$$= 0.016 \times \pi m_t \qquad \text{metric} \quad (3.16a)$$

$$= 0.016 \times \frac{\pi}{P_t} \qquad \text{English} \quad (3.16b)$$

Contact Ratio. The contact ratio of a pair of spur or helical gears represents the length of the zone of action divided by the base pitch. The basic equation is

$$\text{Contact ratio} = \frac{\text{zone of action}}{\text{base pitch}}$$

$$\varepsilon_\alpha = \frac{g_\alpha}{p_b} \qquad \text{metric} \quad (3.17a)$$

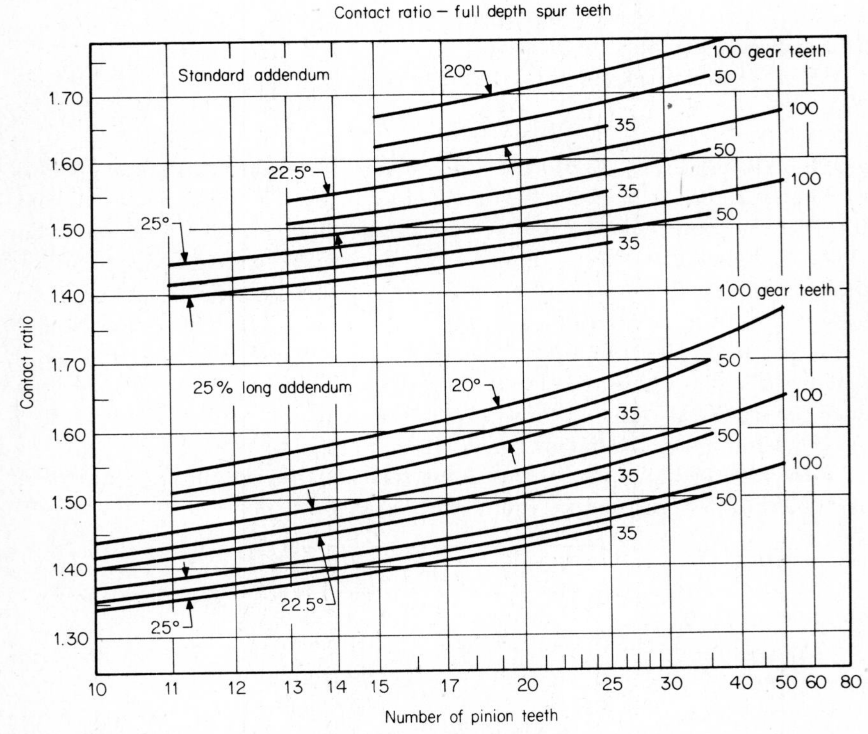

FIG. 3.13 Transverse contact ratios for standard addendum and 25 percent long addendum spur-gear teeth at different pressure angles.

$$m_p = \frac{Z}{p_b} \qquad \text{English} \qquad (3.17b)$$

where g_α or Z = zone of action [Item (19), Table 3.11]
$p_b = \cos \alpha_t \ (\pi m_t)$ for metric
$= \cos \phi_t \ (\pi/P_t)$ for English

Figure 3.13 shows plotted contact-ratio values for involute spur-gear teeth of 20°, $22\frac{1}{2}$°, and 25° pressure angles. Note that the 25 percent long-addendum teeth have somewhat lower contact ratios than standard-addendum teeth. Also note that the 25°-pressure-angle teeth have a much lower contact ratio than 20° teeth.

The term *contact ratio* should be thought of as "average number of teeth in contact." As spur gears roll through mesh, there are either two pair of teeth in mesh or one pair. (A 20° pair with a 1.7 contact ratio never really has 1.7 pair of teeth in contact!)

3.10 Spur-Gear Dimension Sheet

In calculating gear dimensions, it is helpful to use a *dimension sheet* which lists all the items to be calculated. This ensures that all necessary values are calculated, and it is a convenient sheet to file in a design book as a record of different jobs. Table 3.12 shows a recommended dimension sheet for spur gears. The sheet shows how to obtain design values for each item. To illustrate the use of the sheet, numerical values are given for a sample problem.

Several of the dimensions on Table 3.12 require tolerances. In power gearing of small size, a center-distance tolerance of 0.05 mm (0.002 in.) is often used. This affects the backlash about 0.038 mm (0.0015 in.). On control gearing, a closer value would be needed.

The face width of the pinion is usually made a little wider than the gear. It is easier to provide the extra width for error in axial positioning on the pinion than on the gear.

The tolerance on outside diameter is based on whatever tolerance is reasonable to hold in lathe or cylindrical grinding operations. This dimension does not need to be held too close unless accuracy is needed in order to set calipers for close tooth-thickness checking.

The tolerance on root diameter should allow for variation in tool thickness as well as for the worker's error in setting the gear-cutting machine.

Tooth-thickness tolerances should be governed by backlash requirements of the application as well as by Table 3.10 considerations.

The calculation of diameter over pins may be done by the procedure given in Chap. 9, Table 9.2. For a general study of the method of calculation of diameter over pins, Sec. 7-9 of the *Gear Handbook* is helpful.

TABLE 3.12 Spur-Gear Dimensions

Item	Reference	Metric		English	
1. Center distance	Secs. 2.8 to 2.10	181.50		7.145655	
2. Circular pitch	Eq. (1.2)	9.42478		0.37105	
3. Pressure angle	Sec. 3.3	20		20	
4. Working depth	Table 3.6	6.00		0.2362	
5. Module, transverse	Eq. (1.3)	3		—	
6. Diametral pitch, transverse	Eq. (1.3)	—		8.466667	
		Pinion	Gear	Pinion	Gear
7. Number of teeth	Secs. 3.1, 3.2	25	96	25	96
8. Pitch diameter	Eq. (1.4)	75.00	288.00	2.9527	11.3386
9. Addendum	Sec. 3.5	3.54	2.46	0.1394	0.0968
10. Whole depth	Table 3.6	7.05	7.05	0.2775	0.2775
11. Outside diameter	(8) + [2 × (9)]	82.08	292.92	3.2315	11.5322
12. Root diameter	(11) − [2 × (10)]	67.98	278.82	2.6765	10.9772
13. Arc tooth thickness	Sec. 3.6	4.991	4.204	0.1965	0.1655
14. Chordal tooth thickness	Sec. 3.7	5.026	4.243	0.1979	0.1671
15. Chordal addendum	Sec. 3.7	3.62	2.47	0.1397	0.0969
16. Pin size	Table 9.1	5.334	5.334	0.210	0.210
17. Diameter over pins	Table 9.2	83.1905	304.2113	3.2752	11.9768
18. Face width	Sec. 2.8	37.0	35.0	1.45	1.38
19. Form diameter	Table 9.3	71.35	282.65	2.8090	11.1279
20. Roll angle, O.D.	Table 9.3	34.20	23.73	34.20	23.73
21. Roll angle, F.D.	Table 9.3	9.07	17.27	9.07	17.27
22. Base circle, diameter	Table 3.11	70.477	270.631	2.77468	10.6548
23. Minimum root radius	Sec. 3.4	0.84	0.79	0.033	0.031
24. Accuracy	Sec. 5.18	See Note 4			

Notes:
1. See Chap. 4 for gear materials and specifications.
2. See Chap. 8, Problem 4, for an example of spread center design. (This table is for standard center design.)
3. Metric dimensions are in millimeters, English dimensions are in inches. Angles are in degrees (and decimals of a degree.)
4. After the designer has done the load rating and studied Sec. 5.18, accuracy needs may be satisfied by an ISO or AGMA quality level, or the designer may need to write a special recipe for accuracy limits.

Tolerances on tooth accuracy and data on material and heat treatment will be needed (see Secs. 5.18 and 4.10). Usually these data are not shown on the specification sheet unless they can be given by referring to a standard specification. Frequently they are shown only on the part drawing.

In many cases it is desirable to make layouts of pinion or gear teeth to see what they will look like. This can be done by calculating the involute part of the tooth profile as a first step, then calculating the root fillet trochoid as a second step. Calculation Tables 9.4 and 9.5 in Chap. 9 show how to do this. The 25-tooth pinion of Table 3.12 is used as an example. Figure 3.14 shows how this tooth was plotted.

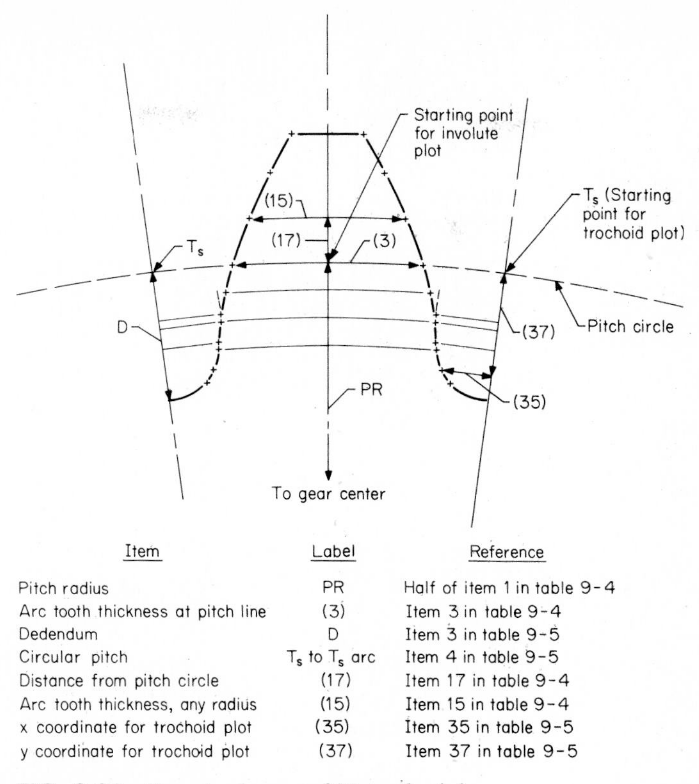

Item	Label	Reference
Pitch radius	PR	Half of item 1 in table 9-4
Arc tooth thickness at pitch line	(3)	Item 3 in table 9-4
Dedendum	D	Item 3 in table 9-5
Circular pitch	T_s to T_s arc	Item 4 in table 9-5
Distance from pitch circle	(17)	Item 17 in table 9-4
Arc tooth thickness, any radius	(15)	Item 15 in table 9-4
x coordinate for trochoid plot	(35)	Item 35 in table 9-5
y coordinate for trochoid plot	(37)	Item 37 in table 9-5

FIG. 3.14 Oversize layout of 25-tooth pinion.

The 25-tooth pinion in Fig. 3.14 looks good. The tip of the tooth is generously wide (should be no trouble in carburizing). The root fillet is generous in curvature, and the base of the tooth is wide. This tooth can be expected to have good beam strength.

3.11 Internal-Gear Dimension Sheet

The dimensions for internal gears may be calculated in a manner quite similar to that just described for spur gears. However, internal gears are subject to two kinds of trouble that do not affect external gears. If the internal gearset is designed for full working depth, the gear may contact the pinion at a lower point on the tooth flank than the cutting tool generated on the involute profile. When internal gearsets have too little difference between the number of teeth in the pinion and the number of teeth in the gear, there

FIG. 3.15 Internal gear of 26 teeth *will not* assemble *radially* with a 19-tooth pinion. Both parts cut to Table 3.13 proportions.

may be *interference between the tips* of the teeth. The interference is most apt to occur as the pinion is moved radially into mesh with the gear.

It is possible to get around the radial-interference difficulty by assembling the set by an *axial* movement of the pinion. The difference between numbers of teeth can be less when this method of assembly is used, but there will still be interference if the difference is too small. Figures 3.15 and 3.16 show radial interference and axial assembly of 19/26 teeth, 20° pressure angle.

The calculations (or layout procedure) that avoid these troubles with internal gears are rather complicated. Instead of presenting the method here, Tables 3.13 and 3.14 will be given to show what dimensions can be safely used with internal gears.

In Tables 3.13 and 3.14, the addendum of the internal gear has been shortened so that the internal gear will contact the pinion no deeper than it would be contacted by a rack tooth with an addendum equal to $2.000m - h_{a1}$ (or $2.000/P_d - a_P$). This makes it possible to manufacture the pinion of an internal gearset in the same way that a pinion would be manufactured to go with an external gear with a large number of teeth. The minimum numbers of teeth for the different methods of assembly are calculated so that the tips clear each other by at least $0.02m$ millimeters (or $0.020/P_d$ inches).

Tables 3.13 and 3.14 are worked out so as to get the most that is possible out of internal gears. Many designers have used internal-gear data which did

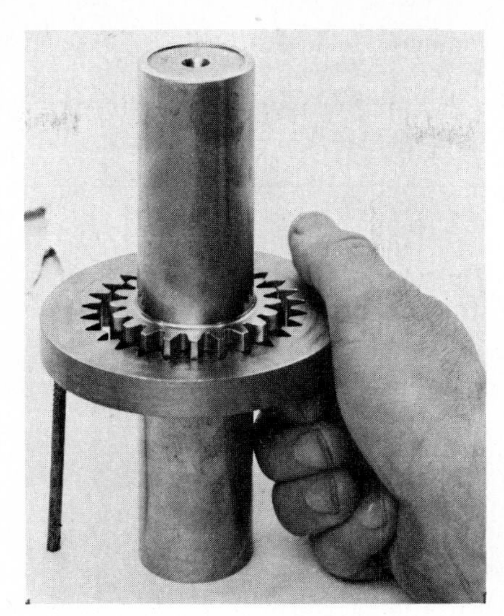

FIG. 3.16 Internal gear of 26 teeth *will* assemble *axially* with a 19-tooth pinion. Both parts cut to Table 3.13 proportions.

not use quite so much working depth and quite so close tooth numbers as are shown in this table. If the design is not critical and center-distance accuracy is not close, it may be desirable not to use quite so low a ratio as would be permitted by the table.

It will be noted that the tables show two addendum values for each number of teeth. The first one is the *minimum* addendum that might be used for the pinion. This addendum has been lengthened only in those cases in which there is danger of undercut. The second addendum has been lengthened to balance tooth strength. The lengthening is not quite so much as layouts of the teeth might indicate, but it is about the right amount to use considering the fact that the quality of material in the gear may not be quite as good as that in the pinion. Also, the stress concentration at the root of the internal-gear tooth is apt to be high. In general, the *minimum* addendum should be used *when the gear drives the pinion*, and the *maximum* addendum should be used *when the pinion drives the gear*.

The internal gear usually cannot have a clearance of much over $0.250m$ (or $0.259/P_d$) because of the effect of the concave (flaring) sides of the teeth.

The "outside diameter" of an internal is really the *inside diameter*. The inside diameter is obtained by subtracting twice the gear addendum from the pitch diameter.

TABLE 3.13 Addendum Proportions and Limiting Numbers of Teeth for Internal Spur Gears of 20° Pressure Angle

		Min. no. of gear teeth		Gear addendum			
No. of pinion teeth $z_1(N_P)$	Pinion addendum $h_{a1}(a_P)$	Axial assembly $z_2(N_G)$	Radial assembly $z_2(N_G)$	u = min* (m_G = min) $h_{a2}(a_G)$	$u = 2$ ($m_G = 2$) $h_{a2}(a_G)$	$u = 4$ ($m_G = 4$) $h_{a2}(a_G)$	$u = 8$ ($m_G = 8$) $h_{a2}(a_G)$
12	1.350	19	26	0.472	0.510	0.582	0.616
	1.510	19	26	0.390	0.412	0.451	0.471
13	1.290	20	27	0.507	0.556	0.635	0.673
	1.470	20	27	0.419	0.445	0.488	0.509
14	1.230	21	28	0.543	0.601	0.688	0.729
	1.430	21	28	0.447	0.479	0.525	0.548
15	1.180	22	30	0.574	0.642	0.733	0.777
	1.400	22	30	0.470	0.506	0.554	0.577
16	1.120	23	32	0.608	0.688	0.786	0.834
	1.380	23	32	0.487	0.526	0.574	0.597
17	1.060	24	33	0.642	0.734	0.839	0.890
	1.360	24	33	0.505	0.546	0.594	0.617
18	1.000	25	34	0.676	0.779	0.892	0.947
	1.350	25	34	0.516	0.558	0.605	0.628
19	1.000	27	35	0.702	0.792	0.808	0.950
	1.330	27	35	0.539	0.578	0.625	0.648
20	1.000	28	36	0.713	0.802	0.903	0.952
	1.320	28	36	0.550	0.590	0.636	0.658
22	1.000	30	39	0.733	0.821	0.912	0.957
	1.290	30	39	0.577	0.621	0.666	0.688
24	1.000	32	41	0.750	0.836	0.920	0.960
	1.270	32	41	0.599	0.644	0.687	0.709
26	1.000	34	43	0.766	0.849	0.926	0.963
	1.250	34	43	0.620	0.666	0.709	0.729
30	1.000	38	47	0.792	0.870	0.936	0.968
	1.220	38	47	0.654	0.702	0.741	0.761
40	1.000	48	57	0.836	0.903	0.952	0.976
	1.170	48	57	0.718	0.764	0.797	0.814

*Minimum $u = z_2/z_1$ minimum for axial assembly.

The tooth thickness of the pinion is usually adjusted for the amount of long addendum which the pinion has. The gear-tooth thickness is obtained by subtracting the pinion thickness and backlash from the circular pitch. No consideration is given to gear addendum in figuring gear-tooth thickness. This is a result of the fact that the gear addendum has been arbitrarily stubbed to avoid tip interference. The pinion thickness for a full-depth

TABLE 3.14 Addendum Proportions and Limiting Numbers of Teeth for Internal Spur Gears of 25° Pressure Angle

No. of pinion teeth $z_1(N_P)$	Pinion addendum $h_{a1}(a_P)$	Min. no. of gear teeth		Gear addendum			
		Axial assembly $z_2(N_G)$	Radial assembly $z_2(N_G)$	$u = \min$* ($m_G = \min$) $h_{a2}(a_G)$	$u = 2$ ($m_G = 2$) $h_{a2}(a_G)$	$u = 4$ ($m_G = 4$) $h_{a2}(a_G)$	$u = 8$ ($m_G = 8$) $h_{a2}(a_G)$
12	1.000	17	20	0.699	0.793	0.900	0.934
	1.220	17	21	0.601	0.656	0.720	0.740
13	1.000	18	22	0.718	0.810	0.908	0.940
	1.200	18	22	0.622	0.680	0.742	0.761
14	1.000	19	24	0.734	0.824	0.915	0.944
	1.180	19	24	0.644	0.703	0.763	0.782
15	1.000	20	25	0.748	0.837	0.921	0.948
	1.170	20	25	0.659	0.719	0.776	0.794
16	1.000	21	26	0.761	0.847	0.926	0.951
	1.150	21	26	0.679	0.741	0.797	0.815
17	1.000	22	27	0.773	0.857	0.930	0.954
	1.140	22	27	0.694	0.755	0.809	0.826
18	1.000	23	28	0.783	0.865	0.934	0.957
	1.130	23	28	0.708	0.769	0.820	0.837
19	1.000	24	29	0.793	0.873	0.938	0.959
	1.120	24	29	0.721	0.782	0.832	0.848
20	1.000	25	30	0.802	0.879	0.941	0.961
	1.110	26	29	0.741	0.795	0.843	0.859
22	1.000	28	32	0.824	0.891	0.947	0.965
	1.090	28	32	0.765	0.820	0.866	0.881
24	1.000	30	34	0.837	0.900	0.951	0.968
	1.080	30	34	0.782	0.836	0.879	0.893
26	1.000	32	37	0.847	0.908	0.955	0.970
	1.060	32	37	0.806	0.859	0.900	0.914
30	1.000	36	40	0.865	0.921	0.961	0.974
	1.050	36	40	0.829	0.879	0.915	0.927
40	1.000	46	51	0.896	0.941	0.971	0.981
	1.020	46	51	0.880	0.923	0.952	0.961

*Minimum $u = z_2/z_1$ minimum for axial assembly.

pinion is

$$s_1 = \frac{p - j}{2} + (h_{a1} - 1.000m)(2 \tan \alpha) \qquad \text{metric} \qquad (3.18a)$$

$$t_p = \frac{p - B}{2} + \left(a_P - \frac{1.000}{P_d}\right)(2 \tan \phi) \qquad \text{English} \qquad (3.18b)$$

The chordal addendum of the gear is not ordinarily needed unless the gear has a large enough inside diameter to permit tooth calipers to be used. It takes at least a 130-mm (5-in.) inside diameter to allow a person's hand inside the gear to measure tooth thickness. Usually small internals are checked for thickness by using measuring pins between the teeth. In an internal gear, the rise of arc must be subtracted from the addendum. Because of the concave nature of the gear tip, only about two-thirds of the pitch-line rise of arc is effective.

The form diameter of the gear is obtained by adding the allowance for excess involute instead of subtracting it. Thus

$$d'_{f2} = d_\ell + \Delta d_\ell \qquad \text{metric} \quad (3.19a)$$

$$D_f = D_\ell + \Delta D_\ell \qquad \text{English} \quad (3.19b)$$

The limit diameter for internal sets is figured by the same general procedure as that shown for external gears in Table 3.11. However, it is necessary to add instead of subtract. For the internal gear, the following equation should be used:

$$\theta_{r\ell} = \theta_r + (\theta_{ra} - \theta_r)\,\frac{z_1}{z_2} \qquad \text{metric} \quad (3.20a)$$

where $\theta_r = \dfrac{180^\circ \tan \alpha}{\pi}$

$$\varepsilon_{r\ell} = \varepsilon_r + (\varepsilon_{ro} - \varepsilon_r)\,\frac{N_P}{N_G} \qquad \text{English} \quad (3.20b)$$

where $\varepsilon_r = \dfrac{180^\circ \tan \phi}{\pi}$

Once the roll angle at the limit diameter is known, the limit diameter is easily calculated by the method shown in Sec. 3.8.

The cutter that generates an internal gear will usually make a fillet that is almost the same radius of curvature as itself. Generally a cutter for an internal gear will have only about two-thirds of the radius given in Table 3.6.

Table 3.15 shows a dimension sheet for internal gears. Data for a sample problem of an 18-tooth pinion driving a 28-tooth gear is also shown.

The calculation of the diameter *between pins* for the internal gear is somewhat different from the calculation of diameter over pins for an external gear. Table 9.6 in Chap. 9 shows how this is done.

The calculation of the tooth profile of an internal gear is shown in Table 9.8. Figure 9.16 shows a layout of the profile of the 28-tooth internal gear on an enlarged scale. Note that the root fillet area is quite small. (The designer may not want to use this design for this reason—this shows that a design layout is important in the design process.)

The layout of the 18-tooth mating pinion is shown in Fig. 9.17. The pinion looks good.

TABLE 3.15 Internal-Gear Dimensions

Item	Reference	Metric		English	
1. Center distance	Sec. 1.14	15.000		0.590550	
2. Circular pitch	(8) × (7) ÷ π	9.42478		0.371054	
3. Pressure angle	Sec. 3.3	25		25	
4. Working depth	Sec. 3.11	5.51		0.217	
5. Module, transverse	(8) ÷ (7)	3		—	
6. Diametral pitch, transverse	(7) ÷ (8)	—		8.466667	
		Pinion	Gear	Pinion	Gear
7. Number of teeth	Tables 3.13, 3.14	18	28	18	28
8. Pitch diameter	Sec. 1.14	54.00	84.00	2.12598	3.30708
9. Addendum	Sec. 3.11, Tables 3.13, 3.14	3.39	2.12	0.133	0.083
10. Whole depth	Sec. 3.11	7.05	6.26	0.2775	0.2465
11. Outside diameter	(8) + 2 × (9)	60.78	—	2.392	—
12. Inside diameter	(8) − 2 × (9)	—	79.76	—	3.141
13. Root diameter	(12) + 2(10), gear	46.68	92.28	1.837	3.634
14. Arc tooth thickness	Sec. 3.11	4.980	4.240	0.1960	0.1670
15. Chordal tooth thickness	Eq. (3.5)	4.973	4.238	0.1958	0.1669
16. Chordal addendum	Sec. 3.11	3.34	2.12	0.1315	0.083
17. Pin size	Table 9.1	5.3340	5.3340	0.2100	0.2100
18. Diameter over pins	Table 9.2	61.912	—	2.4375	—
19. Diameter between pins	Table 9.6	—	77.092	—	3.0351
20. Face width	Sec. 2.8	27.0	25.0	1.06	1.00
21. Form diameter	Eq. (3.19)	50.035	90.536	1.970	3.564
22. Roll angle, O.D.	Table 9.7	42.195	17.904	42.195	17.904
23. Roll angle, F.D.	Table 9.7	12.185	36.877	12.185	36.877
24. Base circle diameter	(8) × cos (3)	48.941	76.130	1.9268	2.9972
25. Minimum root radius	Sec. 3.11	0.90	0.77	0.035	0.030
26. Accuracy	Sec. 5.18	See Note 3			

Notes: 1. Metric dimensions are in millimeters, English dimensions are in inches, and angles are in degrees.
2. This sheet shows a standard center-distance design.
3. After the designer has done the load rating and studied Sec. 5.18, accuracy needs may be satisfied by an ISO or AGMA quality level, or the designer may need to write a special recipe for accuracy limits.

3.12 Helical-Gear Tooth Proportions

A wide variety of tooth proportions have been used for helical gears. In spite of efforts to standardize helical-gear-tooth proportions, there is still no recognized standard. In this section we will consider typical kinds of helical-gear designs and discuss why each kind is used.

In most cases a gear maker will have gear-cutting tools on hand, and so a new design is very often based on existing tools. Hobs can be used to cut different helix angles merely by changing settings and gear ratios in the hobbing machine. For instance, spur-gear hobs are very often used to cut helical gears up to about 30°. If the gear teeth are to be shaped, a shaper cutter is generally needed for each helix angle, and so spur-gear shaper cutters are not usable for cutting helical gears. The guides used on a gear-shaping machine cut a constant *lead* rather than cutting a constant helix angle. As tooth numbers change, the helix angle that is produced by a given guide will change.

The designer of helical gears generally needs certain kinds of tooth proportions to make the gear unit function properly, and this is usually the chief reason for picking certain proportions. Consideration of available cutting tools then becomes secondary. The designer, of course, would hope that a gear shop cutting the design would have tools on hand, but the most important thing would be to make a *good* helical gear design regardless of the availability* of cutting tools.

Table 3.16 shows five kinds of helical-gear teeth, with examples shown for 10°, 15°, 30°, and 35° helix angles. When hobs are available, the normal-section data of the helical gear must agree with those of the hob. After a helix angle is picked, the hob can be put on a hobbing machine to cut gears at this helix angle, and the transverse-section data are obtained. In a helical-gear tooth, the transverse-section data must correlate, of course, with the normal-section data, regardless of how the teeth are made.

When the helical-gear teeth are to be shaped, the shaping-tool design is primarily based on the transverse section. The normal-section data for shaped teeth are calculated the same way as for hobbed teeth.

In Table 3.16, the general-purpose design is typical of relatively standard 20°-pressure-angle spur-gear hobs being used to cut helical gears. The practice of using a spur-gear hob for helical gears is OK when the helical gears are small and narrow in face width. Large, wide-face helical gears need a special tapered hob (see Sec. 6.2). The spur-gear hob without taper would break down too quickly.

The extra-load-capacity tooth proportions are based on 22.5° normal pressure angle and standard depth. These teeth are stronger from a beam-strength standpoint and also from the standpoint of surface durability. The contact ratio is still relatively good, and they will tend to run quite smoothly, although not quite as smoothly as the general-purpose 20°-normal-pressure-angle design.

The high-load-capacity helical-gear tooth, 25° normal pressure angle, tends to have a maximum load-carrying capacity. These teeth do not run quite as smoothly as the designs just mentioned because of the lower contact ratio. However, if tooth profile modifications are properly made, they will run quite well at the design load (teeth modified for a heavy load may run roughly and noisily at light loads).

*See Secs. 6.1 and 6.2 for more details on cutting tools like gear shaper cutters and hobs.

TABLE 3.16 Helical-Gear Basic Tooth Data

Typical use	Normal section data				Transverse section data				Pitch	
	Pressure angle α_n (ϕ_n)	Working depth h' (h_k)	Whole depth h (h_t)	Edge radius r_{a0} (r_T)	Helix angle β (ψ)	Pressure angle α_t (ϕ_t)	Circular pitch p_t (p_t)	Axial pitch p_x (p_x)	Module m_t	Diametral pitch (P_t)
General purpose	20	2.000	2.350	0.350	10	20.2836	3.1901	18.092	1.015427	0.984808
	20	2.000	2.350	0.350	15	20.6469	3.2524	12.138	1.035276	0.965926
	20	2.000	2.350	0.350	30	22.7959	3.6276	6.283	1.15470	0.866025
	20	2.000	2.350	0.350	35	23.9568	3.8352	5.477	1.220775	0.819152
Extra load capacity	22.50	2.000	2.300	0.325	10	22.8118	3.1901	18.092	1.015427	0.984808
	22.50	2.000	2.300	0.325	15	23.2109	3.2524	12.138	1.035276	0.965926
	22.50	2.000	2.300	0.325	30	25.5614	3.6276	6.283	1.15470	0.866025
	22.50	2.000	2.300	0.300	35	26.8240	3.8352	5.477	1.220776	0.819152
High load capacity	25	2.000	2.250	0.300	10	25.3376	3.1901	18.092	1.015427	0.984808
	25	2.000	2.250	0.300	15	25.7693	3.2524	12.138	1.035276	0.965926
	25	2.000	2.250	0.300	30	28.300	3.6276	6.283	1.15470	0.866025
	25	2.000	2.250	0.300	35	29.6510	3.8352	5.477	1.220776	0.819152
Special for low noise	18.2377	2.000	2.400	0.400	10	18.50	3.1901	18.092	1.015427	0.984808
	17.9105	2.000	2.400	0.400	15	18.50	3.2524	12.138	1.035276	0.965926
	16.1599	2.000	2.400	0.400	30	18.50	3.6276	6.283	1.15470	0.866025
	15.3275	2.000	2.400	0.400	35	18.50	3.8352	5.477	1.220776	0.819152
Special for very low noise	17.2500	2.200	2.575	0.375	10	17.50	3.1901	18.092	1.015427	0.984808
	16.9384	2.200	2.575	0.375	15	17.50	3.2524	12.138	1.035276	0.965926
	15.2727	2.200	2.575	0.375	30	17.50	3.6276	6.283	1.15470	0.866025
	14.4817	2.200	2.575	0.375	35	17.50	3.8352	5.477	1.22076	0.819152

Notes: All angles are in degrees. For the metric system, all dimensions are in millimeters. Multiply by normal module for dimensions of other than 1 module. For the English system, all dimensions are in inches. Divide by normal diametral pitch for dimensions of other than 1 normal diametral pitch.

Module in normal section is 1.000 for metric system.

Diametral pitch is 1.000 in normal section for English system.

In high-horsepower designs running at high speed, it is often desirable to use a special tooth design to get quiet operation. (A good example would be 10,000 kW going through a helical gearset at a pitch-line speed of 100 m/s or higher.)

The fourth grouping in Table 3.16 shows examples of special helical-gear-tooth proportions for low noise.

In a few cases the helical-gear application may be so critical that a very special design is justified.

The fifth grouping in Table 3.16 shows some examples in which a relatively low pressure angle is used and the teeth are made deeper than standard depth (the standard working depth for spur or helical gears is usually thought of as 2.000 times the module in the normal section). Helical-gear teeth made to the fifth grouping will not have maximum load-carrying capacity, but they will still have relatively good load-carrying capacity. The design, of course, is biased toward low noise rather than toward maximum torque capacity for the size of the gears.

The designs at 10° and 15° helix angles are preferred for single helical gears because the thrust load is relatively low. It is usually possible to use a face width that is at least as much as the axial pitch. (To get the full benefit of *helical* tooth action, the face width should equal at least two axial pitches.) When the gears are made double helical, there is no thrust load, because the thrust of one helix is opposed by an equal and opposite thrust from the other helix.

Double-helix gears should be made with at least 30° helix angle, and preferably they should have around 35° helix angle. At helix angles this high, it is possible to get several axial pitches within the face width of each helix. This is beneficial for quiet running. The full benefit of helical-tooth action can be obtained quite readily with double-helix gears. Note the double helical design illustrated in Fig. 3.17. There are over five axial pitches per helix.

In a double-helix-gear design, the usual design practice is to position the gear axially with thrust bearings, then permit the pinion to *float* axially so that the load is divided evenly between the two helices. There may be resistance to axial float resulting from friction in coupling devices. If there is enough resistance to axial movement, the division of load in a double helical gear may be impaired. A 30° helix angle, or higher, is needed in the double

FIG. 3.17 Helical gearset used to drive a 1750-kW generator at 1200 rpm. Turbine speed is 10,638 rpm. (*Courtesy of Transamerica DeLaval, Trenton, NJ, U.S.A.*)

helical design to ensure that resistance to axial movement from coupling can be quite readily overcome (it would be a design mistake—in most cases—to use a 15° helix angle for a double helical set).

The relation between the normal and transverse pressure angles of helical gears is given by the following equation:

$$\tan \alpha_t = \frac{\tan \alpha_n}{\cos \beta} \qquad \text{metric} \qquad (3.21a)$$

$$\tan \phi_t = \frac{\tan \phi_n}{\cos \psi} \qquad \text{English} \qquad (3.21b)$$

3.13 Helical-Gear Dimension Sheet

Table 3.17 shows a helical-gear dimension sheet. All the tooth dimensions which will ordinarily be needed are shown on this sheet. In some low-cost applications, items like roll angles, form diameter, and axial pitch may not be required.

The face-width dimensions should be based on the load-carrying requirements, as discussed in Sec. 3.27. Also, it should be remembered that the wider the face width, the harder it is to secure accuracy enough to make the whole face width carry load uniformly. In addition to these considerations, the designer should consider the fact that a certain amount of face width is required to get the *benefit of helical-gear action.* General experience indicates that it takes at least two axial pitches of face width to get full benefit from the overlapping action of helical teeth. In critical high-speed gears where noise is a problem, the designer should aim to get four or more axial pitches in the face width. If the face width is less than one axial pitch, the tooth action will be in between that of a spur gear and a true helical.

Helical pinions should have enough addendum to avoid undercut. Equation (3.2) can be used to calculate the number of teeth at which undercut just starts on a helical pinion. Two pressure angles have to be used, though, to get the right answer. In calculating the h_{fx} dimension, the normal pressure angle α_n is used. In calculating z, the transverse pressure angle α_t is used. Helical pinions can go to lower numbers of teeth without undercut than can spur pinions. It is seldom that helical gearing requires long and short addendum to avoid undercut.

In general, there is not so much need to use long and short addendum to balance strength between pinion and gear in helical gearing as in spur gearing. Low-hardness helical gearing usually has strength to spare and is in no danger of scoring trouble. Wear in the form of pitting is the main thing that limits the design. In this situation, a long-addendum pinion meshing

TABLE 3.17 Helical-Gear Dimensions

Item	Reference	Metric		English	
1. Center distance	Secs. 2.8, 2.10	187.9026		7.39774	
2. Normal circular pitch	Eq. (1.8)	9.4248		0.371054	
3. Normal pressure angle	Sec. 3.12, Table 3.16	20		20	
4. Working depth	Table 3.16	6.00		0.236	
5. Helix angle	Sec. 3.12	15		15	
6. Transverse pressure angle	Eq. (3.21)	20.64689		20.64689	
7. Module, normal	Eq. (1.9)	3		—	
8. Normal diametral pitch	Eq. (1.10)	—		8.466667	
		Pinion	Gear	Pinion	Gear
9. Number of teeth	Sec. 3.13	25	96	25	96
10. Pitch diameter	Eqs. (1.4), (1.5)	77.6457	298.1595	3.05692	11.73856
11. Addendum	Sec. 3.13	3.00	3.00	0.118	0.118
12. Whole depth	Table 3.16	7.05	7.05	0.2775	0.2775
13. Outside diameter	(10) + 2 × (11)	83.65	304.16	3.293	11.974
14. Root diameter	(13) − 2 × (12)	69.55	290.06	2.738	11.419
15. Normal arc tooth thickness	Sec. 3.6	4.617	4.617	0.1818	0.1818
16. Chordal tooth thickness	Eq. (3.5)	4.594	4.609	0.1809	0.1815
17. Chordal addendum	Eq. (3.4)	3.047	3.014	0.1200	0.1185
18. Ball size	Table 9.1	5.33401	5.33401	0.210	0.210
19. Diameter over balls	Table 9.9				
20. Face width	Secs. 3.12, 3.13	78	77	3.07	3.03
21. Form diameter	Table 9.3	73.393	293.338	2.8894	11.5487
22. Roll angle, OD	Table 9.3	32.68	24.87	32.68	24.87
23. Roll angle, FD	Table 9.3	8.17	18.60	8.17	18.60
24. Base circle diameter	(10) × cos (6)	72.6586	279.0091	2.86057	10.98458
25. Hand of helix	Sec. 1.13	RH	LH	RH	LH
26. Lead	(2) × (9) ÷ sin (5)	910.364	3495.796	35.8410	137.6295
27. Minimum root radius	Sec. 3.13	0.89	0.78	0.035	0.030
28. Accuracy	Sec. 5.18	See Note 3			

Notes: 1. Metric dimensions are in millimeters, English dimensions are in inches, and angles are in degrees.

2. This sheet shows a standard center-distance design. See Sec. 8.1 for an example of a special "spread center" design.

3. After the designer has done the load rating and studied Sec. 5.18, accuracy needs may be satisfied by an ISO or AGMA quality level, or the designer may need to write a special recipe for accuracy limits.

with a short-addendum gear offers only a slight advantage over equal addendum on both members. In high-hardness helical gearing where the pinion has a low number of teeth and the ratio is high, it may be desirable to use about the same ratio between pinion addendum and gear addendum as would be used for spur gears. In this case, Fig. 3.5 may be used as a guide.

The minimum root fillet radius of a helical gear is not usually specified on the drawing. This is a hard dimension to check because you cannot get a good projection view of the fillet without cutting out and mounting a section* of the gear. If beam strength is not critical, then it is not necessary to hold a close control over root-fillet curvature. It is good judgment, though, to require that all cutting tools have as much radius as possible.

The equation for the minimum radius of curvature in the root fillet of a helical gear is

$$\rho_f = \frac{r_{a0} - (h_f - r_{a0})^2}{d_p/(2\cos^2\beta) + (h_f - r_{a0})} \qquad \text{metric} \qquad (3.22a)$$

where $h_f = h - h_a$

r_{a0} = edge radius of generating rack

$$\rho_f = \frac{r_T + (b - r_T)^2}{d/(2\cos^2\psi) + (b - r_T)} \qquad \text{English} \qquad (3.22b)$$

where $b = h_t - a$

r_T = edge radius of generating rack

Although Eq. (3.22) is based on the generating action of a rack, the designer can use it for any type of helical-gear manufacture on the assumption that other methods of tooth cutting can meet the same minimum radius value.

The shape of helical teeth in the *normal section* is almost exactly the same as that of a spur gear with a larger number of teeth. For instance, the 25-tooth helical pinion on a 77.6457-mm pitch diameter shown on the sample dimension sheet would be matched in tooth contour by a spur pinion of 27.74 teeth on an 83.220-mm pitch diameter with a 20° pressure angle.

The matching number of teeth in a spur gear is called the *virtual* number of teeth. The virtual number of spur teeth is equal to the number of helical teeth divided by the cube of the cosine of the helix angle. See Table 9.11.

3.14 Bevel-Gear Tooth Proportions

The proportions of straight bevel, Zerol† bevel, and spiral bevel gears can quite logically be considered together. The Gleason Works of Rochester, N.Y., has done an excellent job of standardizing the designs of these kinds of gears. Their work is generally accepted by the gear industry, and in time it

*The section cut is normal to the helical tooth. The minimum radius specified is, of course, in the normal section.

†Trademark registered in the U.S. Patent Office by the Gleason Works of Rochester, NY, U.S.A.

usually becomes part of the standards of the American Gear Manufacturers Association. The material in this section and the next three sections is taken from the (latest) revised editions of Gleason bevel-gear systems for straight, spiral, and Zerol bevel gears.

The pressure angles and tooth depths generally recommended for bevel gears are given in Table 3.18. The whole depth specified is sometimes slightly exceeded by the practice of rough-cutting some pitches a small amount deeper than the calculated depth to save wear on the finishing cutters.

The various Gleason systems have the amount of addendum for the gear and the pinion worked out so as to avoid undercut with low numbers of teeth and balance the strength of gear and pinion teeth. In each case, though, there is a limit to how far the system will go. Table 3.19 shows the minimum numbers of teeth that can be used in different combinations.

TABLE 3.18 Bevel-Gear Proportions

Kind of bevel gear	Size range: Module m_t	Size range: Diametral pitch P_t	Pressure angle α (or ϕ)	Working depth h' (or h_k)	Whole depth h (or h_t)
Straight	25.4–0.40	1–64	20°	2.000	$2.188 + \frac{0.05}{m_t}$ or $0.002P_t$
Spiral	25.4–1.27	1–20	20°	1.700	1.888
	25.4–1.27	1–20	16°	1.700	1.888
Zerol	5–0.40	5–64	20°	2.000	$2.188 + \frac{0.05}{m_t}$
	5–0.80	5–32	$22\frac{1}{2}$°	2.000	or
	5–1.27	5–20	25°	2.000	$0.002P_t$

Notes:
1. For metric design, the values are multiplied by the module to get the working depth and the whole depth.
2. For English design, the values are divided by the diametral pitch to get the working depth and the whole depth.
3. To protect fine pitches, a *constant* value is *added* to the whole depth. This is done for all pitches, but it is not very significant on large pitches. The value is 0.05 mm or 0.002 in.
4. Examples for straight bevel:

	5 module	1 module
Working depth	10.00 mm	2.000 mm
Whole depth	10.99 mm	2.238 mm

TABLE 3.19 Minimum Tooth Numbers for Bevel Gears

Kind of gear	Pressure angle	No. of pinion teeth	Min. no. of gear teeth
Straight bevel	20°	13	31
		14	20
		15	17
		16	16
Spiral bevel	20°	12	26
		13	22
		14	20
		15	19
		16	18
		17	17
Zerol bevel	20°	15	25
		16	20
		17	17
	$22\frac{1}{2}$°	13	15
		14	14
	25°	13	14
		13	13

In spur- and helical-gear work, the amount of addendum for the *pinion* is first determined. Then what is left of the working depth is used for the gear addendum. In bevel-gear practice, just the opposite procedure is used. The *gear* addendum is determined first.

Table 3.20 shows the amount of gear addendum recommended for bevel gears.

Since bevel gears and bevel pinions usually have different addendums, it

TABLE 3.20 Gear Addendum for Bevel Gears

Kind of bevel gear	Metric	English
Straight or Zerol	$0.540m_t + \dfrac{0.460m_t}{u^2}$	$\dfrac{0.540}{P_d} + \dfrac{0.460}{P_d m_G^2}$
Spiral bevel	$0.540m_t + \dfrac{0.390m_t}{u^2}$	$\dfrac{0.540}{P_d} + \dfrac{0.390}{P_d m_G^2}$

Note: The *pinion* addendum is obtained by subtracting the gear addendum from the working depth.

is necessary to use different tooth thicknesses for the two members. The standard systems worked out by the Gleason Works adjust the tooth thicknesses so that approximately equal strength is obtained for each member. The adjustment of the tooth thickness is accomplished by a factor called k. This k should not be confused with the K *factor* used as an index of tooth load. The k values can be read from Figs. 3.18 to 3.21.

The thicknesses of bevel-gear teeth are calculated for the large ends of the teeth. It is customary to calculate the circular thicknesses of the teeth *without allowing any backlash.* In straight bevel gearing, chordal tooth thicknesses are calculated *with backlash.* The chordal thicknesses of a straight-bevel-gear tooth can be measured with tooth calipers.

The formula for the gear circular tooth thickness of any kind of bevel gear is

$$s_2 = \frac{p_t}{2} - (h_{a1} - h_{a2}) \frac{\tan \alpha_t}{\cos \beta} - km_t \qquad \text{metric} \qquad (3.23a)$$

$$t_G = \frac{p_t}{2} - (a_P - a_G) \frac{\tan \phi_t}{\cos \psi} - \frac{k}{P_d} \qquad \text{English} \qquad (3.23b)$$

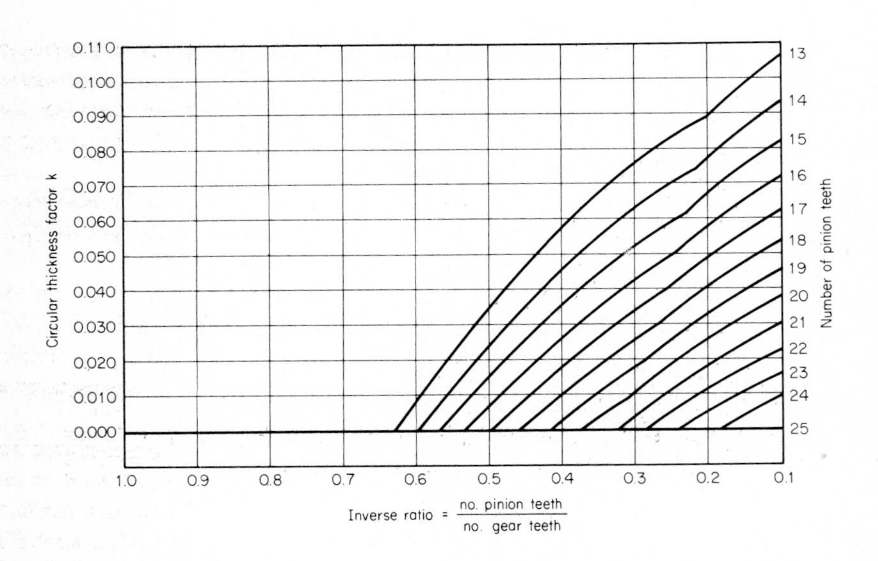

FIG. 3.18 Circular thickness factor for straight bevel gears with 20° pressure angle.

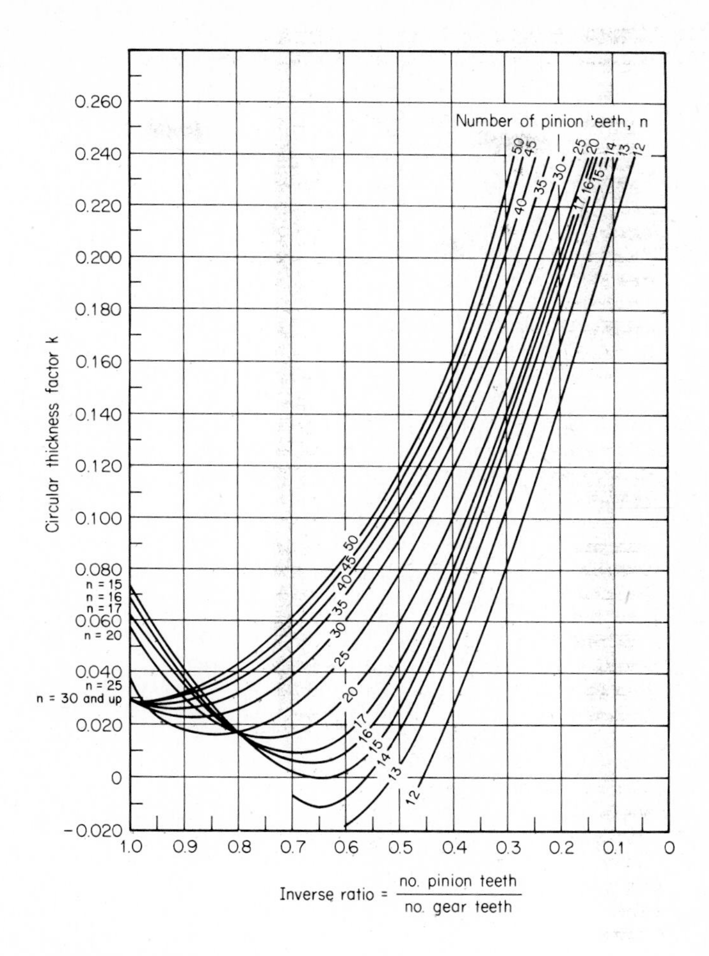

FIG. 3.19 Circular thickness factor for spiral bevel gears with 20° pressure angle and 35° spiral angle. LH pinion driving clockwise or RH pinion driving counterclockwise.

where k is the circular tooth thickness factor given by the appropriate curve for straight, Zerol, or spiral bevel gears. See Figs. 3.18 to 3.21.

The recommended amount of backlash for bevel gearsets when they are assembled ready to run is given in Table 3.21. In instrument and control gearing, it may be desirable to use values even lower than those shown. Conversely, some high-speed gears and gears mounted in casings with a material different from that of the gear may require more backlash.

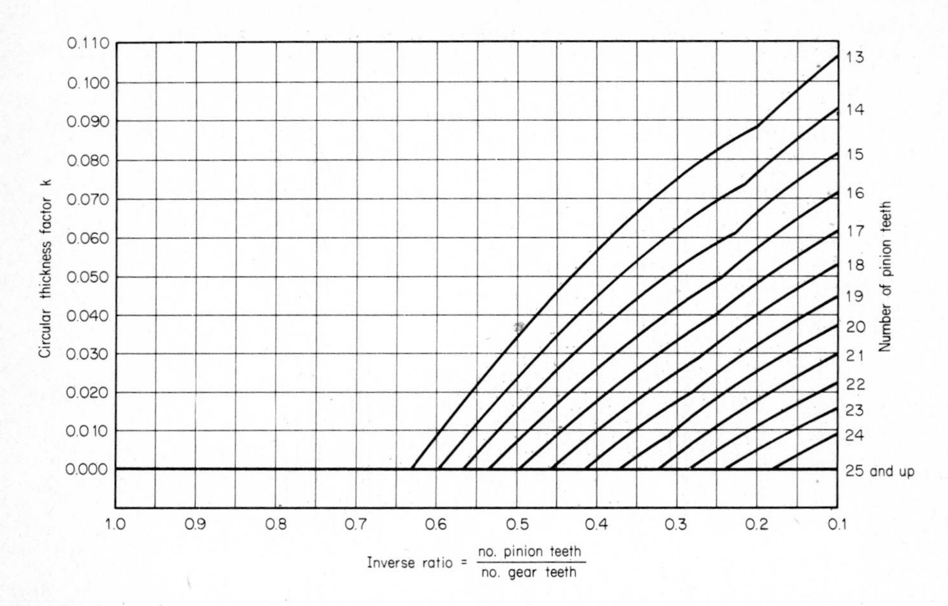

FIG. 3.20 Circular thickness factor for Zerol bevel gears with 20° pressure angle operating at 90° shaft angle.

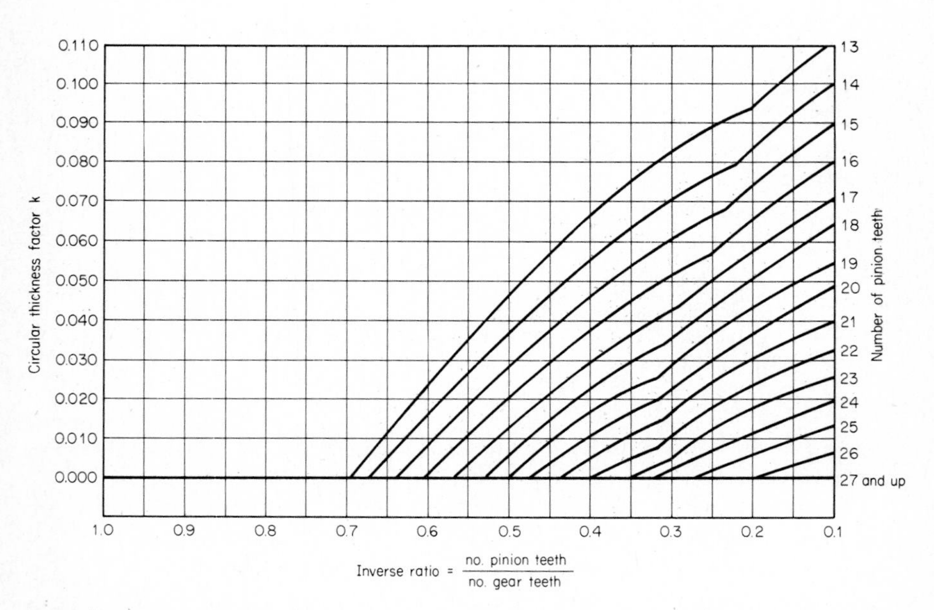

FIG. 3.21 Circular thickness factor for Zerol bevel gears with 25° pressure angle operating at 90° shaft angle.

TABLE 3.21 Nominal Backlash for Bevel Gears at Tightest Point of Mesh

Tooth size range		Backlash for low accuracy		Backlash for high accuracy	
Module m_t	Diametral pitch P_d	millimeters	inches	millimeters	inches
25–20	1.00–1.25	1.14–1.65	0.045–0.065	0.51–0.76	0.020–0.030
20–17	1.25–1.50	0.89–1.40	0.035–0.055	0.46–0.66	0.018–0.026
17–14	1.50–1.75	0.63–1.1	0.025–0.045	0.41–0.56	0.016–0.022
14–12	1.75–2.00	0.51–1.0	0.020–0.040	0.36–0.46	0.014–0.018
12–10	2.00–2.50	0.46–0.76	0.018–0.030	0.30–0.41	0.012–0.016
10–8.5	2.50–3.00	0.38–0.63	0.015–0.025	0.25–0.33	0.010–0.013
8.5–7.2	3.00–3.50	0.30–0.56	0.012–0.022	0.20–0.28	0.008–0.011
7.2–6.3	3.50–4.00	0.25–0.51	0.010–0.020	0.18–0.22	0.007–0.009
6.3–5.1	4.00–5.00	0.20–0.41	0.008–0.016	0.15–0.20	0.006–0.008
5.1–4.2	5.00–6.00	0.15–0.33	0.006–0.013	0.13–0.18	0.005–0.007
4.2–3.1	6.00–8.00	0.13–0.25	0.005–0.010	0.10–0.15	0.004–0.006
3.1–2.5	8.00–10.00	0.10–0.20	0.004–0.008	0.076–0.127	0.003–0.005
2.5–1.6	10.00–16.00	0.076–0.127	0.003–0.005	0.051–0.102	0.002–0.004
1.6–1.2	16.00–20.00	0.051–0.102	0.002–0.004	0.025–0.076	0.001–0.003

3.15 Straight-Bevel-Gear Dimension Sheet

A dimension sheet for calculating straight-bevel-gear-tooth data is given in Table 3.22. This sheet gives several formulas not previously discussed. These can be tried out quite readily by working through numerical calculations for the sample design that is shown in the table.

The backlash allowance in item (20) of the table is taken from Table 3.21. The designer should consult the text in Sec. 3.6 and then decide whether or not special requirements of the application might make it desirable to depart from standard backlash.

The corrections for chordal tooth thickness and chordal addendum are made by these equations:

Chordal tooth thickness

Metric | English

$$\bar{s}_2 = s_2 - \frac{(s_2)^3}{6(d_{p2})^2} - \frac{j}{2} \qquad t_{cG} = t_G - \frac{t_G^3}{6D^2} - \frac{B}{2} \tag{3.24}$$

$$\bar{s}_1 = s_1 - \frac{(s_1)^3}{6(d_{p1})^2} - \frac{j}{2} \qquad t_{cP} = t_P - \frac{t_P^3}{6d^2} - \frac{B}{2} \tag{3.25}$$

TABLE 3.22 Straight-Bevel-Gear Dimensions

Item	Reference	Metric		English	
1. Circular pitch	(8) × π ÷ (7)	15.7079		0.61842	
2. Pressure angle	Sec. 1.15	20		20	
3. Working depth	Table 3.18	10.00		0.3937	
4. Shaft angle	Assumed to be 90°	90		90	
5. Module	(8) ÷ (7)	5.000		—	
6. Diametral pitch	(7) ÷ (8)	—		5.080	
		Pinion	Gear	Pinion	Gear
7. Number of teeth	Table 3.19	16	49	16	49
8. Pitch diameter	Sec. 2.11	80.00	245.00	3.1496	9.6457
9. Pitch angle	Sec. 1.15, Table 3.23	18.08	71.92	18.08	71.92
10. Outer cone distance	Table 3.23	128.87	128.87	5.074	5.074
11. Face width	Secs. 2.11, 3.15	40.00	40.00	1.575	1.575
12. Addendum	Table 3.20	7.05	2.95	0.278	0.116
13. Whole depth	Table 3.18	10.99	10.99	0.433	0.433
14. Dedendum angle	Table 3.23	1.73	3.55	1.73	3.55
15. Face angle	Table 3.23	21.63	73.65	21.63	73.65
16. Root angle	Table 3.23	16.35	68.37	16.35	68.37
17. Outside diameter	Table 3.23	93.41	246.83	3.678	9.718
18. Pitch apex to crown	Table 3.23	120.31	37.20	4.737	1.465
19. Circular tooth thickness	Eq. (3.23)	9.514	6.194	0.3745	0.2438
20. Backlash	Table 3.21, Sec. 3.6	0.13–0.18	0.13–0.18	0.005–0.007	0.005–0.007
21. Chordal tooth thickness	Eqs. (3.24), (3.25)	9.43	6.13	0.3712	0.2413
22. Chordal addendum	Eqs. (3.26), (3.27)	7.32	2.96	0.2882	0.1165
23. Tooth angle	Table 3.23	2.75	2.67	2.75	2.67
Limit point width	Sec. 3.15				
24. large end	Table 9.12	3.30	3.63	0.130	0.143
25. small end	Table 9.12	2.31	2.54	0.091	0.100
26. Tool point width	Table 9.12	1.65	1.78	0.065	0.070
27. Tool edge radius	Table 9.12	0.63	0.63	0.025	0.025

Notes: 1. Metric dimensions are in millimeters, English dimensions are in inches, and angles are in degrees.
2. For more complete data, see Gleason dimension sheet, Table 9.12.

Chordal addendum

Metric / English

$$\bar{h}_{a2} = h_{a2} + \frac{(s_2)^2 \cos \delta'_2}{4d_{p2}} \qquad a_{cG} = a_G + \frac{t_G^2 \cos \Gamma}{4D} \tag{3.26}$$

$$\bar{h}_{a1} = h_{a1} + \frac{(s_1)^2 \cos \delta'_1}{4d_{p1}} \qquad a_{cP} = a_P + \frac{t_P^2 \cos \gamma}{4d} \tag{3.27}$$

where j = backlash in millimeters for metric
B = backlash in inches for English

The *tooth angle* is a machine setting used on a Gleason two-tool straight-bevel-gear generator. See Table 3.23 for the definition of this angle.

The *limit-point width* is the maximum width of the point of a straight-sided V tool which will touch the sides and bottom of the tooth at the small end. The tool actually used must not be larger than this dimension, but it may be a small amount less.

The *tool advance* corresponds to the 0.05 mm or 0.002 in. in the whole-depth formula. (See Table 3.18.) This dimension sets the tool deeper and increases the clearance along the length of the tooth.

Table 3.22 gives the calculations for bevel gears mounted on a 90° shaft

TABLE 3.23 Calculation of Bevel-Gear Body Dimensions

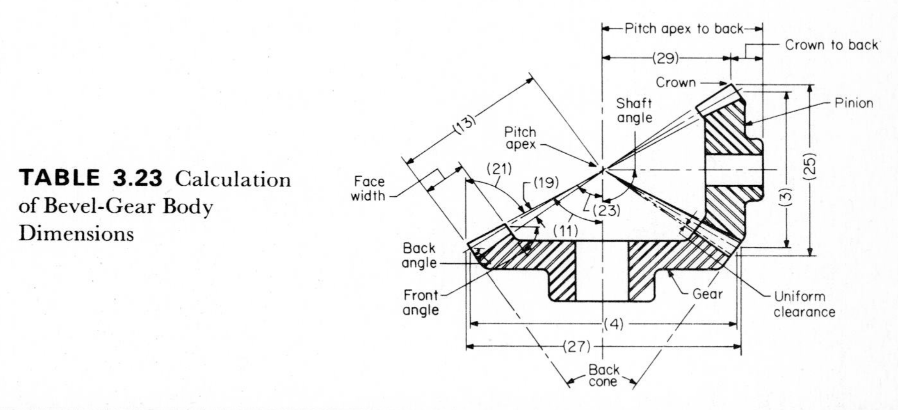

1. No. pinion teeth	16	22. Pinion RA, (10) − (16)	16.3322
2. No. gear teeth	49	23. Gear RA, (11) − (19)	68.3464
3. Pinion, pitch diameter	80.00	24. 2.0 (5) × cos (10)	13.4035
4. Gear, pitch diameter	245.00	25. Pinion OD, (3) + (24)	93.4035
5. Pinion addendum	7.05	26. 2.0 (6) × cos (11)	1.8314
6. Gear addendum	2.95	27. Gear OD, (4) + (26)	246.8314
7. Working depth	10.00	28. 0.50 × (4) − (5) sin (10)	120.3117
8. Whole depth	10.99	29. Pinion pitch apex to crown	(28)
9. (1) ÷ (2)	0.326531	30. 0.50 × (3) − (6) sin (11)	37.1957
10. Pinion PA, arctan (9)	18.0834	31. Gear pitch apex to crown	(30)
11. Gear PA, 90° − (10)	71.9165		
12. 2 sin (10)	0.620804	For straight bevels only:	
13. Outer cone distance, (3) ÷ (12)	128.8652	32. Pinion circular thickness	9.514
14. (8) − (5)	3.94	33. Pressure angle	20°
15. (14) ÷ (13)	0.030575	34. 0.50 × (32) + (14) tan (33)	6.19104
16. Pinion ded. angle, arctan (15)	1.7512	35. 57.30 ÷ (13)	0.44465
17. (8) − (6)	8.04	36. Pinion tooth angle, (34) × (35)	2.7528
18. (17) ÷ (13)	0.062391	37. Gear circular thickness	6.194
19. Gear ded. angle, arctan (18)	3.5701	38. 0.50 × (37) + (17) tan (33)	6.02332
20. Pinion FA, (19) + (10)	21.6535	39. Gear tooth angle, (35) × (38)	2.6782
21. Gear FA, (16) + (11)	73.6677		

Notes: 1. These calculations are for straight, spiral, or Zerol bevel gears on a 90° shaft angle.
2. The abbreviations used are: PA = pitch angle; FA = face angle; RA = root angle; OD = outside diameter.

angle only. If bevel gears are to be mounted on some other angle, special calculations have to be made. Gleason data references at the end of the book may be consulted to get information beyond the scope of this book. A complete Gleason dimension sheet for the bevel gears in Table 3.22 is given as Table 9.12.

The face width of straight bevel gears should not exceed 32 percent of the outer cone distance nor exceed 3.18 times the circular pitch. These rules may be rounded off to 30 percent of the face width and 3 times the circular pitch for convenience. If either rule is exceeded by much, there is apt to be trouble in making and fitting the teeth properly. Real load-carrying capacity will probably be lost as a result of poor running fits when bevel teeth gears are made wider in face width than the rules just mentioned will allow.

3.16 Spiral-Bevel-Gear Dimension Sheet

Table 3.24 shows the relatively simple design sheet that is used for spiral bevel gears. Control of the spiral bevel gear's geometry is obtained by controlling the machine settings of the machine used to make the gears and by testing each gear with standard *test* gears.

Table 3.21 is used as a design guide for backlash of spiral bevel gears. In general, all the backlash is subtracted from the pinion thickness.

Table 3.24 should be used only for spiral bevel gears on 90° shaft angle. The standard spiral angle is 35°.

The *mean* circular thickness shown in item (20) is the tooth thickness at the midsection (midway for the face width). The dimensions in the midsection are all smaller (due to the conical shape of a bevel gear) than they are at the large end. The relation of midsection to large end is

$$\frac{\text{Midsection}}{\text{Large end}} = \frac{2.0 \times \text{outer cone distance} - \text{face width}}{2.0 \times \text{outer cone distance}} \tag{3.28}$$

If the face width is 30 percent of the cone distance, this ratio will come out to be 0.850. This means the mean tooth thicknesses will be about 85 percent of the thicknesses at the large end.

The tooth thicknesses shown in Table 3.24 for the 16/49 spiral bevel set have been reduced from the theoretical to allow a minimum backlash for precision spiral bevel teeth. The sum of the tooth thicknesses is less than the mean circular pitch by the backlash. (The mean circular pitch for the example is 13.2700 mm or 0.5224 in.)

The data shown in Tables 3.22 and 3.25 (Zerol) have been calculated by computer at the Gleason Works. They do not agree exactly with the data given in the Gleason references at the end of the book. With somewhat more complex calculations—handled easily in a large computer program—the proportions can be modified to give best results for the planned method of manufacture. A slightly tilted root-line taper, for instance, is often used to

TABLE 3.24 Spiral-Bevel-Gear Dimensions

Item	Reference	Metric		English	
1. Circular pitch	(9) × π ÷ (8)	15.7079		0.61842	
2. Pressure angle	Sec. 1.17	20		20	
3. Spiral angle	Sec. 3.16	35		35	
4. Working depth	Table 3.18	8.30		0.327	
5. Shaft angle	Assumed to be 90°	90		90	
6. Module	(9) ÷ (8)	5.00		—	
7. Diametral pitch	(8) ÷ (9)	—		5.080	
		Pinion	Gear	Pinion	Gear
8. Number of teeth	Table 3.19	16	49	16	49
9. Pitch diameter	Sec. 2.11	80.00	245.00	3.1496	9.6457
10. Pitch angle	Table 3.23	18.08	71.92	18.08	71.92
11. Outer cone distance	Table 3.23	128.87	128.87	5.074	5.074
12. Face width	Sec. 3.16	38	38	1.496	1.496
13. Addendum	Table 3.20	5.91	2.38	0.233	0.094
14. Whole depth	Table 3.18	9.22	9.22	0.363	0.363
15. Dedendum angle	Table 3.23	1.13	2.83	1.13	2.83
16. Face angle	Table 3.23	20.92	73.05	20.92	73.05
17. Root angle	Table 3.23	16.95	69.08	16.95	69.08
18. Outside diameter	Table 3.23	91.26	246.48	3.593	9.704
19. Pitch apex to crown	Table 3.23	120.67	37.74	4.751	1.485
20. Mean circular tooth thickness	Sec. 3.16	8.13	5.04	0.320	0.1984
21. Backlash	Sec. 3.16, Table 3.21	0.13–0.18	0.13–0.18	0.005–0.007	0.005–0.007
22. Hand of spiral	One LH, other RH	LH	RH	LH	RH
23. Function	Design choice	Driver	Driven	Driver	Driven
24. Direction of rotation	Design choice	CCW	CW	CCW	CW
25. Cutter diameter	Table 9.13	190.5	190.5	7.50	7.50
26. Cutter edge radius	Table 9.13	0.63	0.63	0.025	0.025

Notes: 1. Metric dimensions are in millimeters, English dimensions are in inches, and angles are in degrees.
2. For more complete data, see Gleason dimension sheet, Table 9.13.

allow maximum tooling-point widths. This achieves the best tool life and the largest fillet radii (for decreased bending stresses).

On large production jobs, using Gleason machine tools, it is advisable to obtain a complete summary of design and manufacturing dimensions from the Gleason Works. These dimension sheets show considerably more data than the basic engineering data. Also, computations at the Gleason Works are carried out on a large computer. Small variations to favor a particular job can be made very readily. As examples, the following dimension sheets are given in Chap. 9:

Table 9.12 Straight Bevel (matches Table 3.22)
Table 9.13 Spiral Bevel (matches Table 3.24)
Table 9.14 Zerol Bevel (matches Table 3.25)

TABLE 3.25 Zerol-Bevel-Gear Dimensions

Item	Reference	Metric		English	
1. Circular pitch	(8) × π ÷ (7)	7.8540		0.30921	
2. Pressure angle	Sec. 1.16	20		20	
3. Working depth	Table 3.18	5.00		0.197	
4. Shaft angle	Assumed to be 90°	90		90	
5. Module	(8) ÷ (7)	2.500		—	
6. Diametral pitch	(7) ÷ (8)	—		10.160	
		Pinion	Gear	Pinion	Gear
7. Number of teeth	Table 3.19	32	98	32	98
8. Pitch diameter	Sec. 2.11	80	245.00	3.1496	9.6456
9. Pitch angle	Table 3.23	18.08	71.92	18.08	71.92
10. Outer cone distance	Table 3.23	128.87	128.87	5.074	5.074
11. Face width	Sec. 3.17	32	32	1.260	1.260
12. Addendum	Table 3.20	3.53	1.47	0.1390	0.0579
13. Whole depth	Table 3.18	5.47	5.47	0.2154	0.2154
14. Dedendum angle	Table 3.23	1.37	3.28	1.37	3.28
15. Face angle	Table 3.23	21.37	73.28	21.37	73.28
16. Root angle	Table 3.23	16.72	68.63	16.72	68.63
17. Outside diameter	Table 3.23	86.71	245.91	3.414	9.681
18. Pitch apex to crown	Table 3.23	121.41	38.60	4.780	1.520
19. Mean circular tooth thickness	Sec. 3.17	3.92	2.86	0.1543	0.1126
20. Backlash	Sec. 3.17, Table 3.21	0.05–0.10	0.05–0.10	0.002–0.004	0.002–0.004
21. Cutter diameter	Table 9.14	152.4	152.4	6.00	6.00

Notes: 1. Metric dimensions are in millimeters, English dimensions are in inches, and angles are in degrees.
2. For more complete data, see Gleason dimension sheet, Table 9.14.

Spiral bevel gears should not have a face width exceeding 30 percent of the outer cone distance.

3.17 Zerol-Bevel-Gear Dimension Sheet

The Zerol bevel gear has curved teeth like the sprial bevel gear, but its spiral angle is 0°. The dimension sheet (Table 3.25) is similar in form to the one used for spiral bevel gears, but the dimensions have numerical values more like those used for straight bevel teeth.

The mean tooth-thickness values shown in Table 3.25 are similar to those just discussed in Sec. 3.16 for spiral bevel gears. They are for the middle of the face width, and they have been reduced to allow an amount of backlash for precision gears.

The dedendum angle for Zerol bevels has a small amount added to the angle that would be obtained using the method shown in Table 3.23 for bevel-gear-body dimensions. This added amount, in degrees, can be obtained from the following:

$$\Delta \text{ dedendum angle} = A - B - C \qquad \text{degrees} \tag{3.29}$$

where A is

Pressure angle	A value	
	Metric	English
20°	$111.13 \div z$	$111.13 \div N_c$
$22\frac{1}{2}$°	$81.13 \div z$	$81.13 \div N_c$
25°	$56.87 \div z$	$56.87 \div N_c$

Number of crown teeth:

Metric	English
$z = 2.0(R_a \div m_t)$	$N_c = 2.0 P_d A_o$

The value B is the same regardless of pressure angle:

Metric	English
$B = \dfrac{25.2(d_{p1} \sin \delta_2')^{0.50}}{zb}$	$B = \dfrac{5(d \sin \Gamma)^{0.50}}{N_c F}$

The value C is also the same regardless of pressure angle:

Metric	English
$C = 5.918 \div (z \times m_t)$	$C = (0.2333\ P_d) \div N_c$

FIG. 3.22 Crossed-helical gears in a small mechanism. The driver is steel and the driven gear is nylon.

Zerol bevel gears are quite frequently used in critical instrument work. For this kind of work, it is frequently necessary to use almost no backlash. If the gears are to be used for general-purpose work, Table 3.21 may be used as a design guide for backlash.

The dedendum angles shown in Table 3.25 are made to suit the Duplex method of cutting Zerol bevel gears. This is a rapid method of cutting which allows both pinion and gear to be cut spread-blade (both sides of a tooth space are finished simultaneously). Present machine capacity limits the use of the Duplex method to cut gears approximately 2.5 module (10 pitch) and finer and to ground gears approximately 4 module (6 pitch) and finer. The minimum number of pinion teeth is 13.

Table 3.25 is for use only when the shaft angle is 90°. Angular Zerol bevel gears require special calculations. The face width of Zerol bevel gears should not exceed 25 percent of the outer cone distance.

3.18 Hypoid-Gear Calculations

The hypoid gear quite closely resembles a spiral bevel gear in appearance. The major difference is that the pinion axis is offset above or below the gear axis. In the regular bevel-gear family, the axis of the pinion and that of the gear always intersect. The hypoid type of gear does not have intersecting axes. Since this kind of gear is basically different from the bevel gear, hypoid gears are not ordinarily called hypoid bevel gears. Instead, they are just called hypoid gears. From a manufacturing standpoint, though, they are cut or ground with the same kinds of machinery that are used to make spiral bevel gears.

Hypoid gears can be more readily designed for low numbers of pinion teeth and high ratios than can spiral bevel gears. The Gleason Works recommends the following minimum numbers of teeth for formate* pinions:

Ratio	Minimum number of pinion teeth
$2\frac{1}{2}$	15
3	12
4	9
5	7
6	6
10	5

The calculations involved in designing a set of hypoid gears are quite long. A calculation sheet of about 150 items must be calculated to get all the

*Formate pinions are pinions which are matched to run with formate gears. Formate gears are cut without any generating action.

answers needed. About 45 items on the sheet must be worked through on a trial basis, then repeated two or three times until assumed and calculated values check. With the advent of computers, hypoid-gear calculations became much easier, since they could be programmed.

In view of the large amount of material needed to explain hypoid-gear calculations, it is not possible to present the method here. Those interested in obtaining hypoid-gear designs should either consult a manufacturer of hypoid gears or study the hypoid-gear-design information published by the Gleason Works. A practical approach for most jobs is to get a hypoid dimension sheet made by the Gleason Works.

3.19 Face-Gear Calculations

The pinion of a face gearset can be designed in just the same manner as a spur or helical pinion would be designed. The pinion should have enough addendum to avoid being undercut. Equation (3.2) may be used to check a design to see if it is in danger of undercutting. The meshing action of the face gear with the pinion is somewhat similar to that of a rack meshing with the pinion. The involute profile of the pinion should be finished accurately to a deep enough depth to permit the pinion to mesh with a rack.

One of the principal design problems in face gears is to calculate the *face width*. Since the face-gear teeth run across the end of a cylindrical blank instead of across the outside diameter, the length of the tooth sets an inside diameter and an outside diameter. The face-gear tooth changes its shape as you move lengthwise along the tooth. The *minimum* inside diameter is determined by the point at which the undercut portion of the gear profile extends to about the middle of the tooth height. The *maximum* outside diameter is established by the point at which the top land of the tooth narrows to a knife-edge. In general, it is good design practice to make the face width of the gear somewhat shorter than these two extremes.

Table 3.26 shows some recommended proportions for spur face gears of 20° pressure angle. A ratio of less than 1.5 is not generally recommended. The diameter constants are used to calculate the limiting outside and inside diameters of the gear as follows:

Metric	English	
$d_{a2} = \varepsilon_o z_2 m_t$ $\varepsilon_o = m_o$	$D_o = \dfrac{m_o N_G}{P_d}$	(3.30)
$d_{i2} = \varepsilon_1 z_2 m_t$ $\varepsilon_1 = m_i$	$D_i = \dfrac{m_i N_G}{P_d}$	(3.31)

TABLE 3.26 Tooth Proportions and Diameter Constants for Face Gears, 20° Pressure Angle

No. of pinion teeth	Pinion addendum	Pinion tooth thickness	Gear addendum	Gear diameter constants							
				Ratio = 1.5		Ratio = 2		Ratio = 4		Ratio = 8	
z_1 (N_P)	h_{a1} (a_P)	s_1 (t_P)	h_{a2} (a_G)	ε_o (m_o)	ε_i (m_i)	ε_o (m_o)	ε_i (m_i)	ε_o (m_o)	ε_i (m_i)	ε_o (m_o)	ε_i (m_i)
12	1.120	1.790	0.700	...	...	1.221	1.020	1.221	0.960	1.221	0.945
13	1.100	1.745	0.760	1.202	1.064	1.202	1.015	1.202	0.959	1.202	0.945
14	1.080	1.700	0.820	1.187	1.062	1.187	1.011	1.187	0.958	1.187	0.944
15	1.060	1.660	0.880	1.174	1.052	1.174	1.007	1.174	0.957	1.174	0.944
16	1.040	1.620	0.940	1.161	1.051	1.161	1.004	1.161	0.956	1.161	0.944
17	1.020	1.580	0.980	1.156	1.041	1.156	1.000	1.156	0.955	1.156	0.944
18	1.000	1.570	1.000	1.150	1.039	1.150	0.997	1.150	0.954	1.150	0.943
	1.250	1.752	0.750	1.176	1.042	1.176	0.999	1.176	0.955	1.176	0.943
20	1.000	1.570	1.000	1.144	1.030	1.144	0.991	1.144	0.953	1.144	0.943
	1.250	1.752	0.750	1.166	1.032	1.166	0.993	1.166	0.953	1.166	0.943
22	1.000	1.570	1.000	1.140	1.022	1.140	0.987	1.140	0.952	1.140	0.943
	1.200	1.715	0.800	1.156	1.024	1.156	0.988	1.156	0.952	1.156	0.943
24	1.000	1.570	1.000	1.133	1.015	1.133	0.983	1.133	0.951	1.133	0.942
	1.200	1.715	0.800	1.150	1.017	1.150	0.984	1.150	0.951	1.150	0.943
30	1.000	1.570	1.000	1.121	1.001	1.121	0.975	1.121	0.949	1.121	0.942
	1.150	1.680	0.850	1.131	1.001	1.131	0.975	1.131	0.949	1.131	0.942
40	1.000	1.570	1.000	1.109	0.986	1.109	0.966	1.109	0.946	1.109	0.941
	1.100	1.640	0.900	1.113	0.986	1.113	0.966	1.113	0.946	1.113	0.941

Notes: For metric design, the dimensions are in millimeters and are for 1 module.
For English design, the dimensions are in inches and are for 1 diametral pitch.

In Eqs. (3.30) and (3.31), z_2 and N_G are the number of face-gear teeth. The constants m_o and m_i may be read from Table 3.26.

The maximum usable face width of the gear is

Metric	English	
$b_2 = \dfrac{d_{a2} - d_{i2}}{2}$	$F_G = \dfrac{D_o - D_i}{2}$	(3.32)

The face width of the pinion is usually made a little greater than that of the gear to allow for error in axial positioning of the pinion.

The face gear is cut with a pinion-shaped cutter that has either the same number of teeth as the pinion or just slightly more. If the cutter has slightly more teeth, the gear tooth will be "crowned" slightly, and contact will be heavy in the center of the face width, with little or no contact at the ends of the teeth. The face gear is never cut with a cutter that has a smaller number of teeth than the pinion. If it were, contact would be heavy at the ends and hollow in the center—a very unsatisfactory condition.

When the pinion of a face gearset has less than 17 teeth, it is necessary to reduce the cutter outside diameter to keep the top land of the cutter from becoming too narrow. If the land is too narrow, the cutter will wear too fast at the tip. It should be noted that the combinations shown in Table 3.26 have a working depth of less than 2.000 when the pinion has less than 17 teeth. Also, the pinion tooth thickness is increased more than might be expected for the amount of long addendum. These things are done to make it possible to design cutters for the gear with a reasonable top land.

The whole depth of the face gear is

$$h = h_{a1} + h_{a2} + c \qquad \text{metric} \quad (3.33a)$$

$$h_t = a_P + a_G + c \qquad \text{English} \quad (3.33b)$$

where c is the clearance. A reasonable value for gear clearance is $0.25m_t$ (or $0.25/P_d$).

The pinion may be made to the same whole depth as that given in Table 3.6, or the depth may be adjusted to agree with the gear. The choice usually depends on what tools are on hand to cut the pinion.

The face-gear-tooth thickness can be obtained by subtracting the pinion thickness plus backlash from the circular pitch. Since the gear tooth is tapered, this value does not mean much. The size of face-gear teeth is usually controlled by measuring backlash when the face gear is assembled in a test fixture with a master pinion.

The profile of the face gear cannot be measured in presently available checking machines. The shape of the tooth can be checked only by contacting the tooth with the tooth of a mating pinion. The shape of the pinion tooth *can* be checked in an involute machine. In figuring the roll angle of the pinion at the form diameter, Table 3.11 does not apply. Instead, the roll angle at the limit diameter is

$$\theta_{r\ell} = \theta_{r1} - \frac{360h_{a2}}{\pi d_{p1} \sin \alpha_t \cos \alpha_t} \quad \text{degrees} \qquad \text{metric} \quad (3.34a)$$

$$\varepsilon_{r\ell} = \varepsilon_{rP} - \frac{360a_G}{\pi d \sin \phi_t \cos \phi_t} \quad \text{degrees} \qquad \text{English} \quad (3.34b)$$

After the pinion roll angle of the limit diameter is obtained, the pinion form diameter and roll angle of the form diameter may be obtained in the usual manner.

The top and bottom of the face-gear tooth are defined by *axial* dimensions. The addendum and whole-depth dimensions of the gear are used in figuring these axial dimensions.

3.20 Crossed-Helical-Gear Proportions

The elements of a crossed-helical gear are the same as those of a parallel-helical gear. The biggest difference in the calculations is that the crossed-helical gears meshing together may not have the same pitch, the same pressure angle, or the same helix angle. The only dimensions that are necessarily the same for both members are those in the *normal section.* By comparison, a mating parallel-helical gear and pinion have the same dimensions in both the transverse and normal planes.

Most designers favor making crossed-helical gears with deeper teeth and lower pressure angles than parallel-helical gears. This is done to get a contact ratio equal to or greater than 2. Since the crossed-helical gear has only point contact instead of contact across a face width, its load-carrying capacity and its smoothness of running are much improved by having a design which gives a contact ratio of 2 or better. When the ratio is this high, there will be either two or three pair of teeth in contact at every instant of time as the teeth roll through mesh. If the contact ratio were less than 2, there would be one interval of time when only a single pair of teeth was carrying the load.

There is no trade standard for crossed-helical-gear-tooth proportions. Many manufacturers use crossed-helical gears only occasionally. To save tool cost, they frequently design and cut crossed-helical gears with the same hobs or other tools used for parallel-helical gears. This practice will usually give a workable design, but it will not give the load-carrying capacity and smoothness of running that can be obtained with tooth proportions designed for crossed-helical gears.

Table 3.27 shows a recommended set of proportions for the design of crossed-helical gears. These proportions have been used with good results in many high-speed applications.

Figure 3.22 (see page 3.57) shows an example of crossed-helical gears in a small mechanism. Since the crossed-helical gear is not critical on center-distance accuracy or on axial position, it is very handy to use when the power is low and costs are critical.

The proportions shown in Table 3.27 will give a contact ratio greater than 2 for all combinations of teeth where undercut is not present. The minimum number of *driven* teeth needed to avoid undercut is 20. This same number holds for all four combinations shown in the table.

The minimum number of *driver* teeth needed to avoid undercut is

Helix angle of driver	Minimum number of teeth
45°	20
60°	9
75°	4
86°	1

One of the first two combinations shown in Table 3.27 should be used when both members are to be either shaved or hobbed. Both these operations are difficult to perform when the helix angle is above 60°. When very high ratios are needed or there is need for a large-diameter driver, the last two combinations become attractive.

TABLE 3.27 Tooth Proportions for Crossed-Helical Gears

Normal module $m_n = 1$

Normal circular pitch $p_n = 3.14159$ mm

(Normal diametral pitch $P_{nd} = 1$
Normal circular pitch $p_n = 3.14159$ in.)

Helix Angle		Normal pressure angle	Addendum	Working depth	Whole depth
Driver β_1 (ψ_1)	Driven β_2 (ψ_2)	α_n (ϕ_n)	h_a (a)	h' (h_k)	h (h_t)
45°	45°	14°30′	1.200	2.400	2.650
60°	30°	17°30′	1.200	2.400	2.650
75°	15°	19°30′	1.200	2.400	2.650
86°	4°	20°	1.200	2.400	2.650

Note: The addendum, working depth, and whole depth values are for 1 normal module (metric) in millimeters or for 1 normal diametral pitch (English) in inches.

The whole depth shown does not allow a very large root fillet radius. In crossed-helical gears, root stresses are not high, and so a full fillet radius is not needed. Long and short addendum is sometimes used in crossed-helical gear design, but there is not much need for it. Since the strength of the teeth is not a problem in most cases, there is no need to juggle addendums either

TABLE 3.28 Crossed-Helical-Gear Dimensions

Item	Reference	Metric		English	
1. Center distance	$[(9)_{\text{driver}} + (9)_{\text{driven}}] \div 2$	100.725		3.9655	
2. Normal circular pitch	Design choice (Note 4)	7.853982		0.309212	
3. Normal pressure angle	Table 3.27	17.50		17.50	
4. Working depth	Table 3.27	6.00		0.236	
5. Module, normal	(2) ÷ 3.14159265	2.500		—	
6. Normal diametral pitch	3.14159265 ÷ (2)	—		10.160	
		Driver	Driven	Driver	Driven
7. Number of teeth	Sec. 3.20	12	49	12	49
8. Helix angle	Eqs. (1.23), (1.28)	60° RH	30° RH	60° RH	30° RH
9. Pitch diameter	$(7) \times (2) \div [\pi \times \cos (8)]$	60.00	141.451	2.3622	5.5689
10. Addendum	Table 3.27	3.00	3.00	0.118	0.118
11. Whole depth	Table 3.27	6.63	6.63	0.261	0.261
12. Outside diameter	(9) + 2.0 × (10)	66.00	147.45	2.598	5.805
13. Root diameter	(12) − 2.0 × (11)	52.74	134.19	2.076	5.283
14. Normal tooth thickness	Sec. 3.6	3.88	3.88	0.1525	0.1525
15. Chordal tooth thickness	Eq. (3.5)	3.88	3.88	0.1525	0.1525
16. Chordal addendum	Eq. (3.4)	3.02	3.02	0.1188	0.1188
17. Face width	Sec. 3.20	27	19	$1\frac{1}{16}$	$\frac{3}{4}$
18. Lead	(2) × (7) ÷ sin (8)	108.828	769.690	4.2846	30.3028
19. Base circle diameter	See Note 2	48.508	130.4024	1.9098	5.1339
20. Accuracy	Sec. 5.18	See Note 5			

Notes:

1. Metric dimensions are in millimeters, English dimensions are in inches, and angles are in degrees.
2. Base circle diameter = cos (transverse pressure angle) × (9), and tan (transverse pressure angle) = tan (3) ÷ cos (8)
3. The shaft angle is assumed to be 90° for this table, and the helix angles are assumed to be of the same hand for both members of the set.
4. Table 13-10 of the *Gear Handbook* provides information for the sizing of crossed-helical gears. After a preliminary size is chosen, a rating estimate for the set may be made with the help of Sec. 3.30 in this chapter.
5. After the designer has done the load rating and studied Sec. 5.18, accuracy needs may be satisfied by an ISO or AGMA quality level, or the designer may need to write a special recipe for accuracy limits.

to balance strength between two members or to avoid undercut and permit the use of a smaller number of driver teeth and a resultant coarser pitch.

Table 3.28 shows a dimension sheet and a sample problem for calculating crossed-helical gears. It is based on a 90° shaft angle, and helix angles of like hand for each member.

The exact face width needed on crossed-helical gears depends on how far the point of contact moves as the teeth roll through mesh. When the set is new, the arc of action will be a little longer than two normal circular pitches. After the set has worn in, there will be meshing action over about three or slightly more normal circular pitches.

Table 3.28 shows the pinion face width to be equivalent to a *projection* of three normal circular pitches plus an increment. The added increment keeps contact away from the ends of the tooth and allows for error in axial positioning and variation in the amount of wear. For 2.5 normal module (10 pitch), this increment should be at least 6.3 mm (1/4 in.). For 5 module ($5P_{nd}$), this increment should be at least 9.5 mm (3/8 in.).

3.21 Single-Enveloping-Worm-Gear Proportions

Like crossed-helical gearing, worm gearing seldom has two mating members with the same module (diametral pitch). The *axial* pitch of the worm equals the *circular* pitch of the gear. Also, both members have the *same* normal circular pitch.

In the past, it has been quite common practice to make the tooth proportions a function of the circular pitch (or axial pitch). An addendum of $1m_n$ ($1/P_{nd}$)—which is standard in many kinds of gears—is equivalent to $0.3183p_n$, where p_n is the normal circular pitch in either millimeters or inches.

With low lead angles and only one or two worm threads, it has been quite customary to use an addendum of $0.3183p$, a working depth of $0.6366p$, and a whole depth equal to the working depth plus $0.050p$.

With multiple threads and high lead angles, it is necessary to use quite high pressure angles. It is necessary to shorten the addendum and working depth to avoid getting sharp-pointed teeth and to keep out of undercut trouble. If the tooth proportions are based on the circular pitch of the gear, a high lead angle like 45° may require that the addendum and working depth be cut back to about 70 percent of the values mentioned above. However, if the tooth proportions are based on the normal circular pitch, the addendum will stay in about the right proportion to the lead angle. For instance, $0.3183p_n$ at a 45° lead angle is equal to $0.2250p$.

In the fine-pitch field, AGMA standard 374.04 covers fine-pitch worm

TABLE 3.29 Tooth Proportions for Single-Enveloping Worm Gears

	No. worm threads z_1 (N_w)	Cutter pressure angle α_0 (ϕ_c)	Addendum h_a (a)	Working depth h' (h_k)	Whole depth h (h_t)
Index or holding mechanism	1 or 2	14°30′	$0.3183p_n$	$0.6366p_n$	$0.700p_n$
Power gearing	1 or 2	20°	$0.3183p_n$	$0.6366p_n$	$0.700p_n$
	3 or more	25°	$0.286p_n$	$0.572p_n$	$0.635p_n$
Fine-pitch (instrument)	1–10	20°	$0.3183p_n$	$0.6366p_n$	$0.7003p_n + 0.05$*

*0.05 is for metric system. Add 0.002 in. for English system.

Note: The addendum, working depth, and whole depth values are for 1 normal module (metric) in millimeters or for 1 normal diametral pitch (English) in inches.

gearing in considerable detail. This standard bases the proportions of fine-pitch worm gears on the normal circular pitch. There are no generally accepted trade standards for the proportions of medium-pitch worm gears. From a practical standpoint, it is best to base the proportions of all sizes of worm gears on the normal circular pitch.

Table 3.29 shows recommended proportions for three general kinds of applications. The fine-pitch design is the same as that given in AGMA 374.04. The design for index and holding mechanisms represents average shop practice.

3.22 Single-Enveloping Worm Gears

Low-lead-angle worm gearsets are frequently self-locking. This means that the worm cannot be driven by the gear. The set will "hold" when the worm has no power applied to it.

The exact lead angle at which a worm will be self-locking depends on variables like the surface finish, the kind of lubrication, and the amount of vibration where the drive is installed. Generally speaking, though, self-locking occurs if the lead angle is below 6°, and it may occur with as much as 10° lead angle.

The pressure angle of the tool shown in Table 3.29 is the pressure angle of a straight-sided conical milling or grinding wheel used to finish the worm threads. The normal pressure angle of the worm is a small amount less than this value. The equation for the normal pressure angle is

Metric	English	
$\alpha_n = \alpha_0 - \Delta\alpha$	$\phi_n = \phi_c - \Delta\phi$	(3.35)

where

$$\Delta\alpha = \frac{90 d_{p1} \sin^3 \gamma}{z_1 (d_{p0} \cos^2 \gamma + d_{p1})} \qquad \Delta\phi = \frac{90 d \sin^3 \lambda}{N_W (d_c \cos^2 \lambda + d)} \tag{3.36}$$

The angle $\Delta\alpha$ ($\Delta\phi$) is in degrees, the lead angle is γ (λ), the worm pitch diameter is d_{p1} (d), and the cutter pitch diameter is d_{p0} (d_c).

Table 3.29 allows more clearance than the old figure of $0.050p$. This is in line with the practice of putting more generous tip radii on tools.

The pitch diameter of the worm usually represents a compromise among several considerations. If the worm is small compared with the gear, the lead angle will be high and efficiency will be good. However, the face width of the gear will be small, and there may be trouble getting the bearings close enough together to prevent bending of the small worm. A large worm compared with the gear gives lower efficiency, but it may be possible to use a large enough bore in the worm to permit keying it on its shaft instead of making it integral with the shaft.

An approximate value for the worm mean pitch diameter is

$$d_{p1} = \frac{a^{0.875}}{2.2} \qquad \text{metric} \tag{3.37a}$$

$$d = \frac{C^{0.875}}{2.2} \qquad \text{English} \tag{3.37b}$$

It is believed that this value gives a good practical size for the worm, considering all the factors mentioned. Of course, if the designer is not primarily interested in the efficient transmission of power, it is possible to depart widely from Eq. (3.37) and still get satisfactory operation. The worm pitch diameter may range from $a^{0.875}/1.7$ to $a^{0.875}/3$ ($C^{0.875}/1.7$ to $C^{0.875}/3$) without substantial effect on the power capacity.

If the worm addendum equals the gear addendum, the mean worm diameter is actually the pitch diameter.

In the fine-pitch field, the efficiency and power-transmitting ability of a given size set are usually not too important. For this reason, no particular effort has been made to proportion the worm pitch diameter to an equation like (3.37). AGMA standard 374.04 lists a series of standard axial pitches and a series of standard lead angles. Indirectly, this results in a series of standard pitch diameters. The axial pitches range from 0.75 to 4.0 mm (0.03 to 0.16 in.), and the lead angles range from 30′ to 30°. A considerable amount of tabulated data is given in the standard for each of the combinations shown.

The lead angle of the worm is equal to the helix angle of the worm gear when the shaft angle is 90°. The lead angle may be calculated from any of the following relations:

$$\tan \gamma = \frac{d_{p2}}{d_{p1}u} \qquad \text{metric} \qquad (3.38a)$$

$$\tan \gamma = \frac{p_x z_1}{\pi d_{p1}} \quad \text{or} \quad \sin \gamma = \frac{p_n z_1}{\pi d_{p1}} \qquad \text{metric} \qquad (3.38b)$$

$$\tan \lambda = \frac{D}{dm_G} \qquad \text{English} \qquad (3.38c)$$

$$\tan \lambda = \frac{p_x N_W}{\pi d} \quad \text{or} \quad \sin \lambda = \frac{p_n N_W}{\pi d} \qquad \text{English} \qquad (3.38d)$$

In the Eqs. (3.38), p_x is the axial pitch and u (m_G) is the number of gear teeth divided by the number of worm threads.

In the opinion of the author, it is wise to not use more than 6° *lead angle per thread.* For instance, if the lead angle is 30°, there should be at least five threads on the worm. If too few threads are used, the problem of designing tools and producing accurate curvatures on the worm threads and on the gear teeth becomes too critical for good manufacturing practice.

In general, the number of teeth on the gear should not be less than 29. As an exception, the number can be reduced to 20 when the cutter pressure angle is 25° and the lead angle does not exceed 15°. The number of teeth on the gear and the number of threads on the worm should be picked to get a *hunting ratio.* This is particularly important in worm gearing, because the hob for generating the gear should have the same number of threads as the worm.

Different designers use several different means to get the worm-gear face width and the worm-gear outside diameter. A simple method which is always safe and which will utilize practically all the worm-gear tooth that is worth using is to make the face width equal to (or just slightly greater than) the length of a tangent to the worm pitch circle between the points at which it is intersected by the worm outside circle. The worm-gear maximum diameter is made just large enough to have about 60 percent of the face width *throated.* This design is shown as design *A* in Fig. 3.23. Design *B* shows an alternative that has been widely used for power gearing. Design *C* shows a nonthroated design which may be used for instrument or other applications in which maximum power transmission is not an important design consideration.

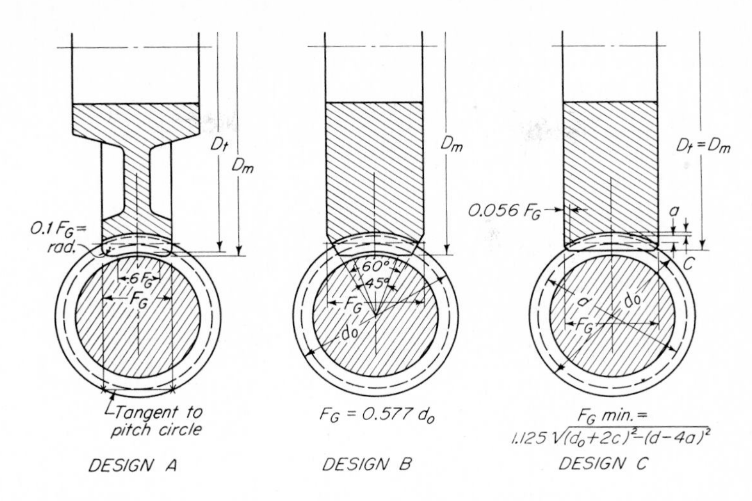

FIG. 3.23 Worm-gear design examples. (Dimensions shown have English system symbols.)

The profile of the worm will have a slight convex curvature when it is produced by a straight-sided milling cutter or grinding wheel. Section 6.4 shows how to calculate the normal-section curvature of the worm.

In worm gearing, it has been customary to obtain backlash by thinning the worm threads only. The worm-gear teeth are given a design thickness equal to half the normal circular pitch (when equal addendums are used for the worm and the worm gear). Generally speaking, worm gears require more backlash than do spur or helical gears. Quite often a steel worm and a bronze gear are housed in a cast-iron casing. The temperature of the set may change quite considerably during operation because of the high sliding velocity of the worm threads. Differential expansions can easily cause an appreciable change in backlash. Except for slow-speed control gears, the design should provide enough backlash to keep the gears from binding at any speed or temperature condition under which the set may have to operate.

Table 3.30 shows a dimension sheet for single-enveloping worm gears and the solution of a sample problem.

3.23 Double-Enveloping Worm Gears

Although several types of double-enveloping worm gears are mentioned in gear literature, one type is at present much more widely used in industry than any other type. This is the Cone-Drive gear, produced by Cone Drive Operations, a division of Ex-Cell-O Corporation. The material in this sec-

TABLE 3.30 Single-Enveloping-Worm-Gear Dimensions

Item	Reference	Metric		English	
1. Center distance	Sec. 2.12	249.565		9.82537	
2. Axial pitch of worm	$\pi \times (10)_G \div (9)_G$	25.00		0.98425	
3. Cutter pressure angle	Table 3.29	25°		25°	
4. Worm lead angle	Eq. (3.38)	25°		25°	
5. Working depth	Table 3.29	14.42		0.568	
6. Module, transverse	(2) ÷ 3.141593	7.95775		—	
7. Diametral pitch, transverse	3.141593 ÷ (2)	—		3.191858	
8. Normal circular pitch	(2) × cos (4)	22.6577		0.892035	
		Worm	Gear	Worm	Gear
9. Number of teeth	Sec. 3.22	5	52	5	52
10. Pitch diameter	Sec. 3.22	85.327	413.803	3.3593	16.2914
11. Addendum	Table 3.29	7.21	7.21	0.284	0.284
12. Whole depth	Table 3.29	15.86	15.86	0.625	0.625
13. Outside diameter	(10) + 2.0 × (11)	99.75	428.22	3.927	16.859
14. Maximum outside diameter, gear	Sec. 3.22	—	435.35	—	17.140
15. Root diameter	(13) − 2.0 × (12)	68.03	396.50	2.677	15.609
16. Normal tooth thickness	Sec. 3.22	10.88	11.32	0.428	0.446
17. Chordal addendum	Eq. (3.4)	7.27	7.27	0.2865	0.2865
18. Face width	Sec. 3.22	115.0	54.20	4.52	2.13
19. Pressure angle change	Eq. (3.36)	0.5559	—	0.5559	—
20. Normal pressure angle	Eq. (3.35)	24.4441	—	24.4441	—
21. Tool to produce the worm. Straight-sided milling cutter. 150 mm (5.905 in.) diameter.					
22. Accuracy		See Note 3			

Notes:
1. The helix angle of the worm gear is the same as the lead angle of the worm when the shaft angle is 90°.
2. If the worm is to be hardened and ground, then the tool definition in (21) should state the diameter of the grinding wheel and the form of grinding wheel.
3. There are some individual company standards for the accuracy of worm gearing, but there are no generally recognized trade standards at this time (1983).
4. Metric data is in millimeters, English data is in inches, and all angles are in degrees.

tion is based on the Cone-Drive design of double-enveloping worm gear. Other types of double-enveloping worm gears are in use, but the Cone-Drive type is produced in such large quantities in the United States that it seems most appropriate to cover this type only in this book.

Table 3.31 shows the proportions recommended by Cone Drive for double-enveloping worm gears.

The pitch diameter of the worm should be approximately $a^{0.875}/2.2$ ($C^{0.875}/2.2$). This is the same value as that given by Eq. (3.37). The worm

TABLE 3.31 Tooth Proportions for Double-Enveloping Worm Gears

Normal pressure angle α_n (ϕ_n)	Addendum h_a (a)	Working depth h' (h_k)	Whole depth h (h_t)
20°	$0.225p_n$	$0.450p_n$	$0.500p_n$

root diameter is

$$d_{f1} = d_{p1} + 2h_{a1} - 2h_1 \qquad \text{metric} \quad (3.39a)$$

$$d_R = d + 2a_P - 2h_{tP} \qquad \text{English} \quad (3.39b)$$

If this value comes out less than $a^{0.875}/3$ ($C^{0.875}/3$), the worm pitch diameter should be increased so that the root diameter is not less than this value.

In picking numbers of threads, the designer should not have more than about 6° *per thread* lead angle for sets of 125 mm (5 in.) or less center distance.

The number of gear teeth should be picked so as to give a hunting ratio if possible. This is not quite so important as with single-enveloping worm gears. It is further recommended that the relation of the number of gear teeth to the center distance be as follows:

Center distance		
mm	in.	Number of gear teeth
50	2	24–40
150	6	30–50
300	12	40–60
600	24	60–80

The axial pressure angle of any kind of worm is determined by the relation

$$\tan \alpha_x = \frac{\tan \alpha_n}{\cos \gamma} \qquad \text{metric} \quad (3.40a)$$

$$\tan \phi_x = \frac{\tan \phi_n}{\cos \lambda} \qquad \text{English} \quad (3.40b)$$

For double-enveloping worm gears, the lead angle which is used is at the *center* of the worm.

The base-circle diameter of the double-enveloping worm gear can be determined by layout, or it can be calculated by

$$d_{b2} = d_{p2} \sin (\alpha_x + \Delta\alpha) \qquad \text{metric} \quad (3.41a)$$

$$D_b = D \sin (\phi_x + \beta) \qquad \text{English} \quad (3.41b)$$

where $\sin \Delta\alpha = p_x/2d_{p2}$ (metric) or $\sin \beta = p_x/2D$ (English).

The active part of the worm face width should almost equal the base-circle diameter. Usually the face width of the worm is made a little shorter. Thus

$$b_1 = d_{b2} - 0.03a \qquad \text{metric} \quad (3.42a)$$

$$F_w = D_b - 0.03C \qquad \text{English} \quad (3.42b)$$

TABLE 3.32 Double-Enveloping-Worm-Gear Dimensions

Item	Reference	Metric		English	
1. Center distance	Sec. 2.12	253.558		9.9826	
2. Axial pitch of worm*	$\pi \times (10)_G \div (9)_G$	25.40		1.000	
3. Normal pressure angle	Table 3.31	20		20	
4. Worm lead angle*	Eq. (3.38)	25		25	
5. Working depth	Table 3.31	10.36		0.406	
6. Module, transverse	$(2) \div \pi$	8.0851		—	
7. Diametral pitch, transverse	$\pi \div (2)$	—		3.141593	
8. Normal circular pitch	$(2) \times \cos (4)$	23.020		0.906308	
		Worm	Gear	Worm	Gear
9. Number of teeth	Sec. 3.23	5	52	5	52
10. Pitch diameter	Sec. 3.23	86.69	420.42	3.413	16.552
11. Addendum	Table 3.31	5.18	5.18	0.203	0.203
12. Whole depth	Table 3.31	11.51	11.51	0.453	0.453
13. Outside diameter	From layout	115.57	445.64	4.550	17.545
14. Throat diameter	$(10) + 2 \times (11)$	97.05	430.78	3.819	16.958
15. Root diameter	Eq. (3.39)	74.03	—	2.913	—
16. Normal tooth thickness	Sec. 3.23	8.99	13.82	0.354	0.544
17. Axial pressure angle	Eq. (3.40)	21.88020	—	21.88020	—
18. Base circle diameter	Eq. (3.41)	—	168.39	—	6.63
19. Face width	Sec. 3.23	160.3	66.7	$6\frac{5}{16}$	$2\frac{5}{8}$
20. Face angle	From layout	45	$87\frac{1}{2}$	45	$87\frac{1}{2}$
21. Accuracy	See Note 3				

*At the center of the worm.

Notes:
1. The helix angle of the worm gear is the same as the lead angle of the worm when the shaft angle is 90°.
2. Metric data are in millimeters, English data are in inches, and all angles are in degrees.
3. There are no trade standards for accuracy of double-enveloping worm gears. Cone Drive can be consulted for appropriate accuracy limits.

In general, the face width of the gear is made slightly less than the root diameter of the worm.

The thicknesses of worm threads and gear teeth are controlled by side-feeding operations. It is customary to make the worm thread equal to 45 percent of the axial circular pitch and the gear tooth equal to 55 percent of the normal circular pitch, provided that the tool design will permit and gear strength is critical. Backlash is subtracted from the worm thread thickness. For average applications, the following amounts of backlash are reasonable:

Center distance		Backlash	
mm	in.	mm	in.
50	2	0.08–0.20	0.003–0.008
150	6	0.15–0.30	0.006–0.012
300	12	0.30–0.50	0.012–0.020
600	24	0.45–0.75	0.018–0.030

Table 3.32 is a dimension sheet for calculating double-enveloping worm gears. The solution of a sample problem is shown on the dimension sheet.

GEAR-RATING PRACTICE

After the gear-tooth data have been calculated, it is necessary to calculate the capacity of the gearset. Since the design was started from an estimate (see Chap. 2), it may be that the first design which is worked out in detail is too small or too large.

Once all the gear-tooth data have been calculated, it is possible to use design formulas to determine a *rated* capacity of the gearset. This rated capacity should be larger than the *actual* load which will be applied to the gearset.

In some fields of gearing, there are well-established trade standards in regard to the rating of gearsets. Sometimes these are quite conservative. In a few unusual cases, a trade standard may rate a gearset as able to carry more load than it really will carry. It must be recognized that a trade standard is based on the general level of quality that representative members of the industry can produce. This *quality* includes the accuracy of the gear teeth, the accuracy with which the gears are positioned in their casings, and the quality of the materials from which the gears are made. Manufacturers who cannot live up to the *normal* level of quality for a particular kind of gears cannot expect their gears to safely carry the full ratings allowed by a trade standard. Likewise, manufacturers who can build gearing of appreciably better quality than the general level of the trade might expect that their gears would be able to carry somewhat more load than that allowed by a trade standard.

As a general rule, in checking gear capacity, it is wise to first check the design using general formulas for tooth strength and durability. Then, if the application falls into the field of a particular trade standard, it should be checked against the trade standard. If the design meets both tests, it is probably all right. In this part of the chapter, we shall consider both general formulas and trade standards for rating gears.

3.24 General Considerations in Rating Calculations

Gear designers make rating calculations to establish that a given gear design is suitable in size and in quality to meet the specified requirements of a gear application. (The buyer of a gear unit or the user of a gear unit may also make rating calculations to check the design being bought or used.)

Rating calculations are concerned with more than direct load-carrying capacity. All three of these somewhat different concerns tend to apply:

1 Has the rating been calculated correctly with a *good* formula, and have all the *right* assumptions and decisions been made in regard to materials, material quality, and geometric quality?

2 Does the design calculate a suitable rated power, length of life, and degree of reliability to satisfy a *specified formula* in the business contract or one established and *recognized* in normal trade practice? For instance, AGMA formulas cover many gear applications. There is a legal obligation in many projects, both in the United States and worldwide,* to meet all applicable AGMA standards.

3 Will the gear unit meet its *normal rating capacity* in the power package using the gears? In a power system there are often situations in which gears are prematurely damaged by undefined overloads, misalignments, unexpected temperature excursions, or contamination of the lubricant by some foreign material (water, ash, chemical vapors at the site, etc.).

The designer needs to rate the gears to meet the application. In a new application with unknown hazards, an appropriate gear rating may not be possible until several prototype units have been in service for a substantial period of time. A reliable gear rating may not be practical until

*In an international project, the gears might be built in Europe and installed in South America. If the project was insured or financed by U.S. interests, there would probably be a contract requirement that the gears meet AGMA standards, even though they were not built in the United States.

enough development work has been done and enough field experience acquired to prove out a gear design suitable for the hazards of the application. (See Chap. 7 for a discussion of things that may be problems in power packages.)

Somewhat aside from the mechanics of making gear-rating calculations and the concerns of contract requirements and application hazards is the fact that there is a shortage of good technical data and specifications to closely control all the things that go into a rating.

In earlier times, the mechanical designer tried to calculate a *safe* stress. It was thought that all parts with less than the safe stress limit would perform without failure. Gears, bearings, and many other mechanical components have a *probability* of failure. A safe stress is in reality only a stress at which the probability of failure is low.

Theoretical gear design has now shifted to using stress values based primarily on some level of probability of failure. Unfortunately, the data available to set probability of failure are still rather limited. This problem is compounded by the fact that a system of probability of failure versus stress needs to be tied into a system of material quality grades.

Material quality grades are still not very clearly defined. AGMA established *two grades* of quality for aircraft gears in the 1960s. In the 1970s, two grades were established for vehicle gears. As this is being written, work is under way to establish grades for high-speed gearing used with marine and land turbine units.

Generally speaking, there is about a 20 to 25 percent change in load-carrying capacity as you go from Grade 1 to Grade 2 material. In a fully developed gear grading system, there should probably be more than two grades of material (at least three), and the material specifications of each grade should be more closely defined than is now the case. The designer who is going to shift a rating up or down 20 percent for material grade certainly needs some rather clear-cut definitions of what must be achieved to qualify the material for its designated grade. (See Sec. 4.10 for detailed information on material quality.)

In earlier times, failure by tooth breakage meant a broken tooth, and failure by pitting meant a substantial number of "destructive" pits. Recent work shows that both of these criteria of failure are inadequate. An aircraft gear with some small cracks in the root found at overhaul has usually "failed." It is not safe to use the part if the cracks are above a certain size in a critical location, so the gear is scrapped—even if it *might* run another 1000 hours.

At the other extreme, an industrial gear may have a whole layer of material pitted away from the lower flank and still be able to run for several more years. In this case, failure by pitting only comes when so much metal has worn away and load sharing between teeth has become so bad that the teeth break.

A further design complication comes from the fact that gear teeth may work-harden in service and may polish up rough tooth surfaces. The designer used to design gears based on the hardness of the part and the finish and fit of the part when it left the gear shop. Now the final finishing of the gear teeth and the final metallurgical character of the tooth surface are often established in service.

The data on how to allow for improvements in finish and fit and for work hardening is still rather limited. Recent technical papers* have shown quantitative data that indicate that a 2 to 1 improvement in finish and a change in hardness of 100 points Vickers or 100 BHN are not uncommon in lower-hardness gears running at medium to low pitch-line velocities.

Calculation Procedure. The calculation begins with a requirement that a gearset must handle a specified power at a given input speed. In a simple rating calculation, the preliminary sizing of the unit has established these things:

Power to be transmitted, in kilowatts (kW) or horsepower (hp)

Rotational speed of pinion

Number of pinion teeth and number of gear teeth

Face width

Pitch diameters of pinion and gear

Pressure angle (normal pressure angle for helical gears)

Size of teeth by module or diametral pitch

Helix angle

Hours of life needed at rated load

The first calculation step is to get the *tangential driving load*. The pinion torque is calculated first, then the torque is converted to a tangential force acting at the pitch diameter.

The torque is

$$\text{Pinion torque} = \frac{\text{power} \times \text{constant}}{\text{pinion rpm}}$$

$$T_1 = \frac{P \times 9549.3}{n_1} \qquad \text{metric} \quad (3.43a)$$

*Material presented by P. M. Nityanandan at the June 1982 IFToMM gearing committee meeting in Eindhoven, Holland, was very revealing in regard to the performance of low-hardness gears in India. (IFToMM is the International Federation for the Theory of Machinery and Mechanisms.)

$$T_P = \frac{P \times 63{,}025}{n_P} \qquad \text{English} \quad (3.43b)$$

In the metric equation, the power P is in kilowatts, and the calculated torque will be in newton-meters (N · m). For the English equation, the power is in horsepower, and the answer will be in inch-pounds (in.-lb).

The tangential driving force is

$$W_t = \frac{T_1 \times 2000}{d_{p1}} \quad \text{N} \qquad \text{metric} \quad (3.44a)$$

$$W_t = \frac{T_P \times 2.0}{d} \quad \text{lb} \qquad \text{English} \quad (3.44b)$$

The geometry factor for strength is usually read from a table or a curve sheet. Section 3.26 gives typical values. The overall derating factor may be read from a table or calculated. Section 3.27 covers overall derating for strength. The geometry factor durability is covered in Sec. 3.28, while overall derating for durability is in Sec. 3.29.

The bending and contact stresses can now be calculated. Before checking whether or not these stresses are permissible, the designer must make some further determinations. The life cycles required for the pinion and for the gear need to be known, and an estimate of which quality grade of material will be used needs to be made. Also, the level of *reliability* needed for the application should be determined.

The loading cycles are

$$n_{c1} = \text{pinion rpm} \times \text{hours life} \times 60 \times \text{no. contacts} \qquad (3.45)$$

$$n_{c2} = \text{gear rpm} \times \text{hours life} \times 60 \times \text{no. contacts} \qquad (3.46)$$

In the above equations, a pinion driving three gears would have three contacts per revolution. Likewise, if five planet pinions drive a single gear, there would be five contacts per revolution of the gear. This kind of situation is common in epicyclic gears. A single pinion driving a single gear has one contact per revolution. (The gear also has one contact for each revolution it makes.)

In general, two quality grades can be considered possible. These are:

Grade 2

The best quality obtainable with an appropriate choice of material composition, and processing that is close to optimum. Usually there is extra cost for the best quality.

Grade 1

A quality of material that is good, but not optimum. This could be considered a typical quality from gear makers doing good industrial work at competitive costs.

For highly critical work in space vehicles, or highly sensitive applications, a Grade 3 quality can be considered. This might be thought of as essentially perfect material made under such rigid controls that there is relatively absolute assurance that the highest possible perfection is obtained. Obviously, the very high cost Grade 3 gears will carry more stress—or will have higher reliability at the same stress—than Grade 2 gears. Grade 3 gear data will not be given in this book. It is too complex and limited in usage.

In regard to reliability, these general concepts should be kept in mind:

Reliability level		
L.1	Fewer than one failure in 1000	Seldom used
L1	Fewer than one failure in 100	Typical gear design
L10	Fewer than one failure in 10	May be used in vehicle gears
L20	Fewer than one failure in 5	Expendable gearing
L50	Fewer than one failure in 2	Highly expendable gearing

The L.1 level has been used in some highly critical aerospace work (particularly space vehicles). L1 is typical of industrial turbine work, helicopter work, and high-grade electric motor gearing. Vehicle gears for land use have tended to be in the L1 to L10 range. Home tools, toys, gadgets, etc., may be in the L20 area, or even up to L50.

If there is a limited amount of laboratory test data, and an *average* curve is drawn through failure points, the curve will be around L50. (It takes much test data and field experience to determine where a stress level that is equivalent to an L1 level of reliability can be located.)

3.25 General Formulas for Tooth Bending Strength and Tooth Surface Durability

The rating formulas for gear-tooth strength and gear surface durability have become very long and difficult to handle in many of the rating standards of the American Gear Manufacturers Association (AGMA), the International Standards Organization (ISO), and other trade groups. In this work, short and simple formulas will be used. In the Appendix, Chap. 9, the complete formulas are given in Sec. 9.9.

The short formulas group all variables into essentially three factors:

An index of load intensity, with dimensions

A geometry factor, dimensionless

A derating factor, dimensionless

The load-intensity evaluation is based on all real numbers that relate the size of the gears to the power being carried by the gears.

The geometry factor evaluates the shape of the tooth. This involves pressure angle, helix angle, depth of tooth, root fillet radius, and proportion of addendum to dedendum.

The derating factor handles all the things that tend to reduce the load-carrying capacity. (Concentrations of too much load at spots on the surfaces of some teeth reduce the average load allowable, since failure can be avoided only when the most overloaded spots are still within safe limits.)

The derating factor handles nonuniform load distribution across the face width and in a circumferential direction. It also handles dynamic overloads due to spacing error and the masses of the pinion and gear meshing together, and other things—quality related—such as surface finish effects, overload effects due to nonsteady power, and variations in metal quality between very large gears and small gears.

Strength Formula. The simplified general formula for tooth bending stress of spur, helical, and bevel* gears is

$$s_t = K_t U_\ell K_d \qquad \begin{matrix} \text{N/mm}^2, & \text{metric} \\ \text{psi}, & \text{English} \end{matrix} \tag{3.47}$$

where

K_t = geometry factor for bending strength

$$= \frac{\text{constant} \times \cos \text{helix angle}}{J \text{ factor}} \qquad \text{(see Sec. 3.26)}$$

U_ℓ = unit load, index for tooth breakage

$$= \frac{W_t}{bm_n} \quad \text{N/mm}^2 \qquad \text{metric} \tag{3.48a}$$

$$= \frac{W_t P_{nd}}{F} \quad \text{psi} \qquad \text{English} \tag{3.48b}$$

K_d = overall derating for bending strength

$$= \frac{K_a K_m K_s}{K_v} \qquad \text{(see Sec. 3.27)} \qquad \text{metric or English}$$

Individual items in the above equations are defined in Table 3.33, along with many other items used in load-rating equations.

Durability Formula. The simplified general formula for tooth-surface

*See the subsection "Rating Bevel Gears" at the end of this section. Also, see Fig. 2.21 for the method of determining the unit load on a bevel gear.

TABLE 3.33 Gear Terms, Symbols, and Units Used in Load Rating of Gears

Term	Metric		English		Reference or formula
	Symbol	Units	Symbol	Units	
Module, transverse	m or m_t	mm	—	—	Metric tooth size
Module, normal	m_n	mm	—	—	$m_n = 25.4 \div P_{nd}$
Diametral pitch, transverse	—	—	P_d or P_t	in.^{-1}	English tooth size
Diametral pitch, normal	—	—	P_{nd}	in.^{-1}	$P_{nd} = 25.4 \div m_n$
Center distance	a	mm	C	in.	Fig. 2.14
Face width	b	mm	F	in.	Fig. 1.18
Face width, effective	b'	mm	F_e	in.	Eq. (3.69)
Pitch diameter	d_p	mm	d	in.	Fig. 2.10
of pinion	d_{p1}	mm	d	in.	Eq. (1.3)
of gear	d_{p2}	mm	D	in.	Eqs. (1.4), (1.13)
of driver (crossed-helical)	d_{p1}	mm	D_1	in.	Eq. (3.64)
of driven (crossed-helical)	d_{p2}	mm	D_2	in.	
Throat diameter, worm	d_{t1}	mm	d_t	in.	Eq. (3.75)
Ratio (tooth)	u	—	m_G	—	No. gear teeth ÷ no. pinion teeth
Pressure angle, normal	α_n	deg	ϕ_n	deg	Eq. (3.64)
Pressure angle, transverse	α_t	deg	ϕ_t	deg	Fig. 1.18
Helix or spiral angle	β	deg	ψ	deg	Fig. 1.19
Lead angle	γ	deg	λ	deg	Fig. 1.19
Rotational speed, pinion or worm	n_1	rpm	n_P or n_W	rpm	Eq. (3.43)
Rotational speed, gear	n_2	rpm	n_G	rpm	Eq. (3.71)
Sliding velocity	v_s	m/s	v_s	fpm, fps	Eqs. (3.68), (3.70), (3.75)
Power	P	kW	P	hp	Eq. (3.43)
Torque	T	N · m	T	in.-lb	Eq. (3.43)
Torque on pinion	T_1	N · m	T_P	in.-lb	Eq. (3.43)
Tangential load or force	W_t	N	W_t	lb	Eqs. (3.44), (3.69)
Dynamic load	W_d	N	W_d	lb	Eq. (3.60)
in normal plane	W_n	N	W_n	lb	Eq. (3.67)
Unit load	U_ℓ	N/mm^2	U_ℓ	psi	Eqs. (3.48), (3.73)
Number of load cycles	n_c	—	n_c	—	
for pinion	n_{c1}	—	n_{cP}	—	Eq. (3.45)
for gear	n_{c2}	—	n_{cG}	—	Eq. (3.46)
Reliability level	L	—	L	—	End of Sec. 3.24
K factor, pitting index	K	N/mm^2	K	psi	Eqs. (3.49), (3.50)
Stress on tooth surface	s	N/mm^2	s	psi	Eq. (3.65)
Bending stress (strength)	s_t	N/mm^2	s_t	psi	Eq. (3.47)
Contact stress (surface)	s_c	N/mm^2	s_c	psi	Eq. (3.49)
Overall derating factor					
for bending strength	K_d	—	K_d	—	Sec. 3.25, Eq. (3.55)
for surface durability	C_d	—	C_d	—	Sec. 3.29, Eq. (3.62)
Geometry factor					
for bending strength	K_t	—	K_t	—	Secs. 3.25, 3.26
for surface durability	C_k	—	C_k	—	Secs. 3.25, 3.28
Application factor					
for bending strength	K_a	—	K_a	—	Sec. 3.27 subsection
for surface durability	C_a	—	C_a	—	Sec. 3.29

TABLE 3.33 Gear Terms, Symbols, and Units Used in Load Rating of Gears (*Continued*)

Term	Metric		English		Reference or formula
	Symbol	Units	Symbol	Units	
Size factor					
for bending strength	K_s	—	K_s	—	Sec. 3.27 subsection
for surface durability	C_s	—	C_s	—	Sec. 3.29 subsection
Dynamic load factor					
for bending strength	K_v	—	K_v	—	Sec. 3.27 subsection, Sec. 3.30
for surface durability	C_v	—	C_v	—	Secs. 3.27, 3.29
Load-distribution factor					
for bending strength	K_m	—	K_m	—	Sec. 3.27 subsections
(face width effects)	K_{mf}	—	K_{mf}	—	Eqs. (3.56), (3.57), (3.58)
(transverse effects)	K_{mt}	—	K_{mt}	—	Eq. (3.56)
for surface durability	C_m	—	C_m	—	Sec. 3.29
(face width effects)	C_{mf}	—	C_{mf}	—	Sec. 3.27 (aspect ratio)
Modulus of elasticity	x_E	N/mm²	E	psi	Eq. (3.65)
Wear-in amount	e_w	mm	e_w	in.	Table 3.39
Mismatch error	e_t	mm	e_t	in.	Eq. (3.57)
Material and type constant	C_p	—	C_p	—	Eq. (3.61)
Wear load	—	—	W_w	lb	Eq. (3.63)
Aspect ratio	m_a	—	m_a	—	Sec. 3.27 subsection
J factor (geometric strength)	J	—	J	—	Alt. to K_t, Sec. 3.26
I factor (geometric pitting)	I	—	I	—	Alt. to C_k, Sec. 3.28
Contact ratio	ε_α	—	m_p	—	Sec. 3.28
Flash temperature index	T_f	°C	T_f	°F	Eq. (3.77)
Gear body temperature	T_b	°C	T_b	°F	Eq. (3.77)
Geometry constant	Z_t	—	Z_t	—	Eq. (3.77)
Surface finish constant	Z_s	—	Z_s	—	Eq. (3.77)
Scoring-criterion number	Z_c	°C*	Z_c	°F*	Eq. (3.77)
Oil-film thickness (EHD)	h_{min}	μm	h_{min}	μin.	Eq. (3.82)
Effective surface finish	S'	μm	S'	μin.	Eq. (3.87)
Lambda ratio	Λ	—	Λ	—	Eq. (3.88)

*Z_c is not a *temperature*, but becomes a *change of temperature* when multiplied by Z_t and Z_s.

Notes: 1. Abbreviations for units are as follows:

Metric system		English system	
mm	millimeters	in.	inches
deg	degrees	deg	degrees
rpm	revolutions per minute	rpm	revolutions per minute
m/s	meters per second	fpm	feet per minute
		fps	feet per second
kW	kilowatts	hp	horsepower
N	newtons	lb	pounds
N · m	newton-meters	in.-lb	inch-pounds
N/mm²	newtons per square millimeter	psi	pounds per square inch
°C	degrees Celsius	°F	degrees Fahrenheit
μm	microns (10^{-6} m)	μin.	microinches (10^{-6} in.)

2. See Table 3.2 for terms, symbols, and units used in the calculation of gear dimensional data.

durability of spur, helical, and bevel* gears give the contact stress:

$$s_c = C_k\,(KC_d)^{0.50} \qquad \begin{matrix} \text{N/mm}^2, & \text{metric} \\ \text{psi}, & \text{English} \end{matrix} \qquad (3.49)$$

where

C_k = geometry factor for durability

$$= \text{constant} \times \left[\frac{1}{I}\,\frac{(\text{ratio}+1)}{\text{ratio}}\right]^{0.50} \qquad \text{(see Sec. 3.28)}$$

K = K factor, index for pitting

$$= \frac{W_t}{bd_{p1}}\left(\frac{u+1}{u}\right) \qquad \text{metric} \qquad (3.50a)$$

$$= \frac{W_t}{Fd}\left(\frac{m_G+1}{m_G}\right) \qquad \text{English} \qquad (3.50b)$$

C_d = overall derating for durability

$$= \frac{C_a C_m C_s}{C_v} \qquad \text{(see Sec. 3.29)} \qquad \text{metric or English}$$

In most long-life power gearing, the size of the gear drive (center distance and face width) is determined by the durability formula. The calculated contact stress must not exceed the allowable stress for the number of cycles of life required and the quality (grade) of material used. The allowed stress is adjusted for the permissible risk of failure (L1, L10, etc.).

The gear-strength calculations are used primarily to determine what size of tooth (module or pitch) is needed to keep the bending stress within allowable limits for the number of cycles of life required, the quality of the material, and the permissible risk of failure.

An exception to this occurs when gears with a very high torque rating are needed for a low number of cycles. (Final drive vehicle gears are often in this situation.)

The gear size may be set primarily by gear-strength considerations. The gears may suffer some degree of surface failure and still run satisfactorily for the needed life. Generally speaking, gear teeth that suffer surface damage in less than 1 million (10^6) cycles of high torque cannot keep on running for more than about 100 million (10^8) cycles, even if the continuous torque is rather light. Turbine gearing, for instance, generally has to run more than a billion (10^9) cycles. Turbine gears cannot have surface damage due to a high torque at low cycles and be expected to last for many years of operation.

Much gear research work is being done in the 1980s to set accurate values for all the variables needed to accurately rate gears. The 1980 ASME paper by Winter and Weiss, for instance, gives a good summary of German work at the Technical University of Munich. Some very good comparisons of pro-

*See the subsection "Rating Bevel Gears" at the end of this section. Also, see Fig. 2.21 for the method of determining the K factor on a bevel gearset.

posed ISO rating formulas and current AGMA standards are given in the 1980 ASME papers by Imwalle, Labath, and Hutchinson of the United States and by Castellani of Italy.

In writing this section on rating formulas and the next five sections on factors in the rating formulas, I have decided to follow this strategy:

- The general formulas and their principal terms will be given in a manner that should remain unchanged for many years.

- Some items that are being changed—and perhaps will continue to change for many years—will be given in numerical values that are conservative for the gearing design practice of the last 20 years (1960 to 1980). The reader will be given practical guidance in what to use in rating gears, but obviously may be able to find better numerical values to use as worldwide gear research and field experience give more information about how to evaluate all of the many things that enter into gear rating.

- This book will endeavor to give the reader a means of determining the approximate size of gears and gear teeth needed to handle a desired rating.* Whenever recognized trade standards or contract specifications are involved, the final sizing and design of the gears should be adjusted to meet these obligations. (In general, gears sized by the principles in this book should not need much adjustment to fit contract obligations. If a contract would allow significantly smaller or weaker gears, the designer should review the field experience available and decide whether or not going beyond the recommendations given here is reasonable.)

- In many areas, not enough is known to rate the gears with any great confidence that the rating is really right. This is particularly true in Regime I lubrication conditions. (See Sec. 2.4 for a discussion of lubrication regimes.) If extensive field experience is not available to verify a gear-rating procedure, it is generally necessary to do initial factory and field testing of prototype units to prove their specified ratings before going into production of the units.

Rating Curves of Stress versus Cycles. The following rating curves are presented as general guides to the gear designer:

Figure 3.24	covers allowable bending stress† for short cycles.
Figure 3.25	covers allowable bending stress† for long cycles.

*See Chap. 7 for a discussion of gear ratings and of possible factors other than the basic rating which may cause failures.

†The bending stress that is considered in Figs. 3.24 and 3.25 is a unidirectional stress for normal gear action. When gear teeth are subject to loading in two directions, such as a planet in an epicyclic set that is loaded on both sides of the teeth, the rating must be *reduced for reverse bending*. An approximately correct rating can be obtained by multiplying the allowable bending stress by 0.70 before comparing it to the calculated stress.

Figure 3.26	covers contact stress for Regime II lubrication and short cycles.
Figure 3.27	covers contact stress for Regime III lubrication and long cycles.

These curves are somewhat different from the presently published curves used in gear standards. They reflect the concept that high loads in fewer than 10^7 cycles can cause microscopic metal damage that makes the gear tooth unable to run for 10^9 cycles or longer. They also take into account regimes of lubrication and the *change in slope* of the stress versus cycles curves for durability.

There are not enough good data in the gear trade to plot a set of curves like those in Figs. 3.24 to 3.27 with a high degree of confidence. The data shown are intended to represent as good a judgment as can be determined, given the present (1982) state of the gear art. Hopefully, more research work and field experience in the 1980s will make it possible to have better data.

These curves are intended to be used with the load histogram manner of design and an obligation to control the scoring problem. See Sec. 8.8 for

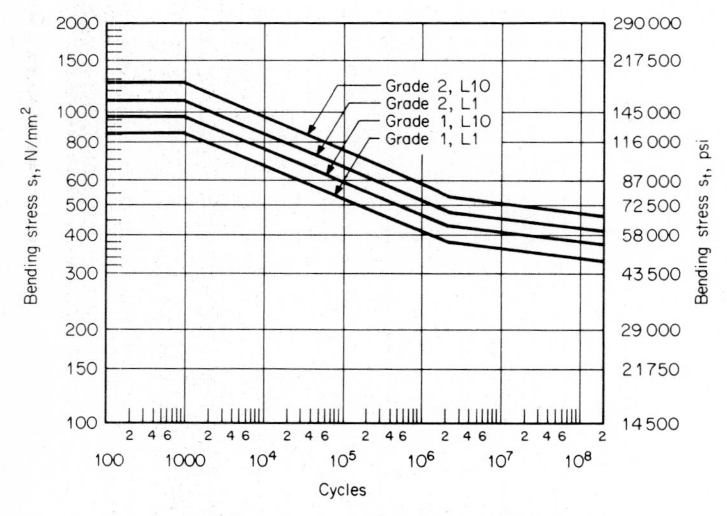

Note: These curves are drawn for full-hardness carburized gears at 60 HRC minimum hardness—700 HV. See Sec. 4.6 for comments on the load-carrying capacity of nitrided gears.
These curves are for unidirectional tooth loading.
If teeth are subject to reverse bending (idlers, planets, etc.), multiply allowable bending stress by 0.70.

FIG. 3.24 Bending stress for a short-life design.

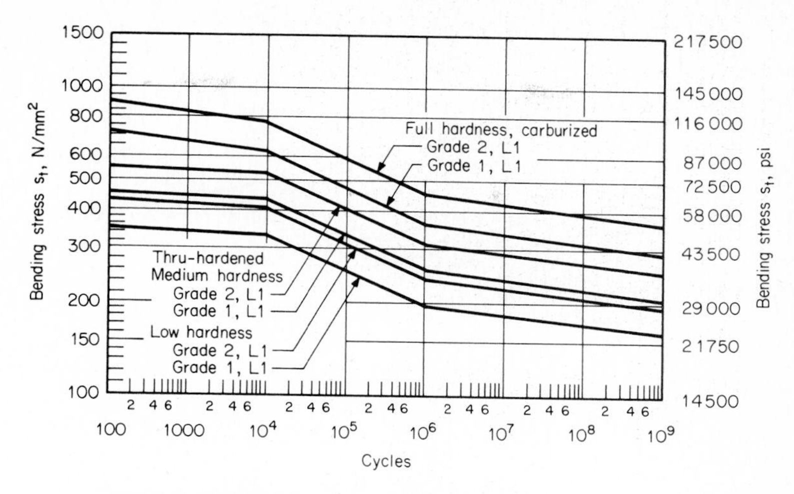

Note: Full hardness is 60 HRC – 700 HV minimum.
Medium hardness is 300 HB–320 HV minimum.
Low hardness is 210 HB–220 HV minimum.
These curves are for unidirectional tooth loading.
If teeth are subject to reverse bending (idlers, planets, etc.), multiply allowable bending stress by 0.70.

FIG. 3.25 Bending stress for a long-life design.

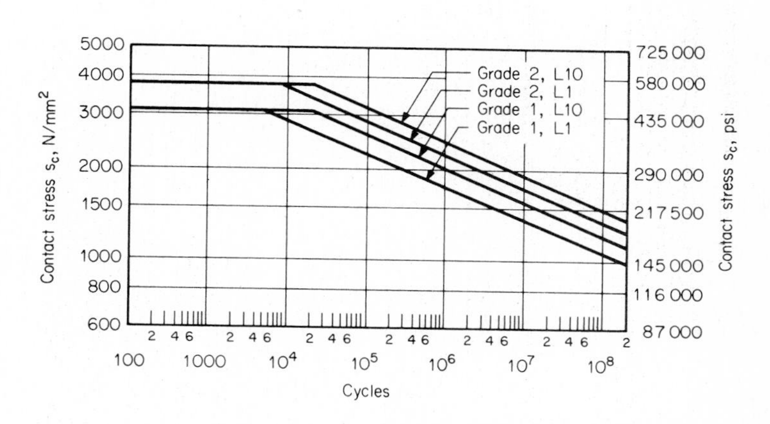

Note: These curves are drawn for full-hardness carburized gears at 60 HRC minimum hardness – 700 HV. See Sec. 4.6 for comments on the load-carrying capacity of nitrided gears.

FIG. 3.26 Contact stress for Regime II and a short-life design.

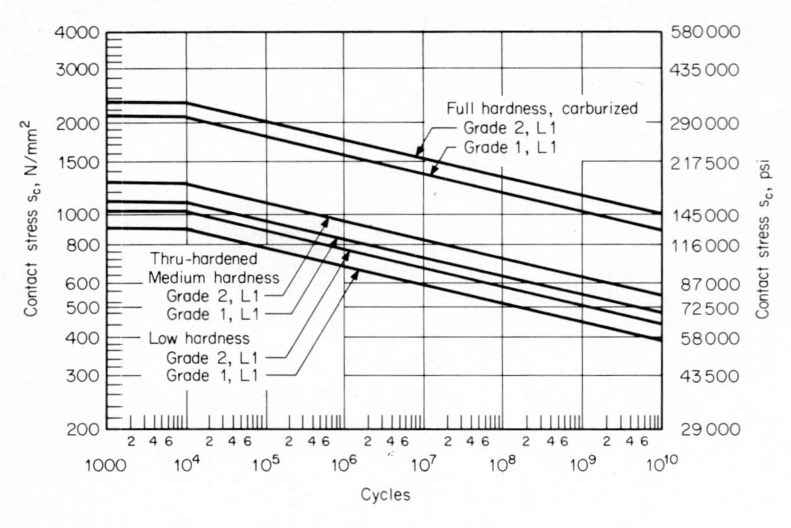

FIG. 3.27 Contact stress for Regime III and a long-life design.

more on the load histogram method, and see Sec. 3.31 for a discussion of how to handle the scoring hazard.

Rating Bevel Gears. When the intensities of tooth loading for bevel gears (*K* factor and unit load) are calculated by the method shown in Fig. 2.31, the values obtained are comparable to those of spur and helical gears. This is very helpful in preliminary design work when a decision as to whether the body shape of the gears should be cylindrical or conical has not yet been made.

As a general rule, a reasonable *K* factor on a bevel gear tends to be about equal to that on a matching spur or helical gear with the same hardness, quality, and pitch-line speed. The unit load may be somewhat less, since it is harder to get a large root fillet radius on a bevel gear than on a matching spur or helical gear.

Size is another factor. Large bevel gears need more derating for size than do cylindrical gears.

With these factors in mind, this book was written with the plan that the basic calculations for surface compressive stress and bending stress of bevel gears would be handled the same way and use the *same allowable stresses* as those for spur and helical gears.

In the period from 1940 to 1980, bevel-gear-rating equations were put together differently than those for spur and helical gears. Furthermore, the allowable stress values were different. The trend now, in the 1980s, is to use similar formulas and to bring the stress values together. (Seemingly the stress values would be the same if they were *true* stresses. Of course, as Sec. 2.1 points out, the stresses used in gear rating are not really true values. They are "stress numbers" that have been established by experience in developing gear ratings.)

The geometry factors and the derating factors for bevel gears in this book follow quite closely the general practice developed in the United States over the last 20 years. Using Eq. (3.47) for strength and Eq. (3.49) for surface durability and the definitions of all the factors in Secs. 3.25 through 3.29 results in calculated stresses for bevel gears that generally come out high compared with the allowable stresses in Figs. 3.24 through 3.27. Sample calculations show that for bevel gears known to be satisfactory in service, calculated stresses predict quick failure. This is a serious problem. *How should bevel gears be rated?*

In time, there will be adjustments in the geometry and the derating factors for both bevel and cylindrical gears. Quite likely, these changes, plus some adjustments in the stress curves, will make it possible to use the same stresses for both bevel and cylindrical gears. It would seem, though, that it will take until about 1990 for this process to run its course.

For those using this book, the best plan is the following:

Establish initial designs by the methods shown here, but cross-check these with applicable AGMA standards, proven experience in bevel-gear work, and recommendations by the Gleason Machine Division in Rochester, New York, U.S.A.

Keep in mind that this book does not cover ratings of bevel gears for aerospace work or for vehicle gears. Only industrial bevel gears are covered.

Strength of bevel gears is more critical than that of cylindrical gears. Lower numbers of pinion teeth are advisable, particularly on fully hardened gears. The strength rating is often the controlling rating for bevel gears, whereas the durability rating is generally controlling for cylindrical gears.

The bending stress of a bevel gear calculated by Eq. (3.47) can generally be divided by an *adjustment factor* of 1.4 before it is compared with the strength rating curves of Fig. 3.25.

The surface compressive stress of a bevel gear calculated by Eq. (3.49) can generally be divided by an *adjustment factor* of 1.25 before it is compared with the durability rating curves of Fig. 3.27.

3.26 Geometry Factors for Strength

The geometry factor for strength is a dimensionless factor that evaluates the shape of the tooth, the amount of load sharing between teeth, and the stress concentration in the root area. AGMA has standard procedures for handling this factor. The ISO standards now being developed have somewhat different procedures. Chapter 2, Sec. 2.3, gave a general background on how gear-tooth strength has been handled in the past.

The geometry factors for strength presented in this section are based on AGMA 226.01. This standard shows the procedures for determining J factors and, in addition, shows many graphs of J-factor values for different gear designs. Although the ISO is developing a somewhat different method for determining geometry factors for strength, the AGMA system has worked quite well in practice and is well accepted in the gear trade.

In this book simplified calculation methods are used, and a K_t factor—rather than a J factor—is used in the strength formulas. The relation of K_t to J is

$$K_t = \frac{1.0}{J} \qquad \text{spur gears} \qquad (3.51)$$

$$K_t = \frac{\cos\text{ (helix angle)}}{J} \qquad \text{helical gears} \qquad (3.52)$$

$$K_t = \frac{1.0}{J} \qquad \text{straight or Zerol bevels} \qquad (3.53)$$

$$K_t = \frac{\cos\text{ (spiral angle)}}{J} \qquad \text{spiral bevels} \qquad (3.54)$$

Since the strength factor is dimensionless, it can be used equally well in metric and English calculations.

Lack of Load Sharing. Normally the strength of spur-gear teeth is calculated on the basis of the teeth sharing load at the first point of contact and at the last point of contact. This is why the critical load is taken at the highest point of single-tooth contact. If the teeth are not cut accurately enough to share load, they may still wear in enough so that load sharing exists before there have been many stress cycles.

In some cases, the accuracy may be poor enough or the metal hard enough so that essentially no useful load sharing is achieved. If this happens then the geometry factor for strength should be determined with *full load* taken at the tip of the tooth. Table 3.34 gives some typical strength factors for full load taken at the tip. Table 3.35 gives some guideline information as to how much error it takes to cause a failure of load sharing.

Calculations for helical gears and bevel gears are not often made for the condition where load sharing does not exist. In general, these gears are

TABLE 3.34 Geometry Factors K_t for Strength of Spur Gears Loaded at the Tip

	20° pressure angle			25° pressure angle		
No. teeth	1.25 add.	1.00 add.	0.75 add.	1.25 add.	1.00 add.	0.75 add.
12	3.95	—	—	3.10	3.70	—
15	3.77	4.50	—	2.97	3.51	—
18	3.66	4.29	—	2.88	3.34	—
25	3.52	3.97	—	2.77	3.09	—
35	3.40	3.70	4.12	2.67	2.92	3.20
50	—	3.57	3.85	—	2.79	2.99
100	—	3.39	3.51	—	2.66	2.75
275	—	3.26	3.29	—	2.58	2.61

Notes: 1. It is assumed that a pinion with 1.25 basic addendum meshes with a gear of 0.75 addendum and that the tooth thicknesses are adjusted for the change in addendum.

2. It is assumed that a 1.00-addendum pinion meshes with a 1.00-addendum gear and that the tooth thicknesses are standard.

3. These data are for extra-depth teeth cut with a relatively full radius fillet (whole depth 2.35 to 2.40).

TABLE 3.35 Limiting Error in Action for Steel Spur Gears

Load intensity per unit of face width		Dimensional error on line of action between contact points			
		Teeth share load		Teeth fail to share load	
Metric W_t/b, N/mm	English W_t/F, lb/in.	Metric, mm	English, in.	Metric, mm	English, in.
100	571	0.005	0.0002	0.013	0.0005
200	1142	0.008	0.0003	0.020	0.0008
300	1713	0.010	0.0004	0.030	0.0012
400	2284	0.013	0.0005	0.041	0.0016
600	3426	0.020	0.0008	0.061	0.0024
1000	5710	0.033	0.0013	0.076	0.0030
1600	9140	0.050	0.0020	0.122	0.0048

Notes: 1. The error values above are useful only as rough guides. Perfect load sharing, of course, can only occur with perfect accuracy. The meaning of "teeth share load" is that reasonably good load sharing can be expected. The meaning of "teeth fail to share load" is that very little useful load sharing can be expected unless the teeth wear enough to remove most of the error.

2. The "error on the line of action" may be either profile error or spacing error, or some combination of the two. Adjacent spacing error is usually the most troublesome.

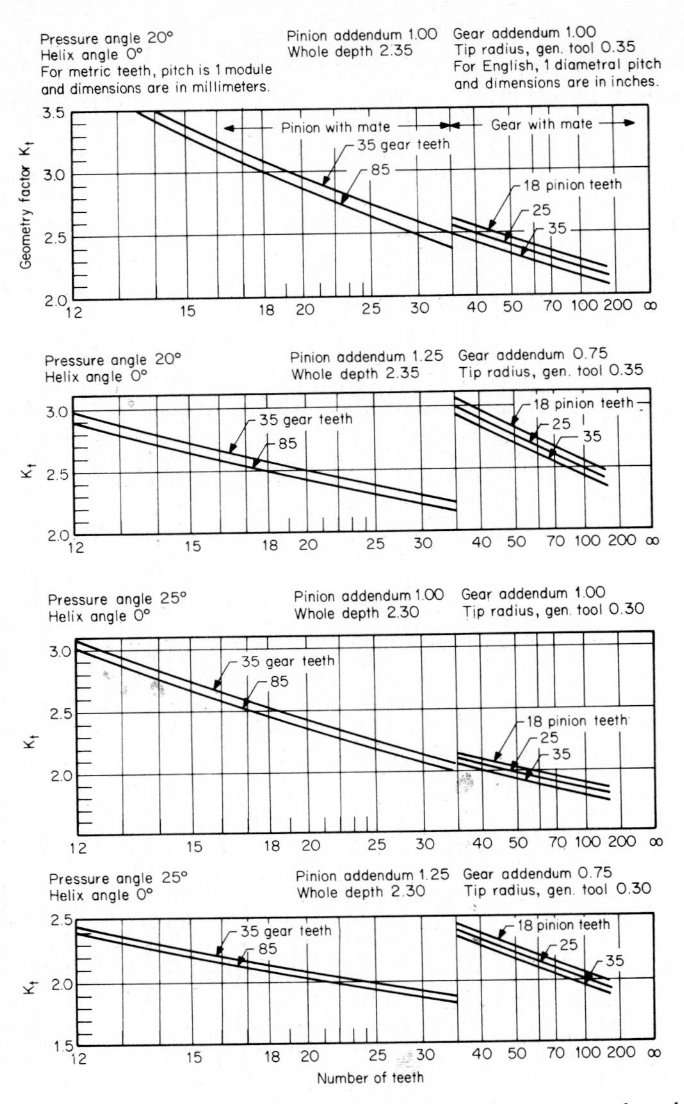

FIG. 3.28 Geometry factors for strength of spur gears based on the highest point of single tooth loading (HPSTC).

either made accurately enough to share load or lapped until a satisfactory contact pattern is achieved. (If they can't be fitted so that they contact properly, they may be rejected.) Inaccurate low-hardness gears may wear and cold-flow enough to develop relatively good contact patterns—and good load sharing—early in their service life.

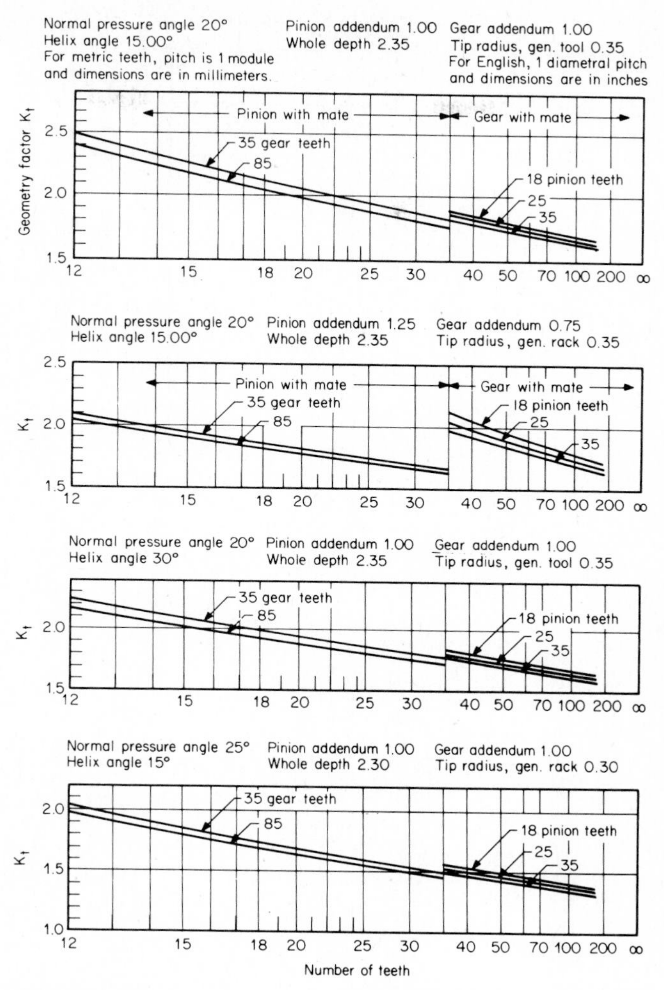

FIG. 3.29 Geometry factors for strength of helical gears based on tip loading and sharing of load between teeth in the zone of contact.

Helical Gears with Narrow Face Width. A good helical gear should have enough face width so that contact ratio in the axial plane is at least 2. If the face width is narrow relative to the pitch diameter of the pinion or if the helix angle is quite low (like 8° or less), the axial contact ratio may be less than 1. How should the strength of a helical pinion or gear be calculated when the axial contact ratio is only 0.50?

When the axial contact ratio is less than 1.0, the helical gear can best be

TABLE 3.36 Geometry Factors K_t for the Strength of Bevel Gears

No. pinion teeth	No. gear teeth	Straight bevels		Spiral bevels	
		Pinion	Gear	Pinion	Gear
15	20	5.00	5.75	4.93	4.93
	35	4.48	5.56	3.79	3.79
	50	4.35	5.49	3.21	3.21
	100	3.79	4.90	2.57	2.57
20	20	5.04	5.04	4.45	4.45
	35	4.25	5.00	3.62	3.63
	50	4.15	4.90	3.05	3.05
	100	3.57	4.35	2.48	2.48
25	25	4.61	4.61	3.80	3.80
	35	4.11	4.67	3.48	3.48
	50	3.95	4.61	2.94	2.94
	100	3.42	4.00	2.42	2.42
35	35	4.14	4.14	3.13	3.13
	50	3.75	4.20	2.78	2.78
	100	3.16	3.66	2.35	2.35
50	50	3.71	3.71	2.64	2.64
	100	2.95	3.33	2.29	2.29

Notes:
1. The values in this table are subject to change as refinements are made in the procedure to determine stress intensity due to bending load on gear teeth.
2. This table is based on the normal design and manufacturing procedure recommended by the Gleason Works. In many cases there will be reason to modify the actual design, and this will tend to cause changes in the geometry factors from the "guideline" values given.
3. The straight bevel data are for Coniflex bevel gears having 20° pressure angle.
4. The spiral bevel data are for 20° pressure angle, 35° spiral angle bevel gears.
5. The geometry factors for Zerol bevel teeth tend to be the same as those for straight bevels.

thought of as in an intermediate zone between a helical gear and a spur gear. At an axial contact ratio of 0.50, a close approximation of the geometry factor for strength can be taken midway between the value for a spur gear and the value for a helical gear. Appendix D of AGMA 226.01 shows how to derive the J factor for helical gears, either wide face width or narrow face width. This standard can be used to get data beyond those given in this section.

Geometry Factors for Strength for Some Standard Designs. The geometry factors for strength have been calculated and plotted on curve sheets for several standard designs of spur and helical gears. See Figs. 3.28

and 3.29. The method used was that of AGMA 225.01. The data shown agree with tabulated data in AGMA 170.01.

Although much design practice is based on AGMA 225.01, it is not known with certainty that the geometry factors are just right. Recent work by Drago (1981) has shown evidence that rim thickness is important and that the true stress may not agree exactly with a stress determined by AGMA 225.01.

The ISO method does not agree with the AGMA method. In particular, the relation of spur teeth to helical teeth is different. Work by Castellani (1980) and by Imwalle et al. (1981) has brought this out.

In the author's opinion, Figs. 3.28 and 3.29 give results that are reliable as long as gear rims are reasonably thick and centrifugal forces are low. When gear research work provides better values, they will probably not be very different from those shown.

Geometry factors for the strength of bevel gears are given in Table 3.36. These are used when the unit load is calculated for the middle of the bevel tooth. See Fig. 2.21.

3.27 Overall Derating Factor for Strength

The overall derating factor evaluates all the things that tend to make the load higher than it should be for the load being transmitted. Specifically, the factor is

$$K_d = \frac{K_a K_m K_s}{K_v} \tag{3.55}$$

where K_a = application factor
K_m = load-distribution factor
K_s = size factor
K_v = dynamic load factor

Each of these factors is explained in the following subsections. The numerical values given should be considered as somewhat typical of what is being used, but not necessarily precise values for any given situation. Most of them are based on experience as much as on theoretical logic. Experience, of course, tends to be an *average* of known data. Anything that is an average represents the mean of a range of actual values. Also, the *known* data may be somewhat limited compared with the unknown data—which would have given a different value, had they been known.

Another problem is that much data has been accumulated in the past on gears that were not too high in power and had low-hardness gear teeth.

These parts were not too large in size, and the lower hardness was helpful in letting the teeth wear in to accommodate manufacturing errors. As gears get larger in size, they are more difficult to make with good quality; if they are much harder, the teeth have very little tendency to wear in during service.

A good example of this kind of change has occurred in mill gearing. Certain mill gearing formerly transmitted around 1000 kW and used gearing around 300 HV (280 HB). In recent gears, the power has gone up to 3000 kW, and much gearing is being built with surface hardnesses over 600 HV (550 HB). In this case, past derating practices need modification to handle the new situation, but the bulk of the experience in the gear trade was accumulated in earlier years on the smaller, lower-hardness gears. How can the gear trade quickly obtain the experience needed to design new products out of the range of older products?

The derating values given in this section must be considered as general guides. AGMA and other organizations will write new standards. In a particular contract job, the buyer may specify that the gearing must meet certain design standards of AGMA (or others). Since derating is so critical and so potentially variable, the gear designer should endeavor to meet these objectives:

Any contract design specifications should either *be met* or variations negotiated.

The design should *look reasonable* by the logic of this book and other books applicable to the gear job at hand.

If the organization building the gears has no good depth of experience in making gears of the size, the hardness, or the kind required, the job should be *considered developmental* until adequate experience is obtained. This involves things like bench testing of components, factory testing of whole units at full load and full speed for some millions of contact cycles, and then a field evaluation of a few prototype production units under actual field service conditions. (A design standard is useful, but it does not remove the need for gear builders to obtain a good depth of experience in the product they are making.)

Application factor K_a. This factor evaluates *external* factors that tend to apply more load to the gear teeth than the applied load W_t. A rough-running prime mover and/or a rough-running piece of driven equipment can seriously increase the effect of the applied load. On an instantaneous basis, the torque being transmitted may be fluctuating considerably. The transmitted torque is then just the *mean* value of the torque fluctuations.

Other things like accelerations and decelerations, rudder turns on a ship, engine misfiring, power-system vibrations, etc., enter into the application factor.

TABLE 3.37 Typical Application Factors K_a for Power Gearing

Prime mover			
Turbine	Motor	Internal combustion engine	Driven equipment
			Generators and exciters
1.1	1.1	1.3	Base load or continuous
1.3	1.3	1.7	Peak duty cycle
			Compressors
1.7	1.5	1.8	Centrifugal
1.7	1.5	1.8	Axial
1.8	1.7	2.0	Rotary lobe (radial, axial, screw, and so forth)
2.2	2.0	2.5	Reciprocating
			Pumps
1.5	1.3	1.7	Centrifugal (all service except as listed below)
2.0	1.7	—	Centrifugal—boiler feed
2.0	1.7	—	High-speed centrifugal (over 3600 rpm)
1.7	1.5	2.0	Centrifugal—water supply
1.5	1.5	1.8	Rotary—axial flow—all types
2.0	2.0	2.3	Reciprocating
			Blowers
1.7	1.5	1.8	Centrifugal
			Fans
1.7	1.4	1.8	Centrifugal
1.7	1.4	1.8	Forced draft
2.0	1.7	2.2	Induced draft
			Paper industry
1.5	1.5	—	Jordan or refiner
1.3	1.3	—	Paper machine, line shaft
—	1.5	—	Pulp beater
			Sugar industry
1.5	1.5	1.8	Cane knife
1.7	1.5	2.0	Centrifugal
1.7	1.7	2.0	Mill
			Processing mills
—	1.75	—	Autogenous, ball
—	1.75	—	Pulverizers
—	1.75	—	Cement mills
			Metal rolling or drawing
—	1.4	—	Rod mills
—	2.0	—	Plate mills, roughing
—	2.75	—	Hot blooming or slabbing

Notes: 1. The values given are illustrative. As more experience is gained, new application factors will be established in the gear trade.

2. The values given may vary in a multistage drive. Experience and study will often show that the first stage needs a different application factor than that needed for the last stage.

3. The power rating and the kind of gear arrangement affect the application factor. The values given here represent somewhat average situations. (Be wary of new gear designs of high power. The old experience on application factors may be wrong for the new situation.)

In the past, the *service factor* was somewhat similar to the application factor. The service-factor concept, though, involved life and reliability as well as overloads. The best present practice treats life on the basis of cycles and reliability on a probability of failure basis. The application factor is used, and service factor is not used.

The application factor is determined by experience. An application factor of 1.0 is best thought of as a perfectly smooth turbine driving a perfectly smooth generator at an always constant load and speed. If another application has to have the load reduced 2 to 1 so that the same gears will last as long as in the ideal turbine/generator application, then the application factor is 2.0.

Table 3.37 gives application factors for a range of gear applications.

Load Distribution Factor K_m. This factor evaluates nonuniform load distribution across the face width and nonuniform load distribution in the meshing direction (transverse plane).

The general formula is

$$K_m = K_{mf} K_{mt} \tag{3.56}$$

The transverse effect is evaluated in some of the ISO standards that are in process of approval at this time. AGMA has not yet made a definitive study of K_{mt}. If the gear teeth fit reasonably well, the effect of K_{mt} is relatively small and will be taken care of by making K_{mf} appropriately large. The data given in this book anticipate that a value of 1.0 will be used for K_{mt}.

The factor K_{mf} should evaluate all the effects which may be due to the following:

Helical spiral of pinion does not match helical spiral of mating gear (helix error effect).

The pinion body bends and twists under load so that there is a mismatch between the pinion and the gear teeth (deflection effects).

The pinion axis, under load, is not parallel to the gear axis. Or, in bevel gears, the pinion axis is not at a 90° angle to the gear axis—when designed for 90° axis angle (positioning error effects, under load).

Centrifugal forces distort the shape of the pinion or gear and mismatch the teeth (centrifugal effects).

Thermal gradients distort the shape of the pinion or gear and mismatch the teeth (thermal effects).

Deliberate design modifications, such as crowning, end easement, or helix correction, concentrate the load in one area and relieve the load in another area. This is usually done to lessen the effect of one of the preceding items, but it is an effect in itself (design effects).

The listing just given shows why load distribution is one of the most complex subjects in gear design. A few years ago a proposed standard method of handling all these variables had about 150 pages—and it was found that it did not adequately cover all the possible situations!

Effects of Helix Error and Shaft Misalignment. In this section, some limited data will be given on misalignment effects that are due to error in matching the helical spirals and on deflection errors that are due to the aspect ratio of the pinion. Table 3.38 gives some target values that the designer should try to meet. (Instead of figuring how high the K_m is when all tolerances and deflections are allowed for, figure how close the tolerances and the deflections must be held to get a reasonable value of K_m.)

TABLE 3.38 Some Target Values of K_m for Spur and Helical Gears

Hardness of gear set and load per unit of face width	Face width 50 mm (2 in.)	100 mm (4 in.)	250 mm (10 in.)	750 mm (30 in.)
High hardness (675 HV)				
$W_t/b = 100 \quad (W_t/F = 571)$	1.7	1.9	—	—
$W_t/b = 300 \quad (W_t/F = 1713)$	1.4	1.6	1.8	—
$W_t/b = 800 \quad (W_t/F = 4568)$	1.2	1.3	1.6	1.8
Medium hardness (300 HB)				
$W_t/b = 100 \quad (W_t/F = 571)$	1.5	1.6	1.8	—
$W_t/b = 300 \quad (W_t/F = 1713)$	1.2	1.3	1.6	1.8
$W_t/b = 800 \quad (W_t/F = 4568)$	1.1	1.2	1.4	1.5
Low hardness (210 HB)				
$W_t/b = 100 \quad (W_t/F = 571)$	1.3	1.4	1.5	1.6
$W_t/b = 300 \quad (W_t/F = 1713)$	1.1	1.2	1.4	1.5
$W_t/b = 800 \quad (W_t/F = 4568)$	1.0	1.1	1.2	1.3

Notes: 1. These values assume that the accuracy is adjusted, with high-hardness gears being more accurate than low-hardness gears.
2. For gears over 100 mm face width, it is assumed that each set is matched or fitted to get an acceptable contact pattern at full load.
3. It is assumed that the low-hardness gears wear in (or cold-flow the metal) to improve the contact. This happens to a lesser extent with medium hard gears, and almost no useful wear-in occurs with high-hardness gears.

Figure 3.30 shows the approximate face-load-distribution factor as a function of mismatch error e_t and intensity of loading. The curves were plotted, up to $K_{mf} = 2.0$, from the relation

$$K_{mf} = \left(\frac{10{,}000b}{W_t} \times e_t\right) + 1 \qquad \text{metric} \qquad (3.57a)$$

$$K_{mf} = \left(\frac{1{,}450{,}000F}{W_t} \times e_t\right) + 1 \qquad \text{English} \qquad (3.57b)$$

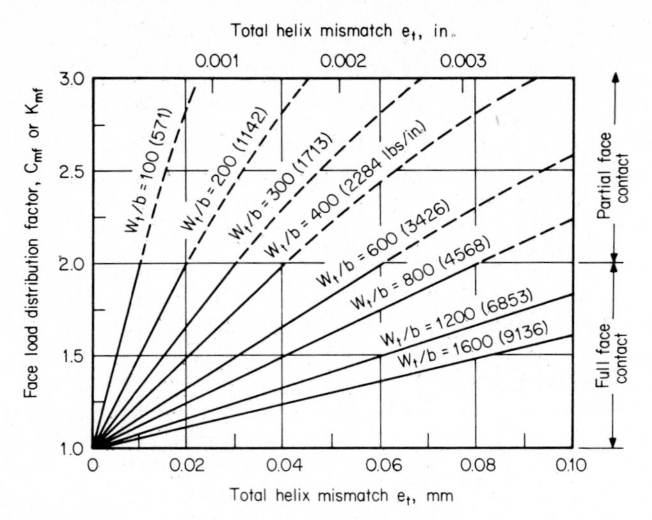

FIG. 3.30 Approximate load-distribution factors K_{mf} from combined effects of helix mismatch and shaft misalignment.

In Eq. (3.57), W_t is in newtons for the metric calculation and in pounds for the English calculation. The face width and error are in millimeters for the metric calculation and in inches for the English calculation. The answer is dimensionless.

The basis for Eq. (3.57) is that the total mesh deflection is

$$\text{Mesh deflection} = \frac{\text{stiffness constant} \times \text{face width}}{\text{load}}$$

$$= \frac{20{,}000b}{W_t} \qquad \text{metric} \qquad (3.58a)$$

$$= \frac{2{,}900{,}000F}{W_t} \qquad \text{English} \qquad (3.58b)$$

When K_{mf} is over 2.0, the error is great enough to make the face width in contact *less than* the total face width. The equation for the face-load-distribution factor then becomes

$$K_{mf} = \left(\frac{40{,}000be_t}{W_t}\right)^{0.50} \qquad \text{metric} \qquad (3.59a)$$

$$= \left(\frac{5{,}800{,}000Fe_t}{W_t}\right)^{0.50} \qquad \text{English} \qquad (3.59b)$$

The choice of a stiffness constant of 20,000 N/mm^2 (2,900,000 psi) deserves some comment. Tests of gear teeth show that this is a good average value for typical gear designs. If it is in error, it is more apt to be a little low than a little high. In a limited amount of testing, I have found 23,000 N/mm^2 to be typical for high-strength tooth designs.

In earlier years, values like 2,000,000 psi and even 1,000,000 psi have been used. (2,000,000 psi is equivalent to about 14,000 N/mm^2.) These values seemed to give reasonable correlation with results observed in practice. The reason they did was that either the teeth tended to wear in to develop a good fit or the gears were flexible enough in their mountings to shift so that the contact was better than it should have been, based on errors and true stiffness of teeth.

The problem with this design approach is that large gears and very hard gears shift scarcely at all, and they don't wear in, either. Therefore, it is best to make a relatively true calculation of K_{mf}. If there is wear-in or gear-body shifting, this can more appropriately be allowed for by determining the compensating amounts directly and then subtracting them from the helix error.

Table 3.39 shows amounts of wear-in e_w that might be expected. There is

TABLE 3.39 Approximate Wear-in Amounts e_w That May Be Realized with Appropriate Lubricants and a Good Break-in Procedure

Material hardness		Initial misfit in helix width							
		0.023 mm (0.0009 in.)		0.038 mm (0.0015 in.)		0.064 mm (0.0025 in.)		0.010 mm (0.004 in.)	
HV	HB	mm	in.	mm	in.	mm	in.	mm	in.
Regime I—less than 1 m/s (200 fpm) pitch-line velocity									
210	200	0.015	0.0006	0.023	0.0009	0.038	0.0015	0.050	0.0020
320	300	0.0125	0.0005	0.020	0.0008	0.030	0.0012	0.038	0.0015
415	400	0.010	0.0004	0.018	0.0007	0.023	0.0009	0.030	0.0012
530	500	0.0075	0.0003	0.0125	0.0005	0.015	0.0006	0.025	0.0010
675	600	0.005	0.0002	0.0075	0.0003	0.0125	0.0005	0.020	0.0008
Regime II—around 5 m/s (1000 fpm) pitch-line velocity									
210	200	0.0125	0.0005	0.018	0.0007	0.025	0.0010	0.030	0.0012
320	300	0.010	0.0004	0.015	0.0006	0.020	0.0008	0.025	0.0010
415	400	0.0075	0.0003	0.0125	0.0005	0.015	0.0006	0.020	0.0008
530	500	0.005	0.0002	0.0075	0.0003	0.0125	0.0005	0.015	0.0006
675	600	0.0025	0.0001	0.005	0.0002	0.010	0.0004	0.0125	0.0005
Regime III—over 20 m/s (4000 fpm) pitch-line velocity									
210	200	0.0075	0.0003	0.010	0.0004	0.0125	0.0005	0.015	0.0006
320	300	0.005	0.0002	0.0075	0.0003	0.010	0.0004	0.0125	0.0005
415	400	0.005	0.0002	0.005	0.0002	0.0075	0.0003	0.010	0.0004
530	500	0.0025	0.0001	0.0025	0.0001	0.005	0.0002	0.0075	0.0003
675	600	0.0025	0.0001	0.0025	0.0001	0.0025	0.0001	0.005	0.0002

relatively little good data on wear-in of gears, and so this table should be considered a good opinion on what is likely to happen rather than the results of any study in depth.

Aspect-Ratio Effects. The relative slenderness of the pinion is called the *aspect ratio*. The aspect ratio m_a is the contacting face width of the pinion divided by the pitch diameter. For double helical pinions, the best practice is to use the total face width (the width of the two helices plus the gap between the helices).

When the aspect ratio approaches 2.0, both single helical and double helical pinions bend and twist enough to tend to develop relatively high K_{mf} values. Figure 3.31 shows a plot of K_{mf} against the aspect ratio for both single helical and double helical pinions. This curve sheet was drawn to fit these assumptions:

The teeth are cut to true and exactly matching helix angles.

The pinions and gears are straddle-mounted on bearings, and the bearings are a reasonable distance from the tooth ends.

There is no wear-in to compensate for deflection.

An approximation formula was used to get the deflection. The deflection was taken as an error and converted to K_{mf} by the formulas just discussed. Since deflection is proportional to load intensity, the answer in K_{mf} is the same regardless of the load intensity.

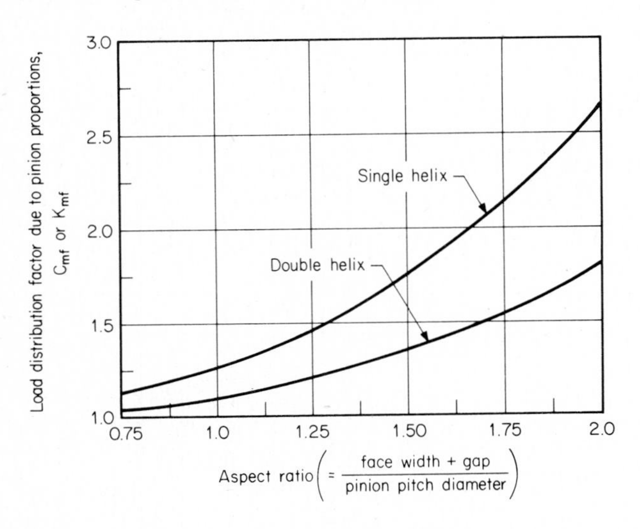

FIG. 3.31 Effect of pinion bending and twisting on load distribution across the face width.

Figure 3.31 makes it look like the double helix does better than the single helix. This is really not so, because of the gap. When a single-helix pinion and a double-helix pinion have the same working face width, the K_{mf} value tends to be about the same.

The high K_{mf} value for an aspect ratio around 2.0 can be reduced considerably by helix modification. In general, helix modification (also called *helix correction*) should be given strong consideration when the aspect ratio of single helical pinions exceeds 1.15 or that of double helical pinions exceeds 1.60.

The problem of K_{mf} begins to look rather formidable from all the foregoing. Some things can be done, though, to improve the situation for spur and helical gears. (Bevel gears are discussed next.)

- If the aspect ratio is under 1.15 and the pinion and gear are straddle-mounted in their bearings, there should be no serious effect from bending and twisting. Of course, if the pinion is overhung, special calculations will be needed to find the overhung deflection, even with an aspect ratio of 1.0.

  The main problem when the aspect ratio is under 1.15 is manufacturing error.

- If the aspect ratio is over 1.5, the bending and twisting effects need to be calculated. Helix correction is apt to be needed. When helix correction is made, the pinions are generally fitted to their gears so that under no load (or very light load), the contact pattern is open where the teeth have been relieved. Using special measuring techniques, the amount the teeth are open can be measured.

  If the pinion does not match its gear properly, it can be reshaved or reground. (In some cases, bearings may be shifted slightly to fix the fit.) When the fitting job is done, the desired mismatch to compensate for deflection has been achieved, and manufacturing errors in cutting teeth or boring cases have been taken care of.

- When the aspect ratio is quite low—like 0.25 or less—there is often a tendency for the gear (or both pinion and gear) to deflect or shift so as to distribute the load relatively evenly, even when an appreciable helix mismatch exists. Tests and observations may reveal that a pair of gears that would have a K_{mf} of around 2.5 may actually run with a *real* K_{mf} of only 1.4! It is beyond the scope of this book to present engineering analysis data on how gears can deflect sideways or shift on their mountings to achieve a substantial reduction in K_{mf} (or C_{mf}). The designer should be alert for this possibility and test new designs thoroughly so that any favorable reduction in K_{mf} can be noted and used.

  As a matter of interest, it is quite common for vehicle transmission gears to have a low aspect ratio and a favorable tendency to run at much lower K_{mf}

values than a simple calculation based on helix errors and tooth load per unit of face width would indicate.

- Helical gears are loaded on an inclined line that runs from the top of the tooth to the limit diameter. Under misaligned conditions, the area of high loading is localized, and the developed field of stress in the tooth root is not as severe as it would be for a spur gear.

It is often practical to use a somewhat lower K_{mf} for helical gears than for spur gears when the aspect ratio is low. For high-aspect-ratio gears, K_{mf} is generally considered to be equal to C_{mf}, the durability factor for misalignment effects.

Load Distribution Factor K_m for Bevel Gears. Bevel gears are generally made with the following design controls:

The face width is 0.30 or 0.25 of the outer cone distance (an aspect-ratio control).

The teeth are cut or ground so that the tooth contact is localized. A slight crown is introduced to compensate for small errors in tooth making and in mounting the bevels on their cone axes.

The bevel gears are tested in special contact-checking machines. If the fit is not right, the bevel gears are either rejected or lightly lapped to make the fit acceptable. If the misfit is more than what lapping can correct, the pinion or gear may be recut or reground to bring the tooth fit on the tester under control.

The result of these special practices and controls is to make it much easier to establish reasonable load-distribution factors for bevel gears than for spur or helical gears.

Table 3.40 shows the general pattern of load-distribution factors for bevel

TABLE 3.40 Load-Distribution Factors for Bevel Gears, K_m and C_m

Application	Both members straddle-mounted	One member straddle-mounted	Neither member straddle-mounted
General industrial	1.00–1.10	1.10–1.25	1.25–1.40
Vehicle	1.00–1.10	1.10–1.25	—
Aerospace	1.00–1.25	1.10–1.40	1.25–1.50

Notes: 1. These values are based on setting the position on the cone element very close to the right position. For instance, if a bevel gear with 25 mm (1 in.) face width was out of position about 0.15 mm (0.006 in.), a K_m value of 1.05 would increase to about 1.8!

2. These values are based on the face width not exceeding 25 mm. Industrial bevel gears are made in rather large sizes. Figure 3.32 shows how the load-distribution factor tends to increase as the face width increases.

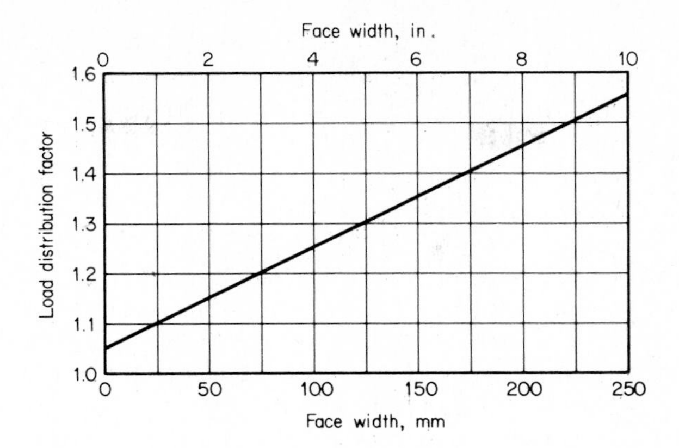

FIG. 3.32 Load-distribution factor for bevel gears, K_m or C_m. This curve is applicable for straddle mounting only and industrial units.

gears. The *same* load-distribution factor is generally used for both strength and durability rating calculations ($K_m = C_m$).

Industrial bevel gears are often made in large sizes. In general, both members are straddle-mounted. Figure 3.32 shows the general trend for the increase in mounting factor as the parts get larger and there is more difficulty in controlling the accuracy.

The mounting factors for bevel gears are right for the *rated* load. The reason for this is that the localized contact is developed to suit the rated torque. If the bevels are operated at lower than rated torque, the mounting factors tend to increase because the fit is not right. This is not too critical, though, because the torque generally decreases faster than the load-distribution factor increases.

A serious problem can occur when a bevel set has to handle very high overload torques for a small number of cycles (like 10^5) and then must run for a large number of cycles (like 10^9) at rated torque. In such a case, the design needs to be biased to fit the dangerous overload torque. At rated torque, the load distribution will not be as good as it should be, and a higher than normal load-distribution factor will be needed.

Size Factor K_s. The size factor derates the gear design for the adverse effect of size on material properties. Large gears may have the same hardness as small gears, but the material may not be as strong or fatigue-resistant. Inclusions or other flaws in the steel tend to be more numerous in a large stressed area than in a small stressed area.

The making of gears involves pouring ingots, forging ingots, quenching and normalizing of forgings, hardening and tempering of gears, etc. All these operations can be done with better control on small parts than on very large parts.

The size factor tends to go up to around 2 in going from rather small gears to very large gears—when all the adverse effects of size are considered. Fortunately, some things can be done to decrease the effect of size.

If the steel used is chosen to have enough alloy content, a much better heat-treating response can be obtained. Also, if temperatures or other variables are somewhat out of control, the richer-alloy steels are more *forgiving* of less than optimum conditions.

Figure 3.33 shows size factors for the strength of spur, helical, and bevel gears. The bevel curve is not the one normally used in older standards. The old curve had a unity value for a very large tooth and a 0.5 value for a small tooth. This was compensated for by using about one-half the allowed stress in bending for bevel teeth as for spur and helical teeth. The new trend is to use the same allowed stresses for spur, helical, and bevel teeth. This is done by making the size factor greater than unity as *size* becomes detrimental.

The dashed curve for spur and helical gears represents the author's viewpoint on what *should be* done in an *average* situation. For more on size-factor policy, see Sec. 3.29.

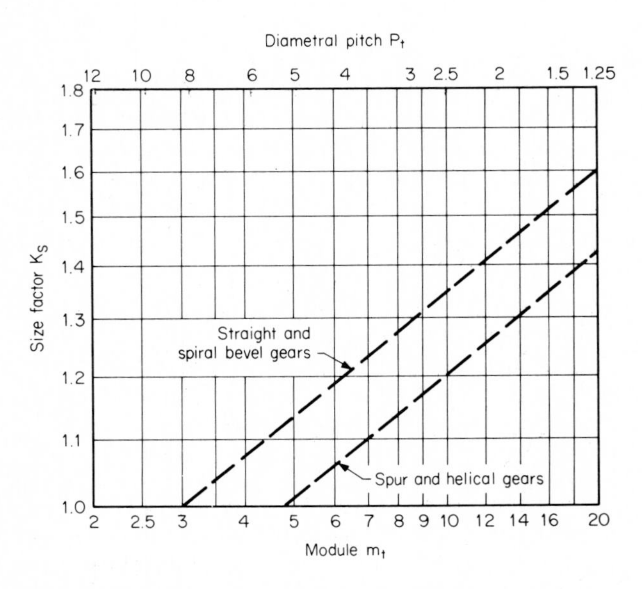

FIG. 3.33 Size factor for the strength of spur, helical, and bevel gears.

Dynamic Load Factors K_v and C_v. The dynamic factor makes allowance for overload effects generated by a pair of meshing gears. If both members of the gear pair were perfect, a uniform angular rotation of one member would result in a uniform angular rotation of the other member. The ratio of the number of gear teeth to the number of pinion teeth would be the exact ratio of the two angular velocities.

Gear teeth are never perfect, although a high-precision pair of gears is much more perfect than a low-precision or "commercial" accuracy pair. The tooth errors result in a *transmission error* which makes the ratio of input speed to output speed tend to fluctuate. On an instantaneous basis, each member of the gear pair is constantly going through slight accelerations and decelerations. This results, in turn, in dynamic forces being developed because of the mass of the pinion and its shaft and the gear and its shaft.

Tooth errors in spacing, runout, and profile cause transmission error. Helix errors influence transmission error because of their indirect effect on load sharing between teeth and their effect on the stiffness constant for the mesh.

The dynamic factor is used as a derating factor to compensate for the adverse effect of the dynamic load caused by tooth errors. The dynamic factor does not handle dynamic overloads caused by the driving or driven machinery. The application factors K_a and C_a are used to handle dynamic loads unrelated to gear-tooth accuracy.

The equation for dynamic factor is

$$K_v = C_v = \frac{W_t}{W_d + W_t} \qquad \text{metric or English} \qquad (3.60)$$

where C_v = dynamic factor for durability
W_t = transmitted load, newtons or pounds
W_d = dynamic load, newtons or pounds

Equation (3.60) makes the dynamic factor for strength the same as the dynamic factor for durability. The definition used for dynamic load is unrelated to the kind of trouble that the load can cause when it is too great. Excessive dynamic loads are a hazard to gear-tooth strength, gear-tooth surface durability, and gear-tooth scoring resistance.

For AGMA calculations of bending stress or contact stress, it has been customary to put the dynamic factor in the *denominator*, whereas the other derating factors are put in the *numerator*. This makes a high dynamic factor come out to some value like 0.50 instead of 2.0. The new ISO work puts the dynamic factor in the numerator. In this book, AGMA practice will be followed.

Figure 3.34 shows dynamic factors for spur and helical gears. A range of

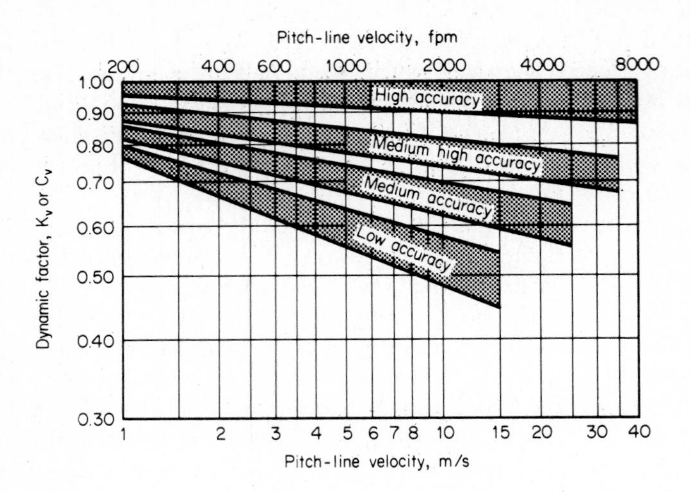

FIG. 3.34 Dynamic factor for strength and durability for spur and helical gears.

values is shown for four general levels of gear accuracy. These levels can be described as follows:

A. High accuracy

Generally ground gears. May be gears hobbed or shaved to very close limits and then precision-shaved. The tooth design provides good profile modification and helix modification (across the face width). Tooth spacing (both tooth-to-tooth and accumulated), profile (both slope and modification), helix (crown, end easement, and/or allowance for bending and twisting), gear runout, and gear surface finish (smoothness and lack of waviness) are held to very close limits. The modifications in profile and helix are based on a *single load* that is reasoned to be the significant load determining the rating.

B. Medium high accuracy

Ground or shaved gears, but quality is a significant step lower than that outlined above.

C. Medium accuracy

Gears are precision-finished by hobbing or shaping. Modifications in profile or helix are either not made or made without close control. This is the best that skilled gear people can do by taking extra time for finishing and using the most suitable machine tools of 1970–1980 capability.

D. Low accuracy

Gears are hobbed or shaped to normal practice. Profile modifications are either not made or not made with close control. Machine tools used are good, but may not have the accuracy capability of the newest types.

These levels of accuracy cannot be tied closely to AGMA 390.03 limits. Some requisite quality items are not specified in AGMA 390.03, and some are not set to match the latest machine tool capability. As a rough guide, though, high accuracy is like AGMA quality level 12 or 13, and medium accuracy is like AGMA quality level 8. DIN quality grade 5 is in the high-accuracy range. (See Sec. 5.18 for more on gear accuracy.)

The range shown in Figure 3.34 is typical of the practice that has been followed successfully for many years. A gear designer can judge how closely every accuracy item is apt to be held in gears that will be made to a given design. If the gears are going to be extra good for the way they are made, then there is reason to go to the top of the range.

Figure 3.34 stops low-accuracy gears at a pitch-line velocity of 15 m/s (3000 fpm) and medium-high-accuracy gears at 35 m/s (7000 fpm). Generally speaking, these kinds of gears are not apt to be used at higher speeds, although they might give satisfactory service. (If a low-accuracy gear is run too fast, there is apt to be trouble with noise and vibration, besides the uncertainty as to whether or not the gear unit will perform as well as its rating would anticipate.)

High-accuracy gears (and super-high-accuracy gears) are being used with relatively good success at pitch-line velocities up to 200 m/s (40,000 fpm). What dynamic load is appropriate for high-precision gears in the 40- to 200-m/s speed range?

High-speed gears must be made very precisely. In general, the dynamic load factor will be quite low—from 0.85 to 0.95. To get the best results, the teeth need to be helical, with enough face width and axial contact ratio to get two axial crossovers.

The following values represent the author's opinion on what may be expected in high-speed gearing:

Helical, axial contact ratio over 2.0, truly high precision in all details

$$K_v = C_v = 0.95$$

Helical, axial contact ratio of 1.0, truly high precision

$$K_v = C_v = 0.90$$

Helical, high precision, but profile and helix corrections not made

$$K_v = C_v = 0.85$$

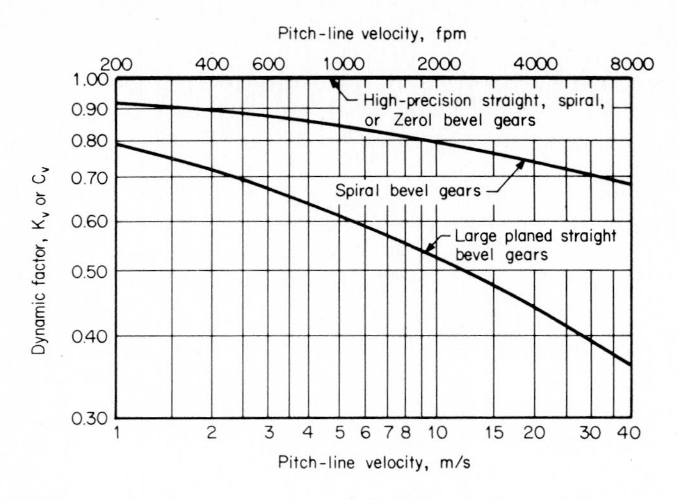

FIG. 3.35 Dynamic factor for strength and durability for bevel gears.

Spur, truly high precision in all details. (The high-speed spur gear needs to be narrow in face width to run above 40 m/s. Generally the upper limit for spur gears is around 20 m/s.)

$$K_v = C_v = 0.85$$

The dynamic load factors for bevel gears are shown in Fig. 3.35. The curves represent the practices that were followed successfully during the 1960–1980 period. The values plotted are the same as those shown in AGMA bevel-gear standards and in publications of the Gleason Works.

Straight bevel gears are not often used above 10 m/s (2000 fpm) pitch-line velocity. If they are not cut to precision accuracy and fitted for the best contact pattern, the dynamic factor should be read from the second or third curve.

Spiral bevels that are finished by cutting and fitted for a good contact pattern should use the dynamic factor given by the second curve.

Some further discussion of dynamic load is given in Chap. 9. See Sec. 9.2 for this material.

3.28 Geometry Factors for Durability

The geometry factors for durability evaluate the shape of the tooth and the amount of load sharing between teeth. AGMA and ISO have procedures for evaluating these factors. The material in this section is based on AGMA methods.

The I factors shown in AGMA standards are geometry factors, but not the same kind as those used in this book, with one exception: The C_k factor given in AGMA 170.01 for spur and helical vehicle gears is the same kind.

The relation of C_k to I is

$$C_k = \frac{C_p}{12.043}\left(\frac{1}{I}\frac{u}{u+1}\right)^{0.50} \quad \text{metric} \quad (3.61a)$$

$$= \frac{C_p}{1.00}\left(\frac{1}{I}\frac{m_G}{m_G+1}\right)^{0.50} \quad \text{English} \quad (3.61b)$$

where C_p = constant for material and gear type
= 2300 for steel spur or helical gears
= 2800 for steel straight, spiral, or Zerol bevel gears
I = dimensionless constant defined in AGMA standard 215.01 (see AGMA 218.01 for additional information covering special cases)
u = metric symbol for tooth ratio
m_G = English symbol for tooth ratio

Figure 3.36 shows geometry factors for the durability of spur gears of standard-addendum and 25 percent long-addendum pinion designs for both 20° and 25° pressure angles. These geometry values are based on the most critical stress being taken at the lowest point of single tooth contact (LPSTC).

The choice of the lowest point is felt to be more conservative than determining the stress at the pitch line. If the number of pinion teeth is over 25 and the contact ratio is 1.7 or higher, there is not much practical difference between stresses taken at the lowest point of single tooth contact and those taken at the pitch line.

Figure 3.37 shows geometry factors for helical-gear teeth of 15° and 30° helix angles and normal pressure angles of 20° and 25°. The critical stress is determined by an AGMA method that allows for load sharing in the zone of action. It is assumed that the axial contact ratio is 2.0 or more (minimum of two axial crossovers). If the axial contact ratio is only 1.0, the geometry factors will increase by a small amount. AGMA 218.01 has provision for calculating this special case. If the axial contact ratio is less than 1.0, the helical gear approaches the spur gear. (At an axial contact ratio of 0.5, the character of the gearset is about halfway between the character of a spur gear and that of a helical gear.)

Table 3.41 shows geometry factors for the durability of bevel gears. These values are based on I factors that were recommended in the 1970s and early 1980s in AGMA standards and in publications of the Gleason Works.

It seems likely that gear research will develop values for the durability geometry factors that are somewhat more complex and therefore more accurate than those given in Figs. 3.36 and 3.37 and in Table 3.41. There is not

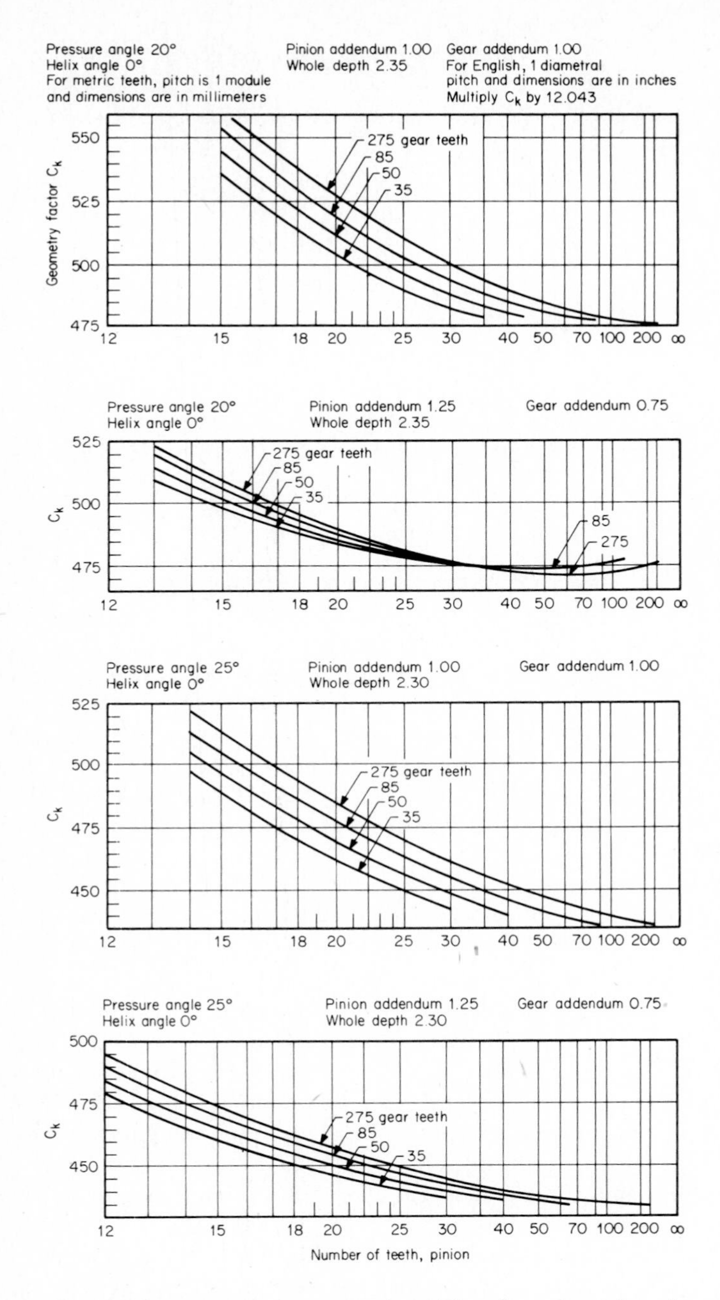

FIG. 3.36 Geometry factors for durability of spur gears based on the lowest point of single tooth contact (LPSTC).

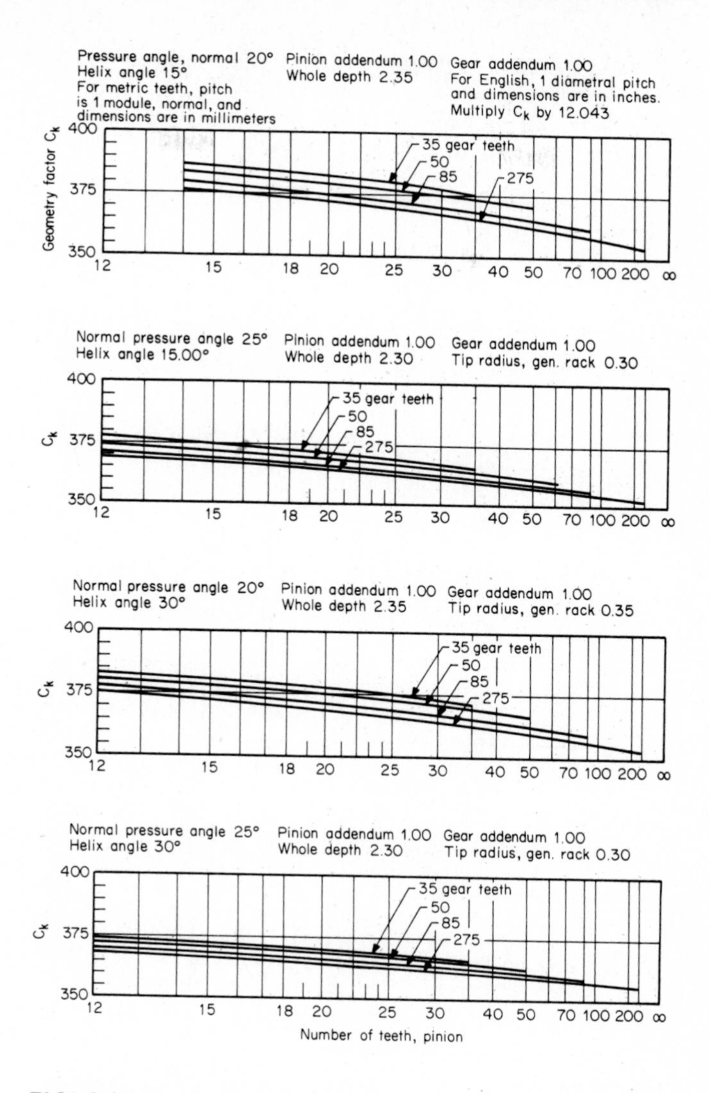

FIG. 3.37 Geometry factors for durability of helical gears based on tip loading and sharing of load between teeth in the zone of contact.

much chance, though, that they will change by any large amount. Experience in the gear trade over the 1960 to 1980 time period shows that the geometry constants for surface durability determined by AGMA methods are quite good.

TABLE 3.41 Geometry Factors C_k for Durability of Bevel Gears

No. pinion teeth	No. gear teeth	Straight bevels	Spiral bevels
15	20	8433	7780
	35	8731	7281
	50	8967	6837
	100	8752	6260
20	20	7952	7537
	35	8102	7285
	50	8315	6803
	100	8144	6283
25	25	7766	7379
	35	7808	7251
	50	7935	6742
	100	7766	6271
35	35	7565	6956
	50	7593	6627
	100	7317	6222
50	50	7353	6458
	100	6989	6121

Notes:
1. These values are subject to change as refinements are made in the procedure to determine stress intensity due to bending load on gear teeth.
2. This table is based on the normal design and manufacturing procedure recommended by the Gleason Works. In many cases there will be reason to modify the actual design, and this will tend to cause changes in the geometry factors from the "guideline" values given here.
3. The straight bevel data are for Coniflex bevel gears with a 20° pressure angle.
4. The spiral bevel data are for 20° pressure angle, 35° spiral angle bevel gears.
5. The geometry factors for Zerol bevel teeth tend to be the same as those for straight bevels.

3.29 Overall Derating Factor for Surface Durability

The overall derating factor evaluates all the things that tend to make the load higher than it should be for the torque being transmitted. The factor is

$$C_d = \frac{C_a C_m C_s}{C_v} \qquad \text{metric or English} \qquad (3.62)$$

where C_a = application factor. Generally C_a is taken to be the same as K_a. See Sec. 3.27.

C_m = load distribution factor. This factor is generally taken to be the same as K_m. See Sec. 3.27. In some special cases, K_m may justifiably be lower than C_m.

C_s = size factor. This factor is not the same as K_s.

C_v = dynamic factor. This factor is the same as K_v. See Sec. 3.27.

Since the overall derating for surface durability is rather close to being the same as the overall derating factor for strength, Sec. 3.27 should be read for general information and for specific data on the factors that are the same in derating for strength and for durability.

Size Factor C_s. From a surface durability standpoint, face width is probably the best way to evaluate the detrimental effect of size. (For tooth breakage, tooth size seems to be the best measure of the size effect.)

The size factor for durability (like that for strength, discussed in Sec. 3.27) is intended primarily for derating gears for the fact that large pieces of steel tend to have more flaws and are more difficult to forge and heat-treat for ideal metallurgical properties than are small pieces of steel.

Since 1966, AGMA standards have acknowledged the need for a size factor in the rating formula for durability of spur and helical gears. However, no numerical values have yet been agreed upon and written into standards. It is left to each designer to assign an appropriate value when large gears cannot be made with metal quality comparable with that of the small gears that were used to set basic allowable stresses in the standards.

For bevel gears, AGMA did set a size factor C_s, with numerical values, in AGMA 216.01A. This 1966 standard, though, deviates from spur and helical practice in that the detrimental effect of size is not handled by a factor greater than unity. Instead, a factor near unity is given to a large gear and a factor of 0.5 to a small gear. This, in effect, says that the *large gear* is the *standard* of reference and gives the small gear credit for being better than the large gear. The more usual AGMA philosophy is that the most is known and made right with the small gear, and it should be the standard of reference. Large gears are then derated for the fact that their size tends to give imperfections that reduce the amount of stress that can be carried.

AGMA 420.04, issued in 1975 to cover spur, helical, and spiral bevel gears, shows a minimum C_s value of 1.0 for spur and helical gears, but it does show C_s values less than 1.0 for spiral bevel gears (the same as AGMA 216.01A).

Figure 3.38 shows a plot of size factors for durability versus face width. The spiral bevel curve is worked out to place the unity value on the small gear and derate the large gear (rather than uprate the small gear). This change was made for this book by shifting the allowable contact stress so that the value used is right for the small gear at $C_s = 1.0$.

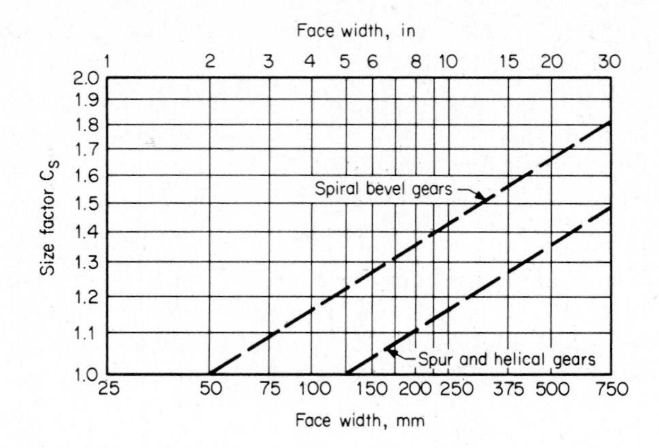

FIG. 3.38 Size factor for durability of spur, helical, and spiral bevel gears.

The size factor—by AGMA definition—does include "area of stress pattern." This variable shifts more in going from small to large bevel gears than it does in spur or helical gears. This has to do with the way the teeth are made and fitted. (It must be kept in mind that bevel teeth are on the surface of a *cone*, while spur and helical teeth are on a *cylinder*.)

The size factor for spiral bevel gears changes about 2 to 1 in going from a small gear to a large gear. The dashed curve for spur and helical gears changes about 1.5 to 1 in going from a small gear to a very large gear. The relative difference is essentially due to the geometric difference between bevel gears and helical gears.

The curve for C_s for spur and helical gears in Fig. 3.38 is shown dashed. It is not based on any AGMA standard. Instead, the curve represents the author's opinion of what can normally be expected in good industrial gear manufacture. Here are the considerations:

Up to 125 mm (5 in.) face width, it should be possible to pick a steel and process it well enough to have essentially no size effect. $C_s = 1.0$.

Above 125 mm face width, it becomes increasingly difficult to avoid size effects. A gearset with about 400 mm (16 in.) face width is apt to have a pinion around 400 mm pitch diameter mating with a gear in the range of 1600 mm (64 in.) pitch diameter. Metallurgical studies* of gears of this size generally show quality degradations ranging from small to very serious. A size derating of 1.3 for a gear with 400 mm face width seems to be about average for industrial gear manufacture around the world by

*See Sec. 4.10.

those skilled in the gear art. (Those unskilled may, of course, do much worse.)

In the aerospace field, great skill and effort are used to keep gear metallurgical quality under close control. Aerospace people could probably make gears up to 250 mm face width without any noticeable size effects. (Most aerospace gears are less than 125 mm face width.)

Marine gears are made in face widths up to 1000 mm (40 in.). Marine practice for ocean-going ships is highly specialized. An appropriate size derating for a 1000-mm marine drive might be around $C_s = 1.20$.

3.30 Load Rating of Worm Gearing

The complete worm-gear family comprises:

Crossed-helical gears (nonenveloping)

Cylindrical worm gearing (single-enveloping)

Double-enveloping worm gears

This section will cover methods for estimating the load-carrying capacity of each of the three family members. The method for crossed-helical gears will follow the work of Earle Buckingham. This method gives reasonable results and is a good guide. There are no trade standards on crossed-helical gears. Since Buckingham's work is all in English units, the synopsis given here will be in English symbols and units only. (Readers can probably best check the reference by sticking to English units.)

The rating for cylindrical worm gearing will follow AGMA 440.04. This is a good guide developed over many years. Not much change can be anticipated in the immediate future.

The rating for double-enveloping worm gears will follow AGMA 441.04. This again gives good guidance and will probably not change much in the immediate future.

The rating of all kinds of worm gearing is primarily based on surface durability. Tooth strength is usually not much of a risk—unless abnormally small threads or teeth are used. For this reason, strength is handled on a very approximate basis. The set is *sized* from the durability estimates.

Crossed-Helical-Gear Durability. Crossed-helical gears are generally rated only by a surface-durability formula. With point contact, not enough load can be carried to cause much danger of tooth breakage. The method presented by Earle Buckingham is a handy general formula for crossed-helical gears which gives very reasonable results. The first step is to calculate a *wear load* W_w:

$$W_w = A^6 B^3 K Q \tag{3.63}$$

Factors A and B depend on the ratio of the radii of curvature of the profiles of the driver and driven. The radius of curvature of the driver is

$$R_{c1} = \frac{D_1 \sin \phi_n}{2 \cos^2 \psi_1} \tag{3.64}$$

The radius of curvature of the driven member is determined by a similar equation. The pitch diameter of the driver is D_1, and the normal pressure angle is ϕ_n. The helix angle is ψ.

Table 3.42 shows the constants A^6 and B^3.

The constant K is *not* the same as the K factor discussed in Chap. 2. This K is

$$K = 29.7662 s^3 \left(\frac{1}{E_1} + \frac{1}{E_2} \right)^2 \tag{3.65}$$

The value s is the stress on the tooth surface, and E is the modulus of elasticity.

The value Q is a ratio factor.

$$Q = \left(\frac{R_{c1} R_{c2}}{R_{c1} + R_{c2}} \right)^2 \tag{3.66}$$

The allowable K for crossed-helical gears that Buckingham recommends is given in Table 3.43.

It should be noted that Table 3.43 shows quite a difference in capacity

TABLE 3.42 Factors for Rating Crossed-Helical Gears

Curvature ratio R_{c2}/R_{c1}	A^6	B^3	$A^6 B^3$
1.000	0.560	1.000	0.560
1.500	1.302	0.449	0.583
2.000	2.411	0.252	0.609
3.000	6.053	0.112	0.678
4.000	11.620	0.064	0.744
6.000	30.437	0.0292	0.889
10.000	106.069	0.0108	1.141

TABLE 3.43 Load-Stress Factors for Crossed-Helical Gears

Pinion (driver)	Gear (driven)	s, psi	K, lb
With initial point contact			
Hardened steel	Hardened steel	150,000	446
Hardened steel	Bronze, phosphor	83,000	170
Cast iron	Bronze, phosphor	83,000	302
Cast iron	Cast iron	90,000	385
With short running-in period			
Hardened steel	Hardened steel	—	446
Hardened steel	Bronze, phosphor	—	230
Cast iron	Bronze, phosphor	—	600
Cast iron	Cast iron	—	770
With extensive running in			
Hardened steel	Hardened steel	—	446
Hardened steel	Bronze, phosphor	—	300
Cast iron	Bronze, phosphor	—	1200
Cast iron	Cast iron	—	1500

with running in. A little wear at light load tends to broaden the point of contact considerably.

The calculated wear load in Eq. (3.63) should be compared with the *dynamic load* in the *normal plane.* If the torque on the driver is T_1, the transmitted load in the normal plane is

$$W_n = \frac{2T_1}{D_1 \cos \psi_1 \cos \phi_n} \tag{3.67}$$

If a high degree of accuracy is obtained, it is usually possible to keep the dynamic load on crossed-helical gears within about 150 percent of the transmitted load in the normal plane. The calculated wear load should be enough less than the transmitted load to allow for dynamic-load effects and to allow for any application factor that may be appropriate for the job.

There is little conclusive information to go on to judge the limiting rubbing velocity that can be handled by spiral gears of different materials. In the author's opinion, hardened steel on bronze will handle the most speed. With ordinary materials and good commercial accuracy, the rubbing speed should probably not exceed 30 m/s (6000 fpm). The author has used special bronze material in combination with a case-hardened and ground driver to handle rubbing speeds up to 50 m/s (10,000 fpm) in aircraft and steam-turbine applications. The other material combinations shown in Table 3.43 should probably not be used above a rubbing speed of 20 m/s (4000 fpm) in ordinary applications.

The sliding or rubbing velocity may be calculated by the formula

$$v_s = \frac{0.262 n_1 D_1}{\sin \psi_1} \quad \text{fpm} \tag{3.68}$$

where n_1 is the rotational speed of the driver in rpm.

A special word of caution should be added. The crosswise rubbing in crossed-helical sets tends to *destroy* the EHD oil film. This means that these gears can get into more trouble than other worm gears, bevel gears, or regular helical gears when the oil is thin or surface finishes are poor. Those using crossed-helical gears need past experience or test-stand results to make sure that the choice of lubricant and the quality of the tooth-surface finishes are appropriate for the application.

Cylindrical-Worm-Gear Durability. The load-carrying capacity of worm gearsets may be estimated from the general formula given below. Since this formula has been developed more by experience than by rational derivation, it is more reasonable to calculate tangential load capacity than it is to calculate stress and compare the calculated stress to allowable stress. The general formula for cylindrical worm gearsets is

$$W_t = \frac{K_s d_{p2}^{0.8} b' K_m K_v}{75.948} \quad \text{N} \qquad \text{metric} \tag{3.69a}$$

$$W_t = K_s D^{0.8} F_e K_m K_v \quad \text{lb} \qquad \text{English} \tag{3.69b}$$

where K_s = materials factor (see Table 3.44;* this is different from the K_s size factor)

d_{p2} or D = worm-gear pitch diameter, mm or in.

b' or F_e = effective face width, mm or in. (not to exceed 2/3 of the worm pitch diameter)

K_m = ratio correction factor, dimensionless (see Table 3.45)

K_v = dynamic factor, dimensionless (see Table 3.46)

The sliding velocity is

$$v_s = \frac{d_{p1} n_1}{19{,}098 \cos \gamma} \quad \text{m/s} \qquad \text{metric} \tag{3.70a}$$

*Tables 3.44 through 3.47 are extracted from AGMA Standard Practice for Single and Double Reduction Cylindrical-Worm and Helical-Worm Speed Reducers (AGMA 440.04, 1971), with the permission of the publisher, the American Gear Manufacturers Association, Suite 1000, 1901 North Fort Myer Drive, Arlington, Virginia 22209, U.S.A.

TABLE 3.44 Material Factor K_s for Cylindrical Worm Gears

For units of 75 mm (3 in.) center distance to about 1 meter (40 in.) center distance

Gear pitch diameter				
mm	in.	Sand cast	Static chill cast	Centrifugal cast
65	2.5	1000	—	—
75	3	960	—	—
100	4	900	—	—
125	5	855	—	—
150	6	820	—	—
175	7	790	—	—
200	8	760	1000	—
250	10	715	955	—
375	15	630	875	—
505	20	570	815	—
635	25	525	770	1000
760	30	—	740	985
1015	40	—	680	960
1270	50	—	635	945
1775	70	—	570	920

For units with less than 75 mm (3 in.) center distance

Center distance		
mm	in.	Maximum K_s value
12	0.5	725
25	1.0	735
38	1.5	760
50	2.0	800
63	2.5	880
75	3.0	1000

Notes: 1. For bronze worm gear and steel worm with at least HV 655 (HRC 58) surface hardness.

2. See Chap. 4 for worm-gear-material data.

3. Sliding velocity not to exceed 30 m/s (6000 fpm); worm speed not more than 3600 rpm.

$$v_s = \frac{0.2618 d n_W}{\cos \lambda} \quad \text{fpm} \qquad \text{English} \qquad (3.70b)$$

where n_1 or n_W = rotational speed of worm, rpm

γ or λ = lead angle of threads at mean worm diameter, degrees

TABLE 3.45 Ratio Correction Factor K_m for Cylindrical Worm Gears

Ratio u (m_G)	K_m	Ratio u (m_G)	K_m
3.0	0.500	14.0	0.799
3.5	0.554	16.0	0.809
4.0	0.593	20.0	0.820
4.5	0.620	30.0	0.825
5.0	0.645	40.0	0.815
6.0	0.679	50.0	0.785
7.0	0.706	60.0	0.745
8.0	0.724	70.0	0.687
9.0	0.744	80.0	0.622
10.0	0.760	90.0	0.555
12.0	0.783	100	0.490

TABLE 3.46 Velocity Factor K_v for Cylindrical Worm Gears

Sliding velocity		Velocity factor	Sliding velocity		Velocity factor
m/s	fpm	K_v	m/s	fpm	K_v
0.005	1	0.649	3.0	600	0.340
0.025	5	0.647	3.5	700	0.310
0.050	10	0.644	4.0	800	0.289
0.10	20	0.638	4.5	900	0.272
0.15	30	0.631	5.0	1000	0.258
0.20	40	0.625	6.0	1200	0.235
0.30	60	0.613	7.0	1400	0.216
0.40	80	0.600	8.0	1600	0.200
0.50	100	0.588	9.0	1800	0.187
0.75	150	0.558	10.0	2000	0.175
1.00	200	0.528	11.0	2200	0.165
1.25	250	0.500	12.0	2400	0.156
1.50	300	0.472	13.0	2600	0.148
1.75	350	0.446	14.0	2800	0.140
2.00	400	0.421	15.0	3000	0.134
2.25	450	0.398	20.0	4000	0.106
2.50	500	0.378	25.0	5000	0.089
2.75	550	0.358	30.0	6000	0.079

After the allowable value of W_t is determined, an output power capacity (at an application factor of 1) can be determined from

$$P = \frac{W_t d_{p2} n_2}{19{,}090{,}800} \quad \text{kW} \qquad \text{metric} \quad (3.71a)$$

$$= \frac{W_t D n_G}{126{,}000} \quad \text{hp} \qquad \text{English} \quad (3.71b)$$

where n_2 or n_G = gear speed, rpm.

The *available* output power from the worm gearset alone has to be divided by a service factor to make allowance for the smoothness or roughness of the driving and driven equipment. In worm-gear practice, this factor is still a *service factor*, since it also allows for the amount of time the unit is to be operated. As was explained in Sec. 3.27, the latest practice for spur and helical gears is to use an *application factor* instead of a service factor. The application factor considers roughness of connected equipment but does not evaluate life cycles or hours of operation.

Table 3.47 shows typical service factors. These were extracted from AGMA 440.04.

If input power is needed, the output power must have added to it the losses in the gearbox. These losses come from friction on the gear teeth, bearing losses, seal losses, and losses due to oil churning. The relation is

Input power =

power used by driven machine + sum of all losses (3.72)

The calculation of worm-gear efficiencies is too complex to be included in this book. The *Gear Handbook*, in Chaps. 13 and 14, gives a considerable amount of data on gear efficiency for all kinds of gears (including worm gears).

Worm gears are used with materials other than a bronze gear and a steel worm. There are no trade standards for these other materials. Some rough guidance as to what these other materials might be expected to do is given in Table 3.48.

The strength of worm-gear teeth is not well established. Since strength is usually not critical, there has not been any extensive research activity to establish calculation means and allowable bending stresses. (Some worm-gear builders have done a considerable amount of testing to establish data for their own products.)

A unit load can be calculated for worm gears:

$$U_\ell = \frac{W_t}{b' m_n} \quad \text{N/mm}^2 \qquad \text{metric} \quad (3.73a)$$

$$= \frac{W_t P_{nd}}{F_e} \quad \text{psi} \qquad \text{English} \quad (3.73b)$$

TABLE 3.47 Service Factors for Cylindrical Worm-Gear Units

Prime mover	Duration of service per day	Driven machine load classification: Uniform	Moderate shock	Heavy shock
Electric motor	Occasional 1/2 hour	0.80	0.90	1.00
	Intermittent 2 hours	0.90	1.00	1.25
	10 hours	1.00	1.25	1.50
	24 hours	1.25	1.50	1.75
Multicylinder internal combustion engine	Occasional 1/2 hour	0.90	1.00	1.25
	Intermittent 2 hours	1.00	1.25	1.50
	10 hours	1.25	1.50	1.75
	24 hours	1.50	1.75	2.00
Single-cylinder internal combustion engine	Occasional 1/2 hour	1.00	1.25	1.50
	Intermittent 2 hours	1.25	1.50	1.75
	10 hours	1.50	1.75	2.00
	24 hours	1.75	2.00	2.25
	Following service factors apply for applications involving frequent starts and stops			
Electric motor	Occasional 1/2 hour	0.90	1.00	1.25
	Intermittent 2 hours	1.00	1.25	1.50
	10 hours	1.25	1.50	1.75
	24 hours	1.50	1.75	2.00

Notes: 1. Time specified for intermittent and occasional service refers to total operating time per day.
2. Term "frequent starts and stops" refers to more than 10 starts per hour.

where W_t = tangential load, N (metric) or lb (English)
b' = effective face width, mm (metric)
F_e = effective face width, in. (English)

$$m_n = \frac{p_x \cos \gamma}{3.14159} \quad \text{(metric)}$$

$$P_{nd} = \frac{3.14159}{p_x \cos \lambda} \quad \text{(English)}$$

Table 3.49 gives some rather approximate values for unit load. Generally there is no problem if the unit load is less than the values shown (providing no unusual shock loads are present).

Double-Enveloping-Worm-Gear Durability. The load-carrying capacity of double-enveloping worm gears is calculated as the input horse-

TABLE 3.48 Guide to Approximate Material Capacity for a Variety of Worm-Gear Material Combinations

Material		Durability constant	Speed range, rubbing
Worm	Worm gear	K_s	velocity
Steel, 53 HRC minimum	Bronze, phosphor	600	Up to 30 m/s (6000 fpm)
Steel, 35 HRC minimum	Bronze, phosphor	600	Up to 10 m/s (2000 fpm)
Steel, 53 HRC minimum	Bronze, super manganese	1000	Up to 2 m/s (400 fpm)
Steel, 53 HRC minimum	Bronze, forged manganese	700	Up to 10 m/s (2000 fpm)
Cast iron	Cast iron	700	Up to 2 m/s (400 fpm)
Cast iron	Bronze, phosphor	600	Up to 10 m/s (2000 fpm)

power by a simplified empirical formula:

$$P = \frac{0.7457 n_1 K_s K_m K_a K_v}{u} \quad \text{kW} \qquad \text{metric} \qquad (3.74a)$$

$$= \frac{n_W}{m_G} K_s K_m K_a K_v \quad \text{hp} \qquad \text{English} \qquad (3.74b)$$

TABLE 3.49 Approximate Values of Unit Load for Cylindrical Worm Gears

Material combination		U_ℓ, psi	
Worm	Worm gear	Running	Static
Steel, hardened	Bronze, phosphor	1350	5,500
Steel, hardened	Bronze, super manganese	3200	12,500
Steel, hardened	Bronze, forged manganese	1800	7,000
Cast iron	Cast iron	1000	5,500
Cast iron	Bronze, phosphor	1350	5,500

Notes: 1. The hardened steel worm will usually be HV 655 or HRC 58 to get surface durability. Some slow-speed worm gears may use through-hardened steel worms. These have less surface durability. It is assumed that the hardened steel worm will at least have HV 345 or HRC 35 hardness.

2. These values assume an average contact ratio of only 1.5. Many worm-gear designs will have a higher contact ratio and therefore somewhat higher unit load capability.

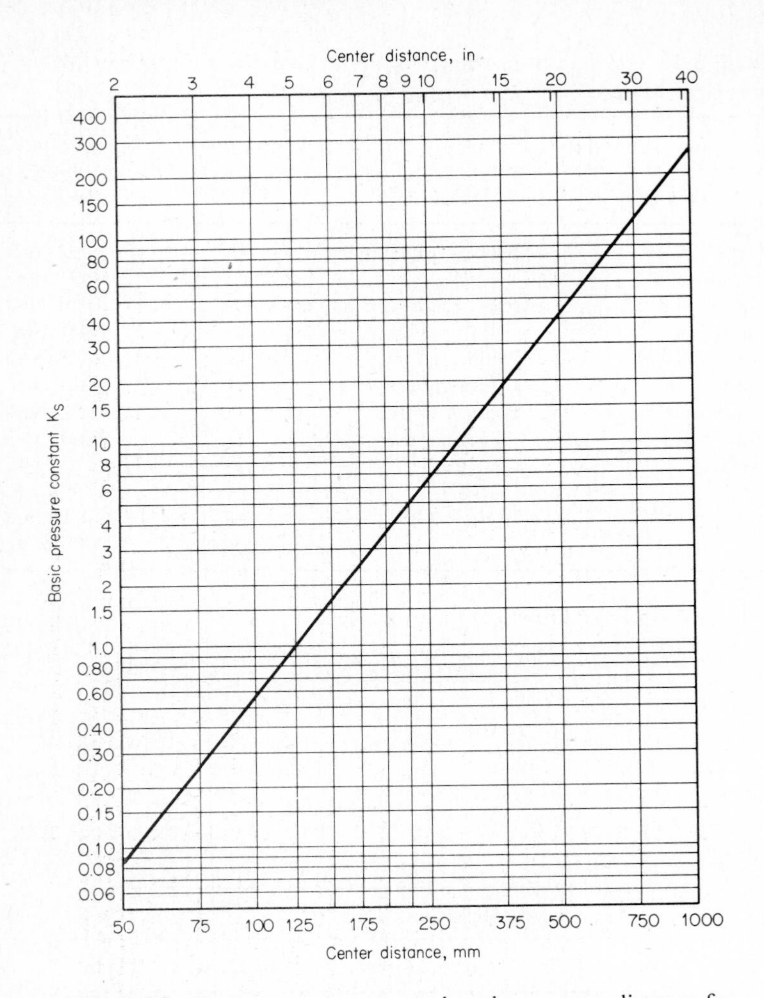

FIG. 3.39 Basic pressure constant based on center distance for standard-design double-enveloping worm gears.

where n_1 or n_W = worm speed, rpm

$$u \text{ or } m_G = \text{ratio} = \frac{\text{no. gear teeth}}{\text{no. worm threads}}$$

K_s = pressure constant based on center distance (see Fig. 3.39)

K_m = ratio correction factor (see Table 3.50*)

*Tables 3.50, 3.51, and 3.52 are extracted from AGMA Standard Practice for Single, Double and Triple-Reduction, Double-Enveloping Worm and Helical-Worm Speed Reducers (AGMA 441.04, 1978), with the permission of the publisher, the American Gear Manufacturers Association, Suite 1000, 1901 North Fort Myer Drive, Arlington, Virginia 22209, U.S.A.

TABLE 3.50 Ratio Correction Factor K_m for Double-Enveloping Worm Gears

Ratio u (m_G)	K_m	Ratio u (m_G)	K_m
3.0	0.380	14.0	0.720
3.5	0.435	16.0	0.727
4.0	0.490	20.0	0.737
4.5	0.520	30.0	0.746
5.0	0.550	40.0	0.748
6.0	0.604	50.0	0.750
7.0	0.632	60.0	0.751
8.0	0.665	70.0	0.752
9.0	0.675	80.0	0.752
10.0	0.690	90.0	0.753
12.0	0.706	100	0.753

K_a = face width and materials factor based on center distance (see Table 3.51)

K_v = velocity factor based on rubbing or sliding speed (see Fig. 3.40)

The sliding speed of double-enveloping worm gears is

$$v_s = \frac{d_{t1} n_1}{19{,}098 \cos \beta} \qquad \text{m/s} \qquad \text{metric} \qquad (3.75a)$$

$$v_s = \frac{0.2618 d_t n_W}{\cos \psi} \qquad \text{fpm} \qquad \text{English} \qquad (3.75b)$$

where d_{t1} or d_t = worm throat diameter (see Fig. 1.31)
n_1 or n_W = worm rpm
β or ψ = worm-gear helix angle

The output power can be obtained by subtracting all the losses from the input power. Thus

$$\text{Output power} = \text{input power} - \text{sum of all losses} \qquad (3.76)$$

AGMA 441.04 shows the standard method of calculating the ratings for double-enveloping worm gears. In Table 7 of this standard, overall efficiency values are given for a wide range of standard designs. The rating data shown above are extracted from this standard. Those designing double-enveloping worm gears should use this standard to obtain more data than can be covered in this book.

TABLE 3.51 Face Width and Materials Factors for Standard Design Double-Enveloping Worm Gears

Center distance		
mm	in.	Materials factor K_a
50.8	2.000	0.620
63.5	2.500	0.684
76.2	3.000	0.755
88.9	3.500	0.780
101.6	4.000	0.855
127.0	5.000	0.934
152.4	6.000	1.014
177.8	7.000	1.073
203.2	8.000	1.113
254.0	10.000	1.175
304.8	12.000	1.250
381.0	15.000	1.281
457.2	18.000	1.328
533.4	21.000	1.368
609.6	24.000	1.398
660.4	26.000	1.411
711.2	28.000	1.425
762.0	30.000	1.438
812.8	32.000	1.445
863.6	34.000	1.453
914.4	36.000	1.460
965.2	38.000	1.469
1016.0	40.000	1.476

In double-enveloping-worm-gear practice, the service factors are based on the shock in the system. (There is no particular difference between an electric motor drive and a turbine.) The usable power is the power obtained from Eq. (3.74) divided by the service factor. Table 3.52 shows service factors extracted from AGMA 441.04.

Comparison of Double-Enveloping and Cylindrical Worm-Gear Rating Procedures. There are several significant differences in practice. A wider variety of design practices are used for cylindrical worm gears. This has led to the use of more general-purpose formulas rather than highly specialized formulas.

To help keep the reader from getting confused over the data presented, these comparisons are worth noting:

Item	Comparison
Power	Cylindrical ratings are based on output power. Double-enveloping ratings are based on input power.
Size	The worm-gear pitch diameter is the primary size quantity for cylindrical worm-gear units. The double-enveloping units use center distance as the primary size quantity.
Materials	Several materials are in general use for the worms or worm gears of cylindrical worm units. Double-enveloping worm-gear units usually use through-hardened steel worms and chill-cast or centrifugally cast bronze gears. For each center distance and speed, there is essentially only one choice of material. (This explains why the "material factor" is handled indirectly as a function of center distance and rubbing speed.)
Design flexibility	Cylindrical worm-gear practice allows some flexibility in regard to worm pitch diameter for a given center distance and some flexibility on other design variables. For double-enveloping worm gears, all variables are tied quite closely to the center distance and the desired ratio.

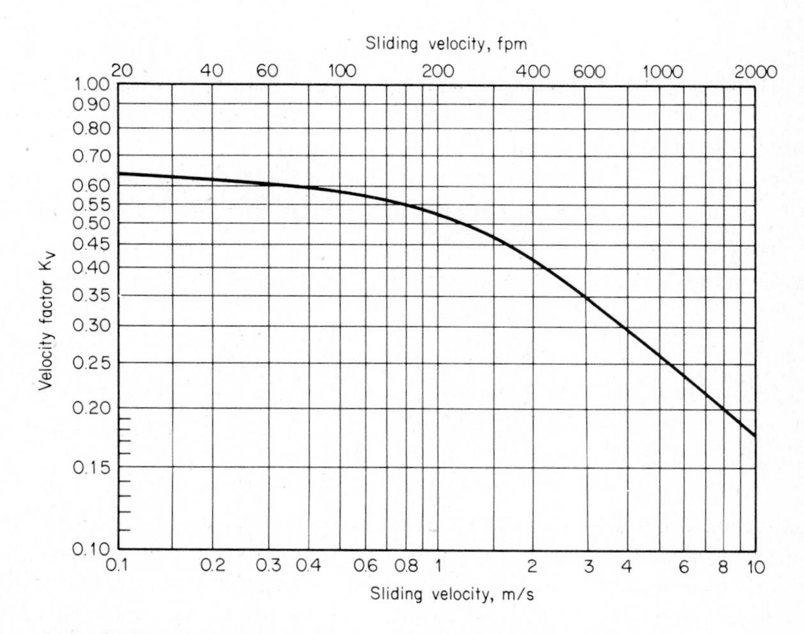

FIG. 3.40 Velocity factor for double-enveloping worm gears.

TABLE 3.52 Service Factors for Double-Enveloping Worm Gears

Hours/day	Uniform	Moderate shock	Heavy shock	Extreme shock
1/2	0.6	0.8	0.9	1.1
1	0.7	0.9	1.0	1.2
2	0.9	1.0	1.2	1.3
10	1.0	1.2	1.3	1.5
24	1.2	1.3	1.5	1.75

3.31 Design Formulas for Scoring

The problem of designing gears to resist scoring is still not completely solved. Section 2.5 gave the historical background of PVT and flash-temperature calculations.

Much work has been done in recent years on elastohydrodynamic (EHD) calculations of oil-film thickness and the possible relation of gear-tooth surface roughness to EHD oil film.

The best that can be done at present (1984) is to estimate the *hazard* of scoring. There is no positive assurance that gears that are calculated to be quite good will not score, and gears that are calculated to be somewhat poor may still perform satisfactorily. The best procedure is to calculate the scoring risk and then plan to handle it by either design changes to lessen the scoring risk or special development of the gearset and its lubrication system to handle a latent scoring hazard.

This section will give two design approaches. One is based on flash temperature and *hot scoring;* the other is based on oil-film thickness and *cold scoring*.

Hot Scoring. A general design formula for spur and helical gears is

$$T_f = T_b + Z_t Z_s Z_c \tag{3.77}$$

where T_f = flash temperature index, °C or °F
T_b = gear body temperature, °C or °F
Z_t = geometry constant, dimensionless
Z_s = surface finish constant, dimensionless
Z_c = scoring criterion number, °C factor or °F factor

The body temperature is hard to measure, but it can be measured with thermocouples and a means of getting the reading out of the rotating part (by slip rings or by miniature radio). In well-designed gears with oil nozzles delivering enough* oil, the temperature rise of the gear body (over the

*See the *Gear Handbook*, Chap. 15, for general information on gear lubrication methods.

incoming oil temperature) ought not to exceed the following values:

25°C (45°F) for aerospace power gears

15°C (27°F) for turbine gears

The geometry constant Z_t was defined in Sec. 2.5, Eq. (2.46). If the teeth have no tip relief, Z_t should be calculated for the tips of the pinion and the gear, since the hazard of scoring will be highest at the tips. Table 3.53 gives some representative values of Z_t for tip conditions.

High-performance gears with teeth 2.5 module (10 diametral pitch) or larger are generally given a *standard* profile modification. With profile modification, the most critical point for scoring is generally at the start of modification.

Table 3.54 shows a design guide for profile modification worked out by

TABLE 3.53 Geometry Constant for Scoring Z_t at the Tip of the Tooth

Pressure angle α_t or ϕ_t	No. pinion teeth z_1 or N_P	No. gear teeth z_2 or N_G	Pinion addendum h_{a1} or a_P (for $m = 1.0$ or $P_d = 1.0$)	Gear addendum h_{a2} or a_G (for $m = 1.0$ or $P_d = 1.0$)	Z_t At pinion tip	Z_t At gear tip
20°	18	25	1.0	1.0	0.0184	−0.0278
	18	35	1.0	1.0	0.0139	−0.0281
	18	85	1.0	1.0	0.0092	−0.0307
	25	25	1.0	1.0	0.0200	−0.0200
	25	35	1.0	1.0	0.0144	−0.0187
	25	85	1.0	1.0	0.0088	−0.0167
	12	35	1.25	0.75	0.0161	−0.0402
	18	85	1.25	0.75	0.0107	−0.0161
	25	85	1.25	0.75	0.0104	−0.0112
	35	85	1.25	0.75	0.0101	−0.0087
	35	275	1.25	0.75	0.007	−0.0072
25°	18	25	1.0	1.0	0.0135	−0.0169
	18	35	1.0	1.0	0.0107	−0.0168
	18	85	1.0	1.0	0.0074	−0.0141
	25	25	1.0	1.0	0.0141	−0.0141
	25	35	1.0	1.0	0.0107	−0.0126
	25	85	1.0	1.0	0.0069	−0.0103
	12	35	1.25	0.75	0.0328	−0.0160
	12	85	1.25	0.75	0.0500	−0.0151
	18	85	1.25	0.75	0.0056	−0.0095
	25	85	1.25	0.75	0.0082	−0.0073
	35	85	1.25	0.75	0.0078	−0.0060
	35	275	1.25	0.75	0.0056	−0.0048

Note: When proper profile modification is made, the risk of scoring is probably more critical at the start of modification than at the tip of the tooth. Values of Z_t at the approximate start of modification are given in Figs. 3.41 to 3.44.

TABLE 3.54 Depth to Start of Profile Modification for General-Purpose Gears

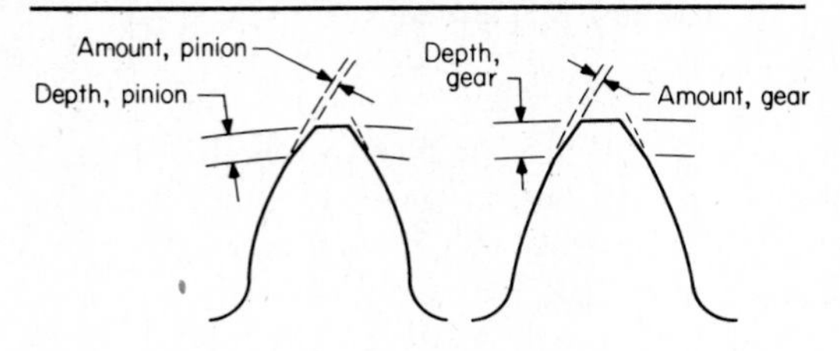

Schematic diagram to show locations of amount of profile modification and depth of profile modification on a pinion and on a gear.

Normal pressure angle	Pinion (driver)	Gear (driven)
20°	0.400	0.450
$22\frac{1}{2}$°	0.365	0.415
25°	0.325	0.375

Notes: 1. The depth shown is in millimeters for 1 module, normal, or in inches for 1 normal diametral pitch. For other size teeth, multiply depth by normal module for metric, or divide depth by normal diametral pitch for English.

2. In some cases, manufacturing considerations lead to putting all the modification on the pinion. If this is done, the modification that might have been put at the gear tip is put at the pinion form diameter. In this case, a diameter for start modification can be calculated for the *gear*. Then as a next step, Table 9.16 formulas can be used to find the diameter on the *pinion* that matches this diameter. This matching pinion diameter is then used as a start of modification diameter for the lower flank of the pinion.

the author for general-purpose gearing with moderately heavy loads. (This guide may not be appropriate for highly critical aerospace power gears or the most critical vehicle gears—more on this in Sec. 8.2.)

The values of Z_t that match the modification depth shown in Table 3.54 are plotted in Figs. 3.41 to 3.44. See Sec. 9.14 for a general method to determine Z at any point on the profile.

A standard amount of modification for general design can be set:

$$\text{Gear-tip modification} = \frac{6.5 C_m W_t}{10^5 b} \quad \text{mm} \quad \text{metric} \quad (3.78a)$$

$$= \frac{4.5 C_m W_t}{10^7 F} \quad \text{in.} \quad \text{English} \quad (3.78b)$$

$$\text{Pinion-tip modification} = \frac{4.1 C_m W_t}{10^5 b} \quad \text{mm} \qquad \text{metric} \qquad (3.79a)$$

$$= \frac{2.8 C_m W_t}{10^7 F} \quad \text{in.} \qquad \text{English} \qquad (3.79b)$$

where C_m is the load-distribution factor for surface durability.

The factor Z_s allows for surface finish conditions. This is a most difficult variable to determine. With much test-stand experience, a manufacturer can determine reasonable values for calculation purposes. On a new product, one must consider the finish achieved in the shop, the initial wear-in (which may considerably improve the effective finish, from a scoring standpoint), and the beneficial effects of lubricant additives. (Special oils and additives may be used to condition the surfaces of gears critical to scoring.)

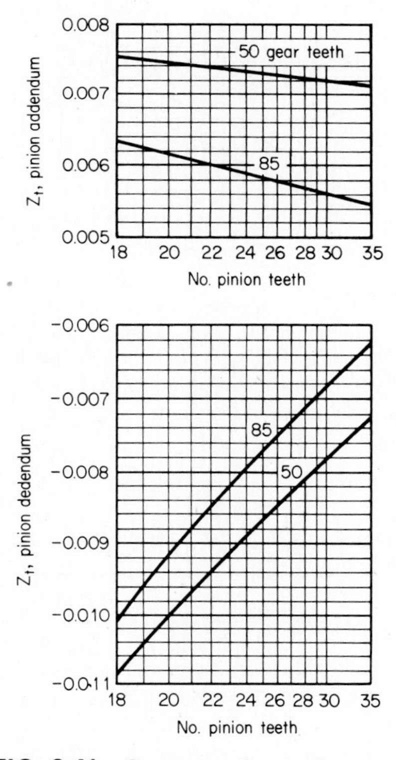

FIG. 3.41 Geometry factor for scoring, Z_t, at the start of standard profile modification. Full depth, 20° pressure angle spur gears. Pinion addendum 1.00, gear addendum 1.00.

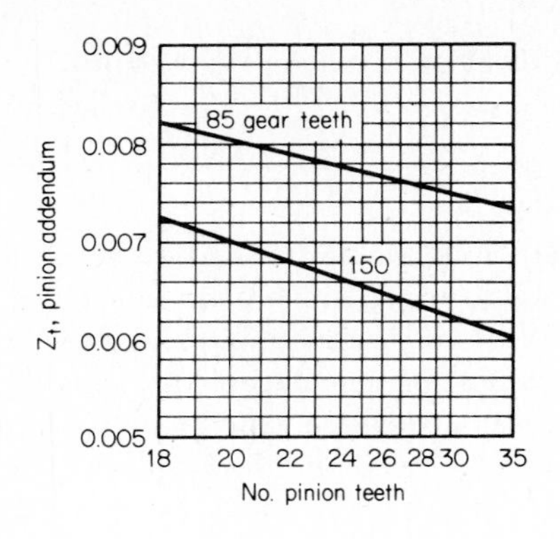

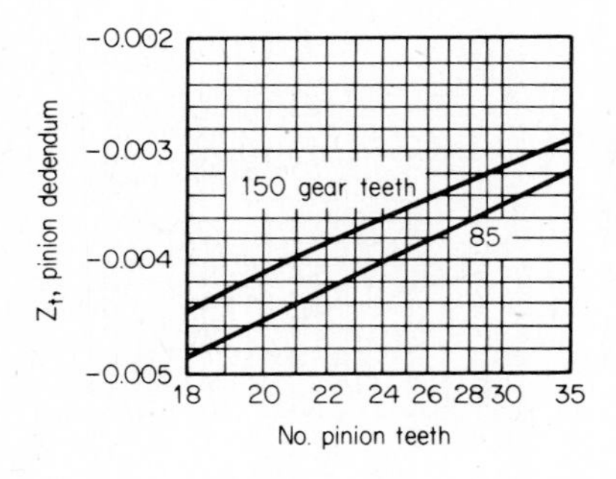

FIG. 3.42 Geometry factor for scoring, Z_t, at the start of standard profile modification. Full depth, 20° pressure angle spur gears. Pinion addendum 1.25, gear addendum 0.75.

The following values represent a rough guide for Z_s:

Initial finish, AA	Z_s	Comment
0.3 μm (12 μin.)	1.2	Usually honed, after finish ground
0.5 μm (20 μin.)	1.5	Fine finish; some break-in needed
0.75 μm (30 μin.)	1.7	Good finish; special break-in needed (for Z_s to equal 1.7)
1 μm (40 μin.)	2.0	Nominal finish; extensive break-in needed (for Z_s to equal 2.0)
1.5 μm (60 μin.)	2.5	Poor finish; special wear-in procedure should be used (then $Z_s = 2.5$ is possible)

The factor Z_c is the scoring criterion number. This index of scoring risk was presented in Sec. 2.5, Eq. (2.44). This factor will be given in somewhat more detail here.

$$Z_c = \left(\frac{W_{te}}{b}\right)^{0.75} (n_1)^{0.5} \left(\frac{m_t^{1/4}}{1.094}\right) \qquad \text{°C factor} \qquad \text{metric} \qquad (3.80a)$$

$$= \left(\frac{W_{te}}{F}\right)^{0.75} (n_P)^{0.5} \left(\frac{1}{P_t^{0.25}}\right) \qquad \text{°F factor} \qquad \text{English} \qquad (3.80b)$$

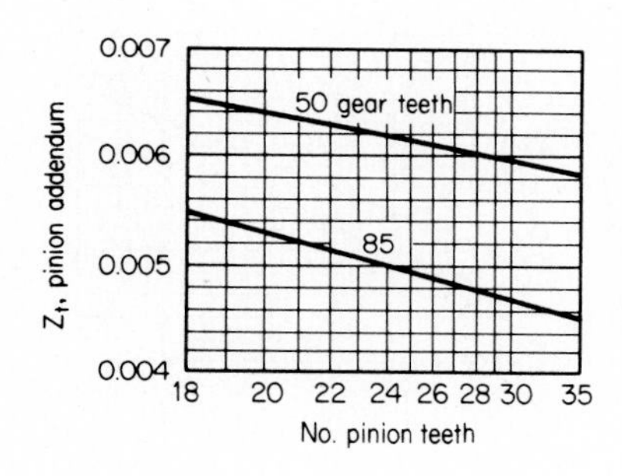

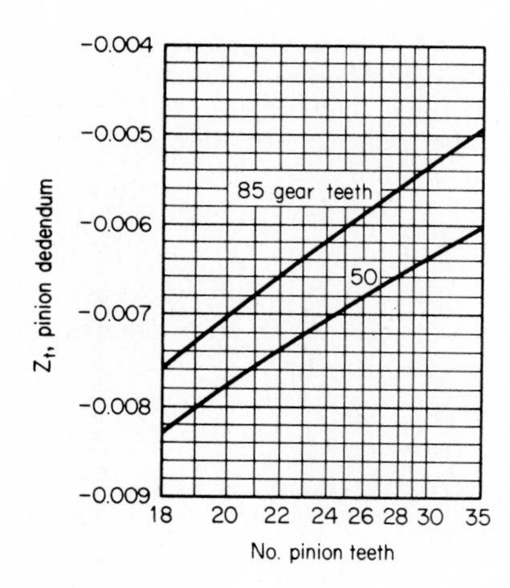

FIG. 3.43 Geometry factor for scoring, Z_t, at the start of standard profile modification. Full depth, 25° pressure angle spur gears. Pinion addendum 1.00, gear addendum 1.00.

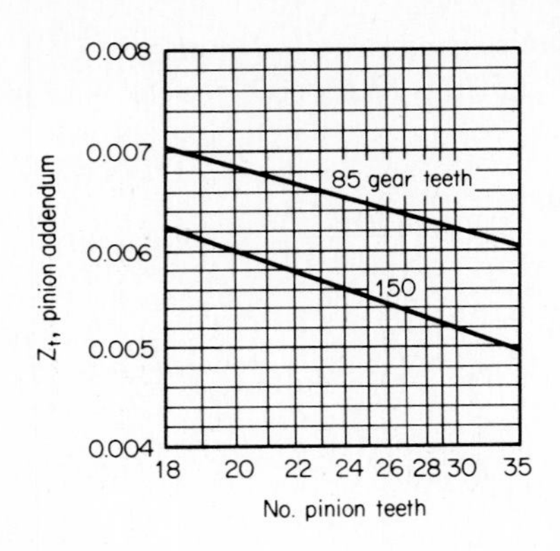

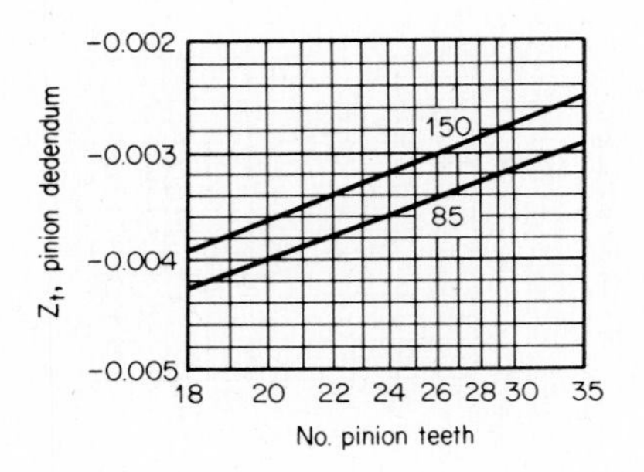

FIG. 3.44 Geometry factor for scoring, Z_t, at the start of standard profile modification. Full depth, 25° pressure angle spur gears. Pinion addendum 1.25, gear addendum 0.75.

where W_{te} = tangential load that is applied to a point on the profile in danger of scoring, newtons (metric) or pounds (English)
b and F = face width, mm or in.
n_1 and n_P = pinion rpm
m_t = module, transverse
P_t = transverse diametral pitch

The load applied at the start of profile modification should generally be the *full* load. For spur gears with modification, the design is generally worked out so that the start of modification becomes a real highest point of single-tooth loading. For helical gears, the design may have a high enough transverse contact ratio to keep the maximum effective load somewhat below the full load. (Usually doing an extensive analysis of load sharing to find out if the helical tooth merited less than full load at the start of modification is not worth the trouble.)

If the teeth are unmodified, close to full load may be applied at the tooth tips. The spur gear, unmodified, would only get about 50 percent load at the tip—since two pair of teeth are sharing the load. However, scoring is a hazard at the position of the *worst* tooth-to-tooth spacing error. At this position, the tooth tip may get full load because the spacing error prevented load sharing. Then the few worst teeth may score, and the scoring may wear away enough metal to restore load sharing. If the scoring is not too bad, it may heal up, and then the unit may run without further scoring.

For both spur and helical gears that are unmodified, a simple and conservative design practice is to take full load at the tooth tips when figuring the scoring risk.

The load distribution across the face width also enters into the choice of load. If $C_m = 1.5$, then the load W_{te} should be 50 percent higher. Scoring, of course, is most apt to happen at the end of the face width that is overloaded. To sum it up:

$$W_{te} = W_t \times C_m \times \text{percent load for profile position} \qquad (3.81)$$

Some values of the flash temperature and a rough guess as to the probability of scoring are given in Table 3.55.

Cold Scoring. Cold scoring occurs when the EHD oil film is small compared with the surface roughness, and the lubricant does not have enough additives to prevent scoring as the asperities on the contacting gear-tooth surfaces abrasively wear.

TABLE 3.55 Flash Temperature Limits T_f and Scoring Probability

	Risk of Scoring			
	Low		High	
	°C	°F	°C	°F
Synthetic oil				
Mil-L-7808	135	275	175	350
Mil-L-23699	150	300	190	375
Mineral oil				
Mil-O-6081, grade 1005	65	150	120	250
Mil-L-6086, grade medium	160	325	200	400
SAE 50 motor oil with mild EP	200	400	260	500
Mil-L-2105, grade 90 (SAE 90 gear oil)	260	500	315	600

The first design step is to calculate an approximate EHD oil-film thickness, h_{min}. A relatively exact calculation of h_{min} is quite complicated and requires special data about the oil. (Paraffinic oils have somewhat different data than napthenic oils.)

A simple, but approximate, calculation for the minimum oil film at the pitch line will be given. The calculation will be given in English units only. The answer, of course, can easily be changed into metric units.

$$h_{min} = \frac{44.6 r_e (\text{lubricant factor})(\text{velocity factor})}{(\text{loading factor})} \tag{3.82}$$

where r_e = effective radius of curvature at pitch diameter

$$= \frac{C \sin \phi_n}{\cos^2 \psi} \frac{m_G}{(m_G + 1)^2} \tag{3.83}$$

$$\text{Lubricant factor} = (\propto E')^{0.54} \tag{3.84}$$

$\propto$ = lubricant pressure—viscosity coefficient, in.^{2}/lb (see Table 3.56)

E' = effective elastic modulus for a steel gearset

$$= \frac{\pi}{2} \frac{E}{(1 - \nu^2)}$$

$$= 51.7 \times 10^6 \text{ psi}$$

since E = 30,000,000 psi

ν = Poisson's ratio = 0.3

$$\text{Velocity factor} = \left(\frac{\mu_0 u}{E' r_e}\right)^{0.70} \tag{3.85}$$

μ_0 = lubricant viscosity at operating temperatures, cP (centipoises); see Table 3.56

u = rolling velocity,* in./second

$$= \frac{\pi n_P d \sin \phi_t}{60}$$

d = pinion pitch diameter

n_P = pinion rpm

ϕ_t = transverse pressure angle

$$\text{Loading factor} = \left(\frac{W_t}{F E' r_e}\right)^{0.13} \tag{3.86}$$

W_t = tangential load, lb

F = face width, in.

*At the pitch line.

TABLE 3.56 Nominal Lubricant Properties

Kind of oil	Temperature °C	Temperature °F	Viscosity, cP	Lubricant pressure-viscosity coefficient, in.^{2}/lb
Mil-L-7808	100	212	3.6 min.	0.000105
	71	160	5.5 min.	0.000115
Mil-L-23699	100	212	5.0 min.	0.000105
	71	160	8.0 min.	0.000115
Mil-O-6081, grade 1005	100	212	5.0 min.	0.000075
Mil-L-6086 grade medium	100	212	8.0 min.	0.000096
	71	160	17.0 min.	0.000110
SAE 30 motor oil	100	212	11.5 min.	0.000096
SAE 50 motor oil	100	212	17 min.	0.000096
SAE 90 gear oil	100	212	16.5 min.	0.000096
	71	160	45 min.	0.000110
SAE 140 gear oil	100	212	35 min.	0.000096

Note: The SAE oils vary somewhat in viscosity limits in different trade applications. For instance, the minimum for SAE 90 gear oil may be as low as 15 cP and SAE 140 may be as low as 25 cP.

The answer, h_{min}, comes out in microinches (μin.). This value can be changed to microns (μm) by dividing by 39.37.

Figure 3.45 shows some plotted values of h_{min} for a heavy vehicle oil, SAE 90 gear oil, and for a light synthetic oil, Mil-L-23699, that is used in the aerospace field. Note that the cold synthetic oil gives less oil-film thickness than the hot vehicle oil.

Table 3.57 shows a general study of how oil-film thickness changes with gear size, gear-tooth load, and pitch-line velocity. Note that pitch-line velocity is by far the most important variable. This table was made for an oil that might be used with medium-speed industrial gears.

After the minimum EHD oil-film thickness is determined, it can be compared with the surface finish of the gear teeth by Fig. 3.46. The surface finish to be used is not the finish before the gears have operated, but the effective finish after they have been given whatever break-in or wear-in treatment is intended.

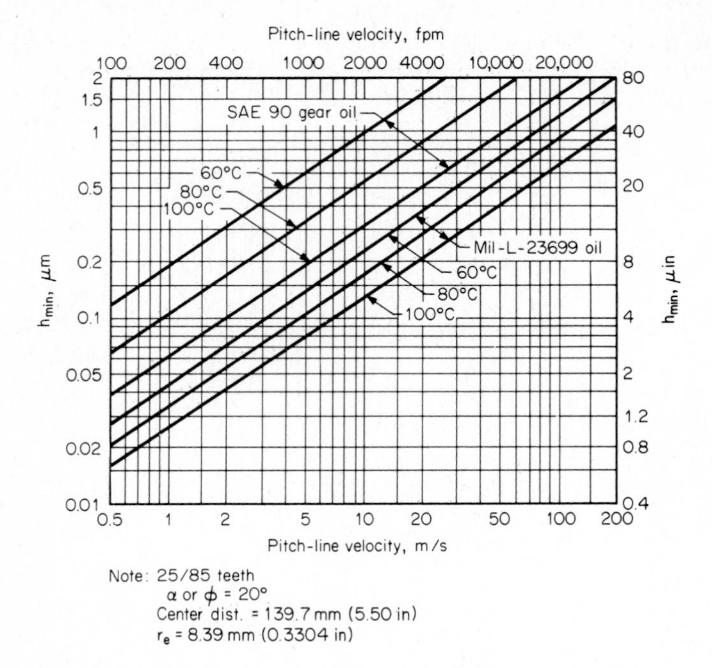

FIG. 3.45 Approximate EHD oil-film thickness for a heavy mineral oil used in vehicles and a light synthetic oil used in aircraft. Note size of gearset.

The effective finish for a pair of gears running together is

$$S' = (S_1^2 + S_2^2)^{0.50} \tag{3.87}$$

where S_1 = finish of one gear after break-in, arithmetic average
S_2 = finish of mating gear after break-in, arithmetic average

The ratio of film thickness to surface finish is

$$\Lambda = \frac{h_{\min}}{S'} \tag{3.88}$$

This ratio, which can be called the *lambda ratio*, is usually over 1.0 for Regime III conditions. In Regime II, it will tend to be less than 1.0, with usual values around 0.4 to 0.8. In Regime I, the lambda ratio is often around 0.1 to 0.3.

Since the lambda ratio varies considerably, the best way to estimate probable gear running conditions is to use a diagram like Fig. 3.46. (Gear builders can plot their own Fig. 3.46 once they gain considerable experience in the application of their gears.) The secret, of course, to successful gear application over all regimes of lubrication is to make up for small lambda ratio values by appropriately strong additives in the oil.

In general, these conclusions hold:

Regime	Conclusion
I	A mild anti-wear oil or a straight mineral oil will probably be OK. No serious hazard of cold scoring.
II	Moderate hazard of cold scoring. Need an anti-wear oil or an EP oil.
III	High hazard of cold scoring. Need a strong EP oil.

TABLE 3.57 Approximate EHD Minimum Oil-Film Thickness for Mil-L-6086 Oil (Similar to AGMA 2, SAE 30 Motor Oil or ASTM 315 Oil)

Gear mesh			h_{min}, μm				h_{min}, μin.			
Temperature		K factor,*	Pitch-line speed, m/s				Pitch-line speed, fpm			
°C	°F	N/mm²	0.5	2.5	10	50	100	500	2000	10,000
Small gear unit†										
60	140	1.38	0.053	0.163	0.44	1.33	2.08	6.41	17.5	52.4
		4.14	0.045	0.141	0.38	1.15	1.80	5.56	15.17	45.4
		13.8	0.039	0.120	0.33	0.98	1.54	4.75	12.97	38.8
80	176	1.38	0.031	0.097	0.26	0.79	1.24	3.82	10.42	31.2
		4.14	0.027	0.084	0.23	0.69	1.08	3.31	9.03	27.1
		13.8	0.023	0.072	0.20	0.58	0.92	2.83	7.72	23.1
100	212	1.38	0.021	0.065	0.18	0.53	0.83	2.56	6.98	20.9
		4.14	0.018	0.056	0.15	0.46	0.72	2.22	6.05	18.1
		13.8	0.015	0.048	0.13	0.39	0.61	1.89	5.17	15.4
Large gear unit‡										
60	140	1.38	0.086	0.265	0.72	2.15	3.4	10.43	28.4	85.1
		4.14	0.073	0.229	0.62	1.87	2.9	9.04	24.6	73.8
		13.8	0.063	0.196	0.53	1.60	2.5	7.73	21.0	63.0
80	176	1.38	0.051	0.157	0.43	1.28	2.01	6.20	16.9	50.61
		4.14	0.044	0.136	0.37	1.11	1.74	5.38	14.6	43.89
		13.8	0.038	0.116	0.32	0.95	1.49	4.59	12.5	37.5
100	212	1.38	0.034	0.105	0.29	0.86	1.35	4.16	11.3	33.97
		4.14	0.029	0.092	0.25	0.75	1.17	3.61	9.8	29.5
		13.8	0.025	0.078	0.21	0.64	1.00	3.08	8.37	25.18

*1.38 N/mm² = 200 psi; 4.14 N/mm² = 600 psi; 13.8 N/mm² = 2000 psi.

†r_e = 8.39 mm = 0.3304 in.

‡r_e = 41.96 mm = 1.652 in.

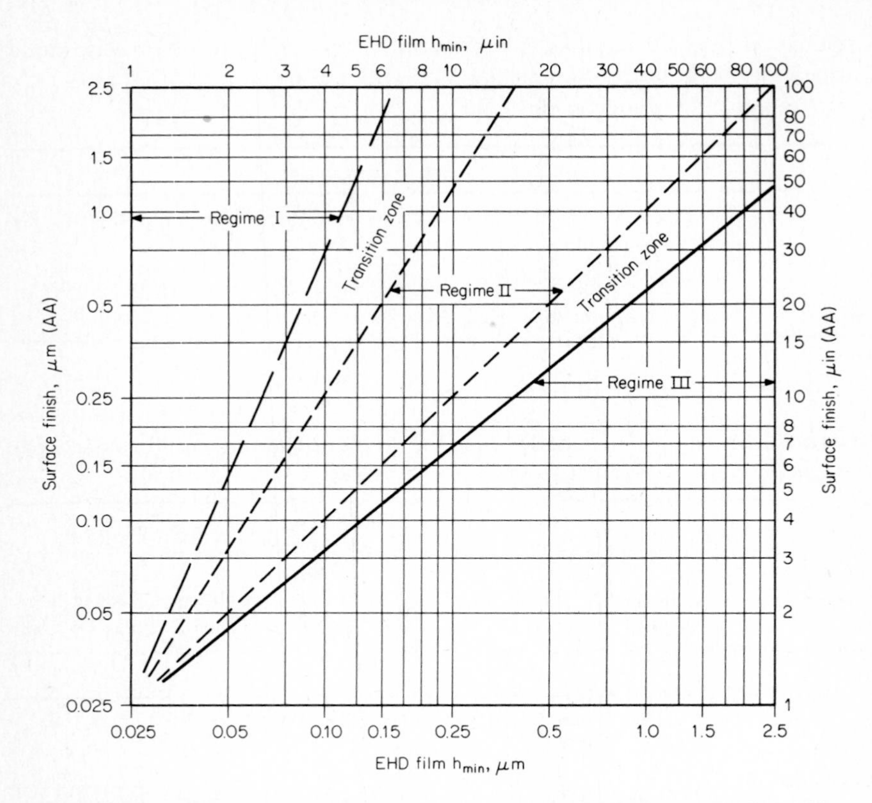

FIG. 3.46 Regimes of lubrication are determined by minimum EHD oil-film thickness and effective surface finish.

Design Practice to Handle Scoring. In most cases, gears are sized to meet durability requirements. Then the tooth size is made large enough to meet tooth-strength requirements. Gear sizing is seldom done to meet scoring requirements.

The usual procedure is to establish the gear design and then *check the design* for scoring hazard. What can the designer do if:

1 There is a serious risk of hot scoring?

2 There is a serious risk of cold scoring?

In the case of hot scoring, the most effective things to do are to improve the surface finish and to use a more score-resistant oil.

Using smaller gear teeth and changing the addendum proportions may be of some help. (Note in Figs. 3.41. to 3.44 how the Z_t value changes as more or less long addendum is put on the pinion.)

A higher pressure angle or a special profile modification can also help (note Problem 6 in Chap. 8), as can better tooth accuracy (note data on tooth accuracy in Sec. 5.18).

If a design is marginal and all the obvious things have been done, it may be necessary to copper-plate or silver-plate the teeth. A very thin deposit of copper or silver is quite effective in preventing scoring. Large turbine gears, running at very high speeds, are routinely plated with copper or silver to control the scoring hazard. Some gear drives for large propeller-driven aircraft have had to use silver-plated teeth.

If cold scoring is the hazard and the gears are in Regime I or in the transition zone to Regime II, the situation may be rather critical. The most obvious thing to do is to use a strong EP oil. (The chemical additives in the extreme pressure oil tend to make a *chemical* film that will substitute for the EHD film that is missing.)

In Regime I, and to a lesser extent in Regime II, the gears tend to machine themselves in service. A gear pair with a 2-μm finish when it left the factory may, in a few days of running, wear in a new surface that is as smooth as 0.5 μm (in the direction of sliding).

This means that it is critical to use an extra-strong EP oil during the break-in period. Also, the gears should not be operated at maximum torque or maximum temperature while they are wearing in. If the wear-in is accomplished without serious damage to the profiles, then the gears can often run for years without the need for a special EP oil.

When cold scoring is a hazard, it is helpful to use as heavy an oil as possible and to use the right amount of profile modification.

In conclusion to this section, it should be said that experience is *most important* in handling scoring problems. If gears score on the test stand or in the field, it is usually possible to try different improvements in lubrication and in the way the gear teeth are finished. Sometimes the *pattern* of grinding or cutting marks can be changed, with much improvement in scoring resistance. Sometimes an oil specialist can recommend a change in lubricant or a lubricant additive that will clear up the scoring problem. Sometimes a change in the heat-treatment procedure used in making the gear teeth will result in a more score-resistant tooth surface. Each builder of gears for applications with high scoring hazard needs to learn a "recipe" for making gears that will survive without undue scoring trouble.

3.32 Trade Standards for Rating Gears

Sections 3.24 to 3.30 gave general methods for determining gear load-carrying capacity. The reader was probably surprised to note that the load-carrying capacity is quite *elastic*. If one assumes that a high degree of accuracy is obtained in the gearing and that the driving and driven apparatus do not impose shock, one obtains a large amount of capacity for a given size of gearset. On the other hand, if poor accuracy and rough-running apparatus are assumed, the calculated capacity becomes quite low. In a sense, the general rating formulas require the designer to use considerable judgment in evaluating all the factors that affect the capacity of a given design.

In contrast, standard rating formulas are usually not elastic. They give a definite answer.

Standards are established by a technical group which meets to discuss the intensity of loading that their field experience has shown to be safe and conservative. In some cases, the degree of quality on which a standard is based is spelled out in the standard. In many cases, though, not all the things that contribute to the quality of a gear are precisely defined. A newcomer in a given gear field may have to scout around to find out just how good the gears that are being made by established manufacturers in the field are.

The principal groups writing general trade standards for gears are:

The American Gear Manufacturers
Association (AGMA)
1901 North Fort Myer Drive, Suite 1000
Arlington, Virginia 22209, U.S.A.

International Standards Organization
(ISO)
(Secretariat address)
DIN · Kamestrasse 2-8
D-5000 Köln
German Federal Republic

Deutsches Institute für Normung
(DIN)
Berlin 30 and Köln 1
German Federal Republic

The standards for gear design or for gear rating may be written to cover a broad field, or they may be product standards for a limited area of usage. For instance, a "mother" standard on gear rating will tend to cover the principles and practice for rating the surface durability and strength of all kinds of spur and helical gears. This kind of standard will often give more than one method for determining a variable. A "product" standard will cover only a limited field of usage. The product standard will be quite specific on how to rate the gears. The principle is that the product standard is derived from the mother standard, and so it can be much shorter and more specific. In a limited field, those who are building and using the gears should have rather good experience to judge what is correct for good technical practice.

Product standards on gear units cover a number of things beyond the capacity of the gear teeth. Frequently the capacity of a set has to be limited by the capacity of the casing to radiate and conduct heat away. The kind of lubrication, the kind of materials, the kind of bearings, and the amount of the service factor are some of the other things that may be specified in gear standards.

The material in this book covers many of the things that are in trade standards. However, a designer who wishes to design a gear in accordance with a particular standard should get a copy of the standard and study every detail of it. Standards are like legal documents. All the fine print must be read and followed before one can claim to be acting in accordance with the standard.

Purchase contracts frequently specify standards or other details of gear-unit design. A builder of gears under contract is, of course, obligated to meet the contract. What should be done if some requirement relating to the gears seems unreasonable or impractical, or if it allows gears to be built that have too much risk of failure? (This book is intended to be conservative and to alert the reader to risks in gear making—hence a gear contract may allow things that do not agree with this book.)

If this book is more conservative than some gear standard or some contract provision, the gear builder or gear buyer would be well advised to consider whether or not there is enough proven experience to justify going beyond the recommendations given here. In the last analysis, it is proven experience that sets the design. Certainly, progress is being made in all aspects of the gear art. It is to be expected that there will be many situations in which there is enough experience and technical know-how to go beyond things in this book.

3.33 Vehicle-Gear-Rating Practice

Vehicle-gear designers are always under great pressure to make their gears both small and inexpensive. A gear failure is not too serious, because there is not much risk to the safety of the vehicle driver. Expensive equipment is not tied up by a failure, as it is when gears in a power plant or a ship fail. However, failures cannot be allowed to happen very often, or the vehicle will get a reputation for being poorly designed. Also, the customer-complaint charges may become serious.

The vehicle designer needs to know quite precisely where the danger point is in loading the gears. There are two good sources of information. Since vehicles are built in very large quantities, a large amount of statistical data are available. These can be collected and plotted to give design curves which are quite reliable for the limited field of gear work for which they apply.

The second source of information is the product experience of individual manufacturers. After many thousands of transmissions and rear ends have been built and put into service, the builder finds out which parts are weak and which parts are stronger than they need to be. If the weak spots are doctored, the rating of the gears can usually be increased. In many cases, automotive manufacturers have been able to improve their gear drives at about the same rate as engine horsepower has been increased. Present-day vehicle engines are much more powerful than they were 20 years ago. In general, though, the gear drives are not larger. They are just made with better accuracy and better materials.

In 1976, AGMA issued Standard 170.01. This is a design standard for spur and helical vehicle gears. The standard defines two quality grades, Grade 1 and Grade 2. Grade 2 steel is specified to be cleaner, harder, and having a better metallurgical structure than Grade 1. The standard shows compositions of low-alloy, medium-alloy, and high-alloy steel. The text explains that the higher-alloy steels are required as the gears become larger and the vehicle is subjected to more severe duty requirements.

AGMA 170.01 gives typical derating factors for different vehicle applications. Table 3.58 shows a sampling of these factors.

The design stress limits shown in AGMA 170.01 are adjusted for Grade 2 or Grade 1 material, and also adjusted for a probability of failure of L10 or

TABLE 3.58 A Sampling of Overall Derating Factors from AGMA 170.01*

Application		Overall derating factor	
		Medium precision	Medium-high precision
Final drive	Off-highway	1.2	1.0
	Truck	1.4	1.2
Shifting transmission	Off-highway	1.5	1.3
	Truck	1.6	1.4
	Passenger car	1.7	1.5
Epicyclic	Off-highway	1.7	1.6
	Passenger car	—	2.0

*Extracted from AGMA 170.01, "Design Guide for Vehicle Spur and Helical Gears" (1976) with the permission of the publisher, the American Gear Manufacturers Association, Suite 1000, 1901 North Fort Myer Drive, Arlington, VA 22209, U.S.A.

TABLE 3.59 Design Stress Limits Shown in AGMA 170.01

No. stress cycles	Bending stress				Contact stress			
	Grade 2		Grade 1		Grade 2		Grade 1	
	L10	L1	L10	L1	L10	L1	L10	L1
	Metric, N/mm²							
10^3	1270	1170	980	880	—	—	—	—
10^4	960	880	750	690	—	3270	3450	2860
10^5	760	690	570	520	3100	2620	2690	2240
10^6	580	520	450	410	2480	2140	2140	1790
2×10^6*	530	480	410	370	—	—	—	—
10^7	530	480	410	370	2000	1720	1690	1400
10^8	530	480	410	370	1650	1380	1310	1100
	English, psi (multiply by 1000)							
10^3	185	170	142	128	—	—	—	—
10^4	140	128	109	100	—	475	500	415
10^5	110	100	83	76	450	380	390	325
10^6	84	75	65	59	360	310	310	260
2×10^6*	77	70	60	54	—	—	—	—
10^7	77	70	60	54	290	250	245	203
10^8	77	70	60	54	240	200	190	160

*The bending stress data show no slope after 2×10^6 cycles. However, the standard concedes that a shallow slope may be needed and suggests a drop of 34 N/mm² (5000 psi) in going from 2×10^6 cycles to 10^8 cycles.

Notes:
1. These limits are for short life (2×10^8 maximum).
2. Some micro damage can be tolerated at cycles below 10^6.
3. These limits are for operation in Regime II.
4. Data in the table are extracted from AGMA 170.01, "Design Guide for Vehicle Spur and Helical Gears" (1976) with the permission of the publisher, the American Gear Manufacturers Association, Suite 1000, 1901 North Fort Myer Drive, Arlington, VA 22209, U.S.A. The notes are by the author and were not in AGMA 170.01.

L1. An L10 designation means that 10 out of 100 gears might fail prematurely by the mode of failure for which the stress level is given.

Table 3.59 shows the design stress limits in tabular form. (The standard presents the values in curve form.)

Vehicle-gear design is characterized by two things:

Very severe loads are permitted at low numbers of cycles (less than 10^7). This means that the teeth are apt to have some surface or subsurface damage from the high loading. The damage may take the form of micro-cracking, surface cold work, or small amounts of pitting. This kind of damage is not expected to result in failure before 10^8 cycles, provided the gear meets the design limits. At 10^8 cycles the gear may be definitely damaged, and it may be quite unfit to run for 10^9 or 10^{10} cycles.

In general, vehicle gears operate under Regime II conditions. To meet their design ratings, they must have appropriate lubricants that have the right viscosity and appropriate additives. Because of Regime II conditions, the load that can be carried on the surface of the tooth drops rather rapidly as the number of cycles increases.

In general, vehicles are built in large quantities. This makes it practical (on a new design) to build a few gear drives that are made just as small as possible by vehicle criteria. The first few drives are then extensively tested. The test results will probably show some failures. In general, design modifications are made to improve the design without changing the overall size. With improvements, the design will pass the test satisfactorily, and it is then ready to go into initial production. After a unit has been in production for a period of time, field results may show a need for further design improvements.

The design improvements might include any one or all of the following things:

Change to a higher-alloy steel or improve the heat-treating practice to get better hardness and metallurgy.

Change the profile modification or the helix modification to get better fit.

Change the pitch of the teeth, the pressure angle, or the tooth proportions to get better geometric conditions.

Improve the accuracy of the teeth, or improve the bearing and casing structures that support the gears.

Use a better lubricant and/or a better means of cooling the gears when they are running under the worst heavy-loading, hot-day conditions.

3.34 Marine-Gear-Rating Practice

The gears used to drive large ships are almost all helical. The gears are so large that it is difficult to case-harden them and retain enough dimensional accuracy to permit finish grinding. The high speed and long life requirements of marine gears make it necessary to grind the gears after casecarburizing. In some cases the smaller marine gears (epicyclic marine gears, for instance) are cut, shaved, or ground before nitriding, then nitrided with such overall skill and control of the manufacturing process that they can be put into service after final hardening without any grinding in the final hard condition.

There has been considerable use of through-hardened gears for marine service that are precision-cut and shaved or ground. These gears have no case and are essentially uniform in hardness throughout the tooth area.

The gear drive on a large ship is a very important piece of machinery. Ship owners want the gearing to be good enough to stay in service for something like 20 to 30 years. The gears run at fairly high speeds, so the lifetime cycles may get up to 10^{10} or even higher. If a gear drive on a ship were to fail, there would be a chance that a storm might be in progress, and the ship might be blown onto the rocks and wrecked. There is also the risk that a ship with disabled gears might be so long in getting into port that a perishable cargo would be lost.

The design of gearing for ships tends to be very conservative. Those who purchase gear drives frequently control the conservatism of the design by specifying maximum K-factor and unit-load values. As an example, a large ship using medium-hard gears might have gears designed to meet values like the following:

First stage

High-speed pinions Hardness 262–311 HB

High-speed gears Hardness 241–285 HB

K factor not to exceed 0.86 N/mm^2 (125 psi)

Second Stage

Low-speed pinions Hardness 241–285 HB

Low-speed gears Hardness 223–269 HB

K factor not to exceed 0.69 N/mm^2 (100 psi)

Those who operate large ships almost always insure the ship. Those who write insurance for ships or for machinery on the ship need independent certification of the capability and condition of the ship or the piece of equipment under consideration. This kind of work is ordinarily handled by organizations that are commonly called *classification societies*. These groups are concerned with the power rating of gears, the quality of gears, and the character of the drive system associated with the gears. This latter concern involves things like propeller shaft bearings, mountings for turbines, and hull deflections under different sea conditions.

The classification societies are involved in approving new designs, as well as evaluating machinery in service. Each of them tends to have rules pertaining to gear rating. A marine-gear designer will often find that a design is required by contract to meet the rules of a designated classification society.

The names and addresses of the principal classification societies are:

American Bureau of Shipping
45 Broad St.
New York, N.Y. 10004 U.S.A.

Bureau Veritas
31 Rue Henri-Rochefort
Paris 17e France

Det Norske Veritas
Veritasveien 1 Høvik
Oslo, Norway

Germanischer Lloyd
Postfach 30 20 60
2000 Hamburg 36
West Germany

Lloyds Register of Shipping
71, Fenchurch St.
London, EC3M 4BS
England

As this book is being written (1984), neither AGMA or ISO has issued standards for marine-gear rating. However, both organizations are working on marine standards and have material in draft form. It is to be expected that new standards for rating marine gears will be issued in the early 1980s.

3.35 Oil and Gas Industry Gear Rating

The gears used in the oil and gas industry need high reliability. Power gearing often handles power from 1000 kW to as much as 30,000 kW. A compressor or generator drive system will often be required to run 20,000 to 30,000 hours before overhauling, and have a total life requirement of 50,000 to 100,000 hours. At an overhaul, seals and couplings, and sometimes bearings, might be replaced. It is generally expected that the gears themselves will last for the total design life. (Sometimes a gear or pinion will last for the total design life, but some rework of teeth or journal bearing surfaces may be required during the life.)

Very often, fast-running turbines drive the gear units in this field. The total life cycles of gear parts are often in the area of 10^{10} to 10^{11} cycles.

The high-speed-gear standard that has been in use for a considerable period of time is AGMA 421.06 (and its predecessors back to 421.01). The large power gears all have pitch-line speeds that make them come under a high-speed-gear standard.

In October 1969, Dudley presented a paper, AGMA 159.02, recommending some changes in the factors used in this standard. This paper made a particular point of the higher reliabilities needed in gears for the oil industry and advocated a more conservative design approach. A general revision of AGMA 421.06 has been in process for the last few years and is now quite close to being approved and ready to issue.

In the meantime, the American Petroleum Institute (API) became concerned with the reliability of power gears and issued a short standard of their own in 1977. Special rating controls were put into API Standard 613, along with other material relating to the design and manufacture of gears.

Table 3.60 shows some material extracted from API Standard 613. The "material index number" is really the K factor when the application factor is equal to 1. In most cases, though, API recommends an application factor greater than 1, and so the real K factor is obtained by dividing the material index number by the application factor.

In some cases, large power gears used in the oil and gas industry heat to the point where the fit of the teeth is considerably affected by thermal distortions, and the body temperature of the pinion may be over 50 degrees hotter than the incoming oil. Thermal problems are being handled, but no trade standards have yet been developed. Section 7.16 of this book has further material on this subject. The 1972 ASME paper by Martinaglia gives some very worthwhile engineering data relative to thermal behavior of high-speed gears.

TABLE 3.60 Some Design Limits Extracted from API Standard 613

	Material index number		Bending stress number	
Kind of material	N/mm^2	psi	N/mm^2	psi
Carburized				
HRC 59	3.10	450	269	39,000
HRC 55	2.83	410	248	36,000
Through-hardened teeth				
HB 300	1.38	200	179	26,000
HB 220	0.90	130	145	21,000

Notes:
1. When the material index is divided by the application factor, it becomes a design K factor.
2. The bending stress equation used by API has the application factor in it and an overall derating factor of 1.8.
3. API uses the term "service factor." The values used, though, are appropriate for the new AGMA definition of application factor. (API sets their limits low enough to handle about 10^{10} cycles, and so their so-called SF values are really application factors.)
4. Extracted from API 613, "Special-Purpose Units for Refinery Services" (1977), with permission of the American Petroleum Institute, Refining Dept., 2101 L Street, Northwest, Washington, DC 20037, U.S.A.

3.36 Aerospace-Gear-Rating Practices

Aerospace gears must be very light in weight for the loads carried, and yet they must be very reliable. Many of the gears are so important to the operation of the aircraft that a broken tooth would cause an aircraft to crash.

The life of an aircraft gear at full torque may vary anywhere from about 10^6 to 10^9 cycles.

Laboratory and bench tests are used extensively to provide design data for aircraft gears. New aircraft engines are so expensive to design and build that it is worth doing a lot of work to develop component parts before they are put into an engine. The stakes are high. A small reduction in the volume and weight of a gearbox could result in one manufacturer's engine being accepted for production contracts and another's being rejected. Gear failures in the field can cause all aircraft using the particular design to be grounded until the questionable gearing is replaced.

Under laboratory conditions, gears will perform best of all. Usually the quality is better than that obtained in large-quantity production. Test stands usually provide a gear with better lubrication and alignment than the worst of the engines that the gears will have to run in.

When the load-carrying capacity of a gear has been determined in a test stand, it is necessary to reduce that capacity for use in an actual engine. Allowances must be made so that even the poorest gear operating in the worst engine will not fail.

New engines are given extensive testing in engine test cells to demonstrate that they will meet design requirements. Then, if they appear to be satisfactory, they are flight-tested. After this the engine may be approved for use in commercial or military aircraft. Aircraft-gear designers are usually free to use any design formula that looks good to them, but their gears—to be successful—must go through the development and testing procedure just described.

In propeller aircraft, the gear unit is generally considered to be a part of the engine package. Many small propeller-driven aircraft are used for pleasure, but relatively few are now used to carry passengers. Jet-engine aircraft usually use no main power gearing, but have a considerable amount of gearing in accessory drives. The smaller military cargo planes do use propellers and propulsion gears.

A large new use of aerospace gearing is in helicopters. Helicopters are used for commercial purposes, and they have a major use in the Army. A typical Army helicopter will have one or two main rotor drives, and each main rotor drive will have about three stages of gearing. The first stage of gearing is often built into the turbine engine package and furnished with the engine. The second and third stages are generally in a gear unit furnished with the helicopter. The helicopter gears work rather hard most of the time. Even when the helicopter is loitering, the helicopter rotor must provide lift to support the weight of the helicopter.

The widely used design guide for aerospace gearing is AGMA 411.02. This standard recognizes two grades of material and lists derating factors for several kinds of applications. Stress levels are given for both grades of material.

The Grade 2 material is a high-quality, high-alloy steel of the AISI 9310 type. It is specified to have very good cleanness, high hardness, and a very good metallurgical structure. The Grade 1 steel may be carburized 9310, or it may be a somewhat similar steel if appropriate hardness and quality can be obtained. It may be air-melt rather than vacuum-melt. Not quite so high a hardness is specified.

Nitriding steel of the Nitralloy 135 type is permitted for Grade 1, provided that the teeth are not larger than 2.5 module (10 pitch). The nitride case is thin, even with rather long nitriding time. The standard reflects concern that the case depth may not be adequate for Grade 1 levels of tooth loading if the teeth are larger than 2.5 module.

Table 3.61 shows some of the overall derating factors given in AGMA 411.02. Table 3.62 shows the design stress limits given in AGMA 411.02 for different numbers of cycles. These stress limits are intended to go with an L1 probability of failure. At the time this standard was written, the gear trade

TABLE 3.61 A Sampling of Overall Derating Factors from AGMA 411.02

<table>
<tr><th colspan="2" rowspan="2">Application</th><th colspan="2">Overall derating factor</th></tr>
<tr><th>Medium-high precision</th><th>High precision</th></tr>
<tr><td rowspan="2">Main propulsion drive gears</td><td>Continuous</td><td>1.8</td><td>1.2</td></tr>
<tr><td>Take-off and early climb</td><td>1.5</td><td>1.0</td></tr>
<tr><td colspan="2">Power take-off accessory gears</td><td>2.1</td><td>1.5</td></tr>
<tr><td colspan="2">Auxiliary power units</td><td>2.1</td><td>1.5</td></tr>
</table>

Note: Extracted from AGMA 411.02, "Design Procedure for Aircraft Engine and Power Take-off Spur and Helical Gears" (1966) with permission of the publisher, the American Gear Manufacturers Association, Suite 1000, 1901 North Fort Myer Drive, Arlington, VA 22209, U.S.A.

TABLE 3.62 Design Stress Limits Shown in AGMA 411.02

No. stress cycles	Bending stress		Contact stress	
	Grade 2	Grade 1	Grade 2	Grade 1
	Metric, N/mm²			
1	1103	965	2296	2041
10^4	827	710	2296	2041
10^5	627	538	2034	1793
10^6	489	414	1779	1586
10^7	448	379	1551	1379
10^8	414	352	1358	1207
10^9	379	324	1193	1069
10^{10}	345	303	1041	938
	English, psi			
1	160,000	140,000	333,000	296,000
10^4	120,000	103,000	333,000	296,000
10^5	91,000	78,000	295,000	260,000
10^6	71,000	60,000	258,000	230,000
10^7	65,000	55,000	225,000	200,000
10^8	60,000	51,000	197,000	175,000
10^9	55,000	47,000	173,000	155,000
10^{10}	50,000	44,000	151,000	136,000

Notes:
1. These stress limits are based on a probability of failure of 1 in 100 (L1).
2. These limits are intended for long life; no micro damage is expected at cycles below 10^6.
3. These limits are for operation in Regime III.
4. Extracted from AGMA 411.02 "Design Procedure for Aircraft Engine and Power Take-off Spur and Helical Gears" (1966) with the permission of the publisher, the American Gear Manufacturers Association, Suite 1000, 1901 North Fort Myer Drive, Arlington, VA 22209, U.S.A.

had not recognized the different regimes of lubrication. It is now acknowledged that these data were developed from test and field experience that was essentially all in Regime III. Recent work in the aerospace field has shown that some situations get into Regime II—even when the gears are relatively fast-running power gears. The gears subject to intermittent duty in controlling flaps and tail rudders on large aircraft are quite often in Regime II. So far no industry standards have been developed for aerospace gears in Regime II.

The aerospace field is somewhat like the vehicle field. The industry standards, in both cases, are really intended as design guides rather than rigid rules. They show what is being achieved by those who are relatively skilled in the gear art and serve as a guide for new designs. The new design, though, is usually made as small as the designer dares to make it.

As was said earlier in this section, the new design has to be proven by a considerable amount of testing on the ground and in the air. Frequently, design modifications are made to improve the fit of the gears or the quality of the material in the gears. Profile modifications are very important, as is surface finish. The lubrication system must work well. Generally the oil is specified, and it is not possible to solve gear problems by using a heavy oil or one with more additives. Aircraft are apt to travel all over the world, and so they have to use the lubricants stocked at airfields. Also, an aircraft may start in the Arctic and a few hours later be operating under hot desert conditions. Usually the oil for the gears has to be the same oil used by the turbine engine. Relatively thin diester oils are the usual standard for aerospace gearing. These oils stand hot temperatures quite well, and are thin enough for the equipment to operate in most arctic conditions. The additives in the oil are mild, but they are sufficient for Regime III operation under favorable conditions.

chapter 4

Gear Materials

A wide variety of steels, cast irons, bronzes, and phenolic resins have been used for gears. In recent years new materials such as nylon, titanium, and sintered iron have also become important in gear work. Designers might well become hopelessly confused when faced with so many different gear materials, except that there are good and specific reasons for using each of the materials that have been adopted for gears. As their outstanding characteristics, the steels have the greatest strength per unit volume and the lowest cost per pound. In many fields of gear work, some kind of steel is the only material to consider.

The cast irons have long been popular because of their good wearing characteristics, their excellent machinability, and the ease with which complicated shapes may be produced by the casting method.

The bronzes are very important in worm-gear work because of their ability to withstand high sliding velocity and their ability to wear in to fit hardened-steel worms. They are also very useful in applications in which corrosion is a problem. The ease with which bronze can be worked makes it a good choice where small gear teeth are produced by stamping or by drawing rod through dies.

The phenolic resins are used in various combinations to produce laminated gears with remarkably good load-carrying capacity in spite of the low physical strength of the material. In general, these materials are about thirty times as elastic as steel. (Their deformation per unit load is about thirty times that of steel.) Their "rubbery" nature makes them operate with less shock due to tooth errors and allows their teeth to bend enough to make more teeth contact and share load than in metal designs. Some of these materials can stand quite high sliding velocities.

In this chapter we shall study all the kinds of gear materials just mentioned. Condensed information will be given to define the composition, heat treatment, and mechanical properties of these materials. To help with the language of materials, a short glossary is given in Table 4.1.

TABLE 4.1 Glossary of Metallurgical and Heat-Treating Nomenclature

Aging A change in an alloy by which the structure recovers from an unstable or metastable condition produced by quenching or by cold working. The degree of stable equilibrium obtained for any given grade of steel is a function of time and temperature. The change in structure consists of precipitation and is marked by a change in physical and mechanical properties. Aging which takes place slowly at room temperature may be accelerated by an increase in temperature.

Annealing A broad term used to describe the heating and cooling of steel in the solid form. The term *annealing* usually implies relatively slow cooling. In annealing, the size, shape, and composition of the steel product and the purpose of the treatment determine the temperature of the operation, the rate of temperature change, and the time at heat. Annealing is used to induce softness, to remove stresses, to alter physical and mechanical properties, to remove gases, to change the crystalline structure, and to produce a desired microstructure.

Austenite In steels, the gamma form of iron with carbon in solid solution. Austenite is tough and nonmagnetic and tends to harden rapidly when worked below the critical temperature.

Austenitic steels Steels which are austenitic at room temperature.

Brinell hardness A hardness number determined by applying a known load to the surface of the material to be tested through a hardened-steel ball of known diameter. The diameter of the resulting permanent indentation is measured. This method is unsuitable for measuring the hardness of sheet or strip metal.

Carburizing Diffusing carbon into the surface of iron-base alloys by heating such alloys in the presence of carbonaceous materials at high temperatures. Such treatments, followed by appropriate quenching and tempering, harden the surface of the metal to a depth proportional to the time of carburizing.

Case hardening Hardening the outer layer of an iron-base alloy by a process that changes the surface chemical composition, followed by an appropriate thermal treatment. Carburizing and nitriding are typical case-hardening techniques. Induction heating and then hardening of the outer layer of metal is another form of case hardening.

Cold working Permanent deformation of a metal below its recrystallization temperature. Some metals can be hot-worked at room temperature, while others can be cold-worked at temperatures in excess of 1000°F.

Ductility The property of a metal that allows it to be permanently deformed before final rupture. It is commonly evaluated by tensile testing in which the amount of elongation or reduction of area of the broken test specimen, as compared with the original, is measured.

Elastic limit Maximum stress to which a metal can be subjected without permanent deformation.

Endurance limit The maximum stress to which material may be subjected an infinite number of times without failure.

Ferrite Iron in the alpha form in which alloying constituents may be dissolved. Ferrite is magnetic, soft, and acts as a solvent for manganese, nickel, and silicon.

Flame hardening Hardening an iron-base alloy by using a high-temperature flame to heat the surface layer above the transformation temperature range at which austenite begins to form, then cooling the surface quickly by quenching. This process is usually followed by tempering. An oxyacetylene torch is often used in flame hardening.

Grain size The grain-size number is determined by a count of a definite microscopic area, usually at 100× magnification. The larger the grain-size number, the smaller the grains.

Grains Individual crystals in metals.

Hardenability The property that determines the depth and distribution of hardness induced by quenching. The higher the hardenability value, the greater the depth to which the material can be hardened and the slower the quench that can be used.

Hardness A property of materials which is measured by resistance to indentation.

Heat treatment A general term which refers to operations involving the heating and cooling of a metal in the solid state for the purpose of obtaining certain desired conditions or properties. Heating and cooling for the prime purpose of mechanical working are not included in the meaning of the definition. Gear metal heat treatments include heating in a furnace followed by quenching, flame hardening, and induction hardening.

Inclusions Particles of nonmetallic materials, usually silicates, oxides, or sulfides, which are mechanically entrapped or are formed during solidification or by subsequent reaction within the solid metal. Impurities in metals.

Induction hardening Hardening of steel by using an alternating current to induce heating, followed by quenching. This process can be used to harden only the surface by using high-frequency current, or it can through-harden the steel if low frequency is used. Induction hardening is a fast process which can be controlled to produce the desired depth and hardness in a localized area and with low distortion.

Jominy test The Jominy test is used to determine the end-quench hardenability of steel. It consists of water-quenching one end of a 1-in.-diameter bar under closely controlled conditions and measuring the degree of hardness at regular intervals along the side of the bar from the quenched end up.

Martensite A microconstituent in quenched steel characterized by an acicular, or needle-type, structure. It has the maximum hardness of any structure obtained from the decomposition of austenite.

TABLE 4.1 Glossary of Metallurgical and Heat-Treating Nomenclature (*Continued*)

Modulus of elasticity The ratio, within the elastic limit, of the stress to the corresponding strain. The stress in pounds per square inch is divided by the elongation of the original gage length of the specimen in inches per inch. Also known as Young's modulus.

Nitriding Adding nitrogen to solid iron-base alloys by heating the steel in contact with ammonia gas or other suitable nitrogenous material. This process is used to harden the surface of gears.

Normalizing A process in which a steel is heated to a temperature above the transformation range and subsequently cooled in still air to room temperature.

Pearlite The lamellar aggregate of ferrite and cementite resulting from the direct transformation of austenite at the lower critical point.

Quenching Rapid cooling by contact with liquids, gases, or solids, such as oil, air, water, brine, or molten salt.

Residual stress Stresses remaining in a part after the completion of working, heat treating, welding, etc., due to phase changes, expansion, contraction, and other phenomena.

Rockwell hardness A hardness number determined by a Rockwell hardness tester, a direct-reading machine which may use a steel ball or a diamond penetrator.

Secondary hardening An increase in hardness developed by tempering high-alloy steels after quenching, usually associated with precipitation reactions.

Stress relief A process of reducing internal residual stresses in a metal part by heating the part to a suitable temperature and holding it at that temperature for a proper time. Stress relieving may be applied to parts which have been welded, machined, cast, heat-treated, or worked.

Tempering A process that reduces brittleness and internal strains by the reheating of quench-hardened or normalized steels to a temperature below the transformation range. A **draw** treatment is a tempering treatment that is hot enough to reduce hardness.

Tensile strength The maximum load per unit of original cross-sectional area carried by a material during a tensile test.

Through hardening Increasing the hardness of a metallic part by a process that hardens the core material as well as the surface layers, with the hardness uniform throughout the whole gear tooth and the metal immediately adjacent to the gear tooth.

Transformation range The temperature range within which austenite forms in ferrous alloys.

Yield point The load per unit of original cross section at which a marked increase in deformation occurs without any increase in load.

Note: Most of the definitions in this table were extracted from Chap. 10 of the *Gear Handbook*. For more details on materials terminology and practices, see this reference.

STEELS FOR GEARS

There are a number of steels used for gears, ranging from plain carbon steels through the highly alloyed steels and from low to high carbon contents. The choice will depend upon a number of factors, including size, service, and design. The following discussions should serve as a guide in selecting steels.

4.1 Mechanical Properties

In designing gears, the mechanical properties of the material are of some interest to the designer from a comparative standpoint, but they cannot be used directly in calculating the load-carrying capacity. As was pointed out in Sec. 2.1, the calculated stresses on gear teeth are not necessarily the true stresses in the material. Moreover, tensile properties—the most commonly published mechanical properties of a material—are determined by loading small bars in simple tension. The gear tooth is a different geometric shape with a more complex stress pattern, and therefore the actual properties of the material as a gear can best be determined by testing the material in the *shape of a gear tooth.* The allowable stresses for rating gears (see Secs. 3.24 and 3.25) are based on test and field experience with *gears* rather than on the mechanical properties of the material as determined by routine laboratory tests. Gear materials and treatments can be most readily discussed, however, on the basis of simple mechanical properties. The mechanical properties are valuable indirectly in that they indicate how gears made of a particular material might be expected to perform. Figure 4.1 is a rough guide to the tensile properties of steel.

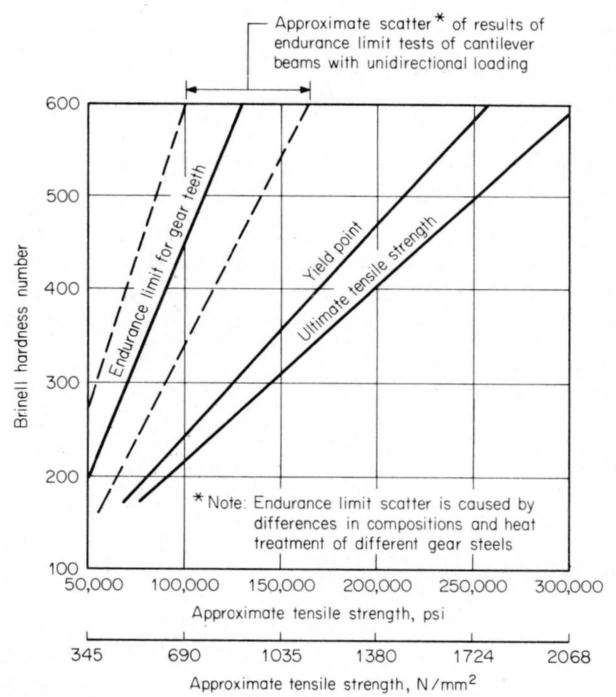

FIG. 4.1 Approximate tensile properties of steel.

In gear terminology, some steels are considered to be *alloy* steels and some are considered to be *plain carbon* steels. The steels used for gears tend to vary from those with a small amount of alloys to steels rich in alloys. From a practical standpoint, the steels that are considered to be plain carbon usually have some alloy content, like manganese and silicon. The steels that are normally thought of as alloy steels usually have chromium, nickel, and molybdenum as well as manganese and silicon.

There is a general feeling in the gear trade that alloy steels are inherently stronger and more fatigue-resistant than the so-called plain carbon steels. The real situation is rather complex. If two steels have equal hardness and each has the same tempered martensitic structure, then the ultimate strength, the yield strength, and the endurance strength will be essentially the same—in a small piece of the metal.

The alloy content helps out in several very important ways:

The cooling rate in quenching can be considerably slower. This makes it possible to get a good metallurgical structure in the larger gears. (A large gear with a low alloy content does tend to be weaker because a good metallurgical structure is not obtained.)

Gears with high alloy content can be carburized with too rich or too lean a carburizing atmosphere and still come out fairly good. Nickel in particular makes heat-treating operations less sensitive to precise control.

Certain alloy combinations are helpful in developing fracture toughness. (With these combinations, a small crack grows very slowly, or perhaps ceases to grow. This is important in gears that suffer some surface damage but could run a long time if the surface damage did not lead to tooth breakage.)

In general, the impact properties are considerably improved by alloy content. Nickel and molybdenum are particularly valuable for impact strength. (Many gears suffer occasional heavy shock loads and therefore need good impact strength.)

The overall situation is that the composition of the steel used in gears is very important. A *poor choice of alloy content* has often led to early failure in gears built with good precision and sized large enough to meet appropriate design standards.

4.2 Heat-Treating Techniques

Gear steels are heat-treated for two general purposes. First, they must be put in condition for proper machinability. Second, the necessary hardness, strength, and wear resistance for the intended use must be developed. Steel in the as-rolled or as-forged condition may be coarse-grained in structure and nonuniform in hardness as a result of uncontrolled cooling after the forging or rolling operations. Therefore, a heat treatment followed by controlled cooling is used to develop the type of metallurgical structure most suited to the subsequent machining operations. Gear forgings of carburizing steels are usually *normalized* or *normalized and tempered* to develop a uniform microstructure and reduce their tendency to distort during later hardening operations. Normalizing consists of heating the steel to well above the critical temperature and somewhat above the final hardening temperature, followed by an air cool.

Another treatment similar to normalizing is *annealing*. The part to be annealed is heated above the critical range, just as in normalizing, but it is cooled at a slow rate either by controlling the furnace cooling rate or by allowing the furnace and load to cool off together with the doors closed. Slow cooling in the furnace usually produces a pearlitic or lamellar structure which provides good surface finishes after machining. An interrupted or *cycle annealing* produces a spheroidized structure which often has maximum machinability.

Steel parts are hardened by quenching and tempering to develop the combination of strength, toughness, hardness, and wear resistance that may be needed to make the part function properly in use. Proper hardening consists of cooling the steel from above the critical temperature quickly enough to form a fully hardened structure and to prevent the formation of undesired structures, which could occur at intermediate temperatures if the cooling rate is too slow. Table 4.2 shows the important temperatures that must be observed with different kinds of steel. Table 4.3 shows the critical cooling rates for steels made to the minimum composition range for each kind of steel. The size of round that will through-harden in a mild quench and the hardness obtained with 60 percent martensite formation are also shown in Table 4.3. Table 4.4 shows the approximate cooling rates needed to get a high level of metallurgical quality in gears.

The steels listed in Tables 4.2 and 4.3 are those which are commonly used for gears. The compositions* of these steels that have been established by the American Iron and Steel Institute are given in Table 4.5. (Somewhat modified compositions are often used. When buying gear steel, note the exact composition being specified or offered.)

The exact composition of a steel may vary somewhat from one steel company to another or from steels used in vehicles to those used in aircraft. For instance, a designer who wants to use 4340-type steel in aircraft gears should specify an *aircraft composition*. The aircraft composition tends to have closer ranges for each alloy element, and there is more control of *trace elements*.

*The steels with an "EX" are relatively new steel compositions. They are in use, but a final designation has not been made.

TABLE 4.2 Heat-Treating Data for Typical Gear Steels

AISI No.	Normalizing temperature, °F	Annealing temperature, °F	Hardening temperature, °F	Carburizing temperature, °F	Reheat temperature, °F	M_s temperature,* °F
1015	1700	1600	—	1650–1700	1400–1450	
1025	1650–1750	1600	1575–1650	1500–1650		
1040	1650–1750	1450	1525–1575			
1045	1600–1700	1450	1450–1550			
1060	1550–1650	1400–1500	1450–1550	—	—	555
1118	1700	1450	—	1650–1700	1650–1700	
1320	1600–1650	1500–1700	—	1650–1700	1450–1500	740
1335	1600–1700	1500–1600	1500–1550	—	—	640
2317	1650–1750	1575	—	1650–1700	1450–1500	725
2340	1600–1700	1400–1500	1425–1475	—	—	555
3310	1650–1750	1575	—	1650–1700	1450–1500	655
3140	1600–1700	1450–1550	1500–1550	—	—	590
4028	1600–1700	1525–1575	—	1600–1700	1450–1500	750
4047	1550–1750	1525–1575	1475–1550			
4130	1600–1700	1450–1550	1550–1650	—	—	685
4140	1600–1700	1450–1550	1525–1625	—	—	595
4320	1600–1800	1575	—	1650–1700	1425–1475	720
4340	1600–1700	1100–1225	1475–1525	—	—	545
4620	1700–1800	1575	—	1650–1700	1475–1525	555
4640	1600–1700	1450–1550	1450–1550	—	—	605
4820	1650–1750	1575	—	1650–1700	1450–1500	685
5145	1600–1700	1450–1550	1475–1525			
52100	—	1350–1450	1425–1600	—	—	485
6120	1700–1800	1600	—	1700	1475–1550	760
6150	1650–1750	1550–1650	1550–1650	—	—	545
8620	1600–1800	1575	—	1700	1425–1550	745
9310	1650–1750	1575	—	1650–1700	1425–1550	650
EX 24	1650–1750	1600	1600	1650–1700	1500–1550	830
EX 29	1650–1750	1600	1600	1650–1700	1500–1550	830
EX 30	1650–1750	1550	1600	1650–1700	1500–1550	830
EX 55	1650–1750	1525	1600	1650–1700	1500–1550	790

*The M_s temperature is the temperature at which martensite forms.

TABLE 4.3 Hardenability Data for Typical Gear Steels
(Data based on minimum composition range except where noted)

AISI No.	Hardness of 60% martensite, HRC	Critical cooling rate, °F per second at 1300°F	Size of round that will through-harden, in.	Mildly agitated quenching medium
		Through-hardening steels		
1045	50.5	400*	0.50†	Water
1060	54	125*	1.20†	Water
1335	46	195	1.00	Water
2340	49	125	0.60	Oil
3140	49	125	0.60	Oil
4047	52	195	1.00	Water
			0.40	Oil
4130	44	305	0.70	Water
4140	49	56	1.00	Oil
4340	49	10	2.80	Oil
5145	51	125	0.60	Oil
52100	60	30	1.30	Oil
6150	53	77	0.80	Oil

AISI No.	Minimum core hardness	Critical cooling rate, °F per second at 1300°F	Size of round that will through-harden, in.	Mildly agitated quenching medium
		Data for core of case-carburizing steels		
1015	15	400†	0.50†	Water
1025	18	400†	0.50†	Water
1118	20	400†	0.50†	Water
1320	20	305	0.70	Water
3310	25	3	3.00	Oil
4028	24	300*	0.80†	Water
4320	32	195	0.40	Oil
4620	30	305	0.20	Oil
			0.70	Water
4820	35	77	0.80	Oil
8620	25	250*	0.80	Water
			0.30	Oil
9310	25	21	1.70	Oil
EX 24	26	195*	0.80	Water
EX 29	32	175*	1.00†	Water
EX 30	35	150*	1.20	Water
EX 55	40	42†	2.00	Oil

*Estimated values.
†Obtained from nominal compositions rather than from minimum of specification range.

TABLE 4.4 Approximate Cooling Rates Needed to Achieve Appropriate Metallurgical Quality for Long-Life, Highly Loaded Gears

Carburizing steel	Core hardness HV10	Time,* s to 600°C (1112°F)	to 400°C (752°F)	200°C (392°F)
4028	339†	3	8	10
8620	339	5	12	28
EX 24	339	6	20	35
4620	339	3	8	10
4320	339	8	22	60
EX 29	339	8	22	60
9310	339	10	35	90
4815	339	6	21	58
EX 30	339	6	21	58
EX 55	390	13	50	125

*Time is from start of quench to the temperature listed.
†339 HV10 is approximately 34 HRC. 390 HV10 is approximately 40 HRC.

International users of this book should be able to find German, Japanese, French, or English steel specifications that are very similar to the American types of steels that are shown. In Chap. 4, the heat-treating temperatures are given in degrees Fahrenheit rather than Celsius. (There isn't room to show both in the tables.) The conversion to Celsius is

$$\text{Degrees Celsius} = \frac{\text{degrees Fahrenheit} - 32}{1.8} \tag{4.1}$$

The hardening temperature of a steel must be slightly above the *critical temperature.* The critical temperature is the temperature at which the steel is completely *austenitized* and ready to undergo the hardening reaction upon quenching. The *critical cooling* rate is the rate of cooling that is just fast enough to produce a fully hardened structure in a particular steel composition.

The M_s *temperature* is the temperature at which the fully hard structure (martensite) first starts to form during the quench. If the cooling rate is slower than the critical rate, other structures (ferrite, pearlite, and upper bainite) may form at intermediate temperatures between the critical temperature and the M_s temperature.

After quenching, steels are usually *tempered* or *stress-relieved.* The tempering operation may be used to reduce the hardness of a part and increase the toughness. By properly adjusting the tempering temperature, a wide range of

TABLE 4.5 Composition of Typical Gear Steels

AISI No.	Chemical composition limits, percent							
	C	Mn	P	S	Si	Ni	Cr	Mo
1015	0.13/0.18	0.30/0.60	0.040	0.050	—	—	—	—
1025	0.22/0.28	0.30/0.60	0.040	0.050	—	—	—	—
1045	0.43/0.50	0.60/0.90	0.040	0.050	—	—	—	—
1060	0.55/0.65	0.60/0.90	0.040	0.050	—	—	—	—
1118	0.14/0.20	1.3/1.6	0.045	0.08/0.13	—	—	—	—
1320	0.18/0.23	1.6/1.9	0.040	0.040	0.20/0.35	—	—	—
1335	0.33/0.38	1.6/1.9	0.040	0.040	0.20/0.35	—	—	—
3140	0.38/0.43	0.70/0.90	0.040	0.040	0.20/0.35	1.10/1.40	0.55/0.75	—
3310	0.08/0.13	0.45/0.60	0.025	0.025	0.20/0.35	3.25/3.75	1.40/1.75	—
4028	0.25/0.30	0.70/0.90	0.040	0.040	0.20/0.35	—	—	0.20/0.30
4047	0.45/0.50	0.70/0.90	0.040	0.040	0.20/0.35	—	—	0.20/0.30
4130	0.28/0.33	0.40/0.60	0.040	0.040	0.20/0.35	—	0.80/1.10	0.15/0.25
4140	0.38/0.43	0.75/1.00	0.040	0.040	0.20/0.35	—	0.80/1.10	0.15/0.25
4320	0.17/0.22	0.45/0.65	0.040	0.040	0.20/0.35	1.65/2.00	0.40/0.60	0.20/0.30
4340	0.38/0.43	0.60/0.80	0.040	0.040	0.20/0.35	1.65/2.00	0.70/0.90	0.20/0.30
4620	0.17/0.22	0.45/0.65	0.040	0.040	0.20/0.35	1.65/2.00	—	0.20/0.30
4640	0.38/0.43	0.60/0.80	0.040	0.040	0.20/0.35	1.65/2.00	—	0.20/0.30
4820	0.18/0.23	0.50/0.70	0.040	0.040	0.20/0.35	3.25/3.75	—	0.20/0.30
5145	0.43/0.48	0.70/0.90	0.040	0.040	0.20/0.35	—	0.70/0.90	—
52100	0.95/1.10	0.25/0.45	0.025	0.025	0.20/0.35	—	1.30/1.60	—
6120	0.17/0.22	0.70/0.90	0.040	0.040	0.20/0.35	—	0.70/0.90	V 0.10 min
6150	0.48/0.53	0.70/0.90	0.040	0.040	0.20/0.35	—	0.80/1.10	V 0.15 min
8620	0.18/0.23	0.70/0.90	0.040	0.040	0.20/0.35	0.40/0.70	0.40/0.60	Mo 0.15/0.25
9310	0.08/0.13	0.45/0.65	0.025	0.025	0.20/0.35	3.00/3.50	1.0/1.40	0.08/0.15
EX 24	0.18/0.23	0.75/1.00	0.040	0.040	0.20/0.35	—	0.45/0.65	0.20/0.30
EX 29	0.18/0.23	0.75/1.00	0.040	0.040	0.20/0.35	0.40/0.70	0.45/0.65	0.30/0.40
EX 30	0.13/0.18	0.70/0.90	0.040	0.040	0.20/0.35	0.70/1.00	0.45/0.65	0.45/0.60
EX 55	0.15/0.20	0.20/1.00	0.040	0.040	0.20/0.35	1.65/2.0	0.45/0.65	0.65/0.80

hardnesses may be obtained. Even when no reduction in hardness is desired, a low-temperaure (250 to 350°F) tempering operation is desirable to reduce stresses in the steel and produce a kind of martensite that is tougher than the kind produced immediately upon quenching.

4.3 Heat-Treating Data

The gear designer should remember that, in most cases, the strength and hardness of the steel gear will depend primarily upon the *skill and intelligence with which the steel has been heat-treated. Improper quenching or tempering at the wrong temperature will completely defeat the designer's selection of the best steel for the job.* Heat treating is still a *skilled art.* The best gears are made by those who study carefully the microstructure of their product and alter their heat-treating technique to get the best possible results.

Table 4.2 gave heat-treating data for some typical gear steels. The values

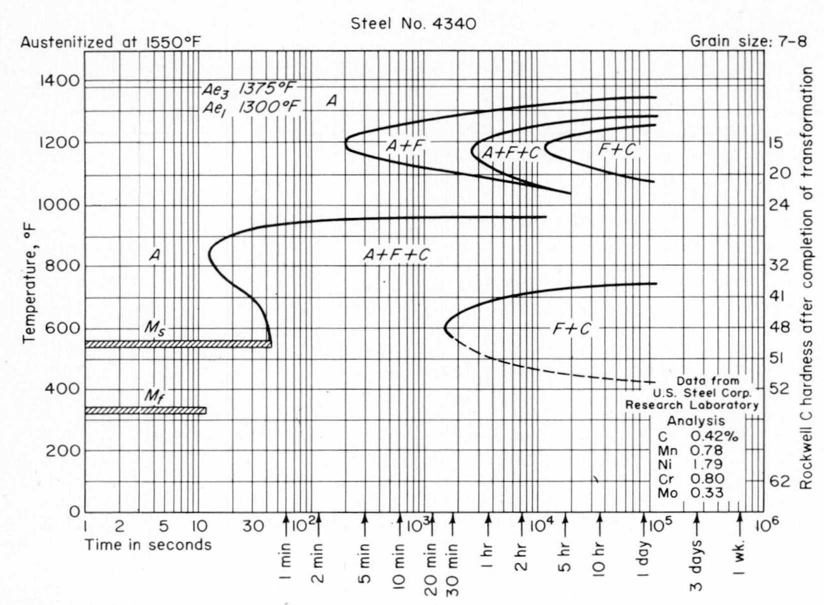

FIG. 4.2 Transformation diagram of AISI 4340. (*Courtesy of International Nickel Co., New York, NY, U.S.A.*)

shown should be considered to be nominal and should be varied in actual practice as experience dictates.

Figure 4.2 shows the way in which structures form during the cooling of 4340 steel. Transformation diagrams such as this one can be obtained from several companies that are involved in steel making. These diagrams are very helpful in developing a suitable heat-treating procedure for a particular steel.

The carbon content of a steel establishes the maximum hardness that can be reached in the fully hardened condition, while the alloying elements determine the critical cooling rate necessary for full hardening and therefore the section thickness that will harden with the quench that is available. For example, plain carbon steels have such high critical cooling rates that they must be water- or brine-quenched to be fully hardened even when the section is relatively small. Alloy steels transform more slowly and can be hardened with an oil quench. In the case of some high-alloy tool and die steels, even cooling in still air will develop high hardness!

End-quench-hardenability curves demonstrate how alloys slow down the reaction rates of steels and give the heat treater time enough to develop full hardness with a mild quench. With large parts made of plain carbon or low-alloy steels, there is a distinct danger of cracking the parts if they are quenched drastically enough to harden completely. On the other hand, a

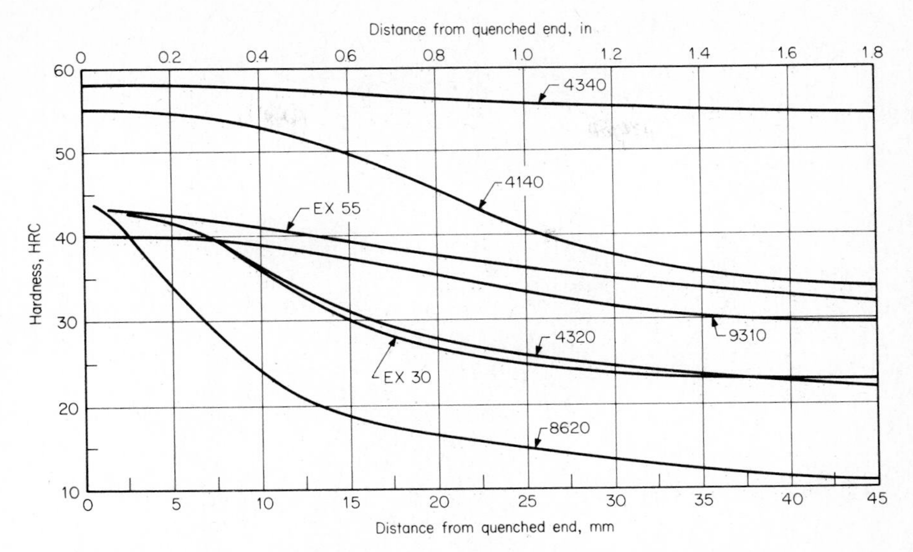

FIG. 4.3 Some typical Jominy curves showing end-quench hardenability.

milder quench may not develop structures with the required strength. In extreme cases, the part may be so large that even with considerable alloy content, it is not practical to use a fast enough quench to develop full hardness. In this case, the designer has to recognize that compromise is necessary, and design with low enough stresses to get by with whatever properties can be obtained in the steel.

Figure 4.3 shows end-quench-hardenability curves for several kinds of gear steels. These data, together with those shown in Tables 4.3 and 4.4, will help the designer choose a steel that will have sufficient hardenability for a specific gear. The designer should also note material quality grades in gear-rating specifications. See Secs. 3.24, 3.33, and 3.36.

4.4 Hardness Tests

The easiest way to determine the approximate tensile strength of a piece of steel is to check its hardness. Gear parts do not always have the same hardness in the teeth as in the rim, web, or hub. One of the best ways for the designer to control the final condition of the heat-treated gear is to specify the hardness of the teeth. In some cases it is desirable to check both the gear teeth and the gear blank for hardness. Small spur-gear teeth can be checked for hardness right on the working flank of the tooth. Figure 4.4 shows how this is done on small aircraft gears.

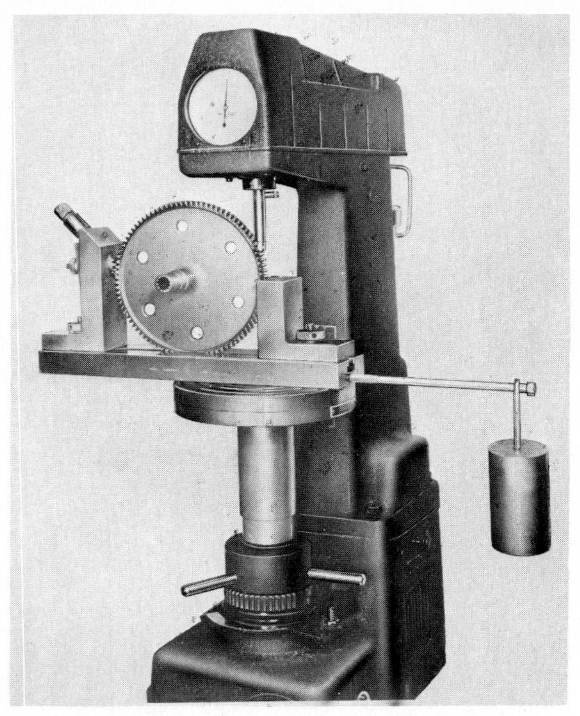

FIG. 4.4 Hardness-checking an aircraft gear near the pitch line of the tooth. (*Courtesy of General Electric Co., Lynn, MA, U.S.A.*)

Table 4.6 shows some of the commonly used hardness checks and the kind of gear for which they are most suited. The amount of load used and the kind of ball or point used to indent the piece being tested are also shown.

The approximate relation between the various hardness-test scales is shown in Table 4.7. The values shown are averages of tests on carbon and

TABLE 4.6 Hardness-Testing Apparatus and Application for Gears

Instrument	Shape and type of indenter	Loading	Recommended use
Brinell	10-mm steel or tungsten carbide ball	3000 kg	For large gears and shafts in range of hardness from 100 to 400 Brinell. (If gears have a hard case, the case depth must be sufficient and the core strength adequate to support the area under test. Rockwell

TABLE 4.6 Hardness-Testing Apparatus and Application for Gears (*Continued*)

Instrument	Shape and type of indenter	Loading	Recommended use
Brinell (*cont.*)			C tests may be used to reveal any error from such irregular conditions.) Brinell tests, when fairly representative of the general hardness, are a good measure of the ultimate tensile strength of the material.
Rockwell C	Diamond Brale penetrator (120° diamond cone)	150 kg	For gears medium to large in size. Range approximately 25 to 68 Rockwell C
Rockwell A	Diamond Brale penetrator (120° diamond cone)	60 kg	For small gears and tips of large gear teeth. Range Rockwell A 62 to 85
Rockwell 30-N	Diamond Brale penetrator (120° diamond cone, special indenter)	30 kg	For small parts and shallow case-hardened parts
Rockwell 15-N	Diamond Brale penetrator (120° diamond cone, special indenter)	15 kg	Lightest Rockwell load. For testing very small parts and checking the working sides of teeth. Check for very thinly case-hardened parts. Rockwell 15-N is used 72-93.
Vickers, pyramid	136° diamond pyramid	50 kg	All applications where piece will not be too heavy for machine. For use in testing hardness of shallow cases, etc.
Scleroscope	Does not indent surface. Diamond-tipped tup bounced on specimen	—	For applications permitting no damage or indentation to surfaces (results not always comparable with indentation hardness tests)
Tukon	Knoop indenter	500–1000 g for practical use	A laboratory instrument used only for finding the hardness of material on pieces of cross sections, e.g., hardness from surface inward, every 0.05 mm (0.002 in.), or hardness of individual microconstituents. All test areas must have flat mirror-polished surfaces. An extremely delicate and precise test. Used for any hardness

TABLE 4.7 Approximate Relation between Hardness-Test Scales

Brinell 3000 kg, 10 mm	Rockwell				Vickers pyramid	Scleroscope (Shore)	Tukon (Knoop)
	C	A	30-N	15-N			
	70	86.5	86.0	94.0	1076		
	65	84.0	82.0	92.0	820	90	840
	63	83.0	80.0	91.5	763	87	790
614	60	81.0	77.5	90.0	695	81	725
587	58	80.0	75.5	89.3	655	79	680
547	55	78.5	73.0	88.0	598	74	620
522	53	77.5	71.0	87.0	562	71	580
484	50	76.0	68.5	85.5	513	67	530
460	48	74.5	66.5	84.5	485	64	500
426	45	73.0	64.0	83.0	446	61	460
393	42	71.5	61.5	81.5	413	56	425
352	38	69.5	57.5	79.5	373	51	390
301	33	67.0	53.0	76.5	323	45	355
250	24	62.5	45.0	71.5	257	37.5	
230	20	60.5	41.5	69.5	236	34	
	Rockwell						
	B		30-T	15-T			
200	93		78.0	91.0	210	30	
180	89		75.5	89.5	189	28	
150	80		70.0	86.5	158	24	
100	56		54.0	79.0	105		
80*	47		47.7	75.7			
70*	34		38.5	71.5			

*Based on 500-kg load and 10-mm ball.

alloy steels. Because of differences in structure, cold-working tendencies, and other factors, there is no exact mathematical conversion between the scales. For this reason, hardness requirements on a gear drawing should be given *only in the scale* by which they will be checked. This will prevent possible ambiguity of hardness specifications.

LOCALIZED HARDENING OF GEAR TEETH

Several methods are used either to case-harden only the gear teeth or to harden the surfaces of gear teeth and leave the inside part of the tooth at an intermediate hardness. Carburizing, nitriding, induction hardening, and flame hardening can all be used to produce gear teeth which are much harder than the gear blank that supports the teeth. Since the tooth surfaces are much more critically stressed than the gear rim, web, or hub, a high-capacity gear can be obtained by fully hardening the gear teeth only.

4.5 Carburizing

Carburizing is the oldest and probably the most widely used process for hardening gear teeth. It consists of heating a 0.10 to 0.25 percent carbon steel at a temperature above its critical range in a gaseous, solid, or liquid medium capable of giving up carbon to the steel. The surface layer becomes enriched in carbon content and therefore is capable of developing a high degree of hardness after quenching.

The concentration of carbon in the surface layer is determined by many factors; if uncontrolled, it may reach 1.20 percent. For best strength and toughness, though, the concentration should be kept under 1.0 percent, preferably around 0.80 to 0.90 percent. Control of the richness of the carbon case is obtained by controlling the richness of the carburizing atmosphere.

The development of the case depends upon the diffusion of carbon into the steel; therefore, time and temperature are the main factors that control the case depth. Steel composition has no great influence on the rate of carbon penetration. Figure 4.5 shows the approximate effect of temperature and time on the depth of case obtained in a gaseous carburizing operation.

Carburized parts may be heat-treated in several ways to achieve a variety of case and core properties. Several of the most important treatments are illustrated in Fig. 4.6 and explained in the table accompanying the chart. For heavy-duty gearing, treatment C generally provides both a good case and a strong core. With only one quench, distortion is minimized. In some high-production gear jobs, it has been possible to get satisfactory gears by directly quenching from the carburizing temperature. The designer should hesitate to use this short-cut method unless there is a steel and a procedure that will produce gears which are *known* (by proper testing) to be good enough for the job.

In the vehicle field, the direct quench method is normally used for carburized gears. The gears are somewhat small, the volume of the production is high, and the facilities used are picked to be just right for the part. All these things tend to make it practical to use direct quench.

In the turbine field, most carburized gears are given a reheat quench. Here the gear parts tend to be fairly large, general-purpose heat-treat equipment is used, and the volume is low. The reheat method seems to give better

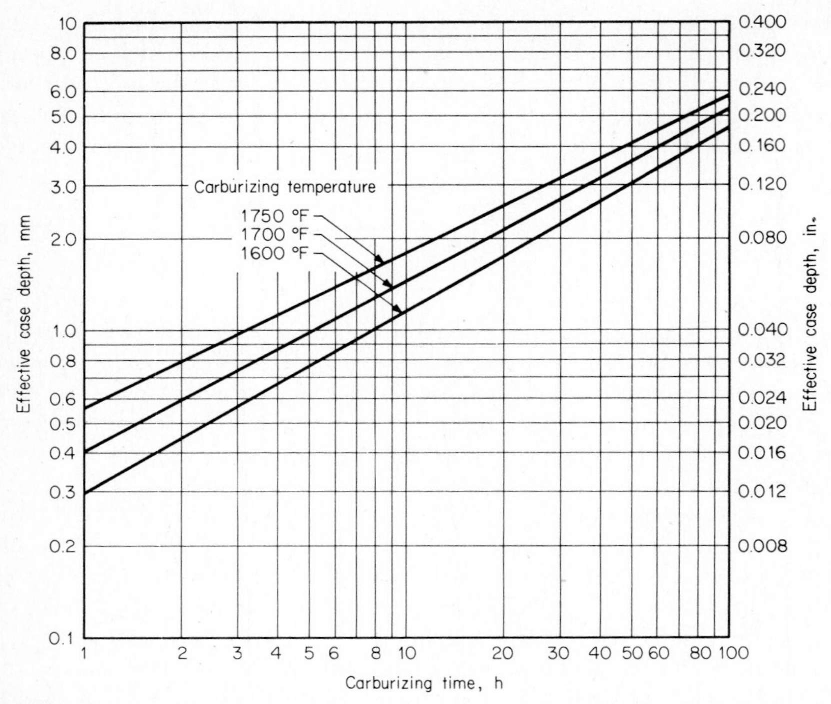

FIG. 4.5 Nominal time and temperature requirements for different case depths.

metallurgical structures and more assurance that the gears can run satisfactorily for 10^9 or 10^{10} cycles. (In the vehicle field, gears seldom run at high loads for more than 10^8 cycles.)

Commonly used carburizing steels are shown in Table 4.3. For best load-carrying capacity, the case should be up to 700 HV (60 HRC), and the core should be in the range of 340 to 415 HV (35 to 42 HRC). Too hard a core promotes brittleness and cuts down the compressive stress which is developed by the slight difference in volume between the case material and the core material. Too soft a core does not provide strength enough to support the high loads that the case can carry. For aircraft work, most designers favor a steel of the AISI 9310 type. The AMS 6260* specification quite closely follows the specification of AISI 9310 (AMS means "aircraft material specification"). This is a nickel-chromium-molybdenum type of steel. Other types of steels which are used for making heavy-duty gears for marine, tractor,

*Most of the critical aircraft gears are made from AMS 6265 steel. This is a vacuum-arc remelt steel of unusual cleanness. Both AMS 6260 and 6265 are 9310 types of steel. (AMS 6260 is an air-melt quality of steel.)

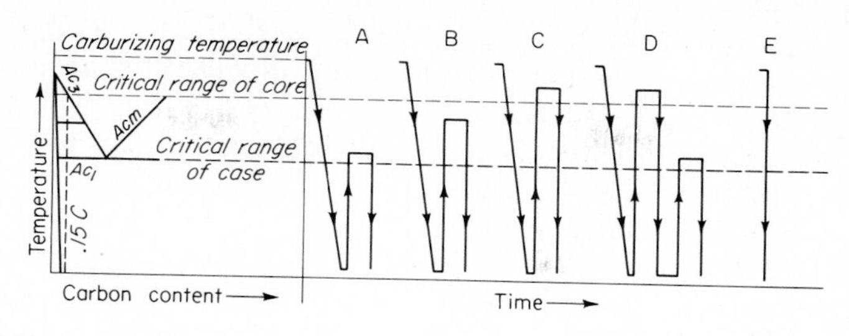

Treatment	Case	Core
A (Best adapted to fine grained steels)	Refined; excess carbide not dissolved.	Unrefined; soft and machineable.
B (Best adapted to fine grained steels)	Slightly coarsened; some solution of excess carbide.	Partially refined; stronger and tougher than (A)
C (Best adapted to fine grained steels)	Somewhat coarsened; solution of excess carbide favored; austenite retention promoted in highly alloyed steels.	Refined; maximum core strength and hardness. Better combination of strength and ductility than (B).
D (Best treatment for coarse grained steels)	Refined; solution of excess carbide favored; austenite retention minimized.	Refined; soft and machineable; maximum toughness and resistance to impact.
E (Adapted to fine grained steel only)	Unrefined with excess carbide dissolved; austenite retained; distortion minimized.	Unrefined but hardened.

FIG. 4.6 Diagrammatic representation of different treatments subsequent to carburization and the case and core characteristics obtained. (*Courtesy of International Nickel Co., New York, NY, U.S.A.*)

railroad, and other applications are the nickel, nickel-chromium, and nickel-molybdenum types. In a few gear applications (usually smaller-sized parts), good load-carrying capacity has been obtained using steels with a low alloy content. On a new job, the designer should do some development work to determine the most suitable type of steel for a given application.

The carburizing cycle brings gears up to a red-hot temperature. When the red-hot gear is quenched, it cools rapidly, but somewhat unevenly. The outer surface, of course, cools the fastest because it is in contact with the quenching medium.

As the steel cools, the structure changes and grows stronger. The unequal cooling rates in different parts of the gear body tend to make the gear change size very slightly and to distort. In addition, the carburized case tends to be slightly larger in volume than the core material. This also contributes to the size change and distortion tendency.

The overall result of this is that the pressure angle of the tooth tends to increase slightly and the helix tends to unwind. There is also a tendency for the bore to shrink, for the part to develop axial and radial runout, and for the outside diameter to become slightly coned. Because of these things, it is necessary either to make allowances for dimensional changes or to grind the part after carburizing. In either event, quenching dies may be helpful in cutting down distortion and reducing the amount of change that must be either allowed for or ground off.

Carburized gears have to have enough surface hardness to resist surface-initiated pitting. The allowable contact stress is based on the surface hardness. Small gears, with about $2\frac{1}{2}$-module (10-pitch) teeth and pitch diameters in the range of about 40 to 300 mm, can be carburized to achieve a surface hardness in the range of 700 to 750 HV (60 to 63 HRC). Larger gears, with 5-module (5-pitch) teeth and diameters going up to 1 meter (40 in.), are more difficult to carburize with optimum results in hardness and metallurgical structure. The design hardness of the medium large gear should generally be in the range of 675 to 725 HV (58 to 62 HRC).

If there are problems in processing carburized gears, the achievable *minimum* surface hardness may be only 600 HV (55 HRC). The problems may come from the parts being rather small or very large. Parts as small as 1 module (25 pitch) or as large as 25 module (1 pitch) are carburized. Either of these sizes is difficult to handle, and the surface hardness may be low.

Besides surface hardness, the carburized pinion or gear needs an adequate case depth. There are subsurface stresses that are strong enough to cause cracks in the region of case-to-core interface if the case is too thin.

The carburized case needs to be deep enough to give adequate bending strength and deep enough to resist case crushing or case spalling. The depth needed for bending strength is a function of the normal module (or the normal diametral pitch), but the depth needed to resist subsurface stresses due to contact loads is a function of the pitch diameter of the pinion, the ratio, and the pressure angle (primarily). Figure 4.7 shows an example of a carburized tooth sectioned to study case and core structure—before finish grinding.

The minimum effective case depth in the root fillet for tooth bending strength may be estimated by this relation:

$$h_{et} = 0.16 m_n \quad \text{mm} \qquad \text{metric} \quad (4.2a)$$

$$= \frac{0.16}{P_{nd}} \quad \text{in.} \qquad \text{English} \quad (4.2b)$$

where m_n = normal module

P_{nd} = normal diametral pitch

The minimum effective case depth on the flank of the tooth for surface

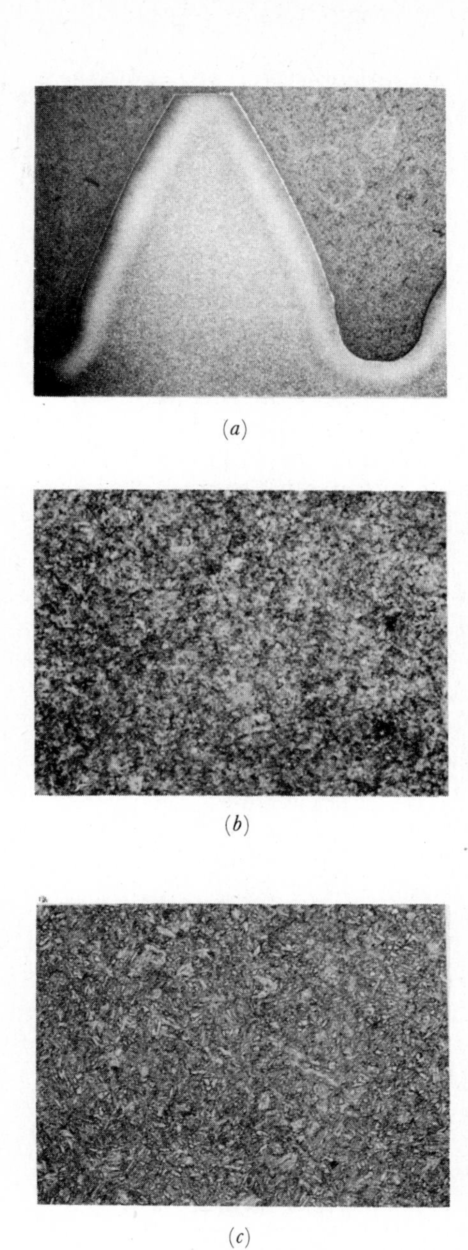

(*a*)

(*b*)

(*c*)

FIG. 4.7 Carburized gear tooth. (*a*) Section about 5×. (*b*) Case structure about 1000×. (*c*) Core about 250×.

durability may be estimated by this relation:

$$h_{ec} = \frac{s_c\, d_{p1} \sin \alpha_t}{48{,}250 \cos \beta_b} \left(\frac{u}{u + 1} \right) \quad \text{mm} \qquad \text{metric} \quad (4.3a)$$

$$= \frac{s_c\, d \sin \phi_t}{7.0 \times 10^{-6} \cos \psi_b} \left(\frac{m_G}{m_G + 1} \right) \quad \text{in.} \quad \text{English} \quad (4.3b)$$

where s_c = maximum contact stress in the region of 10^6 to 10^7 cycles (N/mm^2 for metric, psi for English)
d_{p1} = pinion pitch diameter, mm (metric)
d = pinion pitch diameter, in. (English)
α_t, ϕ_t = pressure angle, transverse, metric, English
β_b, ψ_b = base helix angle, metric, English
u, m_G = tooth ratio, metric, English

Figure 4.8 shows a schematic view of the case on a gear tooth. The minimum thickness needed at region *A* is determined by Eq. (4.3). The minimum thickness needed at region *B* is determined by Eq. (4.2).

If the case is too deep, the depth at region *C* becomes too great. A deep case at region *C* is a hazard because the whole top of the tooth may break off. Generally speaking, the depth at region *C* should not be greater than

$$h_{em} = 0.40 m_n \quad \text{mm} \qquad \text{metric} \quad (4.4a)$$

$$= \frac{0.40}{P_{nd}} \quad \text{in.} \qquad \text{English} \quad (4.4b)$$

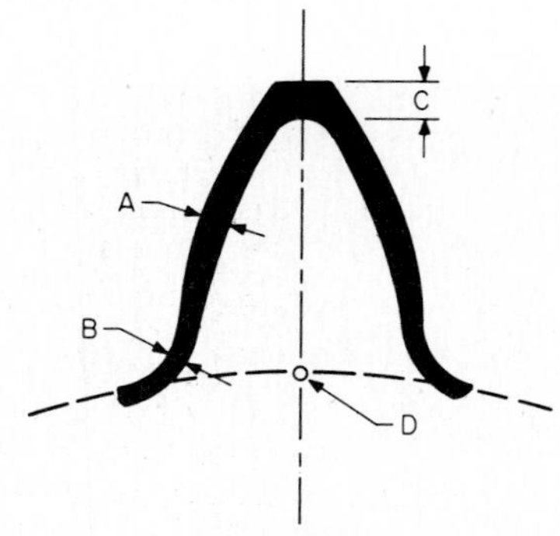

A Flank case thickness
B Root case thickness
C Tip case thickness
D Core hardness taken here

FIG. 4.8 Carburized case pattern. Shaded area is all 510 HV (50 HRC) or higher in hardness. Unshaded area is less than 510 HV (50 HRC).

In carburizing gears, the case depth is customarily specified for region A, with maximum and minimum limits of effective case depth. The *effective* case depth for parts with a minimum surface hardness of at least 675 HV (58 HRC) is taken at the point at which the case is at least HV 510 (50 HRC). For parts with less surface hardness, it is advisable to put the limit point for effective case depth at about 7 HRC points lower than the minimum surface hardness. Thus, the effective case depth for 600 HV (55 HRC) might be taken at HV 485 (48 HRC).

In specifying case depth, a set of values like this needs to be used:

Effective case depth, flank, 0.5 to 0.75 mm (0.020 to 0.030 in.)

Minimum effective case depth, root, 0.4 mm (0.016 in.)

Maximum effective case depth, tip, 1.00 mm (0.040 in.)

The above might be about right for a $2\frac{1}{2}$-module spur pinion, heavily loaded.

The amount of case depth needed for surface durability is illustrated in Fig. 4.9. This figure shows an example of spur gears with 22.5° pressure angle and a tooth contact stress of 1800 N/mm² (261,000 psi) for 5×10^6 cycles. This is typical of a very good vehicle gear, with very high torque at

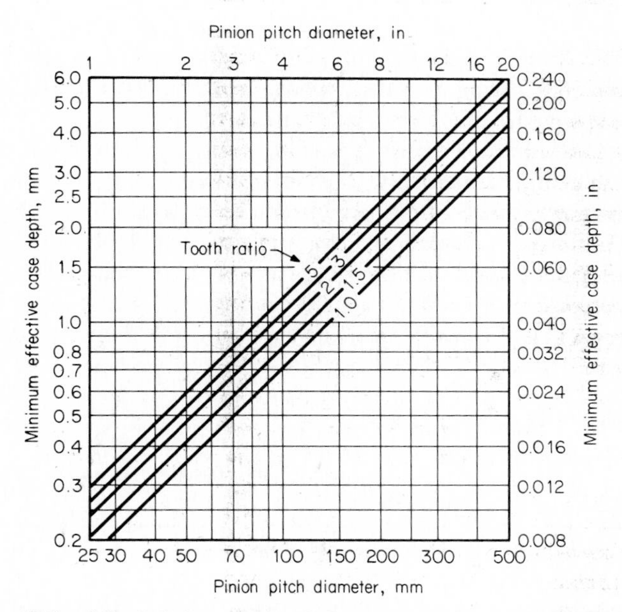

FIG. 4.9 Minimum effective case depth for carburized spur gears of 22.5° pressure angle and a contact stress of 1800 N/mm² (261,000 psi) for not over 10^7 cycles.

relatively slow pitch-line speed. The faster-running turbine gears, for instance, would have lower design stresses in the region of 10^7 cycles and still lower stress levels at a rated load in the region of 10^9 or 10^{10} cycles.

At the present time, more research work is going on to determine all the variables that affect the required case depth. Those designing gears should be alert to new requirements that may appear in trade standards. Equations (4.2) and (4.3) should be considered typical of gear-design knowledge in the early 1980s.

4.6 Nitriding

Nitriding is a case-hardening process in which the hardening agents are nitrides formed in the surface layers of steel through the absorption of nitrogen from a nitrogenous medium, usually dissociated ammonia gas.

Almost any steel composition will absorb nitrogen, but useful cases can be obtained only on steels that contain appreciable amounts of aluminum, chromium, or molybdenum. Other elements, such as nickel and vanadium, may be needed for their special effects on the properties of the nitrided steel. The gear steels most commonly nitrided are shown in Table 4.8. The temperatures used and the hardnesses obtained are shown in Table 4.9.

A nitride case does not form as fast as a carbon case. Figure 4.10 shows the nominal relation between nitriding time and case depth obtained. Nitriding, like carburizing, is a diffusion process, but because the rate of penetration is slower, the time cycles are quite long.

Nitriding is conducted in sealed retorts in an atmosphere of dissociated ammonia at temperatures between 930 and 1000°F. The modern practice is to start the process with 30 percent ammonia dissociation for the first several hours, then to allow dissociation to increase to 85 percent. At the lower dissociation rate, a weak and brittle layer of overly rich nitrides is formed as a surface layer about 0.05 mm (0.002 in.) deep. This is called a *white layer* because it etches out white in a micrograph. The higher dissociation rate that is used at the end of the cycle allows most of the excess nitrides to diffuse

TABLE 4.8 Nitriding Gear Steels

Steel	Carbon	Manganese	Silicon	Chromium	Aluminum	Molybdenum	Nickel
Nitralloy 135	0.35	0.55	0.30	1.20	1.00	0.20	—
Nitralloy 135 modified	0.41	0.55	0.30	1.60	1.00	0.35	—
Nitralloy N	0.23	0.55	0.30	1.15	1.00	0.25	3
AISI 4340	0.40	0.70	0.30	0.80	—	0.25	1
AISI 4140	0.40	0.90	0.30	0.95	—	0.20	—
31 Cr Mo V 9	0.30	0.55	0.30	2.50	—	0.20	—

TABLE 4.9 Nominal Temperatures Used in Nitriding and Hardnesses Obtained

Steel	Temperature before nitriding, °F	Nitriding, °F	Hardness, Rockwell C	
			Case	Core
Nitralloy 135*	1150	975	62–65	30–35
Nitralloy 135 modified	1150	975	62–65	32–36
Nitralloy N	1000	975	62–65	40–44
AISI 4340	1100	975	48–53	27–35
AISI 4140	1100	975	49–54	27–35
31 Cr Mo V 9	1100	975	58–62	27–33

*Nitralloy is a trademark of the Nitralloy Corp., New York, N.Y.

into the metal, leaving only traces of a white layer. Figure 4.11 shows examples of nitride cases on spline and gear teeth.

For best results, parts to be case-hardened by nitriding should be rough-machined and then quenched and tempered. The tempering temperature is usually between 1000 and 1150°F. After heat treatment, the part is finish-machined, stress-relieved at about 1100°F, and then nitrided.

Since the nitriding temperature is lower than the original tempering temperature of the steel, hardening occurs with a minimum of distortion. The method is therefore suitable for complex parts such as gears that can be machined while in the medium-hardness region and then hardened without

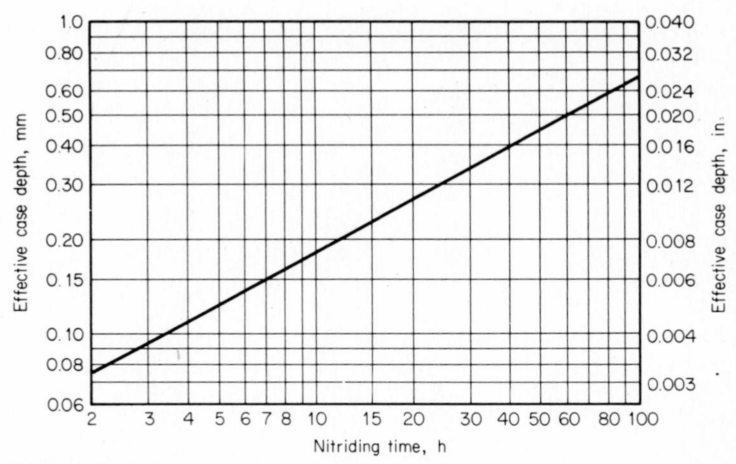

FIG. 4.10 Nominal time required for different nitride case depths. Note: Under the most favorable conditions, about 40 percent more case depth is possible.

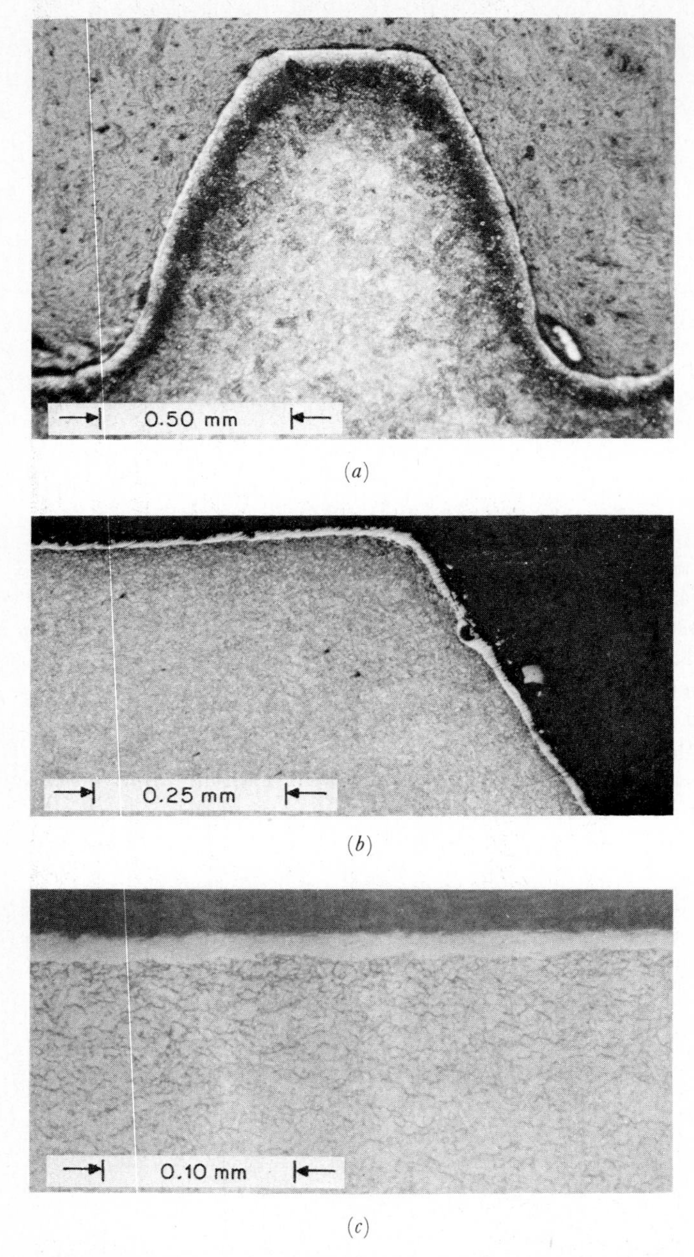

FIG. 4.11 Examples of nitrided gear tooth structures. (*a*) Small spline, Nitralloy 135M. White layer 0.03 mm (0.0012 in.). Case depth 0.41 mm (0.016 in.). (*b*) Medium size, internal spline 4340. White layer 0.01 mm (0.0004 in.). Case depth 0.38 mm (0.015 in.). (*c*) Part of 5-module gear tooth, 31 Cr Mo V.9. White layer 0.016 mm (0.0006 in.). Case depth 0.65 mm (0.026 in.).

enough distortion to require grinding. Parts that are too flimsy to stand a quench and draw without serious distortion can often be successfully brought up to full hardness by nitriding.

The formation of nitrides in the case causes the steel to expand, and, as in carburized cases, a favorable compressive stress is developed. This also results in a slight overall growth of the part. In spur gears this is manifested by an increase in outside diameter and in the diameter over pins. As an example, a 2-module (12-pitch) spur gear with a lightweight web showed an average increase in outside diameter of 0.13 mm (0.005 in.) and a 0.20-mm (0.008-in.) growth in diameter over pins. The pressure angle tends to decrease slightly. (This is just the opposite to the change in profile caused by case-carburizing.)

In general there is no distortion of the gear blank, provided that the blank was thoroughly tempered and stabilized before nitriding. If the blank has residual stresses before nitriding, the many hours at nitriding temperature will relieve these stresses and cause the part to warp.

The tendency for the nitride case to grow produces a "cornice" effect, or an overhang of quite brittle material on sharp corners and edges of parts, unless precautions have been taken to break such corners with a small radius before nitriding. If the controlled dissociation method of nitriding is not used, it is usually advisable to grind or lap off the white layer [0.08 mm (0.003 in.) nominally] after nitriding. It is also advisable to take precautions to avoid decarburization on areas to be nitrided. A very weak and brittle case is produced on decarburized steels or on steels that have not been properly quenched and tempered prior to nitriding.

If the steel contains aluminum, a nitrided case is relatively harder and inherently more brittle than a carburized case. Under high pressures, it may crack and spall because of either too little case depth or too weak a core material under the case. In general, nitrided gears need almost as much case as shown in Fig. 4.9, but with the coarser pitches, it is not possible to get the required depth. In severe load applications, some help can be obtained by using the Nitralloy N type of material. This material goes through a *precipitation hardening* of the core during the nitriding cycle. This gives the case added support and may, to some extent, compensate for the case being too thin on coarse-pitch gears.

The nitrided gear—because of its high hardness—resists scoring and abrasion better than other types of gears. Tests of 2.5-module (10-pitch) and finer nitrided gears have shown that with proper nitriding technique, just as heavy loads could be carried on a nitrided tooth* as on a good case-carburized tooth. In cases where shock loading is present, or where the pitch

*This statement assumes that the nitrided case is the *same* hardness as the carburized case and that the governing load was one for 10^7 cycles or more (not a very high initial load for less than 10^6 cycles).

is medium to coarse, most designers have found that other types of hardened gears would stand more loading than the nitrided gear.

Nitride Case Depth. The case depth needed for nitrided gears seems to be less than that needed for carburized gears. The logic of nitride case depth is still not understood too clearly. The 1980 ASME paper by Young* has a good review of the theory of case depth for nitrided gears and a summary of much practical experience in making large nitrided gears.

From the standpoint of tooth breakage, the nitride case does not generally give a high degree of strength. For spur teeth in the range of 4 module (6 pitch) to 10 module ($2\frac{1}{2}$ pitch), nitriding has some value in increasing the surface load-carrying capacity, but the beam strength has to be based almost entirely on the core hardness of the tooth. Equation (4.2) is a good approximation of the case depth needed if the *nitrided case*—instead of the core—is to govern the beam strength of the nitrided tooth. It can be seen from Fig. 4.10 that it takes about 55 hours nitriding time to get a case depth of 0.48 mm (0.019 in.). Equation (4.2) shows that a 3-module spur tooth needs a case depth of about 0.48 mm if the case is to control the beam strength. This means that a very long nitriding time is needed if teeth larger than 3 module are going to get much beam-strength help from the nitride case.

From the standpoint of surface durability, the situation is also rather critical on nitride case depth. A pinion of 150-mm (6-in.) pitch diameter running with a gear of 450 mm (18 in.) needs about 1.5 mm (0.060 in.) case depth when carburized and designed to carry a load of 1800 N/mm^2 (261,000 psi). There is some limited experience that says nitride case depth does not need to be quite as deep as carburized case depth to handle the same load. If this is true, the nitride case depth—in the author's opinion—would need to be at least 85 percent of the values given by Eq. (4.3).

The net result is that only small pinions (less than 100 mm) will be able to have enough nitride case depth to carry as much load as their surface hardness would indicate.

Many large pinions (and their mating gears) are nitrided and used successfully in turbine-gear applications. How do they get by with a very thin case for their size?

The answer seems to lie in using a surface loading that is *lower* than what the surface hardness could handle, but with *subsurface* stresses that are within the capability of the core material. The *ASME Wear Control Handbook* shows a simplified method of subsurface stress analysis. (See the chapter "Gear Wear" by Dudley, pages 798–802. Refer to Ref. 130.)

If the nitrided gear has a core hardness of at least HV 335 (HRC 34), the subsurface capability of the material underneath the case should be able to handle a surface loading up to about 1000 N/mm^2 (145,000 psi).

*Consult the reference section at the end of the book for complete data on this paper.

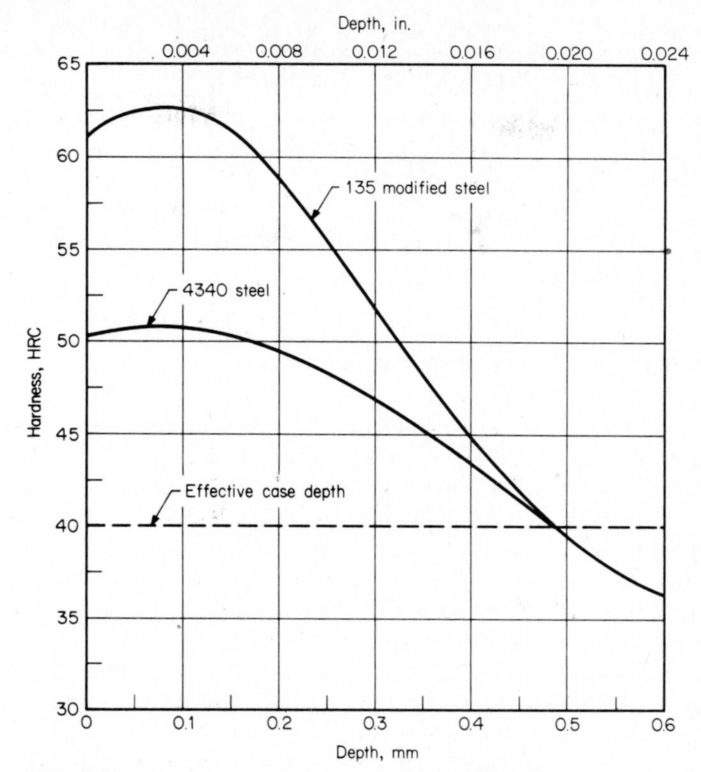

FIG. 4.12 Examples of two steels nitrided for a total time of 45 hours. 4340 is a low-chromium steel. 135M is high-chromium and aluminum steel.

In actual practice, nitrided turbine gears tend to be designed for surface loading in the range of 900 to 1000 N/mm^2 (130,000 to 145,000 psi). This means that they can get by with a much thinner case than Eq. (4.3) would indicate—providing they have *good* core hardness. (See Ref. 62.)

For nitrided gears, the effective* case depth based on HV 395 (40 HRC) seems to work best. The low-chromium nitriding steels develop a surface hardness of only about HV 515 (50 HRC). They need a much lower case determination point than do carburized steels. The aluminum types of nitriding steels and the high-chromium nitriding steels develop hardness comparable to carburized steels. The shape of their case hardness curves, though, is such that most of the hard metal is above HRC 40. Figure 4.12 shows two actual examples. Note how well the effective case is defined by the HRC 40 point.

*If the nitrided gear has a core hardness approaching HV 395 (40 HRC), then a higher value, such as 446 HV (45 HRC), must be used for effective case depth.

To conclude this section, it should be said that more gear research is needed to fully define all the criteria relative to the case depths needed for nitrided and carburized gears. The subject of failure by subsurface stress needs more study and more controlled laboratory tests. The ongoing work of Fujita in Japan is a good example of the pioneering research needed to understand how cased parts fail. The work of Sharma, Breen, and Walter has been most helpful in providing initial guidelines for designing gears with a consideration of the subsurface stress. (See references at the end of the book.)

4.7 Induction Hardening of Steel

High-frequency alternating currents can be used to heat locally the surface layers of steel gear teeth. Since the gear body remains relatively cold during the induction hardening, it serves as a fixture to maintain the dimensional accuracy of the induction-hardened teeth. The surface layers of metal undergo some plastic upsetting as they are heated because of the restraint of the cold blank. Upon hardening, the surface layers of metal undergo some expansion due to the volume increase of the hardened metal. There are thus two conflicting tendencies in induction hardening. One is a tendency for the part to shrink, and the other is a tendency for the part to expand. If the right technique is used with the right steel on the right pitch of teeth, good residual compression can be obtained. If the cycle is not just right, damaging residual tension stresses can result. Some gear manufacturers have developed proprietary processes for induction hardening of certain kinds of gears which enable them to build induction-hardened gears similar in strength to case-carburized or nitrided teeth. Many manufacturers have not been able to build induction-hardened gears with as much capacity as case-hardened gears. Designers of induction-hardened gears should plan on running enough experiments to develop just the right kind of cycle for the particular pitch and size of blank they are concerned with.

Induction-hardened gears have some tendency to warp. Usually there is no change in tooth profile, but there may be a "coning" of the outside diameter, axial runout, and radial bumps or hollows near holes in the web or near spokes in the wheel. Fortunately, much can be done to control induction-hardened-gear distortion by changes in blank design and changes in the induction-heating technique.

Both plain carbon and alloy steels are used for induction-hardened gears. Carbon content is usually either 0.40 or 0.50 percent. If a very fast cycle of heating is used, the choice of alloy will depend on the time that is required for the steel to austenitize. A small gear may be brought to the upper critical temperature in as little as 4 seconds.

FIG. 4.13 High-frequency power source and quenching machine for induction-hardening gears. (*Courtesy of General Electric Co., Lynn, MA, U.S.A.*)

The hardness pattern obtained with induction hardening will depend on the alloy used, the amount of power per square inch of gear surface, the heating time, the frequency, and the pitch of the tooth. Figure 4.13 shows a special machine for induction-hardening gears in a coil. Figure 4.14 shows some examples of hardness patterns obtained in very-high-capacity gear teeth.

The induction-hardening current may be obtained from motor-generator sets, spark-gap oscillators, or vacuum-tube oscillators. The power and frequency presently available from these sources are as follows:

Source	Power, kW	Frequency, cycles per second
Motor-generator	5–1,000	5,000–12,000
Spark-gap oscillator	2–15	10,000–300,000
Vacuum-tube oscillator	2–100	300,000–1,000,000

(a) (b)

FIG. 4.14 Hardness patterns obtained with induction-hardened gear teeth. (*a*) 2-module (12-pitch) pinion. (*b*) 10-module (2.5-pitch) pinion.

The amount of power required to harden a gear is very hard to estimate. It depends upon the efficiency of the coil, the amount of preheat used, and the amount of time that can be spent heating the gear without having too much distortion. Table 4.10 shows some random examples of power used on different gear sizes in regular production work.

Table 4.10 shows that quite large amounts of power are required to induction-harden gears when a coil is wrapped around the whole gear. Many designs cannot be induction-hardened simply because equipment with power enough to handle them is not available.

Fine-pitch gears require very high frequency for best results, while coarse-pitch gears require low frequency. If the wrong frequency is used, the heat may be developed below the teeth (fine pitch) or only in the tooth tips (coarse pitch). Table 4.11 shows the frequencies generally recommended.

TABLE 4.10 Power and Time Required to Induction-Harden Spur Gears

Power, kW	Gear size				Tooth size		Approximate heating time, seconds
	Diameter		Face width				
	mm	in.	mm	in.	m	P_d	
25	12	0.50	12	$\frac{1}{2}$	$1\frac{1}{4}$	20	5
25	50	2.0	6	$\frac{1}{4}$	$2\frac{1}{2}$	10	10
25	50	2.0	25	1	$2\frac{1}{2}$	10	50
50	25	1.0	6	$\frac{1}{4}$	$1\frac{1}{4}$	20	4
50	25	1.0	18	$\frac{3}{4}$	$1\frac{1}{4}$	20	15
50	125	5.0	6	$\frac{1}{4}$	$2\frac{1}{2}$	10	5
50	125	5.0	18	$\frac{3}{4}$	$2\frac{1}{2}$	10	7
100	150	6.0	125	5	8	3	90
100	250	10.0	25	1	$2\frac{1}{2}$	10	12
700	150	6.0	50	2	3	8	6
700	150	6.0	125	5	8	3	20
700	750	30.0	125	5	8	3	130

Note: This table is for hardening the whole gear in one operation.

TABLE 4.11 Frequencies Generally Recommended for Induction Hardening

Module	Diametral pitch	Frequency, cycles per second
0.7	32	500,000–1,000,000
$2\frac{1}{2}$	10	300,000–500,000
5	5	10,000–300,000
10	$2\frac{1}{2}$	6,000–10,000

Induction Hardening by Scanning. During the 1960s and 1970s, methods were developed to induction-harden gear teeth by moving an inductor across the face width of the gear to harden either a single tooth or the space between two teeth. In this way, a large gear could be progressively hardened with a relatively small amount of power.

If a gear had 100 teeth, it would take 100 passes of the inductor across the face width to harden the whole gear. Although this is somewhat time-consuming, the method was quite practical. A carburized gear might require 5 to 10 hours of furnace time, while a nitrided gear might require 50 hours of furnace time. If it took 3 hours to harden a gear by the scanning method, this was not bad. Of course, if the gear could have been induction-hardened by a coil wrapped around the gear, it might have been done in something like 5 minutes.

The scanning method offered the ability to achieve quite close control over the contour that was hardened. Figure 4.15 shows some examples of tests to establish a desired case depth. In the illustration, the *S* values are rates of coil traverse, and the *P* values are power settings. Note the deep case at the left with *S 10"* and *P 4.0* and the thinner case at the right with *S 17.5"* and *P 5.5*. These tests were done with an inductor *between* the teeth.

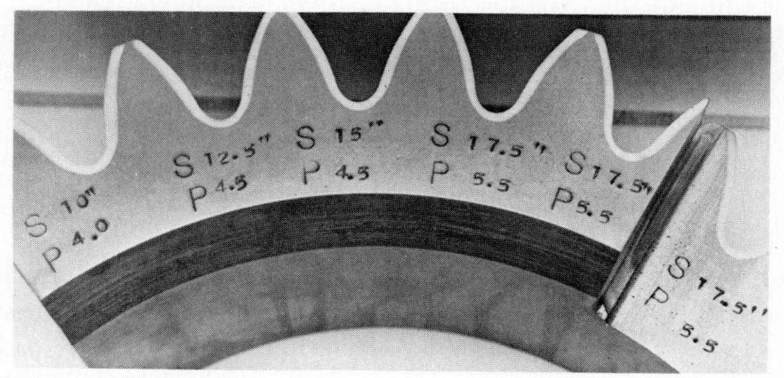

FIG. 4.15 Induction-hardened test piece for case depth. This work was done with a patented submerged inductor by National Automatic Tool Co., Inc., Richmond, IN, U.S.A.

FIG. 4.16 Machine induction-hardening a large internal gear. (*Courtesy of National Automatic Tool Co. Inc., Richmond, IN, U.S.A.*)

The scanning method will do large gears with large teeth. It will do internal gears as well as external gears. The inductor can follow a helical spiral to do helical gears. Figure 4.16 shows a machine doing a large internal gear, while Fig. 4.17 shows a close-up of the mechanism that scans the teeth. Note in this view the guide pin, the inductor, the power lines, and the lines to pass coolant through the inductor.

In some equipment, the gear and the inductor are submerged in coolant while the inductor hardens the teeth. In other equipment, the gear is kept cool by jets of coolant going along behind the inductor; the inductor is not submerged. In some cases, the setup is quite flexible and can be used in a variety of ways to best suit the part being done.

The basics of measuring case depth on teeth hardened by the scanning method are shown in Fig. 4.18. As with the carburized tooth shown in Fig. 4.8, there are three places to check the case and one location for measuring core hardness.

An example of the hardness pattern that may be obtained with the scanning method is shown in Fig. 4.19. Note the rather uniform hardness across the case and then the abrupt drop to core hardness. The effective case depth can be taken at 40 HRC like nitrided gears. (It wouldn't make much difference if it were 45 HRC.)

FIG. 4.17 Close-up view of scanning mechanism on a large induction-hardening machine. Note round guide pin, inductor, electric power cables, coolant lines, and traversing ram. (*Courtesy of National Automatic Tool Co. Inc., Richmond, IN, U.S.A.*)

The scanning method uses frequency values that range from 10 to 300 kHz (a kilohertz is a thousand cyles per second; 10 kHz = 10,000 cyles per second). Table 4.12 shows the nominal range of case depths that can be obtained for different tooth sizes and different frequency values. At a given frequency, the case depth is adjusted by the rate of scanning and the power setting. (Figure 4.15 shows test samples done at 200 kHz on 10-module teeth.)

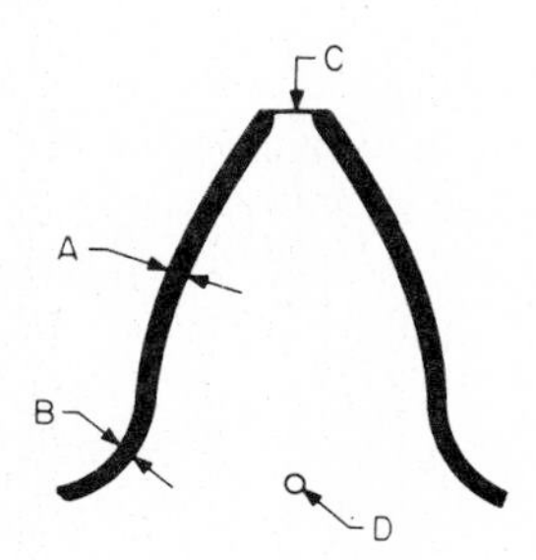

A Flank case thickness
B Root case thickness
C No case at center, top land
D Core hardness taken here

FIG. 4.18 Induction-hardened case pattern by the scanning method of tooth heating.

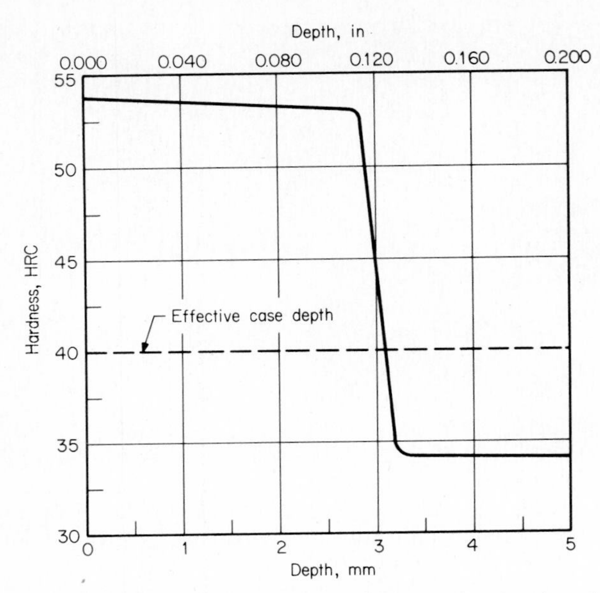

FIG. 4.19 Example of 4340 gear induction-hardened by the scanning method.

The case depth needed with induction-hardened teeth is somewhat greater than that needed for carburized teeth. Since the transition from case to core is not gradual, the case/core interface may not be able to carry as much load as its hardness would indicate. This makes it desirable to get the interface zone deeper into the tooth, where the subsurface stresses are lower.

Load-Carrying Capacity of Induction-Hardened Gear Teeth. The induction-hardened tooth may have about the same load-carrying capacity as a carburized tooth. If the surface hardness is up to about 58 HRC and the pattern of the case is good, a high load-carrying capacity may be achieved by getting an appropriate metallurgical structure and an appropriate residual stress pattern.

The problem, though, is that the *fast* heating and cooling times involved tend to cause considerable variation in both metallurgical structure and the residual stress pattern. The hardness and depth of the case may seem to be right for the job, but the gears may fail prematurely in service because their structure and/or residual stress pattern did not come out right. ("Right" means able to carry the load—not necessarily right from a theory of metals standpoint.)

Pitting is another problem. An induction-hardened tooth may pit, and then a tooth fracture may start at a pit. In many cases, induction-hardened

TABLE 4.12 Scanning Induction Heating Frequency and Case Depth Ranges That Are Practical for Different Sizes of Gear Teeth

Tooth size		Frequency, kHz			
Module	Diametral pitch	300	150	50	10
2.5	10	0.5–1.0 (0.02–0.04)	—	—	—
3	8	0.75–1.25 (0.03–0.05)	—	—	—
4	6	—	0.75–1.5 (0.03–0.06)	0.75–1.5 (0.03–0.06)	—
5	5	—	0.89–1.65 (0.035–0.065)	0.89–1.75 (0.035–0.07)	1.75–2.5 (0.07–0.10)
6	4	—	1.0–1.75 (0.04–0.07)	1.0–2.0 (0.04–0.08)	2.0–2.75 (0.08–0.11)
12	2	—	1.5–2.25 (0.06–0.09)	1.5–2.5 (0.06–0.10)	2.5–3.25 (0.10–0.13)
25	1	—	—	—	2.75–3.5 (0.11–0.14)

Notes: 1. The flank case depths shown are ranges that are practical for tooth size and frequency. The tolerance on case depth should be about ±15 percent. (For 1-mm case, use 0.85–1.15 mm.)
2. The case in the root should be about 70 percent of the case on the flank.
3. The case depths shown above are in millimeters, with equivalent depths in inches shown in parentheses.

gears have shown less capability to survive under moderately serious pitting than have case-carburized teeth. (It is probable that a good choice of an alloy steel and a biased heat-treating procedure can make an induction-hardened tooth able to stand as much pitting without tooth fracture as a good carburized tooth. Past problems with induction-hardened teeth fracturing after pitting were probably due to a lack of understanding of the metallurgy involved on the part of those making the gears.)

In view of the above, the builder of induction-hardened gears needs to develop each design to meet its job requirements. This development involves:

Metallurgical study of sample teeth to verify that the alloy chosen and the induction-hardening cycle will give satisfactory case depth, case pattern, case hardness, and metallurgical structure.

Study of process variables to control uniformity of case from tooth to tooth, from end to end, and from top of tooth to bottom of tooth.

Control study of the induction-hardening machine to maintain its power setting, maintain inductor positioning, avoid over- and under-temperature conditions due to electrical malfunction, etc. (Of particular concern is how to handle a machine stoppage when a gear is partly done without putting a weak spot in the circumference of the gear.)

Verification that the expected load-carrying capacity is achieved by appropriate full-load testing in the factory, and then follow-up observation of gears in service in the field in order to verify that the expected life and reliability is being achieved. (Of particular concern is field damage to the teeth by pitting, foreign material going through the mesh, overloads in transient operating conditions, etc.)

Many experienced builders are producing induction-hardened gears which are very satisfactory for their application. There have been quite a few cases in which inexperienced builders have not understood the complexity of the induction-hardening process and have built gears that have failed prematurely under load ratings that seemed reasonable. With all this in mind, it seems most prudent not to try to establish an industry load rating for induction-hardened gears. Instead, a load rating should become established for a given gearset as the builder acquires enough experience with it to check the manufacturing "recipe" and to acquire adequate knowledge of how the gears stand up in actual service.

4.8 Flame Hardening of Steel

Flame hardening is similar to induction hardening in both results obtained and kinds of steel used. It differs from induction hardening in that the heat is applied to the surface by oxyacetylene flames instead of being generated electrically in a layer extending from the surface to a small distance below the surface. In some cases it is difficult—or impossible—to get the same hardness pattern and fatigue strength by flame as can be obtained by induction hardening.

Special burners have been developed to impinge gas flames simultaneously on all tooth surfaces. Some types of flame-hardening apparatus use electronic control to turn off the gas at precisely the time when the temperature of the part just exceeds the critical temperature.

The flame-hardening process can be used quite handily either to harden the whole tooth or to harden just the working part of the tooth. Where beam strength is critical, the designer can usually improve the tooth strength by hardening the root fillet as well as the working part of the tooth. If wear is the only consideration, hardening the tooth to the form diameter will do the job and reduces the risk of distorting the gear blank.

Figure 4.20 shows some examples of flame-hardened teeth.

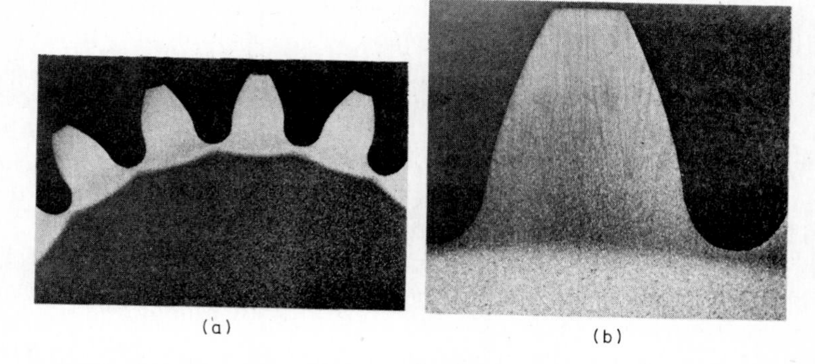

FIG. 4.20 Sections through flame-hardened gear teeth. (*a*) 1.3-module (20-pitch) teeth, 5 ×. (*b*) 4-module (6-pitch) teeth, 5 ×.

4.9 Combined Heat Treatments

In recent years a number of combination heat treatments have been developed. The skilled gear designer can often make use of such heat treatments to get results which are impossible with one procedure alone.

For instance, a double-cycle heat treatment of carburized gears produces a strong, long-wearing case. However, both distortion and time consumed in heat treating may be more than is desired. In some cases it is practical to carburize, quench from the carburizing heat, and draw the gear to medium hardness. Then the teeth can be finished by shaving or light grinding and, as a last step, induction-hardened. This procedure saves furnace time, since induction heating is very rapid. Also, the distortion is appreciably reduced because the whole gear blank does not undergo a high heat and quench after the teeth are finished.

Induction hardening can be done using a furnace preheat and then a period of both high-frequency and low-frequency heating.

The carburizing and nitriding treatments may be combined by using molten salts (or gases) which liberate both available carbon and nitrogen. The heating temperature does not need to be so high as that required for carburizing, and the case formed requires less time than nitriding alone would require. The case is harder, generally, than that obtained by carburizing alone but softer than nitrided cases on steels containing aluminum. In general, this type of treatment does not achieve quite so high a fatigue strength and quite so much pitting resistance as can be obtained with straight carburizing. In automotive gear work, where the cycles at maximum load are not too great, many types of gears have been produced with a cyanide hardening process, and they appear to perform just as well as carburized gears. In aircraft work, where the cycles at maximum load are usually quite large, very little use has been made so far of gears heat-treated by cyaniding or carbo-nitriding.

The gear designer who wants to know what is the *best* hardening process for a particular gear should plan on experimenting with the processes just described. Things like pitch, blank design, steel used, and application requirements all enter into why one heat treatment may work better than others in a particular job.

Hot quenching of gears and other parts may be used to minimize distortion. One such treatment is called *austempering*. It consists of quenching and holding the austenitized gear in a salt bath heated to some temperature below A_{c1}* but above the M_s temperature. A range of hardnesses between 400 and 650 HV (400 and 575 HB) can be developed, depending upon the temperature that is used. An extended time in the quench is required, particularly with the more highly alloyed steels, to permit full transformation. The hardness results are similar to those obtained by a quench and medium-temperature draw, but the structures developed are quite different and generally have better toughness at a given hardness.

Another hot-quench type of treatment is *martempering*. The part is quenched in a bath which is either just above or just below the M_s temperature for a time that is just long enough for all sections of the part to cool down to the bath temperature. Then the part is removed and air-cooled to room temperature. This treatment produces full hardness. After martempering, the part should be given a conventional tempering treatment to the desired hardness. Even if no reduction in hardness is desired, tempering is needed to remove stresses and improve the structure. Austempered pieces, however, do not require further tempering.

The two treatments just described are successful only on parts with small sections or with parts of large sections made of highly alloyed steels. Both are relatively slow quenching processes.

4.10 Metallurgical Quality of Steel Gears

For reliable performance at the design load rating, the gears in a gear unit must have two kinds of *quality* that are suitable for the application:

Geometric accuracy

This involves profile, spacing, helix, runout, finish, balance, etc.

Material quality

This involves hardness, hardness pattern, grain structure, inclusions, surface defects, residual stress pattern, internal seams or voids, etc.

*A_{c1} is the critical temperature of the case.

In the gear trade, the importance of geometric accuracy has been understood ever since the pioneering work of Earle Buckingham on dynamic load effects. AGMA and DIN standards set quality classes for geometric accuracy of gears. This work is continuing. More and better geometric accuracy standards for gear teeth may be expected. (In this book, see Sec. 5.18 for a discussion of gear-tooth geometric accuracy.)

In the field of gear materials, the quality aspect of the material has not received the attention it deserves. The AGMA aerospace gear standard was the first to recognize gear quality with a definition of Grade 1 and Grade 2 material. This standard was first issued in 1955.

The AGMA vehicle gear standard followed this trend in 1976 with definitions of Grades 1 and 2 material for vehicle gears.

In the private sector, several major companies building aerospace or turbine gearing for land use have rather detailed specifications for steel gears showing more than one grade of material and several quality control things to check the gear materials. Gears are passed or rejected for material quality just as they are passed or rejected for their geometric quality.

As time goes on, much more work on gear material quality can be expected. Trade standards that cover at least two grades of material for aerospace, vehicle, turbine, industrial, and mill gear fields of usage are needed. The present definitions used need to be expanded to cover more things and to more precisely define what is *acceptable* and *unacceptable* in each area of gear practice.

The possible gradations in gear-material quality have been thought of in these terms:

Grade 0 **Ordinary quality.**

No gross defects, but no close control of quality items.

Grade 1 **Good quality.**

Modest level of control on the most important quality items. (The normal practice of experienced gear and metals people doing good work.)

Grade 2 **Premium quality.**

Close control on essentially all critical items. (Some extra material expense to achieve better load-carrying capacity and/or improved reliability.)

Grade 3 **Super quality.**

Essentially absolute control of all critical items. (Much extra expense to achieve the ultimate. Has been used in space vehicle work. The need for this level of quality will be rather rare.)

Quality Items for Carburized Steel Gears. The principal items to control for material quality of carburized gears are:

Surface hardness
Core hardness
Case structure
Core structure
Steel cleanness
Surface condition, flanks
Surface condition, root fillet
Grain size
Nonuniformity in hardness or structure

The appropriate controls on these items will not be the same for aerospace gears and vehicle gears. For instance, some retained austenite is generally permissible (or even desired) in vehicle gears. In long-life aerospace or turbine gears, almost no retained austenite is permitted. Cleanness is another item. Certain kinds of dirt are tolerable in vehicle gears when the very high stress is applied for less than 10^7 cycles. Aerospace gears with a heavy design load for over 10^9 cycles are often made with vacuum-arc remelt steel (VAR) to remove essentially all the dirt particles in the steel.

Table 4.13 shows some typical data for long-life, high-speed gears to illustrate the possible differences between Grade 1 and Grade 2 gears. Figure 4.21 shows some metallurgical illustrations of Grade 1 and Grade 2 permissible structures.

As was said earlier, metallurgical quality grades are just being established

TABLE 4.13 General Comparison of Carburized Steel Gear Metallurgical Quality
(For turbine gears but not for vehicle gears)

Quality item	Grade 1	Grade 2
Metallurgy of case	Tempered martensite. Retained austenite 20 percent maximum. Minor carbide network permitted. Some transformation products permitted. Acceptable and unacceptable conditions defined by 1000 × microphotos.	Tempered martensite. Retained austenite 10 percent maximum. No carbide networks. Almost no transformation products such as bainite, pearlite, proeutectoid ferrite, or cementite permitted. Acceptable and unacceptable conditions defined by 1000 × microphotos.

TABLE 4.13 General Comparison of Carburized Steel Gear Metallurgical Quality (*Continued*)

Quality item	Grade 1	Grade 2
Metallurgy of core (at tooth root diameter)	Low-carbon martensite. Some transformation products permitted. Acceptable and unacceptable conditions defined by 250 × microphotos.	Low-carbon martensite. Almost no transformation products permitted. Acceptable and unacceptable conditions defined by 250 × microphotos.
Material cleanness	Air melt (aircraft quality). AMS 2301 E	Vacuum arc remelt (VAR) or vacuum slag process. AMS 2300
Magnetic indications of cracks or flaws on gear teeth	No indications parallel to axis. Not more than 4 surface indications, nonparallel to axis, per tooth, maximum length 4 mm. Not more than 6 subsurface indications, nonparallel to axis, maximum length 5 mm.	No indications parallel to axis. Not more than 2 surface indications, nonparallel to axis, per tooth, maximum length 2 mm. Not more than 3 subsurface indications, nonparallel to axis, maximum length 3 mm.
Forging grain flow	Forgings required for parts over 200 mm (8 in.) diameter. Close grain definition on forging drawing.	Forgings required for parts over 125 mm (5 in.) diameter. Very close grain flow requirements on forging drawing.
Surface defects after carburizing	Surface oxidation not to exceed 0.012 mm (0.0005 in.). Decarburization effects not to exceed 60 HKN (3 HRC).	Surface oxidation not to exceed 0.008 mm (0.0003 in.). Decarburization effects not to exceed 40 HKN (2 HRC).
Minimum hardness of case at surface		
Flank (A)	685 HKN (57.8 HRC)	725 HKN (59.6 HRC)
Root (B)	660 HKN (56.5 HRC)	695 HKN (58 HRC)
Minimum hardness of core at root diameter (D)	30 HRC	34 HRC

Notes:
1. This table shows only a partial amount of the magnetic particle specifications that are needed.
2. Details of acceptable and unacceptable decarburization can be shown by examples of plots of case hardness versus case depth.
3. Maximum case hardness is generally 800 HKN (63 HRC), but it may be specified lower to ensure that the draw treatment after final hardening lowers the hardness slightly and increases the impact strength.
4. The maximum core hardness is generally HRC 41, but it may be made slightly lower to better control the residual stress pattern.

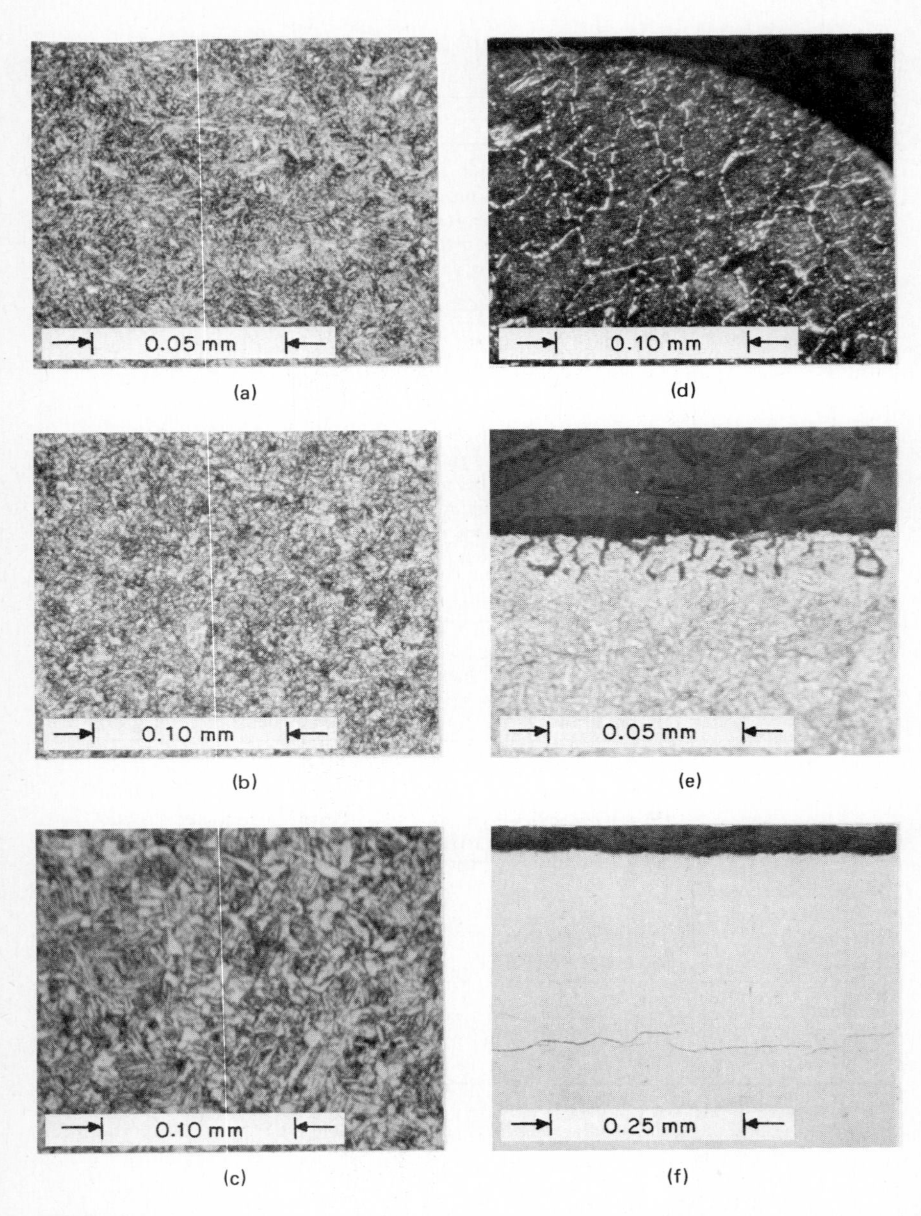

FIG. 4.21 Metallurgical examples, carburized gears. (*a*) Case structure, acceptable for Grade 2 (and Grade 1). (*b*) Core structure, acceptable for Grade 2. (*c*) Core structure, not acceptable for Grade 1. (*d*) Carbide network at tooth tip. Acceptable for Grade 1 but not for Grade 2. (*e*) Intergranular oxide layer, acceptable for Grade 1 but not for Grade 2. (*f*) Subsurface crack. Not acceptable for any grade.

TABLE 4.14 General Comparison of Nitrided Steel Gear Metallurgical Quality
(For small gears heavily loaded or medium large gears with low enough loading to permit nitriding)

Quality item	Grade 1	Grade 2
Metallurgy of case	White layer permitted up to 0.02 mm (0.0008 in.) maximum. Complete grain boundary network acceptable. No microcracks, soft spots, or gross nitrogen penetration areas permitted. Acceptable and unacceptable conditions defined in 500 × microphotos.	No white layer permitted on working surfaces of the tooth, other surfaces 0.02 mm (0.0008 in.) maximum. No microcracks, soft spots, or heavy nitrogen penetration along grain boundaries permitted. Continuous iron nitride network not permitted. Acceptable and unacceptable conditions defined by 500 × microphotos.
Metallurgy of core (at tooth root diameter)	Medium-carbon tempered martensite. Some transformation products permitted. Acceptable and unacceptable conditions defined by 250 × microphotos.	Medium-carbon tempered martensite. Almost no transformation products (bainite and pearlite) or ferrite permitted. Acceptable and unacceptable conditions defined by 250 × microphotos.
Material cleanness	Air melt (turbine quality).	Air melt (aircraft quality). AMS 2301 E
Minimum hardness of case at surface (*A*, *B*):		
Nitralloy 135, 135 M, and N	730 HKN (60 HRC)	740 HKN (60.5 HRC)
31 Cr Mo V 9	700 HKN (58.5 HRC)	725 HKN (59.6 HRC)
AISI 4140, 4340	520 HKN (48.6 HRC)	545 HKN (50.2 HRC)
Minimum hardness of core at root diameter (*D*):		
Nitralloy 135, 135M	31 HRC	34 HRC
Nitralloy N	37 HRC	40 HRC
31 Cr Mo V 9	28 HRC	32 HRC
AISI 4140, 4340	30 HRC	34 HRC

Notes:
1. Magnetic indications are controlled the same for carburized or nitrided parts.
2. Forging grain flow control is about the same as for carburized parts.
3. The maximum case hardness may be specified, but it is not necessary. (No tempering treatment *after* nitriding.)
4. Too high a core hardness is unlikely. (The nitriding treatment *will draw* the core if the parts are too hard before nitriding. This *should be avoided*, as a change in core hardness during nitriding will tend to cause distortion.)

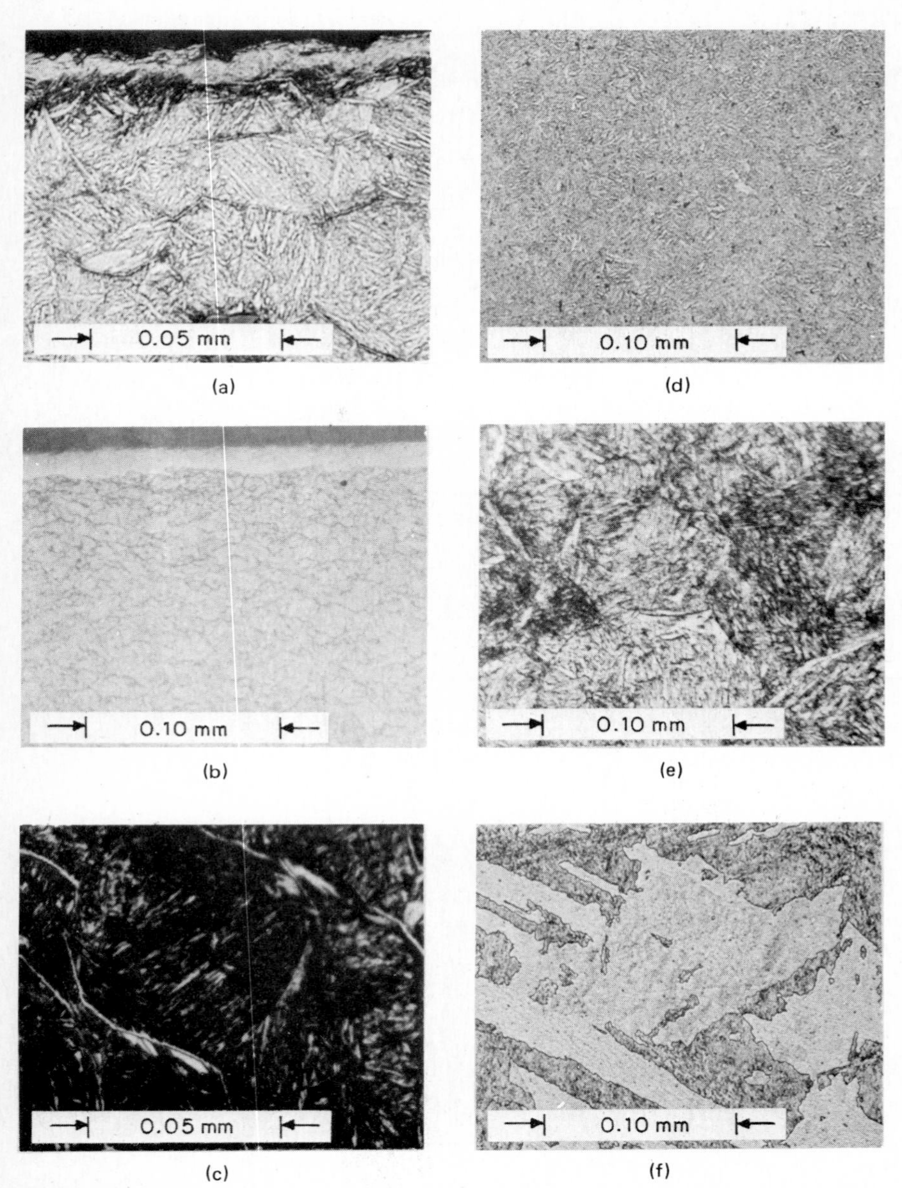

FIG. 4.22 Metallurgical examples, nitrided gears. (*a*) Case structure, thin white layer. Acceptable for Grade 2 by honing off white layer. (*b*) Case structure, thicker white layer but acceptable for Grade 1 without removal. (*c*) Continuous grain boundary nitrides. Not acceptable for Grade 1. (*d*) 4340 core structure, acceptable for Grade 2 (or Grade 1). (*e*) Nitralloy core structure, acceptable for Grade 1 but not for Grade 2. (*f*) 4340 core structure, not acceptable for Grade 1 or 2.

in the gear industry. Table 4.13 and Fig. 4.21 (and Table 4.14 and Fig. 4.22) should be considered as examples of what is involved, not as the author's particular recommendation of exactly what should be done in each field. Much study and work are needed to fully establish material grades in several important fields of gear work.

Quality Items for Nitrided Gears. The same list of items for carburized gears applies to nitrided gears. The nitrided gear tends to have a "white layer" and may have internal cracks as a result of improper nitriding. These things make the actual control of nitrided-gear quality somewhat different from that of carburized gears.

Table 4.14 and Figure 4.22 show concepts of quality grade considerations for nitrided gears.

Procedure to Get Grade 2 Quality. The premium Grade 2 quality requires extra effort and expense. The principal steps that are generally needed are:

1 Choose a steel with enough alloy in it to respond *well* in the heat-treat procedures planned.

2 Check incoming raw material for cleanness. (A certification from the supplier is usually not enough. Take samples and run laboratory tests.)

3 Prove out the heat-treat cycle planned by running one or more test gears. Set time, temperature, location in the furnace, etc., so that sure results can be obtained on the gears.

4 Use a portion of a toothed gear (or a whole gear) as a heat-treat sample, when a batch of gears is done.

5 Do laboratory work on the furnace samples after carburizing or nitriding.

6 Inspect finished gears for cracks and possible improper surface condition by nondestructive methods.

CAST IRONS FOR GEARS

Cast iron has long been used as a gear material. It has special merit, and some disadvantages, derived from its inherent structure and resulting properties. The gray cast irons, especially the alloyed types commonly used for gears, range in strength up to that of low-hardness steel. A newly developed cast iron with spheroidal graphite extends well into the strength range of heat-treated steels.

Cast irons differ from steel in both composition and structure. Their carbon content usually ranges from 2.5 to 4 percent, whereas gear steels contain substantially less than 1 percent carbon. The resulting structural differences, however, are most important. In cast irons as a class, the carbon is predominantly in the free, or graphitic, state, with only a small proportion in the combined, or pearlitic, form. Steels normally contain only the combined form of carbon.

It is the amount, form, and size of the graphite in cast iron which are responsible for its characteristic combination of properties. From the standpoint of mechanical properties, graphite, being weak in itself, reduces ductility, strength, elasticity, and impact resistance; but, on the other hand, it increases the ability of cast iron to damp out vibrations and noise. The graphite also helps cast-iron gear teeth to operate with scanty lubrication.

4.11 Gray Cast Iron

The gray cast irons, either plain or alloyed, are characterized by graphite in the flake form. These flakes act as a source of stress concentration, breaking up the continuity of the steel-like matrix. Figure 4.23 shows the characteristic structure of gray cast iron in comparison with other cast irons.

As cast iron solidifies and cools in the mold, metallurgical changes occur that are similar in many respects to those discussed in the heat treatment of steel. In fact, the mold cooling conditions should be considered a heat treatment—the only one that many gray irons ever receive. The size and distribution of flake graphite are controlled by the relationship between composition and section size, and by several phases of foundry practice. The matrix behaves like steel, and therefore the composition defines the extent of hardening under given cooling conditions. Light sections that cool rapidly are inclined to freeze "white," with the carbon in the form of iron carbide (cementite). Higher carbon and silicon inoculation, and nickel and copper additions, reduce the chilling power and produce graphitic and machinable structures in light sections. High carbon and silicon alone, however, are likely to produce large flakes and weak structures in heavy sections, and so castings with heavy sections are usually made from controlled and inoculated nickel irons.

A pearlitic matrix is highly desirable for a high-strength, wear-resistant iron, and the usual alloying elements—nickel, molybdenum, chromium, and copper—are used to increase the ability of gray-iron matrix to harden to this structure either in the mold or by subsequent heat treatment.

Gray iron has a low modulus of elasticity, varying with the strength level, that ranges from one-third to two-thirds that of steel. For gearing this is an advantage, since it tends to reduce the compressive stress (hertz stress) developed by a given tooth load. It also tends to reduce slightly the beam stress, because the teeth bend more and there is more sharing of load. Gray iron is

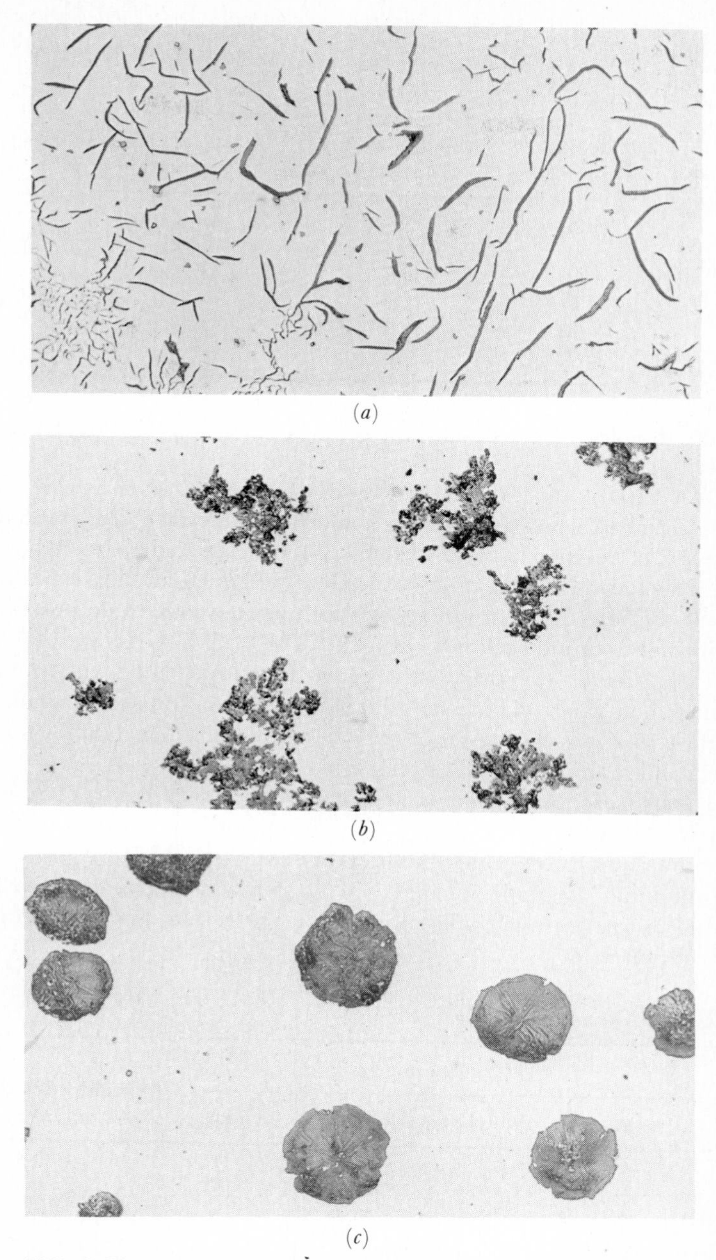

FIG. 4.23 Comparison of structures (all unetched, 250×). Dark particles are graphite. (*a*) Gray iron. (*b*) Malleable iron. (*c*) Ductile iron.

TABLE 4.15 Classes of Gray Cast Iron and Approximate Data for Hardness and Ultimate Tensile Strength

Class number	Brinell hardness, minimum	Tensile strength, psi, minimum
20	155	20,000
30	185	30,000
35	205	35,000
40	220	40,000
50	250	50,000
60	285	60,000

so brittle, though, that it should not be considered in gears subject to severe shock.

AGMA 240.01, the 1972 Gear Materials Manual, gives a wide range of data on steel, cast irons, and certain nonferrous materials. This standard is in the process of revision and, therefore, can be expected to soon have even more and better data than it now has. Gear designers should keep abreast of this work and use the many items of information about trade practices, test bars, normal acceptance limits, etc. In Tables 4.15, 4.16, and 4.17, some general data have been given as a guide, but no attempt will be made to cover the whole range of data now available (or soon to become available).

Table 4.15 shows the classes of gray cast iron and their data for minimum hardness and minimum tensile strength.

Alloy cast irons are needed as size increases and as the part complexity in section thickness increases. Table 4.16 shows some typical alloy cast iron compositions and the expected modulus of elasticity.

The nominal properties of malleable cast iron are given in Table 4.17. This kind of cast iron will take much more shock than gray cast iron. Note the elongation values.

TABLE 4.16 Data on Alloy Cast Irons

Class no.	Composition range			Modulus of elasticity, psi, minimum
	Nickel	Molybdenum	Chromium	
30	0.5–1.0	Optional	0.2–0.4	14×10^6
40	1.0–2.0	Optional	0.3–0.5	16×10^6
50	1.5–2.0	0.3–0.4	Optional	18×10^6
60	2.0–2.5	0.4–0.5	0.20 maximum	20×10^6
70	2.5–3.0	0.5–0.6	0.20 maximum	22×10^6
80	3.0–3.5	0.6–0.7	0.20 maximum	24×10^6

TABLE 4.17 Mechanical Properties of Malleable Iron

Commercial designation	Typical Brinell hardness range	Tensile strength, psi, minimum	Yield strength, psi, minimum	Elongation in 2 in., %, minimum
40010	160–210	60,000	40,000	10.0
43010	160–210	60,000	43,000	10.0
45007	165–220	65,000	45,000	7.0
48005	180–230	70,000	48,000	5.0
50005	180–230	70,000	50,000	5.0
53007	195–240	75,000	53,000	4.0
60003	195–245	80,000	60,000	3.0
70003	205–265	85,000	70,000	3.0
80002	240–270	95,000	80,000	2.0
90001	265–305	105,000	90,000	1.0

4.12 Ductile Iron

Up until 1948 malleable iron was the only type of cast iron available that would provide a useful degree of toughness or ductility. In malleable iron, the free graphite forms from white iron during annealing in clusters of tiny flakes. Malleable iron, as compared with gray iron, has ductility and better yield and elastic properties. Malleable iron has not been used widely for gears, however, because of its poor wear resistance and limitation to parts of relatively light section size.

In 1948 the production of iron with true spheroidal graphite in the as-cast condition was announced. Commercial castings are now widely available. The material is variously referred to as *ductile iron*, *spheroidal-graphite iron*, or *nodular iron*. Figure 4.23, which shows flake graphite in gray iron and spheroidal graphite in ductile iron, clearly demonstrates that the term *nodular iron* is not a completely accurate term to describe the new material.

The spheroidal form of graphite, furthermore, provides a material with a different combination of properties than is possible with malleable iron. Ductile iron may be made by treating a low-phosphorus gray-iron base composition with a magnesium or equivalent additive. It has tensile strengths ranging from 60,000 to 180,000 psi, yield strengths from 45,000 to about 150,000, and elongations up to 25 percent. The modulus of elasticity is about 24×10^6 psi. The standard grades now listed are shown in Table 4.18.

Ductile iron can be made with a high carbon content and still have a low carbide content. It is, therefore, not surprising that both its machinability and its wear resistance are excellent. The combination of strength, toughness, wear and fatigue resistance, and susceptibility to heat treatment offered

TABLE 4.18 Typical Properties of the Different Grades of Ductile Iron

Commercial designation	Recommended heat treatment	Brinell hardness range	Tensile strength, psi, min.	Yield strength, psi, min.	Elongation in 2 in., %, min.
60-40-18	Annealed	140–180	60,000	40,000	18.0
65-45-12	As cast or annealed	150–200	65,000	45,000	12.0
80-55-06	Quenched and tempered	180–250	80,000	55,000	6.0
100-70-03	Quenched and tempered	230–285	100,000	70,000	3.0
120-90-02	Quenched and tempered	270–330	120,000	90,000	2.0

by ductile iron has been of considerable interest to gear designers. It is still early to evaluate all the possibilities of this new material, but it has been used to advantage in applications formerly filled by carbon and alloy through-hardened steels, flame-hardened steel, gray cast iron, and gear bronze.

4.13 Sintered Iron

The art of making metal parts from powdered metals, or sponge metal, is not new. The ancient Egyptians forged tools from sponge iron. Platinum wire was made in the nineteenth century from sponge platinum powder.

During the last few years the art of powder metallurgy has been applied to the making of structural parts, in direct competition with other methods of manufacture. Improvements in the process have made it possible to make many parts by this method, which can compete successfully on a cost-strength basis with other methods of fabrication. Gears made from pressed and sintered iron powder have been made by the millions for such low-cost pieces of machinery as washing machines and food mixers.

The usual base materials for sintered gears are iron or brass metal powders, but when used alone these metals have inherently low strength. They are suitable only for light-duty gearing, for example, in timing devices, small appliances, or toys. Copper-impregnating pressed-iron gears, though, can considerably increase their strength. The impregnation is accomplished by putting a small piece of copper on top of a sintered-iron gear and then heating the gear in an atmosphere-controlled furnace so that molten copper soaks through the porous sintered gear. The copper fills the voids and bonds the material into a strong structure.

Generally accepted trade standards for the composition of powder-metal products have not yet been established. Table 4.19 shows the composition and strength of sintered metals commonly used for gears.

Because of the limitations of die design, only spur gears have been made

TABLE 4.19 Typical Sintered Metals Used for Gears

Type	Tensile strength, psi		% elongation	
	As sintered	Copper-impreg-nated	As sintered	Copper-impreg-nated
Alloy A (iron, 7½% copper)	35,000	70,000	0.8	1.0
Alloy B (iron, 1% copper)	35,000	85,000	0.8	1.0
Alloy C (iron)	20,000	60,000	15	20
Alloy D (80% iron, 20% copper)	30,000	—	20	
High strength (1% carbon, 17% copper, balance iron)	—	85,000	—	1.0

in large quantities by the powder-metal process. Helical gears can be made if the helix is not too large an angle. Blanks for any kind of gear can be made by sintering if the teeth are cut after sintering. There is not much incentive to do this, though, as the biggest cost saving in the sintering process comes from finishing the part by sintering and avoiding the cost of gear tooth cutting.

Sintered gears can carry moderately heavy loads at fairly fast speeds. They resist wear very well, and they are easy to lubricate.

NONFERROUS GEAR METALS

The metals copper, zinc, tin, aluminum, and manganese are used in various combinations as gear materials. The most important, perhaps, is the alloy called *bronze*.

The bronzes have become a widely used family of materials for gears, largely because of their ability to withstand heavy sliding loads. Like cast iron, the bronzes are easy to cast into complex shapes, while certain types are available in wrought forms. Because bronze castings as a rule will be more expensive than cast iron, the designer will select the material primarily for its ability to meet special service requirements. Most gear designers are of the opinion that bronze will withstand high-speed rubbing—such as in a worm gearset—better than cast iron. When the best tin bronzes are compared with the best gray cast irons, the bronzes indeed seem to be superior as a "bearing" material, although individual tests have been recorded in which certain bronzes were found inferior to some cast irons. Even in low-speed applications, bronze may be the most desirable material. Although the tables of hobbing machines do not turn very fast, experience indicates that higher table speeds can be used without danger of scoring when the hobbers have bronze index wheels than when they have cast-iron wheels.

The value of bronze as a bearing material seems to depend upon the fact that the microstructure of the material is made up of two phases, one hard and one soft. It is believed that, when a bronze gear or bearing wears into good contact, the hard constituent of the microstructure has become aligned to fit the rubbing surface and to carry the bearing load. The softer constituent has been soft enough to allow this aligning process to occur.

A number of special alloys are used for die-casting gears. In this type of work, a low-melting-point material with good casting characteristics is essential. Zinc-base alloys such as SAE alloy 903 are very popular. This alloy contains about 4 percent aluminum and about 0.04 percent magnesium, with the remainder zinc. It melts at about 700°F and has a tensile strength of around 40,000 psi. Aluminum-base die castings have about the same tensile strength, but they weigh only about 40 percent as much as the zinc castings. Their melting point is around 1100°F. A good composition for gear work is the aluminum alloy with 10 percent silicon and 0.5 percent magnesium.

4.14 Kinds of Bronze

Like the terms "steel" and "cast iron," "bronze" is really the name of a family of materials that may vary over a wide range of composition and properties. A "bronze" usually is an alloy of copper and tin, as compared with "brass," which is an alloy of copper and zinc. In practice, however, certain bronzes contain both tin and zinc, and the aluminum and manganese bronzes, for example, may contain very little or no tin. It might have been less confusing if these had been called brasses.

The basic bronze is an alloy of 90 percent copper and 10 percent tin that exhibits the desired two-phase structure. The best strength and bearing properties are developed if the hard and soft constituents are finely and intimately dispersed. This is usually accomplished by carefully chilling the casting. See Fig. 4.24*a* for the "delta" constituent.

Zinc is added to copper-tin bronze to increase strength, but at some sacrifice in bearing properties. Nickel also increases strength and has a further beneficial effect on hardness and uniformity of the structure.

Lead added to bronze does not combine with the base metal but remains distributed throughout the casting to act as a solid lubricant, much as graphite does in cast iron. See Fig. 4.24*b* for lead particles in bronze.

Lead is weak; therefore, it softens and weakens the bronze but improves machinability and allows quicker wearing in with a mating part. If bronze is not melted with the proper techniques, the tin may oxidize, and very hard

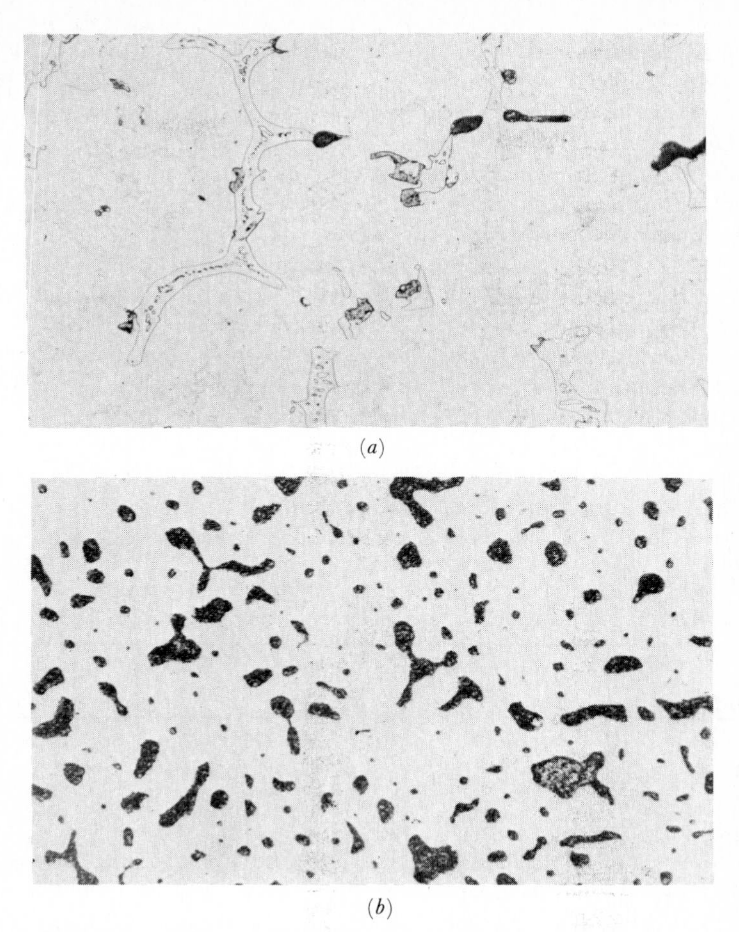

(*a*)

(*b*)

FIG. 4.24 Two typical tin-base worm-gear bronzes (both 250 ×). (*a*) Etched phosphor bronze. Light islands are "delta" constituent, the hard particles in the structure. (*b*) Unetched leaded bronze.

crystals of tin may be formed. These may be as destructive to the bearing surface as emery added to the lubricant! Proper deoxidation will prevent this danger. The tin bronzes deoxidized with phosphor are usually the best for gear applications. The term *phosphor bronze* means literally a bronze deoxidized with phosphor.

Aluminum bronzes are more complex than the copper-tin grades and may not have such good bearing properties. These alloys have a high strength as cast, however, and the strength can be increased by heat treatment. Aluminum bronzes have been used in many gear applications where sliding velocity is not high.

Manganese bronzes have a high zinc content along with smaller amounts of manganese, iron, and aluminum. Their strength far exceeds that of the tin bronzes. Supermanganese bronze has a tensile strength above 100,000 psi. With steel worms of 300 or more Brinell hardness, it makes about the strongest worm-gear combination that can be obtained for slow-speed applications, outside of using steel on steel.

Manganese bronzes are also available as forgings or as cold-drawn or extruded bars. The wrought-manganese bronze is lower in alloy content and strength than the supermanganese bronze, but has surprisingly good bearing properties. Some worm-gear applications with rubbing speeds of up to 50 m/s (10,000 fpm) have been handled with wrought-manganese bronze. It is also suitable for many low-speed, heavy-load applications.

Silicon-alloyed bronzes are available in both cast and wrought forms. Silicon increases strength only moderately in the cast grades, while the wrought forms can be further strengthened and hardened by cold drawing. There has been only limited use of silicon bronze for gears.

Table 4.20 shows some of the nominal compositions, tensile properties,

TABLE 4.20 Types of Gear Bronzes and Typical Examples of Each Type

Type	Composition, %	Strength,* psi	HB (500 kg)	Uses
Bronze (zinc-deoxidized)	Cu 88, Sn 10, Zn 2	ult. 46,000 y.s. 19,000 e.l. 12,000	65	Spur, bevel, worm gears
Phosphor bronze (chill-cast)	Cu 89, Sn 10, Pb 0.25	ult. 50,000 y.s. 22,000	85	Medium-speed worm gears
Nickel phosphor bronze (chill-cast)	Cu 88, Sn 10.5, Ni 1.5, Pb 0.2	ult. 55,000 y.s. 28,000	90	Medium-speed worm gears
Leaded phosphor bronze (sand-cast)	Cu 87.5, Sn 11, Pb 1.5	ult. 50,000 y.s. 22,000	75	High-speed worm gears
Aluminum bronze (sand-cast)	Cu 89, Al 10, Fe 1	ult. 65,000 y.s. 27,000 e.l. 20,000	120	Spur, bevel, low-speed worm gears
Aluminum bronze	Same as above but heat-treated	ult. 95,000 y.s. 60,000 e.l. 50,000	210	Heavy-duty low-speed gears
Supermanganese bronze (sand-cast)	Cu 64, Zn 23, Fe 2.75, Mn 3.75, Al 6.75	ult. 110,000 y.s. 70,000 e.l. 52,000	236	Heavy-duty low-speed gears
Manganese bronze (forged)	Cu 58, Zn 37.5, Al 1.5, Mn 2.5, Si 0.5	ult. 75,000 y.s. 40,000	135	Moderate-load gears. Small high-speed gears
Silicon bronze (sand-cast)	Cu 95, Si 4, Mn 1	ult. 45,000 y.s. 20,000	80	Low-speed gears of moderate load

*ult. = ultimate strength, y.s. = yield strength, e.l. = elastic limit.

and uses of the several kinds of bronze. It should be understood that there are a host of other bronzes which differ somewhat in composition from the typical kinds shown in the table. The strength and hardness values shown are *average* values. There is a considerable spread in properties for each composition, depending upon the size of the part, the rate of cooling of the casting, and the quality of the bronze.

4.15 Standard Gear Bronzes

At the present time, three kinds of copper-tin bronzes are specified as standard materials by AGMA for use in worm-gear applications. AGMA standard 240.01 shows material for cast-bronze gear blanks. Besides copper-tin bronzes, aluminum bronzes and manganese bronzes are shown. The compositions are not given, but expected physical properties are.

Many organizations other than AGMA have set up standards on bronze. The situation is somewhat confused, because there are no standards that are accepted by all bronze users. Frequently contracts will specify that bronze parts are to be made of some kind of bronze that may not be appropriate for the kind of gearing that is required. In such cases, the gear designer should obtain approval to substitute an appropriate gear bronze. Some of the organizations which have set up bronze standards are the U.S. Navy Department, the Naval Aircraft Factory, the U.S. Air Corps, the Society of Automotive Engineers, and the American Society for Testing Materials.

NONMETALLIC GEARS

In early times, gears were often made of wood. At present, few wooden gears are made.* A large quantity of "nonmetallic" gears are used, however. The modern use of nonmetallic gears goes back to the early 1900s, when John Miller conceived the idea of making a gear out of textile fibers held in a state of compression. He patented his idea in 1913. His original gears were made by taking layers of canvas cloth or nonwoven fabric and pressing them between steel plates. The steel plates were bolted together to hold the canvas in a state of compression. Later on, fibers were used instead of cloth, and the gear blank was impregnated with oil. The gear was sold under the tradename Fabroil.

For several years Fabroil, which was made of textile fibers, was the only type of nonmetallic gear in general use. Then another type of nonmetallic gear, made with phenolic resin, appeared on the market. Phenolic resins—

**The Evolution of the Gear Art*, pp. 51 and 52, tells about the making of wooden teeth for gears in the United States in the late 1960s. (See Ref. 9.)

TABLE 4.21 Physical Properties of Nonmetallic Gears

Property	Poly-carbonate	Polyamide	Acetal	Phenolic fabric, LE	
				Cross-wise	Length-wise
Tensile strength, psi × 10^3	9–10.5	8.5–11	10	9.5	13.5
Flexural strength, psi × 10^3	11–13	14.6	14	13.5	15
Elongation, %	60–100	60–300	15–75		
Impact strength, ft-lb per in.	12–16	0.9–2.0	1.4–2.3	1	1.25
Water absorption, % per 24 hr	0.3	1.5	0.4	See Note 2	
Coefficient of thermal linear expansion, °F, in. per in. per °F	3.9	5.5	4.5	1.1	
Heat resistance, °F (continuous)	250–275	250	—	250	
Representative trade names	Lexan	Nylon, Zytel	Delrin	Phenolite, Textolite	

Notes: 1. The tabulated data are average values and should not be used for specifications.
2. The water absorption percentages for phenolic fabric are as follows: 1/8″, 1.3; 1/4″, 0.95; 1/2″, 0.70; and 1″ up, 0.55.
3. This table is courtesy of General Electric Company, Plastics Division, Pittsfield, Mass.

such as the Bakelite invented by Dr. Bakeland—were adopted as a means of holding textile fibers in compression. In these gears, layers of cloth were bonded together with a phenol-formaldehyde resin binder. After processing, the gear blank became a solid structure which did not require metal shrouds and steel studs to hold it together, as Fabroil did.

The cotton-phenolic type of gear belongs to a general class of material called *thermosetting laminates*. In addition to the laminates, several other plastic materials are used for gears. Bakelite and similar plastics are used to injection-mold complete toothed gears. These materials do not have the strength of the laminates, but they are inexpensive and easy to manufacture, and so suitable when large quantities of small, light-duty gears are needed. In the 1960s and 1970s, several remarkable new plastics have appeared on the market. Nylon, for instance, has high strength for a plastic and possesses some good gear properties. Delrin and several other plastic gears are in common use. (See Table 4.21 for general families of nonmetallic gears.)

4.16 Thermosetting Laminates

A wide variety of sheet materials, such as paper, asbestos, cotton fabric or mat, wood veneer, nylon fabric, and glass fabric, may be used in making laminates. The binders may be phenolic resins, melamine resin, or silicones.

The laminates used for gears are generally of cotton fabrics, although paper is used occasionally.

Laminates are made by coating the sheet material with the liquid binder. After drying, the sheets are cut, stacked between metal plates, and bonded to form a board under a pressure of 1000 to 2500 psi at a temperature between 270 and 350°F. Such a board will show directional properties, because the components differ in strength from one direction to another.

The teeth of gears cut from these prelaminated boards will differ in strength, depending upon the position of the teeth with respect to the grain of the board. When the highest strength is needed, it is possible to prepare special gear blanks with the fibers of the laminate running in all possible directions. Then all teeth will have equal strength.

The laminates are sold under a variety of trademarks. Compositions and properties vary considerably. Table 4.21 (extracted from the *Gear Handbook*) shows typical properties for several kinds of nonmetallic gears, including phenolic laminates.

Phenolic-laminated material has several characteristics which make it attractive for gearing. Being nonmetallic, it runs quietly even when meshed with a steel pinion. Nonmetallic gears show very little tendency to vibrate or respond to vibrations.

Nonmetallic gears weigh only about one-fifth to one-sixth as much as steel gears of the same size. Even though their strength is only from one-tenth to one-thirtieth that of steel, it is possible, in some applications, to have nonmetallic gears carry about the same load as a cast-iron gear or low-hardness steel gear of the same size. If both the steel gear and the nonmetallic gear are made to commercial accuracy limits, the effect of tooth errors on the steel gearset is much greater because the teeth deform less under load, and so small errors create severe dynamic overloads in the steel gear teeth. The nonmetallic gear deforms about thirty times more than steel. This ensures good sharing of load between teeth and a low hertz stress as a result of the wide contact band.

Laminated nonmetallic gears have been run together in some applications with only water used as a lubricant. A steel pinion and a laminated gear will often run with less lubrication than a pair of steel gears.

In designing nonmetallic gears, the relatively large tooth deflection creates a problem. The driven gear—because of deflection—has a tendency to gouge the driver at the *first point of contact.* If the driver is a steel or cast-iron gear, this problem is not serious because the nonmetallic driven gear does not have enough hardness to gouge the hard metal. If the driven gear is steel, the gouging tendency can be controlled fairly well by making the driver with a very long addendum and the driven gear with little or no addendum.

For highest load capacity, nonmetallic gears are mated with steel or

FIG. 4.25 Phenolic laminated gear with a steel hub, after testing at a pitch-line velocity of 40 m/s (8000 fpm). (*Courtesy of General Electric Co., Lynn, MA, U.S.A.*)

cast-iron gears. The best wear resistance is obtained when the metal gear of the set has a hardness of 300 Brinell (or more).

In selecting a phenolic laminate, the pitch should be considered. When the teeth are 1.5 module (16 pitch) or coarser, a 15 oz/yd^2 tightly woven duck is about right. Teeth of 1 module (24 pitch) require a fabric base of about $6\frac{1}{2}$-oz duck. Finer-pitch gears use about 3-oz fine cambric.

Laminated nonmetallic gears have been used in a wide variety of applications. A few typical applications are air compressors, automotive timing gears, shoemaking machinery, electric clocks, household appliances, bottling machinery, and calculating machinery. When mated with a good steel gear, sliding velocities up to about 15 m/s (3000 fpm) can be handled. Figure 4.25 shows a gear after testing at 40 m/s (8000 fpm).

TABLE 4.22 Some Properties of FM-10001 Nylon

Tensile strength, psi:	
At −70°F	15,700
At 77°F	10,000
At 170°F	7,600
Modulus of elasticity, at 77°F	400,000
Rockwell hardness (R)	118
Specific gravity	1.14
Mold shrinkage, in. per in.	0.015

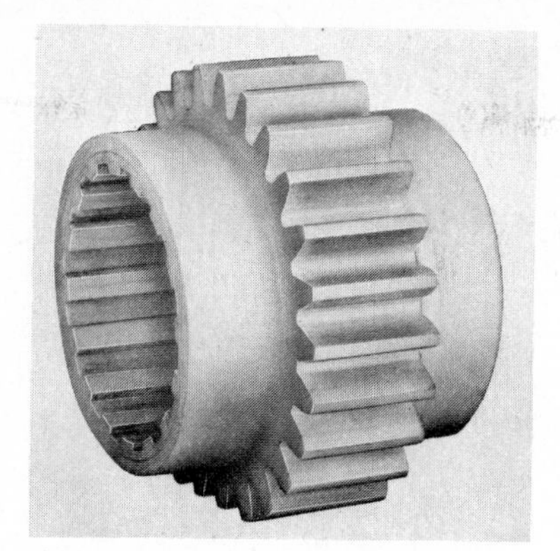

FIG. 4.26 Solid nylon gear after testing at a pitch-line velocity of 40 m/s (8000 fpm) and overload rating. (*Courtesy of General Electric Co., Lynn, MA, U.S.A.*)

4.17 Nylon Gears

One of the newer gear materials is nylon. This versatile plastic material has surprisingly high strength for a molded plastic. It has good bearing properties and considerable toughness.

Nylon may be injection-molded to form a complete toothed gear, or it may be molded in the form of rods or sheets from which gears may be machined. The best accuracy is obtained when the teeth are cut. The lowest cost, of course, is obtained when the complete part is molded.

A commonly used nylon for gears is the du Pont material FM-10001. Some of the properties of this material are shown in Table 4.22.

The values in Table 4.22 indicate that nylon has almost as much strength as the best laminates. Its weight is slightly less than that of the laminates. Nylon will deform under load about 75 times as much as steel!

One of the attractive features of nylon gears is their ability to operate with marginal lubrication. Small nylon gears have been able to run at high speed under light load with no lubricant at all. This is important in some applications, e.g., where a lubricant would soil yarn or film handled by a machine. Nylon gears have worked well in many gear applications, such as in movie cameras, textile machines, food mixers, and timing devices. In some cases, it has been reported that nylon did not stand up well. Tests made by the author with nylon gears running at 40 m/s (8000 fpm) pitch-line velocity and tooth loads up to those carried by low-hardness steel gears indicate that nylon—when properly processed into a well-designed gear—is a surprisingly good gear material. See Fig. 4.26.

chapter 5

Gear-Manufacturing Methods

The many methods of making gear teeth must be considered by the gear designer. The size and geometric shape of the gear or pinion must be within the capacity range of some machine tool. If the lowest competitive cost is to be obtained, then the gear designer must make the gear of a size, shape, and material that will permit the most economical method of manufacture.

The purpose of this chapter is to review all the commonly used methods of making gears. Illustrative data concerning the sizes and kinds of machine tools now available on the market will be given. Design limitations for each method of manufacture will be discussed so that the gear designer will have at least a general idea of what can be done by each method. Some data will be given on how fast gears can be made by each method. This is a controversial subject. The reader should use the data given with caution. They will not fit all situations.

A subject like gear-manufacturing methods is broad enough to require several books. In this chapter it will be possible to tell only a small part of the story. Further information may be found in the references at the end of the book. Gear-manufacturing terms used in this chapter are defined in the glossary Table 5.1.

TABLE 5.1 Glossary of Gear Manufacturing Nomenclature

Broaching A machining operation which rapidly forms a desired contour in a workpiece surface by moving a cutter, called a broach, entirely past the workpiece. The broach has a long series of cutting teeth that gradually increase in height. The broach can be made in many different shapes to produce a variety of contours. The last few teeth of the broach are designed to finish the cut rather than to remove considerably more metal. Broaches are often used to cut internal gear teeth, racks, and gear segments on small gears, and usually are designed to cut all teeth at the same time.

Burnishing A finishing operation which polishes a surface by rubbing.

Casting A process of pouring molten metal into a mold so that the metal hardens into the desired shape. Casting is often used to make gear blanks that will have cut teeth. Small gears are frequently cast complete with teeth by the die-casting process, which uses a precision mold of tool steel and low-melting-point alloys for the gears.

Drawing A metal forming process used to make gear teeth on a small-diameter rod by pulling the rod through a small gear-shaped hole.

Extruding A process that uses extreme pressure to push solid metal through a die of the desired shape.

Generating Any gear-cutting method in which the cutter rolls in mesh with the gear being cut. A generating method allows a straight-sided cutter to cut a curved involute profile into the gear blank.

Grinding A process that shapes the surface by passes with a rotating abrasive wheel. Grinding is not a practical way to remove large amounts of metal, so grinding is used to make very fine-pitch teeth, or to remove heat-treat distortion from large gears that have been cut and then fully hardened. Many different kinds of grinding operations are used in gear manufacture.

Hobbing A precise gear-tooth-cutting operation that uses a threaded and gashed cutting tool called a *hob* to remove the metal between the teeth. The rotating hob has a series of rack teeth arranged in a spiral around the outside of a cylinder (see Fig. 6.9), so it cuts several gear teeth at one time.

Lapping A polishing operation which uses an abrasive paste to finish the surfaces of gear teeth. Generally a toothed, cast-iron lap is rolled with the gear being finished.

Milling A machining operation which removes the metal between two gear teeth by passing a rotating cutting wheel across the gear blank.

Molding A process like casting which involves filling a specially shaped container (the mold) with liquid plastic or metal, so that the material has the shape of the mold after it cools. Injection-molding machines use high pressure to force the hot plastic into steel gear molds.

Punching A fast, inexpensive method of producing small gears from thin sheets of metal. The metal is sheared by a punching die which stamps through the sheet stock into a mating hole.

Rolling A process which rapidly shapes fine gear teeth or worm threads by high-pressure rolling with a toothed die.

Shaping A gear-cutting method in which the cutting tool is shaped like a pinion. The shaper cuts while traversing across the face width and rolling with the gear blank at the same time.

Shaving A finishing operation that uses a serrated gear-shaped or rack-shaped cutter to shave off small amounts of metal as the gear and cutter are meshed at an angle to one another. The crossed axes create a sliding motion which enables the shaving cutter to cut.

TABLE 5.1 Glossary of Gear Manufacturing Nomenclature (*Continued*)

Shear cutting A rapid gear-cutting process which cuts all gear teeth at the same time using a highly specialized machine. This method of cutting gear teeth is no longer used very frequently.
Sintering A process for making small gears by pressing powdered metal into a precision mold under great pressure and then baking the resulting gear-shaped briquette in an oven. Sintering is cost-effective only for quantity production because the molds and tools are very expensive.
Stamping Another word for *punching*.

Figure 5.1 shows a broad outline of the methods used to make gear teeth. Methods which are geometrically similar are grouped together. This figure shows that the gear designer will have to evaluate a large number of methods to choose the most suitable method for each job.

GEAR-TOOTH CUTTING

A wide variety of machines are used to cut gear teeth. As shown in Fig. 5.1, there are four more or less distinct ways to cut material from a gear blank so as to leave a toothed wheel after cutting. The cutting tool may be threaded

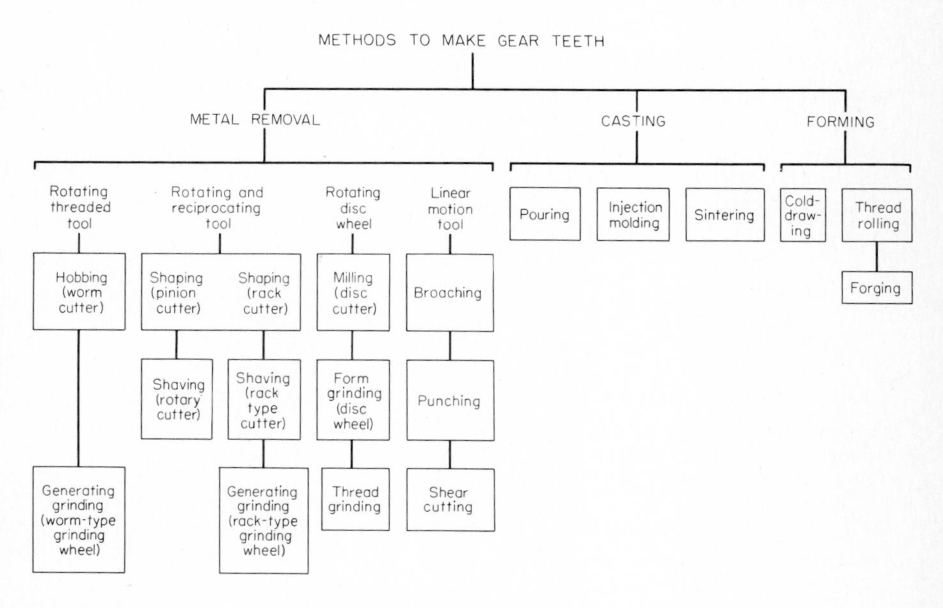

FIG. 5.1 Outline of methods of making gear teeth.

and gashed. If so, it is a *hob*, and the method of cutting is called *hobbing*. When the cutting tool is shaped like a pinion or a section of a rack, it will be used in a cutting method called *shaping*. In the *milling* process, the cutting tool is a toothed disk with a gear-tooth contour ground into the sides of the teeth. The fourth general method uses a tool, or series of tools, that wraps around the gear and cuts all teeth at the same time. Methods of this type are *broaching*, *punching*, and *shear cutting*.

5.1 Gear Hobbing

Spur, helical, crossed-helical (spiral), and worm gears can be produced by hobbing. All gears but worm gears are cut by feeding the hob across the face width of the gear. In the case of worm gears, the hob is fed either *tangentially* past the blank or *radially* into the blank. Figure 5.2 shows how a hob forms teeth on different kinds of gears.

A wide variety of sizes and kinds of hobbing machines are used. Machines have been built to hob gears all the way from less than 2 mm to over 10 m (3/32 to 400 in.) in diameter. Large double-helical gears are frequently hobbed with double-stanchion machines. These hobbers use two cutting heads 180° apart to cut both helices at once. Figures 5.3 to 5.5 show several examples of hobbing.

In designing gears to be hobbed, a number of things must be considered. A hob needs clearance to "run out" at the end of the cut. If the gear teeth come too close to a shoulder or other obstruction, it may be impossible to cut

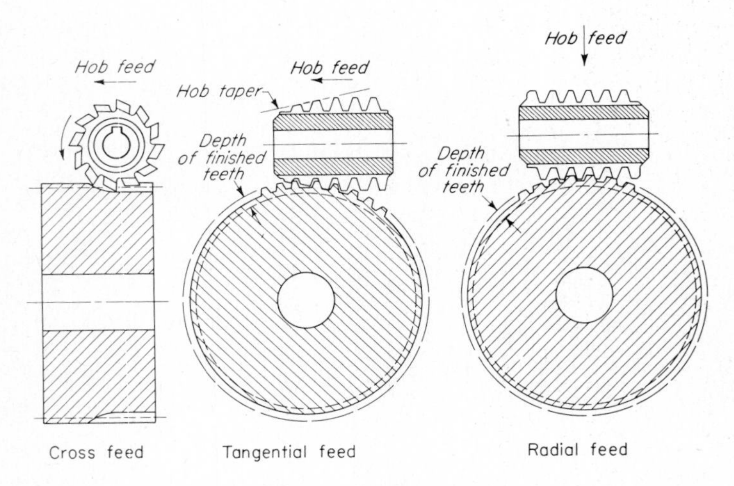

FIG. 5.2 Comparison of different kinds of hobbing.

FIG. 5.3 A tapered hob ready to finish-cut a small helical gear. This picture shows the basics of gear hobbing.

FIG. 5.4 A large coupling hub with external spur teeth that has been precision hobbed on a medium-size hobbing machine. (*Courtesy of Sier-Bath Gear Co., Inc., North Bergen, NJ, U.S.A.*)

FIG. 5.5 A large hobbing machine used to cut precision gears for large ships. (*Courtesy of General Electric Co., Lynn, MA, U.S.A.*)

the part by hobbing. If the gear is double-helical, a gap must be left between the helices for hob runout. The method of calculating the width of this gap is given in Sec. 6.2. If it is not necessary to use the narrowest possible gap, the values shown in Table 5.2 may be used.

Some large hobbers do not have centers to mount the work. In such cases, the gear is normally clamped on its rim. This makes it necessary to provide rim surfaces that are true with the journals of the part. Most of the smaller hobbing machines mount the work on centers. If the part does not have shaft extensions with centers, it is necessary to provide tooling so that the part can be mounted on a cutting arbor with centers.

The hobbing process is quite advantageous in cutting gears with very wide face widths or gears that have a toothed section which is integral with a long shaft. A very high degree of tooth-spacing accuracy can be obtained with hobbing. High-speed marine and industrial gears with pitch-line speeds in the range of 15 to 100 m/s (3000 to 20,000 fpm) and diameters up to 5 m (200 in.) are very often cut by hobbing. A few large mill gears up to 10 meters (400 in.) in diameter are hobbed. (These are not high-speed gears.)

Gears can be finished by setting the hob to full depth and making only one cut. Where highest accuracy is desired, it is customary to make a *roughing* and a *finishing* cut. The roughing cut removes almost all the stock. The finishing cut may remove from 0.25 to 1.0 mm (0.010 to 0.040 in.) of tooth thickness, depending on the size of the tooth.

The time required to make a hobbing cut can be calculated from the following formula:

$$\text{Hobbing time, min} = \frac{\text{no. of gear teeth} \times (\text{face} + \text{gap})}{\text{no. of hob threads} \times \text{feed} \times \text{hob rpm}} \tag{5.1}$$

The reason for adding the gap to the face width is the fact that a hob has to travel a certain distance in going into the cut and coming out of the cut. This extra travel happens to equal the amount of space that is necessary for the gap between helices. Equation (5.1) works with either millimeters or inches for face and feed.

In the past it has been quite customary to use single-thread hobs for finishing and single- or double-thread hobs for roughing. Single-thread hobs give the best surface finish and tooth accuracy. In many cases, though, multiple-thread hobs are used for both roughing and finishing. When gears are shaved or lapped after hobbing, surface finish in hobbing is not quite so important. If the gear has enough teeth and they are not an even multiple of the number of hob threads, hobs with as many as five or seven threads may be quite profitably used. For best results there should be about 30 gear teeth for each hob thread. This would mean that a five-thread hob would not be used to cut fewer than 151 gear teeth. For commercial work of moderate accuracy, the number of gear teeth may be as low as 15 per hob thread.

Hobbing feeds and speeds depend on how well the gear material cuts, the accuracy desired, the size of the gear, and the strength of the hobbing

TABLE 5.2 Nominal Gap Widths

Tooth size		Hob diameter		Gap width					
				15° helix		30° helix		45° helix	
Module, normal	Normal diametral pitch	mm	in.	mm	in.	mm	in.	mm	in.
1.25	20	48	$1\frac{7}{8}$	16	$\frac{5}{8}$	19	$\frac{3}{4}$	19	$\frac{3}{4}$
1.6	16	64	$2\frac{1}{2}$	22	$\frac{7}{8}$	26	1	26	1
2.5	10	76	3	32	$1\frac{1}{4}$	38	$1\frac{1}{2}$	38	$1\frac{1}{2}$
3	8	76	3	35	$1\frac{3}{8}$	48	$1\frac{7}{8}$	48	$1\frac{7}{8}$
4	6	89	$3\frac{1}{2}$	45	$1\frac{3}{4}$	51	2	57	$2\frac{1}{4}$
6	4	102	4	57	$2\frac{1}{4}$	70	$2\frac{3}{4}$	83	$3\frac{1}{4}$
8	3	115	$4\frac{1}{2}$	73	$2\frac{7}{8}$	89	$3\frac{1}{2}$	105	$4\frac{1}{8}$

machine. Table 5.3 shows representative values for three classes of work. The *conservative* values show what would be used when best accuracy was needed. The *high-speed* values are about the highest that can be obtained when machine and hob design receive special attention, and accuracy is not the most important thing. The size of hob will depend on the pitch. Section 6.2 shows standard hob sizes for different pitches.

Table 5.3 is based on a low-hardness steel of 100 percent machinability. For different hardnesses, the cutting speed should be reduced about as follows:

Material	Hardness HV	Hardness HB	Percentage of Table 5.3 speed
Steel	370	350	32
	320	300	40
	205	200	56
Cast iron	180	175	85

The above table is based on hobbers of rugged design cutting parts well within the machine capacity. In many cases it is necessary to reduce feeds and speeds to about 60 percent of the values given to reduce wear on the hob caused by machine vibration.

In the 1960s and 1970s, many advancements were made in machine-tool design and cutting-tool design. The art of gear cutting made notable improvements in both the accuracy and the production rates that could be achieved. Also, the diversity of equipment and methods became much great-

TABLE 5.3 Hobbing Feeds and Speeds

Hob diameter		Feed per revolution: Finishing 1 thread		Roughing 1 thread		Roughing 2 thread		Roughing 3 thread		Speed, rpm		
mm	in.	mm	in.	mm	in.	mm	in.	mm	in.	Conservative	Normal	High
25	1	0.5	0.020	1.3	0.050	0.9	0.035	0.6	0.025	590	870	1150
47	$1\frac{7}{8}$	0.7	0.030	1.5	0.060	1.1	0.045	0.7	0.030	270	370	490
75	3	1.1	0.045	2.2	0.085	1.7	0.065	1.0	0.040	145	210	270
100	4	1.4	0.055	2.5	0.100	1.9	0.075	1.3	0.050	105	150	200
125	5	1.5	0.060	2.5	0.100	1.9	0.075	1.3	0.050	80	115	150
150	6	1.7	0.065	2.8	0.110	2.0	0.080	1.4	0.055	65	95	125
200	8	1.8	0.070	3.0	0.120	2.3	0.090	1.5	0.060	50	70	95

Note: These values are based on AISI B1112 steel, 100% machinability rating.

er than it was in the 1950s. It is not possible in this short book to cover all the latest things in gear hobbing.

To give the reader an appreciation of the state of the art in hobbing (in the early 1980s), Table 5.4 was prepared. This table shows *nominal* production time for a small gearset and a large gearset. It also shows *fast* production time—what can be done using the most advanced hobbers, hobs, and hobbing techniques.

The data shown in Table 5.4 are a composite of survey data collected by the author. This means that the data are somewhat average. It is possible to do even better under the most favorable conditions. (Of course, under poor conditions, Table 5.4 times for either job-shop or fast production will not be achievable.)

TABLE 5.4 Some Examples of Production Time for Hobbing or Milling Gear Teeth

Examples of gearsets	Number of teeth	Module	Face width, mm	Material and hardness	Production time per piece	
					N	F
1	25 102	2 2	32 30	Alloy steel, pregrind cut at Vickers hardness of about 285	5 min 11 min	1.5 min 3 min
2	25 102	2 2	32 30	Alloy steel, preshave cut at Vickers hardness of about 375	15 min 30 min	3 min 6 min
3	25 102	15 15	307 300	Alloy steel, finish hob at Vickers hardness of about 325	6 hr 22 hr	2.5 hr 9 hr
4	25 102	15 15	307 300	Alloy steel, carburized and hardened to Vickers 700. Finish by skive hobbing	4.5 hr 17 hr	1.7 hr 6.5 hr

Notes: 1. The above table is based on spur gears, or helical gears up to 15° helix angle, and 20° pressure angle.

2. The alloy steel would contain chromium, manganese, nickel, and molybdenum. Good examples are AISI 4320 and 4340.

3. Vickers 285 = approximately 270 Brinell hardness
Vickers 375 = approximately 353 Brinell hardness
Vickers 700 = approximately 58.5 Rockwell C

4. Production time to cut:

N Nominal job-shop work. Milling or hobbing teeth, single-start conventional hobs or cutters. Work-holding fixtures and hobbing machines somewhat old and not too well suited to the exact work being done.

F A production hobbing facility doing fast repeat work. Multistart and coated* hobs being used wherever possible. Work-holding fixtures of special design. Most modern, high-performance hobbing machines.

*A popular hard coating for extra performance is titanium nitride (TIN).

Table 5.4 brings out these important considerations:

Fast production work with the best equipment may be three to five times faster than job-shop work with more ordinary equipment.

Finish cutting of the harder steels may take two or three times longer than pregrind cutting of lower-hardness steels.

Skive hobbing fully hardened steels is as fast or faster than finish hobbing medium-hard steels.

5.2 Shaping—Pinion Cutter

Spur, helical, and face gears and worms can be cut with a pinion-type cutter. Either internal or external gears can be cut. Parts from less than 1 mm to over 3 m (1/16 to over 120 in.) may be shaped. Relatively wide face widths may be cut, but in certain cases shaping will not handle as much face width as the hobbing process. For example, a standard 1.25-m (50-in.) gear-shaping machine will have a face-width capacity of 0.2 m (8 in.) regardless of helix angle, but a comparably sized hobbing machine would handle a face width of 0.6 m (24 in.), depending on the helix angle. Figures 5.6 and 5.7 show examples of shaper cutting.

Shaper cutters need only a small amount of cutter-runout clearance at the end of the cut or stroke. Shaped teeth may be located close to shoulders. A cluster gear can be readily shaper-cut where it may be impossible to hob because of insufficient hob-runout clearance. One NC shaper, pictured in

FIG. 5.6. The basics of shaper cutting.

FIG. 5.7 A shaping machine that has just cut a medium-sized double helical gear. (*Courtesy of Fellows Corp., Emhart Machinery Group, Springfield, VT, U.S.A.*)

Fig. 5.11, could conceivably cut a cluster gear in one set-up, depending upon gear data. Double helical gears can be cut with very narrow gaps between helices. In fact, one design of shaper can actually produce a "continuous" double helical tooth.

In designing gears to be shaped, it is necessary to machine a groove as deep as the gear tooth at the end of the face width for runout of the cutter. Normal values for the width of this groove are:

Tooth size		Width of runout groove					
		Spur		15° helix		23° helix	
Module	Diametral pitch	mm	in.	mm	in.	mm	in.
1	24	5	3/16	6	15/64	6.5	1/4
1.8	14	5	3/16	6.5	1/4	7	17/64
2.5	10	5.5	7/32	7.2	9/32	8	5/16
4	6	6.5	1/4	7.2	9/32	8	5/16
6	4	7.2	9/32	9	11/32	9.5	3/8

It is difficult to mount parts between centers while they are being shaper-cut, since the bottom portion must be driven. At least the one end must therefore be clamped to a fixture or gripped by a chuck. Gear parts which are integral with long shaft extensions may be supported at the upper end by a center or steady rest, and a long shaft extension downward may be accommodated by a hole in the base of the machine bed and even by a recessed portion of the machine foundation.

Gear shaping is quite advantageous on parts with narrow face widths. In hobbing, it takes time for the hob to travel into and out of the cut. For helical gears, the hob travel must be increased proportionally. In shaping, there is a minimum of overtravel for spur gears, and this overtravel does not increase for helical gears. For instance, a 2.5-module (10-pitch) gear with 25-mm (1-in.) face width would have an extra travel in hobbing of about 32 mm ($1\frac{1}{4}$ in.). In shaping, the extra travel would be only 5.56 mm (0.219 in.). In this example, the hob would cut across more than twice the face width that a shaper cutter would to do the same part. Furthermore, with the advent of the modern cutter spindle back-off type of machines, it is not uncommon to see stroking rates of 1000 strokes per minute for face widths 25 mm (1 in.) or smaller. In fact, for narrow face widths of 6 mm ($\frac{1}{4}$ in.), high-speed shapers capable of stroking rates of over 2000 strokes per minute are in use. Hydrostatically mounted guide and cutter spindle are necessary because of these high stroking rates.

The time in minutes required to shaper-cut a gear with a disc-type cutter may be estimated by the following formula:

$$\text{Shaping time} = \frac{\text{no. of gear teeth} \times \text{strokes per rev. of cutter} \times \text{no. of cuts}}{\text{no. of cutter teeth} \times \text{no. of strokes* per min}} \tag{5.2}$$

In shaping the coarser pitches, it is necessary to take several roughing and finishing cuts. Table 5.5 shows some nominal sizes of cutters and the number of cuts taken when shaping steel teeth of about 200 Brinell hardness.

Table 5.6 gives some representative values for the rotary feed rate per double stroke. These represent average values which might be used in cutting medium-precision gears.

The number of double strokes per revolution of the cutter can be calculated by

$$\text{Strokes per revolution} = \frac{\text{cutter dia.} \times \pi}{\text{rotary feed rate}} \tag{5.3}$$

*A "stroke" is a cutting stroke and a return stroke. Thus a stroke is really a double stroke.

TABLE 5.5 Nominal Sizes of Shaper Cutters and Number of Shaping Cuts

Tooth size		Cutter diameter		Number of cuts	
Module	Diametral pitch	mm	in.	Roughing	Finishing
1.25	20	50 75	2 3	1 1	1 1
2.5	10	75 100	3 4	1 1	1 1
4	6	100 115	4 4.5	1 or 2 1 or 2	1 1
6	4	100 125	4 5	2 or 3 2 or 3	1 1
12	2	150 175	6 7	2 or 3 2 or 3	1 1

The number of double strokes per minute is calculated from the formula

$$\text{Strokes per minute} = \frac{1000 \times \text{max. cutting speed, m/min}}{\text{stroke length, mm} \times \pi} \qquad \text{metric} \qquad (5.4a)$$

$$= \frac{12 \times \text{max. cutting speed, ft/min}}{\text{stroke length, in.} \times \pi} \qquad \text{English} \qquad (5.4b)$$

TABLE 5.6 Rotary Feed for Each Double Stroke of the Shaping Cutter

Material	Brinell hardness, HB	Machin-ability, %	Rotary feed per double stroke: 1.5 to 2.5 module (10 to 17 DP)		2.5 to 4 module (6 to 10 DP)		4 to 6 module (4 to 6 DP)		6 to 9 module (3 to 4 DP)	
			mm	in.	mm	in.	mm	in.	mm	in.
Steel to be case-hardened	135	100	0.5	0.020	0.5	0.020	0.6	0.024	0.6	0.024
	185	80	0.5	0.020	0.5	0.020	0.6	0.024	0.6	0.024
	220	65	0.3	0.012	0.35	0.014	0.45	0.018	0.5	0.020
Through-hardened alloy steel	172	72	0.4	0.016	0.4	0.016	0.5	0.020	0.6	0.024
	217	55	0.3	0.012	0.35	0.014	0.4	0.016	0.6	0.024
	254	45	0.25	0.010	0.3	0.012	0.3	0.012	0.4	0.016
Plastics	—	130	0.20	0.008	0.3	0.012	0.3	0.012	0.35	0.014

Notes: 1. The above feed values are based on a roughing and a finishing cut for 6 module (4 diametral pitch) and smaller teeth. For larger teeth, up to 10 module, two roughing cuts and one finishing cut are intended.

2. For finishing cuts of high-precision quality, the rotary feed will need to be reduced to get the required finish and the required spacing accuracy.

The cutting speed depends on the face width of the gear, the hardness and machinability of the material, the degree of quality, the cutter material, and the desired cutter life. See Table 5.7.

Just as considerable advancements have been made in hobbing, there have been notable advancements in shaper-cutting gears in the 1960s and 1970s. Perhaps the most notable are:

Numerically controlled machines

Cutter spindle back-off (instead of work table back-off)

Cutter spindle moved hydraulically instead of by mechanical means

New infeed methods

Machine with column that moves and stationary work table (conventional shapers work the opposite way)

Better shaper cutter materials and special hard coatings

These things have led to significant improvements in the precision of shaped gears and considerable improvement in gear shop production of shaped gears.

Figure 5.8 shows the Hydrostroke machine, developed by Fellows Corporation. The details of how the cutter spindle is stroked back and forth by pressurized oil are shown in Fig. 5.9.

The Hydrostroke machine is believed capable of doubling production rates under favorable conditions. It also has the potential to cut some gears so accurately that they do not need to be shaved (or ground) to get a relatively high precision. (The formulas just given for time required to shape gears do not apply to gears shaped on this machine.)

Figure 5.10 shows an example of a high-production machine with a movable column and a stationary work table. Note the special automation tool-

TABLE 5.7 Typical Cutting Speeds for Shaper Cutting

Gear face width		Machinability											
		20%		40%		80%		100%		120%		130%	
mm	in.	m/min	fpm	m/min	fpm	m/min	fpm	m/min	fpm	m/min	fpm	m/min	fpm
200	8	1.5	5	6.4	21	18.6	61	26.5	87	35.4	116	39.6	130
100	4	3.7	12	9.1	30	22.6	74	30.8	101	39.3	129	43.0	141
50	2	6.7	22	12.5	41	26.8	88	35.4	116	43.9	144	47.9	157
30	1.2	9.1	30	15.8	52	31.1	102	39.6	130	47.9	157	51.8	170
20	0.8	11.6	38	19.2	63	35.1	115	43.6	143	51.8	170	55.2	181
13	0.5	15.8	52	24.1	79	40.8	134	49.1	161	57.3	188	60.4	198

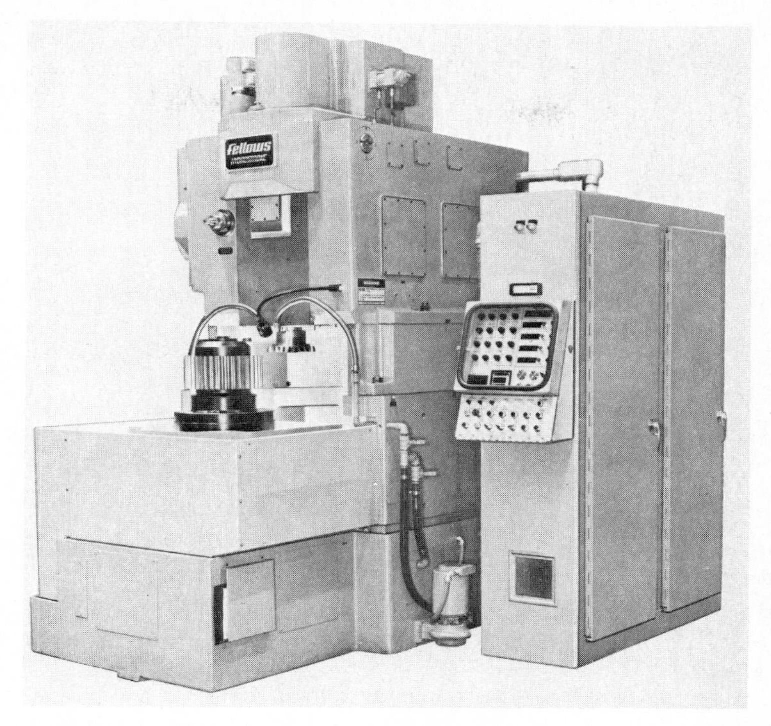

FIG. 5.8 The new Hydrostroke gear-shaping machine. (*Courtesy of Fellows Corp., Emhart Machinery Group, Springfield, VT, U.S.A.*)

ing. Figure 5.11 shows in a schematic fashion how a high-production, moving-column type of machine works. Basic motions are shown in the upper left-hand corner. The drive system is shown in the upper right-hand corner. Note that the drives use dc motors and are infinitely variable. The lower left-hand corner shows a new spiral infeed method.

The machine just described has a cutter spindle back-off system and independent dc motor drives for stroking rates and for rotary and radial feed amounts. This machine provides a significant increase in productivity compared with the older-style table relief shapers that used feed cams and feed-change gears with a single motor.

The special drives resulted in the developing of a new cutting method, sometimes referred to as *spiral infeed*. This cutting method tends to improve chip loading conditions and more evenly distributes tool wear around the cutter.

Table 5.8 shows estimates of production time needed to shape a variety of parts. The time shown tends to be much less than would be obtained by

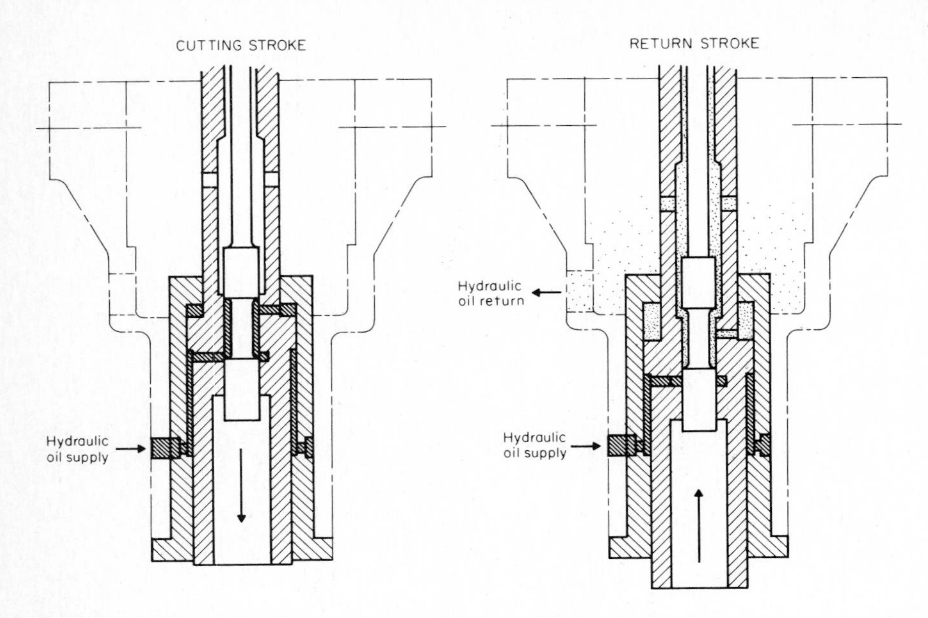

FIG. 5.9 Schematic details showing the principle of the mechanism to reciprocate the cutter in a Hydrostroke gear shaper. (*Courtesy of Fellows Corp., Emhart Machinery Group, Springfield, VT, U.S.A.*)

using the equations in this chapter. The equations, of course, are for job-shop rather than high-production conditions.

The values in Table 5.8 may, of course, be bettered by even more advanced shaping methods—and with somewhat unfavorable conditions, it may not be possible to cut a part as quickly as the table shows.

5.3 Shaping—Rack Cutter

Spur and helical gears as well as racks may be shaped with a rack cutter. Although machines designed to use rack cutters are mostly used for external gears, attachments for cutting internal gears with a pinion-shaped cutter are available.

The generating action is the same as rolling a gear along a mating rack. The rack tool, mounted in a clapper box, reciprocates while the gear rolls past its cutting field. Cutting generally takes place during the downstroke, and the clapper box clears the tool from the work on the upstroke. See Fig. 5.12.

Rack shapers cut only a few teeth in one generating cycle, then index to pick up the next teeth. The number of teeth per generation, the number of strokes per tooth (feed), and the stroking speed are all individually variable. The cutting ram is mounted in long guideways and is driven by a crank motion or, on heavy-duty versions, a multipitch screw.

The rack tool can be likened to one flute of a hob. It is not as expensive as a hob, and it does not require as much runout clearance as a hob. Also, there is no diameter/tooth size restriction, so a single-tooth rack tool can be made as large as the clapper box.

The most popular use for the rack shaper is for coarse pitches, high-hardness material, and narrow-gap double helical gears. It is also ideal for

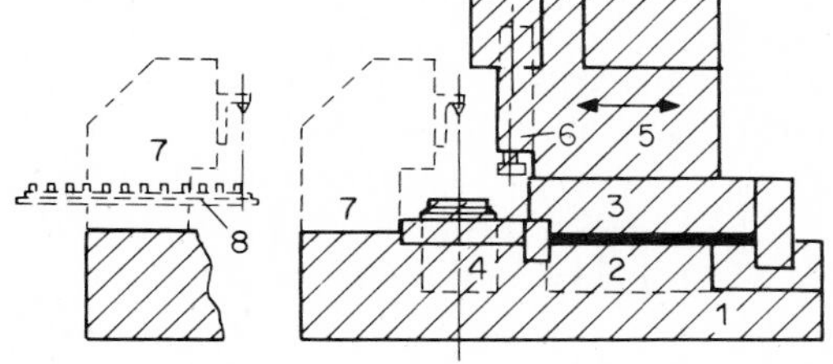

Units of the basic machine
1. Machine bed
2. Radial feed gear train
3. Rotary feed gear train
4. Stationary work table unit
5. Moving machine head
6. Cutter head

Units mounted on machine
7. Work steady-rest
8. Auto-loading system

FIG. 5.10 High-production, numerically controlled (NC) gear-shaping machine. (*Courtesy of Lorenz, a subsidiary of Maag Gear Wheel Co., Ettlingen, German Federal Republic.*)

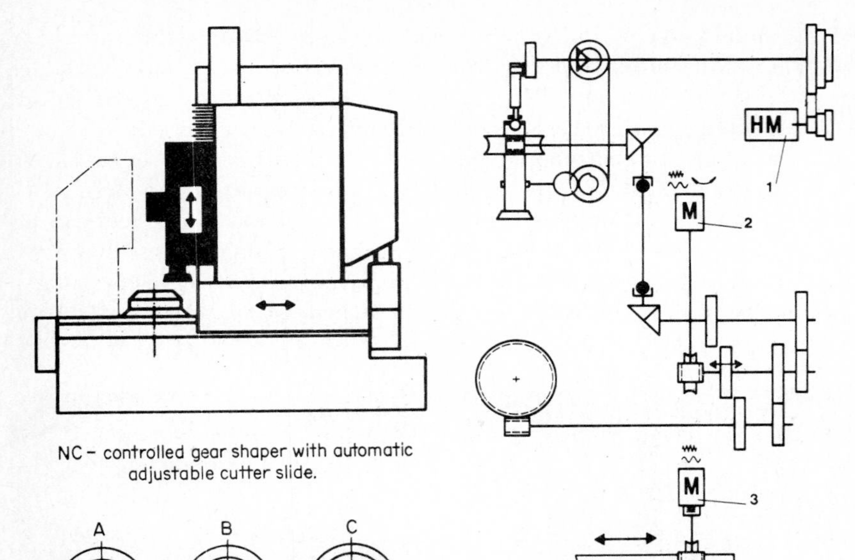

FIG. 5.11 Schematic design of a numerically controlled (NC) gear-shaping machine. (*Courtesy of Lorenz, a subsidiary of Maag Gear Wheel Co., Ettlingen, German Federal Republic.*)

cutting segments, since only the toothed portion must be rolled past the tool. The rack shaper can also machine two- and three-lobe rotors, as a result of the large tool size and large number of strokes per tooth.

Rack shapers are commercially available in sizes that will handle gears all the way from a centimeter (0.4 in.) in diameter up to about 14 meters (45 ft) in diameter. Face widths up to 1.55 meters (61 in.) maximum may be cut. See Fig. 5.13.

Rack shapers are generally built to mount the work in a fixture instead of between centers. Gears with long shaft extensions are usually supported by a steady rest.

The time in minutes required to cut a gear on a rack shaper may be calculated by the following formula:

$$\text{Shaping time} = \text{no. of gear teeth} \times \left(\frac{\text{index time}}{\text{teeth per index}} + \frac{\text{strokes per tooth}}{\text{strokes per min}}\right) \times \text{no. of cuts} \quad (5.5)$$

The indexing time varies from about 0.08 minute on small machines to around 1.0 minute on large machines. When finishing high-precision gears, the machines are indexed once per tooth so that the same tool finishes all the gear teeth, thus preventing tool pitch errors or mounting errors from being transferred to the gear. In roughing, more teeth may be cut per index, depending on the gear diameter and tooth size.

The number of strokes per tooth depends upon the number of teeth in the

TABLE 5.8 Some Production Estimates of Shaping Time Using High-Production Equipment and Techniques

Part	No. teeth	Pitch diameter		Face width		Brinell hardness	Cycle time
		mm	in.	mm	in.		
Auto starter, spur pinion, AISI 4004	10	25.40	1.00	15.9	0.625	165	27.5 seconds
Auto transmission, spur gear, SAE 8620	21	67.3	2.65	17.1	0.673	160	1.6 min
Tractor transmission, helical gear, AISI 1045	27	119.6	4.71	44.5	1.75	140	4.7 min
Truck, spur gear, SAE 5130	55	232.9	9.17	19.1	0.750	225	9.3 min
Truck, spur gear, malleable iron	47	223.8	8.81	15.9	0.625	255	1.67 min
Tractor, spur gear, AISI 4140	55	678.2	26.7	127	5.0	270	110 min
Mach., spur gear, AISI 1552	252	1066.8	42	49.8	1.96	300	72 min
Mach., internal gear, ductile iron	94	477.5	18.8	79.5	3.13	217	37.2 min
Mach., helical spline, 416 stainless	32	58.7	2.31	96.8	3.81	155	12 min

FIG. 5.12 Rack shaping a helical gear. (*Courtesy of Maag Gear Wheel Co., Zurich, Switzerland.*)

gear, the module (pitch), and the gear material. The fewer the strokes, the larger the generating marks on the given tooth. Gears of 100 to 200 teeth have almost straight-line profiles, while smaller numbers of teeth have more profile curvature. For this reason, it is necessary to use more strokes per tooth when finishing gears with small numbers of teeth. In fine pitches, the roughing cuts do not remove too much metal. This makes it possible to use fewer strokes per tooth in roughing than in finishing. In coarse pitches, however, a lot of metal has to be removed in roughing. This makes it necessary to use more strokes per tooth in roughing than in finishing. But with heavy-duty machines, coarse pitch "gashing" is usually done with step-type plunge cutters (Fig. 5.14), which can remove a large volume of material with fewer strokes per tooth. Table 5.9 shows the average practice in strokes per tooth. More strokes may be needed in finishing if highest accuracy is desired, while fewer strokes may suffice in commercial work.

The cutting speed, or number of strokes per minute, is determined by both the size of the machine and the face width. In cutting a very narrow

FIG. 5.13 One of the largest gear-cutting machines in the world. A helical gear 11.9 meters (469.9 in.) in diameter has just been rack-shaped. (*Courtesy of Fuller Company, Allentown, PA, U.S.A.*)

face width, the cutting speed in meters per minute (feet per minute) may be limited by the strokes-per-minute capability. In general, small machines are built to reciprocate much faster than large machines. Rack-type tools are limited to about the same cutting speed in meters per minute as other tools (see Table 5.13), but heavier cuts are possible than with hobs or disc-type shaping tools.

Table 5.10 shows some typical values for number of cuts and strokes per minute for different kinds of work.

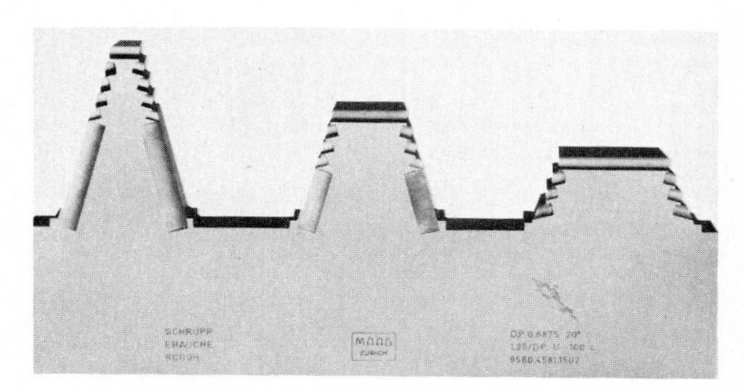

FIG. 5.14 Special rack cutters for the fast, rough cutting of large gears. (*Courtesy of Maag Gear Wheel Co., Zurich, Switzerland.*)

TABLE 5.9 Average Strokes per Tooth for Rack Shaping

No. of teeth	Strokes per tooth											
	Roughing						Finishing					
	2.5 m_t (10 P_t)		4 m_t (6 P_t)		12 m_t (2 P_t)		2.5 m_t (10 P_t)		4 m_t (6 P_t)		12 m_t (2 P_t)	
	Std.	HD	Std.	HD	Std.	HD	Std.	HD	Std.	HD	Std.	HD
15	60	—	103	—	325	175	15	—	22	—	40	39
20	55	—	80	—	295	160	14	—	16	—	30	32
30	50	—	85	50	260	140	11	—	13	12	22	23
50	42	—	75	44	230	130	7.5	—	9	9	16	17
80	38	—	65	38	200	110	7	—	7	7	13	13

Note: Std. = standard machines, HD = heavy-duty machines, m_t = transverse module, P_t = transverse diametral pitch

TABLE 5.10 Number of Cuts and Strokes per Minute for Typical Rack Shaping

Tooth size		Pitch diameter		Number of cuts		
					Finishing	
Module	Diametral pitch	mm	in.	Roughing	Commercial	Precision
1.6	16	100	4	1	1	1
2.5	10	100	4	1	1	1
2.5	10	200	8	1	1	1
4	6	200	8	2	1	2
4	6	1000	40	2	1	2
12	2	1000	40	3	1	2
12	2	2500	100	3	1	2

	Strokes per minute			
	200	80	55	32
Face width, mm (in.)	25 (1)	100 (4)	200 (8)	400 (16)
Cutting speed, m/min (fpm)	13 (42)	27 (90)	27 (90)	27 (90)

5.4 Cutting Bevel Gears

Straight bevel teeth are produced by a generating machine which reciprocates a cutting tool in a motion somewhat like that of a shaper. The tools used do not resemble a pinion or a segment of a rack. The peculiar geometry of the bevel gear makes the use of a special tool to cut each side of the bevel tooth desirable. These tools each have a single inclined cutting edge which generates the bevel gear tooth on one side or the other. The machines achieve a generating motion by rolling the work and the cutter head at a slow rate, while the cutters reciprocate rapidly back and forth. See Fig. 5.15.

The latest models of straight-bevel-gear generators have a design feature which permits the tooth to be cut with a slight amount of crown. A cam can be set so that the cutting tool will remove a little extra metal at each end of the tooth. This makes it possible to secure a localized tooth bearing in the center of the face width.

Bevel gears are overhung from the spindle of the generating machine during cutting. Those designing bevel gears should be careful to make the blank design suitable for mounting in the bevel-gear generator. Frequently it

FIG. 5.15 This view shows the generation of a Coniflex straight bevel gear. Note the two reciprocating tools which travel in a curved path to produce a slight crowning on the teeth. (*Courtesy of Gleason Works, Rochester, NY, U.S.A.*)

is necessary to design the bevel gear as a ring which is bolted onto its shaft after cutting. This gets the shaft out of the way during cutting.

Bevel gears coarser than 1 module (25 pitch) are usually given a roughing and a finishing cut. Where production is high and parts are not over 350 mm (14 in.) in diameter, it is possible to use special high-speed roughing machines which do not have a generating motion. These machines rough faster than the generators, and they save the generators from the wear and tear of roughing. Teeth of 0.8 module (32 pitch) or finer are often cut in one cut. Special Duplete tools are used. These tools have two cutting edges in tandem—one edge roughs and one finishes.

The complications of bevel-gear cutting make it hard to write any general formulas for estimating cutting time. In view of this situation, the best way to give some general information on cutting time is to give a table with cutting time shown for a range of sizes of bevel gears.

Table 5.11 shows the average cutting time for steel gears of about 250 Brinell hardness.

Spiral and Zerol bevel gears are cut with a generating machine that uses a series of cutting blades mounted on a circular toolholder. The toolholder is rotated to cause a cutting action while the work slowly rotates with the toolholder. The rotation of the work with respect to the toolholder causes a generating action to occur. After one tooth space is finished, the machine

TABLE 5.11 Average Time to Cut Straight Bevel Gears

No. of teeth	Pitch-cone angle, degrees	Tooth size		Face width		Time, min	
		Module	Pitch	mm	in.	Roughing	Finishing
12	$8\frac{1}{2}$	1.1	24	9.5	$\frac{3}{8}$	1.1	1.1
20	22	1.1	24	6.4	$\frac{1}{4}$	1.7	1.4
30	45	1.1	24	3.2	$\frac{1}{8}$	2.6	2.1
50	68	1.1	24	6.4	$\frac{1}{4}$	4.3	3.5
80	$81\frac{1}{2}$	1.1	24	9.5	$\frac{3}{8}$	3.4 DI*	6.8
12	$8\frac{1}{2}$	2.5	10	25	1	3.1	3.1
20	22	2.5	10	19	$\frac{3}{4}$	4.5	4.5
30	45	2.5	10	9.5	$\frac{3}{8}$	5.9	6.8
50	68	2.5	10	19	$\frac{3}{4}$	11.3	11.3
80	$81\frac{1}{2}$	2.5	10	25	1	10.3 DI*	20.7
12	$8\frac{1}{2}$	6.4	4	64	$2\frac{1}{2}$	14.4	10.0
20	22	6.4	4	51	2	20.0	14.0
30	45	6.4	4	38	$1\frac{1}{2}$	21.0	16.1
50	68	6.4	4	51	2	50.0	35.0
80	$81\frac{1}{2}$	6.4	4	64	$2\frac{1}{2}$	96.0	66.6

*DI = double index.

FIG. 5.16 Spiral gears up to approximately 1.25 m (50 in.) in diameter are generated on machines employing circular face-mill cutters. (*Courtesy of Gleason Works, Rochester, NY, U.S.A.*)

goes through an indexing motion to bring the cutter into the next tooth slot. See Fig. 5.16.

The line of machines using face-mill cutters will handle gears from 5 mm (3/16 in.) to $2\frac{1}{2}$ meters (100 in.) diameter and teeth from 0.5 module (48 pitch) to 17 module ($1\frac{1}{2}$ pitch). Large spiral gears up to about $2\frac{1}{2}$ meters (100 in.) in diameter can also be cut on a planing type of generator which uses a single tool.

The average time required to cut spiral or Zerol bevel gears may be estimated from Table 5.12. If face widths are less than those shown in the table, there may be some reduction in cutting time, but it will not be in proportion to the reduction in face width. If very high accuracy is required, the time may be longer. No allowance is made for setup time which may be required to adjust the machine to produce the desired tooth contour. The time shown in Table 5.12 is the time required per piece after the machine has produced a few satisfactory pieces. Loading and unloading time are not included.

Several innovations have been made in bevel-gear cutting. Figure 5.17 shows a hypoid gear being cut with a straddle type of cutting tool. Note that the face mill has *two* rows of cutting teeth. This new method cuts gears faster, and it is believed that straddle-cut (or ground) gears have somewhat longer life.

TABLE 5.12 Average Time to Cut Spiral Bevel Gears

No. of teeth	Pitch-cone angle, degrees	Tooth size		Face width		Time, min	
		Module	Pitch	mm	in.	Low production	High production
12	$8\frac{1}{2}$	1.1	24	9.5	$\frac{3}{8}$	2.4	1.2
20	22	1.1	24	6.4	$\frac{1}{4}$	4.0	2.0
30	45	1.1	24	3.2	$\frac{1}{8}$	5.0	2.5
50	68	1.1	24	6.4	$\frac{1}{4}$	10.0	5.0
80	$81\frac{1}{2}$	1.1	24	9.5	$\frac{3}{8}$	16.0	8.0
12	$8\frac{1}{2}$	4.2	6	41	$1\frac{5}{8}$	14.6	4.9
20	22	4.2	6	38	$1\frac{1}{2}$	23.7	7.9
30	45	4.2	6	32	$1\frac{1}{4}$	27.6	9.2
50	68	4.2	6	38	$1\frac{1}{2}$	34.2	11.4
80	$81\frac{1}{2}$	4.2	6	41	$1\frac{5}{8}$	44.8	14.9
12	$8\frac{1}{2}$	8.5	3	83	$3\frac{1}{4}$	34.2	11.4
20	22	8.5	3	83	$3\frac{1}{4}$	57.0	19.0
30	45	8.5	3	83	$3\frac{1}{4}$	78.0	26.0
50	68	8.5	3	83	$3\frac{1}{4}$	130.0	43.3
80	$81\frac{1}{2}$	8.5	3	83	$3\frac{1}{4}$	150.7	50.2

Notes: 1. The 24-pitch gears are assumed to be cut on a Gleason No. 423 Hypoid Generator, the 6-pitch are cut on a No. 641 G-PLETE Generator, and the 3-pitch are cut on a No. 645 G-PLETE Generator.

2. For high production, the completing process is used to finish gear teeth in a single chucking from the solid blank. For lower production requirements, the 5-cut process can be used: rough and finish the gear member, rough the pinion member, then finish each side of the pinion teeth in a separate cutting operation.

Figure 5.18 shows a very large new machine capable of cutting spiral bevel or hypoid gears up to 2.5 meters (100 in.) diameter. This machine will make large gears with large teeth for heavy industrial, marine, and off-the-road vehicle applications.

5.5 Gear Milling

Worms, spur gears, and helical gears may be produced by the milling process. Bevel-gear teeth are sometimes produced by this method, but the geometric limitations of trying to produce accurate bevel teeth by this process greatly restrict its use except for roughing cuts.

Conventional milling machines equipped with a dividing head may be used to mill gear teeth. A slot at a time is milled, and the machine is hand-indexed to the next slot. Several makes of special gear-milling machines, known in the trade as "gear-cutting machines," are on the market.

FIG. 5.17 Straddle-cutting a hypoid gear. (*Courtesy of Gleason Works, Rochester, NY, U.S.A.*)

FIG. 5.18 Large, heavy-duty machine for cutting spiral bevel and hypoid gears. (*Courtesy of Gleason Works, Rochester, NY, U.S.A.*)

These are designed for the sole purpose of cutting gear teeth or clutches and the like with milling cutters. They are usually equipped with automatic indexing equipment.

The machines used to mill worms are a different type from those used to cut gear teeth. The worm-milling machine is essentially a thread-milling machine.

Gear-cutting machines cover the whole range of gear sizes up to more than 5 meters (200 in.) in diameter. Pitches that are coarser than 34 module (3/4 pitch) are often cut with an end mill. Helical rolling-mill pinions in the circular-pitch range of 100 to 200 mm (4 to 8 in.) are often produced by end milling. Figure 5.19 shows a gear being milled. Figure 5.20 shows an end mill used to mill some large gear teeth.

Gear-cutting machines and milling cutters are not so expensive as hobbing machines and hobs or gear shapers and shaper cutters. On the other hand, gear-cutting machines do not produce accuracy comparable with that produced by hobbing and shaping. Some high-precision gears are produced by rough milling followed by hardening and finish grinding.

Parts to be milled must allow room for runout of the cutter at each end of the tooth. Some gear-cutting machines mount the work on centers, while others clamp the work on a fixture. Wide face widths can be milled, and it is usually possible to have fairly long shaft extensions on the gear.

Gear teeth may be milled in one cut, or they may be given a rough cut

FIG. 5.19 Milling a large gear.

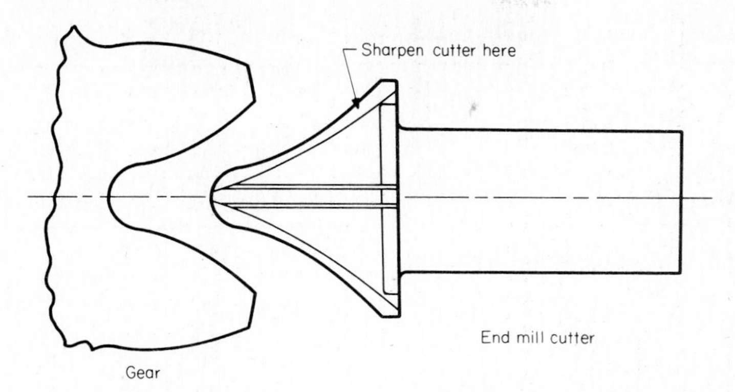

FIG. 5.20 Coarse-pitch spur or helical gears can be cut on a hobbing machine with an end-mill type of cutter.

almost to size and then finish-milled. The time required to make a milling cut can be calculated from the following formula:

Milling time, min

$$= \text{no. of gear teeth} \times \left[\text{index time} + \left(\frac{\text{face} + \text{overtravel}}{\text{feed per min}}\right)\right] \quad (5.6)$$

The index time on automatic machines runs from 0.04 to 0.08 minute per tooth. Hand indexing takes much longer.

The minimum overtravel for milling a spur gear is

$$\text{Overtravel} = 2 \times [\text{depth of cut} \times (\text{cutter dia.} - \text{depth cut})]^{0.5} \quad (5.7)$$

The feed per minute ranges from about 12 to 500 mm/min (1/2 to 20 in./min). The feed rate may be calculated from

$$\text{Feed per min} = \frac{\text{rpm of cutter} \times \text{no. of cutter teeth}}{\text{feed per tooth}} \quad (5.8)$$

The rpm of milling cutters is based on cutting speeds that high-speed steel tools have been able to stand when cutting different materials. Table 5.13 gives some representative values of cutting speeds for different materials and different degrees of care in cutting. The *conservative* values represent the condition where long cutter life is desired, and best accuracy and finish are also sought. The *high-speed* values represent the condition where a rugged machine and cutter are being worked to the limit.

In a few cases, cemented-carbide cutters have been used to make gears instead of high-speed steel cutters. Much higher cutting speeds can be used with carbides, provided that the machine is rugged enough and powerful enough to drive the carbide cutter.

TABLE 5.13 Cutting Speeds for Different Materials

Material	Hardness, HB	Cutting speed					
		Conservative		Normal		High-speed	
		m/min	fpm	m/min	fpm	m/min	fpm
Steel	350	7.6	25	11	35	15	50
	300	11	35	14	45	21	70
	200	17	55	26	85	37	120
Cast iron	250	14	45	18	60	27	90
	175	23	75	30	100	46	150
Bronze	90 (500 kg)	46	150	85	280	122	400
Laminated plastic	—	107	350	168	550	213	700

After the cutting speed is determined, the rpm of the cutter is

$$\text{Rpm of cutter} = \frac{1000 \times \text{cutting speed, m/min}}{0.262 \times \text{outside dia. of cutter, mm}} \qquad \text{metric} \quad (5.9a)$$

$$= \frac{12 \times \text{cutting speed, fpm}}{0.262 \times \text{outside dia. of cutter, in.}} \qquad \text{English} \quad (5.9b)$$

The feed per tooth depends on the finish desired and on how well the material cuts. Some typical values are:

Feed per tooth				Description
Steel material		Cast iron, bronze, or plastic		
mm	in.	mm	in.	
0.05	0.002	0.10	0.004	Conservative
0.08	0.003	0.15	0.006	Normal
0.13	0.005	0.25	0.010	Fast-cutting

There have been important developments in milling just as in hobbing and shaping. Special cutters can be used for very rapid stock removal. With a very rugged machine, precision indexing, and precision cutters, very good accuracy can be achieved.

The milling process is particularly suitable for making racks, especially *large* racks. Figure 5.21 shows the milling of a large rack. Note the special roughing cutter that leads the precision finishing cutter.

FIG. 5.21 Milling large rack segments for a radar antenna application. (*Courtesy of Sewall Gear Mfg. Co., St. Paul, MN, U.S.A.*)

5.6 Broaching Gears

Small internal gears can be cut in one pass of a broach provided that the gear designer does not put the teeth in a "blind" hole. Large internal gears can be made by using a surface type of broach to make several teeth at a pass. Indexing of the gear and repeated passes of the broach can make a complete gear. Gears as large as 1.5 meters (60 in.) in diameter are made by this process.

Racks and gear segments are often made by broaching. The teeth formed by broaching may be either spur or helical.

Present broaching machines and broach-making facilities impose quite definite limits on the size gear that can be made by a one-pass broach. The parts most commonly made range from about 6 to 75 mm (1/4 to 3 in.) in diameter. Parts up to 200 mm (8 in.) in diameter have been made in production by broaching with a one-pass broach. However, when broaches get to this size, they become very costly. It is very difficult to forge, heat-treat, and grind a piece of high-speed steel that is 200 mm (8 in.) in diameter and several feet long and get a hardness of over 62 Rockwell C and an accuracy within 0.005 mm (0.0002 in.). Figure 5.22 shows an example of a small broaching machine.

Broaching is a rapid operation. If the teeth are not too deep or the face

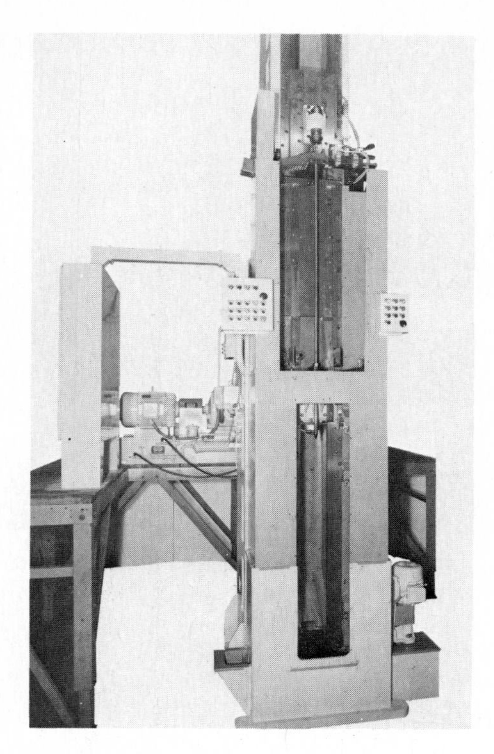

FIG. 5.22 Broaching machine. (*Courtesy of National Broach and Machine, a division of Lear Siegler, Detroit, MI, U.S.A.*)

width too wide, the gear can be cut completely in one pass. The time in minutes for a one-pass broaching cut is

Broaching time

$$= \frac{\text{length stroke}}{12 \times \text{cutting speed}} + \frac{\text{length stroke}}{12 \times \text{return speed}} + \text{handling time} \qquad (5.10)$$

The rate at which a broach can cut will depend on the material being cut and the quality desired. Table 5.14 shows some typical broaching speeds.

On the return stroke, the broach is often moved as fast as the machine will operate. This may be on the order of 9 to 11 m/min (30 to 35 fpm). The handling time for loading and unloading the machine will run about 0.07 to 0.12 minute on a production setup.

The length of the broach stroke will be longer than the cutting portion of the broach, but usually not so long as the overall length. The cutting length

TABLE 5.14 Typical Speed of Broach on the Cutting Stroke

Material	Hardness, HB	Broaching speed					
		Conservative		Normal		High-speed	
		m/min	fpm	m/min	fpm	m/min	fpm
Steel	350	1.2	4	3.0	10	4.9	16
	300	2.4	8	4.9	16	6.1	20
	200	4.9	16	6.7	22	9.1	30
Cast iron	250	4.3	14	6.1	20	7.3	24
	175	5.5	18	7.3	24	9.1	30
Bronze	90	5.5	18	7.3	24	9.1	30

of the broach will depend on tooth depth, face width, and how easily the gear cuts. Table 5.15 shows some typical broach lengths.

A very important development in broaching for the 1970s was the *pot-broaching* technique. Conventional broaching pushes a long broach through the part. Pot broaching moves the part through the broach.

Figure 5.23 shows a tool for *push-up* pot broaching. The parts are pushed through this tool. The tool is made up of a number of small parts with cutting teeth, instead of a very large part with cutting teeth.

Figure 5.24 shows a diagram of a machine for *pull-up* pot broaching. When parts require a long cut, it is mechanically better to pull the parts through the pot broach. This avoids possible buckling of a long pushrod.

The pot-broaching method tends to make the production time much

TABLE 5.15 Typical Broach Lengths

Gear whole depth, in.	Face width, in.	Broach length							
		Free-cutting material				Tough material			
		Cutting portion		Overall		Cutting portion		Overall	
		m	in.	m	in.	m	in.	m	in.
0.250	2	2.2	85	2.5	100				
0.200	1	0.9	35	1.3	50	1.9	75	2.3	90
0.100	1	0.5	20	0.9	35	0.8	30	1.1	45
0.050	1/2	0.15	6	0.25	10	0.25	10	0.5	20

FIG. 5.23 *Push-up* pot-type broach tool. Note parts finished at top and blanks starting at bottom. (*Courtesy of National Broach and Machine, a division of Lear Siegler, Detroit, MI, U.S.A.*)

shorter, and the tool itself is much easier to make. Pot broaching is a high-production method that has come into very substantial use on high-volume jobs. Figure 5.25 shows a good example of pot-broach work.

5.7 Punching Gears

Punching is undoubtedly the fastest and cheapest method of making gear teeth. Unfortunately, punched gears do not have the same degree of accuracy as many of the cut gears, and punching is limited to narrow face widths.

The design of blanks for gears to be punched must suit the process. The

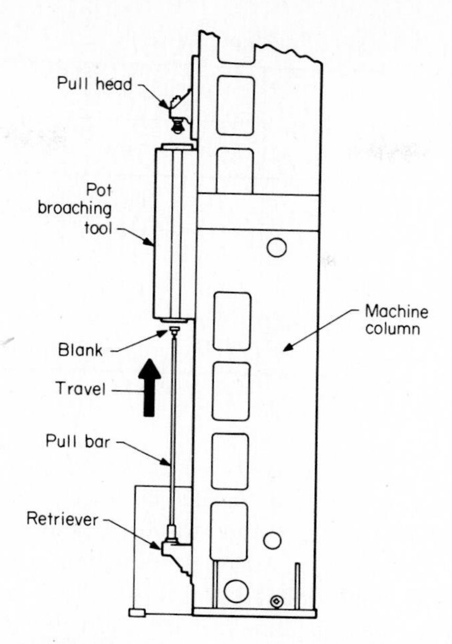

FIG. 5.24 Sketch of broaching machine for *pull-up* pot broaching.

FIG. 5.25 Some small automotive pinions pot-broached at a rate of 195 parts per hour. Right-hand pinion is 2.5 module (10 pitch), and left-hand pinion is 3.17 module (8 pitch).

TABLE 5.16 Typical Punching Rates

Material	Hardness, HB	Thickness, mm	Thickness, in.	Strokes per min
Brass	60	0.5	0.020	300
		2.0	0.080	250
Aluminum	—	0.5	0.020	300
		2.0	0.080	250
Steel	150	0.5	0.020	150
		2.0	0.080	100

punching machines can handle only thin sheet stock. The as-punched gear is a disc-like wafer. It may have a hole in the center. Usually the punched gear needs a shaft. The shaft can be attached to the punching by pressing a piece of rod through the hole in the punching. Punched gears are often mated with pinions that have much wider face widths than the gear. This makes positioning the punched gear precisely at the right distance from the end of the shaft unnecessary. In some cases, though, punched gears must be accurately positioned.

Both external and internal spur gears may be made by punching. Equipment currently in use will handle gears from 6 to 25 mm (1/4 to 1 in.) in diameter. Face widths vary from 0.4 to 1.25 mm (0.015 to 0.050 in.). The face width of the punching should not be greater than two-thirds of the whole depth of the tooth. Only fairly soft materials can be punched. Brass is a popular material for punching. Sheet bronze, aluminum, and steel are also used.

One stroke of a punch can make a punched gear. The punching rate depends on the thickness and hardness of the material as well as on the die life and gear quality desired. Table 5.16 gives some typical punching rates.

5.8 G-TRAC Generating

One of the surprising new developments in gear cutting is the G-TRAC generator, made by the Gleason Works. This machine uses rack-type cutting tools mounted on an endless chain. The gear being cut rolls in mesh with the passing rack teeth in the chain. Figure 5.26 shows the whole machine. Figure 5.27 shows a stack of parts being cut so as to have helical gear teeth.

The G-TRAC machine is intended for high production, low tool cost, and

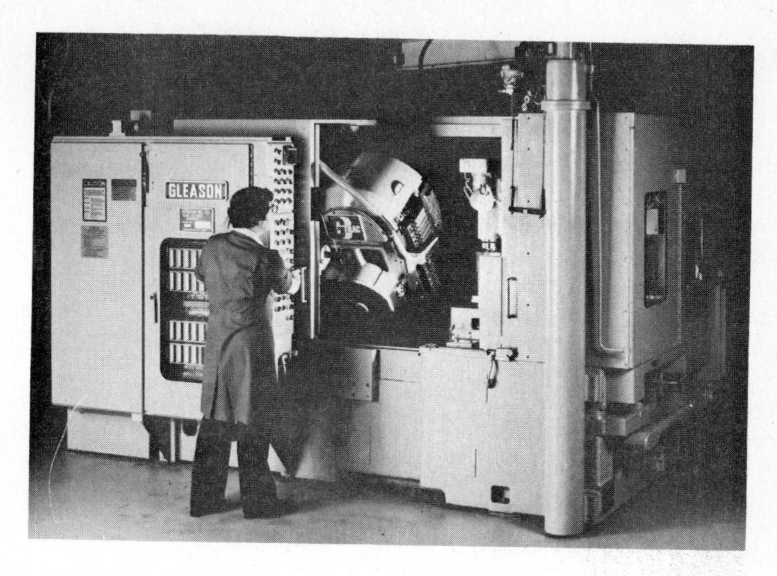

FIG. 5.26 G-TRAC generator. (*Courtesy of Gleason Works, Rochester, NY, U.S.A.*)

FIG. 5.27 Generating helical-gear teeth on a stack of gear blanks by the G-TRAC machine. (*Courtesy of Gleason Works, Rochester, NY, U.S.A.*)

high accuracy. It is possible, though, to use the machine effectively for small production. In this case, a single row of cutting tools is used, and one tooth slot is formed at a time.

The simple rack tools can be made by gear shops that are using the G-TRAC. This feature should make it easy to change tooth module (pitch), tooth pressure angle, or tooth depth when a gear unit is under development. (Normally, gear-cutting tools have to be ordered from a tool-making company, and some months time is lost when new, nonstandard gear tools are needed.)

The concepts of the G-TRAC machine open up several new possibilities in gear machine tools. No doubt more innovative machines for cutting gear teeth will be developed in the 1980s.

GEAR GRINDING

In general, gear grinding is an operation that is performed after a gear has been cut and heat-treated to a high hardness and has had journals or other mounting surfaces finish-ground. Grinding is needed because it is very difficult to cut parts over 350 HB (38 HRC). Since fully hardened steels are needed in many applications and it is often difficult to keep the heat-treat distortion of a cut gear within acceptable limits, there is a large field of gear work in which the grinding process is needed.

In a few cases, medium-hard gears that could be finished by cutting are ground. This may be done to save the cost of expensive cutting tools like hobs, shapers, or shaving cutters; or it may be done to get a desired surface finish or accuracy on a gear that is difficult to manufacture.

In some of the fine pitches, gear teeth may be finish-ground from the solid. For instance, the whole volume of stock removed in making an 0.8-module (32-pitch) tooth is less than the amount of stock removed in finish-grinding a good 4-module (6-pitch) tooth, even when the 0.8-module and 4-module teeth have equal face widths.

Figure 5.1 shows that most of the methods of cutting a gear tooth have a counterpart in a grinding method. Disc cutters are used to mill gear teeth, and disc grinding wheels grind gear teeth. Threaded hobs cut gear teeth, and threaded grinding wheels grind gear teeth. Rack shaping is matched by generating grinders that make a disc wheel go through the motion of a tooth on a rack. There is, however, no cutting counterpart to the dished wheel, base circle generating grinding method.

In the following sections, information is given on how to estimate grinding time. This is a controversial subject which is hard to handle. Things like the hardness of the grinding wheel, the accuracy required of the gear, and the toughness and hardness of the stock being ground all enter into the time required to grind a gear. In general, medium-hard gears which are made by through-hardening steel can be ground faster than carburized gears at full hardness. Also, the less stock left for grinding, the faster the gear can be ground. The grinding times and number of passes required shown in the various tables should be considered as only nominal values, subject to considerable revision either upward or downward in individual cases.

5.9 Form Grinding

Form grinders use a disc wheel to grind both sides of the space between two gear teeth. Their grinding action is very similar to the action of a machine for milling gear teeth. Form-grinding wheels have an involute form dressed into the side of the wheel, while a generating grinding wheel is straight-sided. Figure 5.28 shows a comparison of the two kinds of wheels for the same pinion.

The machines available to form-grind gears can handle external spur gears from about 1 cm (0.4 in.) to about 2 meters (80 in.) in diameter. Internal gears from about 1 meter (40 in.) major diameter to about 50 mm (2 in.) minor diameter can be ground. Some form grinders will grind both spur and helical gears, external or internal gear teeth. Figure 5.29 shows a general-purpose form grinder.

Form-grinding machines usually mount the work on centers. The gear design must provide room for the wheel to run out at each end of the work. Pinions which require an undercut to allow them to mesh with a mating gear without interference cannot be ground with a single grinding wheel.

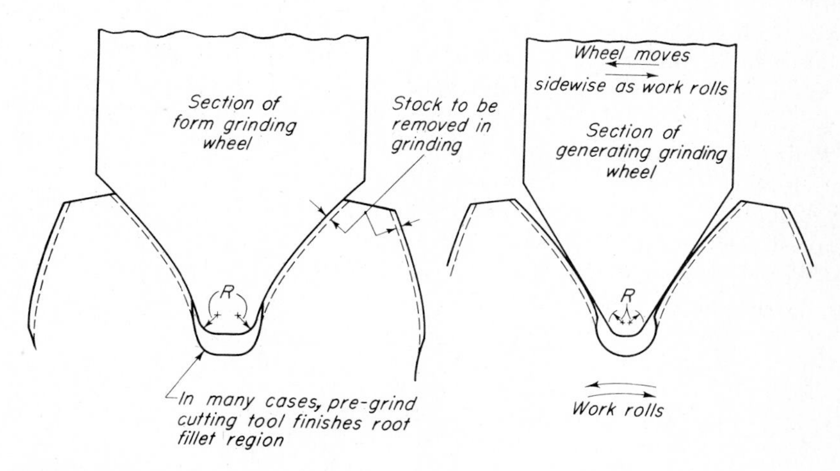

FIG. 5.28 Comparison of form grinding and generating grinding.

FIG. 5.29 An automated general-purpose form-grinding machine capable of doing external or internal gears up to 600 mm (24 in.) pitch diameter and up to 45° helix angle. (*Courtesy of National Broach and Machine, a division of Lear Siegler, Detroit, MI, U.S.A.*)

However, pinions with undercut may be ground with two grinding wheels straddling one or more teeth.

The time required to grind a gear has three parts. These are: (1) time to rough-grind, (2) time to finish-grind, and (3) time to dress the grinding wheel. In addition, there are some handling times, such as time to load the work, time to centralize the grinding stock, time to unload the work, and time to check the work for size.

When ceramic grinding wheels are used, all but the smallest gears will require more than one wheel dressing per gear. The number of dressings required depends upon several factors, of which the principal ones are the number of gear teeth, the grinding-wheel diameter, and the face width. The hardness of the gear and the accuracy required also enter into the picture.

Table 5.17 shows some typical data on number of wheel dressings required and time per dressing. It is assumed that the material is about 60 HRC and that moderate accuracy is required. Face width is assumed to be in these proportions:

Tooth size		Face width	
Module	Pitch	mm	in.
2.5	10	40	1.5
4	6	50	2.0
8	3	100	4.0

TABLE 5.17 Typical Data for Dressing Form-Grinding Wheels

Size of work			Wheel diameter		No. of dressings per gear	Min per dressing
No. of teeth	Module	Pitch	mm	in.		
75	2.5	10	150	6	5	$\frac{3}{4}$
20	2.5	10	150	6	2	$\frac{3}{4}$
75	4	6	300	12	6	1
20	4	6	300	12	2	1
75	8	3	300	12	8	$1\frac{3}{4}$
20	8	3	300	12	3	$1\frac{3}{4}$

The time required for either rough grinding or finish grinding by the form-grinding method may be estimated by Eq. (5.11). In this equation, a cycle is the cutting action that occurs on a single tooth between successive feeds of the grinding wheel. The latest-model form grinders feed down at each end of the stroke while roughing. Thus a *cycle* is only a stroke across the tooth. The older-style machines feed down only once per revolution of the work. On each tooth, the grinding wheel makes a stroke across and back; in this case, a *cycle* includes both strokes.

$$\text{Grinding time, min} = \frac{\text{no. of gear teeth} \times \text{no. of cuts}}{\text{cycles per min}} \tag{5.11}$$

The number of cuts will depend upon the amount of stock left for grinding and the amount removed per cut.

Enough stock must be removed to eliminate both the inaccuracy of the rough-cut gear teeth and the inaccuracy caused by heat-treat distortion. Large gears with thin webs tend to distort more than small gears of solid construction. Quenching dies can be used to limit heat-treat distortion considerably. With care and skill in heat treating, it is possible to hold heat-treat distortion to reasonably low limits.

Table 5.18 shows the general range between low amounts of heat-treat distortion and high amounts. The stock shown on tooth thickness is the *sum* of the amounts left on the two sides of the tooth. The relation between diameter over pins and tooth thickness is only approximate.

The worst condition that can occur before grinding is that the distortion is so bad that some tooth on the gear requires *all the stock to be ground off one side*. If the gear is worse than this, it will not clean up, and the gear might as well be scrapped instead of ground. Assuming that the gear distortion is within the stock allowed, the *maximum* number of cuts is

$$\text{No. of cuts} = \frac{\text{stock left for grinding}}{1/2 \text{ stock normally removed per cut}} \tag{5.12}$$

TABLE 5.18 Amounts of Stock Normally Needed for Grinding

Tooth size		Stock left for grinding							
		Low heat-treat distortion				High heat-treat distortion			
		Tooth thickness		Diameter over pins		Tooth thickness		Diameter over pins	
Module	Pitch	mm	in.	mm	in.	mm	in.	mm	in.
1.6	16	0.13	0.005	0.30	0.012	0.25	0.010	0.64	0.025
2.5	10	0.20	0.008	0.50	0.020	0.38	0.015	0.96	0.038
4	6	0.30	0.012	0.76	0.030	0.64	0.025	1.57	0.062
8	3	0.66	0.026	1.65	0.065	1.14	0.045	2.69	0.106
12	2	1.14	0.045	2.85	0.112	1.90	0.075	4.78	0.188

In Eq. (5.12), the *stock left for grinding* is in terms of tooth thickness. The *normal amount* of stock removed is the amount that would be removed from the tooth thickness if the grinding wheel were cutting on *both* sides. The *minimum* number of grinding cuts is just one-half of that given by Eq. (5.12). In an average case, the number of cuts might be expected to be somewhere about midway between the minimum and maximum number of cuts.

Roughing cuts usually take as much stock per cut as can be removed without burning the work. Finishing cuts take only a small amount of stock, and the last cut may just "spark out," taking almost no stock. Table 5.19 shows the normal amounts of stock removed in form grinding per cut.

The rate at which a form-grinding machine strokes depends upon the face width being ground, the amount of overtravel, the kind of material being cut, and the range of speeds available on the machine. Some of the latest

TABLE 5.19 Stock Removed per Form-Grinding Cut

Tooth size		Rough grinding								Finish grinding	
		Tooth flanks only				Tooth flanks and root					
		45 HRC		60 HRC		45 HRC		60 HRC			
Module	Pitch	mm	in.	mm	in.	mm	in.	mm	in.	mm	in.
2.4	10	0.05	0.002	0.04	0.0015	0.04	0.0015	0.025	0.001	0.012	0.0005
4	6	0.05	0.002	0.04	0.0015	0.04	0.0015	0.025	0.001	0.012	0.0005
8	3	0.06	0.0025	0.05	0.002	0.05	0.002	0.04	0.0015	0.012	0.0005
12	2	0.08	0.003	0.06	0.0025	0.06	0.0025	0.04	0.0015	0.020	0.0008

TABLE 5.20 Typical Cutting Rates for Form Grinders

Face width of gear		Multiple cycles per tooth machine		Single cycle per tooth machine	
mm	in.	Roughing, cycles per min	Finishing, cycles per min	Roughing, cycles per min	Finishing, cycles per min
20	3/4	125	18	26	19
50	2	100	16	23	16
100	4	75	14	18	13
150	6	60	12	15	10
200	8	50	10	13	9

machines on the market can stroke up to 0.35 m/s (70 fpm). They rough out a tooth completely before indexing. This makes it possible to use a much smaller amount of overtravel than would be required if the wheel had to move clear of the work on each stroke to permit indexing.

Table 5.20 shows some typical cutting rates for form grinders. The table is based on a 300-mm (12-in.) grinding wheel for the multiple-cycle machine and a 150-mm (6-in.) wheel for the single-cycle machine. The work is assumed to be 2.5 module (10 pitch). The coarser pitches take slightly longer to grind because of more overtravel. The table is based on 0.25 m/s (50 fpm) for roughing and 0.15 m/s (30 fpm) for finishing for the multiple-cycle machine. For the single-cycle type of machine, roughing speed is assumed to be 0.15 m/s (30 fpm) and finishing speed 0.10 m/s (20 fpm).

Borazon Form Grinding. Gear-tooth grinding has long been done with ceramic wheels such as aluminum oxide or silicon carbide. These wheels have high abrasive performance.

About 1980, new "super abrasives" began to be used to grind* gear teeth. Cubic boron nitride (CBN) is a good example. The popular name for CBN grinding is *Borazon* grinding. Borazon CBN is a trademark of General Electric, U.S.A.

The CBN grinding wheel is being made as a highly precise metal wheel with a single layer of CBN particles galvanically bonded onto the surface. A precisely calibrated grit is used. A 65-μm (0.0025-in.) grit is used for gear finishing, and 100- to 120-μm (0.005-in.) grit is used for gear roughing.

The CBN grinding wheel actually works somewhat like a milling cutter. Each exposed crystal of CBN tends to cut very tiny metal chips. The chips produced by CBN grinding look quite different from the particles produced by a vitrified, ceramic grinding wheel.

*Super abrasives had been used to sharpen hobs and cutters in the 1970s.

It is claimed that the CBN grinding wheel is about 3000 times more wear-resistant than a typical aluminum oxide, ceramic wheel.

Borazon gear-tooth grinding is done quite differently from conventional form grinding with ceramic wheels:

No wheel dressing. (After a considerable amount of gear grinding, the CBN wheel is stripped and replated with a new layer of CBN particles.)

Slow feed. (The wheel progresses slowly across the face width, removing all the stock in one pass.)

Cool grinding. (With plenty of coolant and a free cutting characteristic, the CBN wheel tends to remove stock in a very predictable and controllable manner. Gear-tooth random errors or variations in hardness do not seem to be serious obstacles to the very hard and strong CBN wheel. Local overheating is probably less likely to occur.)

Since the CBN wheel is not dressed, a *different* wheel is needed for each pitch, each number of teeth, and each style of profile modification (or pressure-angle variation). For this reason, the CBN process is less attractive for small-lot production than it is for volume production.

Figure 5.30 shows a form grinder used for Borazon grinding. Figure 5.31 shows a close-up of the grinding wheel and work. Some of the many kinds of parts that can be efficiently ground by the Borazon grinding method are shown in Fig. 5.32.

FIG. 5.30 Form-grinding machine developed for Borazon grinding. (*Courtesy of Kapp Co., Coburg, German Federal Republic.*)

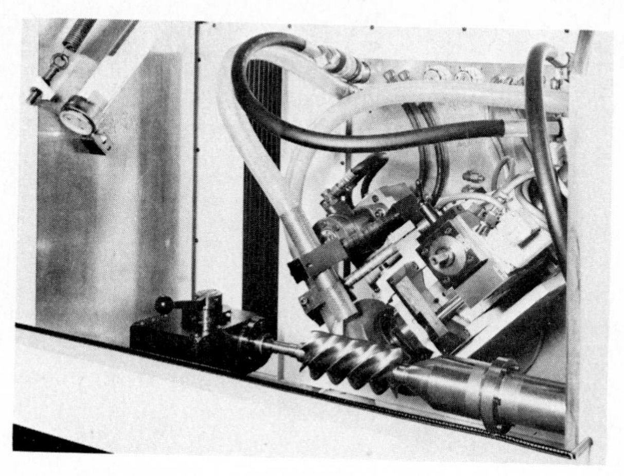

FIG. 5.31 Form grinding a helical-gear part. (*Courtesy of Kapp Co., Coburg, German Federal Republic.*)

FIG. 5.32 Examples of gear parts ground by Borazon form grinding. (*Courtesy of Kapp Co., Coburg, German Federal Republic.*)

5.10 Generating Grinding—Disc Wheel

There are two basic types of generating grinding with disc wheels. One type uses a single wheel which is dressed to the shape of a basic rack tooth. The workpiece is rolled past the grinding area while the wheel reciprocates past the face width. The other type uses two saucer-shaped wheels which are concave toward the tooth flank, so that only a narrow rim contacts the tooth while the workpiece is rolled past the grinding area. Since this latter type of grinder is now made only by the Maag Gear Wheel Company, it will be referred to here as the Maag process, while the dressed-single-wheel type will be referred to as the conical-wheel process.

Conical-wheel grinding machines can handle gears in the range of about 25 mm (1 in.) to 3.5 meters (140 in.) diameter, while the largest Maag machines can handle gears of up to 4.7 meters (184 in.) diameter.

Both types must have room for the grinding wheel to run out at each end of the cut. Smaller machines usually mount the work between centers. Large machines usually mount the work vertically with a fixture. Since the grinding pressure is small, supports are not usually needed.

The generating grinding machines can make both spur and helical external gears. Internal spur and helical gears can be made with one model, which can handle up to 0.85 meter ($33\frac{1}{2}$ in.) base-circle diameter.

The action of a conical-wheel grinding machine is similar to that of a rack shaper using a single point tool. The grinding wheel is dressed to the desired basic rack form and is reciprocated past the face width while the gear rolls past the grinding field on its pitch circle. Because the wheel must maintain a definite form, it must be of a relatively hard bond, and so it requires a coolant to minimize burning of the work. The Maag process is somewhat similar for their larger machines, except that two saucer-shaped wheels form the rack "tooth." The wheel contact area is limited to its outer edge, where wheel wear can be sensed and continuously compensated for by automatic wheel adjustment. Relatively soft bonded wheels are used, so that no coolant is needed.

On the smaller Maag machines, the process is somewhat different. The two grinding wheels are still saucer-shaped and contact the work only at their outer edges, so that wear compensation can be used for soft wheels without coolant. But with the smaller machines, up to 1 meter (40 in.) diameter, the grinding wheels do not form a rack "tooth," but are parallel, and always contact the workpiece involute at a point on a line tangent to the *base* circle. This is known as *zero-degree* grinding because the grinding wheels are set at a pressure angle of 0°. (See Fig. 5.33.) The gear is rolled on the base-circle tangent plane *Y-Y*. The grinding-wheel contact planes are shown as *X-X*, and the contact points are shown as *P*.

Longitudinal corrections are made on all disc-wheel generating grinders

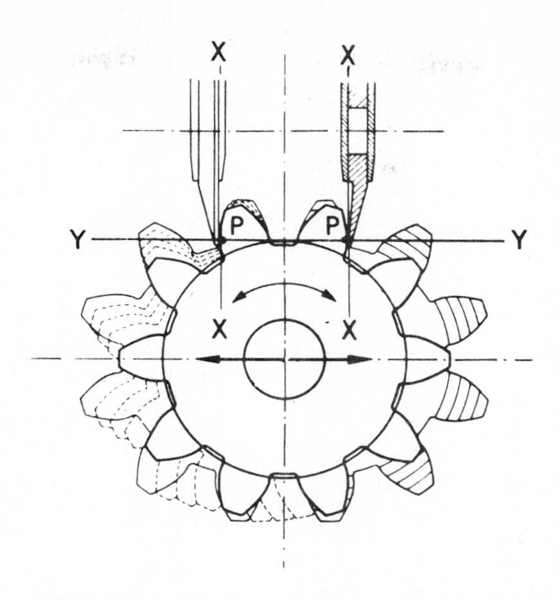

FIG. 5.33 Zero-degree pressure angle grinding with saucer wheels. (*Courtesy of Maag Gear Wheel Co., Zurich, Switzerland.*)

by moving the grinding wheel to cut deeper or shallower as it passes across the face. Profile modifications on conical-wheel machines are made by dressing the wheel. On Maag machines, where there is no wheel "form" to dress, profile modifications are made by moving the wheels to cut deeper or shallower along the profile. Modification by means of wheel movement also allows "topological" modification, in which both profile and helix may be continuously varied across the face width.

The time needed to make gears by generating grinding with disc wheels is made up of essentially the same elements as the time required to form-grind a gear. The time required to dress a grinding wheel (when necessary) may be estimated from Table 5.21. The time in minutes required to do either rough grinding or finishing grinding may be estimated using the following formula:

$$\text{Grinding time} = \text{no. of gear teeth} \times \text{no. of cuts} \times \left(\text{index time} + \frac{\text{strokes per tooth}}{\text{strokes per min}}\right) \qquad (5.13)$$

Equation (5.12) can be used to get the number of cuts for generating grinding as well as for form grinding. In solving this equation, though, Table 5.22 should be used to get the amount of stock that is normally removed per

TABLE 5.21 Typical Frequency and Length of Time Required to Dress Conical Grinding Wheels

Size of work		Wheel dia.		No. of dressings per gear		Min per dressing
mm	in.	mm	in.	45 HRC	60 HRC	
750	30	500	20	4	5	$2\frac{1}{2}$
450	18	300	12	3	4	1
300	12	300	12	3	3	1
150	6	300	12	2	3	$\frac{3}{4}$
50	2	300	12	2	2	$\frac{3}{4}$

cut. Because the amount of stock to be removed does not depend on the method of grinding, this item may be obtained from Table 5.18.

The time required for generating grinding machines to index varies from 0.04 to 0.3 min, depending on the make and size of machine. The strokes per tooth and the strokes per minute vary with machine designs and tooth numbers and face widths.

When the workpiece is lightweight, the machine elements used to generate can also be relatively light. In these cases the workpiece is rolled back and forth very rapidly in generation, while the stroking action is slow. The process lends itself to horizontal mounting of the work. Heavy workpieces need heavy generating elements that cannot be moved rapidly. These parts are mounted vertically and are slowly generated, while the wheel stroking motion is rapid. The result is that vertical machines use many fast passes along the face for each tooth, while horizontal machines use many fast generating motions, but only one pass along the face for each tooth for each cut. Table 5.23*a* shows some typical values for vertical machines, and Table 5.23*b* shows some typical values for horizontal machines.

Figure 5.34 shcws a generating grinding machine of the type that uses a

TABLE 5.22 Typical Amount of Stock Removed per Cut When Generating Grinding

Tooth size		Rough grinding								Finish grinding	
		Tooth flanks only				Flanks and root					
		45 HRC		60 HRC		45 HRC		60 HRC			
Module	Pitch	mm	in.	mm	in.	mm	in.	mm	in.	mm	in.
2.5	10	0.13	0.005	0.08	0.003	0.08	0.003	0.04	0.0015	0.013	0.0005
4	6	0.15	0.006	0.08	0.003	0.08	0.003	0.04	0.0015	0.013	0.0005
12	2	0.23	0.009	0.10	0.004	0.10	0.004	0.06	0.0025	0.020	0.0008

TABLE 5.23a Typical Stroking Rates for Vertical Grinders

Tooth size		Strokes per tooth				Strokes per min		
		Rough grinding		Finish grinding		Face width		
Module	Pitch	15 tooth	75 tooth	15 tooth	75 tooth	50 mm (2 in.)	100 mm (4 in.)	150 mm (6 in.)
2.5	10	30	14	40	20	200	135	90
4	6	35	17	55	28	200	135	90
8	3	40	20	65	35	150	100	65
12	2	45	25	70	50	60	45	30

TABLE 5.23b Typical Stroking Rates for Horizontal Grinders

Tooth size		Generating strokes per minute		Stroking rate (seconds per tooth, per cut), rough grinding*					
				15 tooth—Face width			75 tooth—Face width		
Module	Pitch	15 tooth	75 tooth	50 mm (2 in.)	100 mm (4 in.)	150 mm (6 in.)	50 mm (2 in.)	100 mm (4 in.)	150 mm (6 in.)
2.5	10	120	240	3.5	7.0	10.5	1.8	3.6	5.4
4	6	130	148	2.8	5.6	8.4	2.3	4.6	6.9
8	3	130	75	2.8	5.6	8.4	4.6	9.2	13.8
12	2	110	40	3.5	7.0	10.5	12.0	24.0	36.0

*For finish grinding, multiply seconds per tooth by a factor of 3.

FIG. 5.34 Generating grinding a double helical gear with a conical wheel. (*Courtesy of BHS-Hofler, Ettlingen, German Federal Republic.*)

FIG. 5.35 Close-up view of conical grinding wheel and work. (*Courtesy of BHS-Hofler, Ettlingen, German Federal Republic.*)

FIG. 5.36 Generating grinder using two saucer-shaped wheels on a single helical gear. (*Courtesy of Maag Gear Wheel Co., Zurich, Switzerland.*)

FIG. 5.37 A close-up view of saucer-shaped grinding wheels and work. (*Courtesy of Maag Gear Wheel Co., Zurich, Switzerland.*)

conical wheel. A close-up of the grinding wheel and a double helical gear being ground are shown in Fig. 5.35.

A grinding machine using double saucer wheels is shown in Fig. 5.36. A close-up of the wheel and work is shown in Fig. 5.37.

5.11 Generating Grinding—Bevel Gears

Zerol, spiral, and hypoid gears can be finished by grinding. The machinery available to grind these gears uses a generating motion. The grinding wheel cuts somewhat like a face cutter. The wheel is shaped like a cup rather than like the disc wheels used to grind spur and helical gears. As the bevel gear is ground, the work and the grinding wheel roll through a generating motion. In principle, the grinding wheel acts like one tooth of a *circular* rack which is rolling through mesh with the gear being ground.

Bevel-gear grinding machines index after each tooth space has been ground with the generating motion. The motions of the machine are so smooth that the process appears to be almost as continuous as a hobbing or shaping process.

No feed motion is needed to travel the grinding wheel across the face width of the work. Since the wheel is like a hoop laid across the face width, the whole face width is ground in the same operation. This fact tends to make bevel-gear grinding fast. With spur or helical gears, a feed motion is needed (unless the face width is very narrow). This requires time for both the grinding of the tooth profile and the advance of the wheel across the face width. In bevel gears, the face width is done just as soon as the tooth profile is done.

At the present time, there are several sizes of bevel-gear grinders for general-purpose work on the market. These are more or less universal machines intended to take a range of pitches, ratios, and spiral angles. Many special bevel-gear grinders have been built for the high-production manufacture of a particular gearset.

The designer of bevel gears that require grinding should be careful to design something that is within the range of available machinery, unless the job is important enough to warrant the development of special machine tools.

The capacity ranges of bevel-gear grinders are rather involved. The maximum gear diameter that a machine will do changes rather substantially as the gear ratio changes and as the spiral angle changes. In some cases, bevel gears up to 1 meter (40 in.) can be ground on the larger bevel-gear grinders. Most bevel gears which are ground seem to be in the size range of about 75 mm (3 in.) to 500 mm (20 in.) in diameter.

There are so many complications to bevel-gear grinding that it is desirable for most designers to check with the shop that is to build their gears as soon as they have laid out a preliminary design.

The complications of bevel-gear grinding make it hard to write any for-

TABLE 5.24 Average Time to Grind Spiral Bevel Gears

No. of teeth	Pitch-cone angle, degrees	Tooth size		Face width		No. of passes	No. of dresses	Seconds per tooth	Total time, min
		Module	Pitch	mm	in.				
12	$8\frac{1}{2}$	4	6	41	$1\frac{5}{8}$	4	1	2.7	2.7 per side
20	22	4	6	38	$1\frac{1}{2}$	6	2	2.7	6.4 per side
30	45	4	6	32	$1\frac{1}{4}$	7	2	2.7	10.5
50	68	4	6	38	$1\frac{1}{2}$	8	2	2.7	19.0
80	$81\frac{1}{2}$	4	6	41	$1\frac{5}{8}$	9	3	2.7	33.9
12	$8\frac{1}{2}$	8	3	82	$3\frac{1}{4}$	4	1	4.5	4.1 per side
20	22	8	3	82	$3\frac{1}{4}$	6	2	4.5	10.0 per side
30	45	8	3	82	$3\frac{1}{4}$	7	2	4.5	16.7
50	68	8	3	82	$3\frac{1}{4}$	8	2	4.5	31.0
80	$81\frac{1}{2}$	8	3	82	$3\frac{1}{4}$	9	3	4.5	55.0

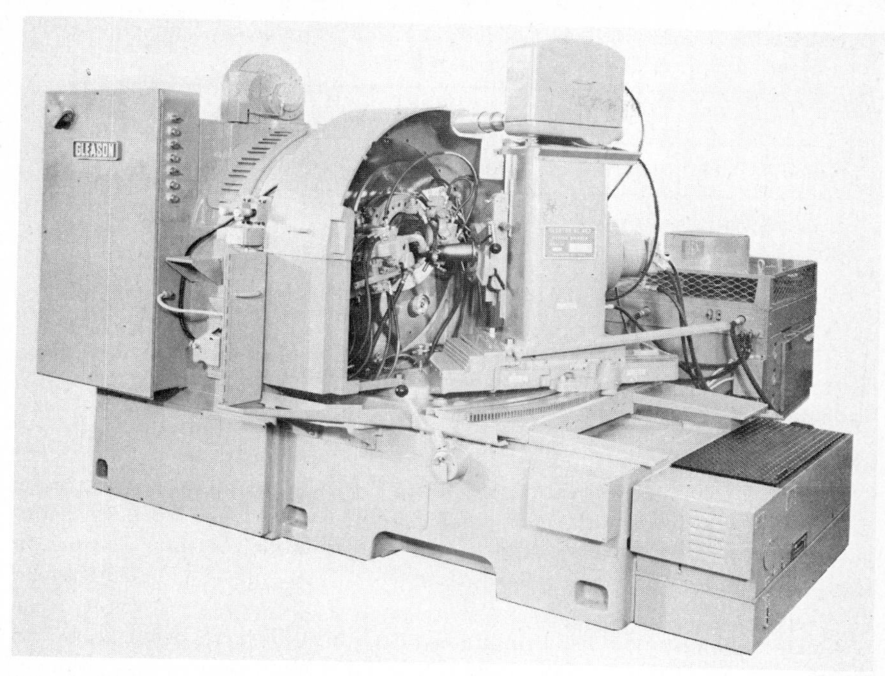

FIG. 5.38 Grinding a spiral bevel gear. (*Courtesy of Gleason Works, Rochester, NY, U.S.A.*)

mula for grinding time. The best way to give information on grinding time appears to be to give a table of approximate times for different combinations. Table 5.24 shows approximate times, assuming that distortion is not serious and that moderate precision is desired.

The total time per piece shown in Table 5.24 includes the automatic wheel-dressing cycle. This is approximately 30 seconds per dress.

Figure 5.38 shows a typical spiral-bevel-gear grinding machine.

5.12 Generating Grinding—Threaded Wheel

Gears can be ground by a grinding machine that uses a threaded grinding wheel. The elements of this kind of machine are very similar to those of a hobbing machine. The process can grind either spur or helical gears, provided they are external.

The threaded-wheel grinding machines are available up to 0.77 meter (30 in.) outside diameter capacity. Either spur or helical, external gear teeth can be ground. Helix angles up to 45° are ground, but the maximum work

TABLE 5.25 Number of Gears Ground per Wheel Dressing and Approximate Overtravel

Tooth size		Face width		Helix angle	Gears per dressing		Overtravel	
Module	Pitch	mm	in.		25 teeth	75 teeth	mm	in.
1.6	16	10	3/8	Spur	200	100	1	1/16
		25	1	15°	100	50	6	1/4
2.5	10	12	1/2	Spur	100	50	2	3/32
		50	2	15°	40	20	6	1/4
4	6	19	3/4	Spur	20	10	3	1/8
		100	4	15°	5	2	9	3/8

diameter has to be considerably reduced. The sizes of teeth produced by this method range from about 0.2 module (120 pitch) to 8 module (3 pitch).

Grinding machines of around 350 mm ($13\frac{3}{4}$ in.) maximum work capacity use threaded grinding wheels about 350 mm in size, while the larger machines of around 0.77-meter capacity use wheels about 400 mm ($15\frac{3}{4}$ in.) in size. The smaller machines (350 mm) are using grinding-wheel speeds up to 1900 rpm.

Gears to be ground with a threaded wheel must allow room for the wheel to run out. (See Table 5.25.)

Several roughing cuts are used to bring the gear down to size. One or more finishing cuts—depending on the finish and accuracy required—are used to finish the gear. In most cases it is not necessary to stop to dress the grinding wheel while a gear is being ground. As Table 5.25 shows, several gears can usually be done before the wheel needs dressing. This table shows some typical numbers of gears ground per wheel dressing and amounts of overtravel.

It takes about 12 min to dress the grinding wheel. Diamond wheels are used to dress threads on the grinding wheel.

TABLE 5.26 Typical Values for Feed and Stock Removal When Grinding with a Threaded Wheel

Tooth size		Feed per revolution of work				Stock removed per cut, roughing or finishing	
		Roughing		Finishing			
Module	Pitch	mm	in.	mm	in.	mm	in.
1.6	16	1.8	0.07	0.63	0.025	0.01	0.0004
2.5	10	1.8	0.07	0.63	0.025	0.01	0.0004
4	6	1.8	0.07	0.63	0.025	0.01	0.0004

The time required to grind a gear by the threaded-grinding-wheel process may be calculated in much the same way as hobbing time is calculated. The time in minutes is

$$\text{Grinding time} = \frac{\text{no. of gear teeth} \times (\text{face} + \text{overtravel}) \times \text{no. of cuts}}{\text{no. of threads} \times \text{feed} \times \text{rpm of wheel}} \tag{5.14}$$

The amount of stock removed with an average cut and the average rates of feed are shown in Table 5.26. The number of cuts may be figured from the stock left to grind, except that extra cuts will be needed to finish the work. The last of these cuts may remove almost no stock.

Wheel wear is quite uniform with the threaded grinding wheel. When one spot gets worn, the wheel is shifted axially to let a new part of the wheel generate the work. This is one of the reasons why a lot of grinding can be done between wheel dressings.

TABLE 5.27 Comparison of Estimated Grinding Times using the Threaded Grinding Wheel Method for High-Precision and Medium-Precision Gears

Tooth size		No. teeth	Face width		Stock to remove		Grinding time, min
Module	Pitch		mm	in.	mm	in.	
High-precision gears (turbine drives)							
2.5	10	25	32	1.25	0.24	0.0095	6.3
2.5	10	102	32	1.25	0.24	0.0095	20.6
2.5	10	102	76	3.0	0.24	0.0095	49.3
5.0	5	25	76	3.0	0.30	0.012	14.3
5.0	5	102	76	3.0	0.38	0.015	65.4
5.0	5	102	152	6.0	0.46	0.018	150.0
Medium-precision gears (vehicle drives)							
2.5	10	25	32	1.25	0.24	0.0095	3.2
2.5	10	102	32	1.25	0.24	0.0095	8.8
2.5	10	102	76	3.0	0.24	0.0095	20.7
5.0	5	25	76	3.0	0.30	0.012	9.1
5.0	5	102	76	3.0	0.30	0.012	24.2
5.0	5	102	152	6.0	0.30	0.012	48.1

Notes: 1. The high-precision gears are ground with a single-thread wheel.
2. The medium-precision gears are ground with a double-thread (two-start) wheel.
3. In all cases, the gears are rough-ground and then finish-ground.

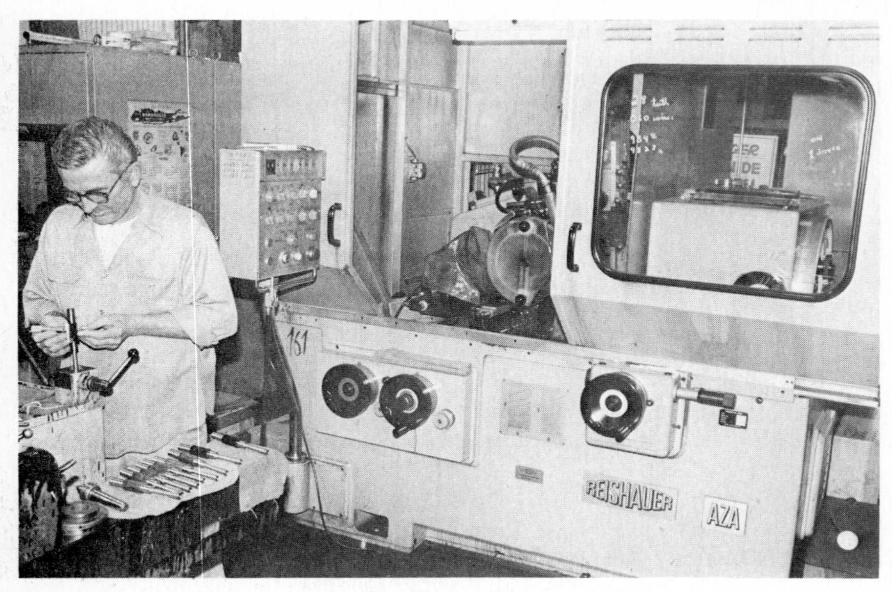

FIG. 5.39 Grinding helical pinions on a threaded grinding wheel machine. (*Courtesy of Sier-Bath Gear Co., North Bergen, NJ, U.S.A.*)

FIG. 5.40 Threaded grinding wheel and helical gear. (*Courtesy of Reishauer Corp., Elgin, IL, U.S.A., and Reishauer Ltd., Zurich, Switzerland.*)

Gear teeth finer than 0.8 module (32 pitch) may be quite satisfactorily ground from the solid. Larger teeth are cut before grinding.

The threaded-wheel grinder is used for high-precision gears. It is also coming into increased use for medium-precision gears which are hardened—and were formerly used without grinding after hardening. Closer quality control and more concern over gear noise make it harder to produce acceptable gears for lower-speed applications. Table 5.27 shows some comparisons of grinding time that may be expected. Note the substantial reduction in grinding time with lower accuracy. These less-accurate gears are adequate for vehicle gears and certain other industrial gears that do not run at high speeds.

Figure 5.39 shows a threaded-wheel grinding machine being used to make high-speed helical pinions. Figure 5.40 shows a close-up of a threaded wheel and a high-speed helical gear.

5.13 Thread Grinding

Single-enveloping worms may be finished by grinding in a thread grinder. Ordinarily worms are milled, hardened, and then ground. In fine pitches—5-mm (0.200-in.) linear pitch and less—it is possible to make the thread complete by grinding. Pitches as coarse as 40-mm (1.60-in.) linear pitch may be ground on available grinding machines. Some grinders limit the lead angle of the worm to 30°, while others will go up to as much as 50°. Worms up to 300 mm (12 in.) outside diameter may be ground with presently available equipment. See Fig. 5.41 for an example of worm thread grinding.

Worm designs to be ground must allow room for a relatively large grinding wheel to run out. A commonly used size of wheel is 500 mm (20 in.).

When the worm grinding wheel has a straight-sided profile, it will produce a worm thread with a convex curvature. This curve is not an involute. The amount of this curvature may be calculated by the method shown in Sec. 6.4. To produce a straight-sided worm thread, a slight convex curvature in the grinding-wheel profile is required.

The time required to grind worm threads may be estimated by the following formula:

Grinding time, min

$$= \frac{\text{no. of threads}}{\text{threads per cut}} \times \left(\text{index time} + \frac{\text{thread length}}{\text{feed rate}} \right) \times \text{no. of cuts} \qquad (5.15)$$

The indexing time runs from about 0.1 to 0.5 min. The developed length of the thread is

$$\text{Length of thread} = \frac{3.14 \text{ worm dia.}}{\text{cos lead angle}} \times \frac{\text{face width}}{\text{lead of worm}} \qquad (5.16)$$

FIG. 5.41 Grinding a large precision index worm. (*Courtesy of Jones and Lamson, Springfield, VT, U.S.A.*)

In fine-pitch worms, it is sometimes possible to use two or three ribs on the grinding wheel and grind all worm threads at once. This saves time.

The number of cuts will depend on both the pitch and the amount of stock left for grinding. Table 5.28 shows the number of cuts and the feed

TABLE 5.28 Number of Cuts and Feed Rates Normally Used in Worm Grinding

Linear pitch		No. of cuts		Feed rate, per min: 250-mm (10-in.) wheel		Feed rate, per min: 500-mm (20-in.) wheel	
mm	in.	Roughing	Finishing	mm	in.	mm	in.
6	0.250	2	1	625	25	1000	40
12	0.500	3	1	500	20	875	35
19	0.750	4	1	375	15	750	30
25	1.000	5	2	300	12	625	25
31	1.250	7	2	250	10	500	20

rates normally used for different pitches of worms. It is assumed that a nominal amount of stock is left for finishing. This would be about 0.25 mm (0.010 in.) on tooth thickness for 12-mm (0.500-in.) linear pitch, and 0.65 mm (0.025 in.) for 32-mm (1.250-in.) linear pitch.

GEAR SHAVING, ROLLING, AND HONING

There are three different ways of finishing involute gear teeth that involve a gearlike tool rolling with the work on a crossed axis:

Shaving

Rolling

Honing

The *shaving* process finishes by cutting. The *rolling* process cold-forms the metal by very small amounts of cold flow on the gear tooth, produced by pressure from the hardened roll. The *honing* process abrasively removes very small amounts of metal from the gear-tooth surfaces.

Gear shaving is strictly a finishing operation. Compared with grinding, shaving is generally a much faster process.

Grinding is not limited to hardness, but shaving is limited to machinable hardnesses. It is usually quite practical to shave gears up to 350 HB (38 HRC). Gears up to 450 HB (47 HRC) have been cut and shaved with fair results. At the higher hardnesses, tool wear is very fast, and special techniques and cutting lubricants are required. Also, the shaving cutter needs to be extra hard.

Shaving is a corrective process. Most people in the trade express the view, "Shaving will not make a bad gear good, but it will make a good gear better!" Shaving readily improves surface finish and reduces gear runout. If the gear and the shaving cutter are properly designed, it is possible to improve profile accuracy considerably. Tooth-to-tooth spacing is improved by shaving, but accumulated spacing error is not changed by a large amount unless the accumulated error comes mostly from eccentricity effects. On narrow-face-width gears, helix errors can be controlled by shaving, but a narrow shaving cutter has little or no control on wide-face gears.

Since shaved gears are not heat-treated between cutting and shaving, there is no heat-treat distortion to clean up, and only a small amount of stock is needed for shaving. Shaved gears are often fully hardened after shaving. When this is done, heat-treat distortion is held to a minimum or controlled in such a manner that uniform distortion results, and this distortion is allowed for in the shaving process.

There are two general methods of shaving, *rotary* shaving and *rack* shaving. The rotary method uses a pinionlike cutter with serrated teeth, while

FIG. 5.42 Shaving an instrument pinion. (*Courtesy of Fellows Corp., Emhart Machinery Group, Springfield, VT, U.S.A.*)

the rack method uses an actual rack with serrated teeth. Figure 5.42 shows rotary shaving, while Figure 5.45 shows rack shaving.

5.14 Rotary Shaving

The rotary shaving cutter has gear teeth ground with a profile that will conjugate with that of the part to be shaved. The cutter teeth are serrated, with many small rectangular notches. As the shaving cutter rotates with the gear, these notches scrape off little shavings of material; hence the name *shaving*. There is no index gearing in the shaving process. Small parts are driven by the cutter that is shaving them, while large parts drive the cutter instead. The shaving cutter is essentially a precision-ground gear made of tool steel. The reason that shaving can produce very high accuracy is that there is an *averaging* action as the cutter rolls with the work. This tends to mask the effect of any slight indexing errors that may have been ground into the cutter.

The shaving cutter does not have the same helix angle in degrees as that of the part it is shaving. This makes the axis of the cutter sit at an angle with the axis of the work. The amount of this crossed-axis angle governs the shaving action. The greater the angle, the more the cutter cuts. The crossed-axis angle causes a cutter tooth to slide sideways as it rolls with the gear tooth. It is this motion that makes the shaving cutter scrape off metal. If shaving cutters were serrated in a radial direction, and the crossed-axis angle were zero, a shaving cutter would not cut at all unless it was reciprocating axially. It so happens that one design of shaving machine does use a rapid reciprocating motion to shave internal gears. In general, shaving cutters do not have any *rapid* reciprocating motion.

Both external and internal gears may be shaved. The gears may be either spur or helical. Small external gears may be shaved by feeding the cutter either parallel to the gear axis or at some angle to the axis. If the cutter is fed at right angles to the gear axis, the cutter must be as wide as or slightly wider than the work. If the cutter is fed in a diagonal direction, there is a relation between the cutter minimum width and the gear face width. When the cutter is fed parallel to the gear axis, there is no geometric requirement on the cutter face width. With this direction of feed, satisfactory results have been achieved by shaving a gear as wide as 0.5 meter (20 in.) face width with a 25-mm (1-in.) cutter.

Figure 5.43 shows a shaving machine for small gears that will shave with the feed at an angle to the axis. A vertical-axis shaving machine is shown in Fig. 5.44. This type of machine is often used for large gears.

Gears which are to be shaved should allow room for the cutter to run out. Shaving-cutter runout is hard to figure, because the cutter sits at an angle with the work and contacts the work on an oblique line. Gears to be shaved are often cut (before shaving) with a cutting tool which has a slight protuberance on its tip. This is helpful because the shaving cutter is not intended to remove metal from the root fillet of the gear. The protuberance on the cutting tool produces a slight relief, or undercut. This undercut allows the tip of the shaving cutter to roll freely instead of hitting a shoulder where the shaving action stops at the bottom of the gear tooth.

Gears to be shaved must have tooth designs that permit sufficient teeth to be in contact with the shaving cutter. Since the cutter either drives or is driven by the work, the gear teeth must be capable of transmitting power smoothly. For instance, shaving standard spline teeth with a 30° pressure angle and a height which is stubbed to 50 percent of full proportions is usually impractical. These teeth do not have enough involute profile to transmit power smoothly when they roll. In general, the pressure angle should be in the range of $14\frac{1}{2}$ to 25°, and tooth height should be at least 75 percent of full depth to permit satisfactory rolling conditions. Clearance in the root fillet should be at least $0.3m_n$ $(0.3/P_{nd})$ to permit a suitable design of a preshaving type of cutting tool.

Spur pinions with small numbers of teeth are somewhat more difficult to shave. There are problems with obtaining good involute when shaving pin-

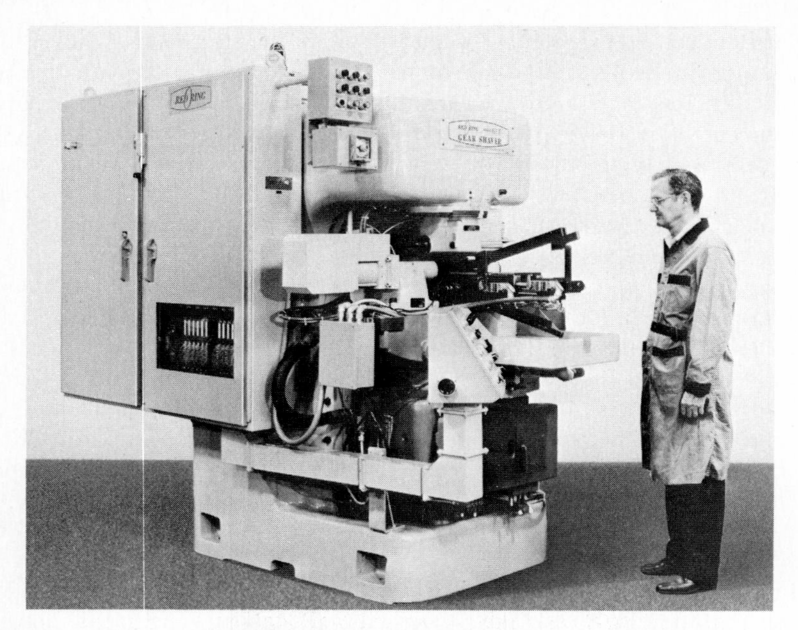

FIG. 5.43 Gear-shaving machine equipped with programmable controller. (*Courtesy of National Broach and Machine Co., a division of Lear Siegler, Inc., Detroit, MI, U.S.A.*)

ions with 10 teeth or fewer. It is also difficult to design a suitable shaving cutter for internal gears with fewer than 40 teeth. When internal gears have 25 teeth, it is just about impossible to get a cutter inside that will shave on the crossed-axis principle.

The time required to shave gears may be estimated by one of two formu-

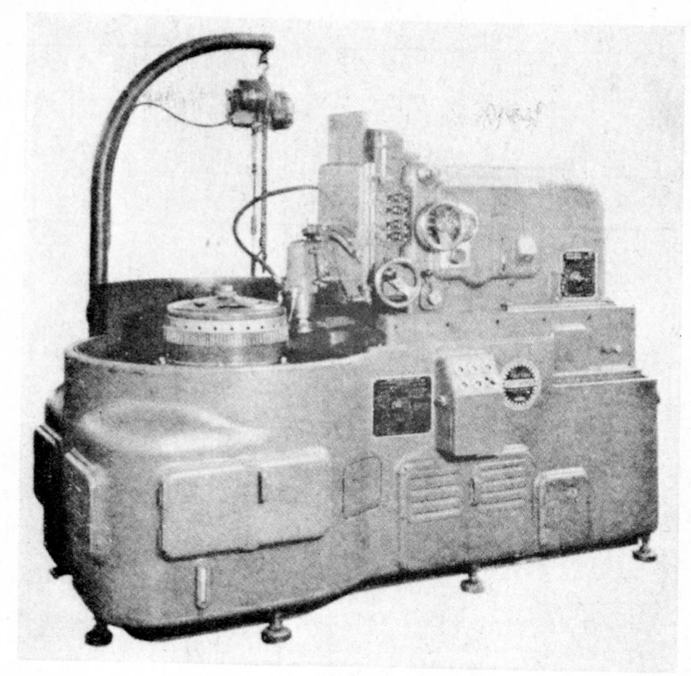

FIG. 5.44 A rotary gear shaver for finishing medium-sized internal and external gears. (*Courtesy of National Broach and Machine Co., a division of Lear Siegler, Detroit, MI, U.S.A.*)

las. If the feed is parallel to the gear axis, Eq. (5.17) should be used. If the feed is at an angle to the axis, Eq. (5.18) is the one to use.

Feed parallel to axis:

Shaving time, min

$$= \frac{0.262 \times \text{pitch dia.} \times (\text{face width} + \text{overtravel}) \times \text{no. of cuts}}{\text{shaving speed} \times \text{feed}} \tag{5.17}$$

Feed at an angle to axis:

$$\text{Shaving time, sec} = \text{time per stroke} \times \text{no. of cuts} \tag{5.18}$$

The overtravel in shaving may be estimated at about $1\frac{1}{2}$ times the cutter width. The face width and pitch diameter in Eq. (5.17) are those of the gear being shaved.

The number of cuts required will depend on the amount of stock left for shaving and the amount taken per cut. Sometimes extra cuts may be needed to secure helix-angle correction. The amount of stock that may be removed in shaving is fairly limited. It is practical to put in only a certain amount of

TABLE 5.29 Amounts of Stock Left for Shaving

Tooth size		Stock left on tooth thickness			
		Minimum (high accuracy)		Maximum (medium accuracy)	
Module	Pitch	mm	in.	mm	in.
1.6	16	0.025	0.001	0.050	0.002
2.5	10	0.038	0.0015	0.075	0.003
4	6	0.050	0.002	0.10	0.004
12	2	0.075	0.003	0.15	0.006

undercut in the preshave cutting. If too much stock is removed, the undercut allowance will be exceeded, and there will be trouble from cutter "bottoming." Table 5.29 shows the approximate amount of stock that may be left for shaving.

The stock removed per cut and the rate of feed depend somewhat on the size of the gear and considerably upon the degree of quality and surface finish desired. Table 5.30 gives some representative values that can be used for estimating purposes.

The rolling velocity of a shaving cutter is generally described as *shaving speed.* The shaving speed, of course, varies considerably depending on the hardness and size of the gear parts being shaved. Some typical values of

TABLE 5.30 Shaving Stock Removal and Feed Rates

Kind of work			Stock removed per cut (on TT)		Cross feed rate per revolution	
Diameter						
mm	in.	Accuracy	Roughing, mm (in.)	Finishing, mm (in.)	Roughing, mm (in.)	Finishing, mm (in.)
150	6	High precision	0.018 (0.0007)	0.008 (0.0003)	0.38 (0.015)	0.15 (0.006)
150	6	Medium precision	0.038 (0.0015)	0.018 (0.0007)	0.50 (0.020)	0.50 (0.020)
600	24	High precision	0.018 (0.0007)	0.008 (0.0003)	0.38 (0.015)	0.20 (0.008)
600	24	Medium precision	0.038 (0.0015)	0.018 (0.0007)	0.63 (0.025)	0.63 (0.025)
2400	96	High precision	0.018 (0.0007)	0.008 (0.0003)	0.38 (0.015)	0.25 (0.010)
2400	96	Medium precision	0.038 (0.0015)	0.013 (0.0005)	0.63 (0.025)	0.38 (0.015)

TABLE 5.31 Seconds per Cycle When Shaving Cutter Is Fed at an Angle to the Gear Axis

Gear diameter		Feed 90° to gear axis		Feed 60° to gear axis		Feed 30° to gear axis	
mm	in.	Commercial	Precision	Commercial	Precision	Commercial	Precision
75	3	28	40	32	45	36	50
150	6	45	65	50	70	54	75
300	12	57	85	63	90	68	95
450	18	70	100	76	105	82	120
600	24	85	125	91	130	97	140

shaving speed are:

Small steel parts, 250 BHN, 25 to 100 mm (1 to 4 in.) in diameter	120 to 150 m/min (400 to 500 fpm)
Large gears, 250 BHN, 1 to $2\frac{1}{2}$ meters (40 to 100 in.) in diameter	90 to 120 m/min (300 to 400 fpm)
Medium gears, 350 BHN, 100 mm to 1 meter (4 to 40 in.) in diameter	75 to 90 m/min (250 to 300 fpm)

When gears are shaved with the cutter traveling at an angle to the axis, the cutter has to be wide enough to shave the whole gear face width in one stroke. This process will not handle as wide work as the parallel method. Typical machinery on the market can handle gears up to 0.6 meter (24 in.) diameter and 100 mm (4 in.) face width by this process. By comparison, when the feed is parallel to the axis, available machinery will handle gears up to 5 meters (200 in.) in diameter and 1.5 meters (60 in.) face width.

The amount of time required to make a stroke (or cut) when the feed is at an angle to the axis depends mostly on the gear diameter. Table 5.31 gives some representative values for different angles of feed.

5.15 Rack Shaving

In rack shaving, the gear to be shaved is rolled back and forth with a rack having serrated teeth. The rack is moved in a direction which is not perpendicular to the gear axis. This gives a crossed-axis effect which makes rack shaving follow the same kind of cutting action as rotary shaving. It is the crosswise sliding that makes the rack cut.

As the work rolls with the reciprocating rack, it is also moved across a portion of the rack so as to equalize the wear of the rack. After each stroke of the rack, the gear is fed in a slight amount.

External spur and helical gears can be shaved by the rack method. Presently available machines will handle gears up to 200 mm (8 in.) diameter

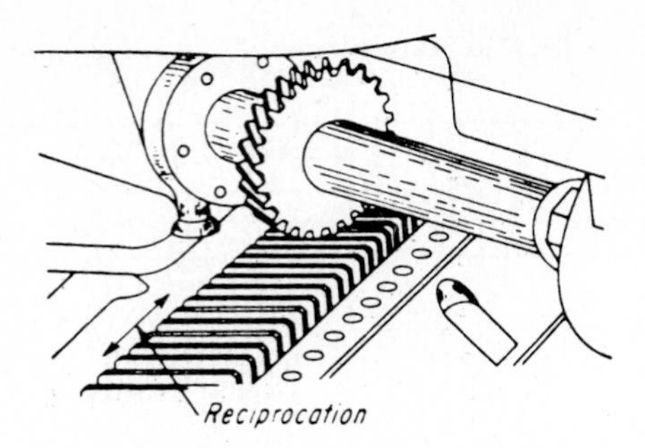

FIG. 5.45 The rack shaving method.

and 50 mm (2 in.) face width. This method of shaving does not lend itself to shaving large parts. The racks used are quite expensive. The rack must be wider than the gear face width, and it must have a length (and stroke) longer than the gear circumference. The rack-shaving process is very rapid, and a very large number of parts are obtained per sharpening of the rack. Rack shaving is quite economical on high-production jobs.

The time required to finish steel gears by rack shaving may be estimated from Table 5.32. The table shows an average time based on a moderate amount of stock left for shaving and material with reasonably good machinability. Special conditions or quality requirements would require proportionally more or less time.

5.16 Gear Rolling

The gear-rolling processes finish the teeth by rolling the gear with a hardened tool that has very precisely ground teeth. This tool is called a *die*. The gear and die are pushed together with a high force.

Figure 5.46 shows the schematic arrangement of single-die rolling. Note the roller steady rests used to transmit the force of the table feed to the work.

TABLE 5.32 Average Amount of Time to Rack Shave Gears

Gear diameter		Time, seconds				
mm	in.	1.6 module (16 pitch)	2 module (12 pitch)	2.5 module (10 pitch)	3 module (8 pitch)	4 module (6 pitch)
25	1	75	72	69	65	60
50	2	73	70	67	63	58
75	3	70	67	64	60	55
100	4	65	62	59	55	50
150	6	58	55	52	48	43
200	8	45	42	39	35	30

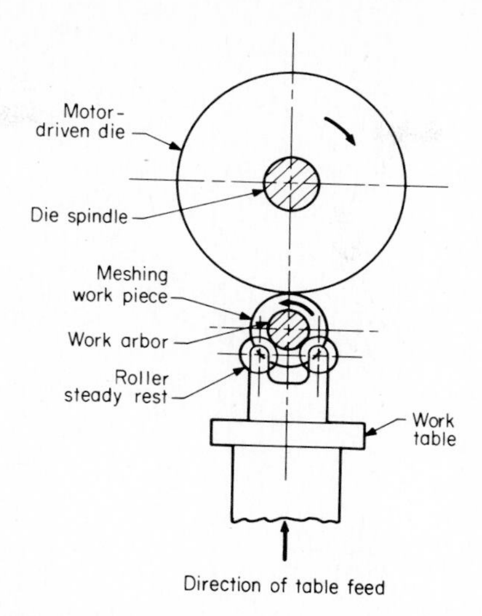

FIG. 5.46 Operating principle of single-die gear-rolling machine. (*Extracted with permission from* Modern Methods of Gear Manufacture, *published by National Broach and Machine Co., a division of Lear Siegler, Inc., Detroit, MI, U.S.A.*)

Figure 5.47 shows a two-die rolling machine. In this case two dies, 180° apart, apply force to the part being rolled. (The part does not need roller steady rests when two dies with equal and opposite forces do the rolling.)

Small parts are generally done with the two-die rolling machine, while large parts are done with the single-die machine. Typical machines roll gears from about 25 mm (1 in.) to 150 mm (6 in.) using two dies. Single-die machines are being used to do gears up to 0.5 meter (19 in.) diameter. The face widths are generally quite narrow [from about 20 mm (0.8 in.) to about 70 mm ($2\frac{3}{4}$ in.)].

Gear rolling on high-production jobs is generally done with the axes parallel. It can, of course, be done with the axes crossed by a rather small angle. It takes less force to do the job with axes crossed, but there is less control of helix accuracy. Also, the rolling time is longer.

In rolling teeth, there is some difficulty with involute accuracy and the quality of the rolled surface. If the gear is too hard or has too much stock left, there is a tendency for slivers of metal to roll over the edges and for there to be folds or flaws around the pitch line. The sliding velocities are *different* on the two sides of the gear being rolled. This fact tends to make the two sides different and to cause trouble at the pitch line, where the sliding velocity reverses. Figure 5.48 shows the characteristic conditions during gear rolling.

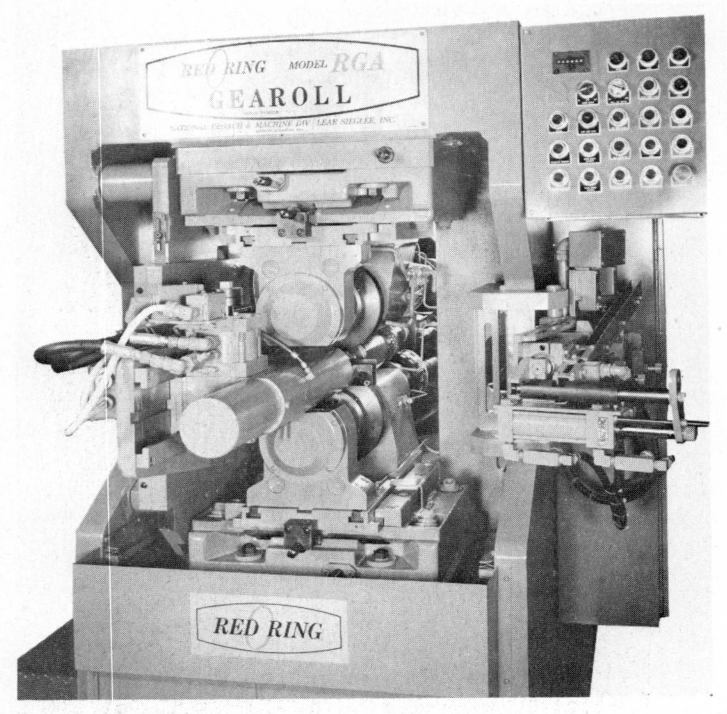

FIG. 5.47 Two-die gear-rolling machine. (*Courtesy of National Broach and Machine Co., a division of Lear Siegler Inc., Detroit, MI, U.S.A.*)

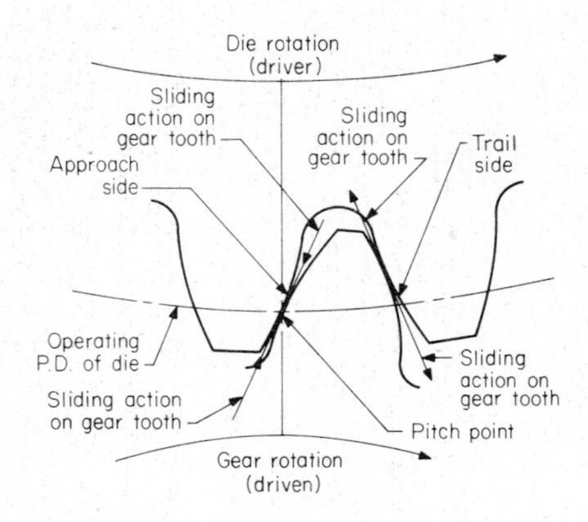

FIG. 5.48 Different sliding directions as a die rolls with a gear.

FIG. 5.49 Gear hones with abrasives bonded to metal and a gear honing arrangement. (*Courtesy of National Broach and Machine Co., a division of Lear Siegler Inc., Detroit, MI, U.S.A.*)

Rolling is successful, though, in spite of the problems just mentioned. These factors will help ensure that the process will work:

The amount of stock left for rolling is small (about one-half of that left for shaving).

The teeth are cut before rolling with a protuberance cutter so that the die can roll clear of the root fillet.

The teeth are usually chamfered at the outside diameter corner.

The gear to be rolled should not be too hard. [A good hardness for rolling is 200 HB (210 HV).]

Rolling jobs are "developed" by experimental rolling, involute checking, and then involute modification of the die to make the involute of the part come out as desired.

The rolling is often *reversed* in direction in order to make the two sides of the gear tooth come out alike.

Gear rolling is fast, and it produces a very smooth, burnished surface finish. In the production of small, high-volume vehicle gears, rolling gears that are going to be carburized and hardened *before* the carburizing process works out well. A low hardness is normal in parts to be carburized, since the final hardness of both case and core material will be established in the carburizing process. Small gears are being made to medium-high-precision accuracy by rolling before carburizing and no grinding after carburizing. (In some cases, such parts may be honed after carburizing.)

To show the relative time involved in shaving, rolling, and honing, the following data from National Broach and Machine are illustrative. These data are for a 25-tooth helical gear with 73.66 mm (2.90 in.) pitch diameter and 16 mm (5/8 in.) face width. Normal pressure angle was 20°, and helix angle was 32°.

Gear shaving:	
Conventional	43 seconds/piece
Diagonal	22 seconds/piece
Gear rolling	10 seconds/piece
Gear honing	21 seconds/piece

5.17 Gear Honing

In the gear-honing process, an abrasive tool with gear teeth is rolled with the gear part on a crossed axis. The force holding the honing tool and work together is very light. The honing tool cuts because of abrasive particles in the composition of the hone or attached to the surface of the hone. The honing is done wet, with an appropriate fluid to serve as a lubricant, a coolant, and a medium to flush away the wear debris from honing.

The gear hone may be a plastic resin material with abrasive grains of silicon carbide. This kind of hone is made by casting in a mold. The hone may be made to medium-precision accuracy and used on gears intended to have medium-high-precision accuracy. The basic accuracy is in the gear before honing. Honing averages the surface and takes off local bumps, scale, etc. Thus the accuracy of the gear is not primarily derived from the hone.

For high-precision gear work, the hone is made to a relatively high precision. It is often possible to get some improvement in involute, helix (lead), and concentricity by careful honing with a precision hone.

Metal hones with bonded-on abrasives are used for fine-pitch gears and for certain medium-pitch gears where a plastic hone might tend to break.

Vehicle gears are often carburized and then run without grinding. These gears are generally shaved or rolled to finish accuracy before carburizing. The final honing operation does these things:

Removes heat-treat scale and oxidation

Removes nicks and bumps from handling (the unhardened gear gets bruised very easily in handling)

Removes some heat-treat distortion

The honed vehicle gear generally runs more quietly. Its load-carrying capacity is higher because of more uniformity in accuracy and smoother tooth surfaces.

High-speed gears used in helicopters and in certain other high-speed turbine applications are generally finish-ground *after carburizing*. Such gears may still need honing to get a very smooth surface finish, so that they will not fail due to scoring. Frequently, such gears need a surface finish better than the grinding machine will produce.

The better the ground finish, the better the honed finish. Some guideline relations are:

Shave or grind to 0.7–0.9 μm (28–36 μin.) finish; hone to 0.4–0.5 μm (16–20 μin.)

Shave or grind to 0.4–0.6 μm (16–24 μin.) finish; hone to 0.25–0.35 μm (10–14 μin.)

Shave or grind to 0.25–0.35 μm (10–14 μin.) finish; hone to 0.15–0.2 μm (6–8 μin.)

When the honed finish must be extra good, the final honing is often done with a rubberlike hone. The hone material is polyurethane. The abrasive is applied as a liquid compound during the honing. The abrasive particles lodge in pores on the hone tooth surface and thereby charge the hone.

The type of honing just described removes almost no stock, and so it has little or no ability to correct involute or helix (lead). The primary purpose of this type of honing is to polish the tooth surface. (In some difficult gear jobs, two-stage honing is used. Normal hones clean up the surface and refine the accuracy. The final finish is obtained by the rubberlike polishing hone.)

Gear-honing machines look like gear-shaving machines. They are special, though, in that they must handle fluids with abrasives, and they must be able to accurately apply very light forces to the hone. Figure 5.49 shows a close-up of a gear-honing operation. The top half of Fig. 5.49 shows some typical hones made of steel and carbide coated.

Gear-honing machines for external gears are readily available for gear sizes up to 0.6 m (24 in.) diameter. Machines for honing internal gears tend to be smaller in capacity, with 0.3 m (12 in.) being typical. The size of teeth commonly honed ranges from 1.2 to 12 module (2 to 20 pitch).

GEAR MEASUREMENT

Those running gear shops find that they need a considerable capability to measure the geometric accuracy of gear teeth. It is not enough to have machinery to cut, grind, and finish gear teeth. Additional machinery is needed to measure gear-tooth spacing, profile, helix, concentricity, and finish.

The gears used in the aerospace field must be rigidly controlled for both geometric and metallurgical quality. The high-speed gears used with turbine engines are almost as critical. A turbine, for instance, that runs at 20,000 rpm will usually be connected to a pinion. In the oil and gas industry, it is normal for the turbine gear drive to be designed for a life of 40,000 hours—at *full-rated* power. A pinion meshing with one gear makes 4.8×10^{10} cycles in 40,000 hours at 20,000 rpm. With a high pitch-line speed and full-rated load, it is obvious that a pinion like this will not last this long if its accuracy is deficient. Precise measurements are needed to verify that each and every item of geometric accuracy is within specification limits.

Vehicle gears do not run as long—total life is often no more than 2×10^8 cycles. The vehicle gear, though, is much more heavily loaded than the turbine gear. In addition, noise and vibration requirements have become quite critical. The vehicle gear does not have to be so accurate as the turbine gear, because it does not run so fast or so long. But the vehicle gear has to meet its own level of accuracy. If it does not, vehicle drives that should last a few years will fail in a few months.

In all fields of gearing, the control of gear accuracy is essential. Since this is the case, it is necessary to present some material on accuracy limits and on machines used to measure gear accuracy.

5.18 Gear Accuracy Limits

The gear designer faces a dilemma when endeavoring to put accuracy limits on a gear drawing. To get high load-carrying capacity and reliability to meet the gear life requirements, each item must be specified very closely. (The *load rating* part of Chap. 3 showed the rather direct relation between accuracy and load-carrying capacity.)

Besides load-carrying capacity, the designer needs to worry about two other things. First, the accuracy called for must be *practical* to meet in the gear shop (or shops) available to do the gear work. Specifying impossible accuracy limits is to no avail. In addition, the gear parts need to be made at *reasonable* cost. In a competitive world, it is not the best gear that is needed. What is really needed is the *lowest-cost* gear that will adequately meet load, life, reliability, and quietness requirements.

To solve the dilemma just given, it is advisable for the gear designer to first consider these things:

Pitch-line velocity

Intensity of loading, length of life, and degree of reliability needed

Requirements as to noise, vibration, or need to run with hot, thin oils

The things just mentioned will guide the designer to the proper *level* of accuracy. Next, the designer needs to consider the machine tools and level of operator skill and discipline that are available to make the gears (*good* trade practice in the product area).

After choosing an appropriate level of accuracy and reviewing manufacturing resources, the designer needs guidelines on the gear trade. Table 5.33 is a brief guide based on the author's experience.

In the gear trade, published standards are used extensively. The most important are AGMA 390.03 and DIN 3963/1978.*

The published standards are revised periodically to cover more quality items and to define items more clearly. Also, the *mix* may change. For instance, the helix accuracy specified for a high-precision gear may be too low to match the profile and spacing accuracy achievable with first-rate grinders. For long-range thinking, it is probably best to think in terms of the six levels described in Table 5.33, then try to find (or establish) a set of accuracy limits that is adequate for the job requirements and practical to meet in the gear shop making the parts.

Many major companies† in the United States have found it necessary to set up their own accuracy limits. In this way they can cover important items

*See Refs. 49 and 107 at the end of the book for complete data on these articles.

†These are primarily companies making helicopter gears or high-speed turbine gears for the oil and gas industry.

TABLE 5.33 Accuracy Levels for Gears

Designation	Description of level	Approximate relation to 1982 trade standards: AGMA 390.03	Approximate relation to 1982 trade standards: DIN 3963/1978
AA Ultra-high accuracy	Highest possible accuracy. Achieved by special toolroom type methods. Used for master gears, unusually critical high-speed gears, or when *both* highest load and highest reliability are needed.	14 or 15	2 or 3
A High accuracy	High accuracy, achieved by grinding, shaving with first-rate machine tools, and skilled operators. Used extensively for turbine gearing and aerospace gearing. Sometimes used for critical industrial gears.	12 or 13	4 or 5
B Medium-high accuracy	A relatively high accuracy, achieved by grinding or shaving with emphasis on production rate rather than highest quality. May be achieved by hobbing or shaping with best equipment and favorable conditions. Used in medium-speed industrial gears and the more critical vehicle gears.	10 or 11	6 or 7
C Medium accuracy	A good accuracy, achieved by hobbing or shaping with first-rate machine tools and skilled operators. May be done by high-production grinding or shaving. Typical use is for vehicle gears and electric motor industrial gearing running at slower speeds.	8 or 9	8 or 9
D Low accuracy	A nominal accuracy for hobbing or shaping. Can be achieved with older machine tools and less skilled operators. Typical use is for low-speed gears that wear into a reasonable fit. (Lower hardness helps to permit wear-in.)	6 or 7	10 or 11
E Very low accuracy	An accuracy for gears used at slow speed and light load. Teeth may be cast or molded in small sizes. Typical use is in toys and gadgets. May be used for low-hardness power gears with limited life and reliability needs.	4 or 5	12

not covered in AGMA or DIN standards, and they can adjust the mix of limits to be right for their kind of gear work.

Figure 5.50 illustrates the principal geometric quality items that need control in gearing. For each item, a method of specifying the item is shown. (Other methods are in use, but the ones shown are believed to be the most popular—and practical—for gear manufacture in the 1980s.)

1. Spacing - The variation in circular pitch from one pair of teeth to a pair immediately adjacent.

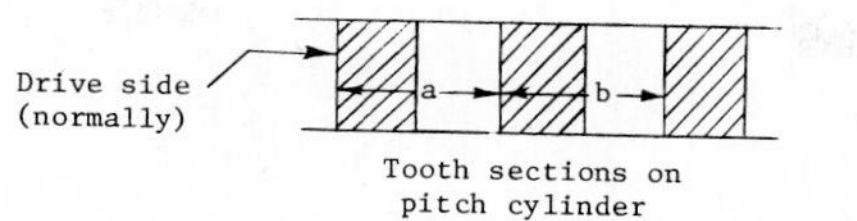

(1) Variation = a - b

(2) Greatest difference in 360°

2. Pitch cumulative - The greatest out of position of any tooth side, with respect to any other tooth side, in the gear circumference.

The shaded area of the sample "K Chart" below shows the range of profile variations allowed by slope and modification tolerances.

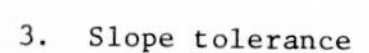

3. Slope tolerance

4. Modification tolerance

5. Irregularity

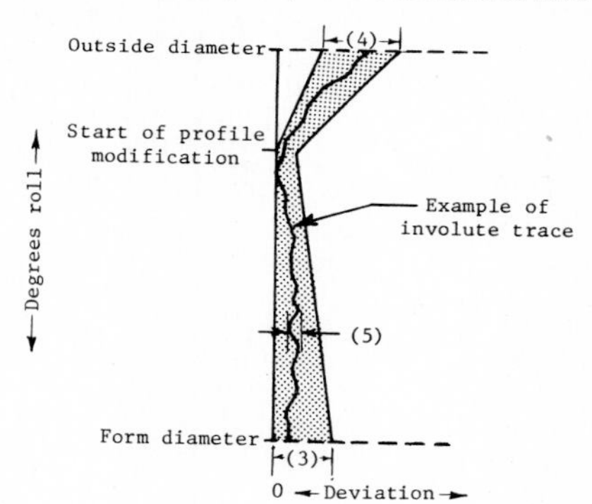

6. Slope tolerance

7. Crown tolerance

8. End easement tolerance

9. Irregularity

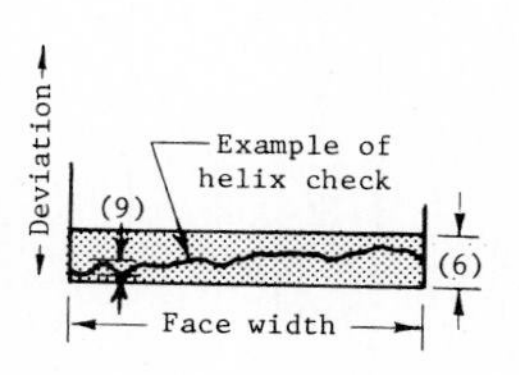

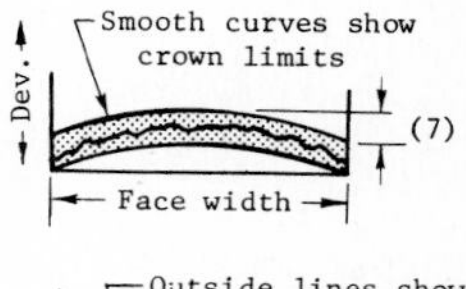

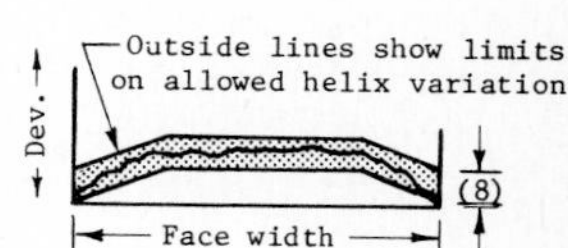

10. Composite T to T - Tooth to tooth variation in center distance, rolling with a master.

11. Composite total - Total variation in center distance, rolling with a master.

12. Profile finish - Arithmetic average finish between form diameter and outside diameter.

13. Root fillet finish - Arithmetic average finish in root (below form diameter).

14. Waviness, working surface - Contour variations in less than 10% of active profile or in less than 5% of face width.

FIG. 5.50 Definitions of gear-tooth geometry tolerances.

TABLE 5.34 Examples of Tolerances for a Range of Gear Sizes and a Range of Quality Levels

	A. High precision			B. Medium-high precision			C. Medium precision		
Quality item	Small gear	Medium gear	Large gear	Small gear	Medium gear	Large gear	Small gear	Medium gear	Large gear
Spacing									
1. Pitch variation (t-to-t)	5 μm (0.0002 in.)	8 μm (0.0003 in.)	10 μm (0.0004 in.)	10 μm (0.0004 in.)	12 μm (0.0005 in.)	20 μm (0.0008 in.)	20 μm (0.0008 in.)	25 μm (0.0010 in.)	35 μm (0.0014 in.)
2. Pitch cumulative	17 μm (0.0007 in.)	23 μm (0.0009 in.)	50 μm (0.0020 in.)	30 μm (0.0012 in.)	48 μm (0.0019 in.)	100 μm (0.0040 in.)	50 μm (0.0020 in.)	90 μm (0.0036 in.)	200 μm (0.0080 in.)
Profile									
3. Slope (total)	7 μm (0.0003 in.)	9 μm (0.00035 in.)	16 μm (0.0006 in.)	13 μm (0.0005 in.)	20 μm (0.0008 in.)	25 μm (0.0010 in.)	25 μm (0.0010 in.)	40 μm (0.0016 in.)	60 μm (0.0024 in.)
4. Modification	10 μm (0.0004 in.)	13 μm (0.0005 in.)	20 μm (0.0008 in.)	20 μm (0.0008 in.)	25 μm (0.0010 in.)	36 μm (0.0014 in.)	36 μm (0.0014 in.)	50 μm (0.0020 in.)	75 μm (0.0030 in.)
5. Irregularities	4 μm (0.00016 in.)	5 μm (0.0002 in.)	7 μm (0.0003 in.)	6 μm (0.00024 in.)	8 μm (0.0003 in.)	10 μm (0.0004 in.)	13 μm (0.0005 in.)	20 μm (0.0008 in.)	30 μm (0.0012 in.)

Helix									
6. Slope	8 µm (0.0003 in.)	12 µm (0.0005 in.)	20 µm (0.0008 in.)	13 µm (0.0005 in.)	20 µm (0.0008 in.)	25 µm (0.0010 in.)	25 µm (0.0010 in.)	40 µm (0.0016 in.)	50 µm (0.0020 in.)
7. Crown	10 µm (0.0004 in.)	—	—	18 µm (0.0007 in.)	—	—	33 µm (0.0013 in.)	—	—
8. End easement	—	12 µm (0.0005 in.)	25 µm (0.0010 in.)	—	25 µm (0.0010 in.)	35 µm (0.0014 in.)	—	50 µm (0.0020 in.)	70 µm (0.0028 in.)
9. Irregularities	4 µm (0.00016 in.)	5 µm (0.0002 in.)	7 µm (0.0003 in.)	6 µm (0.00024 in.)	8 µm (0.0003 in.)	10 µm (0.0004 in.)	10 µm (0.0004 in.)	14 µm (0.0006 in.)	20 µm (0.0008 in.)
Concentricity									
10. Composite (t-to-t)	7 µm (0.0003 in.)	9 µm (0.00035 in.)	15 µm (0.0006 in.)	15 µm (0.0006 in.)	20 µm (0.0008 in.)	28 µm (0.0011 in.)	30 µm (0.0012 in.)	45 µm (0.0018 in.)	60 µm (0.0024 in.)
11. Composite, total	15 µm (0.0006 in.)	20 µm (0.0008 in.)	40 µm (0.0016 in.)	30 µm (0.0012 in.)	50 µm (0.0020 in.)	80 µm (0.0032 in.)	60 µm (0.0024 in.)	90 µm (0.0036 in.)	130 µm (0.0050 in.)
Finish									
12. Profile, AA	0.5 µm (20 µin.)	0.6 µm (24 µin.)	0.8 µm (32 µin.)	0.8 µm (32 µin.)	0.9 µm (36 µin.)	1.0 µm (40 µin.)	1.6 µm (64 µin.)	2.0 µm (80 µin.)	2.5 µm (100 µin.)
13. Root fillet, AA	1.0 µm (40 µin.)	1.2 µm (48 µin.)	1.6 µm (64 µin.)	1.6 µm (64 µin.)	1.8 µm (70 µin.)	2.0 µm (80 µin.)	3.2 µm (126 µin.)	4.0 µm (160 µin.)	5.0 µm (200 µin.)
14. Waviness	1.5 µm (60 µin.)	1.8 µm (70 µin.)	2.0 µm (80 µin.)	2.5 µm (100 µin.)	3.0 µm (120 µin.)	3.5 µm (140 µin.)	5.0 µm (200 µin.)	7.0 µm (280 µin.)	10 µm (400 µin.)

Notes: Small gear is 2.5 module (10 pitch), 50 mm (2 in.) face width, 64 mm (2.5 in.) pitch diameter.
Medium gear is 5 module (5 pitch), 125 mm (5 in.) face width, 250 mm (10 in.) pitch diameter.
Large gear is 12 module (2 pitch), 500 mm (20 in.) face width, 1250 mm (50 in.) pitch diameter.

Table 5.34 shows examples of tolerances for three levels of accuracy and three sizes of gears. This table is based on a survey of key people in the gear trade. It does not agree exactly with any published (or unpublished) accuracy standard. It is hoped that these data will be useful to those studying and setting values for gear accuracy limits.

As a last item, cost needs to be considered. The Fellows Corporation has studied this subject rather thoroughly. They emphasize that the achievement of high accuracy involves several important variables, including:

Machine operator's skill
Blank accuracy, material, and heat treatment
Cutting or grinding tool accuracy
Mounting of cutting tool or grinding wheel
Work-holding fixture accuracy
Accuracy in mounting of work-holding fixture
Production method
Distortion
Inherent capability and condition of machine tool

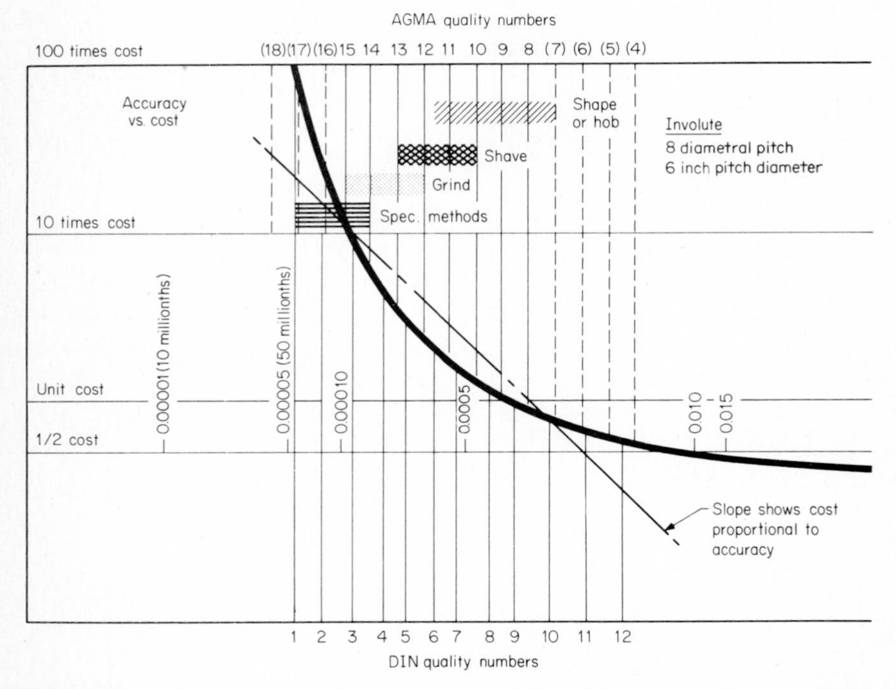

FIG. 5.51 Approximate change in cost of making teeth on a 3-module (8-pitch), 150 mm (6 in.) diameter gear for different degrees of involute accuracy. (*Courtesy of Fellows Corp., Emhart Machinery Group, Springfield, VT, U.S.A.*)

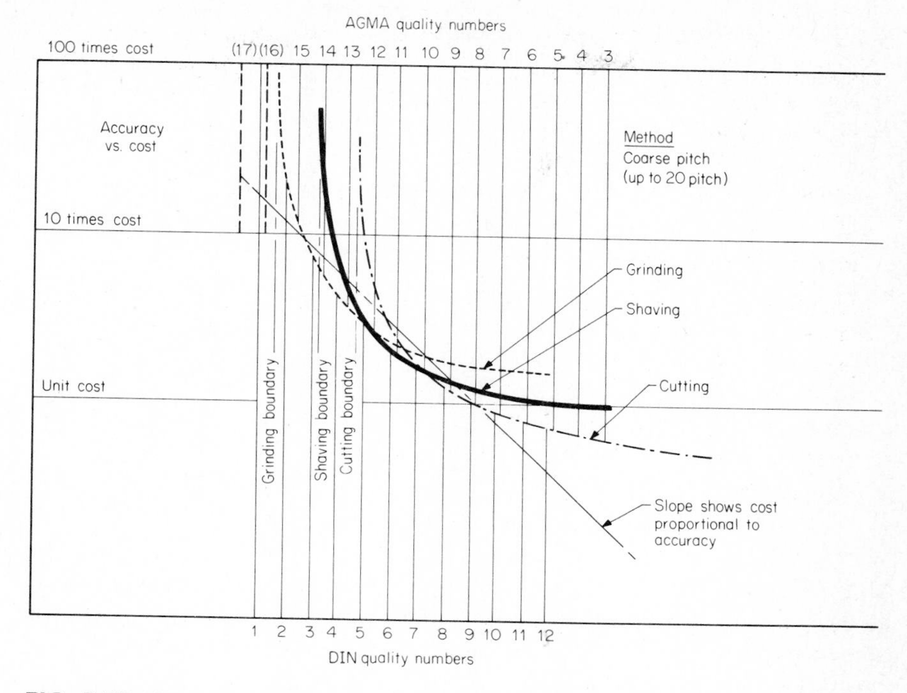

FIG. 5.52 The general trend of the cost of making gear teeth for different manufacturing methods. (*Courtesy of Fellows Corp., Emhart Machinery Group, Springfield, VT, U.S.A.*)

Fellows has released several charts and tables that show cost vs. accuracy trends for fine-pitch and medium-pitch gears and the relative cost of different methods of cutting or finishing gear teeth. Figure 5.51 shows the cost trend as involute accuracy is increased and the range of capability of several gear-tooth-making methods. Note that a change from an AGMA 8 quality number (DIN 9) to an AGMA 15 quality number (DIN 3) involves approximately a *tenfold increase* in cost.

Figure 5.52 shows general cost trends for each method of gear-tooth making. Note that cutting (hobbing or shaping) is the lowest cost for AGMA 8 quality number (DIN 9). However, for AGMA 12 quality number (DIN 5), grinding or shaving is less expensive. (AGMA 12 is very difficult to achieve by cutting.)

An article in the magazine *Design Engineering*, "The Cost of Gear Accuracy," by Doug McCormick, gives a good analysis of gear accuracy needs and manufacturing considerations and the costs involved in obtaining the desired accuracy.

5.19 Machines to Measure Gears

It is possible to make relatively high-accuracy gears without much special measuring equipment. The procedure is along these lines:

Make the gear teeth on good-quality machine tools.

Set up the work accurately and cut or grind with precision cutters or grinding wheels.

Check the runout of the finished gear by measuring runout over pins. (A precision cylindrical pin is put into each tooth space, and radial runout is measured with a high-accuracy indicator which reads to 0.0025 mm or 0.0001 in.)

Contact the mating gears and note how the involute profiles fit and how the helices fit across the face width.

Observe the tooth finish and feel it with your fingernail.

The system just described was widely used in the 1940s. In the 1980s, it is still used in developing countries and by those who make a limited quantity of gears for their own use. It is possible for skilled mechanics with a general understanding of gear quality to handle things so that generally satisfactory results are obtained.

In general, those who build gears for sale on the open market need a machine or machines to measure the prime variables of involute profile, helix across the face width, tooth spacing, tooth finish, and tooth action by meshing with a master gear. Gears cannot be put in quality grades without accurate measurements. End easement, crown, and profile modification cannot be controlled by contact checks alone. (All these items can result in no contact in certain areas. The *gap* in a no-contact situation can be determined only by measurement.)

In medium-production gear shops making gears up to 0.6 meter (24 in.) in diameter, it is usually handiest to have separate machines to check each major variable—for instance, spacing checkers, involute checkers, helix (lead) checkers, master gear rolling checkers, and surface finish checkers. For larger gears up to 2 meters, it is becoming common practice to have one or more general-purpose checking machines that will check involute, helix, spacing, and finish all on the same machine.

It is desirable to use a checking machine of relatively complete capability on a large gear for these reasons:

The large gear is too heavy for one person to lift. It takes a relatively long time to hoist the gear onto the checking machine and get it in position so that it is turning on an exactly true axis.

Gears over 0.6 meter are generally not mass-produced. With lower quantities, the economics of buying separate machines for each kind of check are generally not attractive; it is usually more cost-effective to buy one machine with complete capability.

Figure 5.53 shows a large gear being checked on a machine with complete capability. The equipment in the foreground does the integration to get cumulative tooth spacing from tooth-to-tooth spacing data. Tooth finish data are derived from local parts of involute and helix checks taken at high magnification.

When gears are over 2 meters (80 in.) in diameter, putting the gear on a checking machine becomes rather impractical. The solution to the problem is to take the checking machine to the gear. This may be done with *portable* checking machines that either mount on a machine tool or mount on the

FIG. 5.53 Gear-checking machine for large gears. Spacing, involute, helix, and surface finish are all measured on this type of machine. (*Courtesy of Maag Gear Wheel Co., Zurich, Switzerland.*)

FIG. 5.54 Portable profile-checking head mounted on a grinding machine. (*Courtesy of Maag Gear Wheel Co., Zurich, Switzerland.*)

gear itself. Figure 5.54 shows an example of portable checking equipment temporarily mounted on the bed of a grinding machine. Figure 5.55 shows a portable involute checker mounted on a large marine gear.

The checking of spacing, involute, helix, and finish does not necessarily determine whether or not a gear is a *good* gear. Normally four teeth, 90° apart, are checked. The involute and spacing checks are taken in the center of the face width. The helix is checked at mid height. If just a few teeth are bad, the trouble may be in between the places checked. This possibility is covered by rolling the production gear with a *master* gear.

If the master is as wide as the gear being checked, every bit of tooth surface will be checked. (If the master gear is narrower, the master-gear check can be taken at more than one location across the face width.)

Master-gear checks are *composite* checks. They reveal individual tooth action, and they show the total runout of the gear as a total composite reading (runout plus tooth-action effects).

The machines used for rolling checks are of two types, double-flank and single-flank.

FIG. 5.55 Portable profile-checking head mounted on the rim of a large gear. (*Courtesy of General Electric Co., Lynn, MA, U.S.A.*)

The double-flank machines force the master gear into tight mesh with the gear being checked. The machine reads center distance variation as the gear revolves. Since both flanks touch at all times, the readings show error effects on *both* sides of the teeth. This mixes up errors, and it becomes troublesome when gears are built to high accuracy on the drive side but are allowed to have considerably less accuracy on the essentially nonworking coast side.

The single-flank rolling machines maintain a constant center distance. A small torque keeps the gear and master in contact on the side being measured. The machine measures the change in rotation of one part from a theoretical *uniform* rotation of both parts.

The schematic design of one model of single-flank tester is shown in Figs. 5.56 and 5.57. A single-flank checking machine is shown in Fig. 5.58.

The machines and methods just described apply to parallel-axis gears (involute-helical). Gears on nonparallel axes (bevel gears, worm gears, and

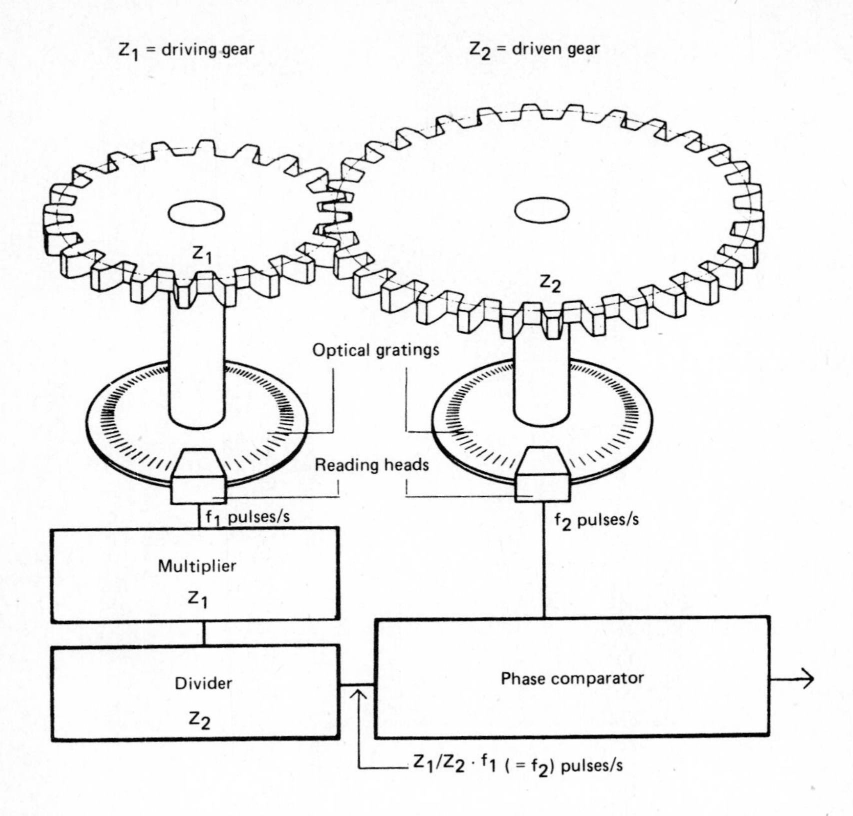

The two motions which are to be compared, either on a single flank tester or in a portable application, are monitored by circular optical gratings. The gratings each give a train of pulses whose frequency is a measure of the angular movements of the two shafts and hence of the gears.

FIG. 5.56 Principle of the Gleason/Goulder single-flank testing machine. (*Reprinted with permission from the SAE technical paper* (*1Q80-920*) "*Testing of Fine Pitch Gears—Single Flank Testing—Double Flank Testing,*" *by Alan M. Thompson, 1980.*)

Spiroid gears) do not have as extensive an array of checking machines, but the logic of using machines to check gears sold on the market is the same. It is not possible to cover checking machine types for these gears in this book. Chapter 23 of the *Gear Handbook* gives a general review of gear-inspection machines and gear-inspection practices for all types of gears (any gear on any axis).

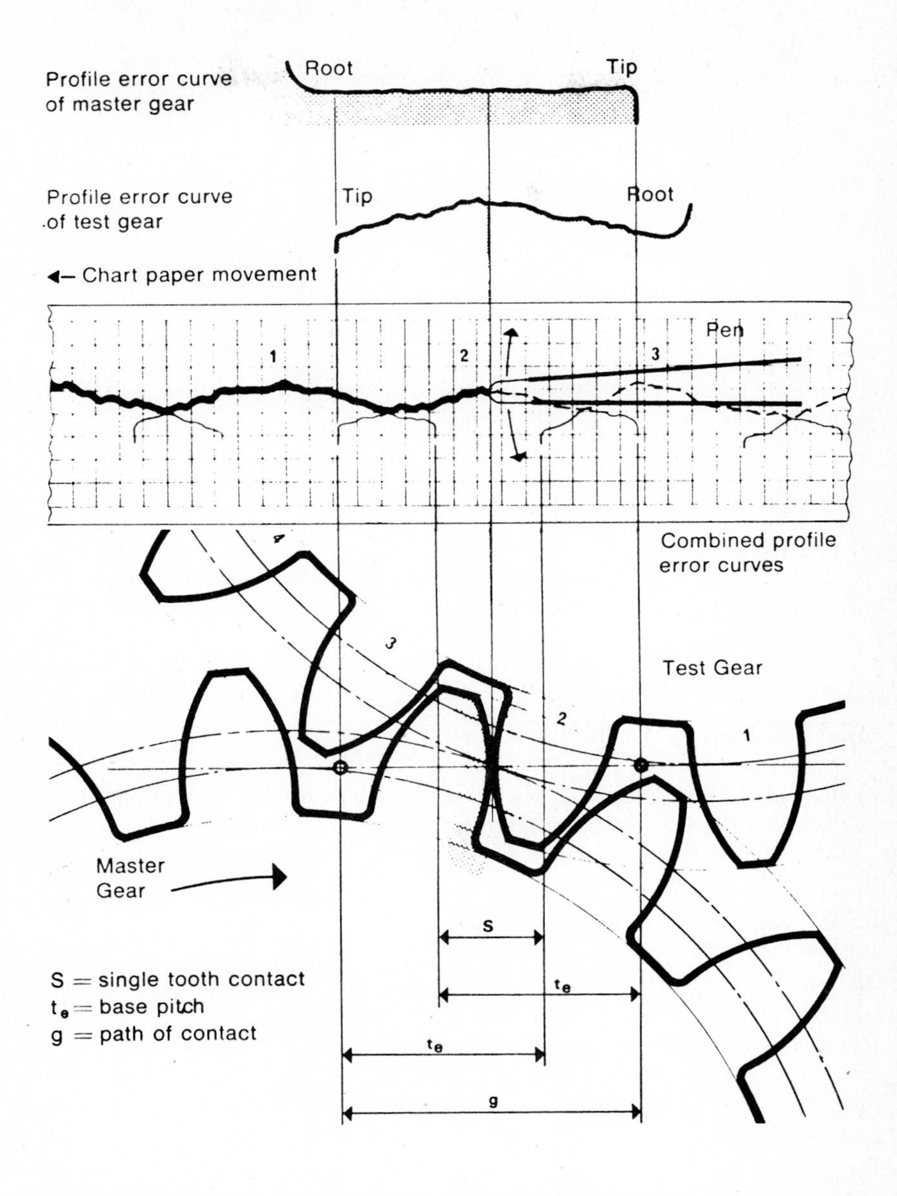

FIG. 5.57 Single-flank error graph. (*Reprinted with permission from the SAE technical paper (1Q80-920) "Testing of Fine Pitch Gears—Single Flank Testing—Double Flank Testing," by Alan M. Thompson, 1980.*)

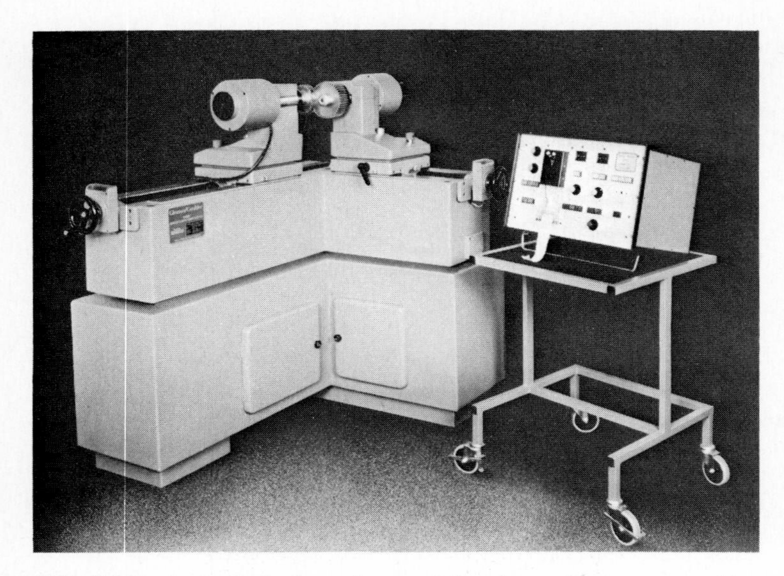

FIG. 5.58 A single-flank testing machine that rolls a master with a gear. (*Courtesy of Gleason/Goulder, Huddersfield, England, a subsidiary of Gleason Works, U.S.A.*)

GEAR CASTING AND FORMING

In this part of the chapter we shall consider some of the ways of making gear teeth other than by metal cutting or grinding.

5.20 Cast and Molded Gears

Although the casting process is most often used to make blanks for gears which will have cut teeth, there are several variations of the casting process that are used to make toothed gears in one operation.

Many years ago, when gear-cutting machines were very limited, it was quite common practice to make a wooden pattern of the complete gear—teeth and all—and then cast the gear in a sand mold. A few old-timers in the gear trade can still recall the days when a "precision" gear was one with cut teeth and an ordinary gear was one with teeth "as-cast." In recent times there has been only very limited use of gears with teeth made by sand casting. In some instances gears for farm machinery, stokers, and some hand-operated devices have used cast teeth. The draft on the pattern and the distortion on cooling make it hard to obtain much accuracy in cast-iron or cast-steel gear teeth.

Large quantities of small gear parts are made by die casting. In the die-casting process, a tool-steel mold is used. The cavity is filled with some low-melting material, such as alloys of zinc, aluminum, or copper. With a precision-machined mold and a blank design that is not vulnerable to irregular shrinkage (such as a spoked wheel), accuracy comparable with that of commercial cutting can be obtained. Complicated gear shapes which would be quite costly to machine can be made quickly and at low cost by the die-casting process. The main disadvantage of the process is that the low-melting metals do not have enough hardness for high load-carrying capacity. In many applications, though, die-cast gears have sufficient capacity to do the job.

Die-cast gears are usually under 150 mm (6 in.) in diameter and from 2.5 module (10 pitch) to 0.5 module (48 pitch). There is no particular reason why larger or smaller gears cannot be made, if dies and casting equipment of suitable size are provided.

A process somewhat similar to die casting is the making of molded-plastic gears. These gears are made in one operation. The raw plastic material is heated in a cylinder to a temperature in the range of 400 to 600°F (depending on the composition). It is forced into a steel mold under pressures as high as 140 N/mm^2 (20,000 psi).

Injection-molding machines now on the market range in size from 30 grams to 10 kg per shot capacity. The cycle time in injection molding is very fast. Machines of 225-gram capacity may make around 100 cycles per hour. One cycle fills a mold. The mold may contain a cavity for one gear, or a half dozen or more parts may be made by filling the cavities in one mold.

The accuracy of injection-molded gears ranges from good to fair. Some plastics are less subject to shrinkage than others. Some—like nylon—absorb water or oil and are subject to distortion through expansion.

Another method of casting gears is the investment-casting process. This process has often been called the "lost-wax" or the "precision" casting process. This process uses a master pattern or die. The master is filled with some low-melting-point metal like a lead-tin-bismuth alloy or some wax or plastic. After this cools, a pattern is formed which is a replica—except for shrinkage allowances—of the part to be made. The pattern is used to form a mold called an *investment*. The investment is made by covering the pattern with a couple of layers of refractory material. The kind of refractory used depends mainly upon the temperature at which the investment will be heated when it is filled with the molten metal. The investment has to be heated to remove the pattern and leave a cavity for pouring. This heating, however, is not nearly so much as the heating which the investment gets when it is filled with the casting material.

The investment process has had only limited use in gear making. Its most apparent value lies in the making of accurate gear teeth out of materials which are so hard that teeth cannot readily be produced by machining. The process can be used with a wide variety of steels, bronzes, and aluminum alloys. With machinable materials, the process would still be useful if the gear was integral with some complicated shape that was very difficult to produce by machining.

5.21 Sintered Gears

Small spur gears may be made by sintering. Small helical gears of simple design may also be made by sintering, provided that the helix angle is not over about 15°.

Machinery presently available will handle parts from about 5 mm (3/16 in.) diameter up to about 100 mm (4 in.) diameter. The sintering process consists of pouring a metal powder into a mold, compressing the powder into a gear-shaped briquette with a broachlike tool which fits the internal teeth of the mold, stripping the mold with another broachlike tool, and then baking the briquette in an oven. It takes about 415 N/mm^2 (60,000 psi) pressure to briquette the larger gears. Presses of 300,000 kg (300 tons) capacity are used for these larger gears.

Pitches in the range of 0.8 module (32 pitch) to 4 module (6 pitch) can be readily sintered. Face widths may range from about 2.5 mm (3/32 in.) to 38 mm (1.5 in.). Smaller face widths are difficult to strip from the mold. Face widths of over 25 mm (1 in.) may give trouble because of loss of briquetting pressure from excessive wall friction.

The sintering process can be used to make a complete toothed gear in one operation. Splines, keyways, double-D bores, crank arms, and other projections may be made by the same sintering operation that forms the gear teeth. By using different powders in the mold, it is even possible to add a thin bronze clutch face integral with one side of the gear!

Sintered gears compare favorably in accuracy with commercial cut gears. The surface finish of sintered gears is usually much better than that of cut gears. The tools that are used to make the briquettes must be lapped to a mirror finish to minimize wall friction.

In most cases, a sintered gear goes through the press only once. The pressing time per gear ranges from 2 to about 15 seconds (depending on the gear size and complexity). The sintering is done in conveyorized furnaces. Since the machinery is almost completely automatic, the operators have to do only such things as fill the powder hopper, transfer trays of green briquettes, gauge pieces for size, and remove finished gears. In spite of the fact that iron powder costs from about 30 cents to as much as $4 per pound, gears made by sintering are frequently cheaper than gears of comparable strength and quality made by other processes. The tools required to sinter gears are very costly but are capable of making a large number of parts. Favorable costs for sintered gears are obtained only when there is enough production to liquidate tool costs adequately. The breakeven quantity may vary from about 20,000 to 50,000 pieces (depending on the complexity of the tools).

5.22 Cold-Drawn Gears and Rolled Worm Threads

Spur pinion teeth may be formed by cold drawing, and worm threads may be rolled. Both these processes are limited in their application. When they can be used, it is possible to get very low costs and a high-strength part.

Cold-drawn pinion stock comes in long rods. These rods have teeth formed in them for their entire length. A rod may be as long as 2.5 meters (8 ft) with a diameter as small as 6 mm (1/4 in.). The pinion rod is chucked in automatic or semiautomatic lathes. Short pinions are rapidly cut off the rod. The pinion may be formed with shaft extensions by turning off the teeth for a distance on each end, or the pinion may be drilled and cut off as a disc with a hole in it to permit mounting on a shaft.

Cold-drawn pinions may be made of any material that has good cold-drawing properties. Carbon steel, stainless steel, phosphor bronze, and many other metals can be used to cold-draw pinions. The extruding operation of making pinion rod is done hot. Only soft, nonferrous metals like brass, aluminum, and bronze can be used for extruding.

Both the cold drawing and the extruding processes use dies to form the pinion teeth.

Pinions from about 3 mm (1/8 in.) to about 25 mm (1 in.) pitch diameter can be made by cold drawing or extruding. The number of teeth should not be less than about 15 nor more than about 24. Tooth size may range from 0.25 module (100 pitch) to 1 module (24 pitch). The teeth should be designed with at least 20° pressure angle and enough addendum to avoid undercut. Sharp corners have to be avoided. The tooth contour should have a full-radius root fillet and a *full radius* at the outside diameter.

The time required to make pinions by the cold-drawing or extrusion process is essentially the time required to cut off each pinion. This ranges from about 2 to 12 seconds, depending on the shaft extensions required and the diameter of the part. The time required to make the teeth is the time required to pull the rod stock through the dies.

Worm threads may be made by cold rolling. The process is very rapid, and it produces a very smooth, work-hardened surface which is quite similar

TABLE 5.35 Typical Production Time to Roll Worm Threads

Pitch diameter		Linear pitch		Threaded length		Pieces per minute	
mm	in.	mm	in.	mm	in.	Hand-fed	Automatic
6.5	0.250	1.2	0.050	9.5	3/8	48	100
9.5	0.375	2.0	0.075	12.5	1/2	48	130
12.5	0.500	2.5	0.100	19	3/4	48	150

to that produced in cold-drawn pinions. Raw stock of 180 HB, for instance, will have a surface hardness equivalent to about 260 HB after rolling. The surface finish may be in the range of 0.25 μm (10 μin.) to 0.75 μm (30 μin.).

The rolling process exerts great pressure on the worm blank. To get a straight worm, it is necessary to use a tooth depth that is not greater than about one-sixth of the outside diameter. To get a satisfactory profile, the worm should have a normal pressure angle of 20° or more. There should be a generous radius in the root fillet and on the thread crest. Lead angles should not exceed 25°.

There is some springback of metal after rolling, and the die used will have a slight generating action because of its finite diameter. To get a symmetrical worm-thread profile of the desired shape, it is often necessary to make the shape of the die slightly different from the shape of the spaces between worm threads.

The time required to roll threads may be estimated from Table 5.35.

chapter 6

Design of Tools to Make Gear Teeth

The design of gear-cutting tools is not necessarily a problem of the gear designer. Usually gear-manufacturing organizations and gear-tool companies will handle the design of tools to make gears.

It often happens, though, that the gear designer has to help out on the tool design. Perhaps a special gear is needed which cannot be readily obtained with conventional tools. Perhaps some work on tool design will show that changes should be made in the gear design to facilitate the tooling. In many cases there is the problem of choosing the proper size or type of tool to best fulfill the requirements of the gear design. Still another problem is the case where tools are on hand from a previous job and someone has to determine whether or not a new design can use these tools.

In this chapter we shall take up some of the more common tool-design problems. Data and calculation methods will be shown so that—if need be—the gear engineer can calculate the dimensions of the cutting tool.

The tool-design data shown in this chapter are of necessity limited. Many special problems involved in designing and manufacturing tools are not discussed here. The gear designer should, wherever possible, secure the services of competent tool designers who specialize in gear-cutting tools. The material in this chapter is intended only as an aid to the *gear designer*, not as a substitute for the services of a tool designer.

6.1 Shaper Cutters

A variety of kinds and sizes of shaper cutters are available on the market. The rack-type shaper machines use rack cutters on external work and pinion cutters on internal work. The pinion-type shaper machines use pinion-shaped cutters on both external and internal gears.

External spur gears usually use a disc type of pinion shaper cutter. Figure 6.1 shows a typical disc-type cutter.

For internal gears, it is frequently necessary to use such small cutters that the disc construction cannot be used. The smallest cutters are usually made shank type. Figure 6.1 shows some typical shaper cutters and their nomenclature. Table 6.1 shows the largest number of cutter teeth that can normally be used with different numbers of internal gear teeth.

There are no official trade standards on shaper-cutter dimensions. Unofficially, though, all the manufacturers are able and willing to work to essentially the same dimensions and tolerances. Table 6.2 shows the most commonly used dimensions for disc and shank cutters.

Shaper cutters frequently have small enough numbers of teeth to cause the base circle to come high on the tooth flank. The region below the base circle may be left as a simple radial flank, or it may be filled in. The filled-in design can be used to break the top corner of the gear tooth being cut. Shaper cutters can be made with a protuberance at the tip. The protuberance cuts an undercut at the root of the gear tooth. This provides a desirable relief for a shaving tool. The protuberance design is also used in some cases to permit the sides of gear teeth to be ground without having to grind the root fillet.

There are a variety of special features that can be provided—and are frequently needed—in shaper-cutter teeth. Figure 6.2 illustrates six different special features.

Figure 6.3 shows some of the design details of a disc shaper cutter. Note that the face of the cutter is shown with a 5° angle. Roughing cutters sometimes have a top face angle as high as 10°. The sides of the cutter have a side clearance of about 2°. The top of the tooth also has a clearance angle. When the pressure angle is 20°, this angle is made about 1.5 times as much as the side clearance angle. The clearance angles and the top face angle are all necessary to make the shaper cutter an efficient metal-cutting tool.

Shaper cutters for finishing work are usually made to a very high degree of precision. Although there are no AGMA standard tolerances for shaper

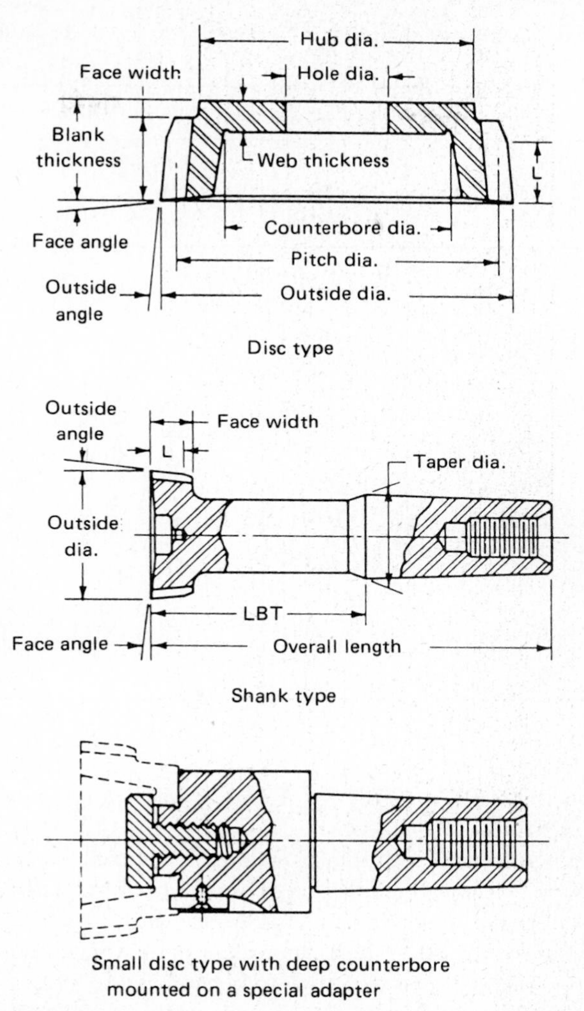

FIG. 6.1 Typical types of shaper cutters and their nomenclature. *(Courtesy of Fellows Corp., Emhart Machinery Group, Springfield, VT, U.S.A.)*

cutters, the standard tolerances of individual tool companies are generally close to being the same. Table 6.3 shows the tolerances that have been published by Barber Colman for five levels of shaper-cutter quality. All values shown are in ten-thousandths of an inch.

Figure 6.4 shows how a shaper cutter cuts an internal gear. The cutter has external teeth and must be small enough to not destroy the corners of

TABLE 6.1 Maximum Number of Shaper-Cutter Teeth for Different Internal Gears

No. of internal teeth	Maximum number teeth in cutter			
	14.5° PA, full depth	20° PA, full depth	20° PA stub, 25° PA full depth	30° PA, fillet root splines
16	—	—	—	9
20	—	—	—	13
24	—	—	10	17
28	—	—	11	21
32	—	10	12	25
36	—	13	14	29
40	14	17	18	33
44	16	21	23	37
48	18	25	27	41
52	21	29	32	45
56	24	34	36	49
60	27	38	40	53
64	30	42	45	57
68	33	46	49	61
72	36	50	53	65
80	44	58	62	73

Note: PA = pressure angle

the internal teeth. See Table 6.1 for the maximum number of cutter teeth that can be used.

Shaper cutters are normally made *external*. They can, however, be made *internal*. Figure 6.5 shows a comparison of an external and an internal shaper cutter. (The internal cutter is often called an *enveloping* cutter.)

When the cutters are small in diameter for the tooth size, they are made integral with a shank. If the face width to be cut is wide, the shank has to be rather long and sturdy. Figure 6.6 shows some shank cutters of rugged design for wider face gears.

Helical gears may be cut with shaper cutters provided that the cutter has an appropriate helix angle and the shaping machine has a helical guide of appropriate lead to twist the cutter as it strokes back and forth. Ordinarily, helical gears are cut with shaper cutters which are sharpened normal to the helix of the cutter tooth. If the helix angle is low, the teeth may be sharpened in the transverse section. Figure 6.7 shows both types.

Herringbone gears of the continuous-tooth type must be cut with a pair of shaper cutters working together. To make the cutting match from both sides, it is necessary to use a cutter with the top face ground normal to the cutter

TABLE 6.2 Typical Dimensions for Shaper Cutters

Tooth size		Approximate pitch diameter		Width		Bore		Counterbore	
Module	Diametral pitch	mm	in.	mm	in.	mm	in.	mm	in.
				Disc type					
9 to 10	$2\frac{1}{2}$ to $2\frac{3}{4}$	150 to 175	6 to 7	32	$1\frac{1}{4}$	70	$2\frac{3}{4}$	105	$4\frac{1}{8}$
2.5 to 6.5	4 to 10	100	4	22	$\frac{7}{8}$	45	$1\frac{3}{4}$	65	$2\frac{9}{16}$
2.5 to 6.5	4 to 10	100	4	22	$\frac{7}{8}$	32	$1\frac{1}{4}$	65	$2\frac{9}{16}$
2.5 to 5	5 to 10	75	3	22	$\frac{7}{8}$	32	$1\frac{1}{4}$	52	$2\frac{1}{16}$
1.7 to 5	5 to 14	75	3	17	$\frac{11}{16}$	32	$1\frac{1}{4}$	52	$2\frac{1}{16}$
1 to 1.6	16 to 24	75	3	22	$\frac{7}{8}$	32	$1\frac{1}{4}$	52	$2\frac{1}{16}$
0.5 to 1.4	18 to 48	75	3	14	$\frac{9}{16}$	32	$1\frac{1}{4}$	52	$2\frac{1}{16}$
				Shank type					
				Shank diameter, large end					
				mm		in.			
2.5 to 3.5	7 to 10	38	$1\frac{1}{2}$	17		$\frac{11}{16}$			
1.6 to 2.3	11 to 16	30	$1\frac{3}{16}$	14		$\frac{9}{16}$			
0.5 to 1.4	18 to 48	25	1	11		$\frac{7}{16}$			

axis. This makes the top face angle 0°, and it makes one side of the cutter tooth have an acute angle and the other side an obtuse angle. These features do not aid the cutting action of the tool, but they are necessary to produce the continuous tooth. Figure 6.8 shows an example of these cutters. Note that a special sharpening technique has produced a good cutting edge even on the obtuse-angle side.

Helical shaper cutters must have the same normal pitch and the same normal pressure angle as the gear they are cutting. Since the axis of the gear and that of the cutter are parallel, the cutter transverse pitch and transverse pressure angle are also equal to those of the gear. The relation of the *hand* of *helix* is as follows:

External gear:
- RH cutter for LH gear
- LH cutter for RH gear

Internal gear:
- RH cutter for RH gear
- LH cutter for LH gear

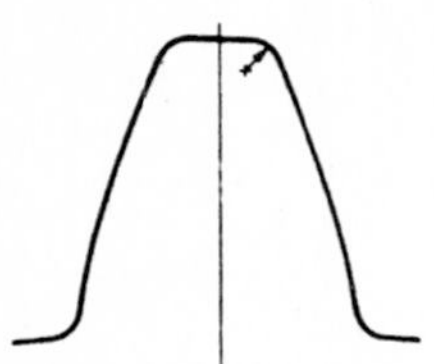

Radius corners
Corners of cutter teeth are radiused to produce a controlled fillet in the root corners of the gear being generated — adds strength to gear and improves tool life.

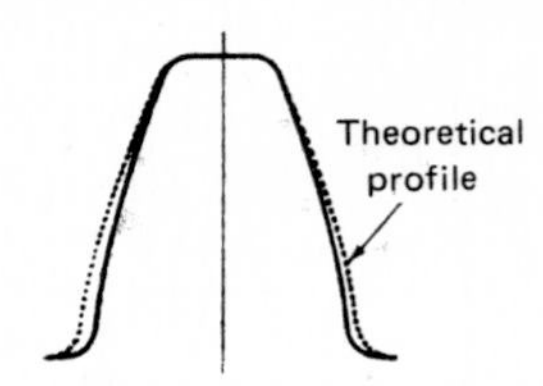

Pressure angle increment
Cutter tooth profile is ground to a slightly lower pressure angle to provide for a constantly increasing amount of stock from root to tip of gear generated — another method of providing relief for subsequent finishing operations.

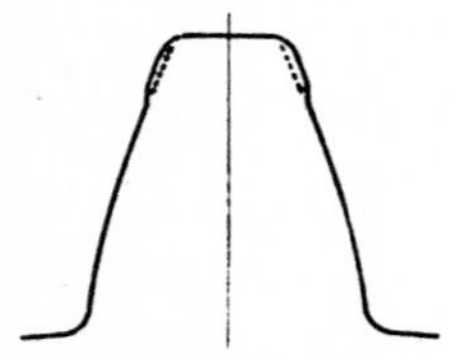

Protuberance tip
Cutter tooth profile is built up on the tip to provide an undercut near the root of the gear being generated — provides relief for subsequent finishing operations.

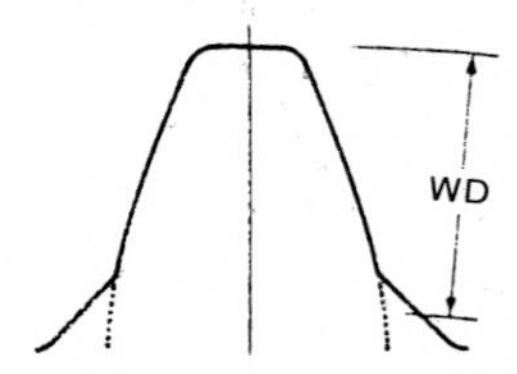

Chambering or semitopping
Root of cutter is filled in to generate a sharp corner break or chamfer on the tips of the gear — minimizes tip build-up during heat treatment due to shaving burrs and nicks incurred in handling.

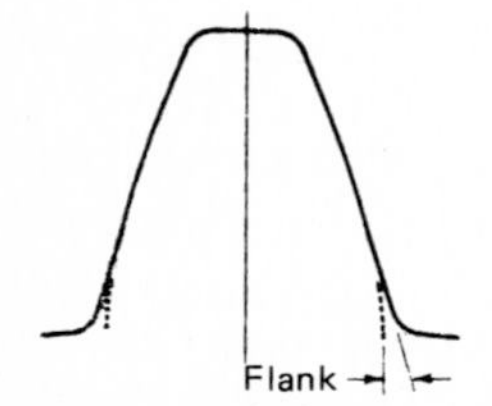

Modifying flank for tip relief
Root or cutter is filled in more gradually than chamfering cutter — removes a small amount of profile from tops of gear teeth — often desirable in high speed gears to minimize noise and heavy tip bearing resulting from tooth deflection under heavy loads.

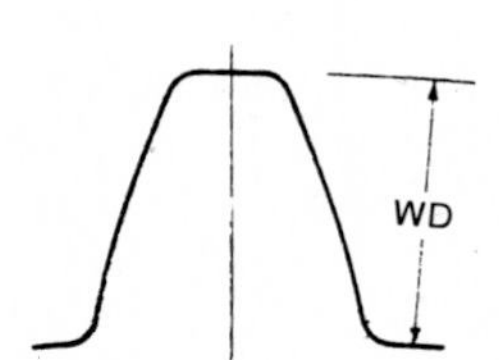

Topping
Cutter tooth depth is ground equal to the whole depth (WD) of the gear tooth. The outside diameter of the gear is "topped" to size when the teeth are cut: More frequently used for fine pitch gearing.

FIG. 6.2 Special features that can be provided in shaper-cutter teeth. *(Courtesy of Fellows Corp., Emhart Machinery Group, Springfield, VT, U.S.A.)*

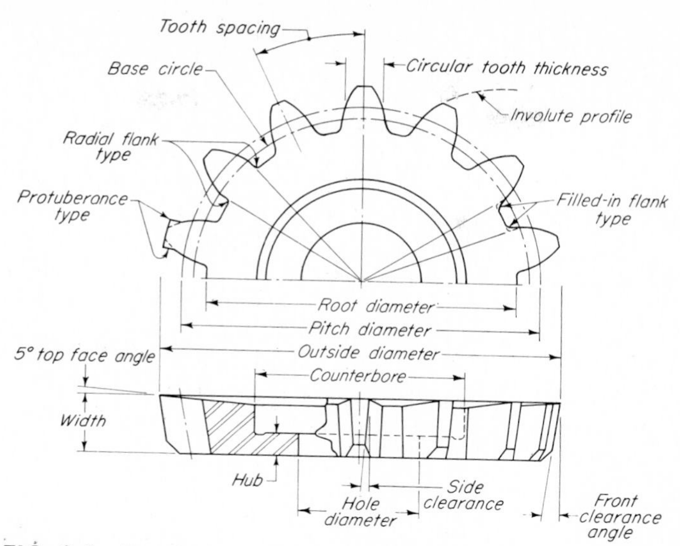

FIG. 6.3 Design details of disc shaper cutter. *(Courtesy of Illinois Tool Works, Chicago, IL, U.S.A.)*

The helix angle that a shaper cutter produces depends on both the lead of the guide and the number of cutter teeth. The helix of the cutter must also agree with the helix angle being cut, or serious "cutter rub" will occur. The formula for the relation of cutter teeth to lead of guide is

$$\frac{\text{No. of teeth in cutter}}{\text{Lead of guide}} = \frac{\text{no. of teeth in gear}}{\text{lead of gear}} \tag{6.1}$$

Shaper cutters do not usually cut the same whole depth throughout their life. A shaper cutter can be designed with a front clearance angle that has such a relation to the side clearance angle that a *certain number* of teeth may be cut to an exact depth and thickness for the life of the cutter. However, if this cutter is used to cut gears of substantially larger or smaller numbers of teeth, the whole depth cut will vary slightly from the design value. If a shaper cutter designed to cut an external gear is used to cut an internal gear of the same tooth thickness, the discrepancy in whole depth may be quite appreciable. In many cases, the designer of a shaper cutter does not know all the numbers of teeth that the cutter may have to cut during its life. This leads the designer to make the front clearance angle large enough so that the cutter usually cuts a little extra on the whole depth. It is usually reasoned that the problem of a little extra depth is less than the problem of having the depth too shallow.

In many high-production jobs, it is desirable to design the shaper cutter

TABLE 6.3*a* Shaper-Cutter Table for Sizes and Tolerances
(Radial Runout and Profile Tolerances, Spur and Helical)

Quality number	Normal diametral pitch	Pitch diameter, in.																Sharpening tolerance side clearance		
		0.5–1.999		2–2.999		3–3.999		4–4.999		5–5.999		6–7.999		8–9.999		10–11.9				
		R	P	R	P	R	P	R	P	R	P	R	P	R	P	R	P	1°	2°	3°
1	1–1.999											38	31	40	31	41	32	280	140	91
	2–2.999									27	21	29	22	30	23	32	23	170	87	58
	3–4.999					18	15	19	15	20	15	22	15	24	15	25	16	130	65	43
	5–7.999	13	11	15	11	16	12	18	12	19	12	20	13	22	13			120	60	40
	8–13.999	12	9	14	9	15	10	16	10	17	10	18	10					116	58	38
	14–19.999	10	7	11	7.5	13	7.5	14	7.5	14	8							65	33	22
2	1–1.999											27	22	29	23	30	23	150	75	50
	2–2.999									19	15	19	15	20	16	22	16	87	43	29
	3–4.999					12	10	13	10	13	10	14	11	15	11	16	11	70	35	23
	5–7.999	10	8	11	8.5	11	8.5	11	8.5	12	8.5	13	9	13	9			54	27	18
	8–13.999	8	6.5	8.5	7	9	7	9	7	10	7	11	7.5					35	17	12
	14–19.999	6.5	5	7	5	7.5	5.5	8	5.5	8.5	5.5							23	12	8
3	1–1.999											19	16	20	16	21	16	87	44	29
	2–2.999									13	10	13	10	14	11	15	11	64	32	21
	3–4.999					8.5	7	9	7	9.5	7.5	10	7.5	11	7.5	11	8	44	22	15
	5–7.999	7	6	7	6	7.5	6	8	6	8.5	6.5	8.5	6.5	9	6.5			32	16	11
	8–13.999	6	4.5	6	5	6.5	5	7	5	7	5	7.5	5.5					26	13	9
	14–19.999	5	3.5	5	4	5.5	4	5.5	4	6	4							22	11	7
4	1–1.999											14	11	15	12	16	12	52	26	17
	2–2.999									9.5	7.5	10	8	10	8	11	8	35	17	12
	3–4.999					6	5	6	5	6.5	5.5	7	5.5	7	5.5	7.5	5.5	26	13	9
	5–7.999	5	4	5	4	5.5	4	5.5	4.5	6	4.5	6.5	4.5	6.5	5			23	11	8
	8–13.999	4	3.5	4.5	3.5	4.5	3.5	5	4	5	4	5.5	4					17	8	6
	14–19.999	3.5	2.5	4	2.5	4	3	4	3	4.5	3							13	6	4
5	1–1.999											11	8	12	8	13	8.5	46	23	16
	2–2.999									7	5.5	7	5.5	7	5.5	7.5	6	29	15	10
	3–4.999					4.5	3.5	4.5	4	4.5	4	5	4	5	4	5.5	4	15	7	5
	5–7.999	4	3	4	3	4	3	4	3	4	3	4.5	3	4.5	3			11	6	4
	8–13.999	3	2.5	3	2.5	3.5	2.5	3.5	2.5	3.5	2.5	3.5	2.5					10	5	3
	14–19.999	2.5	2	2.5	2	3	2	3	2	3	2							8	4	3

Notes: 1. This table was furnished by Barber Colman Co., Rockford, Illinois, USA, as their recommendation for standard shaper cutter tolerances.

2. R = radial runout (numerator pitch)
P = profile tolerance (denominator pitch)
(All readings are in ten-thousandths of an inch)

TABLE 6.3*b* Shaper-Cutter Table for Sizes and Tolerances
(Adjacent and Nonadjacent Indexing Tolerances, Spur and Helical)

Quality number	Normal diametral pitch	Pitch diameter, in.															
		0.5–1.999		2–2.999		3–3.999		4–4.999		5–5.999		6–7.999		8–9.999		10–11.999	
		A	N	A	N	A	N	A	N	A	N	A	N	A	N	A	N
1	1–1.999											7	21	7.5	22	7.5	22
	2–2.999									6.5	16	6.5	17	6.5	17	7	19
	3–4.999					5	12	5	12	5.5	13	5.5	14	5.5	14	5.5	15
	5–7.999	5	9.5	5	11	5	11	5	12	5.5	12	5.5	13	5.5	13		
	8–13.999	4.5	9	4.5	9.5	4.5	10	4.5	10	5	11	5	12				
	14–19.999	4	7.5	4	8	4	9	4	9	4	9						
2	1–1.999											5	15	5	16	5	16
	2–2.999									4.5	11	4.5	11	4.5	12	4.5	13
	3–4.999					3.5	8	3.5	8	4	8.5	4	9	4	9.5	4	9.5
	5–7.999	3.5	7	3.5	7.5	3.5	7.5	3.5	7.5	4	8	4	8.5	4	9		
	8–13.999	3	6	3	6	3	6.5	3	6.5	3.5	7	3.5	7.5				
	14–19.999	2.5	5	2.5	5	3	5	3	6	3	6						
3	1–1.999											3.5	11	3.5	11	4	11
	2–2.999									3	7.5	3	7.5	3.5	8.5	3.5	9
	3–4.999					3	6	3	6.5	3	6.5	3	6.5	3	7	3	7
	5–7.999	3	5.5	3	5.5	3	5.5	3	6	3	6	3	6	3	6.5		
	8–13.999	2.5	5	2.5	5	2.5	5	2.5	5	2.5	5	2.5	5				
	14–19.999	2	4	2	4	2	4	2	4	2	4						
4	1–1.999											2.5	7.5	3	8.5	3	9
	2–2.999									2.5	6	2.5	6	2.5	6	2.5	6.5
	3–4.999					2	4	2	4	2	4.5	2	4.5	2	4.5	2	4.5
	5–7.999	2	4	2	4	2	4	2	4	2	4	2	4.5	2	4.5		
	8–13.999	1.5	3	1.5	3	1.5	3	1.5	3.5	1.5	3.3	2	4				
	14–19.999	1.5	3	1.5	3	1.5	3	1.5	3	1.5	3						
5	1–1.999											2	6	2	6.5	2	6.5
	2–2.999									2	4.5	2	4.5	2	4.5	2	4.5
	3–4.999					1.5	3	1.5	3	1.5	3	1.5	3.5	1.5	3.5	1.5	3.5
	5–7.999	1.5	3	1.5	3	1.5	3	1.5	3	1.5	3	1.5	3	1.5	3		
	8–13.999	1	2	1	2	1	2.5	1	2.5	1	2.5	1	2.5				
	14–19.999	1	2	1	2	1	2	1	2	1	2						

Notes: 1. This table was furnished by Barber Colman Co., Rockford, Illinois, U.S.A., as their recommendation for standard shaper-cutter tolerances.

2. A = adjacent indexing tolerance
N = nonadjacent indexing tolerance (exclusive of runout)
(All readings are in ten-thousandths of an inch)

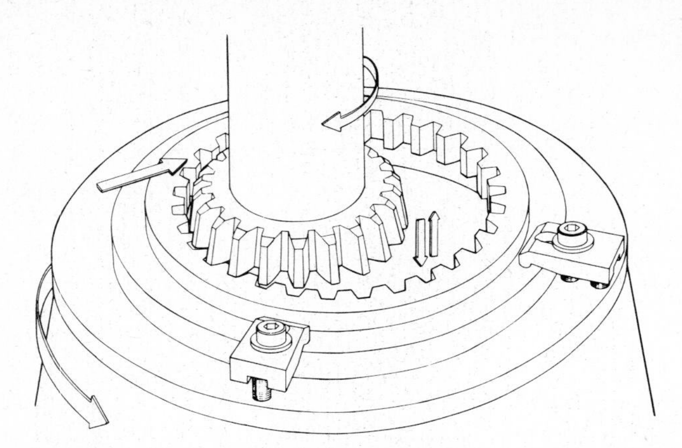

FIG. 6.4 How a shaper cutter cuts an internal gear. *(Courtesy of Fellows Corp., Emhart Machinery Group, Springfield, VT, U.S.A.)*

for a particular gear so that the cutter will do exactly what is wanted throughout its life. This is particularly true when cutters are used to preshave-cut a gear and leave an undercut. The position of the undercut must remain constant within close limits to tie in with the shaving-cutter design.

6.2 Gear Hobs

The gear hob is really a cylindrical worm converted into a cutting tool. Cutting edges are formed by "gashing" the worm with a number of slots.

FIG. 6.5 A comparison of a shaper cutter with external teeth and one with internal teeth. *(Courtesy of Fellows Corp., Emhart Machinery Group, Springfield, VT, U.S.A.)*

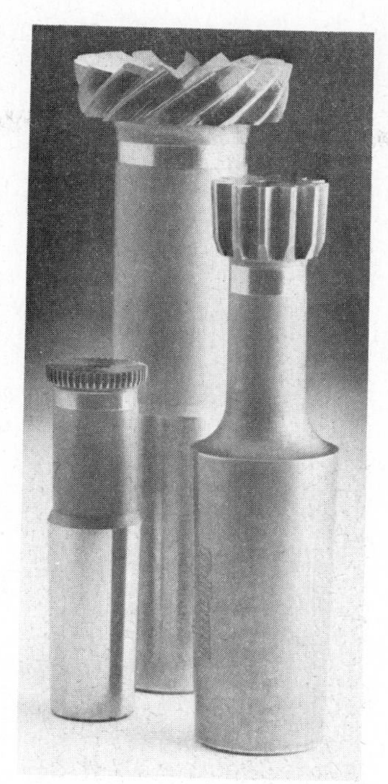

FIG. 6.6 Shank-type cutters for relatively wide face gears. *(Courtesy of Fellows Corp., Emhart Machinery Group, Springfield, VT, U.S.A.)*

FIG. 6.7 Helical-gear cutters for all but low helix angles are sharpened in the normal section. For low helix angles, sharpening may be in the transverse section. *(Courtesy of Fellows Corp., Emhart Machinery Group, Springfield, VT, U.S.A.)*

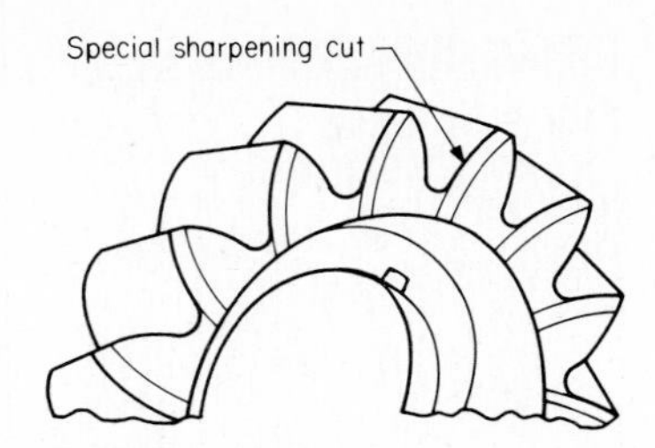

FIG. 6.8 Diagram of top half of a shaper cutter for continuous herringbone teeth. Note special sharpening method which changes original obtuse angle at the corner of the cutter to an angle that will cut.

These slots are usually either *parallel* with the hob axis or *perpendicular* to the worm thread. The teeth of the hob are relieved back of the cutting edge to make an efficient cutting tool. The cutting face may be radial, or it may be given a slight "hook" to improve the cutting action. Usually finishing hobs are radial.

Figure 6.9 shows the design details of a typical spur-gear hob. The involute generating portion of the hob-tooth profile is usually made *straight in the normal section.* Since the thread angle is usually low, this makes the profile come out essentially straight even if the hob is gashed axially instead of normally. Theoretically, the hob should have a slight curvature in its profile to cut a true involute gear. The curvature should correspond to that of an *involute helicoid.* Practically, though, the curvature required is so slight that it is disregarded. Only on multiple-thread hobs of coarse pitch does it become

FIG. 6.9 Typical shell-type hob. *(Courtesy of Barber Colman Co., Rockford, IL, U.S.A.)*

FIG. 6.10 Worm-gear hob with multiple threads and integral with shank. *(Courtesy of Barber Colman Co., Rockford, IL, U.S.A.)*

necessary to grind an involute curve. An involute helicoid may be calculated in the normal section by the method shown in the Dudley and Poritsky AGMA paper P241. (See Ref. 132 at the end of the book.)

Hobs may be made with straight bores, tapered bores, or integral with hob arbors. The *shell* type of hob with a straight bore is the most commonly used type. Taper-bore hobs require more wall thickness than shell hobs. Some companies prefer the taper-bore hob because of the more rigid mounting which the taper provides. Integral-shank hobs are expensive. They are used when the hob diameter has to be made so small that a big enough hole cannot be put through the hob. Very small hob diameters may be required when hob runout space or the gap between helices is limited. Worm-gear hobs sometimes have to be very small to match the diameter of small worms. See Fig. 6.10.

Table 6.4 shows the nominal sizes of shell-type hobs. Taper hobs generally require a smaller bore or a larger diameter than the values given in Table 6.4. Where extra rigidity is required, it is often desirable to put in a larger-diameter hob and support the hob on a larger arbor. For instance, a 10-pitch hob ordinarily has a $1\frac{1}{4}$-in. bore and a 3-in. outside diameter. In cutting high-speed gears to extreme precision, it is desirable to use a 4-in. hob with $1\frac{3}{4}$-in. bore for 10 pitch.

Table 6.4 shows that multiple-thread hobs require larger bores and diameters than single-thread hobs.

Table 6.5 shows some of the commonly accepted tolerances for different classes of hobs. Although about 20 items may be specified in a hob tolerance sheet, the three shown in Table 6.5 are the most important to the user. Lead variation in one turn and hob-profile error both directly affect the profile accuracy of the gear being cut. Other commonly used hob tolerances only indirectly affect the accuracy of the gear.

Helical-gear hobs require a taper when the gear exceeds about 30° helix angle. Even below this angle, a taper is helpful if the gear has over 150 teeth.

TABLE 6.4*a* Typical Dimensions of Shell Hobs, English Dimensions

Diametral pitch	No. of threads	Hole, in.	Outside diameter, in.	Length, in.	Keyway, in.
1	1 or 2	$2\frac{1}{2}$	$10\frac{3}{4}$	15	$\frac{5}{8} \times \frac{5}{16}$
2	1	$1\frac{1}{2}$	$5\frac{3}{4}$	8	$\frac{3}{8} \times \frac{3}{16}$
	2	$1\frac{1}{2}$	$6\frac{1}{2}$	8	$\frac{3}{8} \times \frac{3}{16}$
4	1	$1\frac{1}{4}$	4	4	$\frac{1}{4} \times \frac{1}{8}$
	2	$1\frac{1}{2}$	5	4	$\frac{3}{8} \times \frac{3}{16}$
	3	$1\frac{1}{2}$	$5\frac{1}{2}$	4	$\frac{3}{8} \times \frac{3}{16}$
5	1	$1\frac{1}{4}$	$3\frac{1}{2}$	$3\frac{1}{2}$	$\frac{1}{4} \times \frac{1}{8}$
	2	$1\frac{1}{2}$	$4\frac{1}{2}$	$3\frac{1}{2}$	$\frac{3}{8} \times \frac{3}{16}$
	3	$1\frac{1}{2}$	5	$3\frac{1}{2}$	$\frac{3}{8} \times \frac{3}{16}$
6	1	$1\frac{1}{4}$	$3\frac{1}{2}$	$3\frac{1}{2}$	$\frac{1}{4} \times \frac{1}{8}$
	2	$1\frac{1}{2}$	$4\frac{1}{2}$	$3\frac{1}{2}$	$\frac{3}{8} \times \frac{3}{16}$
	3	$1\frac{1}{2}$	5	$3\frac{1}{2}$	$\frac{3}{8} \times \frac{3}{16}$
8	1	$1\frac{1}{4}$	3	3	$\frac{1}{4} \times \frac{1}{8}$
	2	$1\frac{1}{4}$	$3\frac{3}{4}$	3	$\frac{1}{4} \times \frac{1}{8}$
	3	$1\frac{1}{4}$	4	3	$\frac{1}{4} \times \frac{1}{8}$
10	1	$1\frac{1}{4}$	3	3	$\frac{1}{4} \times \frac{1}{8}$
	2	$1\frac{1}{4}$	$3\frac{1}{2}$	3	$\frac{1}{4} \times \frac{1}{8}$
	3	$1\frac{1}{4}$	$3\frac{3}{4}$	3	$\frac{1}{4} \times \frac{1}{8}$
12	1	$1\frac{1}{4}$	$2\frac{3}{4}$	$2\frac{3}{4}$	$\frac{1}{4} \times \frac{1}{8}$
16	1	$1\frac{1}{4}$	$2\frac{1}{2}$	$2\frac{1}{2}$	$\frac{1}{4} \times \frac{1}{8}$
20	1	$\frac{3}{4}$	$1\frac{7}{8}$	$1\frac{7}{8}$	$\frac{1}{8} \times \frac{1}{16}$
32	1	$\frac{3}{4}$	$1\frac{1}{2}$	$1\frac{1}{8}$	$\frac{1}{8} \times \frac{1}{16}$
100	1	$\frac{3}{4}$	$1\frac{3}{8}$	$\frac{5}{8}$	—

Figure 6.11 shows a typical hob for a helical gear of 250 teeth and 35° helix angle.

The design of the gap between helices on a double helical gear and the hob design are tied to each other. The gap must be wide enough to accommodate both the tapered and full parts of the hob. An *exact* calculation of gap width is quite difficult, but fortunately an approximate solution is usually close enough. The following formula is usually accurate within plus or minus 5 percent:

$$\text{Min. gap} = [h_o(d_o - h_o)]^{0.5} \cos \beta_o + \frac{z_o p_n \sin \beta_o}{\cos \gamma} + \frac{x' \sin \beta_o}{\tan \alpha_n} \quad \text{metric} \quad (6.2a)$$

$$= [h(D_H - h)]^{0.5} \cos \psi_1 + \frac{n_1 p_n \sin \psi_1}{\cos \lambda} + \frac{x' \sin \psi_1}{\tan \phi_n} \quad \text{English} \quad (6.2b)$$

where h_o, h = depth of cut (finishing cut may be less depth than whole depth)

TABLE 6.4*b* Typical Dimensions of Shell Hobs, German Dimensions

Module	Hole, mm	Outside diameter, mm	Length, mm
1	22	50	44
1.25	22	50	44
1.5	22	56	51
1.75	22	56	51
2	27	63	60
2.25	27	70	70
2.5	27	70	70
2.75	27	70	70
3	32	80	85
3.25	32	80	85
3.5	32	80	85
3.75	32	90	94
4	32	90	94
4.5	32	90	94
5	32	100	104
5.5	32	100	104
6	40	110	126
6.5	40	110	126
7	40	110	126
8	40	125	156
9	40	125	156
10	40	140	188
11	50	160	200
12	50	170	215
13	50	180	230
14	50	190	245
15	60	200	258
16	60	210	271
18	60	230	293
20	60	250	319

Notes: 1. Hobs have an end slot rather than a keyway (for the drive).
2. These data are based on DIN 8002, single-thread hobs.

h_t = total depth of cut

d_o, D_H = hob outside diameter (at point doing the cutting)

$\beta_o = \beta - \gamma$, β = helix angle of gear, degrees

$\psi_1 = \psi - \lambda$, ψ = helix angle of gear, degrees

TABLE 6.5 Summary of Hob Lead, Profile, and Tooth Thickness Tolerances

Item	No. of threads	Class	Tooth size											
			1 module (25 pitch)		1.5 module (16 pitch)		2.5 module (10 pitch)		5 module (5 pitch)		8 module (3 pitch)		25 module (1 pitch)	
			μm	10^{-4} in.	μm	10^{-4} in.	μm	10^{-4} in.	μm	10^{-4} in.	μm	10^{-4} in.	μm	10^{-4} in.
Lead variation in one axial pitch of the hob	1	AA	5	2	5	2	8	3	10	4	20	8	—	—
		A	10	4	10	4	13	5	15	6	25	10	64	25
		B	15	6	15	6	18	7	23	9	43	17	90	35
		C	20	8	20	8	23	9	28	11	56	22	115	45
		D	40	16	46	18	50	20	64	25	100	40	150	60
	Multiple	A	10	4	10	4	13	5	15	6	25	10	64	25
		B	18	7	18	7	20	8	25	10	43	17	90	35
		C	25	10	25	10	30	12	38	15	56	22	115	45
		D	—	—	46	18	50	20	64	25	100	40	150	60
Profile error in involute-generating portion of hob tooth (tip relief modification excluded)	1	AA	4	1.7	4	1.7	4	1.7	4	1.7	5	2	—	—
		A	5	2	5	2	5	2	5	2	8	3	25	10
		B	8	3	8	3	8	3	10	4	13	5	40	16
		C	8	3	8	3	8	3	10	4	25	10	64	25
		D	13	5	15	6	20	8	30	12	75	30	200	80
	2	A	5	2	5	2	5	2	8	3	13	5	30	12
		B	8	3	8	3	8	3	13	5	18	7	46	18
		C	8	3	8	3	8	3	13	5	28	11	70	27
		D	—	—	18	7	20	8	30	12	75	30	200	80
	3 or 4	A	5	2	5	2	8	3	8	3	13	5	38	15
		B	8	3	8	3	10	4	13	5	18	7	50	20
		C	8	3	8	3	10	4	13	5	28	11	70	27
		D	—	—	18	7	20	8	30	12	75	30	200	80
Tooth thickness error (minus only)	1 or multiple	AA	25	10	25	10	25	10	25	10	38	15	—	—
		A	25	10	25	10	25	10	25	10	38	15	75	30
		B	25	10	25	10	25	10	25	10	38	15	75	30
		C	38	15	38	15	38	15	38	15	50	20	90	35
		D	50	20	50	20	50	20	50	20	75	30	100	40

Notes: 1. 10^{-4} in. = ten-thousandths of an inch.
2. Hobs are classified by dimensional tolerances as follows:

Classes AA and A = precision ground
Class B = commercial ground
Class C = accurate unground
Class D = commercial unground

$$\gamma, \lambda = \text{lead angle of hob, degrees}$$

$$\sin \gamma, \sin \lambda = \frac{\text{no. hob threads} \times \text{normal circular pitch}}{\pi \times \text{hob pitch diameter}}$$

$$p_n = \text{normal circular pitch}$$

$$z_o, n_1 = \text{number of pitches from hobbing center}$$

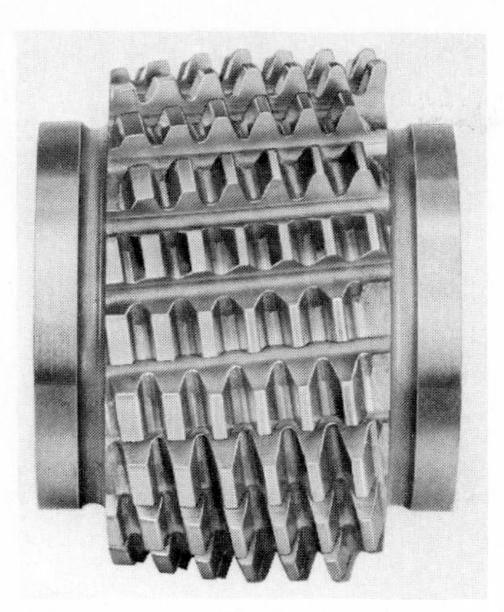

FIG. 6.11 Multiple-thread hob. *(Courtesy of General Electric Co., Lynn, MA, U.S.A.)*

x' = whichever is larger: gear addendum, or gear dedendum minus clearance

α_n, ϕ_n = normal pressure angle, degrees

All linear dimensions above are in millimeters for Eq. (6.2*a*) or in inches for Eq. (6.2*b*).

Figure 6.12 shows schematically how this formula works. The hob must be fed out into the gap between helices until it stops cutting on the helix it was cutting. If it is a roughing cut, it is not necessary to completely stop cutting—the finish cut can take off a little extra at the tooth ends. Frequently large gears are rough-cut to full depth and then finish-cut with a smaller hob and a slightly shallower depth.

As shown in the sketch, the *generating zone* of the hob must just clear the end of the helix. The minimum gap width is determined by the distance needed to keep either the *first full tooth* or *any of the tapered teeth* from hitting the opposite helix. Usually the hob is centered $1\frac{1}{2}$ pitches back from the first full tooth. This makes n_1 equal to 1.5 for the first solution. Since the tooth is a full tooth, h equals h_t, and D_H is the full outside diameter. [This paragraph and Fig. 6.12 are given in English symbols only. The metric equivalents are easily evident in Eq. (6.2).]

After the gap for the first full tooth has been determined, a check should be made to see if any of the tapered teeth require additional gap. As shown in Fig. 6.12, the first tapered tooth has a value of $n_1 = 2.5$, and $h = h_t - a_1$. A series of calculations can be made for different tapered teeth to explore the cutting action of all the tapered teeth.

Sometimes it is desirable to lay out the values calculated, as shown in Fig.

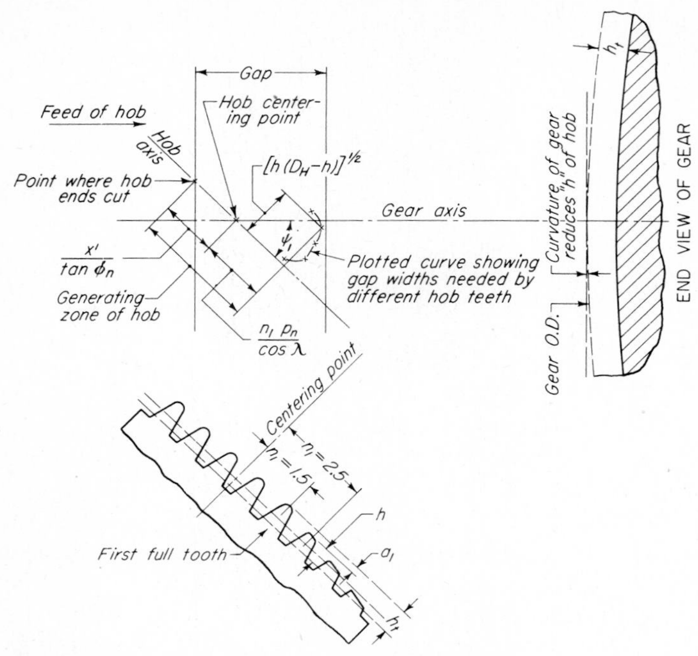

FIG. 6.12 Diagram of hob in gap between helices.

6.12. The curvature of the gear is not taken into account in Eq. (6.2). An end view will show whether the point at which the hob tends to hit the opposite helix is off-center enough to permit the value of h to be reduced an appreciable amount to compensate for the curvature of the gear.

In designing a tapered hob, it is usually desirable to use such an amount of taper that the tapered teeth cut a gap width that is either just equal to that of the first full tooth or *slightly greater* than that of the first full tooth. This ensures that the taper is really doing some work. If the tapered teeth are so short that they do not require as much gap as the first full tooth, they will still do some cutting on the sides of the gear teeth, but they will not be removing the amount of stock that they should.

The end of the hob to be tapered for helical-gear cutting is opposite to that which is sometimes used on large spur gears. For helical gears the rules are:

Conventional hobbing:
- RH hob tapered on LH end, top coming
- LH hob tapered on RH end, top coming

Climb hobbing:
- RH hob tapered on RH end, top coming
- LH hob tapered on LH end, top coming

Worm gears can be hobbed on the same machines used to hob spur and helical gears. Even the same kind of hobs can be used, provided that the work is of the same diameter and tooth profile as the hob. Usually, though, special hobs are required for worm gears. Worm gears which mesh with multiple-threaded worms need *tangential* feed hobbers to eliminate generating flats on the tooth profiles. The tangential hobber has a slow feed in a direction tangent to the gear being cut. The effect of this feed is to shift the center position of the hob continuously during the cut. This shifting makes the hob teeth move into different positions with respect to the gear. The hob cuts as if it had an almost infinite number of cutting edges.

Figure 6.13 shows a worm-gear hob which has just finished cutting a single-enveloping worm gear. Note the long taper on the hob. At the start of the cut, only the taper teeth engage the work. At the end of the cut, the gear is engaging only the full-depth hob teeth. This kind of hob is often called (for obvious reasons) a "pineapple" hob.

The end of the hob to be tapered depends on the direction of feed used on the hobber. For most hobbers, the direction is such as to require:

RH hob to be tapered on RH end

LH hob to be tapered on LH end

There is no handy way of figuring what amount of taper will give the best results on worm-gear hobs. A common practice is to make the length of taper about three times the whole depth and the depth of taper about three-fourths of the whole depth.

FIG. 6.13 Worm-gear hob and worm gear. *(Courtesy of General Electric Co., Lynn, MA, U.S.A.)*

Pineapple hobs are efficient cutting tools but rather expensive. Where production requirements are not great, a much simpler hob can be used if the tangential feed is slowed down. In fact, the tangential type of hobber can generate a complete worm gear with only a single cutting tooth. This scheme has been used quite successfully with cemented-carbide "fly" cutters. With high-speed tool-steel fly cutters, the single cutting edge often gets dull before it finishes a gear. This has led to the use of a hob which has just one tooth for each worm thread. Figure 6.14 shows such a hob. It has five teeth, corresponding to five worm threads. This kind of hob has been called a "pancake" hob.

Worm-gear hobs—no matter what kind—must have about the same diameter as the worm they imitate. Since the hob gets smaller in diameter as it is sharpened, it is necessary to make the new worm-gear hob slightly larger than the worm. The amount of oversize to use has not as yet been standardized. Since any oversize produces error in the gear, the amount of oversize is a function of the amount of error that may be tolerated. If no oversize is used, the hob might cut perfectly when new, but it would have to be scrapped after one sharpening unless the hobbing center distance was held constant and the hob was allowed to cut shallower and thicker teeth after each sharpening. The latter expedient is helpful in some jobs where worms and gears may be sized to fit each other, but it is an awkward way of making gears when the job requires all parts to be essentially the same size and quality.

The amount of hob oversize boils down to a compromise between accuracy and hob life. The more oversize, the more hob sharpenings possible before the hob reaches its "spent" diameter. Usually a hob is considered

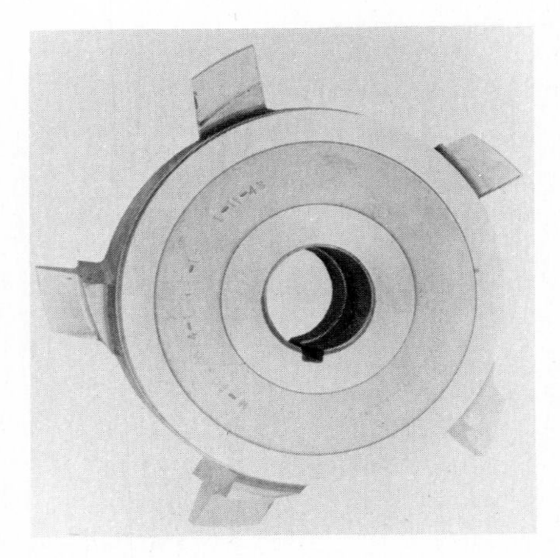

FIG. 6.14 Pancake worm-gear hob.

spent when its diameter is less than that of the worm. *Undersize* damages the accuracy of a hob much more than oversize.

The exact calculation of the effects of hob oversize is too complicated a problem to be treated in this book. For general applications where a quick yardstick is needed, the following formula represents a good limit for hob oversize. High precision can usually be obtained when the hob oversize does not exceed the value given by the formula. If the formula is exceeded, the accuracy will probably be in the commercial class (good enough for many jobs, but not good enough for critical jobs). The formula is

Hob oversize

$$= d_0 - d_{p1} = d_{p1}(0.030 - 0.028 \tan \gamma) \frac{15.24}{p_x + 7.62} \qquad \text{metric} \qquad (6.3a)$$

$$= d_H - d = d(0.030 - 0.028 \tan \lambda) \frac{0.600}{p_x + 0.300} \qquad \text{English} \qquad (6.3b)$$

where d_0, d_H = hob pitch diameter in mm, in.
d_{p1}, d = worm pitch diameter in mm, in.
γ, λ = worm lead angle in degrees
p_x = axial pitch (of worm and hob are equal), mm, in.

The cutting edges of the worm-gear hob must have a curvature that will permit them to lie on an imaginary worm surface which has the same profile curvature as the worm. A curvature which corresponds to that which is cut or ground into the worm must be ground into the hob. Since worms used in the United States usually do not have an involute helicoidal shape, calculations of hob profile must be based on the method used to make the worm (see Sec. 6.4).

The details of designing a hob can best be understood by studying some design problems. Figure 6.15 shows the English design data for a preshave spur-gear hob designed for cutting 10-diametral-pitch gears and pinions which will operate at pitch-line speeds up to 10,000 fpm and loads over 1000 lb per in. of face width. The hob has a full-radius tip. It cuts an extra deep tooth of 0.240 in. When cutting standard addendum gears, it produces a gear-tooth thickness of 0.156 in. This thickness and the depth of 0.240 in. remain constant throughout the life of the hob. It will be recalled that shaper cutters do not produce constant thickness and depth when they are used over a range of tooth numbers. The generating action of the hob is such that tooth numbers do not affect the thickness of the tooth it cuts.

The hob has a protuberance of 0.0014 in. After the gear is shaved down to a design thickness of 0.154 to 0.153 in., the undercut caused by the protuberance blends smoothly into the contour of the gear tooth. The location of the protuberance is made high enough on the hob tooth so that only a small amount of shaving will be required to clean up the gear tooth

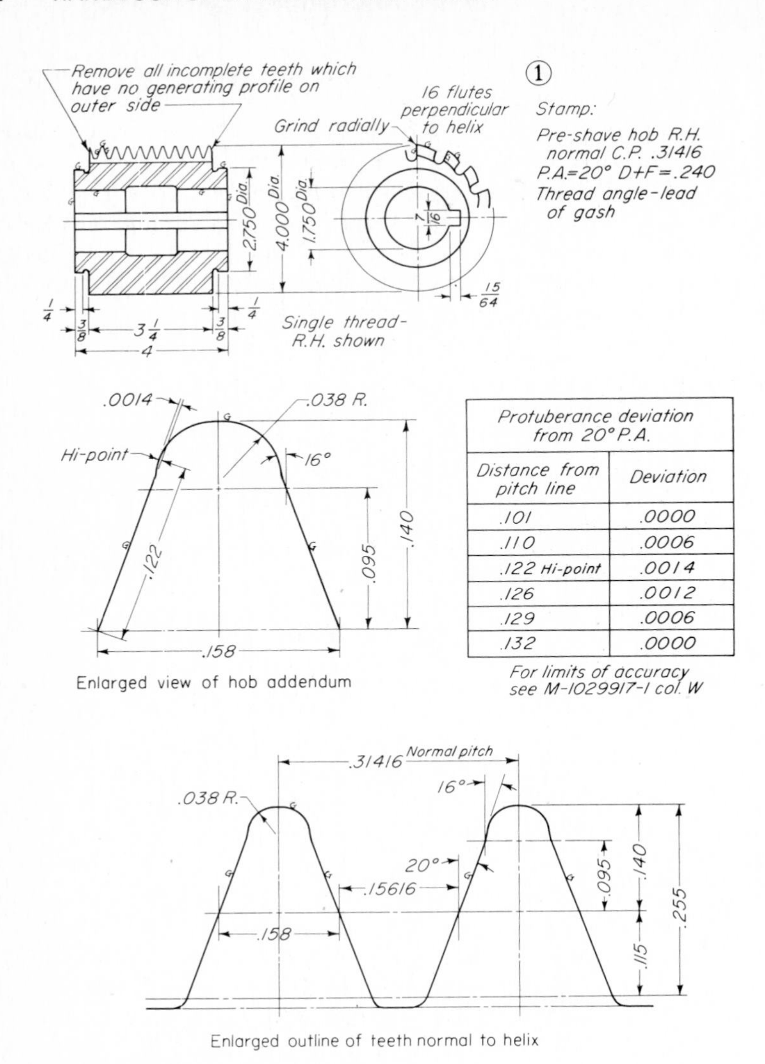

Protuberance deviation from 20° P.A.	
Distance from pitch line	Deviation
.101	.0000
.110	.0006
.122 Hi-point	.0014
.126	.0012
.129	.0006
.132	.0000

FIG. 6.15 Gear hob, preshave.

down to the end of the active part of the involute. Note that the hob is straight for a distance of 0.095 in. above pitch line. Only the first 0.005 in. of the protuberance generates a possible part of the working involute on the gear. The rest of the protuberance cuts in the root fillet of the gear.

The amount of protuberance is controlled mainly by changing the angle on the protuberance. Where 16° is used on this hob, about 18° would be used on a 4-pitch hob with a *Hi-point** of 0.002 in.

**Hi-point* is the point on the protuberance of a hob that cuts the *deepest* undercut on the gear (to be shaved or ground).

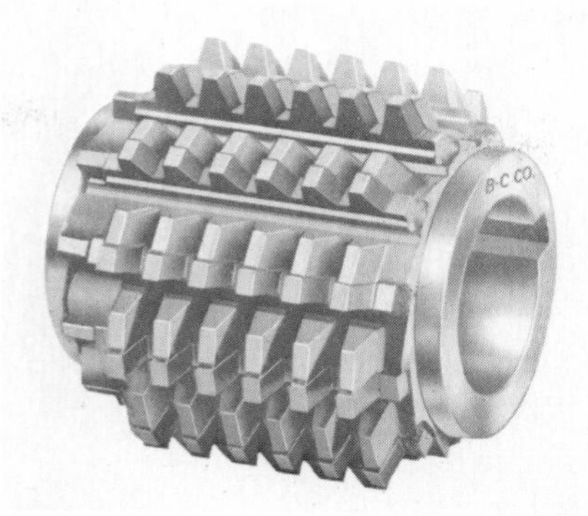

FIG. 6.16 Built-up hob with carbide blades. *(Courtesy of Barber Colman Co., Rockford, IL, U.S.A.)*

In the last 20 years, there have been several important developments in hobs. Three developments that are quite important to the gear industry are these:

A built-up hob. Special hob blades are attached to a body made of less costly material than the blade material.

Special roughing hobs. The special roughing hob is a very efficient tool to remove stock, but it does not produce gear teeth intended to run together.

Skiving hobs. This hob can finish-cut fully hardened gear teeth.

The built-up hobs may have blades brazed to an alloy steel body, or the blades may be mechanically attached. The blade material may be expensive high-speed steel, or it may even be a carbide material. Figure 6.16 shows an example of a built-up hob.

FIG. 6.17 K-Kut roughing hob, U.S. Patent No. 3,892,022. *(Courtesy of Barber Colman Co., Rockford, IL, U.S.A.)*

FIG. 6.18 Dragon roughing hob. *(Courtesy of Azumi Mfg. Co., Osaka, Japan.)*

The larger sizes of built-up hobs may be rebladed. The built-up hob tends to be less expensive (in large sizes) because the body material is not nearly as costly as the blade material. Delivery time may be reduced because a large tool-steel forging is not needed.

FIG. 6.19 Dragon hob roughing a large gear. *(Courtesy of Azumi Mfg. Co., Osaka, Japan.)*

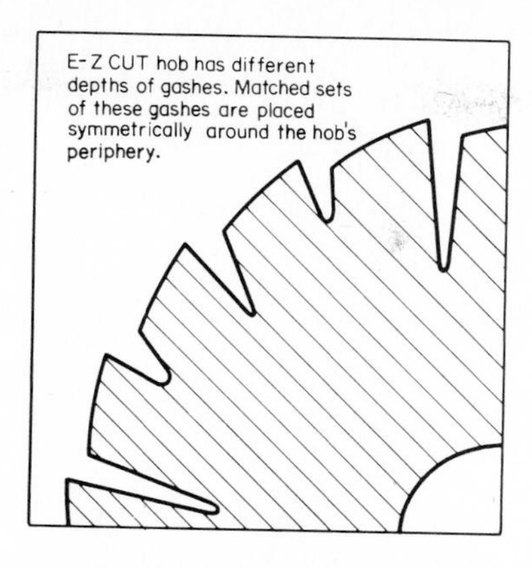

FIG. 6.20 Detail of E-Z Cut hob design, and the E-Z Cut hob. U.S. Patent No. 3,715,789. *(Courtesy of Barber Colman Co., Rockford, IL, U.S.A.)*

The special roughing hobs cut very efficiently. They remove larger chips, and the chips tend to cut and break away in an efficient manner. Figure 6.17 shows a patented K-Kut roughing hob developed by Barber Colman. Figure 6.18 shows the patented roughing hob developed by Azumi, called the Dragon hob. Figure 6.19 shows a Dragon hob cutting a large gear.

The K-Kut hob and the Dragon hob were developed and patented at about the same time. One has a U.S. patent and the other a Japanese

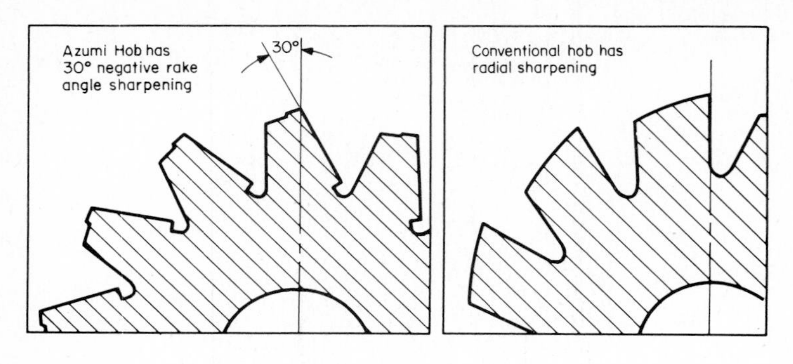

FIG. 6.21 Skiving hob and detail of negative rake angle. U.S. Patent No. 3,786,719. *(Courtesy of Azumi Mfg. Co., Osaka, Japan.)*

patent.* I am told that Barber Colman and Azumi were working independently and did not know details of each other's design until their special roughing hobs were on the market.

Another special patented hob that is very efficient at metal removal is the E-Z Cut hob. This hob will do both roughing and finishing. Figure 6.20 shows this hob and a detail of the design. This hob is intended to be used on very large gears where the cutting time is normally of several days duration.

The skiving hob uses a special carbide blade and a *negative* rake angle of 30°. Figure 6.21 shows a skiving hob and details of the special rake angle. Figure 6.22 shows a skiving hob being set in position to finish-cut a fully

*This patent was pending at the time this manuscript was written (Pat. application No. 48-60104).

FIG. 6.22 Skiving hob being set to finish a large case-hardened gear. Note undercut in gear teeth. Only the sides of gear teeth are skived, not the root fillet. *(Courtesy of Azumi Mfg. Co., Osaka, Japan.)*

hardened gear that was finish-hobbed before hardening with a protuberance type of hob. (The pregrind type of hob can be used as a *pre-skive* hob.)

It is a remarkable achievement, of course, to be able to finish a case-hardened gear by hobbing instead of grinding. In the case where very high accuracy and smooth finish are needed, the hard gear—finished by skiving—may be given a further honing operation or a very light final grind. When a final grind is used, the skiving serves to remove the bulk of the heat-treat distortion, and to remove it in a quicker and more efficient manner than grinding.

6.3 Spur-Gear Milling Cutters

Spur gears can be formed by milling a slot at a time and indexing to the next slot. The milling cutter is made so that its contour has an involute curve matching that of the gear tooth. A cross section through the cutter tooth is the same as that through the *space* between two gear teeth. See Fig. 6.23.

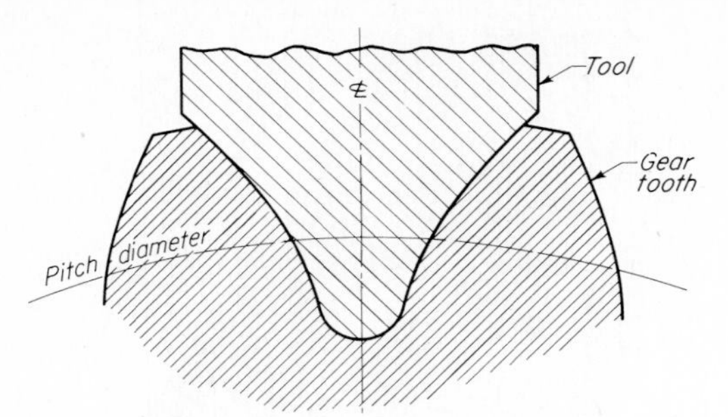

FIG. 6.23 Milling tool fits space between gear teeth exactly after gear is finished.

Standard involute gear cutters are designed to cut a range of gear-tooth numbers. Table 6.6 shows the tooth numbers that standard cutters will cut.

Spur gears cut by involute cutters of the same pitch are interchangeable. The form of the cutter is designed to be correct for the *lowest* number of teeth in the range of the cutter. For instance, a No. 5 cutter has the involute curvature of 21 teeth. If it is used to cut 25 teeth instead of 21 teeth, the curvature will be somewhat too great. However, this is not too serious. Teeth with too much curvature will run together better than teeth with too little curvature.

If close accuracy is desired in form-milled teeth, it is necessary to get a cutter with a curvature which is right for the exact number of teeth. This can be done by purchasing a special single-purpose cutter.

Standard gear cutters are usually not ground. The highest accuracy can be obtained by using both a single-purpose cutter and a ground cutter.

Some companies build standard gear cutters in half numbers. For example, a No. $3\frac{1}{2}$ cutter has a range of 30 to 34 teeth, whereas a No. 4 cutter has a range of 26 to 34.

Gear designers can help themselves by choosing numbers of teeth that tie in with the design values for standard cutters. If a 4 to 1 ratio is desired, tooth numbers of 14 and 56 would be a good choice. A No. 7 cutter would

TABLE 6.6 Standard Involute Gear Cutters

No. 1 is used to cut from 135 teeth to a rack
No. 2 is used to cut from 55 teeth to 134 teeth
No. 3 is used to cut from 35 teeth to 54 teeth
No. 4 is used to cut from 26 teeth to 34 teeth
No. 5 is used to cut from 21 teeth to 25 teeth
No. 6 is used to cut from 17 teeth to 20 teeth
No. 7 is used to cut from 14 teeth to 16 teeth
No. 8 is used to cut from 12 teeth to 13 teeth

be just right for the pinion, and a No. 2 cutter would be within one tooth of being just right for the gear. This would give close accuracy without paying extra for single-purpose cutters.

Where close accuracy is desired in form-milled gear teeth, it is often necessary to make precise layouts of gear and cutter teeth so that both the tool and the work may be checked. Points on the involute profile may be laid out by rectangular coordinates.

The calculation of the cutter profile involves two steps:

The cutter is assumed to be like an *internal* gear tooth that completely fills the space between two external teeth. A series of arc tooth thicknesses are calculated for a series of assumed diameters.

The arc tooth thicknesses are converted to rectangular coordinates based on the point at which the gear pitch diameter intersects the center line of the cutter. These coordinates are plotted to give the cutter profile.

Section 9.6 shows how to calculate the profile of an internal gear tooth, and Fig. 9.16 is an example of a calculated internal tooth profile. This method can be adapted for the design of milling cutter profiles.

Gear milling cutters range in size from $8\frac{1}{2}$ in. diameter and 2 in. bore for 1 diametral pitch to $1\frac{3}{4}$ in. diameter and 7/8 in. bore for 32 pitch. Several kinds of "stocking" cutters are commonly used to rough-cut teeth before finish cutting. Those planning to use gear milling cutters should consult tool vendors' catalogues for further details on the kinds and types of cutters avalable.

6.4 Worm Milling Cutters and Grinding Wheels

On casual observation, one might assume that a milling cutter would produce on a worm a normal section profile that is of the exact same curvature as the normal section of the cutter. However, there is a slight generating action between the cutter and the work. This is caused by the fact that the thread angle of the worm varies from the top to the bottom of the thread. The inclination of the cutter is set to correspond to the thread angle at the *pitch line* of the worm. This means that at the top or bottom of the thread, the cutter will not be tangent to the worm surface in the plane containing the cutter axis (normal section). Since the tangency points do not come in the plane of the normal section, more metal will be removed from the top and bottom of the worm thread than that corresponding to the cutter normal section profile. A straight-sided conical cutter (see Fig. 6.24) will produce a worm thread with a convex curvature in either the normal or the axial sections of the worm. If a straight-sided worm profile is required, the

FIG. 6.24 Worm milling cutter. *(Courtesy of General Electric Co., Lynn, MA, U.S.A.)*

cutter must be formed to a convex curvature which is conjugate with the straight worm.

The amount of curvature produced by the generating action of a milling cutter is rather slight compared with that produced by a hob or a shaper cutter. With low thread angles and fine pitches, the curvature is often almost negligible. With coarse pitches and high thread angles, the amount becomes quite significant. For example, a five-thread worm of 1.250 in. axial pitch and 30° thread angle has about 0.006 in. curvature when cut with a straight-sided cutter. A five-thread worm of 0.625-in. axial pitch has only about 0.001 in. curvature when the thread angle is 15°.

Several kinds of worms have been in common use. When worm threads were made on a lathe, it was quite handy to make the worm profile either straight in the axial section or straight in the normal section. This practice carried over into milled worms, with the result that many designs in current production call for a straight-sided worm. This practice puts a burden on the makers of a milling cutter (or the one who dresses a thread-grinding wheel). They must develop the required curvature in the cutting tool.

Most gear engineers in the United States prefer to use a straight-sided milling cutter or grinding wheel. This puts all the curvature into the worm. This practice makes the job of producing a worm-gear hob somewhat more difficult, since it must have a curvature on the cutting edge corresponding to that of the worm thread. It is reasoned, though, that hob makers are better able to take care of this problem than are makers of milling cutters. Worm-gear hobs have helical gashes in most cases. The combination of gash angle and relief on the sides of the hob tooth would make it necessary to curve the cutting edge of the hob tooth even if the hob had to match a straight-sided worm. Since hob makers cannot escape curvature problems, it is perhaps reasonable to give them the *whole* problem.

In England and in some other countries, worms of involute helicoidal shape are popular. These worms have an involute curve in a transverse section. This design is not handy to work with unless involute generating equipment is available to make worm threads. Such equipment is not generally available in the United States.

Worm-gear designers frequently need to calculate the curvature produced by milling a worm. If a straight-sided cutter is used, the worm thread profile must be calculated before precise data can be put on the worm drawing to check the thread profile. Also, these data are needed to check the worm-gear hob.

Several people have worked on this problem and written technical papers. The references at the end of the book include some of the best work on the worm-cutter problem. The problem is so complicated and takes so many equations to get precise answers that it is not possible to present it in full in this book. As a substitute, a calculation sheet and a sample problem are given. This will give a designer the means of solving for the axial and normal section curvatures of any worm cut by a straight-sided cutter or grinding wheel. The method used is based on the Dudley/Poritsky AGMA paper (1943). More detailed information is available in this reference.

For a sample problem, we shall take a five-threaded worm with 25.00 mm axial pitch. We shall adjust the pitch diameter to give a 25° lead angle. This makes 5° per thread and is about as high a lead angle as should be used with five threads. Using Eq. (3.38), the pitch diameter works out to 85.327 mm. Using the proportions of Table 3.29, we get an addendum of 7.21 mm. Cutter pressure angle is 25°. Normal circular pitch is 22.6577 mm. The worm thread thickness will be 10.88 mm.

The worm thread cutter will have an outside diameter of 150 mm. Subtracting twice the worm dedendum (8.65 mm), we get a cutter pitch diameter of 132.70 mm. The cutter thickness at the pitch line will be equal to the normal circular pitch minus the worm thread thickness. This comes out to 11.7777 mm.

The first step in the calculation will be to determine the angle of rotation of the cutter (θ_2) at which various points on the cutter cut the *deepest* into the worm profile (these are points of tangency with the worm profile). Table 6.7 shows this calculation. Values of Δh may be assumed to give as many points as desired. The five points shown are picked to be one addendum above and below pitch line, at pitch line, and two intermediate points.

After θ_2 has been determined, a second calculation sheet is worked through to get the axial section of the worm. This calculation literally determines the position of a point on the cutter with respect to the *axial* section of the worm. If angles of θ_2 other than the critical value were used, it would be possible to plot the entire cutting curve of a point on the cutter. In fact, a

TABLE 6.7 Calculation of Angle of Rotation for a Straight-Sided Cutter Cutting a Worm

Given data	
1. No. of worm threads	5
2. Pitch diameter of worm	85.327 mm
3. Pitch diameter of cutter	132.7 mm
4. Axial pitch	25.00 mm
5. Shaft angle*	25°
6. Cutter pressure angle	25°
7. Cutter tooth thickness	11.78 mm

Calculation steps					
8. Distance a (assume)	7	3.5	0	−3.5	−7
9. [(2) + (3)] × 0.50	109.0135				
10. Lead = (1) × (4)	125.00				
11. (10) ÷ 2π	19.89437				
12. sin (5)	0.422618				
13. cos (5)	0.906308				
14. tan (6)	0.466308				
15. −1.00 ÷ (14)	−2.14451				
16. (15) × (12)	−0.906308				
17. (15) × (13)	−1.94358				
18. (9) × (13)	98.79978				
19. (9) × (16)	−98.7998				
20. (11) × (12)	8.407723				
21. (11) × (17)	−38.6664				
22. (18) + (20)	107.2075				
23. (22) × (22)	11493.45				
24. (19) − (21)	−60.1334				
25. (24) × (24)	3616.029				
26. (22) × (24)	−6446.75				
27. (7) ÷ 2.00	5.89				
28. (3) ÷ 2.00	66.35				
29. (8) × (14)	3.264154	1.632077	0	−1.63208	−3.26415
30. (27) − (29)	2.625846	4.257923	5.89	7.522077	9.154154
31. r_2 = (28) + (8)	73.35	69.85	66.35	62.85	59.35
32. (30) × (12)	1.109731	1.799476	2.489222	3.178967	3.868712
33. (31) × (16)	−66.4777	−63.3056	−60.1335	−56.9614	−53.7894
34. (32) + (33)	−65.3679	−61.5061	−57.6443	−53.7825	−49.9207
35. (34) × (34)	4272.968	3783.003	3322.865	2892.555	2492.072
36. (35) − (25)	656.9398	166.9747	−293.163	−723.474	−1123.96
37. (23) + (35)	15766.42	15276.45	14816.31	14386.00	13985.52
38. (36) ÷ (37)	0.041667	0.010930	−0.019787	−0.050290	−0.080366
39. (26) ÷ (37)	−.408892	−.422006	−0.435112	−0.448127	−0.460959
40. (39) × (39)	0.167192	0.178089	0.189322	0.200818	0.212483
41. (38) + (40)	0.208859	0.189019	0.169536	0.150528	0.132118
42. $\sqrt{(41)}$	0.457011	0.434763	0.411747	0.387979	0.363480
43. (39) + (42)	0.048120	0.012758	−0.023365	−0.060148	−0.097479
44. Rot. angle = arcsin (43)	2.758124	0.730968	−1.33881	−3.44831	−5.59404

*The shaft angle is usually set to be the same as the worm lead angle.

solution can be obtained by assuming a series of θ_2 values for each line (30) value from Table 6.7 and then plotting individual curves to see which value of θ_2 does the deepest cutting on the worm. In some cases, it may not be possible to get a solution for θ_2 directly from the first calculation sheet. If this happens, a solution can still be obtained by plotting curves for each line (30) value from Table 6.7 and reading values at the point of deepest cutting. The Dudley-Poritsky paper gives further information on this alternative method.

Table 6.8 shows the calculation of the worm axial section. Items (6), (7),

TABLE 6.8 Calculation of Axial Section of Worm Cut with a Straight-Sided Cutter

Given data	
1. No. of worm threads	5
2. Pitch diameter of worm	85.327 mm
3. Pitch diameter of cutter	132.7 mm
4. Axial pitch	25.00 mm
5. Shaft angle	25°

Calculation steps					
6. r_2 (line 31, Table 6.7)	73.35	69.85	66.35	62.85	59.35
7. (line 30, Table 6.7)	2.625846	4.257923	5.89	7.522077	9.154154
8. Rotation (line 44, 6.7)	2.758124	0.730968	−1.33881	−3.44831	−5.59404
9. [(2) + (3)] × 0.50	109.0135				
10. Lead = (1) × (4)	125.00				
11. (10) ÷ 2π	19.89437				
12. sin (5)	0.422618				
13. cos (5)	0.906308				
14. sin (8)	0.048120	0.012758	−0.023365	−0.060148	−0.097479
15. cos (8)	0.998842	0.999919	0.999727	0.998190	0.995238
16. (6) × (14)	3.529584	0.891108	−1.55024	−3.78030	−5.78540
17. (6) × (15)	73.26503	69.84432	66.33189	62.73621	59.06735
18. (12) × (16)	1.491667	0.376599	−0.655160	−1.59763	−2.44501
19. (12) × (7)	1.109731	1.799476	2.489222	3.178967	3.868712
20. (13) × (16)	3.198890	0.807618	−1.40499	−3.42612	−5.24335
21. (13) × (7)	2.379825	3.858989	5.338153	6.817317	8.296481
22. (9) − (17)	35.74847	39.16918	42.68161	46.27729	49.94615
23. (20) + (19)	4.308620	2.607095	1.084227	−0.247151	−1.37464
24. (21) − (18)	0.888158	3.482390	5.993313	8.414942	10.74149
25. [(22) × (22)] + [(23) × (23)]	1296.517	1541.022	1822.896	2141.649	2496.508
26. $\sqrt{(25)}$	36.00719	39.25585	42.69538	46.27795	49.96506
27. (23) ÷ (26)	0.119660	0.066413	0.025395	−0.005341	−0.027512
28. arcsin (27)	6.872482	3.807981	1.455153	−0.305994	−1.57652
29. (28) × π ÷ 180	0.119947	0.066462	0.025397	−0.005341	−0.027515
30. (29) × (11)	2.386278	1.322216	0.505261	−0.106248	−0.547402
31. (30) + (24)	3.274437	4.804606	6.498574	8.308694	10.19409
32. (31) − Z_p*	−3.22414	−1.69397	0	1.810120	3.695519

*Z_p is the value from line 31 in the column in which r_2 equals half of the cutter pitch diameter. In this case, it is the middle column, and Z_p is 6.498574.

and (8) for this calculation are taken from Table 6.7. Items (26) and (32) are the answers. They are rectangular coordinates of points on the axial section profile. Item (26) is a *radial* dimension, while (32) is an *axial* dimension—with 0 at the approximate pitch diameter of the worm. The approximate pitch diameter is used because the point used in the beginning for the pitch point of the cutter does not reach in quite deep enough to give a point on the pitch line of the worm in this calculation.

In general, it is best to check hobs and worms in the *normal* section. This permits the indicator to read normal to the surface being checked instead of at an angle. Table 6.9 shows the calculation of the normal section from the

TABLE 6.9 Calculation of Normal-Section Deviation from Known Axial Section

Calculation steps					
1. (line 32, Table 6.8)	−3.22414	−1.69397	0	1.810120	3.695519
2. Worm pitch diameter × π	268.0627				
3. Lead (line 10, Table 6.8)	125.00				
4. (3) ÷ (2)	0.466309				
5. Lead angle = arctan (4)	25.00006				
6. (line 26, Table 6.8)	36.00719	39.25585	42.69538	46.27795	49.96506
7. (6) ÷ (4)	77.21746	84.18423	91.56031	99.24313	107.1502
8. (3) ÷ 2π	19.89437				
9. (7) + (8)	97.11183	104.0786	111.4547	119.1375	127.0445
10. (1) ÷ (9)	−0.033200	−0.016276	0	0.015194	0.029088
11. arcsin (10), degrees	−1.90258	−0.932579	0	0.870559	1.666876
12. (11) × π ÷ 180	−0.033206	−0.016277	0	0.015194	0.029092
13. (8) × (12)	−0.660620	−0.323812	0	0.302277	0.578776
14. (7) × (10)	−2.56364	−1.37017	0	1.507854	3.116824
15. (13) + (14)	−3.22426	−1.69398	0	1.810132	3.695600

Note: If (15) does not equal (1), this approximation method is not good enough, and a trial-and-error procedure must be used. Assume a new value for (10) and repeat steps (11) to (15), until (15) equals (1).

16. cos (11)	0.999449	0.999868	1.00	0.999885	0.999577
17. (6) × (16)	35.98734	39.25065	42.69538	46.27261	49.94392
18. (6) × (10)	−1.19545	−0.638923	0	0.703126	1.453403
19. sin (5)	0.422619				
20. −(18) ÷ (19)	2.828664	1.511816	0	−1.66373	−3.43904
21. Normal pressure angle from Eq. (3.35)	24.40341				
22. tan (21)	0.453692				
23. (2) ÷ 2π	42.66350				
24. (17) − (23)	−6.67617	−3.41285	0.031882	3.609110	7.280421
25. (24) × (22)	−3.02892	−1.54838	0.014464	1.637424	3.303069
26. (25) + (20)	−0.200258	−0.036565	0.014464	−0.026310	−0.135967
27. cos (21)	0.910659				
28. Deviation = (26) × (27)	−0.182367	−0.033298	0.013172	−0.023959	−0.123820
29. Distance A = (24) ÷ (27)	−7.33114	−3.74767	0.035010	3.963185	7.994673

Note: For deviation curve, plot (28) against (29).

coordinates just obtained for the worm axial section. Items 19 and 23 are rectangular coordinates of the worm normal section.

Machines customarily used to check the profiles of worms are set at an inclination corresponding to the normal pressure angle. Since the curvature of the profile is not great, it is handy to measure the profile by deviations from a straight line. This makes it desirable to continue the calculation to get deviations from a straight line. Items 30 and 31 show the deviations from a straight line set at a normal pressure angle of 24.4072°. This angle was calculated from the cutter pressure angle using Eq. (3.35).

Figure 6.25 shows a plot of the normal section deviations. The solid curve is a plot of items 31 and 32. It will be noted that this curve does not read 0 at the point where A is 0. This is caused by the fact that the axial section was based on an approximate pitch diameter (see above). The dashed-line curve has been moved over by 0.013 mm to correct for this approximation. The

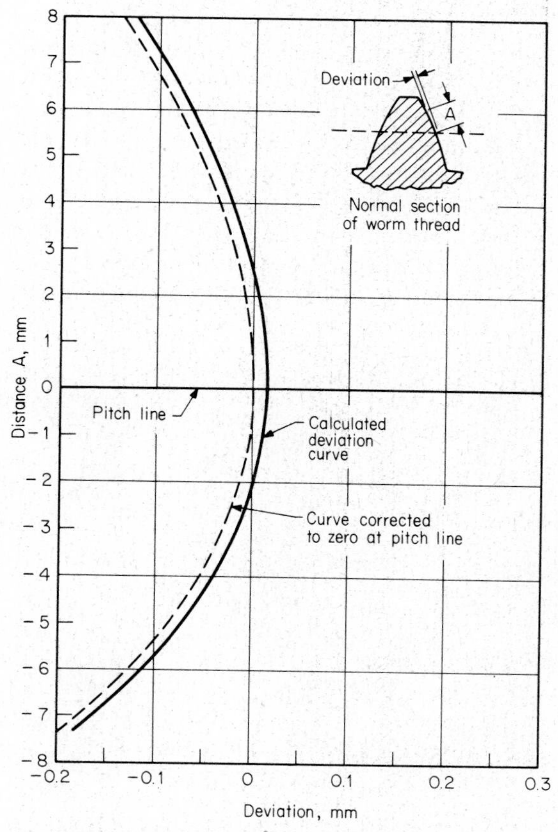

FIG. 6.25 Curvature of worm normal section.

dashed-line curve is the one that should be used for checking. The other curve could be used, but it would confuse the inspectors to have the checking line intersect the surface instead of passing tangent to the surface.

Figure 6.25 shows that the normal section profile has a curvature of about 0.1 mm. Although this is not much distance, it is a significant amount when it comes to the meshing of precision gear teeth. To get a worm that will operate smoothly under high speed and load, it will be necessary to hob its mating gear with a hob which has the same normal section curvature as the worm. The calculation just given is a method of getting both data to check the finished worm and data to check the hob used to finish the worm gear.

6.5 Gear-Shaving Cutters

When gears are made by the shaving process, the gear engineer may have frequent need to study the shaving tool. Essentially this tool represents a gear which has a conjugate tooth action with the part being shaved. The surfaces of the shaving tool are serrated with small rectangular grooves. The cutter is designed purposely to run on a shaft which lacks a few degrees of being parallel with that of the work. The out-of-parallel condition causes the cutter teeth to have a sliding motion across the gear teeth even at the pitch line. It is this sliding motion, together with the serrations and the fact that the tool and work are meshed together at a tight center distance, that causes the tool to "shave" off tiny slivers of material. (See Fig. 6.26 for shaving-cutter examples and Fig. 6.27 for how a shaving cutter works.)

Since the shaving cutter is mounted on a shaft that is not parallel to the

FIG. 6.26 Shaving cutters of different pitches. *(Courtesy of National Broach and Machine, a division of Lear Siegler, Inc., Detroit, MI, U.S.A.)*

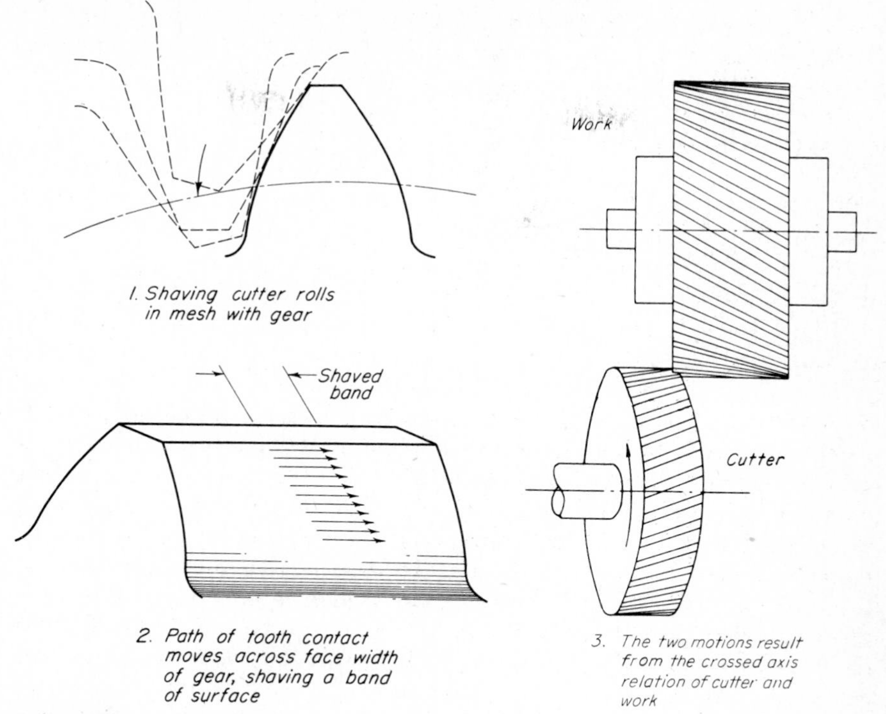

FIG. 6.27 Shaving-cutter action. *(Courtesy of Ex-Cell-O Corp., Tool Products Div., Detroit, MI, U.S.A.)*

gear axis, the teeth of the shaving cutter and the teeth of the work run together like a pair of *crossed-helical* gears. The choice of shaft angle governs the cutting action of the cutter. In general, the higher the shaft angle, the faster the cutter cuts. The best control over helix angle, though, is gained with a low shaft angle.

Since the choice of shaft angle is largely a matter of judgment in weighing different variables, there are no fixed rules. The general practice is about as follows:

Application	Shaft angle, degrees
Spur pinions, under 20 teeth	8–12
Spur pinions, 20 to 35 teeth	10–15
Spur gears	10–15
Helical pinions, narrow face	8–12
Helical gears, narrow face	10–15
Helical pinions, wide face	5–10
Helical gears, wide face	10–15
Internal gears	4–8

At the present time there are no general trade standards for shaving-cutter diameters, bore sizes, or face widths. Each manufacturer develops a practice which may agree in some respects and disagree in others with those of other cutter manufacturers. Light-duty shaving machines for fine-pitch gears up to 100 mm (4 in.) diameter use cutters from about 50 to 75 mm (2 to 3 in.) diameter. Medium-duty shaving machines for gears up to 450 mm (18 in.) use 150- to 280-mm (6- to 11-in.) cutters. Heavy-duty machines for gears up to 1.2 m (48 in.) or more use 175- to 300-mm (7- to 12-in.) cutters. Many shaving-cutter users and manufacturers prefer a 200- to 225-mm (8- to 9-in.) cutter whenever the design permits.

In general, it is desirable to have a "hunting" ratio between the number of cutter teeth and the number of gear teeth. This tends to make it desirable to design shaving cutters with *prime* numbers of teeth. A prime number will hunt with all numbers of teeth except itself. Thus numbers of teeth like 37, 41, 43, 47, 53, 59, 61, 67, 73, etc., are popular for shaving cutters.

The normal circular pitch of a shaving cutter must equal the normal circular pitch of the work. Likewise, the normal pressure angle of the cutter must equal that of the work. Ordinarily the helix angle of the cutter is opposite in hand to that of the work. *When the hands of helix are opposite and the gear is external, the shaft angle is the difference between the helix angles.* With spur gears or low-helix-angle gears, the cutter helix might be designed with either hand for a given hand on the workpiece. *If the hands of the helices are the same and the gear is external, the shaft angle is the sum of the two helix angles.*

The conditions just mentioned usually make it impossible to have the pitch diameter of the cutter come out to some even figure like 200.0 mm or 8.000 in. The designer usually just chooses teeth and shaft angles so that the cutter diameter is very close to the desired diameter.

Shaving cutters are sharpened on their involute surfaces. This makes the cutter change quite appreciably in outside diameter during its life. Like shaper cutters, shaving cutters do not produce the same thickness on the work throughout their life. If the thickness of the work is held constant, the depth that the shaving cutter is fed into the work will vary.

The tendency of the shaving cutter to cut a deeper depth as the teeth are made thinner in sharpening may be controlled by reducing the cutter outside diameter a proper amount each time the cutter is sharpened.

To function properly, the shaving cutter should finish the involute *at least* as deep as the form diameter. Preferably, the cutter should finish the involute close to the diameter that corresponds to the deepest point of undercut left by the preshave tool. Perfect blending of root fillet with shaved profile can be obtained only when the shaving action stops in the middle of the undercut. As the shaving-cutter tip rolls out of mesh, it follows a path which takes it closer to the root diameter of the gear. This movement may cause trouble. The cutter tip may foul either the root diameter or the root fillet of the gear. It is necessary to size the cutter outside diameter so that it will clear the root fillet even when it is at its deepest point of penetration with the gear. This means that the *working depth* of the cutter must be always a certain amount less than the whole depth of the gear.

The calculations necessary to design a shaving cutter are fairly complicated. They will not be given here. For further information on tool design, consult Chap. 22 of the *Gear Handbook*.

6.6 Punching Tools

The tool used to punch gears usually has three working parts: the punch, the die, and the knockout piece. Sheet metal is placed between the die and the punch. The punch has the shape of the gear to be made. For punching an external gear, an external-toothed punch is used. The die has the shape of the stock that is left after the punching is removed from the sheet. An internally toothed die is used for making an external gear.

In punching a gear, the first operation is to feed the sheet metal into the tool. The punch is driven into the die by the ram of the punching machine. This cuts out the gear and leaves it stuck in the die. The punching is removed from the die by a movement of the knockout tool. This tool has a shape very similar to that of the punch. The punching-tool assembly may be so built that spring action both retracts the punching tool and actuates the knockout piece. In this case, the punching machine has to furnish power only for the punching stroke (during which the springs are compressed).

Only thin gears can be punched. The thickness of the sheet stock should not exceed the gear-tooth thickness at the pitch line. As a rule of thumb, the stock should not be thicker than $1.5m_t$ ($1.5/P_d$). This means that a 1-module (25-pitch) gear could be made up to about 1.5 mm (0.06 in.) face width.

The punching operation upsets the metal so that the tooth corners are rounded some on the die end. The face of the tooth is formed by a shearing operation. This shearing is not exactly at 90° to the axis of the gear. This means that a pair of new punched gears cannot be expected to have uniform contact across even their narrow face width. The accuracy of punched gears may be improved by secondary operations. A *shaving* type of punching operation may be used to take a small amount of metal off the gear-tooth faces. A *coining* operation may also be used to improve accuracy. In coining, the punching is rammed into the bottom of a die with so much pressure that the metal flows to conform completely to the shape of the cavity. It is also conceivable that conventional crossed-axis shaving might be used on punched parts. The fact that punched gears are essentially thin wafers pressed on a small shaft is the greatest drawback to shaving. The reactions of the shaving tool would tend to "cock" the gear on its shaft.

FIG. 6.28 Gear punching tool.

The power required to punch gears depends primarily on the cross-sectional area to be sheared. As a rule of thumb, the tonnage capacity of the punching machine should equal at least twice the force calculated as the product of the shear area times the ultimate shear strength. For instance, a 1-in. gear of 1/32-in. thickness would have a shear area at the teeth of about $2.5 \times \pi \times 1$ in. $\times$ 1/32 in., or 0.245 in.^{2}. If the material was steel with 60,000-psi shear strength, a press of about 15 tons capacity would be needed to cut the teeth. Additional power would be required if the gear had a large bore to be cut. All sizes of punching machines up to as large as 2000 tons are on the market. Figure 6.28 shows an example of a gear punching tool.

6.7 Sintering Tools

Before gears are sintered, the metal powder is compressed into a gear-shaped briquette. A complicated and expensive set of tools is required for the briquetting operation. After the briquette is made, it is sintered in an oven. The sintering consists of heating the briquette to a temperature almost up to the melting point. Carefully controlled atmosphere furnaces are used for this operation.

Sintered gears are rather porous. This is an advantage from the lubrication standpoint, but a detriment to the strength of the part. Higher-strength gears can be obtained by filling most of the voids in the part by metal infiltration. This is done by placing a slug of lower-melting metal (such as copper) on top of the briquette when it is placed in the oven. Upon

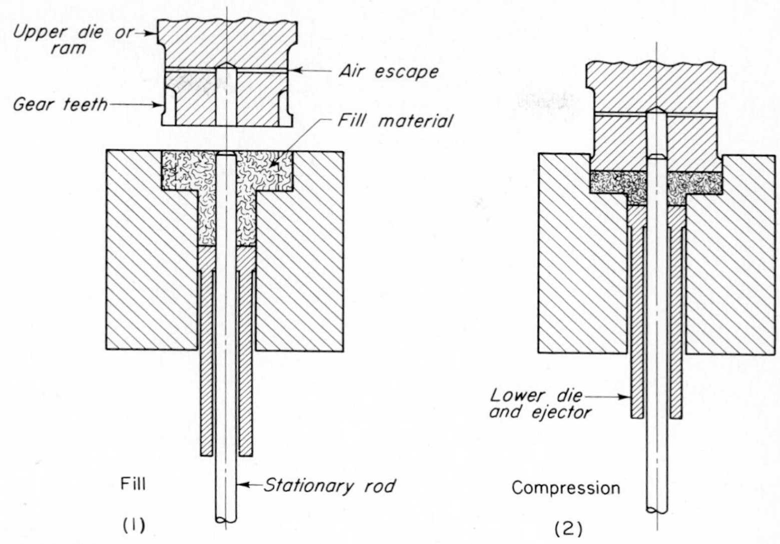

FIG. 6.29 Sintering tools.

heating, the metal slug melts and soaks through the briquette. After heating and cooling, the briquette becomes an impregnated gear.

In making sintered gears, the special tools are used in the briquetting part of the process rather than in the actual sintering.

Figure 6.29 shows in schematic fashion the three tools used to make a briquette. The metal powder is poured into the cavity of a *die barrel.* The floor of the die barrel is the *stripper.* The power is pressed against the stripper by a *ram.* The die barrel has internal teeth, while the ram and the stripper have external teeth.

After the powder is compressed, the briquette is ejected by withdrawing the ram, then pushing the briquette out with an upward stroke of the stripper.

The die barrel is made by broaching internal teeth into a special die steel. After broaching, the die is hardened by furnace heat treatment. The die steel used must be one which will have very little dimensional change upon hardening. Air-hardening types of steel are often used for the die barrel. The ram and the stripper have ground external teeth. Both these pieces are ground slightly larger than the expected size of the die barrel after heat treatment. The die barrel is lapped with a series of about three external toothed laps. This removes slight errors, polishes the die teeth to a mirrorlike finish, and enlarges the die so that the ram and stripper will fit with an almost perfect size-to-size fit.

The teeth of the ram and stripper are designed so that all surfaces can be

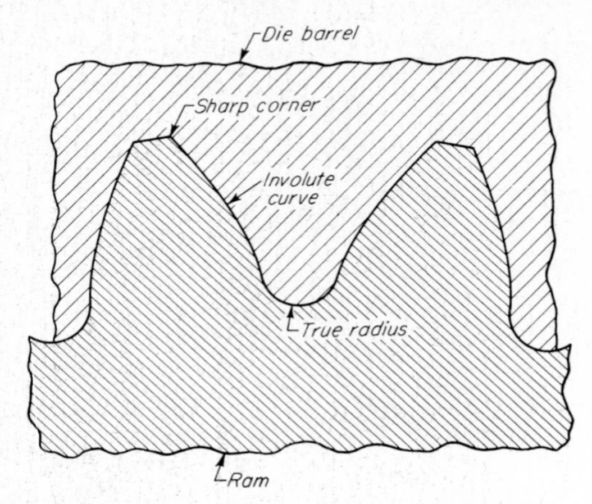

FIG. 6.30 Surfaces of ram and die are ground true and fit with almost no clearance.

ground and measured with great precision. The root fillets are often made as true arcs of circles. This facilitates measurement of root size. Also, it is easy to dress a true circular arc on the tip of a form-grinding wheel. The sides of the teeth are involute curves. No corner radii or chamfers are used at the tips of the teeth. Figure 6.30 shows the way the teeth of the ram and the die fit with each other. To keep the powder from leaking, it is necessary that the tooth surfaces fit so well that no clearance of even as little as 0.01 mm (0.0005 in.) exists anywhere between the contacting tooth surfaces. Great skill and care are required to build a set of sintering tools that will fit on all surfaces with this kind of precision.

chapter 7

The Kinds and Causes of Gear Failures

The previous chapters have covered the selection and design of a gearset. If gear engineering were an *exact* science, information of this type would be all that the designer needed to know. But it is not an exact science. It is both an art and a science. Those who design gears are constantly surprised that some gears run better and last longer than would be expected from the design formulas, while others fail prematurely even when they are operated well within the design limits of the transmitted load. The gear designer needs to be able to evaluate the various causes of gear wear and failure. New gear designs must be based on both textbook logic and practical field experience if the best possible job is to be done.

In studying cases of gear wear and failure, it is very important that the correct analysis be made. Frequently the cause of failure will be something quite different from the amount of transmitted load. An incorrect analysis can lead a designer to make a new gearset larger than it ought to be, and yet the new set may still fail because the real cause of trouble is still uncorrected.

In this chapter we will study the *kinds* of gear failure and the *causes* of gear failure. In a power package, the gear unit is a basic element, taking power from a prime mover and delivering the power to a power-absorbing unit.

Troubles in the gear unit may stem from *power-system* troubles, or they may be localized entirely in the *gear unit.* The investigator needs to be alert to a wide variety of things that may cause failure and then carefully analyze the evidence to sort out what improper thing—or combination of things—led to a failure sequence.

ANALYSIS OF GEAR-SYSTEM PROBLEMS

No matter what the failure is, it is desirable to look at the whole power package and the history of the particular power package in question before proceeding with a detailed study of gear teeth or gear bearings. In this part of Chap. 7, we will analyze the troubles that are essentially gear-system or *geared power package* troubles. The next part will analyze gear-tooth and gear-bearing failures inside the gear unit. The last part will cover some examples of failures.

7.1 Determining the Problem

A malfunction in a geared power system can take many forms. In general terms, one or more of the following may apply:

Problem	Consequences
Broken part	Drive system probably inoperable
Abnormally worn part	Drive system probably operable; may be unfit to continue operation for any appreciable time
Abnormal vibration	Drive system probably operable; may be unfit to continue operation for any appreciable time
Abnormal noise	Drive system operable; may be environmental hazard or prone to early failure
Abnormal part temperature; abnormal oil temperature	Drive system may be operable, but in danger of early failure
Serious oil leakage	Drive system operable, but an environmental hazard; may be in danger of early failure
Part seized in its bearings; part moved out of position and jammed with another part	Drive system will not transmit torque; "inoperable" condition may be more apparent than defect which caused it

Any of the problems listed above may cause a geared system to be investigated for "failure." In a general sense, *failure* should not be thought of as

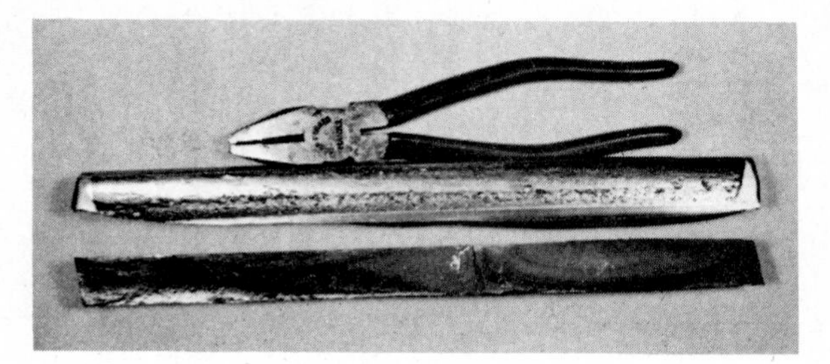

FIG. 7.1 A broken-out helical-gear tooth. Note serious pitting and wear of tooth flank. (The actual size of the tooth can be judged from the standard pliers laid next to the tooth.)

just inability to operate. Rather, failure should be thought of as some unsatisfactory condition which either threatens that a geared system will become inoperable, or poses an environmental disturbance that is considered improper. Of course, there can easily be situations in which one party may consider that the geared machinery is failing to operate properly, and yet that claim is not justified by the generally accepted norms for that particular kind of equipment.

When a gear system breaks down, the real failure may be quite different from the reported failure. For instance, when gear teeth break, investigation may reveal that they were seriously worn long before they broke. The problem then is to discover why the abnormal wear occurred. Figure 7.1 shows a good example of this.

Vibration is another example. A high-speed gear unit may run for months with all modes of vibration within reasonable limits. Then there is an onset of high vibration. Close investigation may reveal small amounts of gear-tooth wear and the development of excessive tooth spacing error. The problem may then be a tooth-wear problem rather than a vibration problem. (The vibration problem is secondary to the tooth-wear problem.) Figure 7.2 shows a tooth spacing situation caused by wear which resulted in severe high-frequency vibration.

In solving gear failures, the available evidence must be sifted to find out what went wrong first. Generally some *one thing* started a chain of events. The problem has been defined when the primary cause of failure has been found and other failure evidence can be considered secondary.

7.2 Possible Causes of Gear-System Failures

When a gear system is not working properly, the cause of the trouble may come from any one of several areas. A good investigator has no *preconceived* idea of the cause, knowing that error or wrong action in any one of five

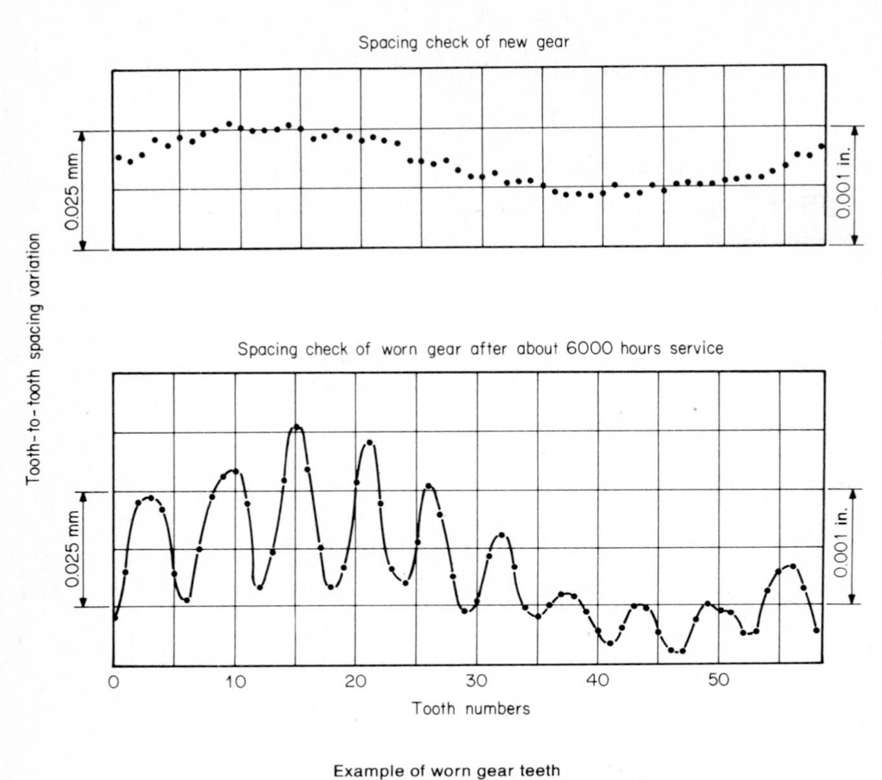

Example of worn gear teeth

FIG. 7.2 A very high speed gear pits and wears. This results in circular pitch variation. Then the result of the several "bumps" per turn of the gear causes severe vibration and shock. The gear unit then fails due to either tooth breakage or bearing failure.

major areas can lead to a gear-system failure. Table 7.1 shows many items in these areas (design, manufacture, installation, environment, and operation) that can cause failure when done improperly.

Some of the things in Table 7.1 are quite obvious, but others tend to be somewhat subtle. Let's take a few examples to illustrate the subtle.

1	Design example.	A two-half gear casing has inadequate dowels. At overhaul, worn dowel holes permit two halves to shift. When the casing is bolted, tight bearings are cramped and gear teeth are misaligned; bearing and/or gear-tooth failure results.
2	Manufacturing example.	In a lightweight casing, bolts are tightened all on one side, then all on the other side. The casing takes a bow, and high-performance (aerospace) gears are misaligned. Scoring occurs immediately in first full load test.
3	Installation example.	Oil pipes from filter to gear unit pick up blowing sand at a desert installation. Failure to carefully clean the pipes just before assembly results in high-speed pinion bearing failures even though a hot-oil flush was used just before the new equipment started up. (The sand was *downstream* from the oil filter.)
4	Environment example.	Gear unit becomes too hot. Gear teeth and bearings wear. Unit runs roughly, and then pinion bearing fails. Fly ash had settled on the gear box. The unit had a splash system and OK thermal rating—provided that the gear casing is clean enough to radiate heat properly.
5	Operation example.	Gear unit drives a "compactor" that is rolling chunks of processed mineral ore. Operators feed ore to the conveyor belt in an erratic manner, with batches of excess material alternating with lean feed areas. The gear unit pits as a result of frequent momentary overloads. Training operators to run the loading machine properly solves the problem, but new gears are needed to replace those damaged by green operators.

TABLE 7.1 Major Areas of Concern When a Gear System Fails

Design	Manufacture	Installation	Environment	Operation
1. Kind of gear (spur, helical, bevel, worm, Spiroid) 2. Design arrangement 3. Tooth design 4. Gear body design 5. Shaft design 6. Bearing design 7. Casing design 8. Seal design 9. Bolting design 10. Lubrication-system design 11. Vibration criticals known and tolerable	1. Tooth accuracy (profile, spacing, lead, concentricity) 2. Tooth material (hardness, composition, cleanliness) 3. Gears (weld quality or casting quality, fit to shaft, balance, etc.) 4. Casings (bore sizes, bore position accuracy; joint flatness and squareness, oil tightness) 5. Assembly (right parts, correct bolt tightening, fits checked)	1. Foundation (adequate rigidity) 2. Alignment (with driving and driven units) 3. Oil system (clean, all connections made, oil filled properly) 4. Instrumentation (temperature, pressure, flow, vibration OK) 5. Bolting (to foundation, flanges, shaft couplings)	1. Air (adequate for cooling, not polluted with fly ash or chemicals) 2. Temperature (not adjacent to hot equipment, extremes of heat and cold within specification limits) 3. Water (adequate protection against rain water, sea water, swamp water) 4. Housekeeping (spare parts or disassembled parts can be cleaned and protected from rust and corrosion)	1. Break-in (may require oil change after short initial run; may require some running at reduced load before maximum load is applied) 2. Operation (meet specification limits on temperature, oil flow, power rating, etc.) 3. Overload (operate without undue extra loading) 4. Misapplication (high-speed idling, run backward, stall at excess torque, etc.) 5. Starting (no undue starting torque or vibration in starting interval)

7.3 Incompatibility in Gear Systems

Perhaps the hardest thing to diagnose in a gear-system failure is an incompatibility situation. In this situation, there is nothing particularly wrong with any of the units or subassemblies that are bolted together. Something tends to fail not because it was made wrong, but because of the behavior of another part of the power package. And, the part that causes the trouble is standing up all right (or at least is runable)!

A good example of this is a coupling between a turbine and a gearbox. The coupling is designed and built to take relatively high misalignment. When it is misaligned, though, the coupling puts varying moments and axial force reactions into the end of the pinion shaft. The pinion radial bearing, adjacent to the coupling, tends to fail because of the coupling disturbance, but the coupling itself survives. The most practical solution may be a better-quality coupling rather than a revised design pinion bearing or an attempt to run the power package with misalignment held to uncomfortably close limits.

Table 7.2 shows some of the more common ways in which incompatibility can lead to trouble or failure in a geared power package.

Table 7.2 shows situations in which the gear unit is in trouble because something is wrong with another part of the drive system. The reverse situation, in which the gear unit gets something else into trouble, is also shown, because this is still a gear problem.

In gear systems, it is necessary that each unit be able to run alone under its rated conditions, but each unit must also be a good neighbor that does not cause neighboring equipment to get into trouble. Thus the things connected to the gear unit need to be tolerable to the gear unit, and the gear unit needs to be tolerable to the other things in the system.

The statement just made is an engineering viewpoint relative to troubleshooting problems in the field. From a business standpoint, the technical responsibility for making a compatible package may lie with the package builder, or it may lie with the builder of a power plant who buys individual pieces of equipment and assembles them into an operating system.

The things in Table 7.2 may be somewhat subtle, just like the things in Table 7.1. As an example, impellers are often overhung on pinion or gear shafts. At speeds of 60,000 rpm, centrifugal force becomes terrific. The pinion-impeller assembly may be balanced just fine at 10,000 rpm. Unfortunately, at 60,000 rpm, centrifugal force is 36 times greater. The impeller will tend to stretch and shift where it is fitted to the pinion. This movement may change the balance enough to create an unsatisfactory running condition for the pinion bearings and the pinion teeth. In cases like this, special design features and special balancing techniques are necessary to achieve satisfactory operation of the high-speed system.

TABLE 7.2 Examples of Incompatibility Situations in a Geared Power System

Vibration	Misalignment	Reactions	Temperature
1. Gear-tooth meshing frequency breaks turbine blades	1. Turbine or diesel engine shifts position as it heats up. Drive to gear unit seriously misaligned or out of position axially	1. Coupling reactions aggravate gearbox bearings	1. Heat of engine exhaust puts thermal distortion into gearbox
2. Reciprocating engine or compressor in trouble with valves or timing. Serious torque pulsations and low-frequency vibration	2. Foundation shift under heavy driven equipment. Gear casing becomes twisted	2. Overhung load on gear output shaft beyond design allowance	2. Hot exhaust of engine too close to air-cooled heat exchanger for package oil system
3. Propeller changed. New vibration mode not tolerable to gear unit	3. Thrust bearing wears in prime mover. Axial shift overloads gear thrust bearing	3. Imbalance of high-speed impeller overhung from pinion prematurely fails pinion bearings	3. Package start-up too quick for thermal equilibrium to be established in gearbox. Bearing seizure due to lack of clearance and/or gear-tooth seizure due to lack of backlash
4. Imbalance in heavy gearing shakes light section of turbine	4. Hull of ship or frame of airplane shifts as cargo load changes. Movement too much for gearbox (beyond design allowance)	4. Heavy vibration-absorbing coupling with multiple pads has a pad in trouble. Severe moment applied to gear shaft, leading to gear-bearing and/or gear-tooth failure	4. Common oil drain from gearbox overloaded with hot, frothy oil from other system equipment. High-speed gears overheat due to gearbox flooding

One more example will show how subtle things can happen even in relatively slow-speed equipment. Most large power packages will have a common oil sump and lubricating oil system supplying oil under pressure to all pieces of equipment. The gearbox oil drain may connect into a long drain line that is draining oil from all the other equipment. Quick trouble can develop if a malfunction like worn seals puts too much oil and foam into the main drain. Oil backs up into the gearbox. Rapid gear overheating and failure can result if large gears start churning oil in a closely fitted gear casing designed for dry-sump operation. A gear unit with a rating over 1000 hp and output speed of only 1200 rpm can be quite vulnerable to this sort of trouble. (Small gear units, around 100 hp with output speed around 500 rpm, may run just fine under wet-sump conditions—in fact, wet-sump design is often used in low-horsepower units.)

7.4 Investigation of Gear Systems

Since there is a rather wide variety of things that may lead to failure in a gear system (or any other system, for that matter), it is desirable to be alert to all the factual circumstances that surround the power system being investigated. Table 7.3 outlines the kinds of information that should be considered.

Table 7.3 covers the many things that would be of concern in investigating the failure of a helicopter gear drive or the gear drive for a piece of major equipment at a petrochemical plant. Of course, not as much information would be available for a small drive used in a minor installation, and hopefully a problem could be solved more easily.

For comparison, the manufacturer of critical gears on a major installation might have involute, spacing, and lead charts for each gear element stored in permanent files under the serial number of the gear unit. If the problem involved small amounts of wear, original inspection charts showing the exact condition of the teeth when new would be very helpful. Hence, the existence of these charts should be ascertained from a review of the quality plan for geometric accuracy. Then, of course, copies of the charts should be obtained.

In low-cost gearing on a minor installation, the manufacturer would probably work to a general quality level rather than routinely making inspection charts. Each production unit might be passed primarily on a visual inspection that the teeth had a reasonably good fit when rolled together with marking colors on the teeth.

The significance of the history has to do with design capability and manufactured quality versus application hazards. If a unit is in a very early stage of development, there may be particular reason to make an in-depth review of the suitability of the design. Perhaps the design is inadequate.

TABLE 7.3 Checklist of Factual Information That May Be Useful in Investigating Gear Failures

Identification	History	Design and manufacturing	Environment
1. Kind of drive system (identify driving and driven equipment)	1. Who designed gear unit, and when	1. Compliance with AGMA specifications	1. Weather (typical and extremes)
2. Serial numbers (of package, of gear unit, of gear or pinion involved)	2. Extent and nature of development test work	2. Compliance with other specifications (bearings, couplings, API, ISO, etc.)	2. Possible pollutants in air
3. Drawing numbers or catalogue numbers (of gear or pinion involved, of bearings, of couplings to gear unit)	3. Number of similar units built	3. Kind of heat treatment for gears	3. Possible exposure to water, mud, wear debris, etc.
4. Geographic (address of site, identification of building or vehicle for each gear unit)	4. Number of units in service	4. Method of finishing gear teeth	4. Proximity of other machinery (consider vibration, heat, and fumes from nearby machines or process equipment)
5. Company names (owner, package builder, gear-unit builder, gear parts makers)	5. Expected or operating TBO	5. Kind of oil and operating temperature limits	5. Nature of foundation or vehicle supporting gear unit
	6. Expected or proven design life	6. Quality plan for geometric accuracy	6. Possible damage in storage, in handling, or in cleaning parts
	7. When unit was built, and when put into service	7. Quality plan for metallurgical control	
	8. Load histogram data	8. Design drawings of each gear and pinion involved	
	9. Frequency of starts	9. Bearing and coupling design data	
	10. Condition of gears at last overhaul or inspection before failure		

On the other hand, if the design has been proven by many units in service with an established TBO (time between overhaul), one must look for something unusual in the particular application or in the environment. Perhaps the load histogram is more severe, or perhaps some environment factor is out of control. Of course, there is always the risk of random manufacturing errors or the risk of an incompatibility problem resulting from a change in the power package configuration outside the gear unit.

Table 7.3 is valuable primarily as a guide to the many kinds of information that may be helpful in conducting investigations of failures in geared power packages.

ANALYSIS OF TOOTH FAILURES AND GEAR-BEARING FAILURES

The first section of this chapter has been concerned with the whole drive system of prime mover, gear unit, and driven unit. This section will take up the gear unit alone and get into the details of gear-tooth and gear-bearing failures.

7.5 Nomenclature of Gear Failure

The various kinds of gear failures and the nomenclature to describe these failures has been standardized by AGMA (American Gear Manufacturers Association).

Although the early work of AGMA described gear-tooth failures rather well, further study and use of AGMA Standard 110.04* led to several refinements and additions. The latest document is an American national standard (ANS B6.12-1964) sponsored jointly by AGMA and the American Society of Mechanical Engineers (ASME).

There are *eighteen* recognized ways in which the surface of a gear tooth may be damaged. There are *three* kinds of tooth breakage. Since several kinds of tooth damage may occur at the same time, it is obvious that the gear engineer who analyzes a set of failed gears will have to carefully note all the items of evidence and then use just the right words to describe the findings. It takes a good detective to unravel gear failures properly.

Figures 7.3 to 7.7 show examples of gear-tooth failures. These photos of actual gear teeth match some of the many kinds of failure shown in the standard on failure nomenclature. Since there are many possible variations in the kinds of tooth failure, it is advisable to keep a copy of the standard handy as a complete reference on this subject.

*See Ref. 60 at the end of the book.

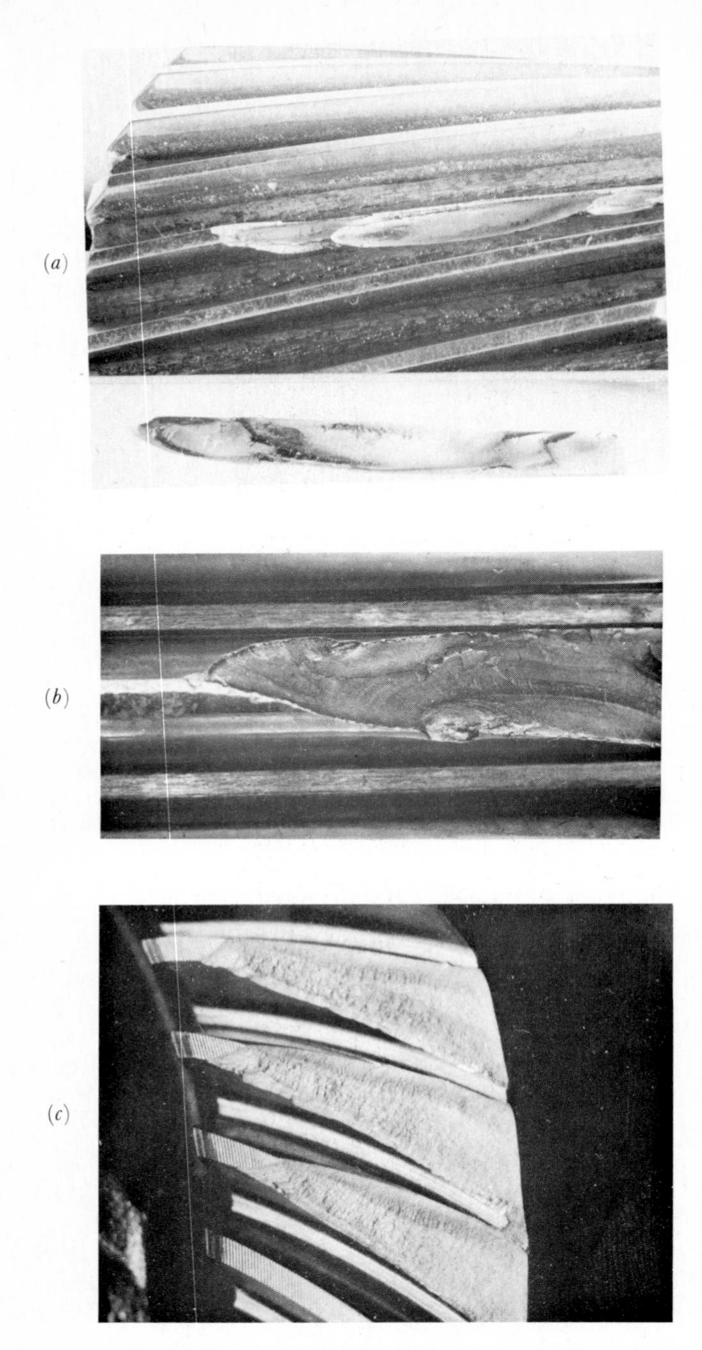

FIG. 7.3 Examples of tooth breakage. (*a*) Helical, 38 HRC. (*b*) Spur, 55 HRC. (*c*) Bevel, 58 HRC. Note the clear-cut "eye" of the break on the spur tooth.

(*a*)

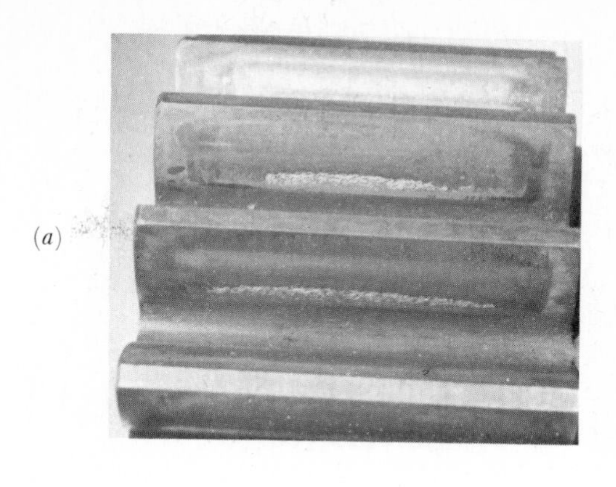

(*b*)

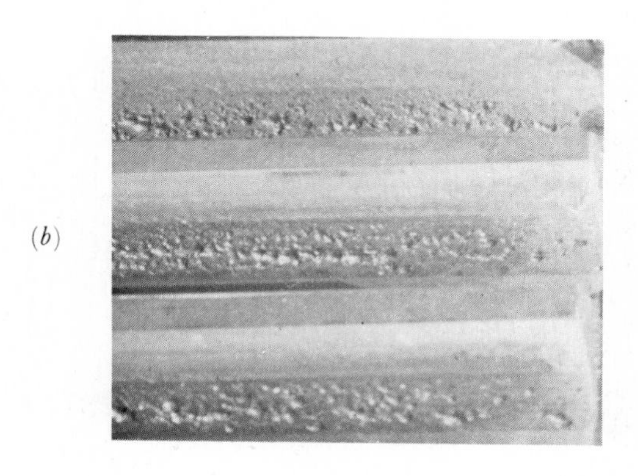

(*c*)

FIG. 7.4 Examples of macro pitting. (*a*) Spur, 60 HRC. (*b*) Helical, 35 HRC. (*c*) Helical, 35 HRC. In general, gears that have *initial* pitting have macro-sized pits. Lower view (*c*) shows ledge wear as a result of macro pitting for thousands of hours.

(a)

(b)

(c)

FIG. 7.5 Examples of gross pitting. (*a*) Helical, 35 HRC. (*b*) Helical, 35 HRC. (*c*) Spur, 60 HRC. This kind of pitting is clearly destructive pitting. Lower view shows both gross pitting and spalling.

FIG. 7.6 Examples of micro pitting. (*a*) Spur, 60 HRC. (*b*) Helical, 60 HRC. (*c*) 1000 × enlargement of section through pits. Until the late 1970s, micro pitting was thought of as "erosion" or "etching." Micro pitting often precedes macro pitting.

(a)

(b)

(c)

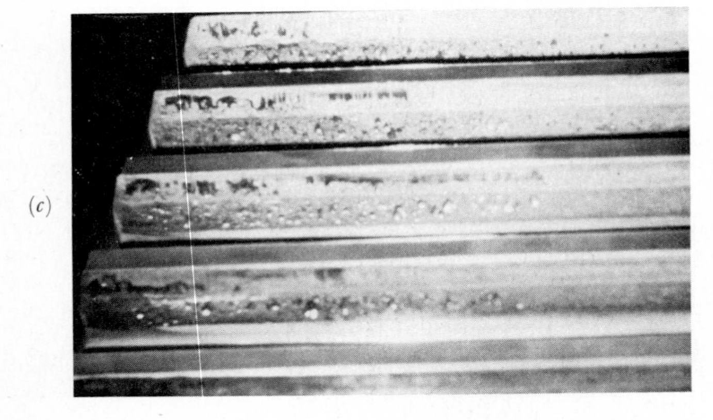

FIG. 7.7 Examples of scoring. (*a*) Spur, 60 HRC. (*b*) Spur, 60 HRC, enlarged. (*c*) Helical, 35 HRC. In the lower view, scoring, macro pitting, gross pitting, and misalignment are all evident.

7.6 Tooth Breakage

When a gear tooth breaks from fatigue, the surface of the fracture is quite smooth. The slow progress of the fracture apparently causes the metal to break like a brittle material. Many years ago it was customary to say that a piece that had failed in fatigue had "crystallized." No doubt the appearance of the break led to this incorrect explanation of fatigue failure. When a broken tooth appears to have had a fatigue failure, there are several things to look for.

Focal Point. There may be evidence of a focal point, or *eye*. This is the point where the break started. If the focal point can be found, some local defect may be located to explain the break. Sometimes a tear or notch in the root fillet may coincide with the focal point. An inclusion or a heat-treat crack may be found at the focal point. If any defect *is* found at the focal point, it is quite likely that this defect is at least partly to blame for the failure.

Fretting Corrosion. During the time that a fatigue break is growing, oil seeps into the crack and is compressed each time the gear tooth goes through mesh. The slight motion of the tooth, coupled with oil and high pressure, will often set up *fretting corrosion* in the crack. Since it takes many hours to set up fretting corrosion, the red stain in a fatigue break indicates roughly the length of time involved in the fracture. When one tooth of a gear breaks by fatigue, it is desirable to examine closely the teeth that are not broken. Frequently red stains can be found seeping out of almost invisible cracks in other teeth. Such evidence indicates that other teeth are about to break.

Evidence of Overload. When a gear tooth breaks from sudden shock or overload, the fracture usually has a stringy appearance. Even though the tooth may be fully hardened, the break will look like fibers of a plastic material which has been wrenched apart. When several consecutive teeth are broken from a gear, usually one or two teeth broke by fatigue. Then, as the gear continued to rotate under torque, the shock of the mating gear jumping across the gap left by the fatigued teeth broke additional teeth. The investigator can often look at a series of broken teeth and find the tooth that failed first.

Teeth that fail by overload frequently will have evidence of surface failure, such as plastic yielding. Since it takes two to four times as much force to fail a tooth by overload as it does to fatigue out a tooth, it is very likely that evidence of the force will show up on the tooth surface. All the teeth in the gear should be studied to see if all or only one or two have evidence of severe surface loading. This will often show the manner in which the severe overload was applied.

Break Location. Gear-tooth fractures ordinarily start in the root fillet. A cantilever beam is weakest at its base. When gear-tooth breaks start at other locations, there is something unusual. Pitch-line pitting will sometimes be severe enough to cause a tooth fracture to start at the pitch line. Sometimes shrink fits or residual heat-treat stresses will cause a break to start in the root midway between two teeth. Case-hardened teeth with too deep a case or too weak a core will sometimes shatter from the pitch line up. The whole upper part of the tooth breaks loose like a cap. Subsurface stresses may cause teeth to break anywhere on the tooth flank.

Break Pattern. Sometimes a tooth will break in an irregular and seemingly unexplainable manner. Often such breaks can be solved by studying the macrostructure of the part. Defects in forging procedure may create lines of weakness which a fatigue crack will follow.

When an end breaks off a gear tooth, this may have some special significance. The most obvious thing to look for is misalignment. Contact markings may show that all the load was being carried on one end of the tooth.

Another likely cause of end breakage is accidental damage to the gear tooth during assembly. A gear dropped on the floor or banged by a crane hook will have some metal which is *upset* above the tooth surface as well as an indentation. If all the upset metal is not carefully scraped or honed away, severe overload will result. Many people think that low-hardness gears will rapidly wear away any bumps caused by careless handling. Unfortunately, this is often not the case. Teeth of steel gears of 200 Brinell hardness have been known to break when the damaged area was only 1.5 mm (1/16 in.) in diameter on a tooth 20 mm (3/4 in.) deep. A raised spot only 0.025 mm (0.001 in.) high will often cause unbearable root stresses.

Notches caused by the unskilled filing of burrs from the ends of teeth may cause end breaks. If the end of the tooth is properly finished, the end is actually slightly stronger than the middle of the tooth. Gears that are well made and well mounted usually—when tested to destruction—break from the middle of the tooth.

Broken gear teeth should always be examined and, if possible, measured for wear. When appreciable wear is present, it is always possible that the wear caused the breakage. In hardened spur gears of high precision, an amount of wear as small as 0.025 mm (0.001 in.) may be enough to double the root-fillet stresses! Helical gears can stand more wear than spur gears because of their overlapping action and the tendency for *uniform* wear. Sometimes as much as 0.8 mm (1/32 in.) can be worn from the surface of medium-hard helical gears without increasing the root stresses too much. Wear on case-hardened gears is doubly damaging to tooth strength. The load on the root fillet is increased, and the thickness of the thin, hard case (which supports most of the root stress) is appreciably reduced.

7.7 Pitting of Gear Teeth

Pitting, like tooth breakage, is a *fatigue* failure. It is almost impossible to make a gear pit without about 10,000 cycles of contact or more. If even more load is applied than the load that will cause pitting in the range of 10,000 to 20,000 cycles, the usual result is that the surface is rolled or peened.

There are several locations where pitting is apt to occur. Helical pinions of medium hardness with 20 or more teeth frequently pit along the pitch line. The mating gear may also pit, but if it is about the same hardness as the pinion and has been heat-treated in the same way as the pinion, it is likely that most of the pitting will be on the pinion.

Pinions are more apt to pit than gears for two reasons. (1) The pinion is ordinarily the *driver*. The directions of sliding are such that sliding is away from the pitch line on the driver and toward the pitch line on the driven member. Figure 7.8 shows how the sliding motion on the driver tends to pull metal away from the pitch line. This leaves the pitch line high and also tends to stretch the metal at the pitch line. On the gear the sliding tends to compress the metal at the pitch line. The cracks that form when a surface is

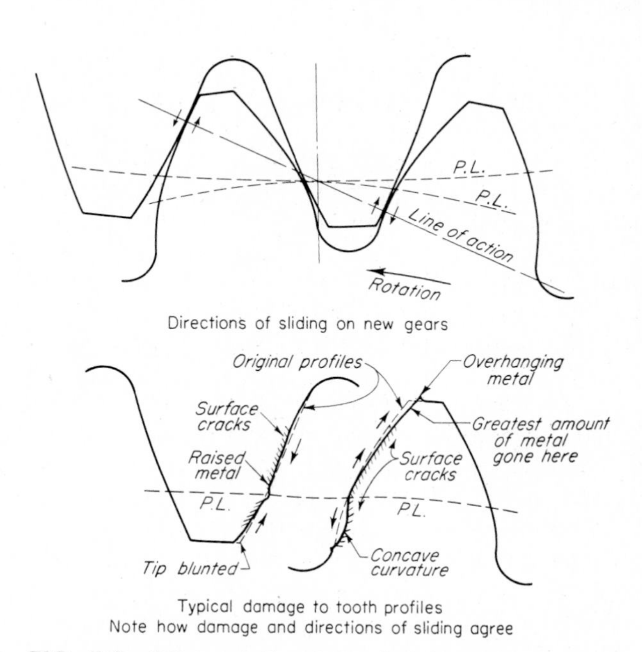

FIG. 7.8 Effects of directions of sliding on gear tooth surfaces when they begin to fail by pitting, wear, or plastic flow of metal.

severely loaded have a tendency to intersect at the pitch line of the driver, while on the driven member they do not. (2) The pinion, being smaller, has more cycles of operation than the gear. The slope of the fatigue curve makes the part with the most cycles the most apt to fail.

When the gear drives the pinion, the cycles favor the pinion failing first, but the sliding action is worst on the gear. Tests made by the author on 4 to 1 ratio helical gears of medium hardness showed that the gear would usually pit first when it was driving the pinion and made of the same hardness material as the pinion!

Spur gears of conventional design have a region of contact where only a single pair of teeth carry all the load. This region usually includes the pitch line, about one-third of the upper part of the dedendum, and about one-third of the lower part of the addendum. At the tips and roots of the teeth there are two pairs of teeth in position to share the load. In most cases the highest calculated hertz stress (contact stress) will occur at the *lowest position on the pinion* at which one pair of teeth carries full load. If this stress is appreciably higher than that at the pitch line, pitting is apt to occur in this region. Because the effects of sliding do not particularly aggravate conditions at this point, pitting will not ordinarily start here unless the stress differential between this point and the pitch line is fairly significant.

The highest hertz stress on the gear will occur in the gear addendum, since it is the gear addendum that contacts the pinion dedendum. For some reason, the pinion usually has more tendency to pit in the dedendum than the gear has a tendency to pit in the addendum. Way* and others have explained this on the basis that oil is *trapped* in surface cracks on the pinion dedendum but is not trapped on the gear addendum. This is based on the pinion's being the driver.

Tests made by the author have shown that the surface of rolls was more apt to fail when the sliding was in a *negative* direction than when it was in a *positive* direction. When negative sliding occurs, the sliding velocity is opposite to the rolling velocity. Negative sliding occurs in the dedendum regions of both the gear and the pinion, while in the addendum regions the sliding is always positive.

When pinions have small numbers of teeth, there is still another danger point on the pinion. At the base circle of the pinion, the radius of curvature of the involute profile is reduced to zero. This means that the stress on the surface tends to approach infinity, even though two pair of teeth may be sharing the load. The net result of carrying heavy load near the base circle is a rapid peening and pitting away of the metal until this critical region stops carrying any appreciable load. On medium- and low-hardness pinions, base-circle pitting may remove enough metal to correct the abnormal stresses, and then the damage may stop. On fully hardened parts, more serious effects

*See Ref. 292 at the end of the book.

may result. The base-circle pitting may leave a bunch of tiny cracks at a critically stressed region on a brittle material. It must be remembered that the tensile stress due to the beam loading of the tooth is high at the bottom of the tooth.

When gears are loaded heavily enough or when local errors are present, pitting may break out almost anywhere on the tooth. Even the addendum region of a driven gear can be made to pit if the applied load is severe enough.

In all the locations discussed above, the pitting may be of the *initial pitting* type, or it may be *destructive pitting*. Pits of the initial pitting type are usually quite small in diameter. On medium-hard parts with 2.5-module (10-pitch) teeth, they are apt to be about 0.4 mm (1/64 in.) in diameter. On 5-module (5-pitch) parts, they may be around 0.8 mm (1/32 in.) in diameter. Destructive pits are usually much larger in size.

It frequently happens that gears which are in trouble with pitting are also in trouble with lubrication. The oil may be too thin or the surface too rough to support a good oil film. There may also be abrasives in the oil. Wear may occur up to the point at which the profile accuracy is appreciably damaged. Then the hertz stresses will be increased, and the tensile stresses due to friction will be high. The combination of effects will make a gear pit under much lighter load than would ordinarily be expected. When investigating pitting, it is always desirable to make accurate measurements of tooth thickness and involute profile. These may be compared with the checks made when the set was new. If serious surface wear is occurring, it is obvious that the control of pitting will require control of the lubrication problem which is causing the wear. (See Secs. 7.9 and 7.16.)

Helical gears that are through-hardened (low to medium hardness) will often pit extensively but still be quite runable. The whole dedendum may become covered with relatively small and uniform pits. The removal of metal by pitting tends to create a "ledge" condition. The dedendum will tend to keep its involute shape, but a layer of metal is gone. If this layer is not too thick, the gears may still have relatively good load-carrying capacity.

A helical gearset may start with some misalignment. The pitting just described will start at one end. Curiously, the pitting of the misaligned gear does not stop in the middle of the face width, but will tend to continue right across the face width. Figure 7.9 shows a good example of this situation.

The general rating practice for through-hardened gears will allow a high enough surface loading to cause pitting when tooth errors, metal quality, or lubricant are somewhat less than what might be desired. Fortunately, it is often possible to get several years of service out of gears that have pitted rather extensively. The user of gears who is confronted with such a situation should be alert to the *severity* of the pitting and the *rate* at which it is progressing. Both items may be either tolerable or intolerable.

Quite often a gearset that has pitting early in its life can be helped.

FIG. 7.9 A misaligned helical gear has pitting which is progressing across the face width. Ledge wear is present at right-hand end. The leading edge of the pitted area shows typical macro pits.

Changes in alignment may be accomplished by bearing adjustment or by realigning the gear unit to driving and driven equipment. A change to a heavier or better type of oil may also be beneficial. Under improved running conditions, the pitted surface may wear and polish a slight amount and thereby *heal* over; a year or so later, the pitting may actually not look as bad as it did when the corrective action was first taken.

7.8 Scoring Failures

Scoring is essentially a lubrication failure. Tears and scratches appear on the rubbing surfaces of the teeth. Unlike fatigue failures, which occur after many cycles of operation, scoring is apt to occur as soon as new gears are first brought up to full load and speed.

Although scoring is a *lubrication* failure, it cannot be blamed on the lubricant in many cases. Frequently the design of the gears or the workmanship in finishing the teeth is such that no lubricant could be expected to make up for the defects in the gears. The gear designer should avoid both high hertz stresses and high sliding velocities at the tips of the teeth. This can be done by proper choice of pitch, addendums, and modification of the involute profile (see Sec. 8.2). Errors in manufacture, such as poor surface finish, waves on the tooth surface caused by erratic action of gear-finishing machines, poor involute profiles, or irregular tooth spacing, all tend to promote scoring.

There are four places at which scoring is apt to start:

1 Where tip of gear contacts root of pinion

2 At lowest point of single-tooth contact on pinion

3 At highest point of single-tooth contact on pinion

4 Where tip of pinion contacts root of gear

In helical gears where the axial overlap amounts to two or more axial pitches, there is no clearly defined position corresponding to the point where single-tooth contact starts and ends on spur gears. However, there may still be two intermediate points that are critical. If tip relief or modification is used, the most critical points may be where the relief ends on the pinion tooth and where it ends on the gear tooth.

After a gear has scored for a short time, the damaged area will frequently extend all the way from the pitch line to the tip and from the pitch line to the root. Along the pitch line itself, there will be a narrow island of metal which will not score. However, this island will soon pit away if the gear is left in service.

Scoring failures are rather hard to analyze. The damage usually spreads so fast that it is impossible to tell just where it started or why it started. When running laboratory tests on scoring, it is quite handy to test a ratio at which the number of pinion teeth divides *evenly* into the number of gear teeth. This makes one particular gear tooth contact with only one pinion tooth. Ordinarily, with a hunting ratio, each gear tooth will contact each pinion tooth. With an even ratio, pitting will break out between some pairs of teeth and not break out on other pairs. This makes it possible to study closely the effect of tooth errors on the tendency to score.

Scoring seems to be considerably influenced by the affinity of one metal for another. It appears that some metals will bond together much more easily than others. Fully hardened steels will generally resist scoring better than medium-hard steels. Low-hardness steels score much more easily than medium-hard steels. In many cases, some benefit has been noted from having the pinion harder than the gear and made of a different kind of steel than the gear. For instance, case-hardened pinions run with a medium-hard gear will frequently make a more score-resistant set than a set in which the pinion and gear are both of the same steel and medium-hard.

There are two degrees of scoring, by definition: *initial scoring* and *severe scoring*. The main difference is that initial scoring occurs for a while and then stops. Severe scoring keeps going until so much metal is removed that the gear teeth finally break off. When scoring first starts, it is difficult to tell whether the scoring is of the initial or the severe variety. If the score marks are quite fine and the scored surface has a kind of smooth, "etched" appearance, there is a good chance that the scoring is of the initial variety. If the surface is rough, with ragged tear marks, there is no doubt that the scoring is of the severe variety.

Scored gears which are stopped before the scoring has progressed too far can often be put back into successful service. The scored areas should be dressed down with a stone or fine abrasive paper to restore some degree of surface finish. When the gears are put back into service, it is desirable to use a higher-film-strength oil—such as one with a good extreme pressure additive or just one of heavier viscosity. Care should be taken to see that the oil-distribution system is *wetting down* all the teeth before they go into mesh. In rare cases, it has been found that the oil was too thick to spread out over the whole tooth surface. The solution to this kind of problem may be to use a thinner oil which will spread more rapidly. Changes in oil-nozzle designs or in oil-pumping systems are often required to overcome gear-scoring problems.

Scoring can often be prevented by careful breaking in of gearsets. It is desirable to run the teeth at light loads and low speeds until the tooth surfaces have polished up. This is particularly beneficial on the lower-hardness steels and on bronzes meshing with steel. Fully hardened steel gears benefit some from running in, but not nearly so much as the softer materials. Tests made on gears of 200 Brinell hardness have shown that careful running in can sometimes reduce an 0.8-μm (32-μin.) machined surface to a 0.25-μm (10-μin.) finish and work-hardened surface equivalent to 250 Brinell hardness. Obviously, changes like this greatly improve a gear's ability to resist scoring.

Scoring is particularly troublesome with high-speed gears running with thin, hot oil. A change to thicker oil or cooler running can be very helpful. If this cannot be done, an improvement in the *character* and *smoothness* of the finish may solve the problem. Helicopter gears are quite often honed after precision grinding to get a kind of finish that will adequately resist scoring under rather difficult service conditions.

Scoring may be a problem with slow-running final drive gears in trucks, tractors, and earth-moving equipment. In these vehicle gears, the problem is a very heavy tooth load and pitch-line speeds so slow that a proper EHD (elastohydrodynamic) oil film is not obtained. This kind of problem is generally solved by using heavy oils and strong EP (extreme pressure) additives. The additives tend to create a chemical film on the tooth surface and/or a chemical reaction with the surface that protects the surface from scoring. (See Secs. 3.31 and 7.15 for more details on lubrication.)

7.9 Wear Failures

According to the dictionary, "wear" means damage caused by use. Under this kind of definition, all kinds of tooth damage, such as pitting, scoring, tooth breakage, and abrasion, might be considered as just different kinds of tooth wear. Most gear engineers consider a worn gear tooth to be one that has had a layer of metal more or less uniformly removed from the surface.

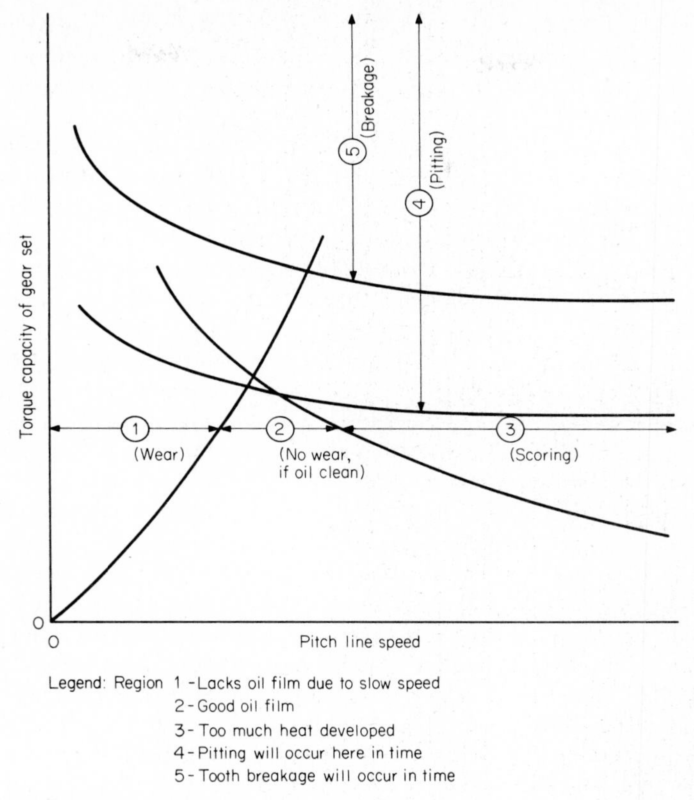

FIG. 7.10 The regions of gear failure.

Damage which does not remove all the surface but instead makes craters or scratches in the surface is generally not called wear. Such damage, of course, is best described as pitting and scoring.

In this section we shall consider the kinds of wear that, by abrasion or other means, remove layer after layer of material from the surface of the tooth. This is the kind of wear that reduces tooth thickness and frequently severely changes the contour of the tooth.

Tests and experiences of the author indicate that all kinds of gear wear fit a logical pattern. Figure 7.10 shows a schematic plot of torque vs. speed for a gearset. The total area is divided into five different regions. Each of these regions is bounded by a failure line of one kind or another.

In Region 1, the gear is not running fast enough to develop a hydrodynamic oil film. The wear is *rapid when measured in terms of metal removed per million contacts* of the tooth. Since the gear is running slowly, the wear may not be particularly fast in terms of wear per hour or per day. The size of

Region 1 can be reduced in most cases by using a thicker oil or by using an oil with a special additive that will make the fluid cling to the gear teeth more tenaciously. Too thin an oil or too rough a surface finish will make Region 1 larger.

The lower part of Region 2 is the ideal place to run a gearset. The speed is high enough to develop a good film. If the oil is free of abrasive foreign material, is noncorrosive, and adheres to the surface properly, a gear can run almost indefinitely in Region 2 without measurable wear.

In Region 3 there is rapid failure. The speed is high enough to produce an oil film, but it shears the oil film so fast that too much heat is developed. The film breaks down, and scoring or welding occurs.

Region 4 is the region in which pitting is apt to occur. Since pitting is a fatigue failure, the size of Region 4 tends to increase with time—more time means more cycles, and more cycles mean a lower load that can be carried at a given speed. Region 4 is also enlarged by poor lubrication conditions. This seems to stem from two causes. Wear damages the tooth profile and causes load to be concentrated near the pitch line. This is one of the regions that is vulnerable to pitting damage. Wear also tends to result in higher local coefficients of friction. A higher friction force means that there is more tendency for the surface to be ruptured with the cracks that cause pits.

Work in the 1970s showed that Region 4 changes rather surprisingly with a substantial change in the "regime" of lubrication. The stress vs. cycles curve for pitting failure changes both slope and location. Figure 7.11 illustrates this tendency in aerospace gearing lubricated with a light synthetic oil. The same general tendency can be noted in slow-speed vehicle gearing when changing from a lighter weight mineral oil to heavier weight oil and when changing from mild EP additives to strong EP additives. (Table 2.6 in Sec. 2.4 presents more information on regimes of lubrication.)

A survey of the gear-wear characteristics of most types of industrial and

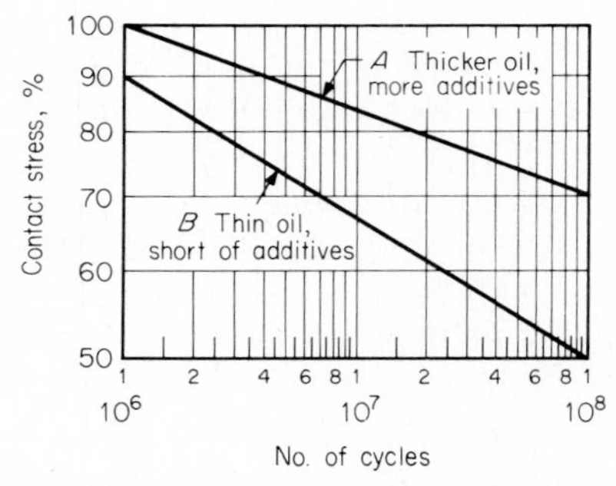

FIG. 7.11 A substantial change in the lubricant may shift the allowable contact stress from curve *B* to curve *A*.

vehicle gears shows that the most common cause of a breakdown of the gear-tooth surface is pitting-related. To say it another way, a worn gear tooth—when closely studied—is very apt to have worn primarily because of some mode of pitting. The successful designer of power gearing will develop a very keen appreciation for all the subtle things involved with the Region 4 boundary.

Region 5 is the region in which tooth breakage is apt to occur. The size of this area is also increased as a function of the length of time the set operates. Breakage is a fatigue failure. The size of Region 5 is increased when wear occurs. Wear makes gears run with more shock and vibration. This is just like increasing the torque. Wear also weakens the tooth by removing metal from the base of the tooth and by acting as a *factor to increase the stress concentration in the root fillet.*

From the foregoing it can be seen that as soon as one kind of gear damage occurs, continued running will make the gear less and less able to resist all the other kinds of gear damage. Frequently a wrecked set of gears will show all kinds of damage, such as abrasive wear, pitting, scoring, peening, wire edging, and tooth breakage. The investigator may be hard pressed to deduce which kind of damage started the fatal chain of events.

The existence of Region 1 can be demonstrated in two different ways. One is to measure the mesh loss of gear teeth. When appreciable torque is applied and held constant over a wide speed range, a curve like Fig. 7.12 will result. The tail at the left-hand side indicates that the oil film has failed and the *coefficient of friction is increasing while speed decreases.* Another way is to measure wear. In one test the author made, a set of precision spur gears was operated for 20 million cycles at a pitch-line speed of 30 m/sec (6000 fpm). Involute measurements showed wear to be less than 2.5 μm (0.0001 in.).

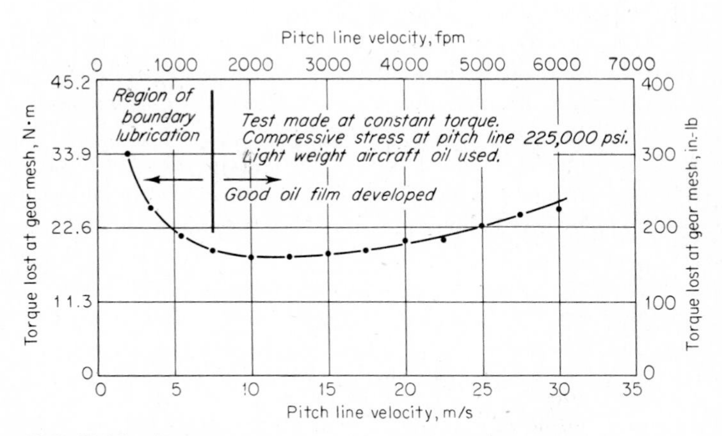

FIG. 7.12 Friction torque as a function of speed.

Then the set was run at 5 m/s (1000 fpm) with the same torque for 5 million cycles. After this shorter, slower run, wear had increased to 13 μm (0.0005 in.).

In high-speed marine and power-plant equipment, it is quite likely that after a year or more of operation, the wear will be so slight that machining marks a few microinches deep will still be visible on the tooth surface. In slow-speed gears such as drive gears on freight locomotives or on winches or hoists, it is not uncommon to see about 1 mm (1/32 in.) of metal worn away in 6 months. It is true that high-speed gears generally have cleaner oils and lighter loads than slow-speed gears. In spite of this, though, the weight of evidence seems to show that well-designed fast-running gears wear less than equally well designed slow-running gears when wear is judged on the amount per million cycles of operation.

Foreign material will, of course, cause wear at any speed. Dirt, sand, and oxides may get into the oil stream. These can cause rapid wear or "lapping" of the gear teeth. Great care must be taken to keep the oil system of a gearset from becoming contaminated. In some kinds of transportation equipment, gear wear is frequently caused by dirt getting into the oil. On the other hand, power-plant gears seldom have this kind of trouble. They are protected from wind, weather, and contacts with soil.

7.10 Gearbox Bearings

If the bearings in a gear unit fail, the gear unit is, of course, failed. From a responsibility standpoint, those technically responsible for gear units are responsible for the gear teeth, the gear bearings, the seals, the oil breather device, the shaft extension splines or keyways, the oil circulation system, etc.

Records that have been kept of the frequency and kind of gear-unit troubles invariably show that about two-thirds of the incidents involve problems with bearing failures or bearing damage. (From a practical standpoint, the gear designer and builder may have to worry more about bearings than about gear teeth!)

The high incidence of bearing problems should not be blamed on the inadequacy of bearings as a mechanical element or on the lack of technical knowledge available in the bearing field. Bearings are involved frequently for two reasons. First, the geometry of the bearing and its fit-up in the gearbox are more complex than gear-tooth geometry and gear-tooth fit-up. Second, the bearings are generally more sensitive to some wrong condition in the application, and they will start to fail sooner than the gear teeth.

Some of the kinds of wrong things that may lead to early bearing troubles are:

The unit is running with foreign material in the oil (iron filings, sand, dirt, water, acid, etc.).

The unit is running too hot.

The unit traveled a *rough* road to the site and incurred damage through vibration and fretting corrosion.

The unit has high vibration (in running).

The unit is misaligned or out of position in an axial direction.

Driving or driven equipment is running poorly (turbine out of balance, reciprocating compressor has some valves stuck, and so on).

Coupling devices between gearbox and connected apparatus are not functioning properly (severe moments or thrusts are being developed).

7.11 Rolling-Element Bearings

Rolling-element bearings like ball bearings, cylindrical roller bearings, tapered roller bearings, and spherical roller bearings are frequently used in gearboxes. These bearings work well at slow speeds. They have low friction losses, particularly at slow speeds, and they position a gear part rather precisely.

At high speeds the friction losses are not so low, and the bearing may have difficulty handling the speed. Figure 7.13 shows a general guide for speed limits on rolling-element bearings. With good lubrication, rolling-element bearings can generally live up to the limits in Fig. 7.13. If the rolling-element bearing is used beyond these limits, the gear designer would be well advised to consider it a special application which a bearing specialist needs to study in depth to make sure that the bearing design features, the accuracy and quality of the bearing, and the lubrication scheme are adequate for the high-speed situation.

Rolling-element bearings are designed against fatigue limits. If a 2000-hour life is needed, a size of bearing may be picked for which calculations—on a surface fatigue basis—predict a 90 percent probability of running this long without serious pitting. This is called a *B-10 life*. A bearing with a B-5 life has a 95 percent probability of running without pitting for the time used in the calculations.

Generally speaking, gear designers know how to make the calculations to pick the right size of bearing. (Frequently, it is desirable to have the specialists at a major bearing company make the calculations and recommend the correct size and style of bearing for a critical gear application.)

When there are troubles in a gearbox with rolling-element bearings, the cause of the trouble is usually something other than that too small a bearing was used for the job. It is usually good practice, though, to review the bearing rating calculations to see if some error might have been made, or if perhaps the real load on a job in production might be higher than that anticipated back in the beginning of a project.

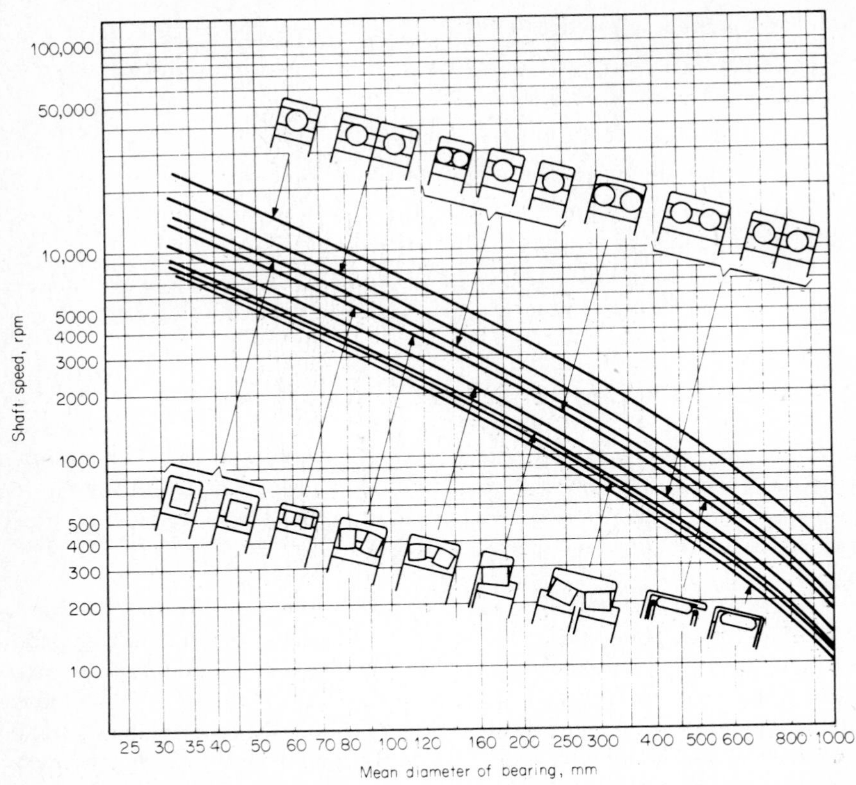

FIG. 7.13 A general guide to when speed becomes critical in rolling-element gear bearings. With special lubrication, very high accuracy, and special materials in cages, rollers, and races, rolling-element bearings can be operated at speeds substantially higher than the limits shown. *(Courtesy of SKF Industries, Inc., King of Prussia, PA, U.S.A.)*

General areas of concern in investigating rolling-element bearings are:

Fit of bearings on shaft or in housing inappropriate.

Bearings not adequately cooled and lubricated.

Bearing internal clearance wrong for the application. (See Fig. 7.14.)

Bearings damaged in shipment, or in assembly, or in overhaul work.

Bearings not made right at the bearing factory.

Foreign material gets into the bearing.

Application of the bearing in the gearbox improper for that style of rolling-element bearing.

Accuracy of the bearing or materials in the bearing not suitable for the high speed of the application. (See Fig. 7.13.)

FIG. 7.14 A rolling-element bearing failure in a gearbox due to improper internal clearance. (Failure occurred in less than 100 hours running time.)

Many kinds of gears will have both a thrust load and a radial load to be carried at a given shaft end. Ball bearings, spherical roller bearings, and tapered roller bearings can all carry both thrust load and radial load. Unfortunately, there are often situations in which the combination of those loads will get bearings into trouble as wear occurs or as thermal changes shift the bearing fit or clearance. Frequently, the best solution may be to use *two* bearings at a shaft end, with one bearing taking only thrust and one bearing taking only radial load. The common design that pairs a ball bearing for thrust with a cylindrical roller bearing for radial load is a good example of this technique.

Table 7.4 shows some of the possible faults that may exist in new bearings bought from a bearing company. The purchaser of rolling-element bearings, in general, receives a mechanical hardware item with amazing accuracy in roundness and perfection in finish for a surprisingly low price. Usually the bearings are made correctly. Once in a while, they are not. If there is a manufacturing fault, it may be present in all bearings in a shipment of a hundred or more, because bearings are usually made on automated or semiautomated machines.

When there is trouble with rolling-element bearings, the investigator should be alert to all the areas of concern mentioned earlier. One of these is a defect in manufacture of the bearings.

Table 7.4 shows some of the manufacturing defects that tend to show up once in a while in new bearings. Roundness, concentricity, and race finish might have been added to the table. Generally these basics are all right.

TABLE 7.4 Defects in Manufacture of Rolling-Element Bearings

Kind of bearing	Kind of defect		
	Races	Rolling elements	Cages
Ball bearing	• Curvature not held closely to design • Hardness too low or too high • Grain size too large • Cleanness of steel not up to specifications	• Balls not all round and of good finish • Missing ball • Nicked ball • Hardness too low • Grain size too large • Cleanness of steel not up to specifications	• Broached with a dull or worn broach • Plating defective • Composition of material out of limits
Roller bearing*	• Guide rail at wrong angle • Finish of guide rail inadequate • Clearance of roller in guide rails too small or too large	• Roller end out of square with roller axis • Roller crown wrong or out of position on roller • Roller corners not rounded properly • Roller ends not finished smoothly	• Shape of pocket wrong to fit roller • Pocket clearance too small or too large • Cage blocks oil entry • Cage not guided adequately

*All the items for ball bearings apply to roller bearings.

Table 7.4 shows some of the other things that may be wrong, and that often require a special investigation to find.

7.12 Sliding-Element Bearings

Sliding-element bearings are used for both radial and thrust loads. In some cases the thrust bearing is integral with the radial bearing; the typical construction is a cylinder with a flange on one end. In many cases, though, the two kinds of bearings are separate. High-speed turbine gearsets used in the oil and gas industry will often have a tilting-pad thrust bearing and split-cylindrical radial bearings.

Sliding-element bearings need a certain amount of speed to run acceptably. In gear applications the load on the bearing is steady, so there is not a fatigue-life problem as with rolling-element bearings. This means that a good sleeve bearing in a gear unit will generally be able to run for many years at high speed without failure. Sliding-element bearings are quite commonly used in turbine applications because of their ability to handle heavy loads and run with high reliability for many years.

If there is going to be trouble with sliding-element bearings in a gear application, the trouble will generally show up early. In fact, a damaged or failed sleeve bearing has often been found on the very first full-speed, full-load test of a new gear design.

Some of the things that can go wrong and cause early sliding-element-bearing failures are:

Foreign material in oil lines or in gearbox passageways gets flushed into the bearings. (The most dangerous locations are *downstream* from the oil filter, but *upstream* from the bearing. The debris gets a chance to lodge in the bearing before it has a chance to lodge in the filter.)

Oil nozzle plugged, or oil passageway not drilled.

Clearance in bearing too small.

Bearing fit to casing or to shafts improper.

Bearings not made correctly at the bearing factory.

Finish, roundness, or cylindricalness of a shaft inadequate for a radial bearing; finish, flatness, or squareness of a thrust runner inadequate for a thrust bearing.

Application of bearing to gearbox improper for that style of sliding-element bearing.

Accuracy of the bearing or materials in the bearing not suitable for the high speed of the bearing.

Like rolling-element bearings, sliding-element bearings are generally made correctly at the factory. Except for those used in automotive gearing, sliding-element bearings are generally not made on highly automated machinery. If something is wrong, it may be limited to a few bearings and represent some random human error or machine misfunction. Table 7.5 shows some of the defects that may occur in new bearings.

One of the problems in Table 7.5 is very simple—a bearing with the wrong direction of rotation. It would seem that this problem would be easy to avoid, but it is really quite troublesome. Bearings at opposite ends of the pinion may need to be made differently, since the thrust faces generally point toward the gear teeth. By simply exchanging the bearings from one end of the pinion to the other end, it is possible—in some gearsets—to end up with the unfortunate situation of two bearings running in the wrong direction.

Presumably the bearings are marked with part numbers, and the assembly drawing shows which part number goes on which end. The bearing

TABLE 7.5 Defects in Manufacture of Sliding-Element Bearings

Kind of bearing	Kind of defect
Full-circle cylindrical	Bore not concentric to O.D. within tolerance Bore or O.D. sizes out of tolerance Bonding of babbitt to backing not sound Composition of babbitt, bronze, or other bearing overlay material not within specification limits Feed grooves or bleeder grooves not accurately made Edges of feed grooves not rounded properly
Split cylindrical	(All the above items apply, plus these below) Bearing made for clockwise rotation, should have been made for counterclockwise rotation or vice versa Curvature of bearing half wrong, so half does not fit casing properly
Tapered-land thrust bearing	Lands not alike or level Ramp curvature out of specification Size and shape of plateau at ramp end too big or too small or misshapen Ramps put in for the *wrong* direction of rotation Feed grooves or bleeder grooves not accurately made Edges of grooves not rounded properly
Tilting pad bearing	Pads not equal height Pad-support pins (or other support mechanism) not fitted properly

maker may put the wrong part number on a bearing, or the mechanic may pick up a bearing of the wrong part number at assembly. Either mistake can lead to a bearing being run in the wrong direction.

Sometimes sliding-element bearings fail after thousands of hours of operation. If the bearing was made correctly and everything fit, what could lead to a delayed failure in a part not subject to fatigue failures?

Some common things that tend to cause service failures of sliding-element gear bearings include:

Wear in gear teeth or couplings causes vibration. A high vibration level fatigues out a bearing that normally would have no fatigue problem. (See Fig. 7.15.)

Shafts and gear teeth rust when a unit is shut down for a long time in a wet climate (or outdoors in a dry climate). Bearings fail due to rusted shafts. Rusted gear teeth may also cause failure due to rough running and wear debris in the oil system.

Oil filters are inadequate or become filled with dirt and then bypass

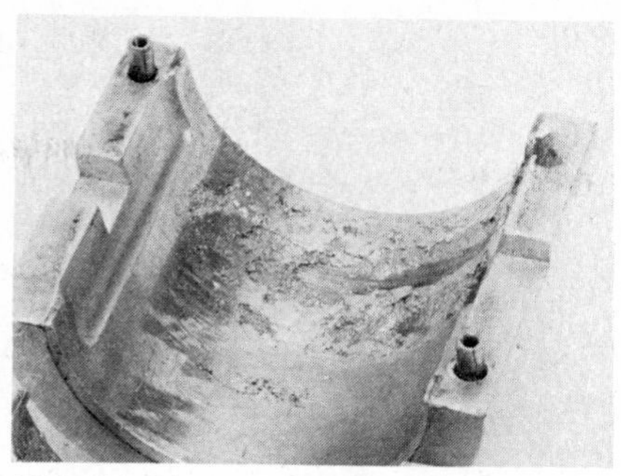

FIG. 7.15 A sliding-element bearing failure in a high-speed gearbox. Excessive system vibration failed the bearing. Gear teeth did not fail, but they were close to failure.

unfiltered and dirty oil. Bearings become contaminated with dirt due to in-service conditions.

The wrong oil is used, or the right oil is used too long. Tarry deposits may plug oil orifices. The lack of antifoam protection may flood a high-speed unit that would normally drain properly and may lead to rapid overheating of bearings and gear teeth.

Careless overhaul of a unit may lead to nicks in journal surfaces, bearings installed with the wrong thrust shims, metering orifices left out of oil feed lines, etc.

SOME CAUSES OF GEAR FAILURE OTHER THAN EXCESS TRANSMITTED LOAD

If a gear unit fails, there is a somewhat natural inclination to believe that it must have been too small to handle the name-plate rating. This may be true, and, of course, a first step in an investigation can be a careful recheck of the power capacity for the size of gear unit involved.

Quite often, though, there is some problem not related to transmitted power. In this part of the chapter, some of the more common things that can go wrong in a gear application will be reviewed.

7.13 Overload Gear Failures

The designer of a gearset usually bases the gear size on a maximum torque and a continuous torque. These are ordinarily based on the amount of power that is being *transmitted* by the gearset under different conditions of operation. It may happen that there are momentary torque fluctuations that are far in excess of the transmitted power.

On ships there is a torque fluctuation each time a propeller blade passes the rudder post. The gearset may have a high-speed turbine driving it, with a large amount of kinetic energy in the turbine rotor. If the ship's power system is not carefully designed, a very nasty torsional vibration may be excited by the slow propeller reacting against the high-speed turbine. Since the gearset is in between, it may be the victim of the conflict between the turbine trying to run at constant speed and the propeller trying to run at a variable speed.

Reciprocating engines driving generators, steam turbines driving air compressors, electric motors driving fans, and a host of other applications are subject to possible trouble from torsional vibration. In all these cases, a good overall engineering design can usually hold the torsional vibration down to reasonable values. The application factors used in gear-rating formulas (see Sec. 3.27) *assume* that torsional vibration has been reasonably well controlled. If this has not been done, then there is the chance that the gears will be rapidly pounded to pieces by torsional vibrations far in excess of the torsional vibrations contemplated by the application factor.

Several things may be done to eliminate torsional vibrations. Changes in shaft stiffness and moments of inertia of rotating elements can change the amplitude and frequency of vibration. The stimulus may be reduced by adding blades or pistons or by making other changes to the device connected to the gearset. Going into the subject of torsional vibrations is beyond the scope of this book.

Another kind of overload is the overload due to *tooth errors*. Tooth errors prevent the masses of the driven and driving apparatus from rotating at uniform velocities. The changes in velocity caused by tooth errors cause momentary overloads. These loads have been commonly called the *dynamic* load. The dynamic load is made up of the transmitted load plus a load increment caused by a tooth error going through mesh. As an error goes through mesh, there is ordinarily an acceleration period and a deceleration period. If the impulse produced is great enough, the teeth may separate on their driving faces, then close back together with an impact. When separation occurs, the greatest overload happens when the teeth come together again.

When gears are run at high enough speeds, the kinetic energy becomes so great that tooth errors cannot change the velocity appreciably. Under this condition, the overload is simply whatever load is required to bend the tooth out of the way (that is, the static load that would cause a deflection corresponding to the tooth error).

Earle Buckingham has published books* which give methods for esti-

*See Refs. 2 and 90 at the end of the book.

mating dynamic loads on all kinds of gears. His work shows that it is quite easy to get a combination of tooth errors, moments of inertia of gears and connected apparatus, and shaft stiffnesses which results in dynamic loads five or six times as great as the transmitted load.

Dynamic load factors used in standard design equations assume relatively low dynamic loads. If designers have enough field experience with a given application, they can determine dynamic load factors which will be quite accurate for the application. It may be hard to calculate dynamic load and get a close check on field experience. The calculator has to assume an amount of error and then can calculate shaft stiffnesses and moments of inertia quite accurately. It becomes difficult, though, to follow the error through mesh and calculate the precise value of the instantaneous load at the worst point. Effects of friction, elastic dampening of the system, and wear are hard to predict. (See Sec. 9.2 for more details on dynamic load.)

When a dynamic overload more than twice the transmitted load is calculated, the designer should try to make changes to reduce the dynamic load. This may be done by using more accurate teeth, reducing masses, using more elastic materials, or changing shaft stiffnesses. One of the greatest values of dynamic-load calculations is that the designer can see which items in the design ought to be changed to reduce the dynamic load.

Another source of gear overloads is imbalance. Heavy parts running at high speed must be dynamically balanced very closely to run properly. In addition, they must be mounted on good foundations. It sometimes happens that a gearset will be tested in the shop on a heavy concrete base. Its balance will be adjusted and it will operate very smoothly. Out in the field, the set may be mounted on a rather weak support. On ships, airplanes, and locomotives, it is always hard to design a good foundation for high-speed apparatus. Vibrations may occur which in time will destroy the tooth accuracy. Then the lack of accuracy can lead to severe dynamic overloads.

7.14 Gear-Casing Problems

Many gear failures are caused by the improper functioning of the gear casing. A gearset depends upon the gear casing, the gear bearings, and flexible couplings to support it properly, to protect it from dirt and moisture, to protect it from reactions of misaligned driving or driven shafts, and to provide nozzles and reservoir capacity to handle a proper circulation of the lubricant.

Providing support for parallel-axis gearing is usually not difficult. Gears on right-angle axes are often hard to support. If one or more members are overhung, deflection of the gear support and shafting may be quite critical. Frequently an overhung gear part will have good contact under average load conditions, but a sudden peak load will cause so much deflection as to throw all the load on one end of the tooth. This can cause a quick failure. Whenever overhung gears show damage at the ends of the teeth, it is desirable to investigate how tooth contact changes as load is increased. It may be necessary to change the tooth design so that all the load is at one end of the tooth under light-load conditions to favor the contact when maximum load occurs. Sometimes even this will not work. When new, the set may have modifications that compensate for deflection. Long running at light load may wear away these modifications. Then, when the severe peak load occurs, there is no modification to protect the teeth from end loading. In this kind of situation, there is no alternative but to design the casing and shafting to provide a stiffer support for the gear teeth.

The gear casing is usually made in at least two halves and bolted together. Dowels are used to position the casings properly before the bolts are tightened. There may be trouble because the dowels are too small or too few, or they become worn. If the dowels do not function properly, serious misalignments of gear teeth or bearings can be the result.

Jackscrews should be provided to disassemble a gear casing. Without jackscrews, a gear casing may become bent or damaged at the joint by pounding and prying on the casing to get it apart. Casings damaged in disassembly are apt to be misaligned when reassembled. They are also apt to have oil leaks.

Bearing wear is another cause of gear failure. Sleeve bearings may gradually increase their clearance. Ball or roller bearings may have inner races that turn on their shafts or outer races that turn in their seats. A gear supported by a pair of either type of bearings may gradually become misaligned by unequal wear of the bearings supporting it. In some configurations, even an equal amount of wear on two bearings will permit misalignment! Slight amounts of bearing wear can be quite serious. A 2.5-module (10-pitch) tooth which is of medium hardness may be seriously distressed by a misalignment of as little as 0.025 mm (0.001 in.) in the face width.

Gear-rating formulas (such as those in Sec. 3.27) allow for misalignment in calculating load-carrying capacity. The gear designer tends to assume that all misalignment is due to errors in machining either the gears or the cases and seldom allows anything for *further misalignment* due to wear of bearings. In many cases, bearings do not wear enough to cause appreciable misalignment. In these cases wear of the gear teeth will improve contact, and there will probably be no trouble due to misalignment. However, if the misalignment increases because of bearing wear, there is often a good chance for gear failure.

When gears fail, the gear bearings are likely to fail also. In such cases the designer should try to deduce whether the bearings failed or wore first, precipitating a gear failure, or whether the gear failure caused the bearings to fail because of overload or because bits of metal from the gear teeth got into the bearing. When both the gear teeth and bearings have failed, it is unlikely that they both failed by coincidence at the same time. One or the other is apt to be to blame for the failure of both.

Gear failures may be caused by malfunctioning of flexible couplings. When a gear with two bearings is connected to a shaft from another device that has two bearings, a flexible coupling is needed to connect the two. In most cases the designer cannot expect that four bearings will be so precisely in line that no flexible joint is required.

Flexible couplings are also needed to allow differential expansions between different pieces of apparatus. Steam turbines, electric motors, generators, pumps, and many other devices are commonly connected to gearsets by flexible couplings.

Flexible couplings may fail just like any other machine element. A failed coupling is not necessarily one that is broken in two. It may have become jammed so that it is no longer flexible. This can lead to the shaft supporting the gear being made to run in a misaligned position because of a reaction being transmitted through the coupling. The gear may also be jammed out of position in an endwise direction. This can upset the tooth contact on worm gears, bevel gears, or double helical gears. Spur gears, however, usually do not suffer from endwise movement unless a difference in face width between the gear and pinion has caused an indentation to be worn into the part with the wider face width.

In the larger sizes and at higher speeds, worn-out couplings will run with quite severe torsional shock and vibration. These things can also cause gear failures.

High-speed gears sometimes get into trouble because the gear tends to churn or "pump" the oil in the casing. Many oils will foam badly when churned too severely by a toothed gear wheel. Oil churning can also rapidly overheat a unit that does not have an oil cooler. The gear casing must provide a means to lubricate the gears adequately, but in addition it must allow the oil to get out of the way of fast-moving gear teeth. Frequently it is necessary to put a sheet-metal shroud around a gear which dips below the oil level. This shroud will keep most of the oil away from the gear when it is running.

7.15 Lubrication Failures

Many gear failures are blamed on the lubricant, when in fact the failure is caused by a faulty mechanical design. Inaccurate teeth, poor surface finishes, lack of profile modification, and overly heavy loads for the strength of the materials may cause failures of the tooth surfaces. [Obviously such failures are not really lubrication failures but rather are design failures (or manufacturing failures)]. It is true that many design failures may be remedied to a certain extent by special lubrication. However, the gear designer can get the best results only with both a *good* mechanical design and a *good* lubricant and lubricating system.

True lubrication failures usually result from one of the following troubles:

1. The lubricating oil does not have the right additives or a strong enough additive package to handle the loads, speed conditions, or temperature of the particular application. A high coefficient of friction and rapid wear is generally the result of inadequate additives.
2. The lubricating oil does not have enough viscosity to develop a suitable oil film between the contacting surfaces. In general, slow-speed gears require rather viscous oil with good chemical additives. Gears above 10 m/s (2000 fpm) can use the thinner oils quite well, and a strong additive package is usually not needed.
3. Heat developed by the gears is not removed quickly enough by the lubricating medium.
4. Wear products and corrosion on the tooth surfaces are not flushed away by the lubricant.
5. The lubricant becomes contaminated with dirt, sand, metal particles, sludge, or acids.
6. The lubricating system does not wet all the tooth surfaces before each surface goes through mesh.
7. Lubricant is not contained; it leaks out, or vaporizes, and escapes. (Loss of oil may result from inadequate vents or seals, leaks in casing joints, inattention to refilling the gearbox with oil, etc.)

In early days, when wooden-toothed gears were common, animal fats were used as lubricants. In modern times, petroleum or "mineral" oils are the most widely used gear lubricants. Modern research has shown that many substances have the ability to lubricate gears. Likewise, many fluids which have the appearance and viscosity of a lubricant may actually have little or no lubricating ability.

Table 7.6 shows some of the fluids that have demonstrated their ability to lubricate gear teeth. This table shows that several kinds of liquids may be used to lubricate gears. To date, petroleum oils have been by far the most widely used gear lubricants.

When there is a suspicion of a lubrication failure, basic lubrication practice for gear units should be reviewed. The next few paragraphs and tables give a brief review of normal practice for industrial, aircraft, and vehicle gears.

TABLE 7.6 Fluids Used to Lubricate Gears

Fluids	Oiliness	Where used
Petroleum oils	Good	All types of gears except under unusual temperature conditions
Diester	Good	Aircraft and military gears with wide temperature ranges
Polyglycol	Good	Some bronze gears, steel gears at very high temperatures
Silicone	Poor	Some extreme-temperature cases, light load
Water	Very poor	Some nonmetallic gears
Phosphates	Good	Aircraft hydraulic equipment

AGMA Standard 250.04 does a good job of specifying petroleum oils for use on various kinds of gears. This standard classifies the oils according to viscosity as measured by a Saybolt universal viscosimeter. The classifications are shown in Table 7.7.

TABLE 7.7 Viscosity Ranges for AGMA Lubricants

Rust and oxidation inhibited gear oils, AGMA lubricant no.	Viscosity range,[a] mm^2/s (cSt) at 40°C	Equivalent ISO grade[b]	Extreme-pressure gear lubricants,[c] AGMA lubricant no.	Viscosities of former AGMA system,[d] SSU at 100°F
1	41.4 to 50.6	46		193 to 235
2	61.2 to 74.8	68	2 EP	284 to 347
3	90 to 110	100	3 EP	417 to 510
4	135 to 165	150	4 EP	626 to 765
5	198 to 242	220	5 EP	918 to 1122
6	288 to 352	320	6 EP	1335 to 1632
7 Comp[e]	414 to 506	460	7 EP	1919 to 2346
8 Comp[e]	612 to 748	680	8 EP	2837 to 3467
8A Comp[e]	900 to 1100	1000	8A EP	4171 to 5098

Note: Viscosity ranges for AGMA lubricant numbers will henceforth be identical to those of ASTM 2422.

[a] "Viscosity System for Industrial Fluid Lubricants," ASTM 2422. Also British Standards Institute, B.S. 4231.

[b] "Industrial Liquid Lubricants—ISO Viscosity Classification." International Standard, ISO 3448.

[c] Extreme-pressure lubricants should be used *only* when recommended by the gear drive manufacturer.

[d] AGMA 250.03, May 1972, and AGMA 251.02, November 1974.

[e] Oils marked Comp are compounded with 3 to 10 percent fatty or synthetic fatty oils.

This table was extracted from AGMA Specification "Lubrication of Industrial Enclosed Gear Drives" (AGMA 250.04, 1981) with the permission of the publisher, the American Gear Manufacturers Association, Suite 1000, 1901 North Fort Myer Drive, Arlington, VA 22209.

Table 7.8 shows the recommended lubricants for industrial gears, while Table 7.9 shows the data for worm gears. Those concerned with gear lubrication problems should study the considerable amount of detailed information given in AGMA 250.04. (See Ref. 61.)

TABLE 7.8 AGMA Lubricant Number[a,b] Recommendations for Enclosed Helical, Herringbone, Straight Bevel, Spiral Bevel, and Spur Gear Drives

Type of unit[c] and low-speed center distance	Ambient temperature[d, e]	
	−10°C to +10°C (15°F to 50°F)	10°C to 50°C (50°F to 125°F)
Parallel shaft (single reduction)		
Up to 200 mm (to 8 in.)	2–3	3–4
Over 200 mm to 500 mm (8 to 20 in.)	2–3	4–5
Over 500 mm (over 20 in.)	3–4	4–5
Parallel shaft (double reduction)		
Up to 200 mm (to 8 in.)	2–3	3–4
Over 200 mm (over 8 in.)	3–4	4–5
Parallel shaft (triple reduction)		
Up to 200 mm (to 8 in.)	2–3	3–4
Over 200 mm to 500 mm (8 to 20 in.)	3–4	4–5
Over 500 mm (over 20 in.)	4–5	5–6
Planetary-gear units (housing diameter)		
Up to 400 mm (to 16 in.) O.D.	2–3	3–4
Over 400 mm (over 16 in.) O.D.	3–4	4–5
Straight or spiral-bevel-gear units		
Cone distance to 300 mm (to 12 in.)	2–3	4–5
Cone distance over 300 mm (over 12 in.)	3–4	5–6
Gear motors and shaft-mounted units	2–3	4–5
High-speed units[f]	1	2

[a] Ranges are provided to allow for variations in operating conditions such as surface finish, temperature rise, loading, speed, etc.

[b] AGMA viscosity number recommendations listed above refer to R&O gear oils shown in Table 7.7. EP gear lubricants in the corresponding viscosity grades may be substituted where deemed necessary by the gear drive manufacturer.

[c] Drives incorporating overrunning clutches as backstopping devices should be referred to the gear-drive manufacturer, as certain types of lubricants may adversely affect clutch performance.

[d] For ambient temperatures outside the ranges shown, consult the gear manufacturer. Some synthetic oils have been used successfully for high- or low-temperature applications.

[e] Pour point of lubricant selected should be at least 5°C (9°F) lower than the expected minimum ambient starting temperature. If the ambient starting temperature approaches lubricant pour point, oil-sump heaters may be required to facilitate starting and ensure proper lubrication.

[f] High-speed units are those operating at speeds above 3600 rpm or pitch-line velocities above 25 m/s (5000 fpm) or both. Refer to Standard AGMA 421, "Practice for High-Speed Helical and Herringbone Gear Units," for detailed lubrication recommendations.

This table was extracted from AGMA Specification "Lubrication of Industrial Enclosed Gear Drives" (AGMA 250.04, 1981) with the permission of the publisher, the American Gear Manufacturers Association, Suite 1000, 1901 North Fort Myer Drive, Arlington, VA 22209.

TABLE 7.9 AGMA Lubricant Number[a] Recommendations for Enclosed Cylindrical and Double-Enveloping Worm-Gear Drives

Type, worm-gear drive	Worm speed[c] (rpm) up to	Ambient temperature[b]		Worm speed[c] (rpm) above	Ambient temperature[b]	
		−10°C to +10°C (15° to 50°F)	10°C to 50°C (50° to 125°F)		−10°C to +10°C (15° to 50°F)	10°C to 50°C (50° to 125°F)
Cylindrical worm[d]						
Up to 150 mm (to 6 in.)	700	7 Comp, 7 EP	8 Comp, 8 EP	700	7 Comp, 7 EP	8 Comp, 8 EP
Over 150 mm to 300 mm (6 to 12 in.)	450	7 Comp, 7 EP	8 Comp, 8 EP	450	7 Comp, 7 EP	7 Comp, 7 EP
Over 300 mm to 450 mm (12 to 18 in.)	300	7 Comp, 7 EP	8 Comp, 8 EP	300	7 Comp, 7 EP	7 Comp, 7 EP
Over 450 mm to 600 mm (18 to 24 in.)	250	7 Comp, 7 EP	8 Comp, 8 EP	250	7 Comp, 7 EP	7 Comp, 7 EP
Over 600 mm (over 24 in.)	200	7 Comp, 7 EP	8 Comp, 8 EP	200	7 Comp, 7 EP	7 Comp, 7 EP
Double-enveloping worm[d]						
Up to 150 mm (to 6 in.)	700	8 Comp	8A Comp	700	8 Comp	8 Comp
Over 150 mm to 300 mm (6 to 12 in.)	450	8 Comp	8A Comp	450	8 Comp	8 Comp
Over 300 mm to 450 mm (12 to 18 in.)	300	8 Comp	8A Comp	300	8 Comp	8 Comp
Over 450 mm to 600 mm (18 to 24 in.)	250	8 Comp	8A Comp	250	8 Comp	8 Comp
Over 600 mm (over 24 in.)	200	8 Comp	8A Comp	200	8 Comp	8 Comp

[a] Both EP and compounded oils are considered suitable for cylindrical-worm-gear service. Equivalent grades of both are listed in the table. For double-enveloping worm gearing, EP oils in the corresponding viscosity grades may be substituted only where deemed necessary by the worm-gear manufacturer.

[b] Pour point of the oil used should be less than the minimum ambient temperature expected. Consult gear manufacturer on lube recommendations for ambient temperatures below −10°C (14°F).

[c] Worm gears of either type operating at speeds above 2400 rpm or 10 m/s (200 fpm) rubbing speed may require force-feed lubrication. In general, a lubricant of lower viscosity than recommended in the above table shall be used with a force-feed system.

[d] Worm-gear drives may also operate satisfactorily using other types of oils. Such oils should be used, however, only upon approval by the manufacturer.

This table was extracted from AGMA Specification "Lubrication of Industrial Enclosed Gear Drives" (AGMA 250.04, 1981) with the permission of the publisher, the American Gear Manufacturers Association, Suite 1000, 1901 North Fort Myer Drive, Arlington, VA 22209.

In many cases it is not possible to follow AGMA lubrication recommendations. Frequently the oil has to lubricate several other things besides the gears in a piece of machinery. The lubrication requirements of these other things may force the choice of lubricant to be something other than that which is best for the gear. For instance, aircraft gas-turbine engines have to be able to start under arctic conditions. This makes it necessary to use a much thinner oil than would ordinarily be used. Whenever thin oils are used, it is necessary to have better tooth accuracy and finish than would otherwise be required. Tooth-profile modifications to compensate for bending also become more important.

Aircraft and helicopter gears usually use a synthetic (diester) type of oil. Although the oil is thin, the load-carrying capacity is quite good. Generally the same oil is used for the engine as the gears. This dictates special properties for the oil. These are the more common oils used:

Mil-L-6086 oil, mineral oil, about 8 cSt (centistokes) at 210°F

Mil-L-7808 oil, synthetic, about 3.6 cSt at 210°F

Mil-L-23699 oil, synthetic, about 5 cSt at 210°F

In vehicle gears, the transmission gears (used to change speed) are normally lubricated with "motor" oils. The wheels are driven by axle gears (also called differential gears or final drive gears when these names are appropriate). These latter units are lubricated with quite heavy oils, generally called gear oils.

Table 7.10 shows the general relation between the viscosity of SAE types of motor oils and gear oils. The motor oils have moderately strong additives. The gear oils—used in high-load, slow-speed gears—tend to have very strong additives of the EP type. Different vehicle builders have studied their special lubricant needs and in many cases have established proprietary specifications for their products.

When thicker than normal oils are used, there is danger of oil-churning trouble or trouble in getting the oil spread across all the contacting surfaces. Also, friction losses and cooling problems become greater.

The problem of removing heat from the gears is well recognized, but there is little exact knowledge to guide either the designer or the troubleshooter. As a general rule of thumb, it takes about 4 liters (1 gallon) of oil per minute to remove the heat developed when 400 hp is transmitted through a gear mesh. This rule assumes that the oil circulates through an oil cooler and that the removal of heat by radiation and conduction is not appreciable. In sets of large size transmitting several thousand horsepower, low friction losses resulting from favorable oil-film conditions may make it OK to use 4 liters (1 gallon) per minute for each 800 hp going through a gear mesh.

TABLE 7.10 Typical Vehicle Gear Lubricants

Designation of oil	Viscosity range, SSU			
	At 0°F (−18°C)		At 210°F (99°C)	
	Min.	Max.	Min.	Max.
Motor oil SAE No.				
5W	—	4,000	—	—
10W	6,000	12,000	—	—
20W	12,000	48,000	—	—
20	—	—	45	58
30	—	—	58	70
40	—	—	70	85
50	—	—	85	110
Gear oil SAE No.				
75	—	15,000	—	—
80	15,000	100,000	—	—
90	—	—	75	120
140	—	—	120	200
250	—	—	200	—

Many small-sized gearsets have no oil coolers. All the heat must be removed from the casing by radiation and conduction. Thermal ratings have been developed by the AGMA for many of these applications. A *thermal rating* restricts the power of a gearset so that the temperature rise of the set will not exceed a safe operating temperature. Some gear casings are made with *fins* to help the heat transfer and thereby permit a higher thermal rating.

Many cases of gear failure result from overheating. Gearsets may become covered with dust or ashes which insulate the set so that it cannot dissipate the heat that it should to meet its thermal rating. Even when oil coolers are used, the tubes may foul with time, and eventually the gearset may be getting oil that is not properly cooled. Poor oil-nozzle design can also cause trouble. The oil nozzle must spread the oil across the face width, and it must allow the oil to contact the gear surface for a slight interval of time before it is thrown off. Some designers claim that the best cooling is achieved when oil is fed into the *outgoing* side of the mesh. With careful nozzle design and testing under full-speed conditions, it is usually possible to put the nozzles on the *incoming* side and achieve satisfactory cooling. In high-speed sets, the incoming side is often preferred because it is more certain that the teeth will be *wet* when they go into mesh. In the most critical high-speed gear units, nozzles put oil on *both* sides of the mesh, with the largest amount going to the outgoing side.

One of the problems of lubricating gears with grease is that wear products or oxides formed by corrosion are not flushed away from the working surfaces. Gears with rough surfaces will tend to wear off the high spots and polish up. This is very desirable, except that if the lubricant becomes full of metal particles, it will start acting as a lapping compound. This sort of trouble may be avoided by running the gears in and then changing to a clean lubricant before shipping the unit.

Sometimes there will be appreciable wear and oxidation even after a unit is run in. Where high pressure and vibration are present, the phenomenon of *fretting corrosion* may occur. Fretting corrosion is ordinarily found more often in ball-bearing fits, spline joints, and hub-on-shaft connections than it is on gear teeth. However, if vibration and pressure are high enough and rubbing velocity is low, this nasty trouble can attack gear teeth. When the lubricant does not flush away the oxides formed by fretting corrosion, there can be very rapid wear. Fretting corrosion is particularly apt to attack a gearset that holds a load for a long period of time in one spot without turning. If oil, moisture, oxygen, and vibration are present, a gearset which is locked under load is very apt to fret a deep groove across the gear teeth at the spot where the teeth are in contact.

It is quite obvious that lubricants must be kept clean to prevent wear. In tractors, trucks, and locomotives, it is very hard to keep wind-blown sand or dirt out of the gear casings. In internal-combustion engines, there may be trouble with the gears because the high temperatures in the cylinders keep breaking down the oil. If the oil is not changed often enough, there may be considerable acid and sludge in the gear lubricant. Gear teeth with high contact pressures cannot tolerate much deterioration of the oil, even though other parts of the engine may still be able to get by when an oil is pretty well worn out.

Wetting down all the contact surfaces is often a problem. High-speed worm gears, in particular, require that all the tooth surfaces be well lubricated before they go into mesh. An oil nozzle may seem to be splashing oil all over the gear teeth. However, when the teeth are moving at high speed, the relative motion of the oil may not hit all teeth. Rapid wear and blackening of the teeth may occur.

When it appears that gear failure is the result of lack of oil wetting, several things may be done. Relocation of oil nozzles or more jets may be the answer. Sometimes it is necessary to use more pressure, so that the oil jet has more kinetic energy to overcome gear windage. A thinner oil which spreads more rapidly may be the answer.

The gear designer can best avoid lubrication failures by studying lubrication schemes that have been used successfully on a similar kind of apparatus in the past. Then if it is necessary to use something different, it is appropriate to test it before it is released for production. Experience is the best teacher when it comes to something as tricky as gear lubrication.

7.16 Thermal Problems in Fast-Running Gears

With high-speed gears, friction with the surrounding air can cause serious overheating. Gear teeth are projections on the surface of a cylinder or cone. When the gear body is turning fast enough, these projections tend to pump air much like the blades on a centrifugal compressor. In meshing gears, the further complication arises that the air that is between teeth must be expelled as the teeth go through mesh. A tooth entering a tooth space comes in and out of the space somewhat like a piston going in and out of a cylinder. The air between gear teeth must be expelled each time a pair of teeth meshes.

Spur teeth in parallel-axis gearing and straight bevel teeth in gearing with intersecting axes do the poorest job of expelling air efficiently. Helical teeth and spiral bevel teeth expel the air in an axial direction as the contact lines move axially across the face width. This is more effective.

As a general guide, spur and straight bevel teeth should not be used when the pitch-line velocity exceeds 50 m/s (10,000 fpm). The air trapping problem would become too troublesome, unless the face width is quite narrow for the module of the teeth. From the standpoints of accuracy and smoothness of meshing, spur teeth and straight bevel teeth are generally used at speeds that do not exceed about 10 m/s (2000 fpm), so air trapping is not usually a problem.

For helical teeth, the severity of the air trapping and related disturbances can be judged quite well by the axial meshing velocity. This velocity is calculated by

Axial meshing velocity = tangential meshing velocity ÷ tan helix angle

$$= \frac{\pi d_{p1} \times n_1}{60{,}000 \tan \beta} \quad \text{m/s} \quad \text{metric} \quad (7.1a)$$

$$= \frac{\pi \times d \times n_P}{12 \tan \psi} \quad \text{fpm} \quad \text{English} \quad (7.1b)$$

where V_t = tangential meshing velocity = pitch circle circumference × rpm
d_{p1}, d = pitch diameter of pinion in mm (or inches)
n_1, n_P = pinion revolutions per minute
β, ψ = helix angle in degrees

When the axial velocity is high, there is a thermal heating problem. The

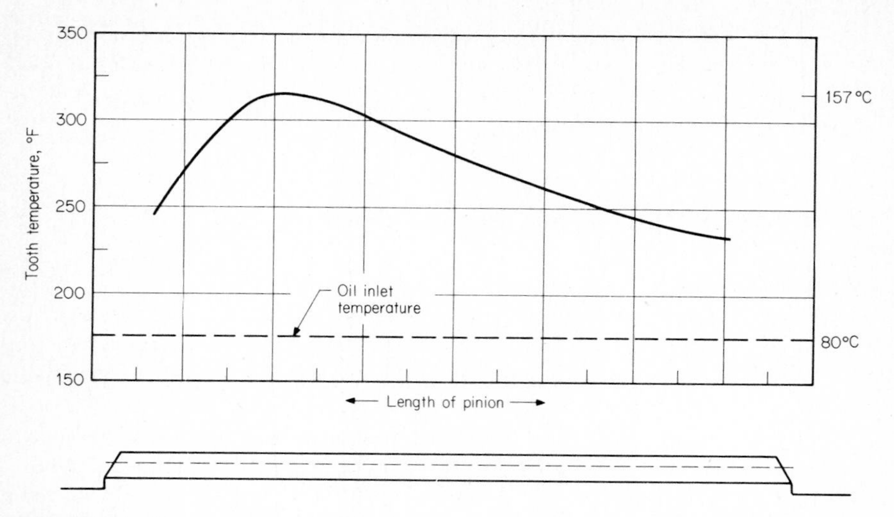

FIG. 7.16 Temperature of pinion teeth across the face width. This is a random example of unpublished test data. Axial meshing velocity exceeded 800 m/s (160,000 fpm).

gear teeth get hot and the temperature across the face width is nonuniform. Figure 7.16 illustrates an example of this situation.

At one end of the face width, the fast-moving air will strike the wall of the gear casing and overheat the casing wall. In a bad thermal situation, the gear teeth may turn blue and the paint on the gear casing may be burned by the casing hot spot.

Gearbox failure can result from thermal trouble by any one of these things:

Carburized gear teeth are overheated enough to soften.

Gear teeth score or pit due to oil-film breakdown on overheated teeth.

The thermal pattern causes enough thermal distortion to seriously alter the tooth-contact pattern. Gear teeth fail as a result of nonuniform load distribution (local overloading).

Thermal distortion of the casing misaligns gears and/or bearings.

The gear bearing which is in the overheated area of the casing fails from overheating.

The severity of the possible thermal troubles can be judged from Table 7.11.

The thermal disturbance is a function of the *square* of the pitch-line velocity. This explains why a 2 to 1 change in speed means going all the way from

TABLE 7.11 Severity of Thermal Problems with Helical Gears

Axial meshing velocity V_x		
m/s	fpm	Severity
400	80,000	No trouble except in very large units where thermal distortion may be enough to require correction. (Need good oil-jet system and generous size casing)
500	100,000	Probably no serious trouble. (Need very good oil-jet system and generous size casing for gear sizes)
700	140,000	Probably have some trouble. May be manageable if gears are not too large and thermal distortions are handled by compensations in tooth fit
850	170,000	Usually difficult to handle. Much skill in tooth compensations needed plus special quality of lubricant
1000	200,000	Probably impractical to handle even with utmost design skill

almost no trouble to almost unmanageable trouble. (The thermal trouble has increased fourfold.)

A speed of 700 m/s (140,000 fpm) is equivalent to around Mach 2! This is a very high speed. Airplane designers are very aware of the thermal heating at Mach 2. Gear designers have their own thermal problems to contend with when meshing gear teeth tend to create high Mach number air velocities.

The axial meshing velocity is, of course, a direct function of the helix angle. Table 7.12 shows the relation of the helix angle to the tangential and axial meshing velocities.

Work in the United States and Europe in the 1960s developed some initial understanding of the thermal problems in fast-running gears. In the

TABLE 7.12 Relation of Helix Angle to Meshing Velocities

Tangential meshing velocity		Axial meshing velocity							
		10° helix		15° helix		30° helix		35° helix	
m/s	fpm	m/s	fpm	m/s	fpm	m/s	fpm	m/s	fpm
100	20,000	567	113,000	373	75,000	173	35,000	143	29,000
125	25,000	709	142,000	467	93,000	217	43,000	179	36,000
150	30,000	851	170,000	560	112,000	260	52,000	214	43,000
175	35,000	992	198,000	653	131,000	303	61,000	250	50,000

FIG. 7.17 Test gears and test bed arrangement for ultra high speed gear testing. *(Courtesy of Ishikawajima-Harima Heavy Industries Co., Ltd., Tokyo, Japan.)*

1970s, much more data was obtained. Figure 7.16 shows a random example of test data on a single-helix gear drive where the axial meshing velocity was high enough to make the situation difficult. Note that gear-tooth surface temperatures are about 77°C (140°F) higher than the inlet oil temperature. The hot spot on the pinion causes the tooth-scoring situation to become critical. The uneven temperature across the face width leads to thermal distortion of the pinion and very poor load distribution, unless the pinion is so made that special helix modifications compensate for the potential thermal mismatch between pinion and gear.

Much of the data on thermal behavior remain unpublished. The subject is very complex, and many gear manufacturers want to get more test data and field experience before publishing papers. Some references are shown, though, at the end of the book. The IFToMM-ASME-AGMA paper by Martinaglia (1972) and the ASME paper by Akazawa et al. (1980) are probably the best papers available now to show test results and to explain some design considerations. (See Refs. 206 and 28.) Figure 7.17 shows a photograph of the test arrangement at Ishikawajima-Harima Heavy Industries Co., Ltd., where data for the Akazawa et al. paper were obtained.

chapter 8

Special Design Problems

The work of gear design involves the solving of special design problems. The designer may learn much about standard gear design practices and then find that most applications tend to need something "special." In this chapter we shall consider some sample problems where special gear-design work is needed. The solutions to these problems will illustrate some of the many calculations that a gear specialist may need to make from time to time.

8.1 Center Distance Problems

It often happens that spur or helical involute gears operate (or should operate) on a center distance that is different from the theoretical center distance.

The first problem is a problem that is old in the gear trade. It is called the *drop-tooth* problem.

We can imagine a simple spur-gear design of a 16-tooth pinion, 20° pressure angle meshing with a 62-tooth gear. The 5-module pinion and gear were made with a standard addendum of 5 mm. The pinion was slightly undercut. Many units are in service. The pinion pits seriously in the first few hundred hours. If it is not replaced, the teeth break. The gears show very little surface distress and appear capable of running 3 to 5 times as long as the pinion. What can be done to fix this design without having to make all new gears?

The solution is to cut 15 pinion teeth on the same blank used to cut 16 teeth. One tooth is dropped. Problem 1 shows the calculations.

PROBLEM 1 Drop-Tooth Design, Fixed Center Distance

GIVEN

16 pinion teeth, 62 gear teeth.

5-module, 20° pressure angle spur gears.

Center distance is 195 mm.

Addendum of pinion and gear are both 5 mm.

REQUIRED

A redesign of the pinion to increase its load-carrying capacity. The new pinions should be able to run with gears on hand with no change in center distance.

SOLUTION

The number of pinion teeth will be changed to 15 by dropping one tooth. The new pinion will have the same outside diameter as the original pinion.

The original pinion pitch diameter, from Eq. (1.3), is

$$\text{Pinion pitch diameter} = 16 \times 5 = 80 \text{ mm}$$

The new tooth ratio, from Eq. (1.7), is

$$\text{Ratio} = 62 \div 15 = 4.133333$$

The operating pitch diameter of the new pinion, from Eq. (1.5), is

$$\begin{aligned}\text{Operating pinion P.D.} &= (2 \times 195) \div (4.133333 + 1.0) \\ &= 75.974031 \text{ mm}\end{aligned}$$

The theoretical pitch diameter of the 15-tooth pinion, from Eq. (1.3), is

$$\text{Pinion pitch diameter} = 15 \times 5 = 75 \text{ mm}$$

The 20° pressure angle of the original pinion came at 80 mm. Now the

20° pressure angle comes at 75 mm. The *spread ratio* for comparing cutting (theoretical) and operating pitch diameters for the 15-tooth pinion is

$$\text{Spread ratio } m' = 75.974031 \div 75 = 1.012987$$

The operating pressure angle can be obtained from these relations:

$$\text{Cos operating P.A.} = \cos \alpha \div m' \qquad \text{metric} \quad (8.1a)$$

$$= \cos \phi \div m' \qquad \text{English} \quad (8.1b)$$

where $$\text{spread ratio } m' = \frac{\text{operating pitch dia.}}{\text{theoretical pitch dia.}}$$

The calculation is

$$\text{Cos operating P.A.} = \cos 20° \div 1.012987 = 0.927645$$

$$\text{Operating P.A.} = 21.929316°$$

The outside diameter of the 16-tooth pinion is

$$\text{Pinion O.D.} = 80 \text{ mm} + 2(5 \text{ mm}) = 90.00 \text{ mm}$$

We need to use this same outside diameter for the 15-tooth pinion, since we will mesh it with the same gear on the same center distance. The operating addendum of the 15-tooth pinion is

$$\text{Pinion addendum} = (90 - 75.9740) \div 2 = 7.01 \text{ mm}$$

CONCLUSION AND COMMENT

The new 15/62 drive will compare with the original drive in this manner:

	Original	Drop-tooth replacement
Teeth	16/62	15/62
Ratio	3.875	4.133
Operating pressure angle	20°	21.9293°
Addendum of pinion	5 mm	7.01 mm
Addendum of gear	5 mm	2.99 mm

The new 15-tooth pinion will have a substantial increase over the old pinion in load-carrying capacity (around 20 percent improvement). A 3 to 1 increase in pinion life is quite certain, and the increase could be more than 5 to 1. The change in ratio is not great.

Figure 8.1 shows a layout comparison of the 15-tooth pinion and the 16-tooth pinion.

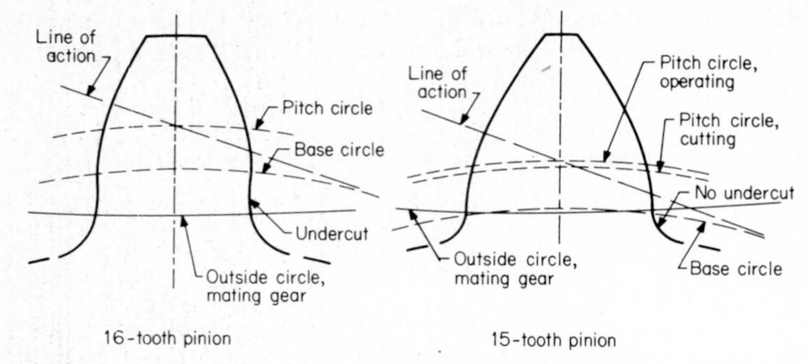

Fig. 8.1 Comparison of the original, undercut, 16-tooth pinion with the replacement 15-tooth pinion. Note the absence of undercut and the sturdy shape of the 15-tooth pinion.

PROBLEM 2 Fixed Center Distance, Standard Tools

This problem is the common one of a fixed center distance and standard cutting tools that cut numbers of teeth that do not match the center distance. It is solved by cutting the parts on pitch diameters that are different from the operating pitch diameters.

GIVEN

Center distance = 154 mm

Ratio = 2 to 1

REQUIRED

A spur-tooth design that can be cut with standard 20° hobs or shaper cutters.

SOLUTION

We will find the module that will allow cutting good gears to run at 154 mm center distance.

The first step is to get the operating pitch diameters.

$$\text{Operating pinion P.D.} = \frac{2 \times 154}{2 + 1} = 102.666666$$

$$\text{Operating gear P.D.} = \frac{2 \times 154}{2 + 1} \times 2 = 205.333333$$

From other considerations (see Sec. 3.1), the number of pinion teeth ought to be in the range of 24 to 28. The shop has old 6-diametral-pitch hobs on hand and new 4-module metric hobs. (They are in the process of changing over from English standard cutting tools to metric standard cutting tools.) The 6-diametral-pitch hobs would cut 24 teeth at a pitch diameter of 4.000 in. or 101.600 mm. The 4-module hobs would cut 25 teeth at a pitch diameter of 100.000 mm. We will use the new metric hobs and 25 teeth.

The theoretical pitch diameters become

$$\text{Pinion P.D.} = 25 \times 4 = 100 \text{ mm}$$
$$\text{Gear P.D.} = 50 \times 4 = 200 \text{ mm}$$

The spread ratio becomes

$$m' = 102.666666 \div 100 = 1.026666$$

The operating pressure angle becomes

$$\alpha' = \arccos\,(\cos 20° \div 1.026666) = 23.753679°$$

We will choose an addendum ratio of 1.1 for the pinion and 0.9 for the gear. (See Table 3.8.) The operating addendum for the pinion and gear are

$$\text{Operating pinion addendum} = 1.1 \times 4 = 4.40 \text{ mm}$$
$$\text{Operating gear addendum} = 0.9 \times 4 = 3.60 \text{ mm}$$

The outside diameters now become

$$\text{Pinion O.D.} = (2 \times 4.40) + 102.666 = 111.47 \text{ mm}$$
$$\text{Gear O.D.} = (2 \times 3.60) + 205.333 = 212.53 \text{ mm}$$

The addendum values for the pinion and gear when hobbing are

$$\text{Theoretical pinion addendum} = (111.47 - 100) \div 2 = 5.735$$
$$\text{Theoretical gear addendum} = (212.53 - 200) \div 2 = 6.265$$

The finishing 4-module hob is designed slightly oversize so that when it is hobbing at full depth, the finished gear will have a reasonable amount of backlash on standard center distance. The hob produces gear teeth with an arc tooth thickness at the 20° pitch line of 6.20 mm (for 0.166 backlash).

The standard 4-module addendum is 4 mm. To cut our spread center gears the hob is held out these amounts:

$$\text{Pinion } \Delta h = 5.735 - 4.00 = 1.735 \text{ mm}$$
$$\text{Gear } \Delta h = 6.265 - 4.00 = 2.265 \text{ mm}$$

The gear teeth will have larger than standard tooth thicknesses at the 20° pitch line:

$$\text{Pinion hobbing TT} = 6.20 + (2 \tan 20° \times 1.735) = 7.463$$
$$\text{Gear hobbing TT} = 6.20 + (2 \tan 20° \times 2.265) = 7.849$$

At the operating pitch diameters, the involute teeth will be thinner. We now need to calculate tooth thicknesses for the operating pitch line (at 23.753679°).

The tooth thicknesses at the operating pitch diameters were calculated by the use of Table 9.4. In step (1) the pitch diameters for cutting were entered. The assumed pressure angle for step (10) was the operating pressure angle 23.7537°. In step (15) the tooth thicknesses at the operating pitch diameters were obtained. They are

$$\text{Arc TT pinion, operating} = 6.573 \text{ mm}$$
$$\text{Arc TT gear, operating} = 5.881 \text{ mm}$$

The circular pitch at 102.6666 mm is

$$CP = (102.6666 \times 3.1415926) \div 25 = 12.90147 \text{ mm}$$

The backlash is

$$BL = 12.90147 - (6.573 + 5.881) = 0.447 \text{ mm}$$

For 4 module, the backlash on standard pitch diameters that went with 6.20 standard TT is

$$(4 \times 3.14159) - (2 \times 6.20) = 0.166 \text{ mm}$$

The increase in backlash is

$$\Delta BL = 0.447 - 0.166 = 0.281$$

If this backlash change is not wanted, it can be controlled by hobbing shallow:

$$\Delta \text{ depth} = \Delta BL \div 2 \tan 20°$$
$$= 0.281 \div 0.728 = 0.385 \text{ mm}$$

The gear can be hobbed shallow by 2/3 of Δ depth, 0.256 mm, and the pinion can be hobbed shallow by 1/3 of Δ depth, 0.128 mm. This will slightly increase the tooth thicknesses and keep the backlash approximately constant. (A small reduction in hobbing depth is tolerable.)

The following tabulation summarizes the results of these calculations.

	Cutting		Operating	
Item	Pinion	Gear	Pinion	Gear
Number of teeth	25	50	25	50
Pitch diameter	100	200	102.6667	205.3333
Module	4	4	4.1066	4.1066
Pressure angle	20°	20°	23.7537°	23.7537°
Outside diameter	111.47	212.53	111.47	212.53
Whole depth*	9.27	9.15	9.27	9.15
Arc tooth thickness at pitch line	7.463	7.849	6.573	5.881
Arc tooth thickness after whole-depth adjustment	7.554	8.031	6.667	6.068

*Standard whole depth for 4 module is 9.4 mm.

PROBLEM 3 Fixed Center Distance, Adjust Helix Angle, Standard Tools
Our next center-distance problem has to do with designing some double-helix gears with 30 to 35° helix angle to go on a center distance of 308 mm. The desired ratio is between 2.8 and 2.9. Again we want to use standard hobs on hand in the shop.

GIVEN

Center distance = 308 mm

Ratio = 2.8 to 2.9

Helix angle 30 to 35°

REQUIRED

A tooth design that can be cut with standard 20° pressure angle hobs.

SOLUTION

We will find a tooth design that can be cut with standard tools. By adjusting the helix angle, we will not need to use spread centers.

The first step is to pick tooth numbers. These are going to be high-speed gears, hobbed and shaved at medium hardness—about HV 320 or HB 300 minimum gear hardness. This leads us to aim for 33 to 37 pinion teeth. (See Sec. 3.1.)

If we had 32° helix and 35 teeth with a ratio of 2.85, we would have these approximate values:

$$\text{Pinion pitch diameter} = \frac{2 \times 308}{2.85 + 1} = 160 \text{ mm}$$

$$\text{Pinion module, transverse} = \frac{160 \text{ mm}}{35} = 4.57$$

$$\text{Pinion module, normal} = 4.57 \times \cos 32^\circ = 3.875$$

The results just obtained indicate that a hob of 4 normal module and 20° normal pressure angle will probably be OK. We will proceed on this basis.

With 35 pinion teeth, a ratio of 2.85 would require 99.75 gear teeth. We could use either 99 or 100 gear teeth. Our choice will be 99.

The ratio now becomes

$$u = \frac{99}{35} = 2.828571$$

The pinion and gear pitch diameters are

$$\text{Pinion pitch diameter} = \frac{2 \times 308}{2.828571 + 1} = 160.89554 \text{ mm}$$

$$\text{Gear pitch diameter} = \frac{2 \times 308}{2.828571 + 1} \times 2.828571$$
$$= 455.10446 \text{ mm}$$

The normal circular pitch is

$$p_n = 4 \times 3.14159265 = 12.566371$$

The transverse circular pitch is

$$\frac{160.89554 \times 3.14159265}{35} = 14.44195$$

This will give a helix angle of

$$\text{Cos helix} = \frac{12.566371}{14.441950} = 0.8701298$$
$$\text{Helix angle} = 29.5262°$$

Our results gave too low a helix angle. Double-helix gears should have at least a 30° helix angle. We will repeat the steps using 33 pinion teeth and 94 gear teeth. (34/97 is out because 97 is a prime number—we can't factor 97 to set up the hobbing machine.)

The ratio now becomes

$$u = \frac{94}{33} = 2.848485$$

The pitch diameters are

$$\text{Pinion pitch diameter} = \frac{616}{3.848485} = 160.06299 \text{ mm}$$

$$\text{Gear pitch diameter} = \frac{616}{3.848485} \times 2.848485 = 455.93701 \text{ mm}$$

The transverse circular pitch now becomes

$$p_t = \frac{160.06299 \times 3.14159265}{33} = 15.23796 \text{ mm}$$

The helix angle is

$$\text{Cos helix} = \frac{12.566371}{15.23796} = 0.824675$$
$$\text{Helix angle} = 34.444403 \text{ degrees}$$

All design objectives have now been met. The tooth numbers of 33/94 have a common factor of 3. This will be OK, since high-speed gears do not wear with Regime III conditions and reasonable tooth loading. (See Sec. 3.2 for a discussion of the hunting tooth issue.)

The transverse pressure angle is

$$\text{Transverse P.A.} = \arctan\,(\tan \text{normal P.A.} \div \cos \text{helix angle}) \quad (8.2)$$

$$\text{Transverse P.A.} = \arctan\,(\tan 20° \div \cos 34.444403)$$
$$= 23.81425°$$

The results of this problem can be summarized as follows:

Item	Cutting and operating data	
	Pinion	Gear
Number of teeth	33	94
Pitch diameter	160.06299	455.93701
Module, normal	4	4
Module, transverse	4.850394	4.850394
Helix angle	34.44440	34.44440
Pressure angle, normal	20°	20°
Pressure angle, transverse	23.81425°	23.81425°

The ratio is 2.8485.
The center distance is 308 mm.

PROBLEM 4 Fixed Design, Standard Tools, Adjust Center Distance for Tooth Proportions

In this problem we consider the situation in which the center distance is not fixed. The desired tooth design is what is fixed. In addition, there is a desire to use standard hobs that are on hand.

GIVEN

Tooth ratio ≐ 2 to 1

Tooth numbers = 24 and 48

The parts are to be pregrind hobbed with 5 normal module, 20° normal pressure angle hobs. The desired helix angle is 12°, and the desired transverse pressure angle is 22.500°. After carburizing, the parts will be finish-ground.

REQUIRED

A design with a spread center distance to give the desired operating, transverse pressure angle.

SOLUTION

The gears will be cut 12° helix angle. The first steps are to find the transverse pressure angle for the hobbing and the transverse module (or pitch) at hobbing.

$$\text{Transverse pressure angle} = \arctan\left(\frac{\tan 20°}{\cos 12°}\right) = 20.410311°$$

$$\text{Transverse module} = \text{normal module} \div \cos \text{helix angle, metric} \quad (8.3)$$
$$= 5 \div \cos 12° = 5.111702$$

Next the spread ratio to get 22.500° operating transverse pressure angle is determined:

$$m' = \frac{\cos 20.410311}{\cos 22.500} = 1.014439$$

The pitch diameters for manufacture (cutting and grinding) are

$$\text{Pinion pitch diameter} = 24 \times 5.111702 = 122.68086 \text{ mm}$$
$$\text{Gear pitch diameter} = 48 \times 5.111702 = 245.36172 \text{ mm}$$

The manufacturing center distance (or theoretical center distance) is

$$\text{Theoretical center distance} = (122.680860 + 245.361720) \div 2.0$$
$$= 184.02129 \text{ mm}$$

The spread center is the theoretical center distance multiplied by the spread ratio:

$$184.02129 \times 1.014439 = 186.67837 \text{ mm}$$

The pinion base-circle diameter is

$$\text{Pinion base diameter} = 122.68086 \times \cos 20.410311$$
$$= 114.97886 \text{ mm}$$

The pinion operating pitch diameter is

$$\text{Operating pinion P.D.} = \frac{2 \times \text{center distance}}{(\text{ratio} + 1)} \quad \text{metric or English} \quad (8.4)$$
$$= \frac{2 \times 186.67837}{(48 \div 24) + 1} = 124.45224 \text{ mm}$$

We can now check whether or not everything was done right by computing the operating transverse pressure angle. It should come out 22.500°.

The calculation is

Operating transverse P.A.

$$= \arccos\left(\frac{\text{pinion B.D.}}{\text{pinion operating P.D.}}\right) \qquad \text{metric or English} \qquad (8.5)$$

$$= \arccos\left(\frac{114.97886}{124.45224}\right) = 22.500021°$$

The result checks OK (within the limits of four-place accuracy). As a final step in defining the gearing, we should get the lead and axial pitch of the pinion.

The pinion lead and axial pitch are

Pinion lead

$$= \frac{\pi \times \text{normal module} \times \text{no. pinion teeth}}{\text{sin helix angle}} \qquad \text{metric or English} \qquad (8.6)$$

$$= \frac{3.14159265 \times 5 \times 24}{\sin 12°} = 1813.227 \text{ mm}$$

Pinion axial pitch

$$= \text{lead} \div \text{no. teeth} \qquad \text{metric or English} \qquad (8.7)$$

$$= 1813.227 \div 24 = 75.55112 \text{ mm}$$

The pinion lead, pinion axial pitch, and pinion base diameter do not change when going from theoretical for manufacture to operating data. (The same, of course, holds true for the mating gear data.)

We will now summarize the results of this problem:

Item	Cutting and grinding		Operating	
	Pinion	Gear	Pinion	Gear
Number of teeth	24	48	24	48
Helix angle	12° RH	12° LH	12.16814°	12.16814°
Module, normal	5	5	5.06900	5.06900
Module, transverse	5.111702	5.111702	5.18551	5.18551
Pressure angle, normal	20°	20°	22.04339°	22.04339°
Pressure angle, transverse	20.41031°	20.41031°	22.5000°	22.5000°
Pitch diameter	122.68086	245.36172	124.45224	248.90449
Base diameter	114.97886	229.95773	114.97886	229.95773
Lead	1813.227	3626.454	1813.227	3626.454
Axial pitch	75.5511	75.5511	75.5511	75.5511
Center distance	184.02129		186.67837	

8.2 Profile Modification Problems

Profile modifications can make spur or helical gears run more quietly and carry more load. Bevel gears are generally cut or ground to achieve a localized contact pattern. The localized contact of the bevel teeth provides some easing of load at the tips of the pinion and gear teeth, which tends to accomplish the same thing as an involute profile modification in spur or helical teeth.

If spacing errors of some magnitude are present, proper profile modification will give the teeth a little clearance at the *first point* of contact. Figure 8.2 shows how a *plus involute* on the pinion will accomplish this.

As shown in Fig. 8.2, a *true* involute design provides no clearance at the first point of contact. If a pair of teeth are spaced too close together, there is a bump as the tooth comes into mesh. With the modification there is a little relief at the first point of contact. This makes the teeth come into mesh smoothly even if an occasional pair of teeth are too close together. The tooth action (with modification) is analogous to sliding a brick down a shingled roof. Without modification, the action is like sliding a brick over an uneven cobblestone street.

When gears are loaded heavily enough, there is appreciable bending. Even if the accuracy is perfect, bending creates interference at the first point of contact. Figure 8.3 shows how this happens.

With heavily loaded teeth, there is also trouble at the *last* point of contact. This comes from the fact that the hertz stress jumps to an extreme value when the full band of contact is broken by the discontinuity of the tooth tip (see Fig. 8.4).

To illustrate the kinds of modification, we shall work out two sample problems. Problem 5 will be for teeth of medium-precision accuracy. Problem 6 will be for teeth of precision accuracy used at high speed.

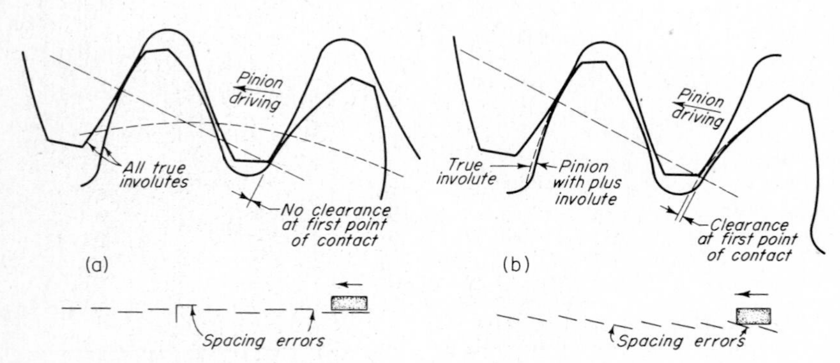

FIG. 8.2 Plus involute provides tip clearance.

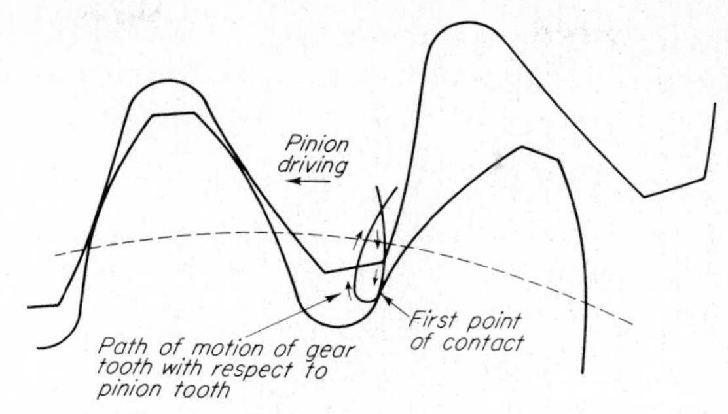

FIG. 8.3 Interference at first point of contact due to tooth bending.

Problem 5 will consider a single helical set of gears having large teeth and running at a typical industrial gear speed. The teeth need long life and high reliability, so they are case-carburized and ground.

PROBLEM 5 Standard Profile Modification

GIVEN

Single helical gearset, 26 and 51 teeth

The teeth are 20 module normal and 20° normal pressure angle

The cutting and operating tooth data are the same

The gearset has a center distance of 787.2 mm (30.9922 in.)

The design is for 700 mm (27.56 in.) face width

The gear unit is designed to handle 4897 kW (6566 hp) at a pinion speed

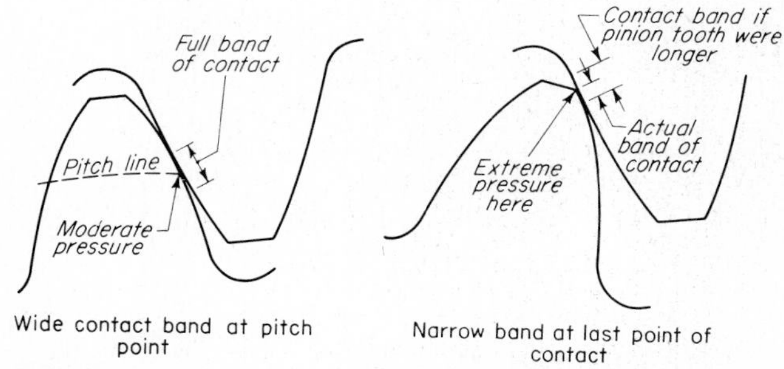

FIG. 8.4 Severe stress caused by discontinuity of tooth tip.

of 150 rpm. This makes the input torque 203,273.6 N · m (1,799,120 in.-lb). This load is relatively constant. A life of 30,000 hours is needed.

REQUIRED

Profile modifications that are reasonably practical to obtain in grinding and that will compensate for tooth errors and tooth deflection. The overall aim is for a smooth-running unit with no tendency for premature distress at the tip of the gear or the tip of the pinion.

SOLUTION

The modifications required are of medium criticalness. With *good* lubrication and *good* metallurgy in the gears, the design is reasonably conservative, provided that the gears, the casing, and the foundation for this unit are accurate enough to provide medium precision. A relatively standard system of profile modification will be used.

The first step is to calculate additional data items. This can be done using the methods illustrated in the preceding sample problems and the data in Secs. 3.5, 3.8, 3.12, 3.13, and 3.25. The results are

Item	Metric		English	
	Pinion	Gear	Pinion	Gear
Number of teeth	26	51	26	51
Pitch diameter	531.62 mm	1042.79 mm	20.9296 in.	41.0546 in.
Module, normal	20	20	—	—
Module, transverse	20.4468	20.4468	—	—
Normal diametral pitch	—	—	1.270	1.270
Pressure angle, normal	20°		20°	
Pressure angle, transverse	20.41031°		20.41031°	
Addendum	22 mm	18 mm	0.866 in.	0.709 in.
Whole depth	47 mm	47 mm	1.850 in.	1.850 in.
Helix angle	12° RH	12° LH	12° RH	12° LH
Face width	710 mm	700 mm	27.95 in.	27.56 in.
Torque on pinion	203,274.6 N · m		1,799,120 in.-lb	
Tangential force	764,733 newtons		171,921 pounds	
Load per unit of width	1092.5 N/mm		6238 lb/inch	
K factor	3.10 N/mm^2		450 psi	
Unit load	54.62 N/mm^2		7922.3 psi	
Revolutions per minute	150	76.5	150	76.5
Pitch-line velocity	4.17 m/s		822 fpm	

The next step is to estimate tooth deflection. At the design load of 1092.5 N/mm (6238 lb/in.), the approximate deflection* will be

$$\text{Mesh deflection} = \frac{\text{tangential load}}{\text{face width}} \times \frac{1}{\text{tooth modulus of elasticity}}$$

$$\Delta x = \frac{W_t}{b} \times \frac{1}{x_{EG}} \quad \text{mm} \qquad \text{metric} \qquad (8.8a)$$

$$= \frac{W_t}{F} \times \frac{1}{E_G} \quad \text{in.} \qquad \text{English} \qquad (8.8b)$$

where Δx = total mesh deflection in the transverse plane, tangent to the pitch circle

x_{EG} = modulus of elasticity for the teeth in mesh

= 20,000 N/mm^2 (approx. value 20° teeth, low helix angle)

E_G = 2,900,000 psi (20,000 N/mm^2 = 2,900,000 psi)

The mesh deflection calculates

$$\Delta x = \frac{1092.5}{20{,}000} = 0.0546 \text{ mm } (0.00215 \text{ in.})$$

A word of explanation on mesh deflection is in order. If we imagine the gear locked against rotation, the mesh deflection comes from the angle that the pinion will rotate when the tooth load is applied. Thus

$$\text{Tan of rotation angle} = \Delta x \div \text{pitch radius of pinion} \qquad (8.9)$$

The stiffness constants for mesh deflection of the teeth have never been known with certainty. Some tests are reported in the technical literature, but the data are still rather limited. The author has had some experience in making these tests. It is difficult to get good data because the gear teeth are very stiff. The value of 20,000 N/mm^2 is a reasonable estimate for design purposes when the teeth are cut to full depth with a generous allowance on the whole depth to accommodate shaving or grinding and there is a generous backlash allowance.

If the 20,000 N/mm^2 is in error, it is probably a little too small. Some data (unpublished) would indicate that this value could be as high as 25,000 N/mm^2 for the design problem under consideration.

In our design problem, the gears are designed with an overall load-distribution factor of 1.85. These are *medium-accuracy* gears. The total helix mismatch can be expected to be around 100 μm (0.004 in.). This much helix misfit makes it necessary to use a fairly high load-distribution factor. (See Fig. 3.30.)

*See the Sec. 3.27 subsection entitled "Effects of Helix Error and Shaft Misalignment."

With a 1.85 load-distribution factor, the *highest* loaded teeth in mesh will deflect about 1.85 times as much as the average deflection. This means that a gear tooth entering mesh (first point of contact) may be out of position by about

$$1.85 \times 0.0546 = 0.101 \text{ mm } (0.004 \text{ in.})$$

We now have a basis for setting the profile modification. At the first point of contact, we want to come fairly close to taking all the load off the tip of the gear. The tip of the gear enters mesh at the pinion *form diameter*. This is a highly critical area for pitting, scoring, and noise generation. Without relief, the gear tip would actually tend to cut into the lower pinion flank. (Note Fig. 8.3.)

At the last point of contact, the conditions are not so critical. At this point, we only need to partially relieve load.

The depth to the start of profile modification may be set by the general design rules of Table 3.54. (If the job is highly critical, the technique of Problem 6 should be followed.)

The diameter for the start of modification on the gear or pinion is

$$\text{Start modification diameter} = \text{O.D.} - 2 \text{ (depth to start)} \qquad (8.10)$$

For our case,

$$\text{Gear O.D.} = 1042.79 + 2(18) = 1078.79 \text{ mm}$$

$$\text{Depth to start} = 0.450 \times 20 = 9 \text{ mm}$$

$$\text{Start modification diameter, gear} = 1078.79 - 2(9) = 1060.79 \text{ mm}$$

$$\text{Pinion O.D.} = 531.62 + 2(22) = 575.62 \text{ mm}$$

$$\text{Depth to start} = 0.400 \times 20 = 8 \text{ mm}$$

$$\text{Start modification diameter, pinion} = 575.62 - 2(8) = 559.62 \text{ mm}$$

The amounts of profile modification can now be set as follows:

Item	First point of contact		Last point of contact	
	Metric	English	Metric	English
Design modification	0.101 mm	0.004 in.	0.063 mm	0.0025 in.
Drawing tolerance limits	−0.084 mm −0.119 mm	−0.0033 in. −0.0047 in.	−0.046 mm −0.081 mm	−0.0018 in. −0.0032 in.
Diameter at start of modification	1060.8 mm	41.76 in.	559.6 mm	22.03 in.
Diameter at end of modification	1078.79 mm	42.47 in.	575.62 mm	22.66 in.

The first point modifications apply to the gear.
The last point modifications apply to the pinion.

The next problem is for a set of high-speed gears that might be used in an aerospace-gear application. The example is similar to Problem 5 with a 26/51 tooth combination and 12°. However, the size of the tooth is 4 module instead of 20 (one-fifth the size). The aspect ratio is much smaller, 0.6 instead of 1.31. The gears and casing will be built to high precision.

PROBLEM 6 Special Profile Modification to Reduce Scoring Risk

GIVEN

Single helical gearset, 26 and 51 teeth

The teeth are 4 module, normal and 20° normal pressure angle

The gearset has a center distance of 157.440 mm (6.1984 in.)

The face width is 63.6 mm (2.50 in.)

The unit is designed to handle 1802.5 kW (2417 hp) at a pinion speed of 10,000 rpm. This makes the input torque 1147.5 N · m (10,156 in.-lb). At this maximum rating, 2000 hours are required. Other ratings are much lower in power.

REQUIRED

Profile modification data. This unit has a high risk of scoring, so the modifications are primarily designed to reduce the scoring hazard.

SOLUTION

Since scoring is critical, the modifications will be worked out on a somewhat different basis from that used in Problem 5.

The first step is to make out a tabulation of tooth data. (This tabulation is like Problem 5 in many respects, since the teeth are scale models of each other. See table on page 8.18.)

The approximate deflection at the design load of 339.4 N/mm (1941 lb/in.) is

$$\Delta x = \frac{339.4}{20{,}000} = 0.017 \text{ mm (0.00067 in.)}$$

These gears will be built to precision accuracy. The low aspect ratio means no serious trouble from bending or twisting. The teeth are small, though, and the load per unit of face width is not high. A load distribution of 1.35 is reasonable to expect. (See Fig. 3.30.)

The tooth modification should be based on a deflection which allows for

Item	Metric		English	
	Pinion	Gear	Pinion	Gear
Number of teeth	26	51	26	51
Pitch diameter	106.32342 mm	208.5575 mm	4.1859 in.	8.2109 in.
Module, normal	4	4	—	—
Module, transverse	4.089362	4.089362	—	—
Normal diametral pitch	—	—	6.35	6.35
Pressure angle, normal	20°		20°	
Pressure angle, transverse	20.41031°		20.41031°	
Addendum	4.4 mm	3.6 mm	0.173 in.	0.142 in.
Whole depth	9.6 mm	9.6 mm	0.378 in.	0.378 in.
Helix angle	12° RH	12° LH	12° RH	12° LH
Face width	65.6 mm	63.6 mm	2.58 in.	2.50 in.
Torque, on pinion	1147.5 N·m		10,156 in.-lb	
Tangential force	21,585 newtons		4852.5 lb	
Load per unit of width	339.4 N/mm		1941 lb/inch	
K factor	4.82 N/mm²		700 psi	
Unit load	84.85 N/mm²		12,325 psi	
Revolutions per minute	15,000	7647.09	15,000	7647.09
Pitch-line velocity	81.58 m/s		16,059 fpm	

the local overload resulting from nonuniform load distribution:

$$1.35 \times 0.017 = 0.023 \text{ mm } (0.0009 \text{ in.})$$

At the first point of contact, the modification makes the load quite light. Tooth-to-tooth spacing errors of up to 0.0075 mm (0.0003 in.) will be allowed. The minimum modification needed can be rationalized as

$$0.80 \times (0.023 + 0.0075) = 0.024 \text{ mm } (0.0010 \text{ in.})$$

The maximum modification at the first point will have to allow for the tolerance in grinding. This would be about 0.010 mm (0.0004 in.) for precision accuracy.

The range is then 0.024 to 0.034 mm profile modification for the tip of the gear. This means that only a very light load is carried at the first point of contact, *even when the worst* spacing errors go through mesh and the worst helix mismatch permitted by the tolerances is present.

At the last point of contact, conditions are slightly less critical. A constant of 0.60 is probably OK:

$$0.60(0.023 + 0.0075) = 0.018 \text{ mm } (0.0007 \text{ in.})$$

The range of modification for the last point is 0.018 to 0.028 mm. This modification is at the tip of the pinion.

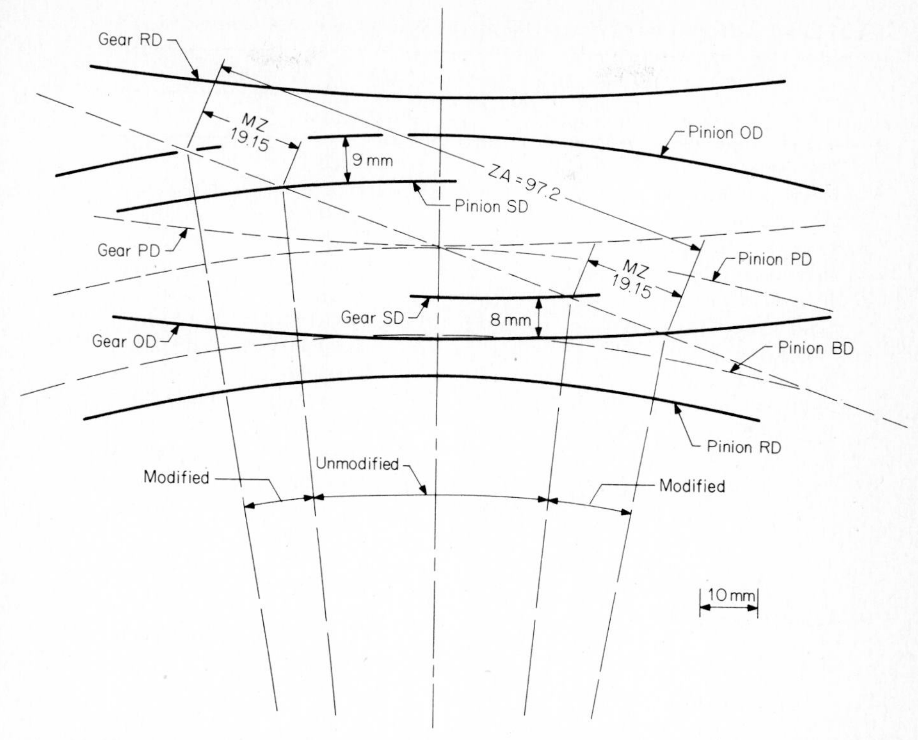

Fig. 8.5 Layout of Problem 6 at 5 times size. One base pitch is unmodified and located in the center of the zone of action.

For smooth tooth action at high speed, the contact zone should have an arc corresponding to one tooth interval that is unmodified. This means that a distance corresponding to one base pitch should be unmodified. The base pitch is

$$\text{B.P.} = 3.14159 \times 4 \times \cos 20.41031 = 11.777 \text{ mm } (0.4637 \text{ in.})$$

To find out where to start the modification, a layout can be made or calculations can be made using the method shown in Table 3.11. For this problem we will make a five times size layout. (Since the teeth of Problem 6 are 5 to 1 smaller than the teeth of Problem 5, a five times size layout is the *same size* as the teeth in Problem 5.)

Figure 8.5 shows the layout just described. All dimensions are laid out five times size. The zone of action ZA scales 97.2 mm. The base pitch at five times size is 58.88 mm.

For this problem we will put the unmodified region in the *center* of the

TABLE 8.1 Calculation of Form Diameter, Roll Angles, and Contact Ratio

	1	2
Data item or operation	Pinion	Gear
1. No. teeth	26	51
2. Pitch diameter	106.3234	208.5575
3. Addendum	4.40	3.60
4. Outside diameter, (2) + 2.0 × (3)	115.123	215.757
5. Pressure angle, transverse	20.41031	20.41031
6. Base diameter, cos (5) × (2)	99.6483	195.4641
7. Gear ratio, $(1)_2 \div (1)_1$	1.96154	1.96154
8. Inverse ratio, 1.0 ÷ (7)	0.509804	0.509804
9. Arccos [(6) ÷ (4)]	30.050867	25.049061
10. O.D. roll, tan (9) × 57.29578	33.147592	26.777214
11. P.D. roll, tan (5) × 57.29578	21.319846	21.319846
12. Addendum roll, (10) − (11)	11.827746	5.457368
13. Pinion roll, $(12)_1 + [(12)_2 \times (7)]$	22.532592	—
14. Gear roll, $(12)_2 + [(12)_1 \times (8)]$	—	11.487200
15. L.D. roll, pinion, (10) − (13)	10.61500	—
16. L.D. roll, gear, (10) − (14)	—	15.290014
17. Arctan [(15) ÷ 57.29578]	10.49599	—
18. L.D. pinion (6) ÷ cos (17)	101.34402	—
19. Arctan [(16) ÷ 57.29578]	—	14.941817
20. L.D. gear (6) ÷ cos (19)	—	202.30438
21. Circular pitch, π × (2) ÷ (1)	12.8471	12.8471
22. Extra involute, 0.016 × (21)	0.2055	0.2055
23. Form diameter, pinion (18) − (22)	101.1385	—
24. Arccos [(6) ÷ (23)]	9.847735	—
25. F.D. roll, pinion = tan (24) × 57.29578	9.945866	—
26. Form diameter, gear (20) − (22)	—	202.0989
27. Arccos [(6) ÷ (26)]	—	14.721915
28. F.D. roll, gr. = tan (27) × 57.29578	—	15.054692
29. Roll per tooth, 360° ÷ (1)	13.84615	—
30. Contact ratio, $(13) \div (29)_1$	1.6273	—
31. Start modification diameter, SD	111.523	212.557
32. Arccos [(6) ÷ (31)]	26.68073	23.13461
33. S.D. roll, tan (32) × 57.29578	28.7926	24.4796

Notes: For metric calculations use millimeter dimensions, and for English calculations use inches. See Sec. 3.9 for cases when (22) may be too much extra involute.

zone of action. This makes the modified zone MZ at each end become

$$MZ = (97.2 - 58.9) \div 2 = 19.15 \text{ mm}$$

We can now scale the radial distance from the diameter at start of modification SD to the outside diameter. The results are

Depth to start of modification, gear = 8 mm $(8 \div 5 = 1.6)$
Depth to start of modification, pinion = 9 mm $(9 \div 5 = 1.8)$

The outside diameters for our problem are

$$\text{O.D. gear} = 208.557 + 2(3.6) = 215.757 \text{ mm}$$
$$\text{O.D. pinion} = 106.323 + 2(4.4) = 115.123 \text{ mm}$$

The diameters at the start of modification are

$$\text{S.D. gear} = 215.757 - 2(1.6) = 212.557 \text{ mm}$$
$$\text{S.D. pinion} = 115.123 - 2(1.8) = 111.523 \text{ mm}$$

In this problem we will do the extra work to convert the profile modification data to an involute profile diagram, commonly called a *K chart.*

We now need roll angles to go with the outside diameters, the diameters at the start of modification, and the form diameter for the pair. Table 8.1 has been worked through to give these values. (See Secs. 3.8 and 3.9 for the equations used in Table 8.1.)

Now that all the data are available, the *K* charts can be made for the pinion and the gear. Figure 8.6 shows these charts. The modifications are between the start modification diameter S.D. and the outside diameter. The region from the form diameter F.D. to the start diameter has a slope tolerance. (For more on tolerances, see Sec. 5.18.)

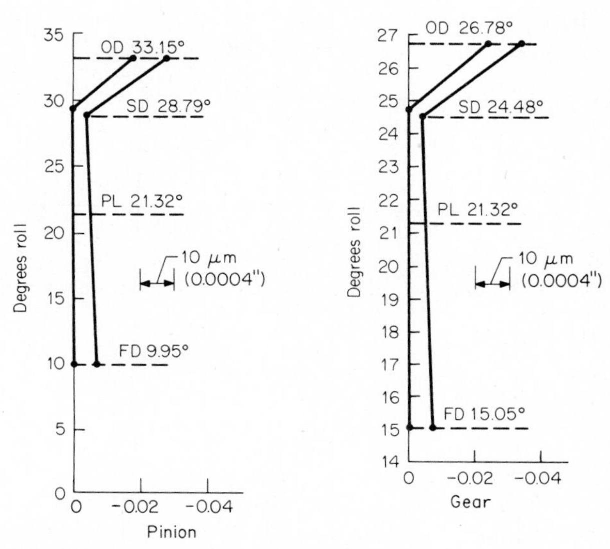

FIG. 8.6 Involute charts for Problem 6.

8.3 Load Rating Problem

Our next problem will involve load rating a set of vehicle gears. The gears in a drive system with a standard engine have been satisfactory. Now a newly developed engine with 40 percent more power capacity is available. It is hoped that the present gear drive can be made somewhat better and that it can be used with little or no change with the new engine.

PROBLEM 7 Load Rating Vehicle Gears

GIVEN

A spur gearset, 18 and 85 teeth.

The teeth are 4 module and 25° pressure angle.

The cutting and operating data are the same.

The center distance is 206 mm.

The pinion addendum is 4.6 mm. Gear addendum is 3.4 mm.

The face width is 40 mm.

The teeth are case-carburized.

REQUIRED

This gearset needs to handle the following load schedule with the new engine. The problem is to evaluate the suitability of the given gearset.

Load condition	Pinion speed, rpm	Pinion torque		Hours	Cycles
		Metric, N·m	English, in.-lb		
Stall engine	(slow)	1200	10,620.9	—	1000
Low* gear	254	920	8,142.7	26	4×10^5
Second gear	300	800	7,080.6	111	2×10^6
Third gear	382	630	5,576.0	127	2.9×10^6
Fourth gear, maximum	573	430	3,805.8	600	2×10^7
Fourth gear, cruise	620	260	2,301.2	2000	7.4×10^7

*A shifting transmission is ahead of this final drive set of gears.

SOLUTION

In the author's opinion, this kind of problem is best solved by a *load histogram* approach that compares calculated tooth stresses with a family of curves showing the estimated capability of the gear material to carry stress.

Table 8.2 shows a load-rating analysis made for the second-gear torque of 800 N · m (7080.6 in.-lb). The geometry factors are obtained from Secs. 3.26 and 3.28. The derating factors are based on vehicle practice. (See Sec. 3.33.)

After the contact stress and the bending stress are obtained, it is easy to obtain the stresses for other torque values. The contact stress is proportional to the square root of torque. The bending stress is proportional to torque. Of course, the derating factors must stay constant if these proportions are to work.

The values of stress for the range of loads are:

Loading condition	Contact stress		Root stress	
	N/mm^2	psi	N/mm^2	psi
Start-up	2097.2	304,200	620.1	90,000
Low gear	1836.3	266,350	475.4	68,960
Second gear	1712.3	248,370	413.4	59,970
Third gear	1519.6	220,400	325.6	47,230
Fourth gear, maximum	1255.4	182,090	222.2	32,230
Fourth gear, cruise	976.2	141,590	134.4	19,490

The next step is to plot the load histograms. Stress is plotted against cycles, *starting with the highest stress* condition. For our problem, stall is the highest, low gear is second highest, and second gear is third highest. The cycles to plot then become

Stall	1000 cycles
Low gear	1000 + 400,000 = 401,000 cycles
Second gear	401,000 + 2,000,000 = 2,401,000 cycles
Third gear	2,401,000 + 2,900,000 = 5,301,000 cycles

Figure 8.7 shows the resulting load histogram for bending, and Fig. 8.8 shows the load histogram for contact stress.

The histograms now reveal which load conditions are most critical. For bending, low gear and second gear are the ones to worry about. For contact stress, it is second gear and third gear.

For our problem, we can assume that it was necessary to have L3 reliability against breakage. This means that any gear in the train of gears would have at least a 97 percent probability of surviving the full load schedule without tooth breakage.

Figure 8.7 shows that Grade 2 material is needed to get the desired reliability in the pinion. If a load histogram had been made for the gear, it would have shown that the lower cycles and lower bending stresses for the gear made it able to get by with Grade 1 material.

TABLE 8.2 Gear-Rating Analysis

Given data				
1. Identification of mesh	2nd gear		2nd gear	
2. Calculation dimensions	Metric		English	
3. Column	1	2	1	2
4. Number of teeth	18	85	18	85
5. Module, normal (cutting)	4.000		—	
6. Diametral pitch, normal (cutting)	—		6.35	
7. Pressure angle, normal (cutting)	25°		25°	
8. Helix angle (cutting)	0°		0°	
Operating data				
9. Center distance	206 mm		8.11024 in.	
10. Face width	42 mm	40 mm	1.6535 in.	1.5748 in.
11. Pinion and gear rpm	200	42.35	200	42.35
12. Input power	16.755 kW		22.469 hp	
Calculation of dimensions				
13. Gear ratio, $(4)_2 \div (4)_1$	4.722222		4.722222	
14. Pitch diameter (cutting)	72 mm	340 mm	2.8346 in.	13.3858 in.
15. Pitch diameter, (operating)	72 mm	340 mm	2.8346 in.	13.3858 in.
16. Spread ratio, $m' = (15) \div (14)$	1.000	1.000	1.000	1.000
17. Tan. P.A. (cutting), tan. (7) ÷ cos (8)	0.4663077		0.4663077	
18. P.A. (cutting), arctan (17)	25°		25°	
19. Cos P.A. (operating), cos (18) ÷ (16)	0.9063078		0.9063078	
20. P.A. (operating), arccos (19)	25°		25°	
21. Addendum	4.60	3.40	0.181	0.134
22. Whole depth	9.12	9.12	0.359	0.359
23. Outside diameter, 2.00 × (21) + (15)	81.20	346.80	3.1966	13.6535
Calculation of rating data				
24. Pinion torque	800 N · m		7080.6 in.-lb	
25. Tangential driving force	22222 N		4995.8 lb	
26. Load per unit face width	555.5 N/mm^2		3172.4 psi	
27. [(13) + 1.000] ÷ (13)	1.2118		1.2118	
28. K factor	9.35		1356.2	
29. C_d (overall derating)	1.4		1.4	
30. C_k (geometry factor)	473.3		5700	
31. s_c (contact stress)	1712.3 N/mm^2		248,370 psi	
32. Unit load	138.87		20,144	
33. K_d (overall derating)	1.3		1.3	
34. K_t (geometry factor)	2.29	2.05	2.29	2.05
35. s_t (bending stress)	413.43	370.09	59,970	53,680
36. Pitch-line velocity	.754 m/s		148.4 fpm	

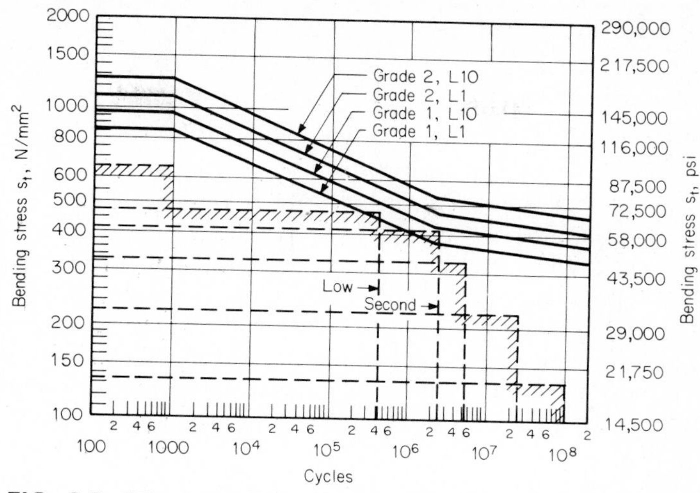

FIG. 8.7 Histogram plot of pinion bending stress for Problem 7. Low gear and second gear are the most critical.

In regard to the hazard of serious pitting, we will assume that L10 reliability is satisfactory. (If 10 percent of the gears are badly pitted, they can be replaced during the life of the unit or continued in service with a considerably increased risk of tooth breakage.)

Figure 8.8 shows that Grade 1 material might be acceptable. Again, a load histogram for the gear would show that the lower cycles helped the gear even though the contact stresses are the same for pinion and gear.

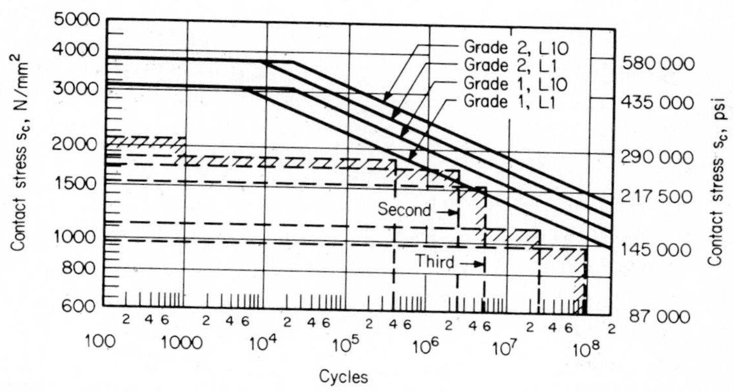

FIG. 8.8 Histogram plot of pinion contact stress for Problem 7. Second gear and third gear are the most critical.

Before deciding what to do, we need to review the probable accuracy of our calculations. There may be trouble from several sources:

The assumed derating factors may be too low (poor mechanical design).

The lubricant may be inadequate.

It may not be possible to get the specified material quality. (Grade 1 was specified, but lack of metallurgical skill and controls yields only Grade 0.)

At the outset it is quite certain that a low derating factor like 1.4 or 1.3 can be obtained only in *heavily* loaded vehicle gears where tooth deflections and wear-in of the surface will give a *good* load distribution across the face width. Our histograms are in some error for the fourth gear, light loads. We can see, though, that fourth gear is not close to governing our design decision, so we will not take the time to redo the histograms for a more accurate derating of the fourth-gear load condition.

In regard to lubrication, low-gear and second-gear conditions have such a low pitch-line velocity that they are close to being out of Regime II operation and into Regime I. Our contact-stress curves in Figure 8.8 are drawn for Regime II. If we really got into Regime I, the contact-stress curves would have a *steeper* slope and this size of gear would not be adequate.

In regard to material, the gear trade is still learning how to control and rate gear quality.* Some manufacturers are making a bona fide Grade 2 quality, but they are apt to be short of knowledge concerning the detrimental effects of either accidental or intentional changes in the details of process procedures. (At any time, Grade 2 in production might lapse into Grade 1.)

With all this in mind, the solution to Problem 7 adds up to this:

1 The load schedule of the new engine requires a *design* for Grade 2 quality. (Even if the product is not as good as the design, it will still probably be somewhat better than Grade 1.)

2 The mechanical design for casings, shafts, bearings, and gear mounting must follow the *best proven* practice for vehicle design. A derating factor of 1.3 for strength will not be obtained at heavy load with a poor design. (Was the old design a good one or marginal with the old engine?)

3 A strong EP† lubricant with high viscosity must be used. Lubrication studies may show that an SAE grade 140 gear oil is needed at the top operating temperature. (If a really good oil can't be used, it is probably best to make new gears that are large enough to survive under Regime I conditions and the increased torque of the new engine.)

*See Sec. 4.10 for a discussion of gear quality grades.

†A strong EP lubricant is generally thought of as being in the API-GL5 classification. For general background information on gear lubricants, Boner's 1964 book *Gear Transmission Lubricants* is excellent. (See references at the end of the book.)

chapter 9

Appendix Material

The first six chapters of this book covered the prime text material: the selection, design, rating, and manufacture of gears. The next two chapters discussed the analysis of gear failures and the handling of certain special problems in gear design.

Chapter 9 is essentially all appendix-type material, with additional explanations and calculations to complement the material in the earlier chapters. The Chap. 9 section titles indicate which chapter is being supplemented.

9.1 Introduction to Gears (Supplement to Chap. 1)

Gears are toothed wheels which have been used for about 3000 years to transmit circular motion or rotational force (torque) from one part of a machine to another. Today gears are used in most machinery, and they range in size from the tiny gears in watch mechanisms to giant 100-ft-diameter gears in radar antennas. Gears are used in pairs, and each gear is usually attached to a rotating shaft. When the teeth of two gears are meshed, rotation of one shaft and its gear causes the other gear and its shaft to rotate also. If the two gears have different diameters, the smaller one (called the *pinion*) will turn faster and with less rotational force than the larger (called the *gear*). Thus gears can be designed to regulate rotational velocity and torque.

For example, suppose a pinion with 10 teeth is connected to the drive shaft of an engine. If this pinion is meshed with a gear with 30 teeth, the pinion will make three complete revolutions for each revolution of the gear. Thus the gear shaft turns only one-third as fast as the pinion shaft. But what is lost in speed is gained in torque, so that the gear exerts three times the angular force of the engine. Obviously this *gear-tooth ratio* (3 : 1 in this example) is very important to a gear designer's work.

Types of Gears. There are a number of different types of gears, each especially suitable for a particular job. The *spur gearset* is the simplest to design and manufacture (except for *friction gears*, which have no teeth at all). The spur gear and pinion both have teeth which run straight across the width of the gear face.* The spur gearset transmits rotary motion and torque from one shaft to a parallel shaft; it is widely used where rotation velocities and torques are relatively low, and cost is an important consideration. The *rack and pinion* (see Fig. 1.18) is a variation of the spur gear in which the gear (rack) is flat rather than round. The rack and its round pinion convert rotation to linear motion or vice versa.

In the usual spur gearset, the gear and pinion will always rotate in opposite directions. If the parallel shafts must rotate in the same direction, there are two solutions: (1) The *internal gearset* (see Fig. 1.20), consisting of one internal gear and one pinion, is used when the two axes are close together and the pinion diameter is not too close to the gear diameter. (2) If there is room between the shafts, an *idler gear* can be mounted on a bearing between the gear and the pinion. The idler gear will rotate freely on its shaft, whereas most gears are locked to their shafts by splines or by small pieces of metal called keys.

The *bevel gear* (see the upper right-hand corner of Fig. 1.7, and Fig. 1.21) is used to transmit rotation from one shaft to a nonparallel shaft. (Perpendicular shafts are most common.) The basic shape of bevel gears is conical, rather than cylindrical. Bevel gears are very common in household appliances and power tools. They are also used to a considerable extent in vehicles, helicopters, and mills.

The straight teeth of spur gears and straight bevel gears tend to make them noisy in operation, since the mating teeth mesh along their whole width all at once. To solve this problem and to obtain gears that can carry a

*See illustrations of gears in Chap. 1. For spur gears, see Figs. 1.7 and 1.18.

higher load, some spur and bevel gears are made with teeth that twist across the *face width*. Spur gears with twisted teeth are called *helical gears* (see Fig. 1.19), because the teeth are made in a helix shape. Bevel gears with twisted teeth are commonly called *spiral bevel gears* (see Fig. 1.23). As helical-gear teeth mesh, the contact between the two gears begins at one end of a tooth and extends gradually in a diagonal line across the width of the tooth. If the face width of the gears is long enough, two or more teeth on each gear will be engaged at all times, and this *overlapping* enables the gears to carry a higher load. Helical gears are smoother and quieter in operation than spur gears, and so they are favored for high-speed applications.

Unfortunately, helical gears convert a portion of the rotational force into a thrust along the gear shaft, which can have an undesirable effect on the shaft bearings. This sideways component of the force, called the *axial thrust load*, occurs in helical gears because the teeth mesh along a diagonal line. When this axial thrust would be a serious problem, it can be eliminated by mounting two gearsets side by side with teeth sloping in opposite directions. This arrangement is referred to as a *double helical gear* (see Fig. 1.11). When the right-hand and left-hand gears are both cut onto a single cylinder, the gear is sometimes called a *herringbone gear*.

Sometimes gears are needed to connect shafts which are neither parallel nor intersecting. For this purpose a variation of the spiral bevel gear, called a *hypoid gear* (see Figs. 1.24 and 1.25), has been developed. The unusual geometry of the hypoid gear allows the pinion to be large and strong even though it has only a few teeth.

Cylindrical helical gears can also be used for nonparallel, nonintersecting shafts, and such gears are called *crossed-helical gears* (see Fig. 1.27). When crossed-helical gears mesh, their teeth meet in only one point at a time, and load-carrying capacity is limited. For this reason, variations have been designed in which the gear is *throated* or curved outward on the edges of its face so that it wraps part way around the pinion like a nut envelops a screw. The small cylindrical pinion is called a *worm*, and the gearset is called a *cylindrical worm gear* or a *single-enveloping worm gear* (see Fig. 1.28). When the worm is not cylindrical, but is throated into an hourglass shape so that it also curves part way around the gear, the result is the *double-enveloping worm gear* (see Fig. 1.30). Crossed-helical gears are sometimes called *nonenveloping worm gears*.

A worm can be designed with only one tooth, or *thread*, which wraps around and around the worm like the thread on a screw. Usually, however, a worm will have several threads. Worm gears provide the easiest way of greatly decreasing or increasing rotation speeds between two shafts, but friction losses can be high as the worm threads slide sideways along the gear teeth.

In practice, gears are used not only in pairs, but also in more complex interactions called *gear trains*. Automatic transmissions in automobiles use *epicyclic* or *planetary gear systems* (see Fig. 2.19). The "sun" or central gear meshes with three "planet" gears. All the planet gears also mesh with an internal "ring" gear. Three different gear ratios can be obtained in an epicyclic* gear train by a clutch system which prevents the rotation of either the sun gear, the internal gear, or the arm which is attached to the three planet gears through bearings.

Gear Design. Designing and manufacturing complex gears which mesh together quietly and efficiently at high speeds and under high loads for millions of cycles requires intricate planning, manufacturing, and testing. If the design of simple spur gears looks like an easy task, try it! There is no better way to learn about gears.

Pretend that you have been asked to design a spur gearset which will reduce the rotational speed of an engine shaft from 40 revolutions per minute (rpm) to 30 rpm. This requires that your gear-to-pinion tooth ratio be 4 to 3. Design your gear and pinion accordingly, and cut them out of heavy paper. Check to see whether the pinion will effectively turn the gear when you pin them through their centers onto a piece of cardboard. This attempt will acquaint you with some of the angles and distances that are familiar tools of the gear designer. For example, the distance between your pins is called, logically enough, the *center distance*.

In your design you might start by drawing a *root circle*, with the idea of drawing your gear teeth sticking out from the root circle. Around this root circle, you'll probably draw a larger *outside circle* so that all the gear teeth will have the same *whole depth*. Then you will decide how many teeth your gear will have, and you will divide 360° by the number of teeth to determine the angle allotted for each tooth. Finally you must design the shape of the tooth, or the *tooth profile*.

After the preliminary design of your gear is finished, a critical question arises: How big should the pinion be?

For two spur gears to mesh properly, it is essential that they have the same *tooth spacing*. But tooth spacing is an ambiguous term on round gears. It sounds logical to define tooth spacing as the distance from the center of one tooth to the center of the next tooth. But do we measure this distance along the outside circle, along the root circle, or somewhere in between? See Fig. 9.1. Unfortunately, "somewhere in between" is the only meaningful choice, since that is where the two gears mesh. The circle that is used is called the *pitch circle*, and the tooth-spacing term *circular pitch* is defined as the circumference of the pitch circle divided by the number of teeth. The pitch-circle circumference cannot be measured directly on a gear, but we can calculate the circumference for a meshed pair of gears.

*See Chap. 3 of the *Gear Handbook* by Darle W. Dudley (McGraw-Hill, 1962) for a general survey of all kinds of gear arrangements, including types of epicyclic gears.

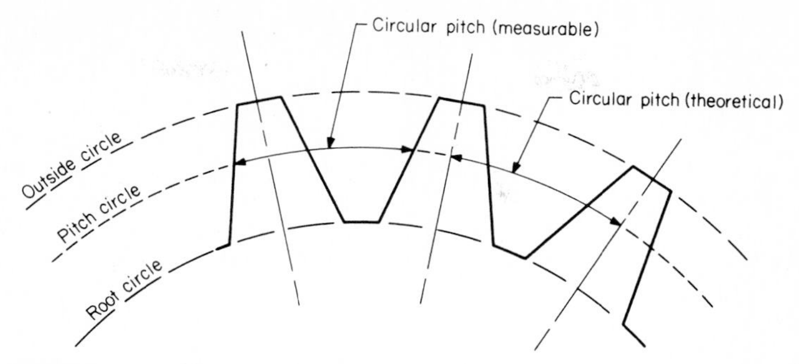

FIG. 9.1 Circular pitch.

The pitch circles of two mounted gears must be *tangent* (just touch each other at a single point, called the *pitch point*), so

$$\text{Center distance} = \text{gear's pitch-circle radius} + \text{pinion's pitch-circle radius} \tag{9.1}$$

We also know that these gears will have the same circular pitch only if the ratio of these two radii is the same as the tooth ratio, so

$$\frac{\text{Radius of gear's pitch circle}}{\text{Radius of pinion's pitch circle}} = \frac{\text{no. of gear teeth}}{\text{no. of pinion teeth}} \tag{9.2}$$

By counting numbers of teeth and measuring the center distance, we can use Eqs. (9.1) and (9.2) to calculate the pitch-circle radii for gear and pinion. The circumference of any circle can be obtained by multiplying its radius by 2π. Dividing the pitch-circle circumference by the number of teeth will then give the circular pitch.

For the gearset you are designing, the gear-tooth ratio is 4/3. Thus the ratio of pitch radii must also be 4/3, i.e., the radius of your pinion pitch circle must be 3/4 the size of your gear's pitch-circle radius.

After many trials with paper gears, you may evolve a design that actually works and that looks something like the gearset in Fig. 9.2. Congratulations! You have learned a lot, and you will have a much easier time absorbing gear-design terminology and equations. However, there are problems with straight-sided tooth profiles like those shown.

First, notice that much of the contact between the two gears is on the leading corners of the *driving gear*. As the gear *wears in*, these corners will tend to round. Such wear is not necessarily detrimental—it may actually improve the running characteristics of the gearset if the break-in period is gentle.

The important difficulty with this design is that the angular velocity of the *driven gear* will not be uniform, even when the angular velocity of the driving gear is uniform. A gear of this design will turn with a slight jerkiness,

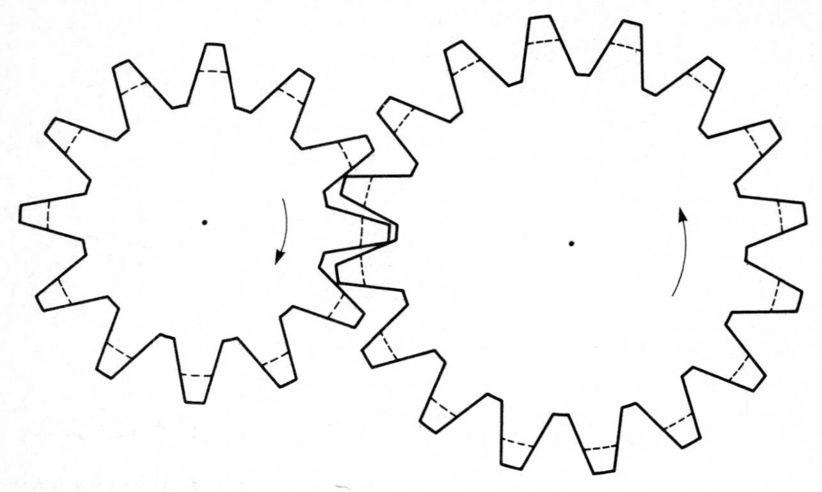

FIG. 9.2 Straight cardboard teeth.

and such nonuniformity is most unwelcome in precision machinery. For this reason, gear teeth usually must have a curved tooth profile. If the tooth curvatures are just right to transmit uniform angular velocity from one shaft to another, the tooth profiles are said to be *conjugate*.

Of the various curves which maintain uniform angular velocity, the easiest for gear manufacturers to produce is called the *involute curve*. You can generate an involute curve by wrapping a string around a circle. The circle you choose will be called the *base circle* of the involute curve. Put a pencil point inside a loop at the end of the string, and slowly unwrap the string while pulling it taut without letting the circle rotate and without letting the string slip. See Fig. 9.3. The curve, $SP_1P_2P\ldots$, which your pencil draws as it is pulled away from the base circle is an involute curve. Notice that at every point, the unwound string lies in a straight line which is tangent to the base circle and also perpendicular to the involute curve at each point. Since

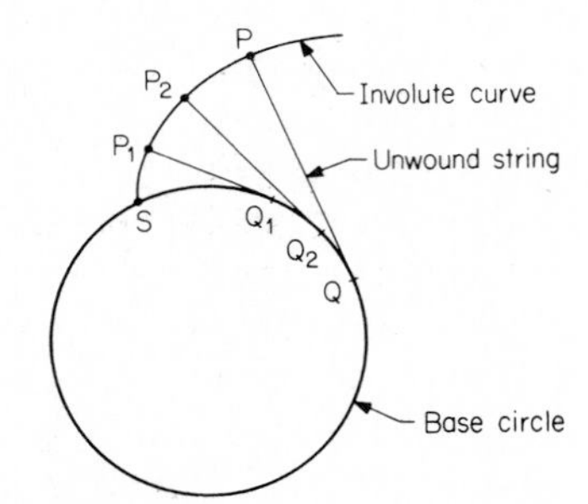

FIG. 9.3 Involute by unwrapping string.

the string didn't change length during the unwinding, the length of string PQ which has been unwound is always equal to the arc length SQ on the base circle. These facts lead directly to the mathematical involute relations of Fig. 2.10 and Sec. 3.8.

Any line perpendicular to the involute tooth profile surface is called a *line of pressure* because it corresponds to the direction of the force whenever the gear driving its mate is in contact at that point. All the lines of pressure for each involute gear tooth are tangent to the base circle (remember the unwound string!). When an involute gear and pinion roll together in mesh, their two lines of pressure through the point of contact *always lie along the same line*. This very special line, called the *line of action*, is tangent to both base circles and contains the pitch point. The point of contact between the pinion and gear is always on this line, moving back and forth as the involute gear teeth roll through mesh.

Before we add an involute curve to our paper gear profiles, let's consider how big we should make the base circle. Figure 9.4 shows two different base circles and the involute profiles that result from each. Base circle c_1 has a radius r_{b1} which is only a little smaller than the pitch-circle radius r. Base circle c_2 is much smaller. The involute curve determined by c_2 is much more slanted at the pitch-line level than involute curve 1. This difference is also reflected in the size of the *pressure angle*, which is defined as the angle at a pitch point between the line perpendicular to the involute tooth surface and the line tangent to the pitch circle.

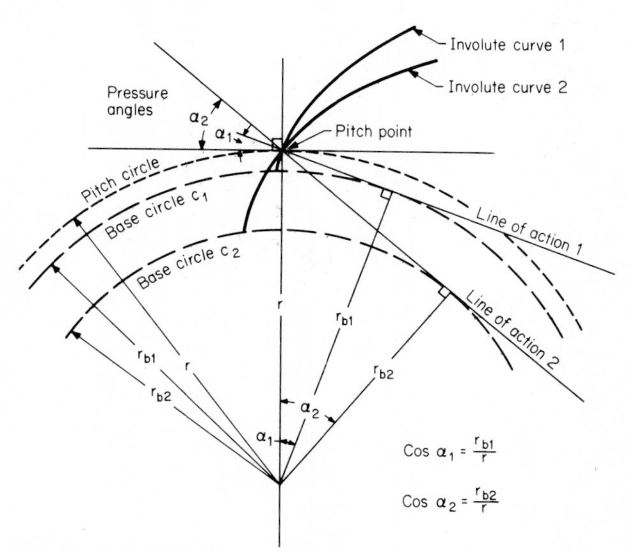

FIG. 9.4 The pressure angle α of an involute gear tooth is determined by the size ratio between the base circle and the pitch circle.

Some simple geometric logic will confirm that the pressure angle α is equal to the *profile angle* between the tangent to the involute profile and the radial line through the pitch point. This profile angle is also equal to the angle labeled α at the center of the circle. It can be seen from the right triangle formed by the unwound string that the cosine of α is equal to the ratio of the base-circle radius to the pitch-circle radius. For Fig. 9.4, the base circle c_1 was chosen to be about 94 percent the size of the pitch circle, so the pressure angle α_1 is about 20° (cos 20° = 0.9397). A pressure angle of 20° is very commonly used in modern gears. The base circle c_2 is only about three-fourths the size of the pitch circle, so the pressure angle α_2 is about 40° (cos 40° = 0.766). If you imagine the other side of the 40° pressure angle tooth, you will see why such a large pressure angle is never used for actual gear teeth. The tooth would be extremely wide at the base, but the two sides would come together at a point before the tooth could reach a workable whole depth. Also, it would be impossible for more than one tooth of the gear to be in contact with a mating gear tooth at the same time, so the gears would not run nearly as quietly or smoothly as 20° pressure angle gears. However, a pressure angle of 25° is sometimes used for fairly low-speed gears which are to be loaded heavily enough to benefit from the extra strength of a wide base.

If we now redesign the tooth profile of our paper gears in Fig. 9.2 to incorporate a 22.5°-pressure-angle involute curve on the mating surfaces and a smooth curve in the root area between the teeth, our gears will look like those shown in Fig. 9.5. Now our gears will mesh together smoothly, and

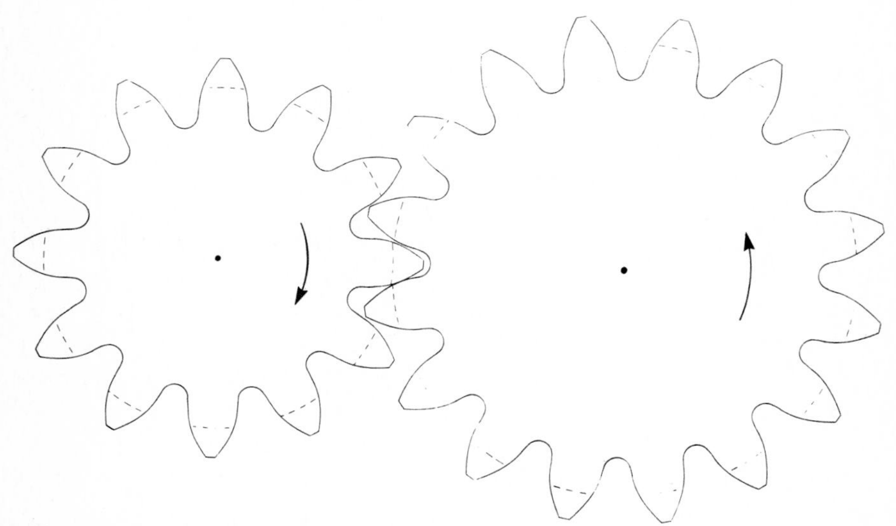

FIG. 9.5 Involute added to Fig. 9.2 teeth.

they are close to the design of some current commercial spur gears, although most gears have more teeth than those shown in this illustration.

9.2 Dynamic Load Theory (Supplement to Chap. 2)

At the IFToMM Gear Committee meeting in Eindhoven, Holland, in June 1983, Dr. Aizoh Kubo* gave an informal presentation covering dynamic load research. Dr. Kubo pointed out that there were really three kinds of "dynamic" load:

1 Fluctuations of input and output torque caused by more or less rough running of the engine making the power and the machine absorbing the power. (A piston engine driving a stone crusher would certainly be a good example of a fluctuating torque situation.)

2 Fluctuations of torque resulting from torsional vibration of the power-transmission system. (A system like a propeller drive on a large ship can have a natural frequency that is excited by the frequency of propeller blades passing the rudder post.)

3 Fluctuations in torque as teeth roll through mesh. This is caused by periodic changes in tooth mesh stiffness and by errors in tooth profile, tooth spacing, and tooth alignment across the face width. (In some badly worn large spur-gear drives, it is possible to feel and hear the disturbance as each tooth goes through mesh.)

These three kinds of errors are handled in gear-design work in the following manner:

Misbehavior of driving and driven equipment is handled by an application factor. (Table 3.37 and Sec. 3.27 give general information on application factors.)

It is necessary to calculate critical torsional frequencies in a power-transmission system and then design and operate the equipment so as to avoid any appreciable operation at or near a critical speed. Fast-running equipment that operates *above* the first critical speed should be brought through the first critical speed quickly and at light load. (See Sec. 7.13 for more discussion of torsional vibration.)

The dynamic load resulting from tooth stiffness effects and tooth errors is handled by a factor called the *dynamic factor*. (See the part of Sec. 2.3 relating to dynamic load. Also see Sec. 3.27 and Fig. 3.34.)

In a private communication of Dec. 31, 1982, Dr. Kubo sent me a short

*Associate Professor, The University of Kyoto, Kyoto, Japan. Dr. Kubo is an IFToMM Gear Committee member.

statement on dynamic load for possible inclusion in this book. In Dr. Kubo's words:

Although a torque applied to a pair of gears is kept constant, momentary overloads act on gear teeth. With progress of meshing, the number of tooth pairs in contact alternates, which results in the periodical change of the rotation of driven gear to the driving gear due to tooth deflection, even if the gears have no tooth errors. When a tooth error goes through mesh, it makes a delay or advance of rotational motion of driven gear to that of the driving gear. These forced changes of rotational movement of gear motion owing to tooth errors and tooth stiffness changes prevent the masses of the driven and driving gears and apparatus from rotating at uniform velocities. The change in velocity causes momentary overloads.

Since most spur gear pairs have contact ratios between 1.3 and 2.0, one tooth pair meshing and two tooth pair meshing alternate cyclically with the progress of meshing. Because the difference of tooth stiffness under one tooth pair meshing and under two tooth pair meshing is large, non-uniform rotational movement of gears, i.e., vibrational excitation owing to tooth deflection, is also large, particularly if no adequate tooth profile correction to obtain uniform rotational movement of gears is made on the spur gears. Consequently the dynamic loads of spur gears without adequate tooth profile correction receive strong mutual influences of tooth stiffness change and tooth errors.

On the other hand, for helical gears with considerably large overlap ratio, the total length of the sum of contact lines on the simultaneously meshing tooth pairs does not change so strongly as for the case of spur gears, and non-uniform rotational movement of gears owing to tooth deflection is in most cases rather small. The vibrational excitation of helical gears is therefore caused mainly by the non-uniform rotational movement of gears owing to tooth errors. In the case of helical gears with large overlap ratio, if tooth error is not the form of undulation which changes in the direction perpendicular to the contact lines on the plane of action, the tooth profile errors are averaged on the contact lines of the simultaneously meshing tooth pairs. And such helical gears can rotate almost uniformly, although they have considerably large profile errors. In this case, dynamic load increment is not large under wide driving speed range, but the tooth suffers from an overload increment caused by the local deflection of tooth pair corresponding to the tooth profile error whose magnitude is different at each part of contact line. In gear rating calculations this statical load increment due to tooth errors of helical gears is often not considered: In many gear rating calculation methods, e.g., AGMA procedure, the sum of both static and dynamic load increment due to tooth errors is usually taken in account by the "dynamic factor" for helical gears. But in some gear rating calculation methods, e.g., ISO/DIS 6336, DIN 3990 procedure, pure dynamic load increment is treated for both spur and helical gears. Consequently the dynamic factors from AGMA and ISO procedures for helical gears of large overlap ratio may show a very large difference between their values (depending on speed and accuracy). By the way, the statical load increment due to tooth errors for helical gears is not well considered in every gear rating method until now, and the use of dynamic factor which considers pure dynamic load increment for the rating calculation of large helical gears without considering the statical load increment due to tooth errors results in an underestimation of real tooth loading in operation.

When the vibration of gears becomes large enough or transmitting load is small enough, driving and driven tooth flanks lose their contact momentarily. Then the tooth flanks collide in the next moment with each other and a large momentary overload acts on the tooth, with a magnitude proportional to the inertia masses of the driving and driven apparatus and to the collision velocity of tooth flanks. The backlash between driving and driven teeth has a very large influence on dynamic overload, when teeth lose their contact.

When gears are run at high enough speeds, the kinetic energy becomes so great that tooth errors and tooth stiffness change cannot change their velocity appreciably. Under such super critical driving speed, the overload is simply whatever load is required to bend the tooth out of the way (that is, the static load which would cause the deflection corresponding to the tooth error).

Figures 9.6 and 9.7 show the two test rigs used by Dr. Kubo and his associates at Kyoto University in Kyoto, Japan, to get dynamic load data. The first illustration shows a back-to-back gear test, while the second shows a power-absorbing type of gear test.

The data obtained from the tests made at Kyoto University are most revealing and interesting. With good instrumentation and a considerable

FIG. 9.6 Circulating torque test rig for dynamic load study. (*Courtesy of Dr. Aizoh Kubo, Kyoto Univ., Kyoto, Japan.*)

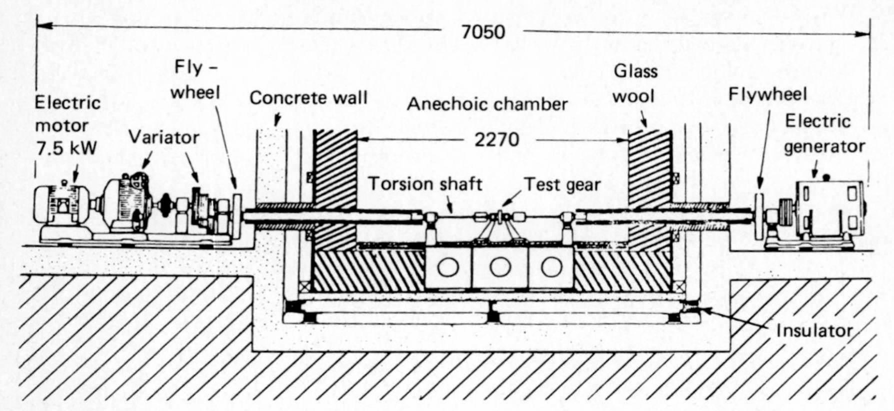

FIG. 9.7 Power-absorbing test rig for dynamic load study. (*Courtesy of Dr. Aizoh Kubo, Kyoto Univ., Kyoto, Japan.*)

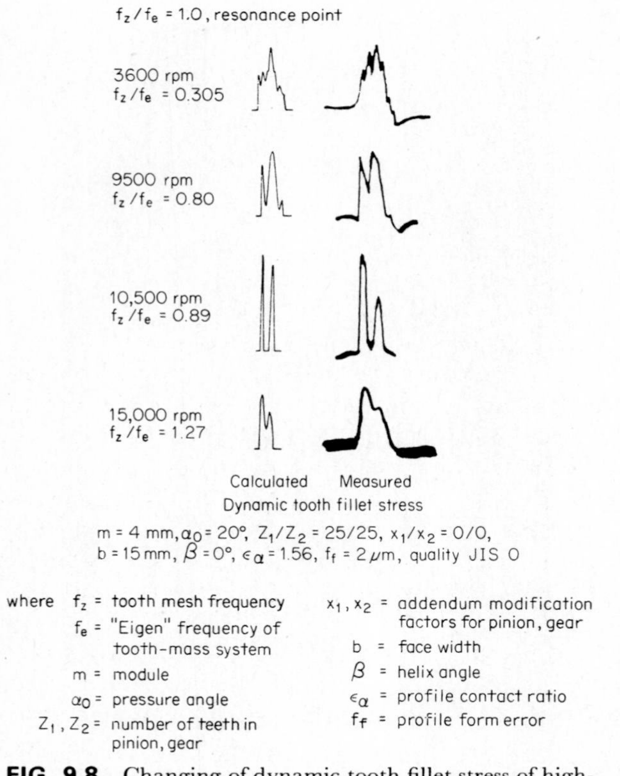

FIG. 9.8 Changing of dynamic tooth fillet stress of high-precision spur gears at different driving speeds.

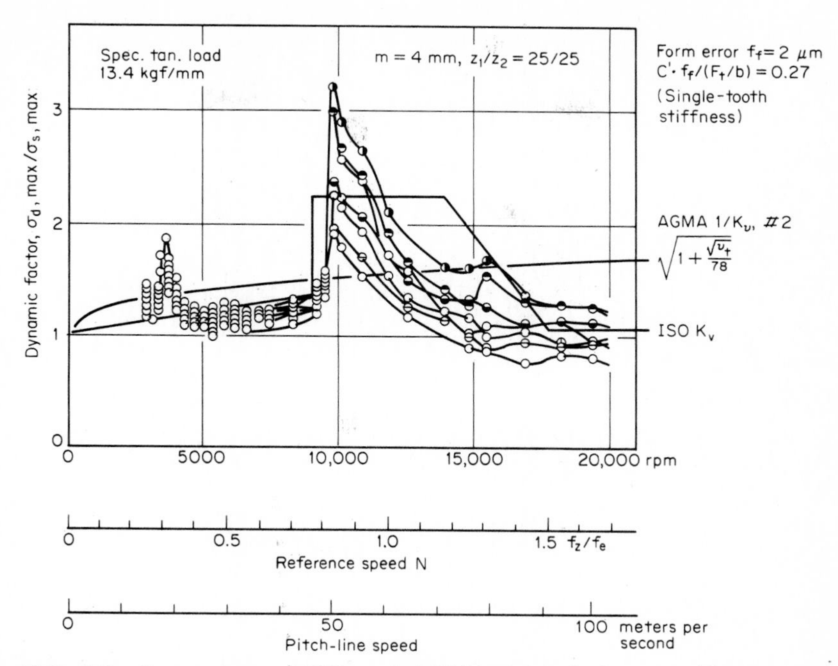

FIG. 9.9 Comparison of ISO and AGMA dynamic factors with measured dynamic factor for fillet stress of high-precision spur gears.

number of tests, it was possible to rather thoroughly explore the dynamic load behavior of typical small gearsets. Figures 9.8 through 9.12 were supplied by Dr. Kubo to show some of his results.

Figure 9.8 shows the general characteristic of the actual data taken. Note how the dynamic load changes as the speed changes.

Figure 9.9 shows a summary of many tests for high-precision spur gears. Note how the dynamic load reaches a peak when there is a vibration resonance between the masses of the two gears in mesh. In Fig. 9.9 this resonance point comes just below 10,000 rpm. Also note the superimposed calculated values for an AGMA dynamic load and an ISO dynamic load.

Figure 9.10 shows a field of data for spur gears of medium quality. The test points are not all shown, but the area bounded by the test points is shown. In this case the relative AGMA and ISO values that would be calculated are shown.

Figure 9.11 shows more data for spur gears. In this case the quality was really poor. Note the very high values of dynamic load. Data such as these teach the gear designer that gear quality is most important. Inaccurate gears are just not capable of running at high speed. They generate so much dynamic overload that the overload will wear out the gears quickly—even when the transmitted overload is relatively small.

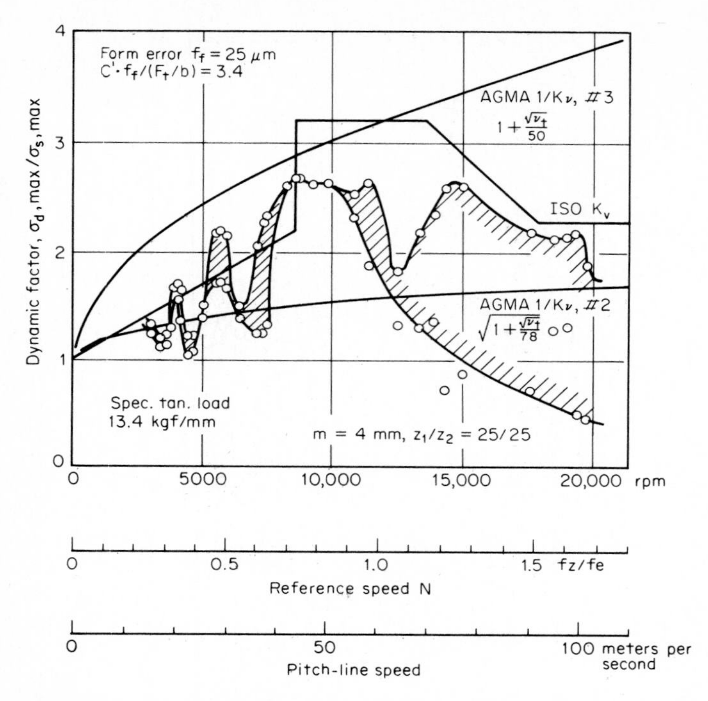

FIG. 9.10 Comparison of ISO and AGMA dynamic factors with measured dynamic factor for fillet stress of spur gears of medium quality.

Figure 9.12 shows the situation for helical gears with relatively high accuracy. Note the rather low values for the dynamic overload. Of course, it should be kept in mind that these tests by Dr. Kubo determined dynamic overload by strain gages mounted in the root fillets of gear teeth. Because the form of tooth fillet stress with progress of gear rotation for helical gears is somewhat different at each individual position of fillet along tooth width, the dynamic overload is difficult to determine by one measurement as shown in Fig. 9.12. But many measurements indicate that the situation of dynamic loading does not differ much from that of Fig. 9.12.

The general conclusion to be drawn from test work on dynamic load is that an exact calculation is nearly impossible. The designer can handle dynamic load by making a reasonable allowance for the effective dynamic load, then specifying close control on gear-tooth accuracy so that relatively small amounts of dynamic load are developed. In addition, it is necessary to operate the gears away from the resonance point, particularly if they are spur gears.

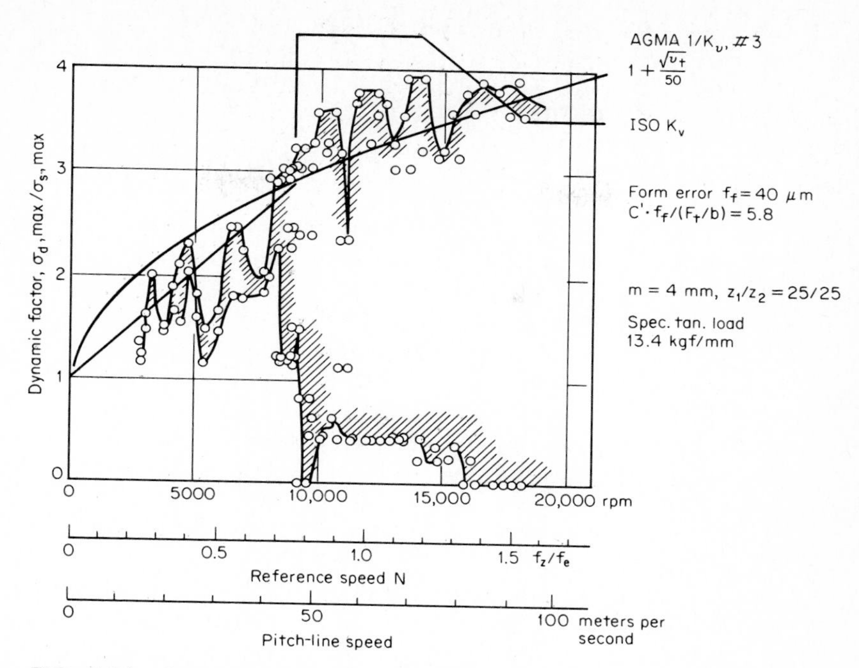

FIG. 9.11 Comparison of ISO and AGMA dynamic factors with measured dynamic factor for fillet stress of spur gears of poor quality.

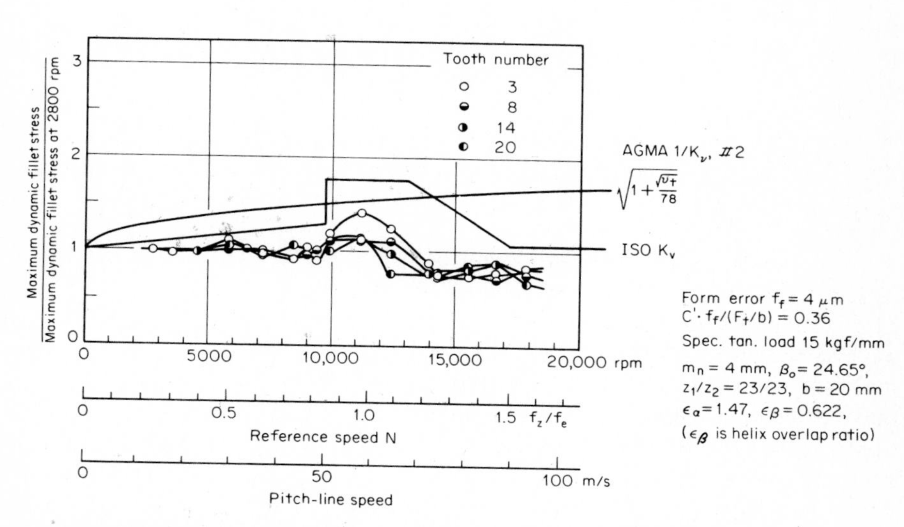

FIG. 9.12 Comparison of ISO and AGMA dynamic factors with measured dynamic factor for fillet stress of high-precision helical gears.

9.3 Highest and Lowest Points of Single-Tooth Contact (Supplement to Chaps. 2 and 3)

Spur gears with 20° pressure angle have contact ratios that are usually in the range of 1.6 to 1.7. Those with 25° pressure angle have contact ratios that are usually in the range of 1.4 to 1.5.

Figure 3.13 shows curves of contact ratio for different numbers of meshing teeth; 20, 22.5, and 25° pressure angles; and both standard addendum design and the design where the pinion is 25 percent long addendum and the gear is 25 percent short addendum. Figure 3.13 is drawn for *standard-depth teeth.* (Working depth is 2.0 × module for metric dimensions or 2.0 ÷ transverse diametral pitch for English dimensions.) The range of Fig. 3.13 goes from a contact ratio of 1.34 for a 10/35 tooth ratio at 25° pressure angle, 25 percent long addendum to 1.78 for a 40/100 tooth ratio, 20° pressure angle, and standard addendum.

Given this, it is evident that in most of the spur-gear designs used in the gear trade, two pair of teeth are in contact when a tooth enters mesh and two pair will be in contact when a tooth leaves mesh. In the middle of the tooth contact area, though, only one pair of teeth will be in mesh. It is only when the calculated contact ratio exceeds 2.0 that two pair of teeth can be in mesh in the middle of the tooth contact area. The general theory of involute spur-gear contact can be expressed as follows:

Contact ratio less than 1.0, only one pair of teeth in contact.

Contact ratio over 1.0 but less than 2.0, two pair of teeth in contact at start and finish of meshing, but one pair of teeth in contact for part of meshing interval.

Contact ratio over 2.0 but less than 3.0, three pair of teeth in contact at start and finish of meshing, but two pair of teeth in contact for part of meshing interval.

Since normal spur-gear designs have a contact ratio over 1.0 but less than 2.0, the locations where contact shifts from one pair of teeth to two pair of teeth have been of much interest to those rating spur gears. It can be theorized that the most critical bending stress should come at the highest point on the tooth at which the tooth has to carry the full transmitted load. It can also be theorized that the most critical contact stress should come at the lowest point on the tooth at which one tooth has to carry the full transmitted load.

In the 1940s and 1950s much bench-test work was done on gear teeth in an attempt to find out whether or not these concepts in rating spur gears were valid. The general answer was that they are valid. [The ASME paper by Seabrook and Dudley (1963) gives an insight into one body of test work that probed the issues just mentioned.]

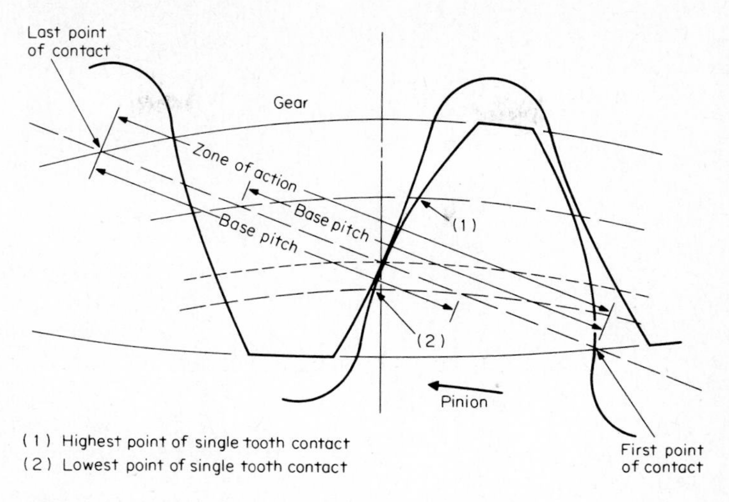

FIG. 9.13 Definition of the highest and lowest points of single-tooth contact for involute spur gears.

In recent years, it has become generally accepted that the changeover points from one pair to two pair of teeth are critical. (It is only in the cases where there is a serious profile error or unusual profile modification that these points are not critical from the standpoint of load-rating calculations.)

Figure 9.13 shows the basic definitions of where the highest and lowest points of single-tooth (single-pair) contact occur. If the pinion drives, the highest point of single-tooth contact is one base pitch away from the first point of contact. (If the pinion is driven, the *first* point of contact becomes the *last* point of contact, and the highest point of single-tooth contact is still at the same place—now one base pitch away from the last point of contact.)

The lowest point of single-tooth contact is one base pitch away from the last point of contact, with the pinion driving.

In Fig. 9.13, point 1 is the highest point on the pinion at which single-tooth contact is carried. This position is often referred to in gear writings as HPSTC.

The lowest point of single-tooth contact in Fig. 9.13 is at point 2. This point is often referred to as LPSTC.

9.4 Layout of Large Circles by Calculation (Supplement to Chaps. 2 and 3)

In making gear-tooth layouts, it is frequently necessary to draw accurate arcs of circles that are quite large. For instance, a 50-tooth gear of 3 module

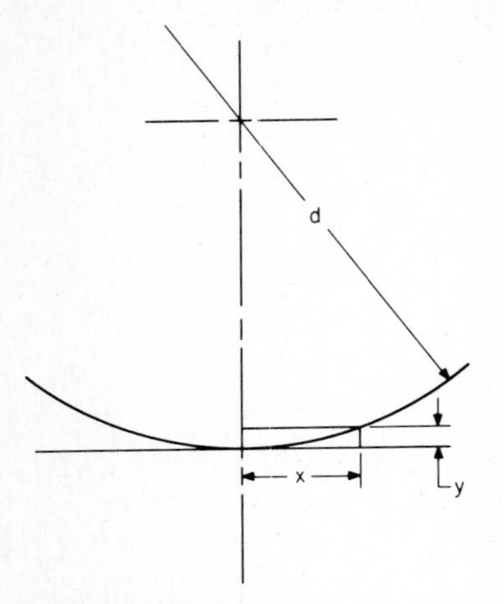

Calculation steps

	1	2	3	4
1. Distance x, mm	25	50	75	100
2. Diameter d, mm	1500			
3. (2) ÷ 2.000	750			
4. (3) × (3)	562500			
5. (1) × (1)	625	2500	5625	10000
6. $[(4) - (5)]^{0.50}$	749.583	748.331	746.241	743.303
7. $y = (3) - (6)$	0.417	1.669	3.759	6.697

FIG. 9.14 Method of calculating points for the layout of large circles.

may be laid out 10 times size. This would make the pitch diameter used in the layout 1500 mm (59.055 in.).

With an ordinary beam compass, it is usually not possible to draw circles, or arcs of circles, greater than about 500 mm (20 in.). How can the gear designer draw accurate arcs of large circles?

The solution to this problem is to calculate the deviation from a straight line for a distance of about 100 mm (4 in.). With the tooth centerline in the center of a sheet of standard paper, it is possible to draw the circular arc for a distance of about 200 mm, with only four guide points on either side of the centerline.

Figure 9.14 shows how four points may be precisely calculated (with a small pocket calculator). The example shown is for a 1500-mm diameter. Note that the fourth point calculates a deviation in the y direction of 6.697 mm. The deviations at the other four x values are

1st point, 25 mm y is 0.417 mm or 6.2%
2d point, 50 mm y is 1.669 mm or 25%
3d point, 75 mm y is 3.759 mm or 56%
4th point, 100 mm y is 6.697 mm or 100%

The percentage values for four evenly spaced points are *essentially constant* for all large circles. Thus calculating the value of the fourth point makes it easy to get the other three points good enough for a layout.

The following list of y deviations at $x = 100$ mm can be used to check calculations or to quickly estimate the deviation of any large-diameter circle from a straight line:

Circle diameter, mm	y deviation, mm at $x = 100$ mm	Circle diameter, mm	y deviation, mm, at $x = 100$ mm
550	18.826	1200	8.392
600	17.157	1500	6.697
650	15.767	1800	5.573
700	14.590	2250	4.453
750	13.579	2800	3.576
850	11.932	3375	2.966
1000	10.102	4000	2.502

The above values, for $x = 100$ mm, can be approximated closely enough for layout purposes by the relation

$$y = \frac{10{,}300}{d} \tag{9.3}$$

9.5 Special Calculations for Spur Gears (Supplement to Chap. 3)

In this section several special calculation procedures that are needed for spur gears will be covered. Other calculation procedures, of course, are covered in Chap. 3.

The supplementary material that will now be discussed covers tooth thickness, involute geometry dimensions, involute profile dimensions, and root fillet trochoid dimensions. Each of these will be covered in a separate subsection.

Tooth Thickness Measurement by Diameter over Pins. It is common practice in the gear trade to check spur gears by taking a measurement over pins. If the part has an even number of teeth, the pins are placed 180° apart. If the part has an odd number of teeth, the pins are placed as near 180° apart as is possible.

In some countries (particularly the United States), standard pin sizes have been established. Gear makers buy standard-size pins to go with the commonly used pitches of teeth. Then there are published tables which make determining the measurement over pins for a standard set of pins and a standard pitch very simple.

Section 24-1 of the *Gear Handbook* by Darle W. Dudley (McGraw-Hill, 1962) gives tables for the measurement of standard external and internal

TABLE 9.1 Pin Sizes Used to Check the Tooth Thickness of Spur Gears

Type of tooth	Pressure angle	Pin diameter constant
External, standard or near standard proportions	$14\frac{1}{2}$ to 25°	1.728 1.920 1.680
External, long-addendum pinion design	$14\frac{1}{2}$ to 25°	1.920
Internal, standard designs	$14\frac{1}{2}$ to 25°	1.680 1.440

Notes: The pin diameters change as the tooth size changes. For metric design, *multiply* the pin size above by the module. For English design, *divide* the pin size by the diametral pitch.

As an example, a 5-module spur tooth would normally use an 8.64-mm pin. A 5-pitch spur tooth would use a 0.3456-in. pin. If the teeth were 5-module and the only standard pin available was the 5-pitch pin, it could be used, since its size is 8.77826 mm, and that is close to the desired size. Calculations by Table 9.2 could be made using the 8.77826 pin size for item (6).

gears. In many cases, though, the pitch may not be standard or the pin size may not be standard. The gear designer then needs to make a special calculation.

Table 9.1 shows the sizes of pins commonly used to check spur gears. These sizes are satisfactory for most gear designs. They are also the sizes that have been standardized in the United States.

The pin size used should touch the involute profile of the gear tooth somewhat above the middle of the tooth height. The top of the pin should stick out beyond the outside diameter of the gear at least a small amount. The bottom of the pin should not go into the gear-tooth space so deeply that it touches the root diameter. These limits on pin size, of course, make it possible to check a gear with several different sizes of pins. Given some choices, the designer should either pick a pin in accordance with Table 9.1 or pick a pin close to the standard size given in Table 9.1.

Table 9.2 shows an operation sheet for calculating the diameter over pins for spur gears. A 25-tooth pinion of 3 module is shown as an example. (The reader can find the basic formulas for pin measurement in Secs. 7-9 and 7-10 of the *Gear Handbook.*)

Calculation of Involute Geometry Values. Table 3.12 shows dimensions for a spur-gear design, giving numerical values for a 25/96 tooth ratio with 3-module teeth. Table 9.3 shows the calculations that need to be made to determine the form diameters, roll angles at the form diameters, and roll

TABLE 9.2 Diameter over Pins for External Spur Gears

Given data				
1. Pitch diameter	75.00			
2. Number of teeth	25			
3. Pressure angle at (1)	20°			
4. Arc tooth thickness at (1)	4.991	4.915		
5. Base circle diameter, (1) × cos (3)	70.47695			
6. Diameter of measuring pin	5.334			
7. 3.14159265 ÷ (2)	0.1256637			
8. Inv. (3) = tan (3) − (3) ÷ 57.29578	0.0149044			
9. (6) ÷ (5)	0.0756843			
10. (4) ÷ (1)	0.0665467	0.0655333		
11. (9) + (10) + (8) − (7)	0.0314717	0.0304583		
12. Inv. angle* for (4), arc inv. (11)	25.3874	25.12653		
Steps				
13. Pressure angle, pin center	25.3874	25.12653	25.45	25.06
14. Inv. (13)	0.0314717	0.0304583	0.0317185	0.0302037
15. (14) − (8)	0.0165673	0.0155539	0.0168141	0.0152993
16. (15) + (7) − (9)	0.0665467	0.0655333	0.0667935	0.0652787
17. Arc thickness, (1) × (16)	4.9910	4.9150	5.009511	4.895900
18. Cos (13)	0.9034296	0.9053723	0.9029606	0.9058647
19. Diameter over pins, (5) ÷ (18) + (6)	—	—	—	—
For odd number of teeth				
20. Cos [90° ÷ (2)]	0.998027	0.998027	0.998027	0.998027
21. [(5) ÷ (18)] × (20)	77.85651	77.68945	77.89695	77.64722
22. Diameter over pins, (21) + (6)	83.19051	83.02345	83.23095	82.98122

*See Table 9.10.

Notes: Normally, (12) is used for (13) in the first column, and then (17) in the first column should equal (4). Other values of (13) are assumed and entered in the remaining columns. Four values are then obtained for tooth thickness versus diameter over pins. Item (19) is for *even* tooth numbers. Calculate (22) if tooth number is odd.

angle at the start of profile modification. In addition, this sheet has a calculation for the contact ratio.

The general theory behind Table 9.3 is given in Secs. 3.8 and 3.9. These sections give equations that could be used in direct calculation. Once the equations are understood, though, it is much simpler in day-to-day work either to use an operation sheet like Table 9.3 or to make a computer routine to carry out the steps in Table 9.3.

In designing spur gears, there is general concern about the relative sizes of the *angle of approach* and the *angle of recess*. Figure 9.15 defines these angles. In the angle of approach the tooth sliding velocity is directed toward the root diameter of the pinion, but the tooth rolling velocity is toward the outside diameter of the pinion. In the angle of recess the rolling velocity continues to be toward the outside diameter of the pinion and the sliding velocity is also toward the outside diameter of the pinion.

TABLE 9.3 Calculation of Form Diameter, Roll Angles, Contact Ratio, and Start Profile Modification for External Gearsets

	Metric		English	
	1	2	1	2
Data item* or operation	Pinion	Gear	Pinion	Gear
*1. Number of teeth	25	96	25	96
*2. Pitch diameter	75.00	288.00	2.9527	11.3386
*3. Addendum	3.54	2.46	0.1394	0.0968
4. Outside diameter, (2) + 2.0 × (3)	82.08	292.92	3.2315	11.5322
*5. Pressure angle, transverse	20°	20°	20°	20°
6. Base diameter, cos (5) × (2)	70.47695	270.6315	2.77463	10.65480
7. Gear ratio, $(1)_2 \div (1)_1$	3.84	3.84	3.84	3.84
8. Inverse ratio, 1.0 ÷ (7)	0.26042	0.26042	0.26042	0.26042
9. Arccos [(6) ÷ (4)]	30.83608	22.49556	30.83802	22.49435
10. O.D. roll, tan (9) × 57.29578	34.204	23.727	34.207	23.726
11. P.D. roll, tan (5) × 57.29578	20.854	20.854	20.854	20.854
12. Addendum roll, (10) − (11)	13.35	2.87	13.35	2.87
13. Pinion roll, $(12)_1 + [(12)_2 \times (7)]$	24.38	—	24.38	—
14. Gear roll, $(12)_2 + [(12)_1 \times (8)]$	—	6.35	—	6.35
15. L.D. roll, pinion, (10) − (13)	9.8196	—	9.8251	—
16. L.D. roll, gear, (10) − (14)	—	17.377	—	17.377
17. Arctan [(15) ÷ 57.29578]	9.72512	—	9.73042	—
18. L.D., pinion, (6) ÷ cos (17)	71.50450	—	2.81513	—
19. Arctan [(16) ÷ 57.29578]	—	16.87215	—	16.87152
20. L.D., gear, (6) ÷ cos (19)	—	282.8049	—	11.13403
21. Circular pitch, π × (2) ÷ (1)	9.42478	9.42478	0.37105	0.37105
22. Extra involute, 0.016 × (21)	0.1508	0.1508	0.00594	0.00594
23. Form diameter, pinion, (18) − (22)	71.3537	—	2.8092	—
24. Arccos [(6) ÷ (23)]	8.99114	—	8.99690	—
25. F.D. roll, pinion = tan (24) × 57.29578	9.07	—	9.07	—
26. Form diameter, gear, (20) − (22)	—	282.6541	—	11.1281
27. Arccos [(6) ÷ (26)]	—	16.77107	—	16.77044
28. F.D. roll, gear = tan (27) × 57.29578	—	17.27	—	17.27
29. Roll per tooth, 360° ÷ (1)	14.4	—	14.4	—
30. Contact ratio, $(13) \div (29)_1$	1.693	—	1.693	—
*31. Start modification diameter SD (see Table 3.54)	80.880	291.570	3.18426	11.47905
32. Arccos [(6) ÷ (31)]	29.38098	21.84605	29.3832	21.84478
33. S.D. roll, tan (32) × 57.29578	32.26	22.97	32.26	22.97

Notes: For metric calculations use millimeter dimensions, and for English calculations use inches. All angles are in degrees. See Sec. 3.9 for cases when (22) may be too much extra involute. Subscript numerals are for column numbers.

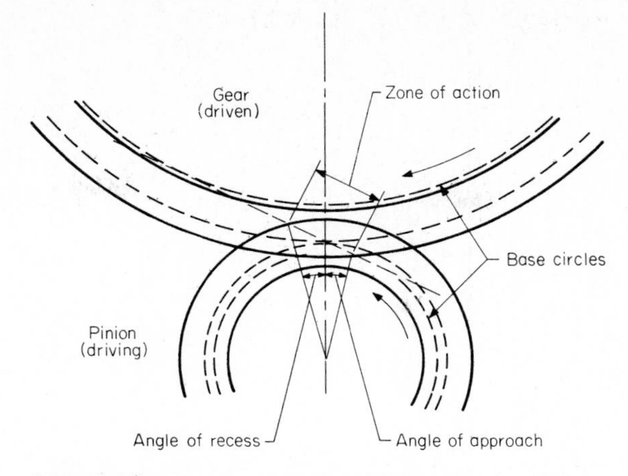

FIG. 9.15 Example of *arc of approach* and *arc of recess.*

TABLE 9.4 Arc Tooth Thickness at Any Diameter, External Spur Gears

Given data	
1. Pitch diameter	75.00 mm
2. Pressure angle at (1)	20°
3. Arc tooth thickness at (1)	5.030 mm

Step A: Solve for the tooth thickness at base diameter.

4. Involute* (2)	0.014904
5. Cosine (2)	0.9396926
6. (4) × (1)	1.117829
7. (3) + (6)	6.147829
8. T.T. at B.D., (5) × (7)	5.777069
9. Base diameter, (5) × (1)	70.47695

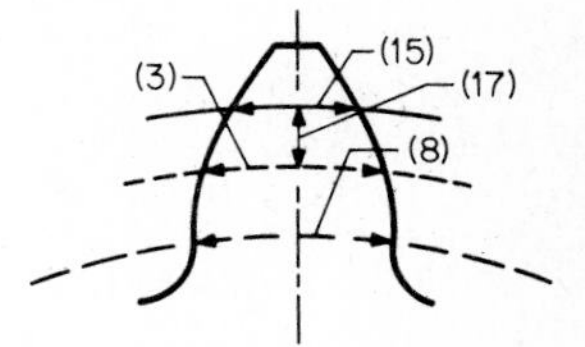

Step B: Solve for a series of tooth thicknesses to study the tooth profile. For any desired diameter, the cosine of the pressure angle at that diameter is

Cos PA at any diameter = base diameter ÷ any diameter

A series of pressure angles is assumed based on diameters of interest. Then calculations are made to get the arc thicknesses (line 15) that go with each diameter.

10. Assumed pressure angles	30.83608	28.24139	24.58019	16.48985	11.80586
11. Cosine (10)	0.858637	0.880962	0.90938	0.95887	0.97885
12. Involute (10)	0.058782	0.04422	0.02841	0.00822	0.00297
13. (12) × (9)	4.142800	3.11653	2.00242	0.57922	0.20907
14. (8) − (13)	1.634269	2.66054	3.77465	5.19785	5.56800
15. Arc TT, (14) ÷ (11)	1.903329	3.02004	4.15080	5.42080	5.68833
16. Any diameter, (9) ÷ (11)	82.08000	80.000	77.5000	73.5000	72.000
17. Δ rad., [(16) − (1)] ÷ 2	3.5400	2.5000	1.2500	−.7500	−1.5000

*The involute of an angle α is defined as: inv α = tan α − (α in radians). If α is in degrees, then: inv α = tan α − ($\alpha \times \pi \div 180$). Involutes can also be read from the involute function table, Table 9.10.

TABLE 9.5 Calculation of Spur-Gear Root-Fillet Trochoid Produced by a Round Corner Hob

Given data	
1. Pitch diameter (as hobbed)	75.00 mm
2. Pressure angle (as hobbed)	20°
3. Dedendum of gear (as hobbed)	3.51 mm
4. Circular pitch (as hobbed)	9.42478 mm
5. Edge radius of hob	1.05 mm
6. Tooth thickness of gear (at pitch line)	5.030 mm
Step A: Solve for some intermediate distances and angles.	
7. Distance to edge radius center, (3) − (5)	2.46
8. Hob tooth thickness, (4) − (6)	4.39478
9. (7) × tan (2)	0.895367
10. (5) ÷ cos (2)	1.117387
11. 0.5 × (8) − (9) − (10)	0.184637
12. [2.0 × (11)] ÷ (1)	0.004924
13. (12) × 180 ÷ π	0.282104

Step B: Solve for points (x, y) on trochoidal path by assuming a series of radius values from mid-dedendum to root radius.

14. Assumed radius values	36.200	36.000	35.600	35.200	35.100
15. (1) ÷ 2.0	37.5				
16. (15) − (7)	35.04				
17. $[(14)^2 - (16)^2]^{0.50}$	9.09057	8.25823	6.28955	3.35237	2.05144
18. Arctan [(17) ÷ (16)], degrees	14.54383	13.26148	10.17601	5.46501	3.35059
19. (18) × π ÷ 180, radians	0.25384	0.23146	0.17760	0.09538	0.05848
20. (17) ÷ (15)	0.24242	0.22022	0.16772	0.08940	0.05471
21. (19) − (20)	0.01142	0.01124	0.00988	0.00599	0.00377
22. (15) × (16) − $(14)^2$	3.56	18.0	46.64	74.96	81.99
23. (15) × (17)	340.8962	309.6837	235.8580	125.7140	76.92894
24. Arctan [(22) ÷ (23)], degrees	0.59832	3.32651	11.18571	30.80654	46.82407
25. $(14)^2 + (5)^2$	1311.543	1297.103	1268.463	1240.143	1233.113
26. (5) × sin (24)	0.01096	0.06093	0.20369	0.53775	0.76572
27. 2.0 × (26) × (14)	0.79384	4.38676	14.50266	37.85745	53.75347
28. $[(25) - (27)]^{0.50}$	36.20426	35.95436	35.41130	34.67398	34.34180
29. (14) − (26)	36.18904	35.93907	35.39631	34.66225	34.33428
30. Arccos [(29) ÷ (28)], degrees	1.66184	1.67067	1.66687	1.49039	1.19875
31. (30) × π ÷ 180, radians	0.02900	0.02916	0.02909	0.02601	0.02092
32. (31) + (21)	0.04043	0.04040	0.03898	0.03200	0.02470
33. (32) + (12)	0.04535	0.04532	0.04390	0.03692	0.02962
34. (33) × 180 ÷ π, degrees	2.59842	2.59660	2.51527	2.11546	1.69708
35. x = (28) × sin (34)	1.64133	1.62886	1.55405	1.27993	1.01704
36. (28) × cos (34)	36.16704	35.91744	35.37718	34.65035	34.32673
37. y = (15) − (36)	1.33296	1.58256	2.12282	2.84965	3.17327
38. point on path = (35), (37)	(1.64, 1.33)	(1.63, 1.58)	(1.55, 2.12)	(1.28, 2.85)	(1.02, 3.17)

When the sliding and rolling velocities are opposite to each other, the tooth surface is much more apt to pit than when they are in the same direction. As a further consideration, the tooth friction makes the pinion run more roughly when the sliding and rolling velocities are opposed.

The designer should tend to favor making the arc of recess longer than the arc of approach, wherever possible. This is particularly important when a small pinion drives a large gear. The small pinion will make several revolutions per turn of the gear, so it is more sensitive to wear than the gear. Also, the small pinion will be rotating several times faster than the large, so the pinion is more subject to vibration trouble.

Arc Tooth Thickness Values. In new design work it is often desirable to plot the complete profile of the gear tooth. This will show the designer what the tooth will look like when it is machined in metal. If the resulting tooth needs changing, it is much better to learn this fact early in the design process than to be surprised at how the teeth look when they are first cut in the shop.

Table 9.4 shows how to calculate the arc tooth thickness of the tooth at any diameter from the base circle to the outside diameter. By calculating a few arc tooth thickness values it is possible to make a layout of the involute part of the tooth profile.

Table 9.4 shows arc tooth thickness values for a 25-tooth pinion, 3 module and 20° pressure angle. This is the same pinion shown in Table 3.12.

Root Fillet Trochoid Calculations. After the involute part of a tooth has been calculated, it may be necessary to calculate the root fillet region. If this region is generated by a hob, there will be a *trochoidal* curve in the root fillet. Table 9.5 shows how to calculate a root fillet trochoid. The same 25-tooth pinion, 3 module and 20° pressure angle, was used for this calculation.

After both the involute part of the tooth and the root fillet part of the tooth have been calculated, it is possible to plot the complete tooth profile. Figure 3.14 shows the 25-tooth profile, which was plotted at an enlarged size from the data in Tables 9.4 and 9.5.

The resulting tooth form in Fig. 3.14 looks good. The width of the tooth at the outside diameter (top land) is generously wide. There would certainly be no difficulty carburizing a tooth with this width of top land.

The root region of the tooth also looks good. There are no sharp curvatures. The relatively gentle curvature should result in a low stress-concentration factor. It should also be easy to design pregrind or preshave hobs with a protuberance tip and then have an easy manufacturing operation to blend the ground or shaved involute profile with the unground root fillet.

9.6 Special Calculations for Internal Gears (Supplement to Chap. 3)

An internal gearset does not involve two internal gears running with each other. This is a geometric impossibility. An internal gearset consists of a pinion with external teeth running with a gear with internal teeth.

TABLE 9.6 Diameter between Pins for Internal Spur Gears

Given data		
1. Pitch diameter	84.00	
2. Number of teeth	28	
3. Pressure angle at (1)	25	
4. Arc tooth thickness at (1)	4.240	4.160
5. Base-circle diameter, (1) × cos (3)	76.12985	
6. Diameter of measuring pin	5.33401	
7. 3.14159265 ÷ (2)	0.11220	
8. Inv. (3) = tan (3) − (3) ÷ 57.29578	0.02998	
9. (6) ÷ (5)	0.07006	
10. (4) ÷ (1)	0.05048	0.04952
11. (7) + (8) − (9) − (10)	0.02164	0.02259
12. Inv. angle for (4), arc inv. (11)	22.54	22.85

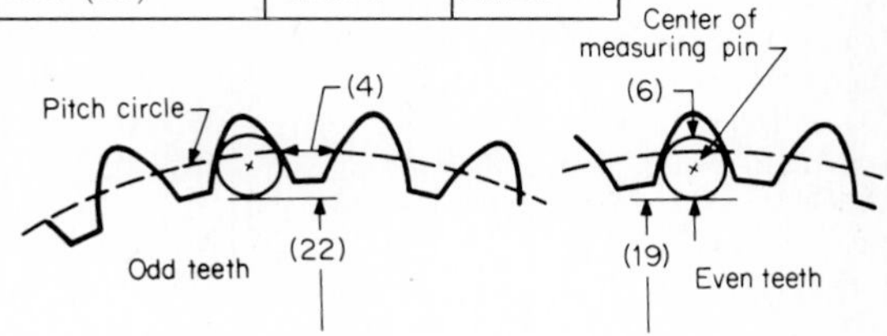

Steps				
13. Pressure angle, pin center	22.54	22.23	22.70	22.85
14. Inv. (13)	0.02164	0.02072	0.02212	0.02258
15. (7) + (8)	0.14218			
16. (15) − (14) − (9)	0.05048	0.05139	0.04999	0.04953
17. Arc thickness, (1) × (16)	4.2403	4.3170	4.1992	4.16045
18. Cos (13)	0.92361	0.92567	0.92254	0.92152
19. Diameter under pins, (5) ÷ (18) − (6)	77.092	76.909	77.188	77.279
For odd number of teeth:				
20. Cos [90° ÷ (2)]	—	—	—	—
21. [(5) ÷ (18)] × (20)	—	—	—	—
22. Diameter under pins, (21) − (6)	—	—	—	—

Notes: Normally, (12) is used for (13) in the first column, and then (17) in the first column should equal (4). Other values of (13) are assumed and entered in the remaining columns. Four values are then obtained for tooth thickness versus diameter between pins. Item (19) is for *even* tooth numbers. Calculate (22) if tooth number is *odd*.

This sample calculation is in the metric system (using millimeters and degrees).

The internal gear is generally checked for tooth thickness with measuring pins, like the external gear. However, the measurement is made *between* pins instead of over pins. Generally the measurement is taken as a "diameter" under two pins placed as near 180° apart as possible.

TABLE 9.7 Calculation of Form Diameter, Roll Angles, and Contact Ratio for Internal Spur Gearsets

Data item* or operation	Metric		English	
	Pinion	Gear	Pinion	Gear
*1. No. of teeth	18	28	18	28
*2. Pitch diameter	54.00	84.00	2.12599	3.30709
*3. Addendum	3.39	2.12	0.133465	0.083465
4. Outside diameter, pinion, (2) + [2.0 × (3)]	60.78	—	2.39291	—
5. Inside diameter, gear, (2) − [2.0 × (3)]	—	79.76	—	3.14016
*6. Pressure angle, transverse	25	25	25	25
7. Base diameter, cos (6) × (2)	48.94062	76.12985	1.92680	2.99724
8. Gear ratio, $(1)_{gear} \div (1)_{pinion}$	1.55556	1.55556	1.55556	1.55556
9. Inverse ratio, 1.0 ÷ (8)	0.64286	0.64286	0.64286	0.64286
10. Arccos [(7) ÷ (4)]	36.36953	—	36.36953	—
11. Arccos [(7) ÷ (5)]	—	17.35275	—	17.35275
12. O.D. roll, pinion, tan (10) × 57.29578	42.19507	—	42.19507	—
13. O.D. roll, gear, tan (11) × 57.29578	—	17.90353	—	17.90353
14. P.D. roll, tan (6) × 57.29578	26.71746	26.71746	26.71746	26.71746
15. Addendum roll, pinion, (12) − (14)	15.47761	—	15.47761	—
16. Addendum roll, gear, (14) − (13)	—	8.81393	—	8.81393
17. Pinion roll, (15) + $[(16)_{gear} \times (8)]$	29.18818	—	29.18818	—
18. Gear roll, (16) + $[(15)_{pinion} \times (9)]$	—	18.76383	—	18.76383
19. L.D. roll, pinion, (12) − (17)	13.00690	—	13.00690	—
20. L.D. roll, gear, (13) + (18)	—	36.66736	—	36.66736
21. Arctan [(19) ÷ 57.29578]	12.79012	—	12.79012	—
22. L.D., pinion, (7) ÷ cos (21)	50.18586	—	1.97582	—
23. Arctan [(20) ÷ 57.29578]	—	32.61786	—	32.61786
24. L.D., gear, (7) ÷ cos (23)	—	90.38498	—	3.55846
25. Circular pitch, π × (2) ÷ (1)	9.42478	9.42478	0.37105	0.37105
26. Extra involute, 0.016 × (25)	0.15080	0.15080	0.00594	0.00594
27. Form diameter, pinion, (22) − (26)	50.03506	—	1.96988	—
28. Arccos [(7) ÷ (27)]	12.00580	—	12.00580	—
29. F.D. roll, pinion, tan (28) × 57.29578	12.18465	—	12.18465	—
30. Form diameter, gear, (24) + (26)	—	90.53577	—	3.56440
31. Arccos [(7) ÷ (30)]	—	32.76668	—	32.76668
32. F.D. roll, gear, tan (31) × 57.29578	—	36.87747	—	36.87747
33. Roll per pinion tooth, 360° ÷ (1)	20	—	20	—
34. Contact ratio, (17) ÷ (33)	1.45941	—	1.45941	—

Notes: 1. Metric dimensions are in millimeters and degrees. English dimensions are in inches and degrees.
2. See Sec. 3.9 for cases where (26) may be too much extra involute.
3. Abbreviations above are: O.D. = outside diameter, P.D. = pitch diameter, L.D. = limit diameter, F.D. = form diameter

Table 9.6 shows the calculation procedure. The numerical example shown is for a 28-tooth internal gear of 3 module and 25° pressure angle. This is the internal gear shown in Table 3.15.

Table 9.7 is a calculation sheet for form diameters, roll angles, and contact ratio. The numerical example shown is for an 18-tooth spur pinion meshing with a 28-tooth internal gear. This is the gearset shown in Table 3.15.

Table 9.8 is a calculation sheet for the arc tooth thickness at any diameter on an internal gear. The numerical data shown are for 28 teeth, 3 module, and 25° pressure angle.

Figure 9.16 shows a layout of the internal gear teeth using the involute profile data from Table 9.8. The root fillet trochoid would be formed by the tip of an internal shaper cutter rather than by the tip of a hob tooth. (Internal teeth are usually cut by shapers.)

TABLE 9.8 Arc Tooth Thickness at Any Diameter, Internal Spur Gearsets

Given data	
1. Pitch diameter	84.00 mm
2. Pressure angle at (1)	25°
3. Arc tooth thickness at (1)	4.240 mm
Step A: Solve for the tooth thickness at base diameter.	
4. Involute (2)	0.029975
5. Cosine (2)	0.906308
6. (4) × (1)	2.51793
7. (3) − (6)	1.72207
8. T.T. at B.D., (5) × (7)	1.56073
9. Base diameter, (5) × (1)	76.12985

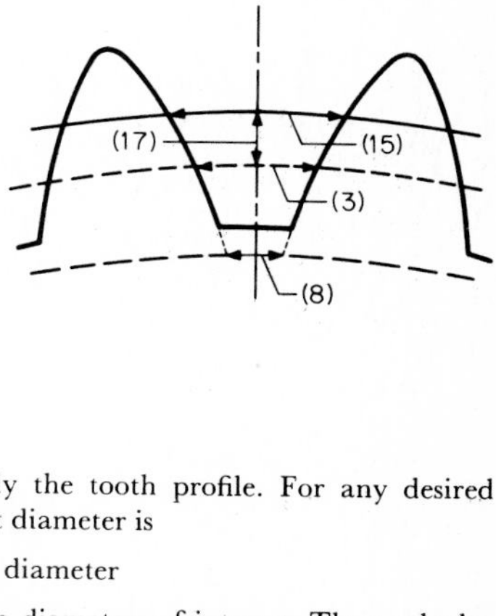

Step B: Solve for a series of tooth thicknesses to study the tooth profile. For any desired diameter, the cosine of the pressure angle at that diameter is

Cos PA at any diameter = base diameter ÷ any diameter

A series of pressure angles is assumed, based on diameters of interest. Then calculations are made to get the arc thicknesses that go with each diameter.

10. Assumed pressure angles	17.35276	21.8	28.9	32.2	34.4128
11. Cosine (10)	0.95449	0.9285	0.8755	0.8462	0.8250
12. Involute (10)	0.00961	0.0195	0.0476	0.0677	0.0844
13. (12) × (9)	0.73184	1.4838	3.6261	5.1570	6.4274
14. (8) + (13)	2.29914	3.0445	5.1868	6.7177	7.9881
15. Arc TT, (14) ÷ (11)	2.4088	3.2790	5.9247	7.9388	9.6827
16. Any diameter, (9) ÷ (11)	79.760	81.993	86.960	89.968	92.280
17. Δ radius, [(16) − (1)] ÷ 2	−2.120	−1.004	1.480	2.984	4.140

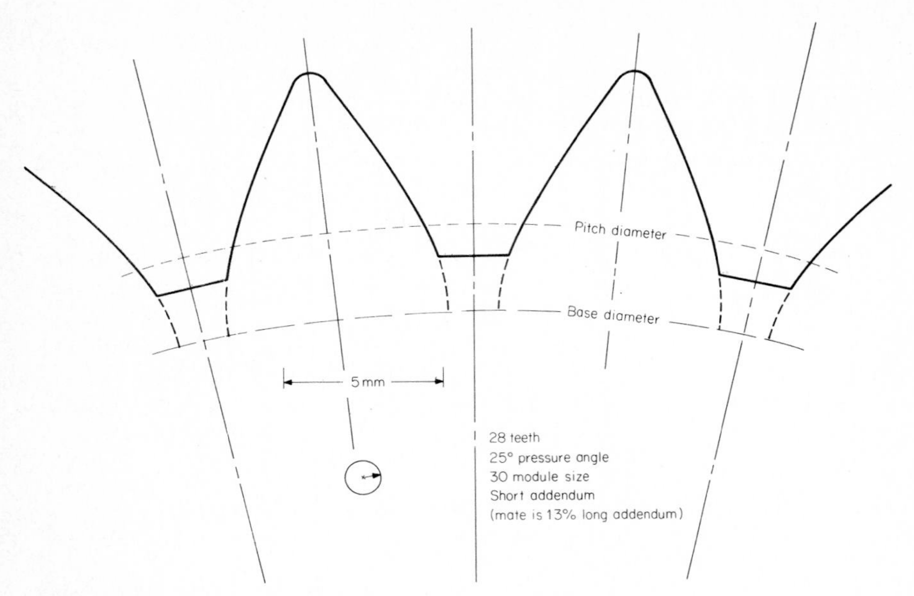

FIG. 9.16 Layout of 28-tooth internal gear.

The example shown in Fig. 9.16 would require a shaper cutter with rather narrow tips on the teeth. The generating action that would produce a trochoid would have to be very limited. For this reason the fillet region of the internal tooth was approximated by an arc of a circle.

Figure 9.16 shows that the internal tooth is not really a good design. The root fillet region is so small that there would be danger of sludge and foreign material collecting and jamming against the outside diameter of the mating pinion. The design could be improved by using a larger number of internal teeth or by using a pressure angle one or two degrees smaller than 25°.

Figure 9.17 shows a layout of the 18-tooth spur pinion intended to mate with the 28-tooth internal gear. The pinion layout looks good. A change in proportions, though, to improve the 28-tooth internal gear would require a change in the 18-tooth pinion also.

If the designer still wants to use 18 teeth meshing with 28 teeth, the first step is to change the 28-tooth gear to get more room in the root region. The changed gear would, of course, require a changed pinion. The new pinion design should then be laid out to see how it looks.

The ratio of 18 to 28 is 1.556. Another way of solving the problem would be to use something like a 23-tooth pinion meshing with a 36-tooth internal gear. This would give a ratio of 1.565, which is almost the same as 1.556. With larger numbers of teeth, the difficulty in the first design would tend to disappear.

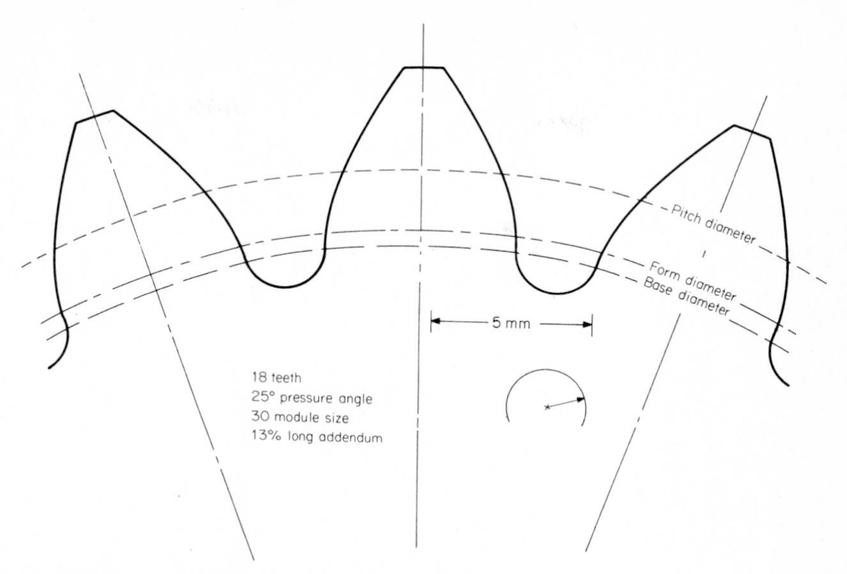

FIG. 9.17 Layout of 18-tooth external pinion.

9.7 Special Calculations for Helical Gears (Supplement to Chap. 3)

The tooth thicknesses of helical gears are often checked by measurement over balls or pins. Theoretically the measurement over balls for helicals can be calculated in a manner similar to that for the measurement over pins for spur gears. Table 9.9 shows a calculation sheet for diameter over balls for a 25-tooth helical pinion and a 96-tooth helical gear. These are the same parts that are shown in Table 3.17.

When the number of teeth is odd, it is not possible to get the balls 180° apart and in the same transverse plane. However, if three balls are used, it is possible to have two balls each 180° apart from the third ball. This is done by putting two balls on one side, one axial pitch apart.

The possibilities just mentioned are all sketched in Table 9.9, and the calculation procedure will handle the two different situations that are possible with an odd number of teeth.

It is often practical to use pins in place of balls on helical teeth. There is a slight geometric error in calculating a diameter over balls and then using this dimension for a measurement of pins. In most helical designs this discrepancy is so slight as to be of no consequence.

Unfortunately, a precise calculation for the measurement of a diameter

TABLE 9.9 Diameter over Balls for Helical Gears

	Pinion	Gear
1. Pitch diameter	77.6457	298.1595
2. Number of teeth	25	96
3. Pressure angle, transverse	20.64689	20.64689
4. Arc tooth thickness, transverse	4.7799	4.7799
5. Base helix angle	14.07610	14.07610
6. Base circle diameter, (1) × cos (3)	72.6586	279.0091
7. Diameter of ball	5.33401	5.33401
8. 3.14159265 ÷ (2)	0.1256637	0.0327249
9. Inv. (3), tan (3) – (3) ÷ 57.29578	0.0164534	0.0164534
10. (7) ÷ (6)	0.0734120	0.0191177
11. (10) ÷ cos (5)	0.0756845	0.0197095
12. (4) ÷ (1)	0.0615604	0.0160314
13. (11) + (12) + (9) – (8)	0.0280346	0.0194694
14. Involute angle for (4), arc involute* (13)	24.47616	21.79269

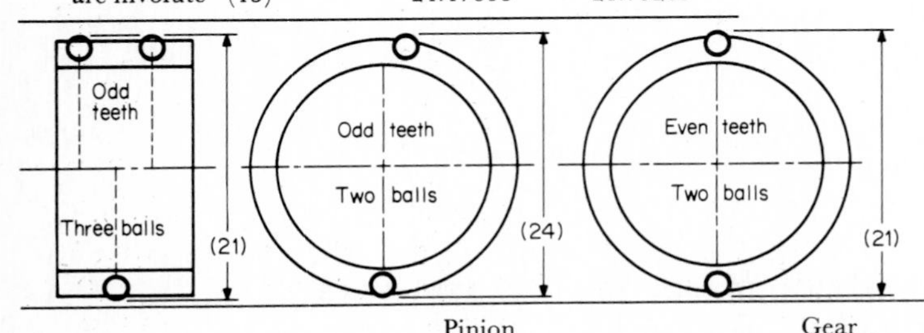

	Pinion	Gear
15. Pressure angle, ball center	24.47616	21.79269
16. Involute (15)	0.0280343	0.0194693
17. (16) – (9)	0.0115809	0.0030159
18. (17) + (8) – (11)	0.0615601	0.0160313
19. Arc thickness, (1) × (18)	4.7799	4.7799
20. Cos (15)	0.910134	0.928533
21. Diameter over balls, (6) ÷ (20) + (7)	—	305.8177
For odd number of teeth:		
22. Cos [90° ÷ (2)]	0.9980267	—
23. [(6) ÷ (20)] × (22)	79.67533	—
24. Diameter over balls, (23) + (7)	85.0093	—

*See Table 9.10 for table of involute functions.

Notes:
1. The arc thickness in the transverse plane, (4), is equal to the arc thickness in the normal plane divided by the cosine of the helix angle (helix angle at the pitch circle).
2. The base helix angle, (5), is determined from the helix of the pitch circle:

   tan base helix = tan pitch helix × cos (pressure angle, transverse)

3. Normally (14) is used for (15) in the first column; then (19) should equal (4). Somewhat different values of the pressure angle are entered into (15) for the remaining columns. This will give four values of tooth thickness versus diameter over balls. Item (21) is for even teeth. Item (24) can be used for odd teeth, but only if two balls are used in a transverse plane. If balls are used in an axial plane, then the *even* calculation must be used for *odd* teeth as well as even teeth.

over pins on helical gears is too complicated to be included in this book. The usual practice in the gear trade has been to make the calculations for balls, then start a product job with both balls and pins of the same diameter available. A few carefully taken measurements will reveal the difference (if any) between the diameter over pins and the diameter over balls for the same part. Once this difference is known, the part can, of course, be checked by diameter over pins, with an appropriate allowance being made for the known difference in reading between pins and balls.

The helical gear can be considered as a gear with two sets of tooth data. One set of data goes with a *transverse* section through the gear teeth. Another set of data goes with a *normal* section through the gear teeth. Things like pressure angle, circular pitch, and tooth thickness change in going from the normal section to the transverse section. The addendum and the whole depth are the same in either section.

The calculations for form diameter, roll angle, and contact ratio are made using transverse-section data, with a helical gear being treated as if it were a spur gear with an infinitesimally small face width (a wafer-thin spur gear). This means that the calculations just mentioned can be made for a helical gear in the same manner that they are made for a spur gear, provided transverse-section data are used.

The profile of a helical tooth is best judged in the normal section. It is conventional practice in the gear trade to make layouts of helical-gear teeth in the normal section, using the technique of a *virtual* spur gear.

The virtual spur gear will have almost exactly the same tooth shape as the helical gear has in its normal section. Table 9.11 shows how to get the needed dimensions of a virtual spur gear which will match the normal section of a helical gear.

The calculation procedure involves these steps:

Convert the normal section of the helical gear to a set of tooth data describing the virtual spur gear. Use the rules of Table 9.11.

Make calculations for the involute part of the virtual spur gear just as if it were a regular spur gear.

Make calculations for the trochoid of the virtual spur gear just as if it were a regular spur gear. (The hob tooth data for a helical gear will match the normal section of the helical gear.)

For what happens when the helical pinion meshes with the helical gear, *do not* use the virtual-spur-gear concept. The involute helical gear is handled by calculations for the real helical gears and their transverse sections.

When a helical gear is cut (or ground) at a pitch diameter different from the operating pitch diameter, the layout of the virtual spur gears is made to match the *normal section for operating conditions*, not the normal section for

TABLE 9.10 Involute Functions (inv $\alpha = \tan \alpha - \text{arc}\ \alpha$)

α	inv α	Diff.	α	inv α	Diff.	α	inv α	Diff.	α	inv α	Diff.
0.0°	.0000000	0	5.0°	.0002222	136	10.0°	.0017941	548	15.0°	.0061498	1262
0.1	00000	0	5.1	02358	142	10.1	18489	559	15.1	62760	1279
0.2	00000	0	5.2	02500	147	10.2	19048	571	15.2	64039	1298
0.3	00000	1	5.3	02647	154	10.3	19619	582	15.3	65337	1315
0.4	00001	1	5.4	02801	158	10.4	20201	594	15.4	66652	1333
0.5	00002	2	5.5	02959	165	10.5	20795	605	15.5	67985	1352
0.6	00004	2	5.6	03124	171	10.6	21400	617	15.6	69337	1369
0.7	00006	3	5.7	03295	177	10.7	22017	629	15.7	70706	1389
0.8	00009	4	5.8	03472	183	10.8	22646	642	15.8	72095	1406
0.9	00013	5	5.9	03655	190	10.9	23288	653	15.9	73501	1426
1.0°	.0000018	6	6.0°	.0003845	196	11.0°	.0023941	666	16.0°	.0074927	1445
1.1	00024	7	6.1	04041	203	11.1	24607	678	16.1	76372	1463
1.2	00031	8	6.2	04244	209	11.2	25285	690	16.2	77835	1483
1.3	00039	10	6.3	04453	216	11.3	25975	703	16.3	79318	1502
1.4	00049	11	6.4	04669	223	11.4	26678	716	16.4	80820	1522
1.5	00060	13	6.5	04892	230	11.5	27394	729	16.5	82342	1541
1.6	00073	14	6.6	05122	237	11.6	28123	742	16.6	83883	1561
1.7	00087	16	6.7	05359	245	11.7	28865	755	16.7	85444	1581
1.8	00103	19	6.8	05604	252	11.8	29620	769	16.8	87025	1601
1.9	00122	20	6.9	05856	259	11.9	30389	782	16.9	88626	1621
2.0°	.0000142	22	7.0°	.0006115	267	12.0°	.0031171	795	17.0°	.0090247	1642
2.1	00164	25	7.1	06382	275	12.1	31966	809	17.1	91889	1662
2.2	00189	27	7.2	06657	282	12.2	32775	823	17.2	93551	1683
2.3	00216	29	7.3	06939	291	12.3	33598	836	17.3	95234	1703
2.4	00245	32	7.4	07230	298	12.4	34434	851	17.4	96937	1725
2.5	00277	35	7.5	07528	307	12.5	35285	865	17.5	98662	1745
2.6	00312	37	7.6	07835	315	12.6	36150	879	17.6	.0100407	1767
2.7	00349	40	7.7	08150	323	12.7	37029	894	17.7	102174	1789
2.8	00389	44	7.8	08473	332	12.8	37923	908	17.8	103963	1810
2.9	00433	46	7.9	08805	340	12.9	38831	923	17.9	105773	1831
3.0°	.0000479	50	8.0°	.0009145	349	13.0°	.0039754	938	18.0°	.0107604	1854
3.1	00529	52	8.1	09494	358	13.1	40692	952	18.1	109458	1875
3.2	00581	57	8.2	09852	367	13.2	41644	968	18.2	111333	1898
3.3	00638	60	8.3	10219	376	13.3	42612	983	18.3	113231	1920
3.4	00698	63	8.4	10595	385	13.4	43595	998	18.4	115151	1943
3.5	00761	67	8.5	10980	395	13.5	44593	1014	18.5	117094	1965
3.6	00828	71	8.6	11375	404	13.6	45607	1029	18.6	119059	1989
3.7	00899	75	8.7	11779	413	13.7	46636	1045	18.7	121048	2011
3.8	00974	79	8.8	12192	423	13.8	47681	1061	18.8	123059	2034
3.9	01053	83	8.9	12615	433	13.9	48742	1077	18.9	125093	2058
4.0°	.0001136	88	9.0°	.0013048	443	14.0°	.0049819	1093	19.0°	.0127151	2081
4.1	01224	92	9.1	13491	453	14.1	50912	1109	19.1	129232	2104
4.2	01316	96	9.2	13944	463	14.2	52021	1126	19.2	131336	2129
4.3	01412	101	9.3	14407	473	14.3	53147	1142	19.3	133465	2152
4.4	01513	106	9.4	14880	483	14.4	54289	1159	19.4	135617	2177
4.5	01619	110	9.5	15363	494	14.5	55448	1176	19.5	137794	2200
4.6	01729	116	9.6	15857	505	14.6	56624	1193	19.6	139994	2226
4.7	01845	120	9.7	16362	515	14.7	57817	1210	19.7	142220	2250
4.8	01965	126	9.8	16877	526	14.8	59027	1227	19.8	144470	2274
4.9	02091	131	9.9	17403	538	14.9	60254	1244	19.9	146744	2300
5.0°	.0002222		10.0°	.0017941		15.0°	.0061498		20.0°	.0149044	

TABLE 9.10 Involute Functions (inv $\alpha = \tan \alpha - \text{arc } \alpha$) (*Continued*)

α	inv α	Diff.	α	inv α	Diff.	α	inv α	Diff.	α	inv α	Diff.
20.0°	.0149044	2325	25.0°	.0299753	3813	30.0°	.0537515	5841	35.0°	.0893423	8589
20.1	151369	2350	25.1	303566	3847	30.1	543356	5889	35.1	902012	8653
20.2	153719	2375	25.2	307413	3882	30.2	549245	5936	35.2	910665	8717
20.3	156094	2401	25.3	311295	3918	30.3	555181	5983	35.3	919382	8783
20.4	158495	2427	25.4	315213	3953	30.4	561164	6032	35.4	928165	8847
20.5	160922	2453	25.5	319166	3988	30.5	567196	6080	35.5	937012	8913
20.6	163375	2479	25.6	323154	4025	30.6	573276	6129	35.6	945925	8979
20.7	165854	2505	25.7	327179	4060	30.7	579405	6177	35.7	954904	9045
20.8	168359	2532	25.8	331239	4097	30.8	585582	6227	35.8	963949	9112
20.9	170891	2558	25.9	335336	4134	30.9	591809	6277	35.9	973061	9179
21.0°	.0173449	2585	26.0°	.0339470	4170	31.0°	.0598086	6326	36.0°	.0982240	9247
21.1	176034	2612	26.1	343640	4207	31.1	604412	6376	36.1	991487	9315
21.2	178646	2640	26.2	347847	4245	31.2	610788	6427	36.2	1000802	9383
21.3	181286	2667	26.3	352092	4282	31.3	617215	6477	36.3	1010185	9452
21.4	183953	2694	26.4	356374	4320	31.4	623692	6529	36.4	1019637	9522
21.5	186647	2722	26.5	360694	4357	31.5	630221	6580	36.5	1029159	9591
21.6	189369	2750	26.6	365051	4396	31.6	636801	6631	36.6	1038750	9662
21.7	192119	2778	26.7	369447	4434	31.7	643432	6684	36.7	1048412	9732
21.8	194897	2806	26.8	373881	4473	31.8	650116	6735	36.8	1058144	9803
21.9	197703	2835	26.9	378354	4512	31.9	656851	6789	36.9	1067947	9875
22.0°	.0200538	2863	27.0°	.0382866	4550	32.0°	.0663640	6841	37.0°	.1077822	9947
22.1	203401	2892	27.1	387416	4590	32.1	670481	6895	37.1	1087769	10019
22.2	206293	2922	27.2	392006	4630	32.2	677376	6948	37.2	1097788	10092
22.3	209215	2950	27.3	396636	4670	32.3	684324	7002	37.3	1107880	10166
22.4	212165	2980	27.4	401306	4709	32.4	691326	7057	37.4	1118046	10239
22.5	215145	3009	27.5	406015	4750	32.5	698383	7110	37.5	1128285	10314
22.6	218154	3039	27.6	410765	4790	32.6	705493	7166	37.6	1138599	10388
22.7	221193	3069	27.7	415555	4832	32.7	712659	7221	37.7	1148987	10464
22.8	224262	3099	27.8	420387	4872	32.8	719880	7277	37.8	1159451	10539
22.9	227361	3130	27.9	425259	4913	32.9	727157	7332	37.9	1169990	10615
23.0°	.0230491	3160	28.0°	.0430172	4956	33.0°	.0734489	7389	38.0°	.1180605	10692
23.1	233651	3191	28.1	435128	4996	33.1	741878	7446	38.1	1191297	10769
23.2	236842	3221	28.2	440124	5039	33.2	749324	7502	38.2	1202066	10847
23.3	240063	3253	28.3	445163	5082	33.3	756826	7559	38.3	1212913	10925
23.4	243316	3284	28.4	450245	5124	33.4	764385	7618	38.4	1223838	11004
23.5	246600	3316	28.5	455369	5166	33.5	772003	7675	38.5	1234842	11082
23.6	249916	3347	28.6	460535	5210	33.6	779678	7733	38.6	1245924	11163
23.7	253264	3378	28.7	465745	5253	33.7	787411	7793	38.7	1257087	11242
23.8	256642	3411	28.8	470998	5297	33.8	795204	7851	38.8	1268329	11323
23.9	260053	3444	28.9	476295	5341	33.9	803055	7911	38.9	1279652	11404
24.0°	.0263497	3476	29.0°	.0481636	5384	34.0°	.0810966	7970	39.0°	.1291056	11486
24.1	266973	3508	29.1	487020	5430	34.1	818936	8031	39.1	1302542	11568
24.2	270481	3542	29.2	492450	5474	34.2	826967	8091	39.2	1314110	11651
24.3	274023	3575	29.3	497924	5518	34.3	835058	8152	39.3	1325761	11734
24.4	277598	3608	29.4	503442	5564	34.4	843210	8214	39.4	1337495	11818
24.5	281206	3642	29.5	509006	5610	34.5	851424	8275	39.5	1349313	11903
24.6	284848	3675	29.6	514616	5655	34.6	859699	8337	39.6	1361216	11987
24.7	288523	3709	29.7	520271	5702	34.7	868036	8399	39.7	1373203	12072
24.8	292232	3744	29.8	525973	5748	34.8	876435	8463	39.8	1385275	12159
24.9	295976	3777	29.9	531721	5794	34.9	884898	8525	39.9	1397434	12245
25.0°	.0299753		30.0°	.0537515		35.0°	.0893423		40.0°	.1409679	

Notes: 1. In the metric system, the pressure angle is α. In the English system, it is ϕ.

2. For angles not shown, the calculation is easy. Inv $\alpha = \tan \alpha - \alpha \div 57.29578$. Use alpha (or phi) in *degrees*.

TABLE 9.11 Virtual Spur Gear to Match Normal Section of a Helical Gear

Item	Helical gear	Virtual spur gear
Number of teeth	Actual number of teeth	$\dfrac{\text{Helical no. teeth}}{\text{cosine}^3\ \text{(helix angle)}}$
Pitch diameter	Actual pitch diameter*	$\dfrac{\text{Helical pitch diameter}}{\text{cosine}^2\ \text{(helix angle)}}$
Tooth thickness	Actual normal-section tooth thickness*	Helical normal-section tooth thickness
Addendum	Actual value*	Helical value
Whole depth	Actual value*	Helical value

*When there are both "cutting" and "operating" data on the drawing, use the operating data values for these items. (See text for a discussion of how operating data are used for virtual-helical-gear layouts.)

cutting conditions. This can be rationalized by the fact that the addendum that meshes is the addendum based on the operating pitch diameter, not an addendum that is valid in cutting only.

Section 9.13 has an example that shows how data are obtained for the normal section for operating conditions, as well as for the normal section for cutting.

9.8 Summary Sheets for Bevel Gears (Supplement to Chap. 3)

When bevel gears are to be manufactured on machines built by the Gleason Works in Rochester, NY, U.S.A., it is common practice to get a summary sheet of tooth data computed by the Gleason Works. These sheets can be obtained at a small charge.

Table 9.12 shows an example of a summary sheet for a straight bevel gearset of 16/49 teeth, 5 module. This is the same set shown in the straight bevel dimension sheet, Table 3.22.

The Gleason summary sheet is quite useful to the gear manufacturer. From a design standpoint, it gives all the tooth geometric data. These data will agree, of course, with the latest design practice recommended by Gleason. (Presumably, the designer will want to use the latest design practice.)

The summary sheet will be based on the kind of machine and the model of machine that is expected to be used in the gear manufacture. (A builder who owns many kinds and models of Gleason machines will need to inform

Gleason which machine or machines are to be used in the manufacture of the particular gearset.)

The summary sheet gives tool data and machine settings. This information is very helpful for the shop engineers who make the bevel-gear processing plans.

The summary sheets will give some values useful in gear-rating equations.

The values given may or may not fit standard rating practices of the various bodies that issue rules on ratings. The designer should consider the rating values on the summary sheet as representing Gleason practice. (The latter part of Chap. 3 covers gear-rating practices and explains how a given gear contract may have specific details that specify how the gear rating is to be computed.)

Table 9.13 shows a summary sheet for spiral bevel gears. This sheet matches the spiral-gear dimension sheet in Table 3.24.

Table 9.14 shows a summary sheet for Zerol bevel gears. It matches the Table 3.25 dimension sheet for a set of Zerol bevel gears.

9.9 Complete AGMA and ISO Formulas for Bending Strength and Pitting Resistance (Supplement to Chap. 3)

During the 1970s, an international technical committee worked on gear-rating formulas and developed a draft of standards for rating the strength and pitting resistance of gear teeth running on parallel axes. The two standards first developed were intended to be "mother" standards for all types of applications. In the late 1970s and early 1980s this work was extended to develop product standards. (Some of the product areas were marine gears, aircraft gears, vehicle gears, and industrial gears.)

The committee doing this work was designated ISO/TC 60/WG 6. This designation means that the work was sponsored by the International Standards Organization. "WG 6" means working group 6 of the general technical committee group 60.

The president (chairman) of WG 6 was (and is) Dr.-Ing. Hans Winter. The handling of proceedings of committee meetings was assigned by ISO to DNA (Deutscher Normenausschuss). Mr. H. Schwarz has been the secretary of the WG 6 committee. His office has provided drafts of the standards and minutes of meetings in several languages.

The gear-rating standards developed by ISO/TC 60/WG 6 are generally referred to as "ISO Standards" in the gear trade. Although draft copies of the proposed ISO Standards have been available for study for several years, these standards are in limited use for international gear work. Some

TABLE 9.12 Dudley Engineering Company Summary Sheet for 16/49 Teeth, Straight Bevel Gearset

STRAIGHT BEVEL GEAR DIMENSIONS NO. M W004474

	PINION	GEAR
NUMBER OF TEETH.	16	49
PART NUMBER		
MODULE	5.000	
FACE WIDTH	40.00	40.00
PRESSURE ANGLE	20D 0M	
SHAFT ANGLE	90D 0M	
TRANSVERSE CONTACT RATIO . . .	1.517	
OUTER CONE DISTANCE.	128.87	
CIRCULAR PITCH	15.71	
WORKING DEPTH	10.00	
WHOLE DEPTH	10.99	10.99
CLEARANCE.	0.99	0.99
PITCH DIAMETER	80.00	245.00
ADDENDUM.	7.05	2.95
DEDENDUM.	3.94	8.05
LIMIT POINT WIDTH.		
LIMIT POINT WIDTH-LARGE END	0.130″	0.143″
LIMIT POINT WIDTH-SMALL END	0.091″	0.100″
STOCK ALLOWANCE.	0.026″	0.030″
MAX. RADIUS-CUTTER BLADES. . .	0.081″	0.089″
MAX. RADIUS-MUTILATION	0.062″	0.069″
MAX. RADIUS-INTERFERENCE	0.048″	0.121″
TOOL EDGE RADIUS.	0.025″	0.025″
MACHINE.	TWO TOOL GENERATOR	
CUTTER DIAMETER.		
BLADE PRESSURE ANGLE		
CUTTER DEPTH DESIGNATION		
BLADE POINT WIDTH	0.065″	0.070″
BLADE EDGE RADIUS.	0.025″	0.025″
AXIAL FACTOR	OUT 0.085	OUT 0.085
SEPARATING FACTOR.	SEP 0.260	SEP 0.028
CONTROL DATA		
PATTERN LENGTH FACTOR.		
PROFILE MISMATCH FACTOR.		

ALL DIMENSIONS ARE IN METRIC UNLESS DENOTED OTHERWISE. ANGLES ARE IN DEGREES (D) AND MINUTES (M).

RELEASED BY— RB

"CONIFLEX" IS A TRADEMARK OF THE GLEASON WORKS

FORM C DATE 8/3/81 TIME 12:1
DATA SHEET FOR CONIFLEX* BEVEL GEARS

		PINION		GEAR
OUTSIDE DIAMETER		93.41		246.83
PITCH APEX TO CROWN		120.31		37.20
CIRCULAR THICKNESS		9.514		6.194
MEAN NORMAL TOP LAND		2.27		3.43
PITCH ANGLE		18D 5M		71D 55M
FACE ANGLE OF BLANK		21D 38M		73D 39M
ROOT ANGLE		16D 21M		68D 22M
DEDENDUM ANGLE		1D 44M		3D 33M
CHORDAL ADDENDUM		7.32		2.96
CHORDAL THICKNESS		9.43		6.13
BACKLASH		MIN. 0.13		MAX. 0.18
TOOTH PROPORTIONS	STD			
FACE IN PERCENT OF CONE DIST				31.040
UNDERCUT	NO			
GEOMETRY FACTOR-STRENGTH-J		0.2373		0.1920
STRENGTH FACTOR-Q		5.74969		2.32077
SIZE FACTOR—KS		0.666		
KI FACTOR		1.3188		
STRENGTH BALANCE DESIRED	STRS			
STRENGTH BALANCE OBTAINED	TPLD			0.189
GEOMETRY FACTOR-DURABILITY-I		0.0756		
DURABILITY FACTOR-Z		3651.26		2086.44
ROOT LINE FACE WIDTH		40.00		40.00
POSITION LOAD APPLICATION	HPT1			
MACHINE SETTINGS—TWO TOOL GENERATOR				
SLIDING BASE		ADV 0.00		ADV 0.00
TOP TOOL HEIGHT		RISE 0.00		RISE 0.00
BOTTOM TOOL HEIGHT		LOWR 0.00		LOWR 0.00
TOOTH ANGLE		2D 45M		2D 40M
TOOL ADVANCE		0.05		0.05
CRADLE TEST ROLL		20D 0M		30D 0M
WORK TEST ROLL		64D 26M		31D 34M
DECIMAL RATIO		0.6873		0.6873
NC/75 RATIO GEARS		47/45 × 50/76		47/45 × 50/76
DEPTH CHECKING DATA—NO. 15 BLANK CHECKER				
CHECKING DIAMETER		72.52		240.01
BACKING	MD –	123.72	MD –	47.65

* FACTORS GIVEN ON THIS DATA SHEET APPLY TO CONIFLEX STRAIGHT BEVEL GEARS WITH LOCALIZED TOOTH BEARING. FOR GEARS CUT WITH NON-LOCALIZED TOOTH BEARING THE STRESSES WILL BE INCREASED 20 to 50 PERCENT

TABLE 9.13 Dudley Engineering Company Summary Sheet for 16/49 Teeth, Spiral Bevel Gearset

SPIRAL BEVEL GEAR DIMENSIONS NO. M S006651

	PINION	GEAR
NUMBER OF TEETH	16	49
PART NUMBER		
MODULE		5.000
FACE WIDTH	38.00	38.00
PRESSURE ANGLE	20D 0M	
SHAFT ANGLE	90D 0M	
TRANSVERSE CONTACT RATIO		1.192
FACE CONTACT RATIO		2.006
MODIFIED CONTACT RATIO		2.333
OUTER CONE DISTANCE		128.87
MEAN CONE DISTANCE		109.87
PITCH DIAMETER	80.00	245.00
CIRCULAR PITCH	15.71	
WORKING DEPTH	8.28	
WHOLE DEPTH	9.22	9.22
CLEARANCE	0.94	0.94
ADDENDUM	5.91	2.38
DEDENDUM	3.32	6.85
OUTSIDE DIAMETER	91.23	246.48
FACE ANGLE JUNCTION DIAMETER		
THEORETICAL CUTTER RADIUS	3.751″	
CUTTER RADIUS	3.750″	
CALC. GEAR FINISH. PT. WIDTH		0.100″
GEAR FINISHING POINT WIDTH		0.100″
ROUGHING POINT WIDTH	0.045″	0.080″
OUTER SLOT WIDTH	0.071″	0.100″
MEAN SLOT WIDTH	0.083″	0.100″
INNER SLOT WIDTH	0.073″	0.100″
FINISHING CUTTER BLADE POINT	0.045″	0.065″
STOCK ALLOWANCE	0.026″	0.020″
MAX. RADIUS-CUTTER BLADES	0.043″	0.074″
MAX. RADIUS-MUTILATION	0.061″	0.076″
MAX. RADIUS-INTERFERENCE	0.045″	0.096″
CUTTER EDGE RADIUS	0.025″	0.025″
CALC. CUTTER NUMBER	3	9
MAX. NO. BLADES IN CUTTER		11.295
CUTTER BLADES REQUIRED	STD DEPTH	STD DEPTH
GEAR ANGULAR FACE—CONCAVE		26D 47M
GEAR ANGULAR FACE—CONVEX		29D 30M
GEAR ANGULAR FACE—TOTAL		31D 52M

ALL DIMENSIONS ARE IN METRIC UNLESS DENOTED OTHERWISE. ANGLES ARE IN DEGREES (D) AND MINUTES (M).

RELEASED BY— RB

FORM M DATE 10/15/82 TIME 16:41

		PINION	GEAR
PITCH APEX TO CROWN..........		120.67	37.74
FACE ANG JUNCT TO PITCH APEX..			
MEAN CIRCULAR THICKNESS......		8.13	5.04
OUTER NORMAL TOP LAND.......		2.18	2.28
MEAN NORMAL TOP LAND........		2.25	2.66
INNER NORMAL TOP LAND.......		2.41	2.36
PITCH ANGLE..................		18D 5M	71D 55M
FACE ANGLE OF BLANK...........		20D 55M	73D 3M
INNER FACE ANGLE OF BLANK.....			
ROOT ANGLE..................		16D 57M	69D 5M
DEDENDUM ANGLE..............		1D 8M	2D 50M
OUTER SPIRAL ANGLE...........			42D 22M
MEAN SPIRAL ANGLE............			35D 0M
INNER SPIRAL ANGLE............			28D 14M
HAND OF SPIRAL...............		LH	RH
DRIVING MEMBER...............	PIN		
DIRECTION OF ROTATION-DRIVER.	REV		
OUTER NORMAL BACKLASH.......		MIN 0.13	MAX 0.18
DEPTHWISE TOOTH TAPER........	TRL		
GEAR TYPE....................			GENERATED
FACE IN PERCENT OF CONE DIST..			29.488
DEPTH FACTOR—K..............			
ADDENDUM FACTOR—C1.........			
GEOMETRY FACTOR-STRENGTH-J..		0.2483	0.2639
STRENGTH FACTOR-Q............		5.78453	1.77692
EDGE RADIUS USED IN STRENGTH.		0.025″	0.025″
CUTTER RADIUS FACTOR-KX......		1.038	
FACTOR......................	MN	0.7856	
STRENGTH BALANCE DESIRED.....	GIVN		
STRENGTH BALANCE OBTAINED...	GIVN		— 0.055
GEOMETRY FACTOR-DURABILITY-I.		0.1254	
DURABILITY FACTOR-Z..........		2932.37	1675.64
GEOMETRY FACTOR-SCORING-G...		0.004934	
SCORING FACTOR-X............		0.3052	
ROOT LINE FACE WIDTH..........		38.00	38.00
PROFILE SLIDING FACTOR........		0.00354	0.00537
RATIO OF INVOLUTE/MEAN CONE..		1.228	
AXIAL FACTOR-DRIVER CW.......		OUT 0.598	OUT 0.050
AXIAL FACTOR-DRIVER CCW......		IN 0.393	OUT 0.156
SEPARATING FACTOR-DRIVER CW.		SEP 0.153	SEP 0.195
SEPARATING FACTOR-DRIVER CCW		SEP 0.476	ATT 0.128
DUPLEX SUM OF DEDENDUM ANG.		3D 58M	
ROUGHING RADIAL..............		3.764″	
INPUT DATA....................	CUTM		1

TABLE 9.14 Dudley Engineering Company Summary Sheet for 32/98 Teeth, Zerol Bevel Gearset

ZEROL BEVEL GEAR DIMENSIONS NO. M Z006652

	PINION	GEAR
NUMBER OF TEETH	32	98
PART NUMBER		
MODULE		2.500
FACE WIDTH	32.00	32.00
PRESSURE ANGLE	20D 0M	
SHAFT ANGLE	90D 0M	
TRANSVERSE CONTACT RATIO		1.463
FACE CONTACT RATIO		
MODIFIED CONTACT RATIO		1.463
OUTER CONE DISTANCE		128.87
MEAN CONE DISTANCE		112.87
PITCH DIAMETER	80.00	245.00
CIRCULAR PITCH	7.85	
WORKING DEPTH	5.00	
WHOLE DEPTH	5.47	5.47
CLEARANCE	0.47	0.47
ADDENDUM	3.53	1.47
DEDENDUM	1.94	4.00
OUTSIDE DIAMETER	86.71	245.91
FACE ANGLE JUNCTION DIAMETER		
THEORETICAL CUTTER RADIUS		
CUTTER RADIUS	3.000″	
CALC. GEAR FINISH. PT. WIDTH		0.070″
GEAR FINISHING POINT WIDTH		0.070″
ROUGHING POINT WIDTH	0.035″	0.050″
OUTER SLOT WIDTH	0.065″	0.070″
MEAN SLOT WIDTH	0.070″	0.070″
INNER SLOT WIDTH	0.062″	0.070″
FINISHING CUTTER BLADE POINT	0.035″	0.040″
STOCK ALLOWANCE	0.027″	0.020″
MAX. RADIUS-CUTTER BLADES	0.037″	0.046″
MAX. RADIUS-MUTILATION	0.063″	0.068″
MAX. RADIUS-INTERFERENCE	0.022″	0.035″
CUTTER EDGE RADIUS	0.015″	0.025″
CALC. CUTTER NUMBER	0	0
MAX. NO. BLADES IN CUTTER		14.781
CUTTER BLADES REQUIRED	STD DEPTH	STD DEPTH
GEAR ANGULAR FACE—CONCAVE		23D 29M
GEAR ANGULAR FACE—CONVEX		25D 2M
GEAR ANGULAR FACE—TOTAL		24D 21M

ALL DIMENSIONS ARE IN METRIC UNLESS DENOTED OTHERWISE. ANGLES ARE IN DEGREES (D) AND MINUTES (M).

RELEASED BY— RB

ZEROL IS A TRADEMARK OF THE GLEASON WORKS

FORM M DATE 10/15/82 TIME 16:46

		PINION	GEAR
PITCH APEX TO CROWN.		121.41	38.60
FACE ANG JUNCT TO PITCH APEX . .			
MEAN CIRCULAR THICKNESS.		3.92	2.86
OUTER NORMAL TOP LAND		1.50	1.88
MEAN NORMAL TOP LAND.		1.72	2.07
INNER NORMAL TOP LAND		1.93	1.85
PITCH ANGLE.		18D 5M	71D 55M
FACE ANGLE OF BLANK.		21D 22M	73D 17M
INNER FACE ANGLE OF BLANK.			
ROOT ANGLE		16D 43M	68D 38M
DEDENDUM ANGLE		1D 22M	3D 17M
OUTER SPIRAL ANGLE			11D 21M
MEAN SPIRAL ANGLE			0D 0M
INNER SPIRAL ANGLE.			– 13D 8M
HAND OF SPIRAL		LH	RH
DRIVING MEMBER.	PIN		
DIRECTION OF ROTATION-DRIVER .	REV		
OUTER NORMAL BACKLASH.		MIN 0.05	MAX 0.10
DEPTHWISE TOOTH TAPER.	DPLX		
GEAR TYPE			GENERATED
FACE IN PERCENT OF CONE DIST . .			24.832
DEPTH FACTOR—K.			
ADDENDUM FACTOR—C1.			
GEOMETRY FACTOR-STRENGTH-J . .		0.2363	0.2330
STRENGTH FACTOR-Q.		12.138	4.01942
EDGE RADIUS USED IN STRENGTH.		0.015″	0.025″
CUTTER RADIUS FACTOR—KX.			
FACTOR	KI	1.3666	
STRENGTH BALANCE DESIRED.	GIVN		
STRENGTH BALANCE OBTAINED . . .	GIVN		0.013
GEOMETRY FACTOR-DURABILITY-I .		0.0785	
DURABILITY FACTOR-Z.		4037.51	2307.15
GEOMETRY FACTOR-SCORING-G . . .		0.002801	
SCORING FACTOR-X		0.2639	
ROOT LINE FACE WIDTH.		32.00	32.00
PROFILE SLIDING FACTOR		0.00228	0.00348
RATIO OF INVOLUTE/MEAN CONE . .		1.383	
AXIAL FACTOR-DRIVER CW		OUT 0.082	OUT 0.082
AXIAL FACTOR-DRIVER CCW		OUT 0.082	OUT 0.082
SEPARATING FACTOR-DRIVER CW .		SEP 0.251	SEP 0.027
SEPARATING FACTOR-DRIVER CCW		SEP 0.251	SEP 0.027
DUPLEX SUM OF DEDENDUM ANG .			
ROUGHING RADIAL.		5.361″	
INPUT DATA.	CUTM		1

countries (outside the United States) have decided to use ISO Standards in their domestic work.

At the date of this writing, 1983, the situation is as follows:

AGMA has just formally approved a new general standard for the rating of gears on parallel axes for both tooth strength and tooth surface durability. Its designation is AGMA 218.01. The older general rating standards, AGMA 210.02, 211.03, 220.02, and 221.02, are now considered obsolete (and replaced by 218.01).

ISO rating work by WG 6 is continuing. Several product standards are being developed. The general standard, ISO/DIS 6336 I-IV, is considered to be finished, but it has not been accepted as the world standard.

The general AGMA and ISO gear-rating equations may be compared as follows:

Total rating stress in bending:

$$s_t = \frac{W_t K_a}{K_v} \frac{P_n}{F} K_m \frac{\cos \psi}{J} \qquad \text{AGMA} \quad (9.4)$$

$$\sigma_F = \frac{F_t}{bm_n} Y_F\, Y_S\, Y_\beta\, K_A\, K_v \cdot K_{F\beta} \cdot K_{F\alpha} \qquad \text{for load at HPSTC}$$

$$\text{ISO} \quad (9.5)$$

$$\sigma_F = \frac{F_t}{bm_n} Y_{Fa}\, Y_{Sa}\, Y_\varepsilon\, Y_\beta\, K_A\, K_v \cdot K_{F\beta} \cdot K_{F\alpha} \qquad \text{for load at tip of tooth}$$

$$\text{ISO} \quad (9.6)$$

Total rating stress for surface durability:

$$s_c = C_p \left(\frac{W_t}{dF} \cdot C_a \cdot \frac{1}{I} \cdot \frac{C_m}{C_v} \right)^{0.5} \qquad \text{AGMA} \quad (9.7)$$

$$\sigma_H = Z_E \left(F_t K_A \frac{1}{d_1 b} \frac{u+1}{u} K_v K_{H\alpha} \cdot K_{H\beta} \right)^{0.5} (Z_H Z_\beta Z_\varepsilon) \qquad \text{ISO} \quad (9.8)$$

Word definitions of all terms in these equations are given in Table 9.15. The AGMA numerical definitions of the terms used are given (for the most part) in Chap. 3. The ISO numerical definitions are too lengthy to be included in this book. The reader who wishes to study ISO proposed standards should obtain original copies from DIN. (They are available in English, German, and French.)

The equations just given do not show size factors like K_s or C_s. Since the *size factor* is often handled by using a value of 1.0 (for small to medium-size gears), it is possible to compare the general equations without getting into the uncertainty of what size factor should be used.

The AGMA and ISO systems do not calculate the *same stress* values for like gears under the same loading. Also, the allowable stress values for a

TABLE 9.15 AGMA and ISO Nomenclature Used in Rating Calculations

AGMA		ISO	
	Bending stress calculation		
s_t	Calculated tensile stress at root of tooth, psi	σ_F	Calculated tensile stress at root of tooth, N/mm^2
W_t	Transmitted tangential load at operating pitch diameter, lb	F_t	Transmitted tangential load at operating pitch diameter, N
K_a	Application factor	K_A	Application factor
F	Contacting face width, in.	b	Contacting face width, mm
P_n	Normal diametral pitch	m_n	Normal module, mm
J	Bending geometry factor	Y_F	Tooth form factor (HPSTC)
K_v	Dynamic factor (derates by being less than 1.0)	K_v	Dynamic factor (derates by being over 1.0)
ψ	Helix angle	Y_β	Helix angle factor
K_m	Load-distribution factor	Y_S	Stress-concentration factor (HPSTC)
		Y_{Sa}	Stress-concentration factor (tip loading)
		Y_{Fa}	Tooth form factor (tip loading)
		Y_ε	Contact ratio factor
		$K_{F\beta}$	Longitudinal load-distribution factor for bending stress
		$K_{F\alpha}$	Transverse load-distribution factor for bending stress
	Contact stress calculation		
s_c	Calculated contact stress, psi	σ_H	Calculated contact stress, N/mm^2
C_p	Coefficient for elastic properties of materials used	Z_E	Coefficient for elastic properties of materials used, $(N/mm^2)^{0.5}$
W_t	Transmitted tangential load at operating pitch diameter, lb	F_t	Tangential load, N
C_a	Application factor	K_A	Application factor
F	Contacting face width, in.	b	Contacting face width, mm
d	Pinion operating pitch diameter, in.	d_1	Pinion pitch diameter, mm
I	Durability geometry factor	$Z_H \cdot Z_\beta \cdot Z_\varepsilon$	Total durability geometry factor
C_v	Dynamic factor for durability (derates by being less than 1.0)	K_v	Dynamic factor (derates by being over 1.0)
C_m	Durability load-distribution factor	$K_{H\beta}$	Longitudinal load-distribution factor, for pitting
		$K_{H\alpha}$	Transverse load-distribution factor, for pitting
		u	$\frac{\text{No. gear teeth}}{\text{No. pinion teeth}}$

defined material in each system are not the same. This makes it somewhat difficult to compare rating results by the two systems. The engineer has to consider:

Which system more correctly calculates the *true* total stress

Which system best knows the *real* ability of a given steel (or other material) to withstand tensile stress or compressive stress in a gear tooth

One of the best ways to compare the two systems is to look at the *load intensity* for gear units in service. True comparisons can be made by calculating the unit load and the K factor. These indexes of tooth loading are calculated in exactly the same way by AGMA and ISO. The calculation is simple, and all variables are directly measurable dimensions or forces.

An excellent comparative study of 54 gear designs was made by D. E. Imwalle, O. A. Labath, and R. N. Hutchinson of The Cincinnati Gear Co., Cincinnati, Ohio, U.S.A. Their results were published in a 1980 ASME paper given at the International Power Transmission & Gearing Conference in San Francisco, CA, U.S.A. This paper shows in considerable detail how to make comparative calculations by AGMA and ISO methods. Calculation results in terms of stress, derating factors, and hardness of steel are compared.

At the same ASME meeting, an excellent analytical study of AGMA and ISO methods for calculating tooth strength was given by G. Castellani and V. P. Castelli. (Castellani is a gear consultant in Modena, Italy, and Castelli is a professor at the University of Bologna, Italy.)

The papers just mentioned, plus other studies made since 1980, show that there are unresolved differences in rating by the two methods. The most serious problems have to do with gear-strength rating. More worldwide gear research and more follow-up evaluation of gears in service are needed to establish better formulas and data on gear materials capabilities. Both AGMA and ISO are continuing their work on gear rating. New or revised rating standards can be expected—at least through the 1980s.

Figure 9.18 shows a comparison of "unit load allowable" for a substantial number of gear designs made by Dennis E. Imwalle and Octave A. Labath. These data were presented and discussed at the IFToMM gear committee meeting in Eindhoven, Holland, in June 1982.

The *allowable unit load* is obtained by first calculating a power rating using an AGMA or ISO calculation method. Then the allowed power rating is used to calculate the unit load and K-factor indexes of tooth loading intensity.

Figure 9.18 shows these comparisons for unit load:

For fully hard helical gears, ISO would allow more load than AGMA 218. (AGMA 218 would allow more than the obsolete AGMA 225.)

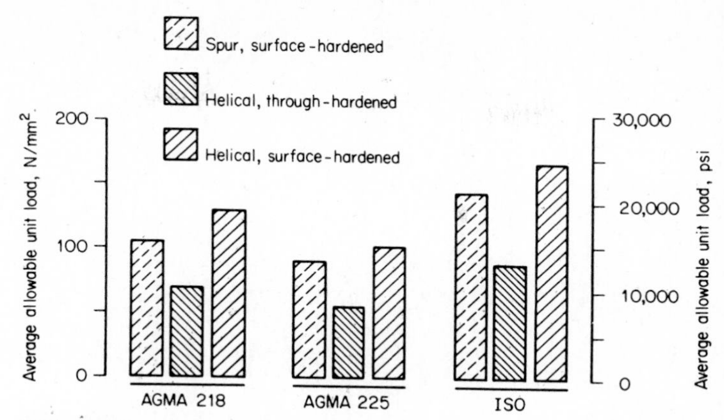

FIG. 9.18 Average allowable unit load, AGMA and ISO. (*Data courtesy of the Cincinnati Gear Co., Cincinnati, OH, U.S.A.*)

For medium-hard helical gears, ISO would again allow more load than AGMA 218.

For fully hard spur gears, ISO would allow more load than AGMA 218.

Spur and helical gears are somewhat closer to the same rating in ISO than in AGMA.

The allowable ratings of Fig. 9.18 are too high for long-life gears of high reliability. (See Chap. 3 for effects of grades of material, levels of reliability, and numbers of cycles like 10^9 or more.)

In a similar fashion, Fig. 9.19 shows allowable K factors for the same group of designs studied by Imwalle and Labath.

Figure 9.19 shows these comparisons:

For fully hard helical gears, ISO and AGMA 218 are close to the same level of loading. (AGMA 218 will allow more load than the obsolete 225.)

For medium-hard helical gears, ISO would allow less load than AGMA 218—or even than the old AGMA 225.

For fully hard spur gears, the allowed ratings are close to the same value. ISO is slightly less than AGMA 218.

The allowable ratings of Fig. 9.19 are too high for long-life gears of high reliability. (See Chap. 3 for effects of grades of material, regimes of lubrication, levels of reliability, and numbers of cycles like 10^9 or more.)

The above comparisons of allowable unit loads and K factors for AGMA and ISO should be considered as generalizations developed by Imwalle and Labath in their published study. Dr. H. Winter, chairman of the ISO/TC

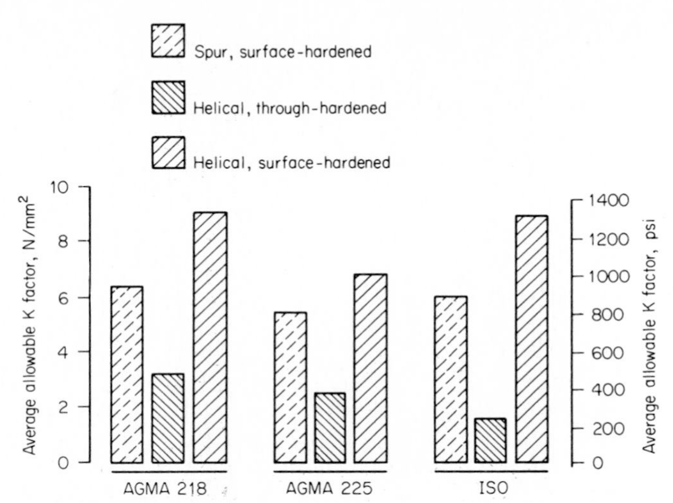

FIG. 9.19 Average allowable K factor, AGMA and ISO. (*Data courtesy of the Cincinnati Gear Co., Cincinnati, OH, U.S.A.*)

60/WG 6 committee, has reminded me that recommended safety factors vary between AGMA and ISO, and the hardness of a through-hardened gear may be somewhat different. Exact comparisons can only be made by studying all the details in individual cases.

9.10 Profile Modification Calculation Procedure (Supplement to Chap. 3)

Profile modifications are generally made to reduce the risk of tooth scoring. Section 3.31 gives general information on how to design gears that may have a scoring hazard. Table 3.54 shows a general guide for depth of the profile modification.

The best procedure is to put profile modification at the tip of the pinion and at the tip of the gear. The involute has less curvature here, and it has more length for an increment of roll angle.

In some cases a gear builder will own a pinion grinding machine capable of making modified involute profiles, but the larger machine that will grind the gear is not equipped to grind a modified involute. What can be done?

The pinion can be made with a modification at the tip and a second modification near the root fillet. This is reasonably practical for pinions with large enough numbers of teeth to keep the form diameter a few degrees of roll away from the base circle. (The base circle is at 0 degrees roll.)

The calculation procedure for this kind of design involves locating a diameter on the pinion that *matches* the diameter at which the involute profile modification might have started on the gear.

Table 9.16 is a calculation sheet that can be used to get a diameter on the pinion matching a diameter on the gear.

The calculation procedure is as follows:

TABLE 9.16 Assume Any Diameter on a Gear and Calculate the Matching Diameter on the Mating Gear.

Basic data (for information only)

Pinion addendum 22 mm
Gear addendum 18 mm

The part chosen for calculation may be either the pinion or the gear. In metric system use millimeters; in English system use inches.

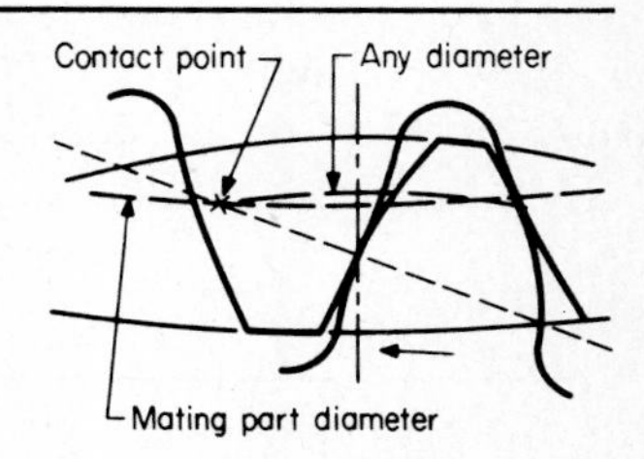

Location	At start modification		At outside diameter	
Column	1	2	3	4
1. No. teeth	51		26	51
2. No. teeth in mate	26		51	26
3. Pressure angle, transverse	20.410311		20.410311	20.410311
4. Pitch diameter	1042.787		531.617	1042.787
5. Any diameter	1060.808		575.620	1078.790
6. Cos (3) × (4)	977.3200		498.2417	977.3200
7. (6) ÷ (5)	0.921298		0.865574	0.905941
8. Arccos (7)	22.88345		30.05169	25.04969
9. Tan (8) × 57.29578	24.18318		33.14869	26.77798
10. Tan (3) × 57.29578	21.31985		21.31985	21.31985
11. (9) − (10)	2.86333		11.82884	5.45813
12. (1) ÷ (2)	1.961538		0.509804	1.961538
13. (11) × (12)	5.61654		6.03039	10.70633
14. (10) − (13)	15.70331		15.28946	10.61352
15. (14) ÷ 57.29578	0.274074		0.266851	0.185241
16. Arctan (15)	15.32694		14.941299	10.49456
17. Cos (16)	0.964433		0.966190	0.983272
18. (6) ÷ (12)	498.2417		977.3201	498.2417
19. (18) ÷ (17)	516.61606		1011.5196	506.71797

Notes:
1. Item (19) is the diameter on the mate that contacts with the diameter on the part, chosen for item (5).
2. If item (5) is the outside diameter of a part, item (19) is the limit diameter of the mating part. (See Columns 3 and 4.)
3. Item (9) is the roll angle of the part to the contact point.
4. Item (14) is the roll angle of the mating part to the contact point.
5. Column 1 is an example showing how to find a start modification diameter on a pinion to match the diameter that might have been used for a modification on the gear.

Determine the diameter at which the profile modification might have started on the gear. Enter this value as "any diameter" in (5).

Fill in the column for the gear number of teeth and the gear pitch diameter.

Show the number of pinion teeth in (2) for the mating part.

Item (19) is the pinion diameter for start of modification—in the dedendum.

The numerical values in Column 1 of Table 9.16 are for the sample problem on scoring shown in Sec. 8.2. If the gear modification had been put on the lower flank of the 26-tooth pinion, the theoretical pinion profile would have had these values, in the metric system:

	Location		
Name	Diameter	Degrees roll	Involute basic value
Limit diameter	506.72	10.49	−0.101
End modification	516.62	15.70	0.00
Pitch diameter	531.62	26.778	0.00
Start modification	559.61	29.30	0.00
Outside diameter	575.62	33.15	−0.063

With both modifications on the pinion, the gear profile would be a theoretical true involute from the limit diameter to the tip radius at the outside diameter.

9.11 The Basics of Gear-Tooth Measurement for Accuracy and Size (Supplement to Chap. 5)

In cartoon style, Fig. 9.20 shows the principal kinds of checks used to determine the geometric accuracy and size of gear teeth. Section 5.18 has already discussed the accuracy of gears needed for different kinds of applications. Figure 5.50 defined gear-tooth tolerances. Some additional discussion is needed to clarify how the checks are taken.

In Fig. 9.20, the upper view on the schematic gear shows a tooth-to-tooth basic checking method. The checking device is set to read zero at the approximate circular pitch of the gear being checked. The first reading might be from the working side of tooth 1 to the working side of tooth 2. The second reading would then be taken from tooth 2 to tooth 3 and the third from tooth 3 to tooth 4. In a similar manner, readings are taken all the way around the gear.

The value that is needed is the *difference* in readings, not the readings

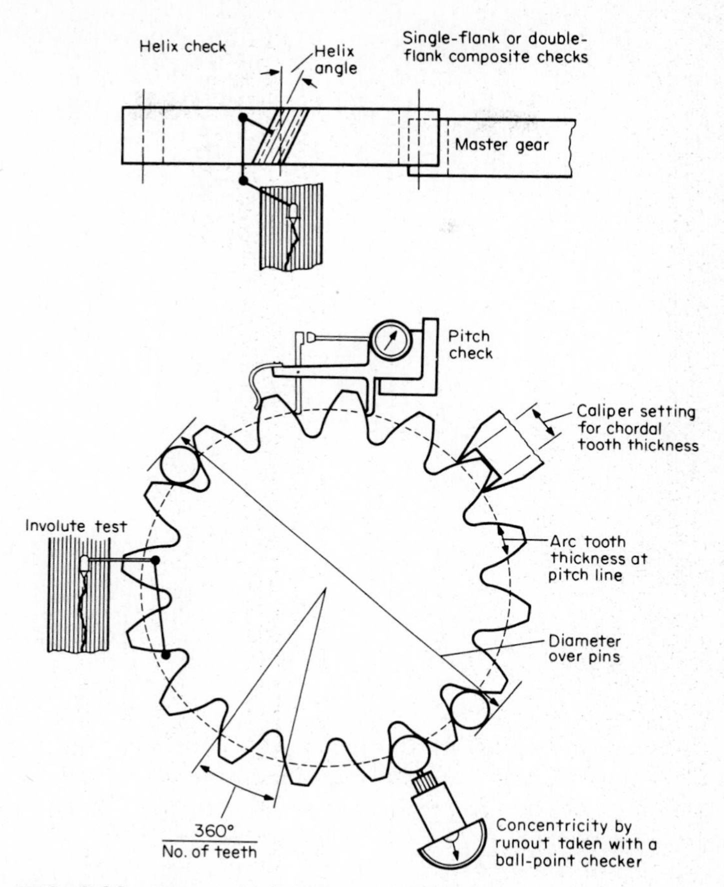

FIG. 9.20 Schematic of different gear-tooth checks.

themselves. The first difference is obtained by subtracting the 1–2 reading from the 2–3 reading. The second difference is obtained by subtracting the 2–3 reading from the 3–4 reading.

In the manner just described, as many differences are obtained as there are teeth on the gear. The drawing limit is the *maximum* difference. If any of the differences in the gear circumference exceeds the drawing maximum, then the gear does not meet the drawing specification.

The cumulative error is obtained directly by setting an angle equal to 360° divided by the number of teeth. This method is shown in the lower part of Fig. 9.20.

At the first tooth, zero is set on the tooth and a reading is taken on the second tooth with an angular setting of 360° divided by the number of teeth. For the third tooth, the angular setting is doubled, and for the fourth tooth

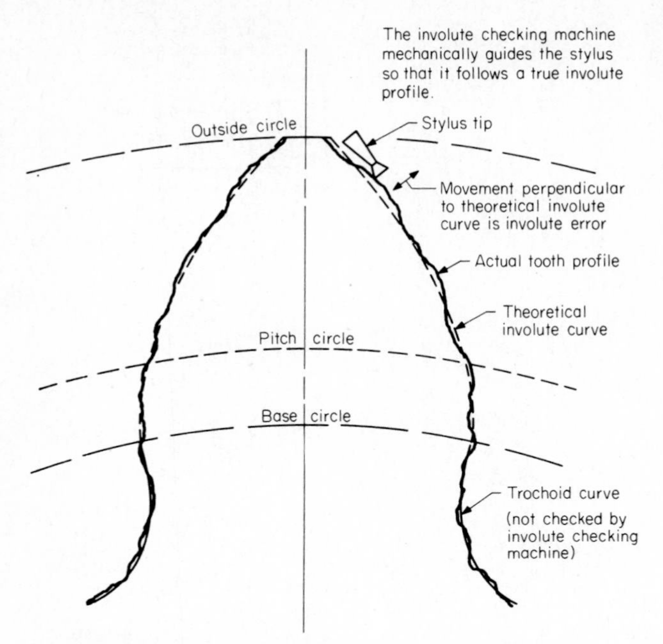

FIG. 9.21 Details of involute check.

the angular setting is tripled. In this manner the out-of-position reading for all teeth is determined with respect to a starting point on one tooth.

In the gear trade, cumulative error is often called *accumulated* error, *index* error, or *out-of-position* error. This error does not compare adjacent teeth. The drawing limit is the greatest amount any one tooth is *out of position with respect to any other tooth.*

The two teeth that determine the cumulative error are often close to 180° apart. In an extreme case, two adjacent teeth could be so much in error that they set the maximum cumulative error. (The reader should carefully note that it takes three adjacent teeth to set a maximum tooth-to-tooth spacing error, while the distance setting a maximum cumulative error can be from two teeth to one-half the total number of teeth in the part.)

The involute check is taken by a stylus that traverses the involute profile. Note the Fig. 9.20 schematic and the details of Fig. 9.21. (Involute variations in Fig. 9.21 are exaggerated.) Involute checks measure slope, irregularity, and waviness, and determine whether or not a specified profile modification was obtained. Note in particular how involute profiles are specified by a *K* chart in Fig. 5.50.

The surface finish may be evaluated in an involute check if the machine will read deviations at 2000 magnification. For involute accuracy, 500 or

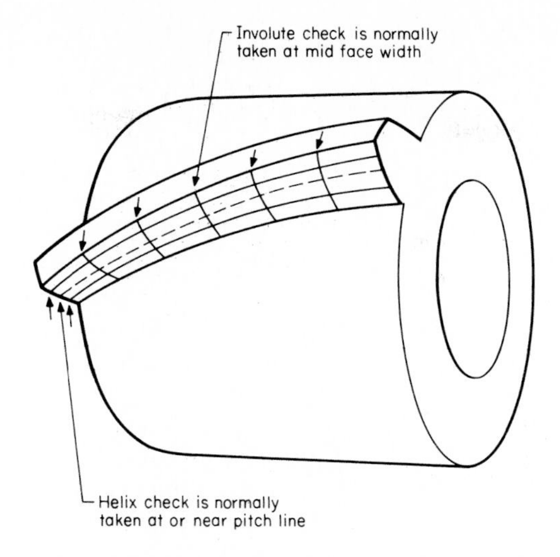

Helix checks and involute checks are sometimes taken at all the locations shown above to get more complete knowledge of the tooth accuracy.

FIG. 9.22 Locations for involute and helix checks.

1000 magnification is normally used for high-accuracy gears. For medium-accuracy gears, 250 magnification may be suitable.

The helix is checked by a stylus moving lengthwise across the tooth. The stylus moves in a helical spiral. If the tooth is spur (0° helix), the stylus moves in a straight line. See upper view of Fig. 9.20.

The concentricity of a gear may be determined using a ball-point checker or by a double-flank check with a master gear; see upper and lower views of Fig. 9.20.

Production gears are generally checked by rolling with a master gear. In a double-flank check, the master gear is spring-loaded to stay in tight mesh with the gear being checked. In a single-flank check, the master gear and production gear roll in mesh, with only one side of the teeth contacting. A timing mechanism determines the *transmission* error. (See Sec. 5.19 for more information on composite checking machines.)

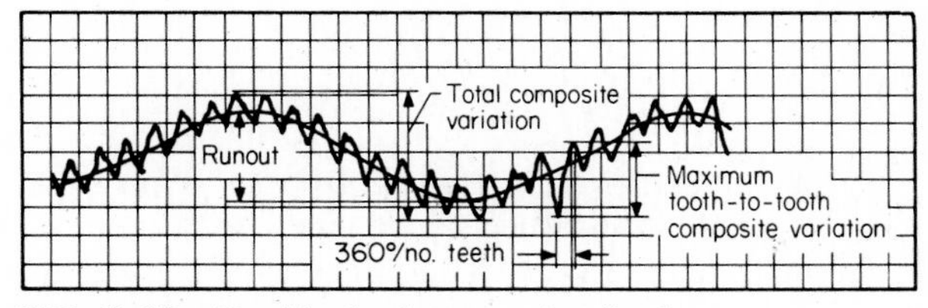

FIG. 9.23 Double-flank composite check.

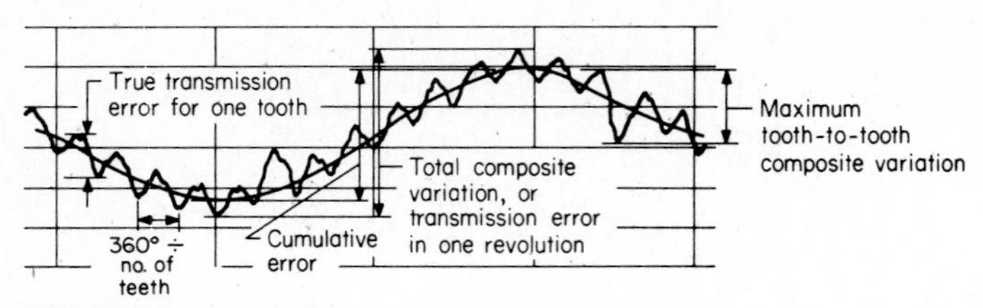

FIG. 9.24 Single-flank composite check.

The tooth thickness of a gear may be measured directly with calipers, or it may be determined indirectly by diameter pins. The sizing of gears may be controlled by double-flank composite checks and center-distance settings corresponding to maximum and minimum tooth thickness specifications.

Figure 9.22 shows locations for involute and helix checks. Normally, four teeth 90° apart are checked. This method finds problems with the teeth on a gear not being alike and any serious effect on involute and helix due to a part being eccentric.

In some cases ends of teeth may have extra involute errors, or the helix at the tooth tip or root may be worse than at the pitch line. Figure 9.22 shows how a grid of checks may be used to more fully explore a gear tooth. (Composite checks with a master gear often find local bad spots by contacting the whole tooth surface.)

Figure 9.23 shows an example of a double-flank composite check using a master gear. Note that the *maximum* tooth-to-tooth composite reading is found and compared with the design specification. Also note that a runout reading is not usually as large as the total composite variation.

Figure 9.24 shows a single-flank composite check. This check shows *transmission* error in a circumferential direction, not *runout*-type errors in a radial direction. The cumulative error is usually less than the total composite variation.

Chapter 23 of the *Gear Handbook* gives a considerable amount of additional information on gear-checking procedures and types of equipment being used. The reader who needs more information than this book can provide should refer to the *Gear Handbook*.

9.12 Shaper-Cutter Tooth Thickness (Supplement to Chap. 6)

Figure 9.25 shows an example of a critical shaper-cutter design. This is a preshave cutter designed to produce the deepest point of undercut at a 360.8324-mm diameter on the gear. The cutter is designed to hold a constant root diameter of 362.255 mm. Curves *A* and *B* show how the cutter

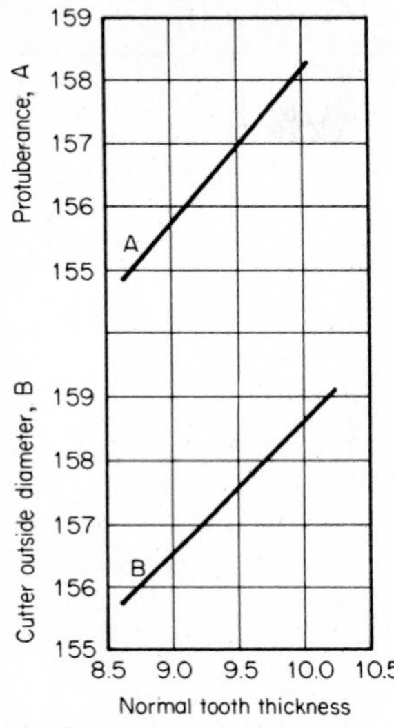

Item		Cutter	Sample
Number of teeth		23	55
Module		6.35	6.35
Pitch diameter		146.05	349.25
Addendum		6.5024	5.080
Whole depth		—	11.5824
Normal pressure angle		25°	25°
Normal circular pitch		19.949	19.949
Depth B&S calipers		6.68	5.03
Chordal	Tooth	10.109	—
thickness	Space	—	10.1854–10.287
Helix angle		0°	0°
Pressure angle		25°	25°

FIG. 9.25 Shaper-cutter design to hold fixed major diameter on internal part.

"Hi-point" of protuberance and the cutter outside diameter must change as the tooth thickness of the cutter is reduced because of sharpening. When the locations of the profile changes are measured by a conventional involute checker, the diameters in the chart are converted to *degrees roll* of the gear. (Table 9.3 shows how to calculate roll angles.)

Table 9.17 shows the calculation sheet that was used to design the shaper cutter in Fig. 9.25. In this case, the gear designer wanted the deepest point of undercut to be about midway between the end of active involute (form diameter) and the root diameter.

The calculations were made by assuming a series of operating pressure angles. A wide enough range of angles must be used to get curves that will cover the change in tooth thickness during the life of the cutter. Roughly, the change in cutter thickness is 0.060 mm per mm of cutter width.

At some time during the life of the cutter, the operating pressure angle is usually the same as the design pressure angle of the gear. When this happens, the cutter is rolling with the gear on the design pitch line of the gear. The cutter designer may choose to design the cutter so that the operating pressure angle runs either lower or higher than theoretical. If the cutter has a small number of teeth, it may be necessary to keep the operating pressure angle high to avoid undercut on the cutter. The smallest fillet on the gear is produced when the operating pressure angle of the cutter is close to the pressure angle at the root of the gear tooth.

TABLE 9.17 Calculation of Design Data for Internal-Gear Shaper Cutter

Cutter data				
1. Number of teeth	23			
2. Pitch diameter	146.05			
3. Transverse pressure angle	25°			
Gear data				
4. Number of teeth	55			
5. Pitch diameter	349.25			
6. Inside diameter	339.09			
7. Root diameter	362.25			
8. Form diameter	359.41			
9. Undercut diameter	360.83			
10. Helix angle	0°			
11. Arc tooth thickness	9.7384			
Calculations				
12. (5) × π ÷ (4)	19.949			
13. (5) − (2)	203.20			
14. (5) × cos (3)	316.528			
Calculation of cutter outside diameter (22) vs. cutter tooth thickness at pitch line (20)				
15. Assume operating pressure angle	25.00°	25.50°	26.00°	26.50°
16. Cos (3) ÷ cos (15)	1.000	1.004124	1.008360	1.012709
17. *Inv (3) − inv (15)	0	−0.001942	−0.003972	−0.006094
18. (12) − (11)	10.2107			
19. (13) × (17)	0	−0.39446	−0.80704	−1.23830
20. (18) + (19)	10.2107	9.81626	9.40368	8.97241
21. (13) × (16)	203.20	204.04	204.90	205.78
22. (7) − (21)	159.05	158.21	157.35	156.47
Calculation of diameter on cutter (31) to produce maximum undercut on gear at (9)				
23. (14) ÷ (9)	0.87722			
24. Arccos (23)	28.69096			
25. (24) − (15)	3.69096	3.19096	2.69096	2.19096
26. Sin (25)	0.064375	0.055664	0.046949	0.038230
27. Cos (25)	0.997926	0.998450	0.998897	0.999269
28. x = (9) × (26)	23.22836	20.08521	16.94053	13.79457
29. y = (9) × (27) − (21)	156.882	156.233	155.533	154.784
30. $(28)^2 + (29)^2$	25,151.4	24,812.0	24,477.6	24,148.3
31. $(30)^{0.5}$	158.5919	157.5183	156.4533	155.3973

*See Table 9.10 for definition of involute function.

Notes:
1. For calculation of diameter on cutter to correspond to a particular diameter on the gear, substitute the particular diameter for (9), and repeat steps (23) through (31).
2. Linear dimensions shown above are all in millimeters, but the calculation procedure is the same when all dimensions are in inches.

The equations for the relation of cutter tooth thickness to outside diameter are shown below. Equations (9.11) and (9.12) were used in Table 9.17.

External gear cutters:

$$s_0 = (p - s) - 2a(\text{inv}\ \alpha_t - \text{inv}\ \alpha_0) \qquad \text{metric} \qquad (9.9a)$$

$$t_c = (p - T) - 2C(\text{inv}\ \phi_t - \text{inv}\ \phi_c) \qquad \text{English} \qquad (9.9b)$$

$$d_{a0} = 2a\left(\frac{\cos \alpha_t}{\cos \alpha_0}\right) - d_r \qquad \text{metric} \qquad (9.10a)$$

$$d_{oc} = 2C\left(\frac{\cos \phi_t}{\cos \phi_c}\right) - D_R \qquad \text{English} \qquad (9.10b)$$

Internal gear cutters:

$$s_0 = (p - s) + 2a(\text{inv}\ \alpha_t - \text{inv}\ \alpha_0) \qquad \text{metric} \qquad (9.11a)$$

$$t_c = (p - T) + 2C(\text{inv}\ \phi_t - \text{inv}\ \phi_c) \qquad \text{English} \qquad (9.11b)$$

$$d_{a0} = d_r - 2a\left(\frac{\cos \alpha_t}{\cos \alpha_0}\right) \qquad \text{metric} \qquad (9.12a)$$

$$d_{oc} = D_R - 2C\left(\frac{\cos \phi_t}{\cos \phi_c}\right) \qquad \text{English} \qquad (9.12b)$$

where s_0 or t_c = cutter tooth thickness at pitch line, mm or in.
p = circular pitch of gear, mm or in.
s or T = tooth thickness of gear at design pitch line, mm or in.
a or C = design center distance, mm or in.
$= \dfrac{d_{p0} + d_p}{2}$, metric, or $\dfrac{d_c + D}{2}$, English, external gear
$= \dfrac{d_p - d_{p0}}{2}$, metric, or $\dfrac{D - d_c}{2}$, English, internal gear
d_{a0} or d_{oc} = outside diameter of cutter, mm or in.
α_t or ϕ_t = transverse pressure angle of gear, degrees
α_0 or ϕ_c = operating pressure angle of cutter, degrees
d_p or D = pitch diameter of gear, mm or in.
d_{p0} or d_c = design pitch diameter of cutter, mm or in.
d_r or D_R = root diameter of gear, mm or in.

When some special feature—such as a protuberance or a chamfering bevel—is needed on a tool, it is desirable to calculate the location of the point on the cutter that will produce this feature on the gear. This permits the cutter profile to be checked any time during its life to see if the cutter is properly formed to produce the gear. This system may even be used to check and see how close a cutter will come to producing a gear it was not designed to cut.

If a point is taken on the cutter instead of on the gear, the calculation may be worked in reverse to see what the cutter does to the gear. For instance, one might take the cutter outside diameter as a starting point and solve for the diameter of a point on the gear that was cut by this point on the cutter. Such a calculation would give the exact location of the end of the involute profile on the gear (which is also the point at which the root fillet starts).

The equations to calculate from a point on one member to a point on the other member are:

External gear cutter (or any two external gears with axes parallel):

$$\cos \alpha' = \frac{d_p \cos \alpha_t}{d'_p} \qquad \text{metric} \quad (9.13a)$$

$$\cos \phi' = \frac{D \cos \phi_t}{D'} \qquad \text{English} \quad (9.13b)$$

$$x = d'_p \sin (\alpha' - \alpha_0) \qquad \text{metric} \quad (9.14a)$$

$$x = D' \sin (\phi' - \phi_c) \qquad \text{English} \quad (9.14b)$$

$$y = 2a\left(\frac{\cos \alpha_t}{\cos \alpha_0}\right) - d'_p \cos (\alpha' - \alpha_0) \qquad \text{metric} \quad (9.15a)$$

$$y = 2C\left(\frac{\cos \phi_t}{\cos \phi_c}\right) - D' \cos (\phi' - \phi_c) \qquad \text{English} \quad (9.15b)$$

$$d' = (x^2 + y^2)^{0.5} \qquad \text{metric or English} \quad (9.16)$$

Internal gear cutter (or internal gearset):

$$y = d'_p \cos (\alpha' - \alpha_0) - 2a\left(\frac{\cos \alpha_t}{\cos \alpha_0}\right) \qquad \text{metric} \quad (9.17a)$$

$$y = D' \cos (\phi' - \phi_c) - 2C\left(\frac{\cos \phi_t}{\cos \phi_c}\right) \qquad \text{English} \quad (9.17b)$$

$$d' = (x^2 + y^2)^{0.5} \qquad \text{metric or English} \quad (9.18)$$

where d'_p or D' = diameter to be cut on gear (or point on either member at which calculation starts)

α' or ϕ' = pressure angle at d'_p or D'

α_0 or ϕ_c = operating pressure angle of cutter

x, y = rectangular coordinates of point on cutter

d' = diameter through point on tool which cuts point on gear (or point on second member corresponding to starting point on first member)

Note that calculations on shaper cutters are carried out just as if the shaper cutter were an involute spur pinion. No account is taken of the fact that the cutter may have a top face angle of 5 or 10°. Since finishing cutters usually have a 5° angle, this feature cannot be ignored. The actual cutting is done by a tooth profile which is equivalent to a *projection of the cutter tooth.* This projection is just the same as a section through an equivalent spur pinion. For this reason calculations can be made on the basis of an equivalent pinion.

If an involute shaper cutter is checked back of the cutting edge, in a plane perpendicular to the cutter axis, it is necessary to take account of the top face angle. This can be done by making a small reduction in the base-circle diameter setting that is used to check the cutter. Usually cutter drawings allow the tool manufacturer to stamp the cutter with a base-circle diameter that allows for the top face angle.

The calculations just described may be used for *helical* as well as spur gears. In calculating a helical job, it is only necessary to keep all dimensions in the *transverse plane.* The tooth action in this plane is the same for either spur or helical shaper cutters. The transverse tooth thickness is equal to the normal tooth thickness divided by the cosine of the helix angle. Usually design drawings will show the transverse pressure angle, but sometimes it is necessary to convert normal tooth thicknesses to transverse tooth thicknesses (which have not been given).

9.13 General Method for Determining Tooth Thicknesses When Helical Gears Are Operated on Spread Centers (Supplement to Chap. 8)

Problem 2 in Chap. 8 showed how to design spur gears to be cut with standard cutting tools and operated on spread centers. The more general problem is that of helical gears designed to run on spread centers. (A spur gear is a helical gear with 0° helix angle.) In this section we will show the general procedure for setting the tooth thickness values of a set of helical gears on spread center.

The method will be shown by going through a step-by-step procedure for an 18/95 teeth gearset cut at 3 normal module, 20° normal pressure angle, and 15° helix angle. This set is to run on a center distance of 180 mm so as to give an operating pressure angle of about 24°.

The first step is to calculate the basic tooth data for both cutting and operating conditions. The several equations given in Chaps. 2, 3, and 8 are used. (Presumably the reader is familiar with these by now.)

The values given below are the basic data for the design:

Item	Pinion	Gear
Number of teeth	18	95
Pitch diameter, cutting	55.90490	295.05366
Normal circular pitch, cutting	9.42478	9.42478
Normal pressure angle, cutting	20°	20°
Transverse pressure angle, cutting	20.64690	20.64690
Helix angle, cutting	15° RH	15° LH
Lead	655.4619	3459.3824
Base diameter	52.31420	276.10272
Center distance, operating	180	180
Pitch diameter, operating	57.34513	302.65486
Transverse circular pitch, operating	10.00861	10.00861
Transverse pressure angle, operating	24.17914	24.17914
Helix angle, operating	15.368364	15.368364
Normal circular pitch, operating	9.65072	9.65072
Normal pressure angle, operating	23.40902	23.40902

The next calculation step is to establish the tooth height dimensions. A 3 normal module tooth has a standard working depth of 6 mm. A whole depth of at least 7 mm and a good-sized root fillet radius are needed for shaving or grinding. With a small number of pinion teeth, the pinion should be made about 25 percent long addendum and the gear about 25 percent short addendum. We will divide the working depth into a pinion addendum of 3.75 mm and a gear addendum of 2.25 mm.

With these decisions made, we can now make a working table dimensioning the tooth height:

Item	Pinion	Gear
Addendum, operating	3.75	2.25
Pitch diameter, operating	57.3451	302.6549
Outside diameter	64.8451	307.1549
Whole depth	7.1	7.1
Root diameter	50.6451	292.9549

The operating circular pitch was 10.0086 mm. Our gears are to be used at a relatively slow pitch-line speed (10 m/s), and there will be frequent torque reversals. This makes it desirable to have a small amount of backlash. We will design for 0.10 to 0.15 mm backlash in the transverse plane. This means that the sum of our design tooth thicknesses should be no greater than 9.9086 mm (10.0086 − 0.10).

With standard-addendum gears, this tooth-thickness sum would be divided approximately evenly between pinion and gear. However, in this case, the pinion addendum will be 0.75 mm longer than standard addendum (3.75 − 3.00). The pinion transverse arc tooth thickness should be about 0.61 larger than standard, and the gear, being 0.75 short, should be about 0.61 thinner than standard. The 0.61 is 0.75 × 2 tan 22°. (22° is about midway between the operating pressure angle of 24.1791° and the cutting pressure angle of 20.6469°.)

The next step is to calculate the tooth thicknesses for the cutting (and shaving) operations. The arc tooth thickness at the cutting pitch diameter is determined by the method of Table 9.18, using the desired operating tooth thickness as a starting point. The normal section arc tooth thickness is obtained by multiplying by the cosine of the helix angle (at the cutting pitch diameter). The results are:

Item	Pinion	Gear
Arc tooth thickness, operating	5.5643	4.3443
Arc tooth thickness, cutting	6.0127	7.3395
Helix angle, cutting	15°	15°
Normal arc tooth thickness, cutting	5.8079	7.0895
Pitch diameter, cutting	55.90490	295.05366

A preshave hob is available to cut these parts. The hob has an addendum of 4.20 mm and a tooth thickness of 4.56 mm. It is 20° normal pressure angle. Its standard cutting depth is 7.20 mm. (2.40 × 3 module = 7.20.)

The dedendum of the pinion during hobbing is

$$\begin{aligned}\text{Pinion dedendum} &= 0.5 \times (\text{pitch diameter} - \text{root diameter})\\ &= 0.5 \times (55.90490 - 50.6451)\\ &= 2.6299 \text{ mm}\end{aligned}$$

When cutting the long-addendum pinion, the hob would use an addendum close to the dedendum of the pinion, which is 2.6299 mm. At 2.6299 mm, instead of 4.20, the hob tooth thickness would be

$$\begin{aligned}\text{Hob tooth thickness} &= 4.56 - 2.0 \tan 20°(4.200 - 2.6299)\\ &= 3.41706\end{aligned}$$

The hob *cuts its own thickness* at the hobbing pitch diameter. We can now subtract the hob tooth thickness from the normal circular pitch to get the normal arc tooth thickness that the chosen hob will produce. This is 9.4248 mm − 3.4171 mm = 6.0077 mm.

Our earlier calculations gave a design value of 5.8079 mm for the pinion normal tooth thickness at the cutting pitch diameter. Since the pinion is to be shaved, we need to add 0.05 mm for shaving stock. We should produce a tooth thickness of 5.8579 at the hobbing operation. The calculations just

TABLE 9.18 Determination of Arc Tooth Thickness at Cutting Pitch Diameter from Design Value at Operating Pitch Diameter

Given data

	Pinion	Gear
1. Pitch diameter	57.34513	302.65486
2. Pressure angle at (1)	24.17914	24.17914
3. Arc tooth thickness at (1)	5.5643	4.3443

Step A: Solve for the tooth thickness at base diameter.

	Pinion	Gear
4. Involute (2)	0.0269747	0.0269747
5. Cosine (2)	0.912269	0.912269
6. (4) × (1)	1.54687	8.16402
7. (3) + (6)	7.11117	12.50832
8. T.T. at B.D., (5) × (7)	6.48730	11.41095
9. Base diameter, (5) × (1)	52.31420	276.1026

Step B: Solve for a series of tooth thicknesses to study the tooth profile. For any desired diameter, the cosine of the pressure angle at that diameter is

cos PA at any diameter = base diameter ÷ any diameter

A series of pressure angles is assumed based on diameters of interest. Then calculations are made to get the arc thicknesses that go with each diameter.

	Pinion	Gear
10. Assumed pressure angles	20.64690	20.64690
11. Cosine (10)	0.935771	0.935771
12. Involute (10)	0.0164534	0.0164534
13. (12) × (9)	0.860746	4.54282
14. (8) − (13)	5.62655	6.86813
15. Arc T.T., (14) ÷ (11)	6.01274	7.33954
16. Any diameter, (9) ÷ (11)	55.90492	295.05359
17. Δ rad., [(16) − (1)] ÷ 2		

finished show that the hob will produce a tooth thickness of 6.0077. We need to hob the pinion teeth about 0.1498 mm thinner (6.0077 − 5.8579 = 0.1498). What do we do now?

The answer is easy. If we sink the hob in 0.2058 mm, it will cut the teeth 0.1498 mm thinner (0.1498 ÷ 2 tan 20° = 0.2058). Our design was set at a whole depth of 7.100 mm. Sinking the hob in for tooth thickness adjustment will give a whole depth of about 7.3 mm (7.100 + 0.206 = 7.306). This is

OK. The original aim in this job was to get a whole depth of at least 7.0 mm. The depth of 7.3 is not too much.

When hobbing the short-addendum gear, the gear dedendum is

$$\begin{aligned}\text{Gear dedendum} &= 0.5 \times (\text{pitch diameter} - \text{root diameter})\\ &= 0.5 \times (295.05366 - 292.9549)\\ &= 1.0494\end{aligned}$$

When cutting the short-addendum gear, the hob will use an addendum of 1.0494 (to match the gear dedendum). At this addendum, the hob tooth thickness will be

$$\begin{aligned}\text{Hob tooth thickness} &= 4.56 - 2.0 \tan 20°(4.200 - 1.0494)\\ &= 2.2665\end{aligned}$$

We subtract 2.2665 from the gear normal circular pitch (9.4248) to get a gear-tooth thickness of 7.1583. We need 0.05 mm shaving stock, and so the gear-tooth thickness that we need to hob is 7.1395 ($7.0895 + 0.05 = 7.1395$).

Our hob will produce 7.1583 mm and we need only 7.1395. The gear teeth will be too thick by 0.0188 mm ($7.1583 - 7.1395$). This problem is quite easy to solve. We will hob the gear slightly deeper than 7.10 mm. An extra depth of 0.026 mm will make the gear-tooth thickness come out just right ($0.0188 \div 2 \tan 20° = 0.0258$ mm). Our approximate whole depth in hobbing will be 7.126 mm. This slight difference in whole depth is of no consequence at all. It is between the 7.100 design whole depth and the 7.200 whole depth normally used for the hob.

The calculation procedure to determine tooth thicknesses for a spread-center helical gearset is finished.

The reader should note that this general procedure will work for spur gears, since they are really just helical gears with 0° helix angle. Also, the procedure shows how to check out a preshave hob. If a pregrind hob is used, the procedure is the same, but the stock allowance for grinding will be much greater than the stock allowance for shaving.

9.14 Calculation of Geometry Factor for Scoring (Supplement to Chap. 3)

In Sec. 3.31 a general equation was given for the calculation of *flash temperature.* This value shows the hazard of hot scoring. A term in the formula is the *scoring geometry factor.* This factor is defined in Eq. (2.46). The historical background of this equation (and others relating to scoring) is given in Sec. 2.5.

In Sec. 8.2, Problem 5 finds the diameters at which profile modifications should start for gears of moderately critical scoring hazard. The problem is

TABLE 9.19 Calculation of Geometry Factor for Scoring

Basic data		
1. Circular pitch, transverse	64.2355	
2. Pressure angle, transverse	20.410311	
3. Cosine (2)	0.937219	
4. Sine (2)	0.348741	
5. Center distance	787.20 mm	
Calculations	**Column 1**	**Column 2**
6. No. teeth	26	26
7. Pitch diameter	531.6156	531.6156
8. Diameter, start modification	559.620	516.616
9. Base diameter, (7) × (3)	498.2417	498.2417
10. (9) ÷ (8)	0.890321	0.964433
11. Arccos (10)	27.08639	15.32692
12. Tan (11)	0.511426	0.274074
13. $\rho_1 = 0.50 \times (9) \times (12)$	127.4069	68.2775
14. (5) × (4)	274.5289	274.5289
15. $\rho_2 = (14) - (13)$	147.1220	206.2514
16. $(13)^{0.50}$	11.2875	8.2630
17. (6) ÷ No. gear teeth*	0.509804	0.509804
18. $[(17) \times (15)]^{0.50}$	8.66045	10.25416
19. (16) − (18)	2.62705	−1.99116
20. 0.0175 × (19)	0.045973	−0.034845
21. $(3)^{0.75}$	0.952535	0.952535
22. (13) × (15)	18744.36	14082.33
23. (13) + (15)	274.5289	274.5289
24. $[(22) \div (23)]^{0.25}$	2.87455	2.67622
25. (21) × (24)	2.73811	2.55026
26. (20) ÷ (25)	0.016790	0.013663
27. $m_t = (1) \div 3.1415926$	20.4468	20.4468
28. $(27)^{0.25}$	2.1265	2.1265
29. $Z_t = (26) \div (28)$	0.00789	−0.006425
For English calculation:		
30. $P_t = 3.1415926 \div (1)$		
31. $(30)^{0.25}$		
32. $Z_t = (26) \times (31)$		

*Number of teeth in the mating gear is 51.

Notes:

1. The diameter at the start of modification is usually critical from a scoring standpoint. If there is no modification of involute profile, the outside diameter of the pinion and the limit diameter of the pinion should be used in item (8) for the scoring geometry factor calculation.
2. This calculation sheet can be used for either metric or English units. Item (29) is the metric answer. Item (32) is the English answer. The same answer should be obtained either way, since Z_t is dimensionless.
3. This calculation only works for diameters on the pinion. When the gear is modified, find the matching diameter on the pinion. (See Table 9.16, Column 1, for an example.)

for a 26/51 tooth mesh of 20 module. We will now show how to calculate the scoring geometry factors at the start of profile modification.

The 26-tooth pinion has a start of profile modification at 559.620 mm (diameter). The profile modification of the 51-tooth gear starts at 1060.808 mm (diameter).

Table 9.19 shows the calculations for the scoring geometry factor. Column 1 determines Z_t at the start of modification near the pinion tip. The answer is 0.00789.

The second column determines the scoring geometry factor near the gear tip. The calculation sheet only works, though, for *diameters on the pinion.* This means that it is necessary to find the diameter on the pinion that matches the start of modification on the gear. Table 9.16 does this operation and is all worked out in Column 1 for our problem. The diameter on the pinion (near root fillet) is 516.616 mm. This diameter matches 1060.808 mm on the gear.

Column 2 of Table 9.19 gives the second Z_t value needed. It is -0.006425.

The method of Table 9.19 is general in nature. If a study of scoring at locations other than the start of profile modification is needed, the Z_t value can be calculated for a series of diameters going from the limit diameter to the outside diameter.

references

Those working in the gear field are not all in agreement on every aspect of designing and building *good* gears. This book gives the author's viewpoint, and (of course) the references given are apt to support the author's viewpoint. In a number of instances though, the references listed here provide different viewpoints from that of the author. The reader should study this book and other appropriate writings and then make an independent decision on the best course to follow in each situation.

For each reference the reader will find two annotations. The first entry is a code which categorizes the reference into one of four groups:

- Code H: A historic paper that provided the first* important technical information on some aspect of gear technology.
- Code G: A general reference book, booklet, or paper that provides supplementary data to what is given in this book.

*Concepts of engineering generally evolve from the incomplete to the complete. "First" is used here in a broad sense to denote an early and influential publication of a new concept or new technical information.

- Code S: A design standard or design guide that may be important in gear design or manufacturing work.
- Code P: A technical paper that provides a viewpoint or specific data which is useful as supplemental information to what is given in this book.

Some references are specifically cited in the text, while other references provide background material for the text but are not discussed in the text. The second annotation specifies which chapter, or chapters, of this text contain material related to the reference.

	Book	Code	Chapter
1	Boner, C. J.: *Gear and Transmission Lubricants*, Reinhold Publishing Corp., New York, 1964.	G	3, 7
2	Buckingham, Earle: *Analytical Mechanics of Gears*, Dover Publications, New York, 1949.	G	1, 2, 3, 5, 6
3	Candee, Allan H.: *Introduction to the Kinematic Geometry of Gear Teeth*, Chilton Company, Philadelphia, 1961.	G	1, 2, 3
4	Castellani, G., and V. Zanotti: *La Resistenza Degli Ingranaggi*, Tecniche Nuove, Milano, 1980.	G	3, 9,
5	Chironis, Nicholas P. (ed.): *Gear Design and Application*, McGraw-Hill Book Company, New York, 1967.	G	1 to 9
6	Colvin, Fred H. and Frank A. Stanley: *Gear Cutting Practice*, 3d ed., McGraw-Hill Book Company, New York, 1950.	G	5, 6
7	Dowson, D., and G. R. Higginson: *Elastohydrodynamic Lubrication*, Pergamon Press Ltd., Oxford, 1966.	H	2, 3
8	Dudley, Darle W. (ed.): *Gear Handbook*, McGraw-Hill Book Co., New York, 1962.	G	1 to 9
9	Dudley, Darle W.: *The Evolution of the Gear Art*, American Gear Manufacturers Assoc., Washington, D.C., 1969.	H	1, 2
10	Dudley, Darle W. (ed.): *Manual de Engranajes*, Compania Editorial Continental, S.A., Mexico, 1973.	G	1 to 9
11	Dudley, Darle W., and Hans Winter, *Zahnrader*, Springer-Verlag, Berlin, 1961.	G	1 to 9
12	Ewert, Richard H.: *Gearing—Basic Theory and Its Application—A Primer*, Sewall Gear Manufacturing Co., St. Paul, 1980.	G	1, 2, 3
13	Henriot, Georges: *Traité Théorique et Pratique des Engrenages* 1, Dunod, Paris, 1979.	G	1 to 9
14	Khiralla, T. W.: *On the Geometry of External Involute Spur Gears*, C/I Learning, North Hollywood, 1976.	G	1, 2, 3

	Book	Code	Chapter
15	Merritt, Henry E.: *Gear Engineering*, Pitman Publishing, London, 1971.	G	1 to 9
16	*Metal Cutting Tool Handbook*, Metal Cutting Tool Institute, New York, 1949.	G	6
17	*Metals Handbook*, Vol. 1: *Properties and Selection: Irons and Steels*, 9th ed., American Society for Metals, Metals Park, Ohio, 1978.	G	4
18	*Modern Methods of Gear Manufacture*, National Broach & Machine Division/Lear Siegler, Inc., Detroit, 1972.	G	4, 5, 6
19	Müller, Herbert W.: *Epicyclic Drive Trains*, Wayne State University Press, Detroit, 1982.	G	3
20	*Nickel Alloy Steels Data Book*, 3d ed., The International Nickel Company, New York, 1965.	G	4
21	Niemann, G., and H. Winter: *Maschinenelemente II*, Springer-Verlag, Berlin, 1983.	G	1 to 9
22	Niemann, G., and H. Winter: *Maschinenelemente III*, Springer-Verlag, Berlin, 1983.	G	1 to 9
23	Parrish, Geoffrey: *The Influence of Microstructure on the Properties of Case-Carburized Components*, American Society for Metals, Metals Park, Ohio, 1980.	G	3, 4, 7
24	Scoles, C. A., and R. Kirk: *Gear Metrology*, Macdonald Technical & Scientific, London, 1969.	G	5, 6
25	Siebert, C. A., D. V. Doane, and D. H. Breen: *The Hardenability of Steels*, American Society for Metals, Metals Park, Ohio, 1977.	G	4
26	Tuplin, W. A.: *Gear Design*, Industrial Press, New York, 1962.	G	1 to 9

	Book	Code	Chapter
27	Ainoura, M., and M. Yonekura: Research on High-Speed-Precision Gear Hobbing with the Carbide Hob and Unique High-Speed Hobbing Machine, presented at the Congres Mondial Des Engrenages, June 22–24, 1977.	P	6
28	Akazawa, M., T. Tejima, and T. Narita: Full Scale Test of High Speed, High Powered Gear Unit—Helical Gears of 25,000 PS at 200 m/s PLV, ASME Paper No. 80-C2/DET-4, 1980.	P	3, 7
29	Almen, J. O.: Facts and Fallacies of Stress Determination, AGMA P225, 1941.	P	2
30	Almen, J. O.: Surface Deterioration of Gear Teeth, Mechanical Wear, *Proc. MIT Conf.*, June 1948.	H	7

	Book	Code	Chapter
31	American Gear Manufacturers Assoc.: Progress Report by Automotive Gearing Committee Sec. II, Scoring Factor (PVT) Values of Gear Teeth, AGMA 101.02A, Oct. 1951.	H	2
32	American Gear Manufacturers Assoc.: Design Procedure for Aircraft Engine and Power Take-Off Bevel Gears, AGMA 431.01, 1964.	S	3
33	American Gear Manufacturers Assoc.: Rating the Strength of Spiral Bevel Gear Teeth, AGMA 223.01, 1964.	S	3
34	American Gear Manufacturers Assoc.: Rating the Strength of Straight Bevel and Zerol Bevel Gear Teeth, AGMA 222.02, 1964.	S	3
35	American Gear Manufacturers Assoc.: Surface Durability (Pitting) Formulas for Straight Bevel and Zerol Bevel Gear Teeth, AGMA 212.02, 1964.	S	3
36	American Gear Manufacturers Assoc.: Design of General Industrial Coarse-Pitch Cylindrical Wormgearing, AGMA 341.02, 1965.	S	3
37	American Gear Manufacturers Assoc.: Design of General Industrial Double-Enveloping Wormgears, AGMA 342.02, 1965.	S	3
38	American Gear Manufacturers Assoc.: Gear Scoring Design Guide for Aerospace Spur and Helical Power Gears, AGMA 217.01, 1965.	S	2, 3, 9
39	American Gear Manufacturers Assoc.: Design Procedure for Aircraft Engine and Power Take-Off Spur and Helical Gears, AGMA 411.02, 1966.	S	2, 3
40	American Gear Manufacturers Assoc.: Rating for the Surface Durability of Spiral Bevel Gears for Enclosed Drives, AGMA 216.01A, 1966.	S	3
41	American Gear Manufacturers Assoc.: Surface Durability (Pitting) of Spur, Helical, Herringbone and Bevel Gear Teeth, AGMA 215.01, 1966.	H	2, 3
42	American Gear Manufacturers Assoc.: Information Sheet for Strength of Spur, Helical, Herringbone and Bevel Gear Teeth, AGMA 225.01, Dec. 1967.	H	2, 3
43	American Gear Manufacturers Assoc.: Surface Temper Inspection Process, AGMA 230.01, 1968.	S	4
44	American Gear Manufacturers Assoc.: Practice for High-Speed Helical and Herringbone Gear Units, AGMA 421.06, 1969.	S	3
45	American Gear Manufacturers Assoc.: Helical and Herringbone Gearing for Rolling Mill Service, AGMA 323.01, 1969.	S	3

	Book	Code	Chapter
46	American Gear Manufacturers Assoc.: Design Practice for Helical and Herringbone Gears for Cylindrical Grinding Mills, Kilns, and Dryers, AGMA 321.05, 1970.	S	3
47	American Gear Manufacturers Assoc.: Information Sheet, Geometry Factors for Determining the Strength of Spur, Helical, Herringbone, and Bevel Gear Teeth, AGMA 226.01, 1970.	S	3
48	American Gear Manufacturers Assoc.: Practice for Single and Double-Reduction Cylindrical-Worm and Helical-Worm Speed Reducers, AGMA 440.04, 1971.	S	3
49	American Gear Manufacturers Assoc.: AGMA Gear Handbook, vol. 1: Gear Classification, Materials and Measuring Methods for Unassembled Gears, AGMA 390.03, 1973.	S	2, 3, 5
50	American Gear Manufacturers Assoc.: Design for Fine-Pitch Wormgearing, AGMA 374.04, 1973.	S	3
51	American Gear Manufacturers Assoc.: Design Manual for Fine-Pitch Gearing, AGMA 370.01, 1973.	S	3
52	American Gear Manufacturers Assoc.: Lubrication of Industrial Open Gearing, AGMA 251.02, 1974.	S	7
53	American Gear Manufacturers Assoc.: Gear-Cutting Tools, Fine- and Coarse-Pitch Hobs, AGMA 120.01, 1975.	S	6
54	American Gear Manufacturers Assoc.: Practice for Enclosed Speed Reducers or Increasers Using Spur, Helical, Herringbone and Spiral Bevel Gears, AGMA 420.04, 1975.	S	3
55	American Gear Manufacturers Assoc.: Design Guide for Vehicle Spur and Helical Gears, AGMA 170.01, 1976.	S	2, 3, 8
56	American Gear Manufacturers Assoc.: Gear Nomenclature (Geometry)—Terms, Definitions, Symbols, and Abbreviations, AGMA 112.05, June 1976.	S	1
57	American Gear Manufacturers Assoc.: Information Sheet—Systems Considerations for Critical Service Gear Drives, AGMA 427.01, 1976.	S	7
58	American Gear Manufacturers Assoc.: Practice for Single, Double-, and Triple-Reduction, Double-Enveloping Worm and Helical-Worm Speed Reducers, AGMA 441.04, 1978.	S	3
59	American Gear Manufacturers Assoc.: AGMA Standard for Metric Usage, AGMA 600.01, March 1979.	S	1 to 9
60	American Gear Manufacturers Assoc.: Nomenclature of Gear Tooth Failure Modes, ANSI and AGMA 110.04, Aug. 1980.	S	7
61	American Gear Manufacturers Assoc.: Lubrication of Industrial Enclosed Gear Drives, AGMA 250.04, 1981.	S	7

	Book	Code	Chapter
62	American Gear Manufacturers Assoc.: Rating the Pitting Resistance and Bending Strength of Spur and Helical Involute Gear Teeth, AGMA 218.01, 1982.	S	2, 3
63	American National Standard: Gear Drawing Standards—Part 1 for Spur, Helical, Double Helical and Rack, ANSI Y14.7.1, 1971.	S	2
64	American National Standard: Gear Drawing Standards—Part 2 for Bevel and Hypoid Gears, ANSI Y14.7.2, 1978.	S	2
65	American National Standard: Gear Drawing Standards—Part 3 for Crossed Helical, Worm, Spiroid and Helicon Gears, ANSI Y14.7.3, 1979.	S	2
66	American National Standard: Gear Drawing Standards—Part 4 for Involute Splines, ANSI Y14.7.4, 1981.	S	2
67	American Petroleum Institute: Special-Purpose Gear Units for Refinery Services, API Standard 613, 1977.	S	3
68	American Standard: Nomenclature of Gear-Tooth Wear and Failure, B6.12-1964 (also AGMA 110.03).	S	7
69	Antosiewicz, M.: New Techniques for Aligning and Maintaining Large Ring Gears, AGMA P159.04, 1981.	P	7
70	Archer, C.: Some Classification Aspects of Marine Reduction Gearing, International Symposium on Gearing and Power Transmissions, Tokyo, Aug. 30 to Sept. 3, 1981, Paper No. d-1.	P	3
71	Barber-Colman Co.: Azumi Skiving Hobs, Rockford, Illinois.	P	6
72	Barish, Thomas: How Sliding Affects Life of Rolling Surfaces, Penton Publishing Co., Cleveland, Ohio, 1960.	P	2, 3
73	Bartz, W. J.: Some Investigations of the Application of EHD Theory to Practical Gear Lubrication, Paper C6/72, Elastrohydrodynamic Lubrication, 1972 Symposium, Sec. I, Mech. E., London.	P	2, 3
74	Benton, M., and A. Seireg: Factors Influencing Instability and Resonances in Geared Systems, ASME Paper No. 80-C2/DET-8, 1980.	P	7
75	Binder, S., and J. C. Mack: Experience with Advanced High Performance Gear Steel, ASME Paper No. 80-C2/DET-77, 1980.	P	4
76	Bloch, Peter: Carbide Milling Surface Hardened Gears, presented at the Congrès Mondial des Engrenages, June 22–24, 1977.	P	5
77	Bloch, Peter: Analysis of Gear Cutting, ASME Paper No. 80-C2/DET-76, 1980.	P	5, 6

	Book	Code	Chapter
78	Blok, H: Les Températures de Surface dans les Conditions de Graissage Sous Pression Extreme, 2d World Petroleum Congress, Paris, 1937.	H	2, 3
79	Bloomfield, B.: Designing Face Gears, *Mach. Des.*, April 1947, pp. 129–134.	H	2, 3
80	Bodensieck, E. J.: A Stress-Life-Reliability Rating System for Gear and Rolling-Element Bearing Compressive Stress and Gear Root Bending Stress, AGMA P229.19, 1974.	P	3
81	Bohle, F.: Toward More Economical Gear Inspection, AGMA P239.05, 1957.	P	5
82	Bohle, F., and O. Saari: Spiroid Gears, AGMA P389.01, 1955.	P	2, 3
83	Borsoff, V. N.: On the Mechanism of Gear Lubrication, *J. Basic Eng.*, Vol. 81, No. 1, March 1959, p. 79.	P	2, 3
84	Borsoff, V. N.: Predicting the Scoring of Gears to Establish the Limits of Load, *Mach. Des.*, Jan. 7, 1965, p. 132.	P	2, 3
85	Bosch, M., and D. Klingelnberg: The Klingelnberg Spiral Bevel Gear Systems, AGMA P129.23, 1977.	P	5
86	Bowen, C. W.: The Practical Significance of Designing to Gear Pitting Fatigue Life Criteria, presented at the Sept. 26–30, 1977 meeting in Chicago, Illinois, ASME Paper No. 77-DET-122.	H	2, 3
87	Breen, D. H.: Fundamental Aspects of Gear Strength Requirements, presented at the AGMA Semi-Annual Meeting in Oak Brook, Illinois, Nov. 3–6, 1974, AGMA 229.17.	P	2, 3
88	Brownlie, K., and I. T. Young: Research, Development and Design for Marine Propulsion Geared Steam Turbines, presented to the Institution of Mechanical Engineers, London, England, 1969.	P	2, 3
89	Bryant, Richard C., and Darle W. Dudley: Which Right-Angle Gear System? *Prod. Eng.*, Nov. 7, 1960.	P	1
90	Buckingham, Earle: Dynamic Loads on Gear Teeth, Report of the ASME Special Research Committee on the Strength of Gear Teeth, American Society of Mechanical Engineers, New York, 1931.	H	2, 9
91	Candee, A. H.: Geometrical Determination of Tooth Form Factor, AGMA P223, 1941.	H	2, 3
92	Candee, A. H., and A. Zamis: Oversize of Wormgear Hobs, AGMA P129.09, 1953.	P	6
93	Castellani, G., and V. P. Castelli: Rating Gear Strength, ASME Paper No. 80-C2/DET-88, 1980.	P	3

	Book	Code	Chapter
94	Castellani, G.: Rating Gear Life, International Symposium on Gearing and Power Transmissions, Tokyo, Aug. 30 to Sept. 3, 1981, Paper No. c-38.	P	3
95	Castellani, G.: l'IFToMM Gearing Committee e la Riunione di Eindhoven, Organi di Trasmissione, Oct. 1982.	P	3
96	Chen, J. H., F. M. Juarbe, and M. A. Hanley: Factors Affecting Fatigue Strength of Nylon Gears, ASME Paper No. 80-C2/DET-104, 1980.	P	3
97	Cheng, H. S., and B. Sternlicht: A Numerical Solution for the Pressure, Temperature and Film Thickness between Two Infinitely Long, Lubricated Rolling and Sliding Cylinders Under Heavy Loads, *J. Basic Eng.*, Sept. 1965.	H	2
98	Chesters, W. T.: Surface Hardening of Large Gears, *J. Iron Steel Inst.*, Vol. 208, Nov. 1970, p. 982.	P	4
99	Climax Molybdenum Co.: EX Steels, Greenwich, Connecticut.	P	4
100	Collins, L. J.: Gears, Their Application, Design and Manufacture, AGMA P109.01, 1947.	P	3, 5
101	Collins, L. J.: Developments in Gear Design and Their Lubrication Requirements, ASTM Tech. Pub. 92, 1949, pp. 9–13.	P	2, 3
102	Coniglio, J. W.: Economics of CNC Gear Gashing vs. Large D. P. Hobbing, presented at the AGMA Fall Technical Meeting in New Orleans, Louisiana, Oct. 11–13, 1982, AGMA P129.26.	P	5, 6
103	Coy, J. J., D. P. Townsend, and E. V. Zaretsky: Dynamic Capacity and Surface Fatigue Life for Spur and Helical Gears, ASME Paper No. 75-Lub-19, 1975.	P	3
104	Crook, A. W.: The Lubrication of Rollers—Part IV, *Phil. Trans. Royal Soc.*, London, Series A 255, 1963 p. 281.	H	2
105	Dawson, P. H.: Effect of Metallic Contact on the Pitting of Lubricated Rolling Surfaces, *J. Mech. Eng. Sci.*, Vol. 4, No. 1, 1962.	P	2, 3
106	DIN: Wälzfräser für Stirnrader, DIN 8002, Jan. 1955, and DIN 3968, Sept. 1960.	S	6
107	DIN: Toleranzen für Stirnrädverzahnungen, DIN 3962 and DIN 3963, Aug. 1978.	S	2, 3, 5
108	Dolan, T. J., and E. I. Broghamer: A Photoelastic Study of the Stresses in Gear Tooth Fillets, *Univ. Illinois Eng. Expt. Sta. Bull.*, No. 335, March 1942.	H	2, 3
109	Drago, R. J., and F. W. Brown: The Analytical and Experimental Evaluation of Resonant Response in High-Speed, Lightweight, Highly Loaded Gearing, ASME Paper No. 80-C2/DET-22, 1980.	P	3, 7

	Book	Code	Chapter
110	Drago, R. J., and R. V. Lutthans: An Experimental Investigation of the Combined Effects of Rim Thickness and Pitch Diameter on Spur Gear Tooth Root and Fillet Stresses, AGMA P229.22, Oct. 1981.	P	3
111	Drago, Raymond J.: An Improvement in the Conventional Analysis of Gear Tooth Bending Fatigue Strength, AGMA P229.24, 1982.	P	3
112	Dudley, D. W.: Graphical Determination of Gear Contact Ratios, *Prod. Eng.*, March 1948, pp. 152–155.	P	3
113	Dudley, D. W.: How to Grind Medium-Pitch Gears, *Am. Mach.*, March 10, 1949, pp. 94–97.	P	5
114	Dudley, D. W.: Modification of Gear Tooth Profiles, *Prod. Eng.*, Vol. 20, Sept. 1949, pp. 126–131.	H	3, 8
115	Dudley, D. W.: Estimating the Weight of Single Reduction Gear Sets, *Prod. Eng.*, May 1950, pp. 84–89.	H	2
116	Dudley, Darle W.: How to Design Involute Splines, *Prod. Eng.*, Oct. 28, 1957, p. 75.	P	2
117	Dudley, Darle W.: When Splines Need Stress Control, *Prod. Eng.*, Dec. 23, 1957, p. 56.	P	2
118	Dudley, D. W.: How Increased Hardness Reduces the Size of Gear Sets, reprinted from the issue of November 9, 1964, *Prod. Eng.*	P	3
119	Dudley, Darle W.: Successes and Failures in Space Gearing, presented at the SAE/ASME Air Transport and Space Meeting in New York, April 27–30, 1964.	P	3, 7
120	Dudley, Darle W.: Elastohydrodynamic Behaviour Observed in Gear Tooth Action, presented to the Institution of Mechanical Engineers, Leeds, England, Sept. 1965.	P	2, 3
121	Dudley, Darle W.: How to Pick Gears for Performance, Mech. Eng., New York, Nov. 1965.	G	1, 2
122	Dudley, Darle W.: Proposed Application Factors for Industrial and High Speed Gearing, presented at the AGMA Semi-Annual Meeting in Denver, Colorado, Oct. 26–29, 1969, AGMA 159.02.	G	3
123	Dudley, Darle W.: The Development of Long Life Epicyclic Gearing for Industrial Gas Turbines, presented to AGMA Semi-Annual Meeting, Oct. 25–28, 1970, St. Louis, Missouri, AGMA 219.07.	P	3
124	Dudley, Darle W.: Vehicle Gearing—A Panel Presentation as Part of *The History and Present Status of AGMA Standards*, AGMA P109.31, 1972.	P	2, 3

	Book	Code	Chapter
125	Dudley, D. W.: Design and Development of Close-Coupled, High Performance Epicyclic Gear Unit for Gas Turbines at 4600-HP Rating and 10:1 Ratio, ASME Paper No. 75-GT-109, 1974.	P	3
126	Dudley, Darle W.: Load Rating Practices of Carburized and Nitrided Gears, presented at the 10th Round Table Conference on Marine Gearing, Brunnen, Switzerland, Sept. 25–26, 1975.	G	4
127	Dudley, Darle W.: High Speed Gear Wear and Damage, presented to the 11th Round Table Conference on Marine Gearing, Chatham, Massachusetts, Oct. 1977.	P	3, 7
128	Dudley, Darle W.: Load Rating of Helical Gears After Wear on the Tooth Flanks, presented at the Congrès Mondial des Engrenages, Paris, France, 1977.	P	3, 7
129	Dudley, Darle W.: Characteristics of Gear Wear, presented at the World Symposium on Gears and Gear Transmissions, Dubrovnik, Yugoslavia, 1978.	G	3, 7
130	Dudley, Darle W.: Gear Wear, *Wear Control Handbook*, ed. by M. Peterson and W. Winer, American Society of Mechanical Engineers, New York, 1980, p. 755.	G	3, 7
131	Dudley, Darle W.: Characteristics of Regimes of Gear Lubrication, International Symposium on Gearing & Power Transmissions, Tokyo, 1981.	G	2, 3, 7
132	Dudley, D. W., and H. Poritsky: Cutting and Hobbing Gears and Worms, presented at AGMA Semi-Annual Meeting, AGMA P241, Oct. 1943.	H	5, 6
133	Poritsky, H., and D. W. Dudley: On Cutting and Hobbing Gears and Worms, Trans. ASME, 1943.	P	5, 6
134	Dudley, Darle W. and Robert E. Purdy: The Quest for the Ultimate in Gear Load Carrying Capacity, Society of Automotive Engineers, Paper No. 670285, 1967.	P	3
135	Dyson, A., H. Naylor, and A. R. Wilson: The Measurement of Oil-Film Thickness in Elastohydrodynamic Contacts. Elastohydrodynamic Lubrication, *Mech. Eng.*, Vol. 180, Part 3B, 1965.	P	2, 3
136	Ehrlenspiel, K.: Statistical Investigation on High-Speed Gear Failures—Possibilities to Reduce Failures, ASME Paper No. 72-PTG-32, Oct. 1972.	P	7
137	Erler, John: Cr-Mo and Cr-Mo-V Nitriding Steels, *Met. Prog.*, Dec. 1966, p. 232.	P	4
138	Ernst, C. E., R. V. Adair, and G. L. Cox: Flame Hardened Ductile Irons, reprinted with supplement from *Mater. Methods*, Nov. 1955.	P	4

	Book	Code	Chapter
139	Errichello, R.: An Efficient Algorithm for Obtaining the Gear Strength Geometry Factor on a Programmable Calculator, AGMA P139.03, 1981.	P	3
140	Faulstich, H. I.: Actual Trend of Development and Application of Large Hobbing Machines, presented at the Congrès Mondial des Engrenages, June 22–24, 1977.	P	5
141	Fellows Corp.: Gear Shaper Cutters, Springfield, Vermont.	P	6
142	Fowle, T.: Gear Lubrication: Relating Theory to Practice, *ASLE Lubr. Eng.*, Vol. 32, No. 1, Jan. 1976.	P	3, 7
143	Francis, Victor, and Joseph Silvagi: Face Gear Design Factors, *Prod. Eng.*, July 1950, pp. 117–121.	P	2, 3
144	Frushour, R. H., and P. E. Grieb: Borazon CBN Application Technology—Today and Tomorrow, presented at the International Tech Conference and Exhibition, Abrasive Engineering Society, 1976.	P	5, 6
145	Fujita, K., and A. Yoshida: Surface Durability of Steel Rollers (In the Cases of Case-Hardened and of Nitrided Rollers), *Bull. JSME*, Vol. 21, No. 154, April 1978, p. 761.	P	3, 4
146	Fujita, K., A. Yoshida, and K. Akamatsu: A Study on Strength and Failure of Induction-Hardened Chromium-Molybdenum Steel Spur Gears, *Bull. JSME*, Vol. 22, No. 164, Feb. 1979, p. 242.	P	3, 4
147	Fujita, K., A. Yoshida, and K. Nakase: Surface Durability of Induction-Hardened 0.45 Per Cent Carbon Steel and Its Optimum Case Depth, *Bull. JSME*, Vol. 22, No. 169, July 1979, p. 994.	P	3, 4
148	Gates, T. S., and J. R. Newman: Modern Methods of Finishing Gears by Shaving, Honing, and Grinding, AGMA P129.16, 1965.	P	5
149	Gauvin, R., P. Girard, and H. Yelle: Investigation of the Running Temperature of Plastic/Steel Gear Pairs, ASME Paper No. 80-C2/DET-108, 1980.	P	3, 7
150	Gleason Machine Division: Straight Bevel Gear Design, Rochester, New York, 1980.	S	3, 9
151	Gleason Works: Zerol Bevel Gear System, Rochester, New York, 1978.	S	3, 9
152	Gleason Works: Installation of Bevel Gears, Rochester, New York, 1980.	P	7
153	Gleason Works: Spiral Bevel Gear System, Rochester, New York, 1980.	S	3, 9

	Book	Code	Chapter
154	Glover, J. H.: How to Construct Ratio and Efficiency Formulas for Planetary Gear Trains, presented at AGMA Semi-Annual Meeting, Oct. 26–29, 1969, AGMA 279.01.	P	3
155	Godfrey, D.: Boundary Lubrication. Interdisciplinary Approach to Friction and Wear, *NASA SP-181*, 1968, p. 335.	P	2, 3
156	Gowens, B. J. McD., and F. E. Porter: Naval Service Experience with Surface Hardened Gears, *Proc. Inst. Mech. Engrs.*, Vol. 184, Part 3 O, Paper 6, 1970.	P	2, 3, 7
157	Graham, R. C., A. Olver, and P. B. Macpherson: An Investigation into the Mechanisms of Pitting in High-Hardness Carburized Steels, ASME Paper No. 80-C2/DET-118, 1980.	P	2, 3, 7
158	Greening, J. H., R. J. Barlow, and W. G. Loveless: Load Sharing on the Teeth of Double Enveloping Worm Gear, ASME Paper No. 80-C2/DET-43, 1980.	P	3
159	Haas, L. L.: Latest Developments in the Manufacture of Large Spiral Bevel and Hypoid Gears, ASME Paper No. 80-C2/DET-119, 1980.	P	5
160	Haizuka, S., C. Naruse, R. Nemoto, and K. Nagahama: Studies on Limiting Load for Scoring of Crossed Helical Gears, *Bull. JSME*, Vol. 24, No. 191, May 1981, p. 863.	P	3
161	Hall, W. F.: Tooth by Tooth Induction Hardening Vehicle Gearing, presented at the AGMA Semi-Annual Meeting in New Orleans, Louisiana, Nov. 4–7, 1973, AGMA 109.34.	P	4
162	Harrison, W. H.: High-Speed Gears: Important Features of Design and Maintenance, *Proc. Instn. Mech. Engrs.*, Vol. 184, Part 3 O, 1969–1970, p. 68.	P	3, 7
163	Hartman, Martin A.: Fuel Additive: A New System and Lubricant for Rocket Engine Gearboxes, *Lubr. Eng.*, March 1962.	P	3, 7
164	Hayashi, Kunikazu, Susumu Aiuchi, and Phan Van Hien: Bending Fatigue Strength of Gear Teeth under Random Loading, ASME Paper No. 77-DET-120, 1977.	P	3, 8
165	Hayashi, Kunikazu, and Takehide Sayama: Load Distribution in Marine Reduction Gears, *Jpn. Soc. Mech. Eng. Bull.*, Vol. 5, May 1962, p. 18.	P	3
166	Henriot, Georges: Reflexions on the Longitudinal Distribution Factor $K_{H\beta}$ of the I.S.O. Procedure, AGMA P209.13, 1981.	P	3, 9
167	Hertz, Heinrich: On the Contact of Solid Elastic Bodies and on Hardness, *J. Math.*, Vol. 92, 1881, pp. 156–171.	H	2, 3
168	Hildreth, R. S.: Grinding and Honing of Gears, AGMA P129.16A, 1965.	P	5

	Book	Code	Chapter
169	Hirt, Manfred: German and American Quality System of Spur, Helical and Bevel Gears—Influence of Gear Quality on Costs and Load Capacity, ASME Paper No. 80-C2/DET-18, 1980.	P	2, 5
170	Hirt, M., and H. Weiss: Increase of Load Capacity by Use of Large Case-Hardened Gears, AGMA P219.11, 1981.	P	4
171	Hlebanja, Jože: Minimale Zähnezahl Bei Doppelseitiger Sondrverzahnungen, Scientific Society of Mechanical Engineers, 4th Budapest Conference on Gears.	P	3
172	Hoffman, B. A.: A Comparison of the AGMA and DIN Quality Systems, AGMA P239.17, 1982.	P	2, 5
173	Howes, M. A. H., and J. P. Sheehan: The Effect of Composition and Microstructure on the Pitting Fatigue of Carburized Steel Cases, Society of Automotive Engineers Paper No. 740222, 1974.	P	3, 4
174	Huntress, Edward A.: A New Way to Cut Gears, *Am. Mach.*, May 1979.	P	5, 6
175	Ichimaru, K., A. Nakajima, and F. Hirano: Effect of Asperity Interaction on Pitting in Rollers and Gears, ASME Paper No. 80-C2/DET-36, 1980.	P	2, 3
176	Imwalle, D. E., O. A. LaBath, and R. N. Hutchinson: A Review of Recent Gear Rating Developments ISO/AGMA Comparison Study, ASME Paper No. 80-C2/DET-25, 1980.	P	3, 9
177	Imwalle, D. E., and O. A. LaBath: Differences Between AGMA and ISO Rating Systems, presented at the AGMA Semi-Annual Meeting in Toronto, Canada, Oct. 10–14, 1981, AGMA 219.15.	P	3, 9
178	Ishibashi, A., and S. Hoyashita: Appreciable Increase in Pitting Limit of a Through Hardened Steel, ASME Paper No. 80-C2/DET-28, 1980.	P	3
179	Ishibashi, A., and S. Tanaka: Effects of Hunting Gear Ratio upon Surface Durability of Gear Teeth, ASME Paper No. 80-C2/DET-35, 1980.	P	3
180	ISO/TC 60: Principles for the Calculation of Load Capacity for Spur and Helical Gears, Part 4, Calculation of Scuffing Load Capacity, Nov. 1977.	P	2, 3
181	Jablonowski, Joseph: Inside Gleason's New Hobber, *Am. Mach.*, March 1982, p. 141.	P	5
182	Jones, T. P.: Fifteen Years Development of High-Power Epicyclic Gears, *Trans. Inst. Marine Engrs.*, Vol. 79, No. 8, 1967, p. 273.	P	3
183	Kelley, B. W.: A New Look at the Scoring Phenomena of Gears, *Trans. SAE*, 1952.	H	2, 3

	Book	Code	Chapter
184	Kelley, B. W.: Gear Hob Tolerancing System, AGMA P129.19, 1974.	P	6
185	Kelley, B. W., and A. J. Lemanski: Lubrication of Involute Gearing, Conference on Lubrication and Wear, Institute of Mechanical Engineering, London, Sept. 1967.	P	3, 7
186	Klimo, V., A. Pažak and J. Chrobák: Tribological Problems of the Mesh of Teeth of Cylindrical Worm Gears, International Symposium on Gearing and Power Transmissions, Tokyo, Aug. 30 to Sept. 3, 1981, Paper No. a-22.	P	3, 7
187	Kojima, Masakazu: The Geometrical Analysis on Gear Skiving of Internal Gears, ASME Paper No. 77-DET-133, 1977.	P	5, 6
188	Kojima, M., and H. I. Faulstich: Computer Aided Skiving of Internal Gears, ASME Paper No. 80-C2/DET-72, 1980.	P	5, 6
189	Krishnamurthy, R., and V. C. Venkatesh: On Pitting Characteristics of Gears, ASME Paper No. 80-C2/DET-26, 1980.	P	2, 3
190	Kron, H. O.: Gear Tooth Sub-Surface Stress Analysis, Congres Mondial des Engrenages, Paper A 10, 1977.	P	3
191	Kubo, Aizoh: On the Dynamic Factor for Gear Strength Calculation, Kyoto University, Kyoto, Japan, July 1980.	P	3, 9
192	Kubo, A.: Estimation of Gear Performance, International Symposium on Gearing and Power Transmissions, Tokyo, Aug. 30 to Sept. 3, 1981, Paper No. c-34.	P	7, 8, 9
193	Kubo, A., T. Aida, and H. Fukuma: Examination of the Dynamic Factor K_v for Gear Strength Calculation Based on the ISO Recommendation ISO TC60/WG6 Document 166 and Comparison between ISO and AGMA Recommendation, Kyoto University, Kyoto, Japan, 1980.	P	3, 9
194	Kubo, A., T. Okamoto, and N. Kurokawa: Contact Stress Between Rollers with Surface Irregularity, ASME Paper No. 80-C2/DET-10, 1980.	P	3, 5
195	Kuehl, Ronald J.: Hobbing & Shaping Notes, Barber-Colman Co., Rockford, Illinois, 1969.	P	5, 6
196	LaBath, Octave A.: Rating Trend Differences Between AGMA and ISO for Vehicle Gears, presented at the AGMA Vehicle Gearing Committee Meeting, Rochester, New York, May 5, 1981, AGMA 209.12.	P	9
197	Laskin, I.: Prediction of Gear Noise from Design Data, AGMA P299.03, 1968.	P	7
198	Leach, E. F., and B. W. Kelley: Temperature—The Key to Lubricant Capacity, presented at the ASLE/ASME International Lubrication Conference, Washington, D.C., Oct. 13–16, 1964.	P	3, 7

	Book	Code	Chapter
199	Lemanski, A. J.: Gear Design, Society of Automotive Engineers Paper No. 680381, July 1968.	G	3
200	Lewis, Wilfred: Investigation of the Strength of Gear Teeth, *Proc. Eng. Club*, Philadelphia, 1893.	H	2
201	Loveless, W. G., and R. J. Barlow: Some Applications of Advanced Instrumentation Techniques to Double Enveloping Worm Gear Testing, presented at the AGMA Semi-Annual Meeting in Atlanta, Georgia, Oct. 17, 1978, AGMA 109.40.	P	3, 7
202	Loy, W. E.: Hard Gear Processing with Azumi Skiving Hobs, AGMA P129.27, 1982.	P	6
203	Lutz, Claude, and B. W. Cluff: An Emerging Technology: Form Grinding with Borazon, presented at the SME International Tool & Manufacturing Engineering Conference in Philadelphia, Pennsylvania, May 19, 1982.	P	5, 6
204	Lynch, D. W., T. J. Snodgrass, and T. T. Woodson: Powder Metallurgy—A New Process for Manufacturing Gears, AGMA P249.02, 1951.	P	4
205	Lynwander, Peter: Gear Tooth Scoring Design Considerations, presented at the AGMA Semi-Annual Meeting in Toronto, Canada, Oct. 12–14, 1981, AGMA P219.10.	P	3, 8
206	Martinaglia, L.: Thermal Behavior of High-Speed Gears and Tooth Corrections for Such Gear, ASME/AGMA International Symposium on Gears & Transmissions, San Francisco, California, Oct. 11, 1972.	H	3, 7
207	Maxwell, J. H.: Vibration Analysis Pinpoints Coupling Problems, *Hydrocarbon Process.*, Jan. 1980, p. 95.	P	7
208	McCormick, Doug: The Cost of Gear Accuracy, *Des. Eng.*, Jan. 1981.	P	5
209	McIntire, W. L., R. C. Malott, and T. A. Lyon: Bending Strength of Spur and Helical Gear Teeth, AGMA P229.11, 1967.	P	3
210	Meng, H. R.: On Problems of Surface Pressure in Gear Load-Carrying Capacity Calculation, International Symposium on Gearing and Power Transmissions, Tokyo, Aug. 30 to Sept. 3, 1981, Paper No. b-27.	P	2, 3
211	Mente, Hans-Peter: Roughing Large Gears by Form Milling or Hobbing, *Ind. Prod. Eng.*, Munich, Nov. 5, 1981.	P	5
212	Merritt, H. E.: Contact Stresses in Crossed-Axis Cylinders and Crossed Helical Gears, *The Engineer*, March 1965, p. 543.	P	3
213	Michaelis, K.: Calculation of Scoring Resistance According to Niemann and Seitzinger for Spur and Helical Gears, ISO 60/6 N126E, 1972.	P	2, 3

	Book	Code	Chapter
214	Milton, Roy: Large Bearing Gears Shape Up, *Mod. Mach. Shop*, Feb. 1983.	P	5
215	Mudd, G. C.: A Numerical Means of Predicting the Fatigue Performance of Nitride-Hardened Gears, *Proc. Inst. Mech. Engrs.*, Vol. 184, 3 O, Paper 12, 1970.	P	3, 4
216	Mudd, G. C., and E. J. Myers: Design Considerations in Large Mill Gears, David Brown Gear Industries Limited, Huddersfield, West Yorkshire, England.	P	3
217	Mudd, G. C., and E. J. Myers: Load Distribution Factors in Proposed AGMA and ISO Rating Procedures, AGMA 219.14, Oct. 1981.	P	3, 7
218	Munro, R. G.: Gear Transmission Error, presented at the AGMA Aerospace Gearing Committee Meeting in Portsmouth, New Hampshire, Aug. 24–25, 1967, AGMA 239.10.	P	5
219	Munro, R. G.: The Interpretation of Results from Gear Measuring Instruments, presented at the British Gear Manufacturers Assoc. Technical Meeting, May 14, 1968.	P	5
220	Murphy, N.: Diagnosing Unsuspected Errors in Shaved Gears, *Mach. Prod. Eng.*, April 23, 1975.	P	5
221	Murrell, P. W.: Developments in High Powered Marine Epicyclic Gearing 30,000 S.H.P. Prototype Trials Results, International Symposium on Gearing & Power Transmissions, Tokyo, 1981.	P	2, 3
222	Nagano, K., and M. Ainoura: A Research on High Speed Hobbing with High Speed Steel Hob, ASME Paper No. 80-C2/DET-50, 1980.	P	6
223	Nagano, K., and M. Ainoura: The Cutting Performance of Tin-Coated High Speed Steel Hob, International Symposium on Gearing and Power Transimssions, Tokyo, Aug. 30 to Sept. 3, 1981, Paper No. a-31.	P	6
224	Nagorny, G. W., and R. A. Stutchfield: Gear Noise—The Generation of Rotational Harmonic Frequencies in Marine Propulsion Gears, AGMA P299.06A, 1981.	P	7
225	Niemann, G., H. Rettig, and G. Lechner: Some Possibilities to Increase the Load-Carrying Capacity of Gears, Soc. of Automotive Engineers, Paper No. 468A, 1962.	P	3
226	Nityanandan, P. M.: Surface Durability of Low Hardness Steel, Gears India Pvt. Ltd., Madras, India, unpublished paper presented at the IFToMM Gearing Committee Meeting in Eindhoven, Holland, 1982.	P	3

	Book	Code	Chapter
227	Oda, Satoshi, and Yasuji Shimatomi: Study on Bending Fatigue Strength of Helical Gears, 1st Report, Effect of Helix Angle on Bending Fatigue Strength, *Bull. JSME*, Vol. 23, No. 177, March 1980, Paper No. 177-16.	P	3
228	Oda, Satoshi, Yasuji Shimatomi, and Nobuyuki Kawai: Study on Bending Fatigue Strength of Helical Gears (2nd Report, Bending Fatigue Strength of Casehardened Helical Gears), *Bull. JSME*, Vol. 23, No. 177, March 1980, Paper No. 177-17.	P	3
229	Oda, Satoshi and Koji Tsubokura: Effects of Addendum Modification on Bending Fatigue Strength of Spur Gears (3rd Report, Cast Iron and Cast Steel Gears), *Bull. JSME*, Vol. 24, No. 190, Paper No. 190-15, April 1981.	P	3
230	Orcutt, F. K.: Experimental Study of Elastohydrodynamic Lubrication, ASLE Paper presented at the Annual Meeting in Detroit, Michigan, May 1965.	P	2, 3
231	Parker, S. C.: Why Borazon?, *Tool.*, Vol. 28, No. 12, Dec. 1974, p. 40.	P	5
232	Pederson, R., and R. L. Rice: Case Crushing of Carburized and Hardened Gears, *Trans. SAE*, 1961, p. 250.	H	3, 7
233	Pfenninger, R., and E. Bartholet: The Trend Toward Gear Grinding, *Manuf. Eng.*, June 1978.	P	5
234	Pittion, B.: Problems in Induction Hardening of Gear Teeth, presented at the Congrès Mondial des Engrenages, Paris, June 22–24, 1977.	P	4
235	Polymer Corp.: Nylatron Nylon Gear Design Manual, Reading, Pennsylvania, 1974.	P	4
236	Poritsky, H., and D. W. Dudley: Conjugate Action of Involute Helical Gears with Parallel or Inclined Axes, *Quar. Appl. Mech.*, Vol. 6, No. 3, Oct. 1948.	G	1, 2
236*a*	Portisky, H.,and D. W. Dudley On Cutting and Hobbing Gears and Worms, Trans. ASME, 1943.		
237	Poritsky, H., A. D. Sutton, and A. Pernick: Distribution of Tooth Load along a Pinion, *J. Appl. Mech.*, Vol. 12, pp. A78-A86, 1945; Vol. 13, pp. A246–A249, 1946.	P	3
238	Radzimovsky, E. I.: How to Find Efficiency, Speed, and Power in Planetary Gear Drives, *Mach. Des.*, June 11, 1959, p. 144.	P	3
239	Reswick, J. B.: Dynamic Loads on Spur and Helical Gear Teeth, *Trans. ASME*, Vol. 77, No. 5, July 1955, p. 635.	P	2
240	Rettig, H., and H. J. Plewe: Lebensdauer und Verschleissverhalten Langsam Laufender Zahnrader, Antriebstechnik 16, No. 6, 1977.	P	2, 3

	Book	Code	Chapter
241	Rice, C. S.: Gear Shaper Cutters, AGMA P129.22, 1977.	P	6
242	Rice, Carl S.: Gear Production Update, *Manuf. Eng.*, April 1979.	P	5, 6
243	Rieger, N. F.: Gear-Excited Torsional Vibrations of Machine Drive Systems, AGMA P109.20, 1968.	P	7
244	Ryder, E. A.: A Gear and Lubricant Tester—Measures Tooth Strength or Surface Effects, *ASTM Bull.*, 148, Oct. 1947, pp. 69–73.	P	3, 7
245	Schaffer, George: Roll-Finishing of Larger Gears, *Am. Mach.*, June 1, 1975.	P	5, 6
246	Schmidt, G. R., W. Pinnekamp, and A. Wunder: Optimum Tooth Profile Correction of Helical Gears, ASME Paper No. 80-C2/DET-110, 1980.	P	3, 8
247	Seabrook, John B. and Darle W. Dudley: Results of a Fifteen Year Program of Flexural Fatigue Testing of Gear Teeth, Trans ASME, 1963.	H	2, 3, 4
248	Seireg, A., and T. Conry: Optimum Design of Gear Systems for Surface Durability, *ASLE Trans.*, Vol. 11, No. 4, Oct. 1968, p. 321.	P	3
249	Sharma, V. K., D. H. Breen, and G. H. Walter: An Analytical Approach for Establishing Case Depth Requirements in Carburized Gears, presented at the Sept. 26–30, 1977 meeting in Chicago, Illinois, ASME Paper 77-DET-152.	H	3
250	Sheehan, J. P., and M. A. H. Howes: The Role of Surface Finish in Pitting Fatigue of Carburized Steel, Society of Automotive Engineers Paper No. 730580, 1973.	P	3
251	Shipley, E. E.: Gear Failure, *Mach. Des.*, Vol. 39, No. 28, Dec. 7, 1969, p. 152.	P	7
252	Shipley, E.: Failure Modes of Gears, ASME paper presented to the forum on Gear Manufacture and Performance, Detroit, Oct. 1973.	P	7
253	Shipley, E. E.: Failure Analysis of Coarse-Pitch, Hardened and Ground Gears, presented at the AGMA Fall Technical Meeting in New Orleans, Louisiana, Oct. 11–13, 1982, AGMA P229.26.	P	7
254	Shotter, B. A.: Experiments with a Disc Machine to Determine the Influence of Surface Finish on Gear Performance, International Conference on Gearing, London, 1958.	P	3, 5
255	Shotter, B. A.: Scuffing and Pitting, Recent Observations Modify the Traditional Concepts, World Symposium on Gears and Gear Transmissions, Dubrovnik, Yugoslavia, 1978.	P	3

	Book	Code	Chapter
256	Sigg, Hans: Profile and Longitudinal Corrections on Involute Gears, presented at the AGMA Semi-Annual Meeting in Chicago, Illinois, Oct. 24–27, 1965, AGMA 109.16.	P	9
257	Smith, J. O.: The Effect of Range of Stress on the Fatigue Strength of Metals, *Univ. Illinois Eng. Exp. Stn. Bull.*, No. 334, 1942.	H	2, 3
258	Smith, J. O. and Chang Keng Liu: Stresses Due to Tangential and Normal Loads on an Elastic Solid with Application to Some Contact Stress Problems, *J. Appl. Mech.*, June 1953, p. 157.	H	2, 3
259	Society of Automotive Engineers, Premium Aircraft-Quality Steel Cleanliness, Aerospace Material Specification AMS 2300B, 1973.	S	2, 3, 4
260	Society of Automotive Engineers, Aircraft Quality Steel Cleanliness, Aerospace Material Specification AMS 2301E, 1974.	S	2, 3, 4
261	Srikanthan, G.: Synthesis of Tooth Profiles for Helical Gears, International Symposium on Gearing & Power Transmissions, Tokyo, 1981.	P	3
262	Stauffer, Robert N.: Gleason's New Gear Hobber Advances Spur and Helical Gear Machining, *Manuf. Eng.*, May 1982, p. 91.	P	5
263	Stolzle, K., H. Winter, G. Henriot, and E. J. Wellauer: German, French, and AGMA Gear Rating Practices, AGMA P229.15, 1970.	P	3
264	Taber, D. S., D. J. Edwards, J. J. Giammaria, and A. Commichau: A Look to the Future in Industrial Gear Lubricants, AGMA P254.30, 1970.	P	7
265	Tarasov, L.P.: Some Factors Influencing the Quality of Ground Gears and Worms, AGMA P109.02, 1948.	P	5
266	Terauchi, Y., H. Nadano, and M. Nohara: Effect of Tooth Profile Modification on Scoring Resistance of Spur Gears, ASME Paper No. 80-C2/DET-19, 1980.	P	3, 8
267	Tersch, Richard W.: Finishing Gear Teeth by Roll-Forming Processes, SME Paper No. MF70-263, 1970.	P	5, 6
268	Theberge, J. E., B. Arkles, P. J. Cloud, and R. Goodhue: Gear and Bearing Designs with Lubricated and Reinforced Thermoplastics, 28th Annual Technical Conference of the Society of the Plastics Industry, Inc., 1973.	P	3, 4, 7
269	Thoma, F. A.: The Load Distribution Factor as Applied to High Speed and Wide Face Helical Gears, AGMA P229.10, 1965.	P	3

	Book	Code	Chapter
270	Thoma, F. A.: Pitting Can Be Caused by Inadequate Lubrication, ASME Paper 77-DET-122 presented at the Sept. 26–30, 1977 meeting in Chicago, Illinois.	P	3, 7
271	Thompson, Alan M.: Testing of Fine Pitch Gears—Single Flank Testing, Double Flank Testing, Soc. of Manufacturing Engineers Paper No. IQ80-920, 1980.	P	5
272	Timken Company: Practical Data for Metallurgists, Canton, Ohio, 1983.	G	4
273	Tobe, Toshimi, and Katsumi Inoue: Longitudinal Load Distribution Factor for Straddle- and Overhang-Mounted Spur Gears, ASME Paper No. 80-C2/DET-45, 1980.	P	3
274	Tordion, G. V.: The Mechanical Impedance Approach to the Dynamics (Torsional Vibrations) of Geared Systems, AGMA P209.04, 1963.	P	7
275	Townsend, Dennis P.: Lubrication Considerations in Gear Design, presented to AGMA meeting in New Orleans, Louisiana on Feb. 11–12, 1971.	P	2, 3, 7
276	Townsend, D. P., and L. S. Akin: Analytical and Experimental Spur Gear Tooth Temperature as Affected by Operating Variables, ASME Paper No. 80-C2/DET-34, 1980.	P	3, 7
277	Townsend, D. P., and E. V. Zaretsky: Endurance and Failure Characteristics of Modified VASCO X-2, CBS 600 and AISI 9310 Spur Gears, NASA Lewis Research Center, Cleveland, Ohio, 1977.	P	4
278	Trapp, Hans-Jurgen: Quality Achievements in Spiral Bevel Gears by the HPG-Method, AGMA P239.16, 1981.	G	5
279	Triemel, J.: Grinding with Cubic Boron Nitride, 14, International Machine Tool Design & Research Conference (MTDC), Manchester, England, Sept. 1973.	P	5
280	Tucker, A.: Dynamic Loads on Gear Teeth Design Applications, ASME Paper 71-DE-1, April 1971.	P	3, 9
281	Tucker, A. I.: Bevel Gears at 203 Meters per Second (40,000 FPM), ASME Paper No. 77-DET-178, 1977.	P	3, 7
282	Tucker, A. I.: The Gear Design Process, ASME Paper No. 80-C2/DET-13, 1980.	P	1, 2
283	Tuplin, W. A.: Dynamic Loads on Gear Teeth, *Mach. Des.*, Vol. 25, Oct. 1953.	P	2, 3, 9
284	Ueno, Taku, K. Terashima, and K. Hidaka: On the Corner Wear of Hob Teeth, presented at the Congres Mondial Des Engrenages, June 22–24, 1977.	P	6

	Book	Code	Chapter
285	Ueno, Taku, Yasutsune Ariura, and Tsutomu Nakanishi: Surface Durability of Case Carburized Gears—On a Phenomenon of "Grey-Staining" on Tooth Surfaces, presented at the ASME meeting Aug. 18–21, 1980, San Francisco, California.	P	3, 7
286	Volcy, G. C.: Deterioration of Marine Gear Teeth, World Congress on Gearing, Paris, 1977.	P	3
287	Volcy, G. C.: Gearing Damages and Ship Structure Flexibility, International Symposium on Gearing and Power Transmissions, Tokyo, Aug. 30 to Sept. 3, 1981, Paper No. d-2.	P	7
288	Wadhwa, S. K.: Computed Geometry Factor for Hobbed Spur Gears, AGMA P229.08, 1964.	H	3
289	Walker, H.: Gear Tooth Deflection and Profile Modification, *Engineer*, Vol. 166, pp. 409–412, 434–436, 1938; Vol. 170, pp. 102–104. 1940.	H	3, 8
290	Walter, G. H.: Computer Oriented Gear Steel Design Procedure, presented at the AGMA Semi-Annual Meeting in Oak Brook, Illinois, Nov. 3–6, 1974, AGMA 109.35.	P	4
291	Way, S.: Pitting Due to Rolling Contact, *Trans. ASME*, Vol. 57, 1935, pp. A49-A58.	H	2
292	Way, Stewart: How to Reduce Surface Fatigue, *Mach. Des.*, Vol. 11, March 1939, pp. 42–45.	P	2, 3
293	Wellauer, E., and G. Holloway: Application of EHD Oil film Theory to Industrial Gear Drives, ASLE/ASME Paper No. 75-PTG-1, Oct. 1975.	P	3, 7
294	Wente, D. E.: Rear Axle Noise Quality Test Stand, AGMA P299.05, 1972.	P	7
295	Wilcox, L. E.: A New Method for Analyzing Gear Tooth Stress as a Function of Tooth Contact Pattern Shape and Position, AGMA P229.25, 1982.	P	3
296	Willis, R. J.: Lightest-Weight Gears, *Prod. Eng.*, Jan. 21, 1963.	H	3
297	Willn, J. E., and R. J. Love: Proportions of Automobile Change Speed Gear Teeth, Report No. 1970/7 of the Motor Industry Research Assoc., 1970.	G	2, 3, 4
298	Winter, H.: Calculation of Slow Speed Wear of Lubricated Gears, AGMA P219.16, 1982.	P	3
299	Winter, Hans, and Masakazu Kojima: A Study on the Dynamics of Geared System—Estimation of Overload on Gears in System, International Symposium on Gearing & Power Transmissions, Tokyo, 1981.	P	3, 7, 9

	Paper, Booklet, or Trade Standard Publication	Code	Chapter
300	Winter, H., and T. Weiss: Some Factors Influencing the Pitting, Micro-Pitting (Frosted Areas) and Slow Speed Wear of Surface Hardened Gears, ASME Paper No. 80-C2/DET-89, 1980.	G	2, 3, 7
301	Winter, H., and H. Wilkesmann: Calculation of Cylindrical Worm Gear Drives of Different Tooth Profiles, ASME Paper No. 80-C2/DET-23, 1980.	P	3, 6
302	Winter, H., and X. Wirth: The Effect of Notches at the Tooth Root Fillet on the Endurance Strength of Gears, ASME Paper No. 77-DET-54, 1977.	H	3
303	Yelle, H., and D. J. Burns: Calculation of Contact Ratios for Plastic/Plastic or Plastic/Steel Spur Gear Pairs, ASME Paper No. 80-C2/DET-105, 1980.	P	3
304	Yelle, H., and D. J. Burns: Root Bending Fatigue Strength of Acetal Spur Gears—A Design Approach to Allow for Load Sharing, AGMA 149.01, 1981.	P	3, 4
305	Yonekura, M., and M. Ainoura: A Research on Finishing Hardened Gears of Large Modules, ASME Paper No. 80-C2/DET-62, 1980.	P	6
306	Young, I. T.: A Wider Scope for Nitrided Gears, ASME Paper No. 80-C2/DET-46, 1980.	P	3, 4
307	Yu, David: The Optimizing Programming Design of the KHV Planetary Gear Driving, International Symposium on Gearing & Power Transmissions, Tokyo, 1981.	P	3
308	Yuruzume, I., and H. Mizutani: Bending Fatigue Tests of High Speed Spur Gears, ASME Paper No. 80-C2/DET-87, 1980.	P	2, 3
309	Zamis, A.: Equations for the Normal Profile of Helical Gears, *Am. Mach.*, Sept. 1947, pp. 82–84.	P	6
310	Zaretsky, Erwin V. and W. J. Anderson: How to Use What We Know about EHD Lubrication, *Mach. Des.*, Vol. 40, No. 26, Nov. 7, 1968, p. 167.	P	2, 3, 7
311	Zrodowski, J. J., and D. W. Dudley: Modern Marine Gears, *Trans. SNAME*, Vol. 58, 1950, pp. 788–814.	P	3, 7
312	Zrodowski, J. J., and A. D. F. Moncrieff: Advanced Precision Shaving Techniques Applied to High Speed Marine Gears, *Trans. SNAME*, Vol. 61, 1953.	P	5, 6

index

Abbreviations (*see* Symbols used in equations; *and specific abbreviation*)
Accuracy:
of concentricity, **2.**66
vs. cost, **5.**73, **5.**78–**5.**79
of derating factors, **3.**93
and dynamic load, **9.**9–**9.**15
effect on load-carrying capacity of, **3.**141–**3.**142, **3.**144, **9.**9–**9.**15
effects of thermal problems on, **3.**149
factors which determine, **5.**78
geometric specifications for, **5.**74–**5.**77
of involute profile, **2.**66
levels of, **3.**106–**3.**107, **5.**73–**5.**74
limits for drawing specifications, **5.**73–**5.**80
maximum obtainable, **2.**65–**2.**67
measurements of (*see* Checking procedures for gear size and accuracy)
obtainable with different methods of manufacturing, **5.**28, **5.**30, **5.**34, **5.**36–**5.**38, **5.**57, **5.**59, **5.**60, **5.**67, **5.**71–**5.**72, **5.**87, **5.**88, **6.**39

Accuracy (*Cont.*):
obtainable with hobbing, **5.**6–**5.**8
required in gear mounting: of bevel gears, **1.**33
in casing, **2.**69, **7.**38
of crossed-helical gears, **1.**41–**1.**42
of double-helical gears, **3.**42–**3.**43
of worm gears, **1.**44–**1.**45, **1.**47
required in gear teeth: of aerospace gears, **1.**21
of control gearing, **1.**11–**1.**12
of marine gears, **1.**17, **1.**19
to prevent scoring, **2.**24, **3.**141
of surface finish, **2.**66
surface-finish specifications for, **5.**75, **5.**77
of tooth alignment, **2.**66, **2.**74
of tooth spacing, **2.**65–**2.**66, **8.**12
of tooth thickness, **2.**66
trade standards on, **2.**66–**2.**67, **5.**73
(*See also* Checking procedures for gear size and accuracy; Derating factors; Distortion of gears)

Addendum:
of bevel gears, **3.**47
chordal, **3.**21–**3.**23, **3.**38, **3.**52
definition of, **1.**2
illustrations of, **1.**29
long, **1.**21, **3.**14–**3.**18
minimum, **3.**15–**3.**16
sample calculation of, **8.**3, **8.**5
shortened for internal gear, **3.**34
for worm gears, **3.**65
(*See also* Tooth proportions)
Aerospace and aircraft gears:
effect of size on quality of, **3.**115
general discussion of, **1.**19–**1.**21
handling high rubbing speeds in, **3.**117
lubrication of, **7.**44
material quality of, **4.**41–**4.**42, **5.**72
number of teeth of, **3.**3
plating of, **3.**141
profile modification of, **8.**17–**8.**21
rating of, **3.**150–**3.**153
reliability level of, **3.**78
scoring problems with, **2.**24
steels for, **4.**7, **4.**18
typical *K* factors of, **2.**46
Aging, definition of, **4.**2
AGMA (*see* American Gear Manufacturers Association)
Aircraft gears (*see* Aerospace and aircraft gears)
AISI (American Iron and Steel Institute), **4.**7
Akamatsu, K., **4.**30, Ref. 146
Akazawa, M., **2.**34, **7.**51, Ref. 28
Alignment accuracy, **2.**66, **2.**74
Alloy steels (*see* Steels for gears)
American Gear Manufacturers Association (AGMA):
address of, **3.**142
formulas for bending strength and pitting resistance, **9.**44
gear-failure standards, **7.**11
gear materials manual, **4.**50
list of standards, Refs. 31–62
lubrication standards, **7.**41
nomenclature of rating, **9.**45
quality numbers, table, **2.**70–**2.**71
quality standards, **3.**75, **4.**41, **5.**73
rating standards: for aerospace gears, **3.**151
comparison with ISO, **2.**13, **3.**83, **3.**93, **9.**10–**9.**15, **9.**37, **9.**44–**9.**48
complexity of, **3.**78
dynamic factor, **3.**105
American Gear Manufacturers Association (AGMA), rating standards (*Cont.*):
geometry factors: for durability, **3.**108–**3.**109
for strength, **3.**88
legal requirement to use, **3.**74, **3.**143
load distribution factors, **3.**96
for marine gears, **3.**148
size factor, **3.**113
for worm gears, **3.**115, **3.**118–**3.**126
American Iron and Steel Institute (AISI), **4.**7
American National Standards Institute (ANSI), **2.**58–**2.**64
American Society of Mechanical Engineers (ASME), **2.**12, **2.**58–**2.**64, **3.**83
AMS (aircraft material specification) steels, **4.**18
Angle of approach and angle of recess, **9.**21–**9.**23, **9.**26
Annealing:
definition of, **4.**2, **4.**7
purpose of, **4.**7
temperatures used in, **4.**8
ANSI (American National Standards Institute), **2.**58–**2.**64
Appliance gears, **1.**7–**1.**8
Application factors, **3.**93–**3.**96, **3.**113
table of, **3.**95, **9.**9
Approach action:
definition of, **3.**2
with long-addendum designs, **3.**17
ASME (*see* American Society of Mechanical Engineers)
Aspect ratio:
definition of, **3.**100
effects of, **3.**100–**3.**102
Austempering, definition of, **4.**40
Austenite, definition of, **4.**2, **4.**42
Automotive gears, **1.**12–**1.**14
case depth of, **4.**23–**4.**24
cyanide hardening of, **4.**39–**4.**40
load distribution factors for, **3.**101–**3.**102
load-rating sample calculation, **8.**22–**8.**26
lubrication of, **7.**44–**7.**46
manufacture of, **5.**70, **5.**71
material quality standards for, **4.**41–**4.**42
number of pinion teeth for, **3.**7
rating practice for, **3.**143–**3.**146
reliability levels of, **3.**78
specifications for, **5.**72
typical *K* factors for, **2.**46

Axial meshing velocity:
calculation of, **7.**47–**7.**49
relation to thermal problems, **7.**49
Axial pitch:
equation for helical gears, **1.**31
sample calculation of, **8.**11
for worm gears, **1.**45, **1.**47, **3.**65, **3.**67
Axial section, definition of, **1.**2
Axial thrust load, definition of, **9.**3
Azumi Manufacturing Co., **6.**25–**6.**27

Backlash:
with bevel gearing, **3.**48–**3.**49, **3.**51, **3.**54, **3.**58
with control gearing, **1.**11
definition of, **2.**2
recommended amounts of, **3.**19–**3.**20
sample calculation of, **8.**6
with worm gearing, **3.**69–**3.**73
Balanced design:
between pinion and gear beam strength, **3.**15–**3.**16, **3.**48–**3.**50
between surface durability and beam strength, **3.**6–**3.**7
Band of contact (*see* Contact band)
Barber Colman Co., **6.**8–**6.**9, **6.**25–**6.**26
Base circle:
of Cone-Drive gear, **3.**71–**3.**72
of involute gear, definition of, **9.**6
Base (circle) diameter, equation for, **3.**27
BD or B.D. (base diameter), **3.**27
Beam strength:
balance between pinion and gear, **3.**15
definition of, **2.**7
effect of fillet radius of curvature on, **3.**12
effect of pressure angle on, **3.**10
(*See also* Strength)
Bearings:
defects in manufacture of, **7.**32, **7.**34
environmental problems with, **7.**28–**7.**29
factors to consider in choice of, **7.**29, **7.**32–**7.**33
failure of, possible causes of, **7.**30, **7.**33–**7.**35
frequency of problems with, **7.**28
kinds of, **7.**32, **7.**34
life expectancy of, **7.**29, **7.**32–**7.**35
potential problems with, **2.**68–**2.**69, **7.**28–**7.**35, **7.**38–**7.**39
responsibility of gear designer for, **2.**68, **7.**28
Bearings (*Cont.*):
rolling-element, **7.**29–**7.**32
sliding-element, **7.**32–**7.**35
Bending of teeth in mesh, **2.**5
Bending strength rating calculations, **3.**78–**3.**153, **9.**44–**9.**48
(*See also* Stress calculations, bending stress)
Bevel gears:
definition of, **1.**2, **9.**2
design for high torque, **3.**103
dimension sheets for, **3.**52, **3.**53, **3.**55, **3.**56
estimating size needed, **2.**47–**2.**51
Gleason Works summary sheets for, **9.**36–**9.**43
hypoid (*see* Hypoid gears)
manufacture of, **5.**23–**5.**26, **5.**51–**5.**53
estimated time for, **5.**24, **5.**26, **5.**52
profile modification of, **5.**23, **8.**12
rating of, **3.**86–**3.**87, **3.**102–**3.**104, **3.**108, **3.**113–**3.**114
spiral, **1.**37–**1.**38, **9.**40–**9.**41
straight, **1.**33–**1.**35, **3.**51–**3.**54, **9.**38–**9.**39
tooth proportions of, **3.**45–**3.**51
Zerol, **1.**36–**1.**37, **9.**42–**9.**43
BL or B.L. (*see* Backlash)
Blok, Harmen, **2.**28, Ref. 78
Bottom land, definition of, **2.**2
Bowen, Charles, **2.**21, Ref. 86
Break-in period (*see* Wear-in)
Breen, D. H., **4.**30, Ref. 249
Brinell hardness:
conversion to other scales, **4.**16
definition of, **4.**2
procedure for measuring, **4.**14
Broaching, **5.**31–**5.**34
definition of, **5.**2
lengths of broaches for, **5.**33
pot, **5.**33–**5.**35
production time for, **5.**32–**5.**33
Broghamer, E. I., **2.**11, **2.**13, Ref. 108
Broken teeth:
definition of, **3.**2
due to deep case, **4.**22
due to excess load, **7.**27
due to shallow case, **4.**20
due to weak and brittle case, **4.**27, **4.**28
effects of tooth dimensions on likelihood of, **3.**10
illustrations of, **7.**3, **7.**12
investigation of, **7.**17–**7.**18
(*See also* Strength; Unit load)

Bronze for gears, **4.**1–**4.**2, **4.**53–**4.**57
  compositions of, **4.**54–**4.**57
    table of, **4.**56
  phosphor, **3.**117, **4.**55
  trade standards for, **4.**57
  in worm gearing, **3.**69, **3.**117
Buckingham, Earle, **2.**12, **3.**115–**3.**116, **4.**41, **7.**36, Refs. 2, 90
Burnishing, definition of, **5.**2

Calculation sheets (*see* Dimension sheets; *and specific entries*)
Cantilever-beam model of gear tooth, **2.**7
Capacity (*see* Load-carrying capacity; Rating calculations)
Carburizing:
  carbon percent required for, **4.**17
  core data after, **4.**9
  definition of, **4.**2
  distortion caused by, **4.**19–**4.**20
  effect of alloy content on, **4.**6
  effect of size on, **4.**20
  factors to control with, **4.**17, **4.**18
  heat treatment after, **4.**19
  metallurgical structure after, **4.**21, **4.**44
  potential problems with, **2.**68, **4.**17, **4.**20
  recommended temperatures for, **4.**8
  of steel gears, **4.**17–**4.**24
  (*See also* Hardening)
Case depth:
  of carburized gears, **4.**20, **4.**22
  of induction-hardened gears, **4.**33–**4.**37
  maximum recommended, **4.**22
  minimum effective, **4.**20–**4.**23
    graph of, **4.**23
  trade standards for, **4.**24
Case hardening:
  definition of, **4.**2
  potential problems with, **2.**67–**2.**68, **3.**146, **4.**27, **4.**39–**4.**40
  (*See also* Carburizing; Flame hardening of steel gear; Induction hardening; Nitriding)
Casings for gears:
  design of, **7.**38–**7.**39
  flexible-coupling problems in, **7.**39
  importance of, **7.**37
  oil churning in, **7.**39, **7.**44
  potential problems with, **7.**37–**7.**39
  requirements for, **2.**69
Cast-iron gears, **1.**9, **4.**1, **4.**47–**4.**53
  ductile, **4.**51–**4.**52
  gray, **4.**47–**4.**50
  sintered, **1.**7, **1.**8, **4.**52–**4.**53, **5.**88–**5.**89
  structures of, **4.**49
Castellani, Giovanni, **2.**13, **3.**83, **3.**93, **9.**46, Ref. 93
Castelli, V. P., **2.**13, **3.**83, **3.**93, **9.**46, Ref. 93
Casting, **5.**86–**5.**89
  definition of, **5.**2
  investment-casting process, **5.**87–**5.**88
CBN (cubic boron nitride), **5.**43
Center distance:
  crossed-helical gear equations for, **1.**43
  definition of, **9.**4
  estimating size needed (*see* Size)
  internal gear equations for, **1.**32
  modification of: to allow use of standard hob, **8.**9–**8.**11
    for helical gearsets, **9.**59–**9.**61
  operating, **1.**29, **8.**9–**8.**11
  special problems relating to, **8.**1–**8.**11
  spur-gear equations for, **1.**28
Certification societies (*see* Classification societies for large ships)
Checking procedures for gear size and accuracy, **5.**72–**5.**86, **9.**50–**9.**54
  for bevel gears, **3.**102, **5.**83–**5.**84
  for measuring: helix, **5.**81, **9.**53
    profile, **5.**81–**5.**83, **5.**85, **9.**52–**9.**53
    runout (concentricity), **5.**80, **5.**82, **9.**53–**9.**54
    surface finish, **5.**80, **5.**81, **9.**52–**9.**53
    tooth spacing, **5.**81, **9.**50–**9.**52
    tooth thickness, **3.**22, **3.**38, **3.**48, **9.**19–**9.**20, **9.**54
    (*See also* Diameter, over pins)
  with minimal equipment, **5.**80
  recommended equipment for, **5.**80–**5.**86
  rolling checks with master gear, **5.**82–**5.**86, **9.**53–**9.**54
  for Spiroid and worm gears, **5.**83–**5.**84
Chordal dimensions, **3.**21–**3.**23, **3.**51–**3.**52
Circular pitch:
  of bevel gears, **1.**35
  of crossed-helical gears, **1.**43
  definition of, **1.**2, **9.**4
  helical-gear equation for, **1.**30
  illustrations of, **1.**29, **9.**5
  spur-gear equation for, **1.**28
  of worm gears, **1.**49, **3.**65

Classification societies for large ships, **3.**147–**3.**148
Clearance, illustration of, **1.**29
Cold drawing, **5.**89–**5.**90
Cold-drawn gear teeth, **1.**6
Cold-rolled gear teeth, **1.**6, **5.**89–**5.**90
Cold working, definition of, **4.**3
Compressive stress:
  increase of: due to carburizing, **4.**18
    due to nitriding, **4.**27
  with induction hardening, **4.**30
  (*See also* Contact stress; Stress calculations)
Concentricity:
  accuracy of, **2.**66
  (*See also* Runout)
Cone-Drive gears (*see* Worm gears, double-enveloping)
Conjugate tooth profiles, definition of, **9.**6
Contact band, width of:
  Blok equation for, **2.**29
  in different regimes of lubrication, **2.**21
  hertz equation for, **2.**15
Contact checks, **2.**69
Contact ratio:
  calculation sheet for, **9.**22, **9.**28
  of crossed-helical gears, **1.**43, **3.**62
  definition of, **3.**31
  equations for, **3.**27, **3.**30–**3.**31
  of helical gears, **9.**33
  sample calculation of, **8.**20
  of spur gears, graph, **3.**30, **9.**15–**9.**17
Contact stress:
  in different regimes of lubrication, **2.**23
  as a function of load intensity, **2.**23–**2.**24
  sample calculation of, **8.**23–**8.**24
  worst-load position of, **2.**18–**2.**19
  (*See also* Hertz stress; Stress calculations)
Control gears, **1.**9–**1.**12, **3.**19–**3.**20
Copper impregnating sintered-iron gears, **4.**52
Copper plating of gear teeth, **3.**141
Cost vs. accuracy, **5.**73, **5.**78–**5.**79
Cost factors in design decisions, **3.**21
  (*See also* Low-cost gears)
Couplings for gearsets, malfunctioning of, **7.**39
CP or C.P. (*see* Circular pitch)
Critical cooling rate:
  definition of, **4.**10
  for plain carbon steels, **4.**12
Critical speeds, **9.**9
  (*See also* Application factors)
Critical temperature, definition of, **4.**10
Crossed-helical gears, **1.**41–**1.**43, **9.**3
  load rating of, **3.**115–**3.**118
  tooth proportions of, **3.**62–**3.**65
Crown, definition of, **2.**2
Cubic boron nitride, **5.**43
Cutting tools:
  for crossed-helical gears, **3.**62
  designing to use standard sizes, **8.**4–**8.**11
  effect on gear design of, **3.**13, **3.**34, **3.**39–**3.**40
  for face gears, **3.**61
  factors in choosing number of cutter teeth, **3.**8, **6.**4
  for hobbing gears, **6.**10–**6.**27
  for hobbing worm gears, **6.**19–**6.**21
  for milling spur gears, **6.**27–**6.**29
  for milling worms, **6.**29–**6.**36
  for shaping gears, **6.**2–**6.**10
    design of, **9.**54–**9.**59
  for shaving gears, **6.**36–**6.**39
Cycles (*see* Life expectancy; Life requirements)
Cylindrical worm gears (*see* Worm gears, cylindrical)

Damage to teeth (*see* Broken teeth; Failure of gears; Pitting; Scoring; Wear)
Dedendum:
  definition of, **1.**2
  illustration of, **1.**29
Deflection of teeth in mesh, **8.**12–**8.**21
  calculation of, **8.**15, **8.**17
  equation for, **3.**98
  resulting in momentary overload, **9.**9–**9.**15
Degrees roll, **3.**23–**3.**29
  (*See also* Roll angles)
Derating, definition of, **3.**2
Derating factors:
  for aerospace gears, **3.**151
  overall: for strength, **3.**79, **3.**93
    for surface durability, **3.**82, **3.**112–**3.**113
  for vehicle gears, **3.**144
  (*See also* Rating; Strength; Surface durability)
Design:
  of cutting tools, **6.**1–**6.**39, **9.**54–**9.**59
  experience factor in, **3.**143
    (*See also* Testing of gears)
  introduction to, **9.**4–**9.**9
  special problems in, **8.**1–**8.**26, **9.**59–**9.**63

Design limits, **2.**5–**2.**6, **2.**32, **5.**73–**5.**80
Design steps:
  choosing dimensions: for aerospace gears, **3.**150
    to handle scoring, **3.**140–**3.**141
    (*See also* Dimension sheets)
  choosing kind of gear, **1.**26
  estimating size needed, **2.**34
  for gear accessories, **2.**68–**2.**69, **2.**74
  layout of gear teeth, **3.**32–**3.**33, **9.**26, **9.**29–**9.**30
  modifications to consider, **3.**146, **3.**153, **8.**1–**8.**26
  specifications needed, **2.**35, **2.**74
    (*See also* Drawings)
Deutscher Normenausschuss (DNA), **9.**37
Deutsches Institute für Normung (DIN):
  address of, **3.**142
  publications of, **5.**73, Refs. 106–107
  quality grades, table, **2.**72–**2.**73
Diameter:
  over balls (helical gears), **9.**31–**9.**33
    calculation sheet for, **9.**32
  form (*see* Form diameter)
  matching: on pinion and gear, **9.**49
    on shaper-cutter and gear, **9.**58
  outside (*see* Outside diameter)
  between pins (internal gears), **9.**27–**9.**29
    calculation sheet for, **9.**27
  over pins, **9.**19–**9.**20
    calculation sheet for, **9.**21
    for helical gears, **9.**31–**9.**33
    for internal gears (*see* between pins, *above*)
    pin sizes, **9.**20
  under pins (*see* between pins, *above*)
Diametral pitch:
  definition of, **1.**2
  equation: for crossed-helical gears, **1.**43
    for helical gears, **1.**30
    for spur gears, **1.**27–**1.**28
  (*See also* Tooth size)
Die-cast gears, **1.**5
Die casting, **5.**87
  (*See also* Casting)
Dimension sheets:
  for bevel gears, **3.**53
    spiral, **3.**55
    straight, **3.**52
    Zerol, **3.**56
  for crossed-helical gears, **3.**64
Dimension sheets (*Cont.*):
  for cylindrical worm gears, **3.**70
  for double-enveloping worm gears, **3.**72
  for helical gears, **3.**44
  for internal gears, **3.**39
  for spur gears, **3.**32
Dimensions:
  of internal gears, **1.**31
  (*See also* Size; Tooth proportions)
DIN (*see* Deutsches Institute für Normung)
Distortion of gears:
  from carburizing, **4.**19–**4.**20
  from casting process, **5.**87
  from combined heat treatments, **4.**39–**4.**40
  from heat treating, **4.**7, **4.**39–**4.**40, **5.**41–**5.**42
  from induction hardening, **4.**30
  of molded plastic, **5.**87
  from nitriding, **4.**25, **4.**27
  from uneven temperature rise during mesh, **7.**50
DNA (*see* Deutscher Normenausschuss)
Dolan, T. J., **2.**11, **2.**13, Ref. 108
Double-enveloping worm gears (*see* Worm gears, double-enveloping)
Double-helical gears, **9.**3
  (*See also* Helical gears)
Drago, R. J., **3.**93, Ref. 110
Draw treatment, definition of, **4.**4
Drawing to form gear teeth, **5.**89–**5.**90
  definition of, **5.**2
Drawings:
  accuracy limits for, **5.**73–**5.**80
  blank dimensions needed for, **2.**55
  data for, **2.**55–**2.**67
  material specifications for, **2.**67–**2.**68
  recommended style, example of, **2.**57
  standard drawing formats (ANS): for cylindrical worm gears, **2.**62
    for double-enveloping worm gears, **2.**63
    for spiral bevel gears, **2.**61
    for Spiroid gears, **2.**64
    for spur and helical gears, **2.**59
    for straight bevel gears, **2.**60
  tolerances for, **2.**65–**2.**67, **2.**70–**2.**73
  tooth data needed for, **2.**56
  (*See also* Layouts)
Drop-tooth problem, **8.**1–**8.**4
Ductility, definition of, **4.**3
Dudley, Darle W., **1.**1, **2.**22, **2.**31, **3.**149, **4.**28, **4.**57*n.*, **6.**13, **6.**31–**6.**33, **9.**16, **9.**19, Refs. 8–11, 112–134

Dynamic factor for load, **3.**93, **3.**105–**3.**108, **3.**113
for bevel gears, **3.**108
graph of, **3.**106
for worm gears, **3.**118, **3.**120
Dynamic load, **2.**5, **2.**12–**2.**13, **2.**35, **3.**117, **7.**36–**7.**37
research on, **9.**9–**9.**15
(*See also* Load)

Edge radius, definition of, **3.**2
Efficiency with different types of gears, **1.**26
EHD (*see* Elastohydrodynamic lubrication)
Elastic limit, definition of, **4.**3
Elastohydrodynamic (EHD) lubrication, **2.**20
in crossed-helical gearsets, **3.**118
effect of hunting ratio on, **3.**8–**3.**9
and scoring, **3.**128, **3.**135–**3.**140
(*See also* Oil-film thickness)
End easement, definition of, **3.**2
Endurance limits:
definition of, **4.**3
for wear, **2.**19–**2.**20
(*See also* Stress calculations, stress-limit tables)
EP (extreme pressure) oils, **2.**23, **3.**141
Epicyclic gears, **1.**31, **2.**42
amounts of backlash for, **3.**20
definition of, **9.**4
Equations:
applying to helical gears, **1.**30–**1.**31
applying to internal gearsets, **1.**32–**1.**33
applying to spur gears, **1.**28–**1.**29
(*See also* Symbols used in equations)
Equipment for checking accuracy, **5.**80–**5.**86
double-flank and single-flank rolling checkers, **5.**82–**5.**86
(*See also* Checking procedures for gear size and accuracy)
Experience factor in gear design, **3.**143
(*See also* Testing of gears)
External gears, definition of, **1.**2
Extruded gears, **1.**5
Extruding process, **5.**89–**5.**90
definition of, **5.**2

Face angle of bevel gears, **1.**34, **1.**35, **3.**52, **3.**53, **3.**55, **3.**56
Face gears, **1.**40–**1.**41
calculations for, **3.**59–**3.**62
definition of, **1.**2
estimating size of, **2.**51
Face width:
of bevel gears, **2.**50, **3.**54, **3.**56, **3.**58, **3.**102
considerations in choosing, **2.**38–**2.**40
of crossed-helical gears, **3.**65
definition of, **2.**2
effect on cutting time, **5.**12
effect on surface durability, **3.**113
estimating size needed (*see* Size)
of face gears, **3.**59–**3.**61
of helical gears, **3.**42, **3.**43
hobbing for wide, **5.**6
illustration of, **1.**29
limits of: for punching, **5.**34, **5.**36, **6.**39
for shaping, **5.**10, **5.**18
for shaving, **5.**61, **5.**66
for sintered gears, **5.**89
and materials factor, **3.**126
of worm gears, **3.**68, **3.**72–**3.**73, **3.**118
Failure of gears:
of aerospace gears, **3.**150
clarification of gear-system problems, **7.**1–**7.**6
definition of, **3.**75–**3.**76, **7.**3
due to bearing failure, **7.**28–**7.**35, **7.**38–**7.**39
due to coupling failure, **7.**39
due to dynamic loads, **7.**36–**7.**37
due to gear-casing problems, **7.**37–**7.**39
due to incompatibility, **7.**7–**7.**9
due to lubrication problems, **7.**22, **7.**24–**7.**28, **7.**39–**7.**47
due to misalignment, **7.**38
due to overheating, **7.**45–**7.**51
due to overloads, vibration, imbalance, **7.**35–**7.**37
due to tooth breakage: illustrations of, **7.**3, **7.**12
investigation of, **7.**17–**7.**18
torque/speed region of, **7.**27
due to tooth surface damage: illustrations of, **7.**13–**7.**16
nomenclature of, **7.**11
pitting, **7.**19–**7.**22, **7.**26–**7.**27
scoring, **7.**22–**7.**24, **7.**26
trade standards on, **7.**11
uniform wear, **7.**24–**7.**28
due to vibration, noise, abnormal wear, **7.**2–**7.**3

Failure of gears (*Cont.*):
  effect of alloy content on, **4.**6
  information needed for investigation of, **7.**9–**7.**11
  kinds and causes of, **7.**1–**7.**51
  probability system (*see* Reliability-level system)
  sequence of wear failures, **2.**14
  torque vs. speed regions of, **7.**25–**7.**26
  (*See also* Broken teeth: Design steps, modifications to consider; Life expectancy; Pitting; Scoring; Surface durability)
Fatigue tests, **2.**5
FD or F.D. (*see* Form diameter)
Fellows Corporation, **5.**78–**5.**79
Ferrite, definition of, **4.**3
Fillet, definition of, **2.**2
Fillet radius of curvature, **3.**9–**3.**10, **3.**12–**3.**14
  calculation sheet for, **9.**24–**9.**25
  of crossed-helical gears, **3.**64
  equation for minimum generated, **3.**13
  with extra-depth teeth, **3.**12
  graph of minimum, **3.**14
  of helical gears, **3.**45, **9.**33
  of internal gears, **3.**38, **9.**30
Finite element method of stress analysis, **2.**13
Flame hardening of steel gears, **4.**38
  definition of, **4.**3
Flank, definition of, **2.**2
Flash temperature:
  calculation of scoring risk, **2.**28–**2.**31, **3.**128–**3.**135
  definition of, **3.**2
Form diameter, **3.**23, **3.**25, **3.**29–**3.**30
  calculation sheet for, **9.**22, **9.**28
  definition of, **2.**2
  equation for, **3.**29
  of helical gears, **9.**33
  of internal gears, **3.**38, **9.**28
  sample calculation of, **8.**20
  significance of, **8.**16
Formulas (*see* Equations)
Fretting corrosion, **7.**17, **7.**46
Friction gears, definition of, **9.**2
Friction resistance of bronze, **4.**53
Fujita, K., **4.**30, Refs. 145–147
Full-depth teeth, definition of, **3.**2, **3.**9
Future needs in gear practice:
  in case-hardening research, **4.**30
  in gear rating, **3.**93
  in manufacture, **5.**38
  in material quality, **4.**41
Gap:
  between double-helical gears, **1.**30
  width of, **6.**14–**6.**18
Gear, definition of, **1.**2, **9.**1, **9.**2
Gear Handbook, Ref. 8
Gear nomenclature, **1.**2, **2.**2, **3.**2–**3.**3, **4.**2–**4.**3, **5.**2–**5.**3, **9.**2–**9.**8
Gear terms, symbols, and units, **1.**3, **2.**3, **3.**4–**3.**5, **3.**80–**3.**81
Gear trains, definition of, **9.**3
  (*See also* Epicyclic gears)
Gears, **9.**1–**9.**9
  aerospace (*see* Aerospace and aircraft gears)
  appliance, **1.**7–**1.**8
  automotive (*see* Automotive gears)
  control, **1.**9–**1.**12, **3.**19–**3.**20
  industrial, **1.**21–**1.**23
  introduction to, **9.**1–**9.**9
  kinds of, **9.**2–**9.**4
  machine-tool, **1.**9
  marine (*see* Marine gears)
  mill, **1.**24–**1.**25, **3.**94
  in oil and gas industry, **1.**23–**1.**24, **3.**148–**3.**149
  radar, **1.**10–**1.**11
  selection of type, **1.**26–**1.**51
  toy, **1.**5
  transportation (*see* Transportation gears)
Generating, definition of, **5.**2
Geometry factors:
  for bending strength, **3.**79, **3.**88–**3.**93
    graphs of, **3.**90, **3.**91
    table of, **3.**89
  for bevel gears, **3.**92, **3.**112
  comparison of AGMA and ISO, **2.**13
  for scoring, **2.**32, **3.**128–**3.**134, **9.**63–**9.**65
    calculation sheet for, **9.**64
  for surface durability, **3.**82, **3.**108–**3.**112
    graphs of, **3.**110, **3.**111, **3.**131–**3.**134
    table of, **3.**129
Gleason Works, **3.**45–**3.**59, **3.**108, **5.**36, **9.**36–**9.**43, Refs. 150–153
Glossary of gear terms (*see* Symbols used in equations; Terminology; Units; *and specific term*)
Grain size:
  definition of, **4.**3
  before heat treatment, **4.**6–**4.**7
Grinding, **5.**38–**5.**59
  amount of stock removed by, **5.**41, **5.**42
  of bevel gears, **5.**51–**5.**53
  after carburizing, **4.**20

Grinding (*Cont.*):
- to control scoring, **3.**141
- definition of, **5.**2
- of fine-pitch gears without cutting, **5.**57
- by form wheel, **5.**39–**5.**45
  - Borazon form grinding, **5.**43–**5.**45
- by generating wheel, **5.**46–**5.**53
- kinds of, **5.**38–**5.**39
- runout required for, **5.**46, **5.**54
- by threaded wheel, **5.**53–**5.**59
- time required for, **5.**38–**5.**41, **5.**43, **5.**47–**5.**49, **5.**52, **5.**55, **5.**57–**5.**58
- of worm threads, **5.**57–**5.**59, **6.**29–**6.**30

G-TRAC generating, **5.**36–**5.**38

Hardenability,
- definition of, **4.**3
- limits of, **4.**13
- for specific gear steels, **4.**9, **4.**13

Hardening:
- by carburizing, **4.**17–**4.**24
- by combined treatments, **4.**39–**4.**40
- critical cooling rate during, **4.**9
- effect of alloy content on, **4.**12
- flame, **4.**38–**4.**39
- induction (*see* Induction hardening)
- by nitriding, **4.**24–**4.**30
- recommended cooling rates for, **4.**10
- recommended speed of, **4.**7–**4.**10
- recommended temperatures for, **4.**8
- through (*see* Through hardening)

Hardness:
- of automotive gears, **1.**13
- Brinell (*see* Brinell hardness)
- of carburized gears, **4.**20
- comparison of test scales, **4.**16
- of core, **4.**9, **4.**29
- definition of, **4.**3
- of die-cast gears, **5.**87
- of different material grades, **4.**42–**4.**45
- increase during wear-in, **3.**76
- induction (*see* Induction hardening)
- of induction-hardened gears, **4.**36
- limits for cutting of gears, **5.**38
- of machine-tool gears, **1.**9
- of marine gears, **1.**18
- of nitrided gears, **4.**29
- nonuniformity of, before heat treatment, **4.**7
- recommended tests of, **4.**13–**4.**16
- Rockwell (*see* Rockwell hardness)

Hardness (*Cont.*):
- of 60 percent martensite steels, **4.**9
- specifications for, **4.**16
- (*See also* Case depth)

Heat treatment:
- after carburizing, **4.**17, **4.**19
- of cast-iron gears, **4.**48
- combinations of, **4.**39–**4.**40
- cooling rates for, **4.**10
- cracking during, **4.**12–**4.**13
- definition of, **4.**3
- effect of alloys on, **4.**6, **4.**12–**4.**13
- before nitriding, **4.**25
- nomenclature of, **4.**2–**4.**3
- recommended temperatures for, **4.**8, **4.**11–**4.**12
- and scoring hazard, **3.**141
- skill needed in, **4.**11, **4.**17
- specifications for, **4.**13, **4.**16, **4.**23
- structures obtained with, **4.**7, **4.**12
- techniques for, **4.**6–**4.**13
- (*See also* Hardening)

Helical gears:
- aspect ratio effects of, **3.**100–**3.**102
- choosing dimensions for, **3.**39–**3.**45
- crossed (*see* Crossed-helical gears)
- definition of, **1.**2, **9.**3
- designing of, to use standard hobs, **8.**7–**8.**9
- dimension sheet for, **3.**44
- dynamic factors of, **9.**10, **9.**13, **9.**15
- estimating size needed of, **2.**36–**2.**47
- external, **1.**30–**1.**31
- internal, **1.**31–**1.**33
- mounting of double-helical gears, **3.**42–**3.**43
- rating narrow-face-width gears, **3.**91–**3.**92
- special calculations for, **9.**31–**9.**36
- tooth thickness calculation for spread-center operation, **9.**59–**9.**63

Helicon gear, **1.**50

Helicopter gears, **3.**150–**3.**151, **5.**71, **5.**73, **7.**24, **7.**44
- (*See also* Aerospace and aircraft gears)

Helix angle:
- of crossed-helical gears, **1.**42–**1.**43
- definition of, **1.**2
- distortion from carburizing, **4.**19
- of external gears, **1.**30, **1.**31
- of internal gears, **1.**32
- measurement of, **5.**81, **9.**53
- modification of, **3.**101, **8.**7–**8.**9
  - to allow use of standard hob, **8.**7–**8.**9

Helix angle, modification of (*Cont.*):
definition of, **3.**2
recommended sizes of, **3.**41–**3.**42
of worm gears, **1.**45, **1.**49
Helix mismatch, effects of, **3.**97–**3.**98
Herringbone gears, **9.**3
(*See also* Helical gears)
Hertz, Heinrich, **2.**14, Ref. 167
Hertz stress:
derivation of, **2.**14–**2.**17
worst-load position of, **2.**19
High-production methods, **1.**5, **1.**7, **1.**13
High-speed gears:
accuracy level required for, **3.**107
close tolerances required for, **2.**65
face width of, **3.**43
hobbing of, **5.**6
lubrication of, **7.**24, **7.**46
regimes of lubrication, **2.**21
number of pinion teeth for, **3.**3–**3.**7
profile modification of, **8.**17–**8.**21
scoring of, **5.**71, **7.**24, **8.**17–**8.**21
spiral bevel vs. Zerol bevel choice, **1.**38
surface finishing of, **5.**71, **7.**24
thermal limits of, **2.**34
thermal problems with, **7.**47–**7.**51
trade standards for, **3.**148–**3.**149
Highest point of single tooth contact (HPSTC), **2.**29, **2.**30, **3.**134, **9.**15–**9.**17
Hirano, F., **3.**8, Ref. 175
Histograms of load intensity, **2.**35–**2.**36, **3.**84, **8.**22–**8.**25
History of gears, **1.**1
Hobbing, **5.**4–**5.**10
advantages and disadvantages of, **3.**15
clearance required for hob, **5.**4–**5.**7
definition of, **5.**2
feeds and speeds, **5.**4, **5.**8
gap widths required for, **5.**7
of helical gears, **3.**39–**3.**40, **8.**7–**8.**9
production time for, **5.**7, **5.**9–**5.**10
Hobs, **6.**10–**6.**27
calculation of gap width required for, **6.**14–**6.**18
dimensions of, **6.**14–**6.**15
kinds of, **6.**12–**6.**13, **6.**19–**6.**20, **6.**23–**6.**27
oversize to allow for sharpening of, **6.**20–**6.**21
profile cut by, **6.**12, **6.**21
recent developments in, **6.**23
root fillet cut by, **9.**26
Hobs (*Cont.*):
special design problems using, **8.**4–**8.**6, **9.**59–**9.**63
tolerances for, **6.**13, **6.**16
typical design problem using, **6.**21–**6.**22
using at less than full depth, **8.**5, **8.**6
using at more than full depth, **9.**62–**9.**63
for worm gears, **6.**19–**6.**21
Honing, **5.**59, **5.**70–**5.**72
time required for, **5.**70
uses of, **5.**71, **5.**72
HPSTC (*see* Highest point of single tooth contact)
Hunting ratio:
definition of, **3.**2
factors in choosing, **3.**8–**3.**9
for worm gears, **3.**68
Hutchinson, R. N., **3.**83, **9.**46, Ref. 176
Hypoid gears, **1.**38–**1.**40, **9.**3
calculations for, **3.**58–**3.**59
estimating size needed, **2.**51

I factors, **3.**109
Ichimaru, K., **3.**8, Ref. 175
Idler gear, **9.**2
IFToMM (International Federation for the Theory of Machinery and Mechanisms), **3.**76*n.*, **9.**9
Imbalance overloads, **7.**37
Imwalle, Dennis E., **3.**83, **3.**93, **9.**46–**9.**48, Refs. 176, 177
Inclusions, definition of, **4.**3
Induction hardening:
definition of, **4.**3
potential problems with, **4.**36–**4.**38
power and frequency needed for, **4.**31–**4.**33, **4.**35, **4.**37
by scanning, **4.**33–**4.**36
speed of, **4.**30–**4.**31, **4.**33
of steel gears, **4.**30–**4.**38
Industrial gears, **1.**21–**1.**23
Injection-molded gears, **1.**5
Interference in meshed gears, **3.**14–**3.**15
due to bending, **8.**12–**8.**13
in internal gears, **3.**34
Internal gears, **1.**31–**1.**33
calculation sheet for, **3.**39
choosing dimensions for, **3.**33–**3.**39
definition of, **1.**2
special calculations for, **9.**27–**9.**30

International Federation for the Theory of Machinery and Mechanisms (IFToMM), **3.**76*n.*, **9.**9
International Organization for Standardization (ISO):
- address of, **3.**142
- comparison with AGMA standards, **9.**10–**9.**15, **9.**37, **9.**44–**9.**48
- formulas for bending strength and pitting resistance, **9.**44
- gear-rating standards, **2.**13, **3.**78, **3.**83, **3.**88, **3.**93, **3.**96, **3.**105, **3.**148, **9.**37–**9.**44
- nomenclature of rating, **9.**45

Involute checks (*see* Checking procedures for gear size and accuracy, for measuring profile)
Involute curve, definition of, **2.**2, **9.**6–**9.**7
Involute equations, **2.**17
Involute function, table of values, **9.**34–**9.**35
Involute geometry calculations, **9.**20–**9.**22
Involute relations, **2.**17, **3.**24
Iron gears (*see* Cast-iron gears)
Ishibashi, A., **3.**8, Ref. 179
ISO (*see* International Organization for Standardization)

J factors, **3.**88
Jominy curves, **4.**13
Jominy test, definition of, **4.**3
Journal surfaces, definition of, **2.**2

K chart, **5.**75, **8.**21
K factor:
- comparison of AGMA and ISO allowable, **9.**46–**9.**48
- definition of, **2.**2, **2.**18, **2.**41–**2.**43
- derivation of, **2.**17–**2.**18
- equations: for bevel gears, **2.**47–**2.**48
  - for spur and helical gears, **2.**43, **3.**82
- for estimating gear size needed, **2.**37, **2.**44–**2.**47
- in histogram plots, **2.**36
- for marine gears, **3.**147
- for oil and gas industry gears, **3.**149
- table of: for bevel gears, **2.**49
  - for spur and helical gears, **2.**45
- typical values for different applications, **2.**46

Knoop hardness test (*see* Tukon hardness test)
Kubo, Aizoh, **2.**12, **9.**9–**9.**15, Refs. 191–194
Kyoto University, dynamic load research at, **9.**9–**9.**15

LaBath, Octave A., **3.**83, **3.**93, **9.**46–**9.**48, Refs. 176, 177
Lambda ratio for regimes of lubrication, **3.**138
Laminates for gears, **1.**8, **4.**2, **4.**58–**4.**60
Lapping, definition of, **5.**2
Layouts:
- of external gear teeth, **3.**32–**3.**33, **9.**26
- of helical gear teeth, **9.**33
- of internal gear teeth, **9.**29–**9.**30
- of large circles, **9.**17–**9.**19
- of profile modification zones, **8.**19
- of root-fillet trochoids, **9.**24–**9.**26
- (*See also* Drawings)

LD or L.D. (*see* Limit diameter)
Lead:
- definition of, **3.**2
- sample calculation of, **8.**11
- of worm, **1.**47

Lead angle:
- definition of, **3.**2
- of worm gears, **1.**43, **1.**45, **1.**47, **3.**65, **3.**67–**3.**68, **3.**71

Lewis, Wilfred, **2.**7–**2.**10, **2.**12, **2.**13, **2.**43, Ref. 200
Lewis formula, derivation of, **2.**7–**2.**9
Life expectancy:
- extending by in-service tooth surface treatment, **3.**148
- extending by use of reheat quench, **4.**17–**4.**18
- of pitted gears, **3.**82
- of vehicle gears, **3.**146

Life requirements:
- of aerospace gears, **3.**150
- of industrial gears, **1.**22–**1.**23, **3.**148–**3.**149
- of marine gears, **1.**19, **3.**147

Lightweight gear units, **1.**19–**1.**20, **2.**39, **2.**41, **3.**150
Limit diameter, **3.**25–**3.**29
- definition of, **3.**2
- equation for, **3.**27

Line of action:
- definition of, **9.**7
- equation for length of, **2.**27, **3.**27

Load:
 axial thrust, **9.**3
 calculation of, **2.**43
  (See also *K* factor: Stress calculations; Unit load)
 dynamic (*see* Dynamic load)
 and gear failure, **7.**25
 tangential driving, **3.**76–**3.**77
 transmitted, **2.**43
 unit (*see* Unit load)
 on vehicle gears, **3.**145–**3.**146
 worst, **2.**9–**2.**10, **2.**18–**2.**19
 (See also *K* factor)
Load-carrying capacity:
 of crossed-helical gears, **1.**41, **3.**115–**3.**118
 design modification to increase, **8.**2–**8.**4
 design specifications for, **2.**35–**2.**36
 determined by field experience, **2.**6, **3.**150
 in different regimes of lubrication, **2.**23–**2.**24
 effect of: accuracy on, **3.**141–**3.**142, **9.**9–**9.**15
  case depth on, **4.**20–**4.**22, **4.**28–**4.**29, **4.**36
  hardness on, **4.**18
  hunting ratio on, **3.**8
  profile modification on, **8.**12
  tooth proportions on, **3.**9–**3.**10, **3.**14, **3.**54
 of induction-hardened gears, **4.**36–**4.**38
 maximizing for helical gears, **3.**40–**3.**41
 of nonmetallic gears, **4.**59, **4.**61
 reduction of, by dynamic loads, **9.**9–**9.**15
 of Spiroid gears, **1.**50
 of worm gears: double-enveloping, **1.**48, **3.**122–**3.**128
  single-enveloping, **1.**44, **3.**118–**3.**122, **3.**126–**3.**128
 (See also *K* factor; Rating calculations; Strength; Stress calculations; Surface durability; Unit load)
Load distribution, **2.**12, **7.**50, **8.**15–**8.**17
 across face width, **2.**4–**2.**5, **2.**38–**2.**39, **2.**47, **3.**96, **3.**135
Load distribution factor:
 for bevel gears, **3.**102–**3.**103
 graph of, **3.**98
 for spur and helical gears, table of, **3.**97
 for surface durability, **3.**113
 for tooth strength, **3.**93, **3.**96–**3.**103
Load rating (*see* Rating)
Load sharing, **3.**88
 (*See also* Contact ratio; Geometry factors; Highest point of single tooth contact; Lowest point of single tooth contact)
Low-cost gears, **1.**5–**1.**7, **1.**50, **3.**63, **4.**61, **5.**34, **5.**36–**5.**38, **5.**87, **5.**89
Lowest point of single tooth contact (LPSTC), **2.**29, **2.**30, **9.**15–**9.**17
LPSTC (*see* Lowest point of single tooth contact)
Lubricant coefficient, **3.**136–**3.**137
Lubricant number recommended by AGMA, **7.**42–**7.**43
Lubricant viscosity ranges, **3.**136–**3.**137, **7.**41, **7.**44, **7.**45
Lubrication:
 of aircraft gears, **7.**44
 during break-in period, **2.**25
 and cooling, **2.**32, **2.**34, **3.**128–**3.**129
 design of systems for, **2.**44, **7.**45–**7.**47
  for high-speed gears, **2.**69
  for Spiroid gears, **2.**54
  for worm gears, **2.**52
 EHD (*see* Elastohydrodynamic lubrication)
 failures of, **7.**40
 fluids used for, **7.**40–**7.**41
 kinds of oils, **2.**23, **3.**137
 of nonmetallic gears, **4.**59, **4.**61
 potential problems with, **7.**39–**7.**47
 regimes of (*see* Regimes of lubrication)
 to remove heat from gears, **7.**44–**7.**45
 requirements for, **3.**139
  with worm gears, **1.**48, **3.**118
 and scoring, **2.**24, **3.**131, **3.**135–**3.**141
 trade standards for, **7.**41
 of vehicle gears, **3.**146, **7.**44–**7.**46, **8.**26
 (*See also* Oils)
Lutthans, R. V., **3.**93, Ref. 110

M_s temperature:
 definition of, **4.**8, **4.**10
 table of, **4.**8
Maag Gear Wheel Co., grinding process of, **5.**46–**5.**47
McCormick, Doug, **5.**79, Ref. 208
Machine-tool gears, **1.**9
 (*See also* Industrial gears)
Manufacturing methods, **5.**1–**5.**90
 broaching, **5.**31–**5.**34
 casting and molding, **5.**86–**5.**89
 chart of, **5.**3

Manufacturing methods (*Cont.*):
cost of different, **5.**79
for different levels of accuracy, **3.**106–**3.**107
for different types of gears: bevel, **3.**102, **5.**23–**5.**26, **5.**51–**5.**53, **9.**36–**9.**43
spiral, **1.**37–**1.**38
straight, **1.**33
Zerol, **1.**36–**1.**37
crossed-helical, **1.**42, **5.**4
face, **1.**41, **5.**10
helical, **1.**30, **5.**4, **5.**10, **5.**16, **5.**26, **5.**31, **5.**39, **5.**46, **5.**53, **5.**61, **5.**65, **5.**88
hypoid, **1.**38
internal, **1.**32, **5.**10, **5.**16, **5.**31, **5.**36, **5.**39, **5.**46, **5.**61, **5.**62, **5.**72
marine, **3.**146–**3.**147
racks, **5.**30, **5.**31
Spiroid, **1.**50, **2.**53–**2.**54
spur, **1.**27, **5.**4, **5.**10, **5.**16, **5.**26, **5.**31, **5.**36, **5.**39, **5.**46, **5.**53, **5.**61, **5.**65, **5.**72, **5.**88, **6.**27–**6.**29
worm, **1.**45, **2.**51, **5.**4, **5.**10, **5.**26, **5.**27, **5.**57–**5.**59, **6.**19–**6.**21
grinding: form, **5.**39–**5.**45
generating: with disc wheel, **5.**46–**5.**51
with threaded wheel, **5.**53–**5.**57
thread, **5.**57–**5.**59
G-TRAC generating, **5.**36–**5.**38
hobbing, **5.**4–**5.**10
honing, **5.**59, **5.**70–**5.**72
milling, **5.**26–**5.**31
punching, **5.**34–**5.**36
rolling and cold drawing, **5.**59, **5.**66–**5.**70, **5.**89–**5.**90
shaping: with pinion cutter, **5.**10–**5.**16
with rack cutter, **5.**16–**5.**22
shaving, **5.**59–**5.**66
sintering, **5.**88–**5.**89
tooth cutting, **5.**3–**5.**38
(*See also* Checking procedures for gear size and accuracy; Cutting tools; *and specific methods*)
Manufacturing nomenclature, **5.**2–**5.**3
Manufacturing trends, **1.**4–**1.**25
Marine gears, **1.**16–**1.**19, **3.**115, **3.**146–**3.**148, **4.**18
Martempering, definition of, **4.**40
Martensite:
definition of, **4.**3
and M_s temperature, **4.**10
production of, **4.**11
Martinaglia, L., **2.**34, **3.**149, **7.**51, Ref. 206
Matching diameter, calculation of:
for pinion and gear, **9.**49–**9.**50
for shaper cutter and gear, **9.**58
Material factor for cylindrical worm gears, **3.**118–**3.**119
Materials for gears, **4.**1–**4.**61
AGMA manual for, **4.**50
bronze (*see* Bronze for gears)
copper plating, **3.**141
factors to consider in choosing, **4.**1–**4.**2
iron (*see* Cast-iron gears)
laminates, **1.**8, **4.**2, **4.**58–**4.**60
nonferrous metals, **4.**53–**4.**57
nonmetallic, **4.**57–**4.**61
nylon, **1.**8, **4.**60–**4.**61
plastic, **1.**5
for punched gears, **5.**36
silver plating, **3.**141
steels (*see* Steels for gears)
(*See also* Metallurgical quality; Worm gears, materials used in)
Measuring of gears (*see* Checking procedures for gear size and accuracy)
Mesh deflection (*see* Deflection of teeth in mesh)
Meshing diameters of pinion and gear, calculation of, **9.**49–**9.**50
Metallurgical nomenclature, **4.**2–**4.**3
Metallurgical quality:
checking procedure for, **4.**47
effect of alloy content on, **4.**6
effect of cooling rate on, **4.**7, **4.**10, **4.**17–**4.**18
effect of gear size on, **3.**113, **4.**20
grades of, **3.**75, **3.**77–**3.**78, **3.**144, **3.**151, **4.**40–**4.**47
importance of, **2.**67–**2.**68, **4.**37
specifications needed for, **2.**68, **3.**75
of steel gears, **4.**40–**4.**47
trade standards on, **3.**144, **3.**151
Metric system, **1.**3
in gear practice, **1.**28
used in this book, **2.**19*n.*, **3.**115
Mill gears, **1.**24–**1.**25, **3.**94
Miller, John, **4.**57
Milling, **5.**26–**5.**31
best uses of, **5.**30
clearance required for, **5.**28
definition of, **5.**2
production time for, **5.**9, **5.**29–**5.**30
Milling cutters, **6.**27–**6.**36
choosing size of, for accuracy, **6.**28–**6.**29

Milling cutters (*Cont.*):
  profile of, **6.**27–**6.**28
    calculation of, **6.**29
  for spur gears, **6.**27–**6.**29
  standard sizes of, **6.**28, **6.**29
  for worm gears, **6.**29–**6.**36
Misalignment of gearset in casing, **7.**38–**7.**39
Modification (*see* Helix angle, modification of; Profile modification)
Module:
  of bevel gears, **1.**33
  of crossed-helical gears, **1.**43, **3.**62
  definition of, **1.**2, **1.**27
  equation for helical gears, **1.**30
  of hypoid gears, **1.**38
  of worm gears, **3.**65
  (*See also* Tooth size)
Modulus of elasticity, **3.**116
  of cast iron, **4.**48
  definition of, **4.**4
Molding, **5.**86–**5.**89
  definition of, **5.**2
  production time for, **5.**87

Nakajima, A., **3.**8, Ref. 175
Nakase, K., **4.**30, Ref. 147
Narita, T., **2.**34, **7.**51, Ref. 28
New gear designs, need for testing of, **3.**94
Nitriding:
  alloys used with, **4.**24
  case depths after, **4.**27–**4.**30
  definition of, **4.**4, **4.**24
  distortion caused by, **4.**27
  potential problems with, **4.**27
  quality control with, **4.**47
  quality grades resulting from, **4.**45–**4.**47
  of steel gears, **4.**24–**4.**30
  structures obtained with, **4.**26, **4.**46
  suitable uses of, **4.**25–**4.**27
  techniques used for, **4.**24–**4.**25, **4.**28
  temperatures used in, **4.**25
  time required for, **4.**24–**4.**25
Nityanandan, P. M., **3.**76*n.*, Ref. 226
Noise of gears:
  effect of pressure angle on, **3.**10
  of marine gears, **1.**18–**1.**19
  reduction by profile modification, **8.**12
  special helical designs to minimize, **3.**41
  of spur gears, **1.**27
Nomenclature (*see* Gear nomenclature; Terminology)
Nonenveloping worm gears (*see* Crossed-helical gears)
Nonmetallic gears, **4.**57–**4.**61
  (*See also* Laminates for gears; Nylon gears; Plastic gears)
Nonparallel-axis gears, **1.**26
Normal section:
  definition of, **1.**2
  of helical gears, **1.**30, **1.**31
Normalizing:
  definition of, **4.**4, **4.**7
  purpose of, **4.**7
  temperatures used for, **4.**8
Number of teeth (*see* Teeth, number of)
Nylon gears, **1.**8, **4.**60–**4.**61

OD or O.D. (*see* Outside diameter)
Oil and gas industry gears, **1.**23–**1.**24, **3.**148–**3.**149
Oil-film thickness, **2.**25, **3.**135–**3.**140
  effects of velocity on, **3.**137–**3.**139
  equation for, **3.**136
  (*See also* Elastohydrodynamic lubrication; Lubrication)
Oils:
  extreme pressure (EP), **2.**23, **3.**141
  properties of, **3.**137–**3.**140
  for temperature extremes, **3.**153
  used with aircraft gears, **3.**153
  (*See also* Lubrication)
Outside circle, definition of, **9.**4
Outside diameter:
  effect on choice of checking equipment of, **5.**80–**5.**81
  illustration of, **1.**29
  limits of: for bevel-gear generators, **5.**25–**5.**26
    for broaching, **5.**31
    for cold drawing and extruding, **5.**89
    for grinding, **5.**46, **5.**52–**5.**54
    for hobbing, **5.**4, **5.**10
    for honing, **5.**72
    for milling, **5.**28
    for punching, **5.**36
    for rolling, **5.**67
    for shaping, **5.**10, **5.**18
    for shaving, **5.**65–**5.**66
Overhung, definition of, **2.**2
Overlapping, definition of, **9.**3
Overload:
  effect of tooth errors on, **7.**36–**7.**37, **9.**9

Overload (*Cont.*):
imbalance, **7**.37
momentary, **7**.35–**7**.37, **9**.9–**9**.15
torsional vibration, **7**.36, **9**.9–**9**.15

PA or P.A. (*see* Pressure angle)
Parallel-axis gears, **1**.26
PD or P.D. (*see* Pitch diameter)
Pearlite:
benefit of, **4**.7, **4**.48
definition of, **4**.4
Pinion, definition of, **1**.2, **9**.2
Pins (*see* Diameter: between pins; over pins)
Pitch (*see* Diametral pitch)
Pitch angle:
of bevel gears, **1**.34, **1**.35, **1**.37
of hypoid gears, **1**.40
Pitch circle, definition of, **9**.4
Pitch diameter:
of bevel gears, **1**.35, **2**.50
of crossed-helical gears, **1**.42–**1**.43
definition of, **1**.2
estimating size needed (*see* Size)
of hypoid gears, **1**.38
illustration of, **1**.29
internal gear equations for, **1**.33
operating, **1**.29, **8**.4–**8**.6, **8**.9–**8**.11
spread ratio, **8**.3
spur gear equations for, **1**.28
worm gear equations for, **1**.47, **1**.49, **3**.67
Pitch point, definition of, **3**.2, **9**.5
Pitch-line velocity, definition of, **2**.2
(*See also* Speeds of gears)
Pitting, **7**.19–**7**.22
causes of, **7**.19, **7**.21, **7**.26–**7**.27, **9**.26
definition of, **3**.2
destructive type of, **7**.21
healing of, **7**.21–**7**.22
of helical gears, **3**.43–**3**.44, **7**.21
illustrations of, **7**.13–**7**.16, **7**.22
initial type of, **7**.21
locations on tooth of, **7**.19–**7**.21, **9**.26
and lubrication problems, **7**.21, **7**.26
sequence of, **2**.20
(*See also* Failure of gears; Surface durability)
Planoid gear, **1**.50
Plastic gears, **1**.5
Poritsky, H., **6**.13, **6**.31, **6**.33, Ref. 132
Power:
through helical gears, **1**.26
Power (*Cont.*):
through industrial gears, **1**.22
through marine gears, **1**.17
through mill gears, **1**.24
through oil and gas industry gears, **1**.23
transmitted, equation for, **2**.43
(*See also* Load-carrying capacity)
Power capacity:
of Spiroid gearsets, **2**.54
of worm gearsets, **2**.52, **2**.53, **3**.121, **3**.123, **3**.125
Pressure angle:
of aerospace gears, **1**.21, **3**.10
of bevel gears: spiral, **1**.38
straight, **1**.35, **3**.46
Zerol, **1**.37
of crossed-helical gears, **1**.43, **3**.62–**3**.63
definition of, **1**.2, **9**.7
distortion: from carburizing, **4**.19
from nitriding, **4**.27
of face gears, **1**.41
factors to consider in choosing, **3**.10, **3**.12, **3**.141
of helical gears, **1**.30, **3**.40–**3**.41, **3**.43
of hypoid gears, **1**.38
illustration of, **1**.29
of internal gears, **9**.30
limit for cold-drawn and extruded stock, **5**.89
limit for rolling worm threads, **5**.90
operating, **1**.28–**1**.29, **8**.2–**8**.6, **8**.9–**8**.11
range for rotary shaving, **5**.61
range in use, **1**.28, **3**.10
of worm gears, **1**.46, **1**.49, **3**.65, **3**.67, **3**.71
Pressure constant for worm gears, **3**.124
Profile accuracy:
of involute profile, **2**.66
(*See also* Checking procedures for gear size and accuracy, for measuring, profile; *K* factor; Surface durability)
Profile modification:
of aerospace gears, **1**.21
amount of, **3**.130–**3**.131
of bevel gears, **5**.23, **8**.12
calculation procedure for, **9**.48–**9**.50
definition of, **3**.2–**3**.3
depth to start, **3**.130
diameter to start (SD), **8**.16, **8**.20–**8**.21, **9**.22
example of *K* chart for, **8**.21
in grinding, **5**.47
of helical gears, **3**.40

Profile modification (*Cont.*):
  layout of zones for, **8.**19
  of machine-tool gears, **1.**9
  on pinion only, **9.**48–**9.**50
  of precision-accuracy gears, **8.**17–**8.**21
  purpose of, **8.**12, **8.**14
  sample problems for, **8.**12–**8.**21
  and scoring, **3.**129–**3.**134, **3.**141, **8.**17–**8.**21, **9.**63–**9.**65
  specifications for, **8.**16, **8.**21
  standard system of, **8.**13–**8.**17
  tolerances on, **8.**18
Proportions (*see* Tooth proportions)
Punched gears, **1.**5
Punching, **5.**34–**5.**36, **6.**39–**6.**41
  definition of, **5.**2
  power required for, **6.**40
  procedure used in, **6.**39
  suitable uses for, **5.**36
  time required for, **5.**36
  tools for, **6.**39–**6.**40

Q factor, **2.**36
  definition of, **2.**2
  use of, for estimating size required: of bevel gears, **2.**47–**2.**51
    of spur and helical gears, **2.**36–**2.**41
Quality grades:
  for geometric accuracy, **3.**106–**3.**107, **5.**73–**5.**74
  for metallurgical quality, **3.**75, **3.**77–**3.**78, **3.**144, **3.**151, **4.**40–**4.**47
Quality tests:
  for geometric accuracy (*see* Checking procedures for gear size and accuracy)
  low-cost, **2.**67
  for metallurgical quality, **4.**47
Quenching:
  definition of, **4.**4
  with dies to minimize distortion, **1.**12, **4.**20
  directly from carburizing temperature, **4.**17
  improper, **4.**11
  mediums for, **4.**9, **4.**12
  methods of, **4.**40
  rate of, **4.**6, **4.**9, **4.**10
  reheat, **4.**17–**4.**18
  tempering after, **4.**4

Rack:
  definition of, **1.**28, **9.**2
Rack (*Cont.*):
  function of, **9.**2
  manufacture of, **5.**30, **5.**31
Radar gears, **1.**10–**1.**11
Radius of curvature:
  of crossed-helical gears, **3.**116
  of root fillet (*see* Fillet radius of curvature)
Rating:
  of bevel gears, **3.**86–**3.**87
  comparison of trade standards on, **9.**37, **9.**44–**9.**48
  graphs of stress vs. cycles, **3.**83–**3.**86
  specifications relating to, **3.**147
  validity of trade standards on, **3.**73–**3.**74, **4.**5
Rating calculations:
  accuracy of, **8.**26
  comparison of procedures for cylindrical and double-enveloping worm gears, **3.**126–**3.**127
  factors to consider in, **3.**74–**3.**76, **3.**83
  load histogram method of, **8.**22–**8.**25
  need for field experience backup of, **3.**74–**3.**75, **3.**83
  sample problem of, **8.**22–**8.**26
  starting point for, **3.**76
  for tooth bending strength, **3.**78–**3.**153, **9.**44–**9.**48
    graphs of allowable stress, **3.**84–**3.**85
  for tooth surface durability, **3.**78–**3.**153, **9.**44–**9.**48
    graphs of allowable contact stress, **3.**85–**3.**86
  trade standards on, **9.**37, **9.**44–**9.**48
  (*See also* Derating factors; Load-carrying capacity; Stress calculations)
Ratio (tooth):
  for crossed-helical gears, **3.**63
  definition of, **1.**2, **1.**29, **9.**2
  for double-enveloping worm gears, **1.**49
  for hypoid gears, **1.**38, **3.**58
  for internal gears, **3.**35–**3.**37
  for Spiroid gears, **1.**51
  (*See also* Hunting ratio)
Ratio correction factor for worm gears, **3.**118, **3.**120, **3.**125
Recess action:
  definition of, **3.**3
  with long-addendum designs, **3.**17
Regimes of lubrication:
  for aerospace gears, **3.**152–**3.**153
  and cold-scoring hazard, **3.**139

Regimes of lubrication (*Cont.*):
definition of, **2.**20–**2.**21
determining factors for, **2.**21–**2.**22, **3.**138–**3.**141
lubrication recommendations for different, **3.**139
for vehicle gears, **3.**146, **8.**26
Reliability-level system, **3.**78, **3.**144–**3.**145
(*See also* Life requirements)
Research on gears:
extent of, **1.**1
(*See also* Future needs in gear practice; Testing of gears; *and specific properties*)
Residual stress, definition of, **4.**4
Rockwell hardness:
conversion to other scales, **4.**16
definition of, **4.**4
test method for determining, **4.**15
Roll angles, **3.**23–**3.**29, **3.**39, **3.**44
calculation sheet for, **9.**22, **9.**28
equations for, **3.**27, **3.**62
of helical gears, **9.**33
sample calculation of, **8.**20–**8.**21
Rolling (method of gear finishing), **5.**59, **5.**66–**5.**70, **5.**89–**5.**90
definition of, **5.**2
recommended uses for, **5.**70
time required for, **5.**70, **5.**90
Root angle of bevel gears, **1.**34, **1.**35, **3.**52, **3.**53, **3.**55, **3.**56
Root circle, definition of, **9.**4
Root fillet (*see* Fillet radius of curvature; Trochoidal root fillet)
Root stress (*see* Stress calculations, for bending stress)
Rubbing velocity (*see* Sliding velocity)
Runout (clearance) (*see specific tooth-cutting methods*)
Runout (concentricity):
definition of, **3.**3
measurement of, **5.**80, **5.**82, **9.**53–**9.**54

Schwarz, H., **9.**37
Scleroscope hardness test, **4.**15, **4.**16
Scoring, **7.**22–**7.**24
calculating risk of, **2.**25–**2.**32, **3.**135
cold, **2.**24–**2.**26, **3.**135–**3.**141
definition of, **2.**24, **3.**3
design formulas for, **3.**128–**3.**141
design procedure to handle, **3.**140–**3.**141, **4.**53–**4.**54, **7.**22, **8.**17–**8.**21
Scoring (*Cont.*):
due to thermal problems, **7.**50
effects of gear materials on, **7.**23
of helical gears, **3.**43
hot, **2.**24–**2.**26, **3.**128–**3.**135, **3.**140–**3.**141
illustrations of, **7.**16
kinds of, **2.**24–**2.**26, **7.**23
and lubrication, **7.**22, **7.**24, **7.**26
prevention of, **7.**24, **8.**17–**8.**21
probable locations on tooth of, **2.**30, **7.**22–**7.**23, **8.**16
problems: with extra-depth teeth, **3.**12
with long-addendum pinions, **3.**17
PVT formula, **2.**26
in Regime I, **2.**25
self-healing of, **3.**135, **7.**23–**7.**24
tooth geometry factor for, **2.**32, **9.**63–**9.**65
of worm gears, **2.**51
Scoring criterion method, **2.**31–**2.**32, **3.**128, **3.**133–**3.**135
Scuffing (*see* Scoring)
SD or S.D. (*see* Profile modification, diameter to start)
Seabrook, John B., **9.**16, Ref. 247
Secondary hardening, definition of, **4.**4
Self-locking worm gears, **3.**66
Service factor, **3.**96, **3.**121, **3.**126
table of, **3.**122, **3.**128
Shaft misalignment, effects of, **3.**97
Shaper cutters:
design of, **6.**2–**6.**11, **9.**54–**9.**59
dimensions of, **6.**5
for helical gears, **6.**4–**6.**5, **6.**7, **6.**12
for internal gears, **6.**3–**6.**4, **6.**10
kinds and sizes of, **6.**2–**6.**4, **6.**10–**6.**11
special features on, **6.**2, **6.**6
trade standards on, **6.**2–**6.**3, **6.**8–**6.**9
whole depth cut by, **6.**7
Shaping, **5.**10–**5.**22
advances in, **5.**14
clearance required for, **5.**10–**5.**11
definition of, **5.**2
design of cutter for, **6.**2–**6.**11, **9.**54–**9.**59
of helical gears, **3.**40
with pinion cutter, **5.**10–**5.**16
popular uses of, **5.**17–**5.**18
production time for, **5.**12–**5.**14, **5.**19, **5.**22
with rack cutter, **5.**16–**5.**22
Sharma, V. K., **4.**30, Ref. 249
Shaving, **5.**59–**5.**66
amount of stock removed by, **5.**64
change in cutter from sharpening, **6.**38

Shaving (*Cont.*):
- choice of cutter size for, **6.**38
- clearance required for, **5.**61, **5.**63
- cutting action in, **6.**36–**6.**37
- definition of, **5.**2
- design of cutter for, **6.**36–**6.**39
- with rack cutter, **5.**65–**5.**66
- with rotary cutter, **5.**60–**5.**65
- shaft angles recommended with, **6.**37
- time required for, **5.**62–**5.**66, **5.**70
- uses of, **5.**59

Shear cutting, **5.**2–**5.**3

Shock in driving and driven apparatus (*see* Dynamic load)

Shore hardness test, **4.**15, **4.**16

Silver plating gear teeth, **3.**141

Single-enveloping worm gears (*see* Worm gears, cylindrical)

Sintered gears, **1.**7, **1.**8, **4.**52–**4.**53, **5.**88–**5.**89

Sintering, **5.**88–**5.**89, **6.**40–**6.**42
- definition of, **5.**3
- procedure used in, **5.**88, **6.**40–**6.**41
- tools for, **6.**41–**6.**42

Size (center distance and face width):
- calculating gear size needed, **2.**5–**2.**6, **2.**34–**2.**54, **3.**82
  - based on K factor, **2.**44
  - of bevel gears, **2.**47–**2.**51
  - of complex gear arrangements, **2.**39–**2.**41
  - of face gears and hypoid gears, **2.**51
  - of helical gears, **2.**36–**2.**47
  - of Spiroid gears, **2.**53–**2.**54
  - of spur gears, **2.**36–**2.**47
  - of worm gears, **2.**51–**2.**53, **3.**67
- change in: during carburizing, **4.**19
  - during induction hardening, **4.**30
  - during nitriding, **4.**27
- effect of, on case hardening, **4.**20
- of marine gears, **1.**16, **1.**18
- of mill gears, **1.**25
- of radar gears, **1.**10, **9.**1
- of transportation gears, **1.**14
- (*See also* Face width; Outside diameter; Size factor in gear rating; Tooth size)

Size factor in gear rating:
- for bevel gears, **3.**113–**3.**114
- for tooth strength, **3.**93, **3.**103–**3.**104
  - graph of, **3.**104
- for tooth surface durability, **3.**113–**3.**115

Sliding, direction of, **9.**21–**9.**23, **9.**26

Sliding velocity, **1.**43, **1.**48
- comparison by gear types, **2.**53

Sliding velocity (*Cont.*):
- for crossed-helical gears, **3.**117–**3.**118
- for cylindrical worm gears, **3.**118–**3.**119
- definition of, **2.**2
- for double-enveloping worm gears, **3.**125

Spacing accuracy, **2.**65–**2.**66, **8.**12

Spalling, **4.**27

Specifications (*see* Checking procedures for gear size and accuracy; Drawings, accuracy limits for; Heat treatment, specifications for; Rating, specifications relating to)

Speeds of gears:
- of aircraft gears, **1.**27
- of industrial gears, **1.**22
- of marine gears, **1.**17
- of mill gears, **1.**25
- of oil and gas industry gears, **1.**23
- of spur gears, **1.**27
- (*See also* High-speed gears)

Spiral angle, **1.**36, **1.**38

Spiral bevel gears (*see* Bevel gears, spiral)

Spiral gears (*see* Crossed-helical gears)

Spiroid gears, **1.**49–**1.**51
- definition of, **1.**2
- estimating size of, **2.**53–**2.**54

Spread center, **8.**9–**8.**11, **9.**59–**9.**61

Spread ratio, **8.**3, **8.**5, **8.**10

Spur gears:
- choosing dimensions and tolerances for, **3.**31–**3.**33
- definition of, **1.**2, **9.**2
- dimension sheet for, **3.**32
- dynamic factors for, **9.**9–**9.**14
- estimating size of, **2.**36–**2.**47
- external, **1.**27–**1.**29
- internal, **1.**31–**1.**33
- special calculations for, **9.**19–**9.**26
- virtual, **9.**33, **9.**36

Stamped gears, **1.**7

Stamping (*see* Punching)

Standards (*see* American Gear Manufacturers Association; International Organization for Standardization; Trade standards)

Steels for gears, **4.**1, **4.**4–**4.**47
- alloys suitable for: induction hardening, **4.**30
  - nitriding, **4.**24, **4.**27, **4.**29
- carburizing of, **4.**17–**4.**24
- chemical composition of specific, **4.**7, **4.**11
- combined heat treatments of, **4.**39–**4.**40

Steels for gears (*Cont.*):
effects of alloy content in, **3.**104, **4.**6, **4.**12, **4.**24
effects of carbon content of, **4.**12, **4.**17
flame hardening of, **4.**38–**4.**39
hardness tests for, **4.**13–**4.**16
heat-treating techniques for, **4.**6–**4.**16
(*See also* Heat treatment)
high-alloy, **1.**20, **4.**6
induction hardening of, **4.**30–**4.**38
low-alloy, **1.**9, **1.**12, **1.**14, **4.**6, **4.**19
mechanical properties of, **4.**5, **4.**6
metallurgical quality of, **4.**40–**4.**47
(*See also* Metallurgical quality)
nitriding of, **4.**24–**4.**30
structures obtained: after carburizing, **4.**21, **4.**44
after flame hardening, **4.**39
after heat treatment, **4.**10, **4.**12–**4.**13
after nitriding, **4.**26, **4.**46
table of commonly used, **4.**8, **4.**9, **4.**11
Stiffness constant, **3.**98–**3.**99, **8.**15
Straddle mount, definition of, **2.**2
Strength:
effect of alloy content on, **4.**6
effect of heat treatment on, **4.**6–**4.**7, **4.**11, **4.**17, **4.**20, **4.**27–**4.**30
rating of (*see* Rating calculations)
of worm gears, **3.**115, **3.**121
(*See also* Beam strength; Stress calculations, for bending stress)
Stress calculations:
for bending stress, **2.**7–**2.**13, **3.**79, **3.**84–**3.**85, **8.**23–**8.**24, **9.**44
for compressive stress, **2.**15–**2.**18, **2.**27
for contact stress, **3.**82, **3.**85–**3.**86, **8.**23–**8.**24, **9.**44
factors involved in, **2.**4–**2.**5, **3.**84, **4.**5
for shear stress, **2.**15
stress-limit tables: for aerospace gears, **3.**152
for case-hardened gears, **4.**28
for oil and gas industry gears, **3.**149
for vehicle gears, **3.**145
(*See also* Histograms of load intensity)
Stress relief:
definition of, **4.**4
before nitriding, **4.**25
Stresses on gear teeth:
from bending, **2.**7–**2.**13, **3.**79
in contacting surfaces, **2.**14, **3.**82
points of maximum, **9.**16–**9.**17
Structure of steel (*see* Steel for gears)
Stub teeth, current use of, **3.**11
Surface durability:
calculations: historical, **2.**14–**2.**24
rating (*see* Rating calculations, for tooth surface durability)
of carburized gears, **4.**20
in different regimes of lubrication, **2.**22
effect of long addendum on, **3.**17–**3.**18
endurance limit idea, **2.**19–**2.**20
factors involved in, **2.**19–**2.**20, **3.**145–**3.**146
of helical gears, **3.**40
of honed gears, **5.**71
of induction-hardened gears, **4.**36–**4.**37
of nitrided gears, **4.**27, **4.**28
redesign to increase, **8.**2–**8.**4
reworking tooth surfaces to increase, **3.**148
of vehicle gears, **3.**145–**3.**146
of worm gears, **3.**115–**3.**128
(*See also* Contact stress; Failure of gears; *K* factor; Pitting; Scoring)
Surface finish:
accuracy of, **2.**66
after cold drawing and rolling, **5.**89–**5.**90
constant for, **3.**128, **3.**131–**3.**132
definition of, **2.**25, **3.**138
after hobbing, **5.**7
after honing, **5.**71
of machine-tool gears, **1.**9
measuring of, **5.**80, **5.**81, **9.**52–**9.**53
and oil-film thickness, **3.**137, **3.**140
and scoring, **3.**128–**3.**141
after sintering, **5.**88
after wearing in, **2.**25, **3.**8, **3.**76, **3.**141
of worm gears, **3.**118
Swaging, definition of, **2.**24
Symbols used in equations, tables of, **1.**3, **2.**3, **3.**4–**3.**5, **3.**80–**3.**81

Tanaka, S., **3.**8, Ref. 179
Teeth:
broken (*see* Broken teeth)
number of: factors to consider in choosing, **3.**3, **3.**6, **3.**7
in high-speed pinions, **3.**3
for hypoid gears, **3.**58
for internal gears, **3.**33–**3.**37, **9.**30
virtual, **1.**35, **3.**45, **9.**33, **9.**36
for worm gears, **3.**68, **3.**71
(*See also* Hunting ratio; *and under* Tooth)
Tejima, T., **2.**34, **7.**51, Ref. 28

Temperature(s), **4.**10
of meshing gears, **3.**128–**3.**129
thermal problems, **3.**149, **7.**44–**7.**51
(*See also* Thermal rating)
used during carburizing, **4.**8
used during heat treatment, **4.**8, **4.**11–**4.**12
used during nitriding, **4.**25
used during tempering, **4.**8, **4.**11, **4.**25
Tempering:
definition of, **4.**4
methods of, **4.**40
before nitriding, **4.**25
purpose of, **4.**10–**4.**11
temperatures used in, **4.**8, **4.**11, **4.**25
(*See also* Quenching)
Tensile strength:
definition of, **4.**4
determination of, **4.**13
graph of, **4.**5
Terminology:
of bevel gears, **1.**33–**1.**34
of face gears, **1.**40
of gear manufacture, **5.**2–**5.**3
of gear metallurgy, **4.**2–**4.**4
of gears, **1.**2–**1.**3, **2.**2–**2.**3, **3.**2–**3.**5, **9.**2–**9.**8
of heat treatment, **4.**2–**4.**4
of helical gears and racks, **1.**30–**1.**31
of internal gears, **1.**32
of Spiroid gears, **1.**50–**1.**51
of spur gears and racks, **1.**28–**1.**29
of worm gears, **1.**45–**1.**46, **1.**48
(*See also* Gear nomenclature; Gear terms, symbols, and units)
Testing of gears:
for accuracy and size (*see* Checking procedures for gear size and accuracy)
aerospace, **3.**150, **3.**153
need for, **2.**5, **3.**54, **3.**94, **3.**141, **4.**5, **4.**30, **4.**37–**4.**38, **4.**47
vehicle, **3.**146
Thermal problems, **3.**149, **7.**44–**7.**51
(*See also* Lubrication, and cooling)
Thermal rating, **2.**32–**2.**34
by AGMA, **7.**45
of worm gears, **2.**52
Thread of worm gear, definition of, **9.**3
Thread grinding of worms, **5.**57–**5.**59
amount of stock removed by, **5.**59
clearance required for, **5.**57
without prior cutting, **5.**57
profile produced by, **5.**57
time required for, **5.**57
Throated gears, definition of, **2.**2, **9.**3
Through hardening, **4.**7
definition of, **4.**4
potential problems with, **2.**68
size limits for, **4.**9
Thrust load on bearings:
from bevel gears, **1.**33, **1.**38
from crossed-helical gears, **1.**41
from face gears, **1.**40
from helical gears, **1.**30, **3.**42, **9.**3
from worm gears, **1.**43–**1.**44, **1.**47
Tolerances:
on gear dimensions, **2.**65–**2.**67, **3.**20–**3.**21, **3.**31–**3.**32, **5.**75–**5.**77
on hobs, **6.**13, **6.**16
minimum obtainable, **2.**65–**2.**67
on profile modification, **5.**75, **8.**18, **8.**21
on shaper cutters, **6.**8–**6.**9
on tooth thickness, **3.**20–**3.**21
Tools:
for cutting gear teeth (*see* Cutting tools; Hobs)
designing to accommodate standard sizes of, **8.**4–**8.**11
for punching, **6.**39–**6.**40
for sintering, **6.**40–**6.**42
standard modules and pitches needed in, **1.**28
(*See also specific manufacturing processes*)
Tooth profile:
of bevel gears: straight, **1.**33–**1.**34
Zerol, **1.**36
of face gears, **1.**41
of helical gears, **3.**45
of internal gears, **9.**29–**9.**30
involute curve, **9.**6–**9.**7
of worm gears, **1.**43, **1.**45, **1.**48, **3.**69
Tooth proportions, **3.**9–**3.**23
for bevel gears, **3.**45–**3.**58
for crossed-helical gears, **3.**62–**3.**65
definition of "full-depth," **3.**2, **3.**9
for face gears, **3.**59–**3.**62
factors involved in choosing depth, **3.**9–**3.**12
for helical gears, **3.**39–**3.**45
operated on spread center, **9.**59–**9.**63
for internal gears, **3.**34–**3.**39
long-addendum, **3.**14–**3.**18
and scoring hazard, **3.**140
for speed-increasing drives, **3.**18
for spur gears, **3.**9–**3.**23
of stub teeth, **3.**11
for worm gears: cylindrical, **3.**65–**3.**69
double-enveloping, **3.**69–**3.**73

Tooth size:
of bevel gears, **1.**33
of crossed-helical gears, **1.**43, **3.**62
factors involved in choosing, **2.**44, **3.**82, **3.**140
of worm gears, **3.**65, **3.**70
(*See also* Diametral pitch; Module)
Tooth spacing:
accuracy of, **2.**65–**2.**66, **8.**12
measurement of, **5.**81, **9.**50–**9.**52
Tooth thickness:
accuracy of, **2.**66
adjustment for long and short addendum, **3.**19
arc, **3.**19–**3.**21
equation for, **3.**19
illustration of, **1.**29
of bevel gears, **3.**48–**3.**51, **3.**54–**3.**56
calculation sheet for, **9.**23, **9.**29
chordal, **3.**21–**3.**23
equation for, **3.**22
illustration of, **1.**29
of face gears, **3.**61
of helical gears operated spread center, **9.**59–**9.**63
of internal gears, **3.**36–**3.**37
measurement of, **3.**22, **3.**38, **3.**48, **9.**19–**9.**20, **9.**54
(*See also* Diameter, over pins)
at operating pitch diameter, **8.**5–**8.**6
of shaper cutter, **9.**47
tolerances on, **3.**20–**3.**21, **3.**31–**3.**32
(*See also* Backlash)
of worm gears, double-enveloping, **3.**73
Top land, definition of, **2.**2
Torque, calculation of, **3.**77–**3.**78
Toys, gears for, **1.**5
Trade standards:
on accuracy, **2.**65, **2.**67
for aerospace gears, **3.**151–**3.**153
for gears, **3.**141–**3.**143
on load rating, **3.**115, **3.**141–**3.**143
for marine gears, **3.**148
for oil and gas industry gears, **3.**148–**3.**149
for vehicle gears, **3.**144
Transformation range:
definition of, **4.**4
diagram of, **4.**12
Transportation gears, **1.**14–**1.**16, **4.**18–**4.**19, **7.**24
(*See also* Automotive gears)
Transverse section:
definition of, **1.**2, **1.**30
Transverse section (*Cont.*):
in helical gears, **1.**30
Trochoidal root fillet, **3.**13, **9.**24–**9.**26, **9.**33
(*See also* Fillet radius of curvature)
TT or T.T. (*see* Tooth thickness)
Tucker, A. I., **2.**12, Ref. 280
Tukon hardness test, **4.**15, **4.**16
Turbine gears:
choosing number of pinion teeth for, **3.**6–**3.**7
in helicopters, **3.**150
metallurgical quality grades for, **4.**42–**4.**43
in oil and gas industry, **3.**148, **5.**72, **5.**73
plating to control scoring of, **3.**141
typical K factors for, **2.**46

Undercut:
definition of, **2.**2
disadvantages of, **3.**14–**3.**15
effect of addendum length on, **3.**14–**3.**15, **3.**17, **3.**46, **3.**65
effect of number of cutter teeth on, **3.**15
effect of pressure angle on, **3.**16–**3.**17
minimum number of teeth to avoid, **3.**16, **3.**43, **3.**47, **3.**63
redesign to eliminate, **8.**2–**8.**4
Unit load, **2.**41–**2.**45
comparison of AGMA and ISO allowable, **9.**46–**9.**47
equations: for bevel gears, **2.**48
for spur and helical gears, **2.**43, **3.**79
for worm gears, **3.**121–**3.**123
table of, **2.**45
Units: **2.**19*n*.
of factors in rating equations, **3.**80–**3.**81
of gear dimensions, **1.**3, **2.**3, **3.**4–**3.**5, **3.**80–**3.**81
used in this book, **2.**19*n*.

Vehicle gears (*see* Automotive gears; Transportation gears)
Velocity factor:
for oil-film thickness, **3.**136–**3.**139
for worm gears, **3.**120, **3.**125, **3.**127
Vibration problems, **7.**36–**7.**37, **7.**39
due to tooth friction, **9.**26
and dynamic load, **9.**9–**9.**15
(*See also* Application factors)
Vickers hardness test, **4.**15, **4.**16
Virtual number of teeth, **1.**35, **3.**45, **9.**33, **9.**36
Virtual spur gear, **9.**33, **9.**36

Walter, G. H., **4.**30, Ref. 249
Warping (*see* Distortion of gears)
Wear:
  allowable, **1.**9
  due to dirty lubricants, **7.**46
  due to lack of oil, **7.**46–**7.**47
  due to pitting, **2.**20
  kinds of, **2.**24–**2.**25, **7.**24–**7.**28
  theory of, **7.**25–**7.**28
  (*See also* Failure of gears; Pitting; Scoring; Surface finish)
Wear-in:
  conditions during, **3.**141
  of crossed-helical gears, **3.**116–**3.**117
  lubrication procedure for, **7.**46
  in Regimes I and II, **3.**141
  table of amounts of, **3.**99
  (*See also* Surface finish)
Wear load of crossed-helical gears, **3.**116–**3.**117
Weight of gearsets, estimating, **2.**36–**2.**41
Weiss, T., **3.**82, Ref. 300
White layer from nitriding, **4.**24–**4.**25, **4.**27
Whole depth:
  definition of, **1.**2
  illustration of, **1.**29
  recommended for bevel gears, **3.**46
  (*See also* Dimension sheets: Tooth proportions)
Willis, R. J., **2.**39, Ref. 296
Winter, Hans, **3.**82, **9.**37, **9.**47, Ref. 300
Worm gears:
  cylindrical, **1.**43–**1.**47, **3.**65–**3.**69, **3.**118–**3.**122, **3.**126–**3.**128
Worm gears (*Cont.*):
  definition of, **1.**2, **9.**3
  dimension sheets for, **3.**64, **3.**70, **3.**72
  double-enveloping, **1.**47–**1.**49, **3.**69–**3.**73, **3.**122–**3.**128
  estimating size needed, **2.**51–**2.**53
  hobs for, **6.**19–**6.**21
  kinds of, **9.**3
  load rating of, **3.**115–**3.**128
  lubricants recommended for, **7.**43
  materials used in, **2.**51, **3.**69, **3.**117, **3.**121, **3.**123, **4.**53
  nonenveloping (*see* Crossed-helical gears)
  self-locking, **3.**66
  single-enveloping (*see* cylindrical, *above*)
  strength of, **3.**115, **3.**121
Worm thread profiles, **6.**29–**6.**31
  sample calculation of, **6.**31–**6.**36

Y factors for bending stress calculations, **2.**9–**2.**10
Yield point, definition of, **4.**4
Yoshida, A., **4.**30, Refs. 145–147
Young, I. T., **4.**28, Ref. 306

Zerol bevel gears (*see* Bevel gears, Zerol)
Zone of action:
  definition of, **3.**3
  equation for, **3.**27

About the Author

Darle W. Dudley, P.E., has been involved in gear technology for over forty years. He is the author of a wide-ranging number of technical papers and five books, including *Practical Gear Design*, the *Gear Handbook*, and *The Evolution of the Gear Art.* As chairman of the AGMA Aerospace Gear Committee for nineteen years, he helped establish the first trade standards for aerospace gearing. In recent years, Mr. Dudley has been very active in various engineering organizations devoted to the gear industry. He is the recipient of many awards for his outstanding contributions to the gear industry, among them the prestigious Edward P. Connell Award and the Golden Gear Award. Mr. Dudley currently heads his own consulting company, Dudley Engineering Co., of San Diego, California.